JOURNAL FOR THE STUDY OF THE NEW TESTAMENT
SUPPLEMENT SERIES
48

Executive Editor, Supplement Series
David Hill

Publishing Editor
David E Orton

JSOT Press
Sheffield

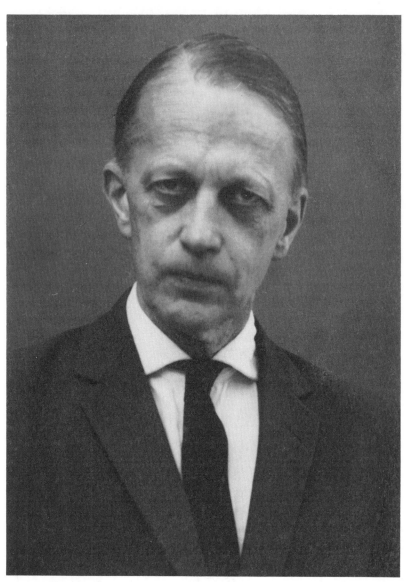

Ernst Bammel

TEMPLUM AMICITIAE

Essays on the Second Temple presented to Ernst Bammel

Edited by
William Horbury

Journal for the Study of the New Testament
Supplement Series 48

E.B.

HVIVSMODI STVDIORVM CVLTORI
PERACVTO INDEFESSO DOCTISSIMO

AMICI DISCIPVLI
D.D.D.

Published by JSOT Press
JSOT Press is an imprint of
Sheffield Academic Press Ltd
The University of Sheffield
343 Fulwood Road
Sheffield S10 3BP
England

Typeset by Sheffield Academic Press and
Printed on acid-free paper in Great Britain
by Billing & Sons Ltd
Worcester

British Library Cataloguing in Publication Data

Templum Amicitiae: essays on the second temple
   presented to Ernst Bammel
   1. Israel. Jerusalem. Temples: Temple of Jerusalem,
   history
   I. Horbury, William   II. Bammel, Ernst   III. Series

   ISSN 0143-5108
   ISBN 1-85075-273-7

CONTENTS

PREFACE

It is a source of pleasure both to me and to many others that
Ernst Bammel should be honoured in this collection of essays
by former pupils (I use the word 'former' with hesitation, since
one continues to learn from him), Cambridge colleagues and
other friends, on the occasion of his sixty-seventh birthday on
20 January 1990. Cambridge, in particular, owes him a debt of
gratitude for the breadth and depth of the scholarship he has
brought to the University, and he has had much to offer especially to research students. Others than those in Cambridge,
however, can benefit from the fruits of his scholarship, which
are available, through his many publications, to all who are
interested in biblical studies and in Judaism in the intertestamental period and the early centuries AD (not that Ernst's
interests are confined to those periods). The bibliography in the
present volume gives an indication of the contribution to
scholarship that has been made by his searching, original and
well-equipped mind; but he will doubtless soon render it out of
date. It is a welcome development that his *kleine Schriften*,
which shed fresh light on numerous problems, are being collected together, revised and published in a series of volumes.

His scholarship is not the only reason for pleasure that he
should be honoured. Mention must also be made of the
warmth of friendship that so many feel towards him.
Although he retired in 1990 from his Readership in Early
Christian and Jewish Studies in the Faculty of Divinity, we are
glad that he will still spend much time in Cambridge, where
his wife Caroline will continue to teach in the same Faculty.

It will be a source of pleasure to Ernst that William Horbury,
whom he supervised as a graduate student years ago, has
edited this volume which Professor D.J.A. Clines has seen
through the Press. If one of the best indications of a scholar's

achievement is the pupils he has trained, then Ernst Bammel has good reason to be satisfied.

John Emerton

ABBREVIATIONS

Adv. Jud.	Chrysostom, *Adversus Judaeos*
Agric.	Philo, *De Agricultura*
Alex.	Plutarch, *Alexander*
Al. Protr.	Clement of Alexandria, *Protrepticus*
Anac.	Epiphanus, *Anacorus*
ANRW	*Aufstieg und Niedergang der römischen Welt*
Ant.	Josephus, *Antiquities of the Jews*
Antiq.	Dionysus of Halicarnassus, *Antiquities*
Anton.	*Antonianum*
Apoc. Abr.	*Apocalypse of Abraham*
Apoc. Ezra	*Apocalypse of Ezra*
Apoc. Mos.	*Apocalypse of Moses*
Apoc. Zeph.	*Apocalypse of Zephaniah*
Apol.	Justin, *Apology*
Ar.	Aristophanes
ARN	*Abot de Rabbi Nathan*
Asc. Isa.	*Ascension of Isaiah*
Ass. Mos.	*Assumption of Moses*
ASTI	*Annual of the Swedish Theological Institute*
ATD	Das Alte Testament Deutsch
Ath.	Athenaeus
A.Z.	Talmud, *Abodah Zarah*
BAR	*Biblical Archaeology Review*
2 Bar.	*2 (Syriac) Baruch*
Barn.	*Epistle of Barnabas*
BASOR	*Bulletin of the American Schools of Oriental Research*
Bek.	Talmud, *Bekorot*
Ber.	Talmud, *Berakot*
BET	Beiträge zur evangelischen Theologie
BETL	Bibliotheca ephemeridum theologicarum lovaniensium
BJRL	*Bulletin of the John Rylands University Library of Manchester*
BK	*Bibel und Kirche*
BM	Talmud, *Baba Meiṣ'a*
BRW	G.B. Winer, *Biblisches Realwörterbuch*
BZAW	Beihefte zur ZAW
BZNW	Beihefte zur ZNW
BZRGG	Beihefte zur ZRGG
Calig.	Suetonius, *Caligula*

CanJT	Canadian Journal of Theology
Cat. Ma.	Plutarch, Cato Maior
CBQ	Catholic Biblical Quarterly
CCL	Corpus christianorum latinorum
CD	Damascus Document
Cher.	Philo, De Cherubim
Cic.	Cicero
CIJ	Corpus inscriptionum judaicarum
Clem.	Clement
1 Clem.	1 Clement
Conf. Ling.	Philo, De Confusione Linguarum
ConNT	Coniectanea neotestamentica
Contra Haer.	Irenaeus, Contra Haereses
Congr.	Philo, De Congressu Eruditionis Gratia
CRINT	Compendia rerum iudaicarum ad novum testamentum
Decal.	Philo, De Decalogo
De div.	Cicero, De divinatione
De Imp. Cn. Pomp.	Cicero, Oratorio de Imperio Cn. Pompei
Dem.	Talmud, Demai
Dem. Ev.	Eusebius, Demonstratio Evangelica
Deus Imm.	Philo, Quod Deus sit Immutabilis
D.H.	Dionysus of Halicarnassus
Dial.	Justin Martyr, Dialogue
Eccl. R.	Ecclesiastes Rabbah
EJ(ud)	Encyclopaedia Judaica
1 En.	1 (Ethiopic) Enoch
Ep.	Epistle
ET	English Translation
ETL	Ephemerides theologicae lovanienses
Exod. R.	Exodus Rabbah
Flacc.	Philo, In Flaccum
FRLANT	Forschungen zur Religion und Literatur des Alten und Neuen Testaments
Fug.	Philo, De Fuga et Inventione
GCS	Griechische christliche Schriftsteller
Gen. R.	Genesis Rabbah
Geog.	Strabo, Geography
Gitt.	Talmud, Gittin
HAT	Handbuch zum Alten Testament
HbNT	Handbuch zum Neuen Testament
HDB	Hastings' Dictionary of the Bible
Hdt.	Herodotus
H.E.	Eusebius, Historia Ecclesiastica
Hist.	Tacitus, Histories
H.N.	Pliny, Historia Naturalis
HNT	Handbuch zum Neuen Testament
Hor.	Horace
H.P.	Theophrastus, Historia Plantarum

HSM	Harvard Semitic Monographs
HTR	*Harvard Theological Review*
HUCA	*Hebrew Union College Annual*
Hul.	Talmud, *Hullin*
ICC	International Critical Commentary
IDB	G.A. Buttrick (ed.), *Interpreter's Dictionary of the Bible*
IEJ	*Israel Exploration Journal*
Inst.	Quintilian, *Institutio Oratoria*
ISBE	*International Standard Bible Encyclopedia*
j.	*Jerusalem Talmud*
JBL	*Journal of Biblical Literature*
JBLMS	*Journal of Biblical Literature Monograph Series*
JJS	*Journal of Jewish Studies*
Jos.	Philo, *De Josepho*
Jos. Asen.	*Joseph and Asenath*
JQR	*Jewish Quarterly Review*
JR	*Journal of Religion*
JRS	*Journal of Roman Studies*
JSJ	*Journal for the Study of Judaism in the Persian, Hellenistic and Roman Period*
JSNTSup	*Journal for the Study of the New Testament* Supplement Series
JSOT	*Journal for the Study of the Old Testament*
JSOTSup	*Journal for the Study of the Old Testament* Supplement Series
JSS	*Journal of Semitic Studies*
JTS	*Journal of Theological Studies*
Jub.	*Jubilees*
KAT	Kommentar zum Alten Testament.
KEKNT	Kritisch–Exegetischer Kommentar zum Neuen Testament
Kel.	Talmud, *Kelim*
Ker.	Talmud, *Keritot*
LAB	*Liber Antiquitatum Biblicarum*
Lad. Jac.	*Ladder of Jacob*
LAE	*Life of Adam and Eve*
LCL	Loeb Classical Library
LD	Lectio divina
Leg. ad Gaium	Philo, *Legatio ad Gaium*
Leg. All.	Philo, *Legum Allegoriae*
Lev. R.	*Leviticus Rabbah*
L.L.	Varro, *De Lingua Latina*
Lys.	Aristophanes, *Lysistrata*
LXX	Septuagint
m.	*Mishnah*
Maas.	Talmud, *Ma'aserot*
4 Macc.	*4 Maccabees*
Mart.	Martial

Mart. Pol.	*Martyrdom of Polycarp*
MDOG	Mitteilungen der deutschen Orient-Gesellschaft
Men.	Talmud, *Menahot*
Merc. Cond.	Lucian, *De Mercede Conductis*
Mid.	Talmud, *Middot*
Midr. Pss.	*Midrash on Psalms*
Midr. Teh.	*Midrash Tehillim (Midrash on Psalms)*
Migr. Abr.	Philo, *De Migratione Abrahami*
Mir.	Phlegon, *Miracula*
MPG	Migne, *Patrologia Graeca*
M.Q.	Talmud, *Mo'ed Qatan*
Mut. Nom.	Philo, *De Mutatione Nominum*
Naz.	Talmud, *Nazir*
NCB	New Century Bible
NEB	*New English Bible*
NHC	*Nag Hammadi Codex(-ices)*
Nid.	Talmud, *Niddah*
NIV	*New International Version*
NovT	*Novum Testamentum*
NovTSup	*Novum Testamentum* Supplements
ns	new series
NTD	Das Neue Testament Deutsch
NTOA	Novum Testamentum et Orbis Antiquus
NTS	*New Testament Studies*
Num. R.	*Numbers Rabbah*
OCCL	P. Harvey (ed.), *The Oxford Companion to Classical Literature*
Od.	*Odes of Solomon*
Ohol.	Talmud, *Oholot*
OTP	J.H. Charlesworth, *The Old Testament Pseudepigrapha*
Paed.	Clement of Alexandria, *Paedagogus*
Paus.	Pausanias
PEQ	*Palestine Exploration Quarterly*
Pes.	Talmud, *Pesahim*
PG	J. Migne, *Patrologia graeca*
Ph.	Philo
PL	J. Migne, *Patrologia latina*
Plant.	Philo, *De Plantatione*
Plin.	Pliny
Plu.	Plutarch
Protev.	*Protevangelium*
PsJ	Pseudo-Jonathan
P–W	Pauly–Wissowa
Quaest. in Exod.	Philo, *Quaestiones in Exodum*
Quaest. in Gen.	Philo, *Quaestiones in Genesin*
Quint.	Quintilian
RAC	*Reallexikon für Antike und Christentum*

RB	*Revue biblique*
Rec.	*Clementine Recognitions*
REJ	*Revue des études juives*
Rer. Div. Her.	Philo, *Quis Rerum Divinarum Heres sit*
RevQ	*Revue de Qumran*
RevSR	*Revue des sciences religieuses*
R.H.	Talmud, *Roš-haš-šanah*
RheinMus	*Rheinisches Museum*
RHR	*Revue de l'histoire des religions*
RhV.	*Rheinische Vierteljahrsblätter*
Rom.	Plutarch, *Romulus*
RQ	*Revue de Qumran*
RSR	*Recherches de science religieuse*
RSV	*Revised Standard Version*
Sanh.	Talmud, *Sanhedrin*
Sat.	Juvenal, *Satires*
SBL	Society of Biblical Literature
SBLDS	SBL Dissertation Series
SBT	Studies in Biblical Theology
SE	*Studia Evangelica I, II, III* (= TU 73 [1959], 87 [1964], 88 [1964], etc.)
Shab.	Talmud, *Shabbat*
Sheb.	Talmud, *Shebi'it*
Sheq.	Talmud, *Sheqalim*
Sib. (Or.)	*Sibylline Oracles*
Sifre Num.	*Sifre on Numbers*
Silv.	Statius, *Silvae*
si v.l.	*si vera lectio*, if the reading is correct
Sim.	Hermas, *Similitudes*
Slav. Enoch	*2 (Slavonic) Enoch*
SNT	Studien zum Neuen Testament
SNTSMS	Society of New Testament Studies Monograph Series
Somn.	Philo, *De Somniis*
Songs R.	*Song of Songs Rabbah*
Spec. Leg.	Philo, *De Specialibus Legibus*
Str.	Strabo
Suet.	Suetonius
Suk.	Talmud, *Sukkah*
SUNT	Studien zur Umwelt des Neuen Testaments
s.v.	*sub verbo*, see under that word
SVT	Supplements to Vetus Testamentum
Syr. Bar.	*Syriac Baruch*
Taan.	Talmud, *Ta'anit*
T. Abr.	*Testament of Abraham*
T(ar)g.	*Targum*
T. Ash.	*Testament of Asher*
T. Benj.	*Testament of Benjamin*
T. Dan	*Testament of Dan*

Tg. Jon.	*Targum Jonathan*
Tg. Neof.	*Targum Neofiti*
Tg. Onk.	*Targum Onkelos*
Tg. Ps.-J.	*Targum Pseudo-Jonathan*
THAT	*Theologisches Handbuch zum Alten Testament*
ThB	*Theologischer Blätter*
ThHkzNT	Theologischer Handkommentar zum Neuen Testament
T. Levi	*Testament of Levi*
TLZ	*Theologische Literaturzeitung*
TN	*Targum Neofiti*
TNTC	Tyndale New Testament Commentaries
Toh.	Talmud, *Tohorot*
TSAJ	Texte und Studien zum antiken Judentum
TU	*Texte und Untersuchungen*
TWAT	G.J. Botterweck and H. Ringgren (eds.), *Theologisches Wörterbuch zum Alten Testament*
TWNT	G. Kittel and G. Friedrich (eds.), *Theologisches Wörterbuch zum Neuen Testament*
USQR	*Union Seminary Quarterly Review*
UT	C.H. Gordon, *Ugaritic Textbook*
Vay. R.	*Vayyiqra Rabbah*
VC	*Vigiliae christianae*
Vg	Vulgate
Vis.	Hermas, *Visions*
VL	*Vetus Latina*
Vit. Mos.	Philo, *De Vita Mosis*
VT	*Vetus Testamentun*
WMANT	Wissenschaftliche Monographien zum Alten und Neuen Testament
WTJ	*Westminster Theological Journal*
WUNT	Wissenschaftliche Untersuchungen zum Neuen Testament
Yeb.	Talmud, *Yebamot*
ZAW	*Zeitschrift für die alttestamentliche Wissenschaft*
ZDPV	*Zeitschrift des deutschen Palästina-Vereins*
Zeb.	Talmud, *Zebaḥim*
ZNW	*Zeitschrift für die neutestamentliche Wissenschaft*
ZRGG	*Zeitschrift für Religions- und Geistesgeschichte*
ZTK	*Zeitschrift für Theologie und Kirche*

THE TEMPLE IN THE BOOKS OF CHRONICLES

H.G.M. Williamson

Several years ago, Ernst Bammel kindly but firmly persuaded me to present a paper on the topic of the temple in the books of Chronicles to his graduate seminar. Since at the time he urged me to publish it, and in view of the subject chosen for this volume in his honour, he will, I hope, be prepared to accept this revised version of what was said on that occasion as a token of admiration and respect.

One of the few points about which all commentators on Chronicles are agreed is that the temple was of central significance to its author. While some aspects of its importance to him will be our primary concern in the bulk of what follows, it may serve as a useful introduction to the subject to remind ourselves of one or two of the devices by which the Chronicler draws attention to the centrality of the temple in his thinking.

To start with a simple example, we may note his introduction to Solomon's reign. Solomon was popularly remembered as a man of wealth and wisdom, and as the one who built the first temple. These three points are grouped together in 2 Chronicles 1.[1]

(a) Verses 2-6 are based on 1 Kgs 3.4, which serves in its context merely as an introduction to the dream which follows. Here, however, the Chronicler has developed the material into a narrative in its own right, in which the

---

1. For other aspects of the significance of 2 Chron. 1 for the Chronicler's portrayal of Solomon, cf. R.B. Dillard, 'The Chronicler's Solomon', *WTJ* 43 (1980), pp. 289-300; 'The Literary Structure of the Chronicler's Solomon Narrative', *JSOT* 30 (1984), pp. 85-93; and *2 Chronicles* (Word Biblical Commentary, 15; Waco: Word Books, 1987), pp. 1-15.

king leads the people in a major act of sacrificial worship. Moreover, he has made it the first recorded incident of Solomon's reign. It thus serves as a pointer to the aspect of the reign which the Chronicler deemed to be of greatest significance and invites us to read the following chapters in its light.

(b) Verses 7-13 represent a radical abbreviation of 1 Kgs 3.5-15 for reasons that need not concern us here.[2] The gift of wisdom to Solomon was, of course, one of the topics most widely remembered about this king. Against his *Vorlage*, however, the Chronicler no longer has the account of the dream at Gibeon followed by the illustrative example of the exercise of Solomon's wisdom in the story of the judgment between the two prostitutes (1 Kgs 3.16-28). In his view, the primary purpose of Solomon's wisdom was not to equip him for civil rule but to enable him to undertake the task of temple-building retold in the following chapters.

(c) A further well-known feature of Solomon's reign was his wealth. In Kings, the details of this come at the end of the faithful part of his reign (1 Kgs 10.26-29), before his fall from grace. The Chronicler, however, has given this paragraph a completely new position in 2 Chron. 1.14-17; clearly, his purpose is again to show how this aspect too of Solomon's glory was channelled into the building of the temple, the account of which follows directly.

What is seen here in miniature in 2 Chronicles 1 is, in fact, largely true of the whole of his preceding narrative. Since clearly we cannot deal with so much material here even in brief, let us again take three representative examples.[3]

First, in the period before the temple was built, its role in the religious life of the people was largely fulfilled by the ark. This

---

2. Cf. my *1 and 2 Chronicles* (NCB; Grand Rapids: Wm B. Eerdmans and London: Marshall, Morgan & Scott, 1982), pp. 195-96.

3. For fuller discussions, cf. especially R. Mosis, *Untersuchungen zur Theologie des chronistischen Geschichtswerkes* (Freiburger theologische Studien, 92; Freiburg: Herder, 1973), pp. 44-124; T.-S. Im, *Das Davidbild in den Chronikbüchern* (Europäische Hochschulschriften, XXIII/263; Frankfurt am Main: Peter Lang, 1985).

may be seen by the facts that the temple was built explicitly to house the ark, that the Chronicler heightens the centrality of the bringing of the ark into the sanctuary at the dedication of the temple (2 Chron. 5.2–6.11), and that he uses the same loaded theological vocabulary of it as he does later of the temple. Now, when 1 Chron. 10.13-14 (the Chronicler's own comment on the reasons for Saul's death) is read in the light of 1 Chron. 13.1-5, the use of the same stereotyped vocabulary strongly suggests that a major contribution to Saul's failure was his neglect of the ark, and that David made the rectification of this abuse one of his first priorities. But then in turn, while David's care for the ark is drawn out to dominate the whole of 1 Chronicles 13–16 (contrast 2 Sam. 6), the Chronicler deliberately introduces a drastic change in the sequence of his *Vorlage* in order to work into the middle of this narrative the events of 1 Chronicles 14. Naturally, this was not meant to be a chronological improvement: in the space of three months (1 Chron. 13.14), even David could hardly have fathered more than thirteen children and still have had the strength to wage two successful campaigns against the Philistines! Rather, these are stereotyped markers of divine blessing for faithful kings. Welten[4] has isolated in particular building, military victory and large families as such tokens in Chronicles, and it is precisely these three that are assembled in 1 Chronicles 14. It is obvious, therefore, that even under the guise of the ark, the temple dominates much of David's reign. Proper attention to it is the source of blessing for the life of the nation.

Second, this same concern is the trigger for the dynastic promise which follows in 1 Chronicles 17. To cut a long story short,[5] the net result of the slight changes which the Chronicler introduces by comparison with 2 Samuel 7 is first to focus the oracle more exclusively on Solomon himself as the temple builder, and secondly to relate the more general conditional

4. P. Welten, *Geschichte und Geschichtsdarstellung in den Chronikbüchern* (WMANT 42; Neukirchen-Vluyn: Neukirchener Verlag, 1973).
5. Cf. my 'The Dynastic Oracle in the Books of Chronicles', in A. Rofé and Y. Zakovitch (eds.), *Essays on the Bible and the Ancient World: Isac Leo Seeligmann Volume* (Jerusalem: E. Rubinstein, 1983), vol. 3, pp. 305-18.

elements in the Deuteronomic forms of the oracle to the one specific condition of Solomon's faithfulness in regard to temple building. It thus emerges that the future of the dynasty is made dependent upon Solomon bringing to completion the work of his father David—David himself being ritually debarred[6] from undertaking the work 'because you have shed much blood upon the earth in my sight' (1 Chron. 22.8).

Third, it now becomes understandable why the rest of the account of David's reign is completely dominated by preparations for the building: site, materials, plans, personnel, political conditions, nothing that can be anticipated is left undone. Even David's extensive military campaigns are reinterpreted as the source for the precious metals that Solomon would need later on (1 Chron. 18.8,[7] 11; 2 Chron. 5.1).

In view of this and much more that could be said, it is obvious that the Chronicler set enormous store by the temple. But why? Wherein did its importance lie? And what kerygmatic purpose did he think would be served by his emphasis?

For many years it has been customary to respond to such questions in terms of the Chronicler's negative polemic. It is contended that his stress on the Jerusalem temple was intended to uphold its legitimacy in face of the claims of other comparable centres, most notably the Samaritan temple on Mount Gerizim. This in turn is linked with an interpretation of his work as a whole as being fundamentally anti-Samaritan in tone and purpose.[8]

---

6. As correctly observed by J. Goettsberger, *Die Bücher der Chronik oder Paralipomenon* (HSAT IV/1; Bonn: Peter Hanstein, 1939), p. 163.

7. For the difficult question of the Chronicler's *Vorlage* here, where the LXX of 2 Sam. 8.8 is closer to Chronicles than to the MT of Samuel, cf. M. Rehm, *Textkritische Untersuchungen zu den Parallelstellen der Samuel–Königsbücher und der Chronik* (Alttestamentliche Abhandlungen, 13, 3; Münster: Aschendorff, 1937), p. 25; H.G.M. Williamson, 'The Accession of Solomon in the Books of Chronicles', *VT* 26 (1976), pp. 351-61 (357f.); R. Braun, *1 Chronicles* (Word Biblical Commentary, 14; Waco: Word Books, 1986), pp. 204-205, *contra* W. Rudolph, *Chronikbücher* (HAT 21; Tübingen: Mohr, 1955), p. 135, and W.E. Lemke, 'The Synoptic Problem in the Chronicler's History', *HTR* 58 (1965), pp. 349-63 (354-55).

8. See the fundamental studies of C.C. Torrey, *Ezra Studies* (Chicago: Chicago University Press, 1910), pp. 208-51, and M. Noth, *Überlieferungsgeschichtliche Studien* (Halle: Max Niemeyer, 1943), pp. 171-80 (=

While such sentiments may still be found in some standard text-books and reference works on the subject, this position has in fact been abandoned by almost all major scholars working in this field during the past fifteen or twenty years. This dramatic turn-around in interpretation has largely focused, however, upon the Chronicler's attitude to the northern kingdom.[9] Less attention has been directed to the consequences which this shift might have for an appreciation of his temple theology. It is appropriate, therefore, to attempt such a reappraisal within the new context which Chronicles studies have established. I shall seek specifically to defend the view that the temple in Chronicles is not a litmus test of an orthodoxy that would exclude the non-conformist but rather a focus of unity for the people of Israel as a whole. We shall then in conclusion test this hypothesis by contrasting it with a different presentation from a slightly later date which in fact comes much closer to the exclusive model so frequently postulated of the Chronicler.

It is often thought to be a good approach in ecumenical discussions to start by going back in time to the common fount in history which unites various groups that may have diverged over lesser issues in subsequent time.[10] In the light of that unity one may then have a better perspective from which to approach those divisions. This, at any rate, is what the Chronicler patently does in his presentation of the temple. His concern is always to link it back by physical ties of unbroken continuity with institutions or settings of far earlier days, before the divisions of the monarchical period, let alone his own

---

The Chronicler's History [JSOTS 50; Sheffield: JSOT Press, 1987], pp. 97-106).

9. In addition to most of the recent works on Chronicles cited elsewhere in this article, cf. H.G.M. Williamson, *Israel in the Books of Chronicles* (Cambridge: Cambridge University Press, 1977); R.L. Braun, 'A Reconsideration of the Chronicler's Attitude toward the North', *JBL* 96 (1977), pp. 59-62; S. Japhet, *The Ideology of the Book of Chronicles and its Place in Biblical Thought* (Jerusalem: Bialik, 1977), pp. 228-333 [Hebrew].

10. See, for instance, S.C. Neill in R. Rouse and S.C. Neill (eds.), *A History of the Ecumenical Movement 1517–1948* (2nd edn; London: SPCK, 1967), p. 726.

much later time, had surfaced. Let us examine two main
examples of this: the temple site and its design.

(a) *The temple site.* The choice of temple site is explained in
1 Chronicles 21, the account of David's census, the consequent
plague and David's purchase of the threshing floor of Ornan
the Jebusite, the point where the plague stopped. In the
Chronicler's *Vorlage*, 2 Samuel 24, the narrative is closely
linked with 2 Samuel 21 for purposes of its own, and it is not
explicitly stated that the threshing floor which David purchased became the future temple site. The text of this chapter
had, we now know, already passed through some intermediate stage of development before it reached the Chronicler.
Nevertheless, it is equally certain that he has himself taken
this development further in ways that are important for our
theme.[11]

First, the closing verses of the passage (21.26–22.1) are his
own addition and, as is his customary method, they provide us
with his interpretation of the foregoing narrative. Here we
find that he aims to establish the divinely willed continuity
between the Mosaic sanctuary and the future Jerusalem
temple. The acceptance of the burnt offering by fire from
heaven not only confirms the choice of the present site, but
establishes a link with the altar of the tabernacle (cf. Lev. 9.24)
and points forward to the similar occurrence at the dedication
of the temple (2 Chron. 7.1). At the same time, although vv.
29-30 are circumstantial, and hence almost parenthetical,
there is a conscious contrast between 'the tabernacle of the

11. For discussion of the textual and literary arguments that lead to
this conclusion, see (in addition to the commentaries) Lemke (above, n.
7), pp. 355-57; E.C. Ulrich, *The Qumran Text of Samuel and Josephus*
(HSM 19; Missoula: Scholars Press, 1978), pp. 156-59; R. Micheel, *Die
Seher- und Prophetenüberlieferungen in der Chronik* (BET 18; Frankfurt am Main: Peter Lang, 1983), pp. 20-23; P.E. Dion, 'The Angel with
the Drawn Sword (II [*sic*!] Chr. 21,16): An Exercise in Restoring the
Balance of Text Criticism *and* Attention to Context', *ZAW* 97 (1985), pp.
114-17; S.L. McKenzie, *The Chronicler's Use of the Deuteronomistic
History* (HSM 33; Atlanta: Scholars Press, 1985), pp. 55-58, 67-71; E.
Nicole, 'Un cas de relecture: 2 Samuel 24 et 1 Chroniques 21', *Ḥokhma*
26 (1983), pp. 47-55; and S. Romerowski, 'A propos de la relecture de
2 Samuel 24 par 1 Chroniques 21', *Ḥokhma* 28 (1985), pp. 54-60.

Lord' with its 'altar of burnt offering' (v. 29) on the one hand, and 'the house of the Lord God' and 'the altar of burnt offering' (22.1) on the other. Sandwiched in between, v. 30, which is rich in allusion to the preceding narrative, reminds us of the divine will which had deflected David away from the tabernacle at Gibeon to this new and unexpected setting.[12] The other relevant aspect of the Chronicler's treatment of this chapter is his characteristic use of typology. Typology in this context, it should be said, does not quite have the force that it does when used between the New Testament and the Old. It is not used to point to one incident or institution as the fulfilment of its shadowlike predecessor; rather, it serves as a cross-reference from one incident to another, inviting the reader to draw parallels and conclusions that go beyond the immediate statement of the text. There are two examples of this procedure in this passage.[13]

Verse 20 has little connection with its *Vorlage* in 2 Sam. 24.20; a number of features, however, suggest that a deliberate comparison with the story of Gideon in Judges 6 has been introduced. The basic theme is the same: the encounter of an angel with one who was threshing wheat and the offering received by supernatural fire, while some points of detail further support the analogy, such as the expressions 'hid themselves', 'he turned', and 'saw' in the sense of 'perceived'. Even

12. It is worth noting in passing that this passage has previously been understood in terms of anti-Samaritan polemic: David's statement in 22.1, which starts זה הוא בית יהוה האלהים, 'this is the house of the LORD God', is said by J.W. Rothstein and J. Hänel, *Kommentar zum ersten Buch der Chronik* (KAT XVIII/2; Leipzig: A. Deichertsche Verlagsbuchhandlung, 1927), pp. 376-77, 385, and by Rudolph (above, n. 7), p. 148, to echo Jacob's statement in Gen. 28.17—מה־נורא המקום הזה אין זה כי אם בית אלהים, 'How dreadful is this place! This is none other but the house of God.' This echo, however, is weak at best (it is not exact, for in Chronicles it refers to the future rather than to present realization) and in any case is not necessarily anti-Samaritan as such: the Samaritans revered Gerizim rather than Bethel. At the most it should be regarded as critical of the pre-exilic northern royal cult, which is not at all the same thing. But, as I have tried to indicate, it is better taken as a positive statement about the future temple site than as a purely polemical outburst.

13. Cf. T. Willi, *Die Chronik als Auslegung* (FRLANT 106; Göttingen: Vandenhoeck & Ruprecht, 1972), pp. 157-58.

if some of this evidence is overplayed, the basic analogy is attractive, for the appearance of the angel to Gideon also led to the establishment of a permanent holy place to the Lord. Moreover, Gideon went on from there to contend for the Lord against Baal; did the Chronicler see in his account a similar development from a Jebusite sanctuary to one consecrated to the Lord? It is, at least, noteworthy that he introduces the term מקום in vv. 22 and 25, for this, as is well known, can have the extended meaning of 'holy site'.[14]

In vv. 22-25, the Chronicler introduces a more significant comparison by patterning David's purchase on Abraham's purchase of the cave of Machpelah from Ephron in Genesis 23. To the underlying similarity of the leading representative of the people of God buying a site for sacred purposes from a member of the indigenous population is added a number of details to make the analogy clear. Most noteworthy is his addition twice of the phrase בכסף מלא, 'at its full price', exactly as at Gen. 23.9 and occurring nowhere else in the OT. Further, against his *Vorlage* he twice uses the verb נתן 'give' for 'buy' in v. 22 as at Gen. 23.4 and 9, has David initiate the conversation (v. 22) as Abraham did at Gen. 23.3f., and in v. 23 he gives added emphasis to Ornan's initial response of wishing to 'give' (twice) the site to David, just as Ephron did with Abraham (Gen. 23.11). Perhaps also the Chronicler's extension of the area to be purchased from the threshing floor to the whole site (vv. 22, 25) was influenced by the similar dispute in Genesis 23 about the cave and the field in which it was found.

Preachers are fond of drawing out lessons from the fact that the cave of Machpelah was the only piece of real estate which the patriarchs secured in the promised land. There is no reason why the Chronicler should not also have been aware of this and made conscious use of the fact in his valuation of the temple site. It became in his view a firstfruit, so to speak, of the land of promise, so that all who revered Abraham as patriarch might feel a bond with this place.

A similar point is made even more obviously in the other passage which centres on the temple site, 2 Chron. 3.1:

14. Cf. A. Cowley, 'The Meaning of מקום in Hebrew', *JTS* 17 (1916), pp. 174-76, and J. Gamberoni, *TWAT*, IV, cols. 1113-24.

Then Solomon began to build the house of the LORD at Jerusalem in Mount Moriah, where the LORD appeared to David his father, which he made ready in the place that David had appointed, in the threshing floor of Ornan the Jebusite.

Mount Moriah is referred to elsewhere only at Genesis 22 as the site where Abraham was commanded to offer up Isaac.[15] The important verses for our present concern are 2 and 14, though they contain several difficulties of their own. It is probable that in their present form they already interpret the narrative as a pointer towards the future temple. Particularly noteworthy is the use in v. 14 of the phrase 'the mount of the LORD', which elsewhere refers to the temple hill (Ps. 24.3; Isa. 2.3; 30.29). Further, the phrase 'as it is said this day' suggests association with a well-known location, and the word-play between 'it shall be provided' (which links back to v. 8 of the narrative) and 'he will be seen' could well be understood in cultic terms. Possible, but less certain, is the argument that if the popular view is right which sees in Genesis 22 an aetiology for the abolition of human sacrifice, then a reference to Jerusalem (apparently the centre of the 'Molek cult', which practised this form of sacrifice) is to be expected.[16] Now, while it is clear that v. 14 is important for determining one aspect of the narrator's purpose, it cannot be divorced from v. 2 in which the mention of Moriah is found. These are the only two verses which suggest that the altar was built on a mountain; the phrase 'one of the mountains of which I shall tell you', by its resemblance to the expression of God's choice of the sanctu-

15. It does not, as was once thought, occur in one of the Khirbet Beit Lei inscriptions; cf. F.M. Cross, 'The Cave Inscriptions from Khirbet Beit Lei', in J.A. Sanders (ed.), *Near Eastern Archaeology in the Twentieth Century* (Garden City: Doubleday, 1970), pp. 299-306; A. Lemaire, 'Prières en temps de crise: les inscriptions de Khirbet Beit Lei', *RB* 83 (1976), pp. 558-68; and P.D. Miller, 'Psalms and Inscriptions', in J.A. Emerton (ed.), *Congress Volume: Vienna 1980* (SVT 32; Leiden: E.J. Brill, 1981), pp. 311-32, *contra* J. Naveh, 'Old Hebrew Inscriptions in a Burial Cave', *IEJ* 13 (1963), pp. 74-92, and J.C.L. Gibson, *Textbook of Syrian Semitic Inscriptions*. Volume 1: *Hebrew and Moabite Inscriptions* (Oxford: Clarendon, 1971), pp. 57-58.

16. See the discussion in G.C. Heider, *The Cult of Molek. A Reassessment* (JSOTS 43; Sheffield: JSOT Press, 1985), pp. 273-77. Heider himself rejects any association of Gen. 22 with the Molek cult.

ary in, for instance, Deuteronomy 12, seems to be making a similar allusion to that in v. 14; and finally, the name Moriah itself may well, by a popular form of etymology, have been understood as 'the vision of the Lord', or the like, and so again be a pointer to one element in v. 14.

In 2 Chron. 3.1 the Chronicler has picked up and made explicit these major interpretative themes from Genesis 22. First, the identity of Moriah with the temple site is, of course, plainly stated. Second, the use of the word 'mount' relates to that feature already noted which seems to have entered Genesis 22 only as an element of interpretation, and third, the description 'where the Lord appeared to David his father' is subtly introduced to link an important feature of Gen. 22.14 ('he will be seen') with the more immediate designation of the temple site in 1 Chronicles 21, analysed above.

It may thus be concluded that the Chronicler's association of the temple site with Moriah is not arbitrary; rather, he has drawn on a tradition which was sufficiently deeply rooted and well established as to have influenced the Genesis text itself.[17] His own contribution is first to spell out what is alluded to in the earlier texts (exactly as was shown above to be the case with his handling of 2 Sam. 24 in 1 Chron. 21), and, second, to link these three episodes together in such a way as to emphasize the continuity of worship at this site and so indirectly to link the temple of his own day with some of the major religious leaders of Israel's past.

For all of these reasons, then, the Chronicler saw in the site of the Jerusalem temple a focus of continuity with the nation's earliest history and one that should therefore override more recent differences. It is, of course, impossible to be sure what was happening in the north at the time that he was writing (mid-fourth century BC), but it appears that it was not much: Shechem was still deserted, as it had been for a century previously, so that clearly it was not yet a revered cult centre; that came only later, in my opinion under the impetus of a division

---

17. For the reasons given above, this conclusion seems more probable than the suggestion that 'Moriah' entered the text of Gen. 22 under the influence of Chronicles itself; cf. R. Kilian, *Isaaks Opferung. Zur Überlieferungsgeschichte von Gen 22* (Stuttgarter Bibelstudien, 44; Stuttgart: Katholisches Bibelwerk, 1970), pp. 31-46.

in the Jerusalem priesthood, a breakaway group from which united with lay northern Israelites to form what we know as the Samaritan community.[18] If this is even approximately correct, it will mean that the later Samaritan characteristic of linking all previous events in Israelite history with Gerizim[19] will be a response to the type of approach attested in Chronicles. The latter may then be seen not as negative polemic, since it had no opposite view to counteract in this sphere, but rather as the positive presentation of a point of unity.

(b) *The temple design.* We have already seen that a connection is made in 1 Chronicles 21 between the Mosaic tabernacle and the Jerusalem temple. This, however, is only one small element in a rich vein concerning the Chronicler's understanding of the temple.

In 2 Chron. 5.5, the Chronicler follows his *Vorlage* in saying that, at the dedication of the temple, 'they brought up the ark, and the tent of meeting, and all the holy vessels that were in the tent'. However the Kings text should be understood,[20] the Chronicler has given it a clear significance of his own by his references to the presence of the Mosaic tabernacle at Gibeon: 1 Chron. 16.39; 21.29; 2 Chron. 1.3-6. The temple has thus become the final resting place not only of the ark, but also of the tabernacle and all its sacred vessels.

Now, in the Chronicler's presentation this is wholly appropriate, for he emphasizes the parallels between the two structures far more than does Kings. We need here only pick out a

---

18. Cf. H.G. Kippenberg, *Garizim und Synagoge* (RVV 30; Berlin: de Gruyter, 1971), and my 'Early Post-Exilic Judaean History', in J.A. Hackett (ed.), *The Bible and the Ancient Near East* (forthcoming).

19. As attested, for instance, throughout the *Memar Marqah*; cf. J. Macdonald, *Memar Marqah. The Teaching of Marqah* (BZAW 84; 2 vols.; Berlin: Alfred Töpelmann, 1963).

20. It is believed by many to betray the hand of a late priestly editor, working in the light of Chronicles. By contrast, R.E. Friedman (*The Exile and Biblical Narrative. The Formation of the Deuteronomistic and Priestly Works* [HSM 22; Chico: Scholars Press, 1981], pp. 48ff.) has argued that it rests on sound historical memory; even if he is right, that does not invalidate discussion of what the significance of this might have been for the Chronicler.

few of the most obvious elements that contribute to this typological patterning.

First, in 1 Chron. 28.11-19, a passage which has no parallel elsewhere,[21] David gives to Solomon the plans for the temple which he is being commissioned to build. The word תבנית, used four times in these nine verses with reference to most aspects of the building, is clearly intended as an echo of the 'pattern' of the tabernacle and its furnishings, shown to Moses on Mount Sinai in Exod. 25.9, 40. There is a difference, however. Unlike the position in Exodus, there is no suggestion in Chronicles that David drew up a plan as a copy of something he had seen. Rather, David says in his summary, 'All this have I been made to understand in writing by the hand of the Lord upon me, all the works of the pattern'. The verse is difficult to construe in detail, but probably implies that David wrote the plans under conscious divine inspiration. It may be suggested, therefore, that since there was so much in common between the basic plan of the tabernacle and the temple, and since they stood in continuous tradition with each other, David did not need to see the heavenly pattern afresh: he could visit it at Gibeon. All he needed to do was to adapt the pattern under inspiration to the new conditions.

Second, it is necessary to do no more than mention that the parallel with the account of the building of the tabernacle is continued in both substance and vocabulary in the next chapter, 1 Chronicles 29, as David first appeals for offerings and the people then respond generously; cf. Exodus 25 and 35.

Third, we should consider the temple builder—Hiram in Kings, but Huramabi in 2 Chron. 2.13-14. Granted the context of a tabernacle–temple typology, it is striking that the list of his skills is amplified in Chronicles to include craftsmanship in materials that Bezalel had to be able to work in for the tabernacle (2 Chron. 2.7, 14; cf. Exod. 35.35). In the light of this, it is likely that the ascription of his mother to Dan in Chronicles rather than Naphtali in Kings is based on the help Bezalel received from Oholiab, who belonged to the tribe of Dan. Furthermore, it has been suggested that the additional *ab* element

---

21. Against attempts to deny this paragraph to the Chronicler, see my *1 and 2 Chronicles*, pp. 181-82.

which the Chronicler has given to his name is also a reflection of the final syllable of Oholiab. Both builders of the tabernacle are thus typologically brought together in the one figure of Huramabi.[22]

Finally, a number of elements in the construction of the temple differ in Chronicles from Kings in ways that agree with the description of the tabernacle. I limit myself here to the most obvious example, the veil of 2 Chron. 3.14. Nowhere else does the OT refer to such a veil in the temple. The suggestion that a sentence to this effect has dropped out of 1 Kgs 6.21 is textually improbable and would contradict 6.31-32 which speaks of doors at this point. Rather, the Chronicler has introduced here a verbal citation from Exod. 26.31 and 36.35.

We are now in a position to suggest, therefore, that as the temple was associated with the patriarchs by its site, so it was associated by its design with Moses. Added to this, a fuller treatment of the subject than is possible here could also catalogue the many passages in which the Chronicler draws attention to the continuity of cultic observance and personnel with those of the Mosaic period.[23] In all this too, he was presenting his contemporaries with a focus for unity. Ark, tent, vessels; associations with Gibeon, and perhaps Shiloh and Shechem too—all these diverse strands, which were potential sources of fragmentation, were now drawn into the one sanctuary.[24] Once again, therefore, it is possible that the later Samaritan tradition of hiding the tabernacle vessels during the present age should be seen in part as a reaction to this viewpoint, the Chronicler's own presentation being intended positively rather than as negative polemic.[25]

22. See further, in addition to the commentaries, Mosis (above, n. 3), pp. 136-47.

23. Cf. S.J. De Vries, 'Moses and David as Cult Founders in Chronicles', *JBL* 107 (1988), pp. 619-39.

24. Cf. J.W. Flanagan, *David's Social Drama. A Hologram of Israel's Early Iron Age* (JSOTS 73; Sheffield: Almond, 1988), p. 212, who writes, 'The terminology and action betray the strength of lingering loyalties for religious centers other than Jerusalem'.

25. Cf. Kippenberg (above, n. 18), pp. 234-54; M.F. Collins, 'The Hidden Vessels in Samaritan Traditions', *JSJ* 3 (1972), pp. 97-116. For the temple vessels as a focus for continuity, cf. P.R. Ackroyd, 'The Temple

Of the many points that ought to be noted from the post-Solomonic chapters in 2 Chronicles, I will mention just two that cannot be left unsaid. First, Abijah's 'sermon on the mount' in 2 Chron. 13.4-12 is not to be regarded as anti-Samaritan temple polemic, as has frequently been maintained. One of its twin foci is the legitimacy of the Davidic dynasty, which would have been an irrelevance in the postexilic debate; then, as Kippenberg (pp. 49f.) has shown, to single out 'the sons of Aaron' for mention would have been to play into the hands of the Samaritans at one of their strongest points. Finally, the point of deepest division between the two later communities—namely, the relative virtues of the locality of their respective sanctuaries—receives no mention here at all. Rather, the speech is to be entirely explained on the basis of its present narrative context where it plays an important role in a somewhat different aspect of the Chronicler's ideology.[26]

The other point is the use and role of the temple as a focus for unity in the reform of Hezekiah. This reform is of the greatest importance to the Chronicler, for in it he presents his solution to the problem of the divided kingdom. With the northern royal house now finally removed, he portrays Hezekiah as a second Solomon[27] over all Israel in a wide variety of spheres. Prominent amongst these are the arrangements which the two kings made for the temple. For instance, in his account of Solomon's building of the temple, the Chronicler singles out eight items and practices as being specifically 'an ordinance in Israel'. In each case, this reference is in addition to Kings. Without going into detail,[28] it may here be stated in summary fashion that in his account of Hezekiah's reformation, the Chronicler (again without parallel in Kings) exactly picks up each one of these eight items. His summarizing conclusion in both cases may serve as our summary of this point too:

Vessels—A Continuity Theme', in *Studies in the Religion of Ancient Israel* (SVT 23; Leiden: Brill, 1972), pp. 166-81.

26. Cf. *Israel in the Books of Chronicles* (above, n. 9), pp. 110-14.

27. Or David and Solomon combined; cf. M.A. Throntveit, *When Kings Speak. Royal Speech and Royal Prayer in Chronicles* (SBLDS 93; Atlanta: Scholars Press, 1987), pp. 121-24.

28. For which see *Israel in the Books of Chronicles*, pp. 119-25.

2 Chron. 8.16   ותכן כל־מלאכת שלמה עד־היום מוסד בית יהוה
2 Chron. 29.35   ותכון עבודת בית־יהוה

Another aspect of this presentation of Hezekiah is his attempt, partially successful, to reunite the hitherto divided tribes of Israel. Careful study reveals, however, that his appeal to the northerners is integrally linked with the temple, both because the invitation is to a centralized celebration of Passover and also because the appeal is couched in terms that suggest that it is to be understood as a paradigm of how to act in conformity with Solomon's prayer of dedication; cf. 2 Chron. 30.6-9. Especially noteworthy here is v. 9, which is drawn from the Kings account of Solomon's prayer (1 Kgs 8.50), but which the Chronicler had earlier omitted from his account of the same event.

While this summary has been both sketchy and compressed, enough has been said to conclude that the Chronicler did not regard Solomon's reign merely as a story from ancient history. By his reworking of some of its central themes in the account of Hezekiah's reign, he showed that many of its characteristics were paradigmatic of national salvation; and central to this paradigm stands the temple as a focus for the reunification of the divided and scattered people of Israel.

As a concluding point, it may be worth noting how distinctive is this viewpoint of the Chronicler's by comparing it with that of another who, in my opinion, worked two or three generations later in the early Hellenistic period and was himself a member of a circle which valued Chronicles sufficiently to have been influenced by it in a number of respects. I refer to the editor of Ezra 1–6, the latest part of Ezra–Nehemiah to have been composed.[29] This editor had some primary sources at his disposal and he worked directly from these; his usual method was to cite the source verbatim and then to construct a narrative join with the next source directly out of its wording. In this, however, it can be shown that he too worked with a strong ideology of continuity: the second temple is continuous

<hr>

29. See my 'The Composition of Ezra i–vi', *JTS* ns 34 (1983), pp. 1-30. This suggestion has recently been challenged by J. Blenkinsopp, *Ezra–Nehemiah* (London: SCM, 1989), pp. 43-44, though I do not find his arguments persuasive.

with the first; its sacred vessels are the same; priesthood and people are pure descendants of the first temple generation, and so on. But to what purpose was this continuity put? Not to the kind of inclusive policy which we have seen characterizes Chronicles, but rather the reverse. The whole drift of the work is to use continuity as a means of excluding some who might at first have been thought to have a rightful claim to participation, whether they are members of the Judaean community (cf. Ezra 2.59-63) or those who come from the northern part of the land (4.1-3). The contrast could scarcely be more marked.

If our view, hinted at earlier, of the rise of the Samaritans proper is approximately correct, and if the first temple was built on Gerizim in the early years of the Hellenistic period, then this all makes admirable sense. During the earlier reforms of Ezra and Nehemiah, it is clear that there were at least two groups in Jerusalem. Particularly amongst the priests and aristocracy, there were those who favoured a fully open attitude to other inhabitants of the land, whether truly Israelites or not. On the other hand, the reform party took a rigorously exclusive view for ideological reasons. During the decades which followed, attitudes vacillated, but tended on the whole to polarize. The Chronicler's programme for reconciliation in the mid-fourth century BC failed, and not long after a group of the assimilationists found themselves forced out. What was more natural than that they should remove to the ancient and sacred site of Shechem to establish a new community more truly representative of Israel as they saw it (cf. n. 18 above)? When eventually they found themselves able to build a temple, the author of Ezra 1–6 compiled his polemical response, asserting emphatically the legitimacy of the Jerusalem sanctuary alone.

Thus we may conclude that at each step of this chequered history, much of which was determined by sociological and political as much as by theological factors, each faction presented an ideology of the temple to bolster its broader programme. Once the Chronicler's attempt at mediation had failed, the map was irrevocably drawn: the temple would not only be claimed as a touchstone of orthodoxy by Jerusalem and Shechem, but also in later years and in different ways by such other breakaway groups as Qumran and even—though here I stray beyond my competence and very much into Ernst Bammel's—by the early Christians.[30]

---

30. Cf. B. Gärtner, *The Temple and the Community in Qumran and the New Testament* (SNTSMS 1; Cambridge: Cambridge University Press, 1965).

THE PRESENCE OF GOD IN THE SECOND TEMPLE
AND RABBINIC DOCTRINE

G.I. Davies

One of the central beliefs of First Temple times is agreed to
have been that God was present in a special sense in the
Jerusalem temple, which could therefore be referred to as his
'dwelling place' (מושב, משכן); e.g. Ps. 132.13. When the temple
was rebuilt in the late sixth century, however, it is commonly
held that such beliefs did not continue, and the change is attributed to an increased emphasis on the transcendence of God
or to the removal of a strong belief in God's presence in
Jerusalem to the realm of eschatological hope, or both.[1] Confirmation of the view I have described is often found in a Talmudic passage (b. Yoma 21b) which lists five things that were
missing from the Second Temple which had been in the First:
the ark (with its cover and the cherubim), the fire from
heaven, the Shekinah, the Holy Spirit and the Urim and
Thummim.

In his valuable monograph *God and Temple* R.E. Clements
presented a view of the matter very like this, but his discussion
included some hints that there may be more to be said.[2] He
pointed out that the book of Joel, which is commonly regarded
as post-exilic, appears to re-assert the belief in a divine presence in the temple: 'and you shall know that I [God] am in the
midst of Israel (בקרב ישראל)' (2.27); 'and you shall know that I

---

1. E.g. W.J.T. Phythian-Adams, *The People and the Presence*
(Oxford, 1942), p. 112, citing J.T. Marshall, in *HDB*, IV, 489 (art. Shekinah); G. Henton Davies, *IDB*, III, 875 (art. Presence of God); S.
Terrien, *The Elusive Presence* (New York, 1978), p. 402.
2. R.E. Clements, *God and Temple* (Oxford, 1965), pp. 123-34.

am the Lord your God, who dwells on Zion, my holy hill (שֹׁכֵן
בציון הר קדשׁי)' (4.17).[3]

> It would not be at all surprising if, after the rebuilding of the
> temple, some Jews resurrected the old attitudes and ideas.
> Indeed it would be surprising if it were otherwise, when we
> remember that the psalms of the first temple were still being
> sung, even if in a different context of worship (p. 128).

He envisages a certain mixture of beliefs, which he finds well
reflected in the theology of the books of Chronicles. Of course
there is a difficulty here in that the temple which the Chronicler purports to be describing is the First Temple, and when
we find him enunciating the 'old' doctrine of the presence of
God in the temple, we cannot be completely sure that he would
have applied it to the temple of his own day.

It is in fact not at all easy to discover what Jews of the Second
Temple period believed on this matter, and we must indeed be
careful not to impose an artificial unity of belief on them. Nevertheless there are a number of texts in addition to those in
Joel, from varied dates and backgrounds, which suggest that a
belief in the divine presence in the Second Temple was much
more widespread than is commonly allowed.

The first is *Psalm 135.21*. There seem to be strong reasons,
which most commentators accept, for regarding this as a post-
exilic composition: they relate to aspects of its language, its
anthological style and the organization of the priesthood.[4] In v.
21 God is described as שֹׁכֵן ירושלם, as clear an indication of a
belief in divine presence as one could require.

The second passage comes from the *Temple Scroll*, and I use
it with some hesitation, because its interpretation is not

---

3. Clements noted the view of A.S. Kapelrud that the book of Joel
belongs to the late pre-exilic period. After his monograph was published W. Rudolph argued strongly for this view (*Joel–Amos–Obadja–
Jona* [KAT XIII/2; Gütersloh, 1971], pp. 24-29), but the arguments for a
later date remain strong (see H.W. Wolff, *Joel und Amos* [BK;
Neukirchen, 1969], pp. 2-4 [ET, pp. 4-6]).
4. E.g. H. Gunkel, *Die Psalmen* (HKAT; Göttingen, 1926), p. 575;
A.A. Anderson, *The Book of Psalms* (NCB; London, 1972), p. 889; H.-J.
Kraus, *Psalmen* (BK; 5th edn; Neukirchen, 1978), p. 1074. A pre-exilic
date is preferred by A. Weiser, *Die Psalmen* (ATD; 4th edn; Göttingen,
1955), p. 545 (ET, p. 789), but without convincing arguments.

entirely certain. In col. 29.7-10, at the end of the laws about the festivals, there is a passage in which God gives certain undertakings about the future. These include the words: 'I will dwell (ושכנת[י]) with them for ever and ever, and I will sanctify my sanctuary with my glory, for I will cause my glory to dwell (אשכין) upon it until the blessed day when I shall create my sanctuary to prepare it for myself for all time...'[5] Although it may surprise us in view of what we know of the Qumran community's antipathy to the Jerusalem temple, it does seem that the passage implies an acceptance of the belief in a divine indwelling in the Second Temple.

In both these passages, as well as Joel 4.17, the verb used is שכן. It is sometimes suggested that this verb denotes a less permanent 'dwelling' of God than ישב; if this were true, its use in post-exilic texts might point to a move away from the strong belief in God's presence in the temple that was characteristic of earlier times. A full review of this issue cannot be given here, but the usage of שכן in the Old Testament gives no support to such an interpretation of its theological use.[6] In the Septuagint κατασκηνόω and related words are often used to render it, but this is not as decisive a clue to its meaning as may at first appear. The Septuagint must not be assumed to represent the understanding of the Old Testament among all Jews of the Second Temple period—we know from other instances how much it was affected by factors which were peculiar to Egypt and its Hellenistic milieu. In any case Michaelis has shown that the verb κατασκηνόω itself by no means carries the connotations of temporary, insecure dwelling, as of a nomad in his tent.[7] In all probability the word was chosen as a result of the equation of the divine משכן with the Tent of Meeting in the Priestly account of Exodus 25ff., and we see here a further

---

5. I here follow the interpretation of Y. Yadin, *The Temple Scroll* (Jerusalem, 1983), I, p. 183 (cf. p. 412), and J. Maier, *Die Tempelrolle vom Toten Meer* (Münich, 1978), pp. 39, 89-90 (ET, pp. 32, 86), as opposed to the view of B. Thiering, *JBL* 100 (1981), pp. 60-61, and B.Z. Wacholder, *The Dawn of Qumran. The Sectarian Torah and the Teacher of Righteousness* (Cincinnati, 1983), pp. 21-24, 46-47, who hold that the שכן statements refer to the eschatological temple.

6. Cf. A.R. Hulst, *THAT*, II, pp. 904-909.

7. *TDNT*, VII, pp. 389-91 (ET, pp. 387-89).

case of the powerful influence of the Septuagint Pentateuch on future translation policy and ordinary usage.

Thirdly, *Matthew 23.21* contains the following statement attributed to Jesus: 'He who swears by the temple swears by it and *by him who dwells in it*' (καὶ ὁ ὀμόσας ἐν τῷ ναῷ ὀμνύει ἐν αὐτῷ καὶ ἐν τῷ κατοικοῦντι αὐτόν).[8] This verse, like much of ch. 23, appears only in Matthew's Gospel, and it is not certain whether it represents the thinking of Jesus himself or only that of Matthew and his church. But either way it shows how the old belief could still be appealed to in the first century AD.

Fourthly, Josephus's account of the final stages of the siege of Jerusalem in AD 70 contains a curious episode which clearly presupposes the presence of God in the Temple up to that point (*War* 6.299). Josephus tells how the priests, on entering τὸ ἔνδον ἱερόν at the Feast of Pentecost, heard a loud noise of movement and then a cry in unison: 'We are leaving this place' (μεταβαίνομεν ἐντεῦθεν).[9] The same story is also reported by Tacitus (*Hist.* 5.13), but he combines it with another portent which Josephus dates to the Feast of the Tabernacles in the same year (*War* 6.293-96): *aperire repente delubri fores et audita major humana vox, excedere deos.* It is possible that the story owes something to Ezekiel's vision of the departure of the divine glory from the First Temple (Ezek. 11.22-25); in any case the assumptions behind it are clear.

The final passage also comes from after the destruction of the Second Temple, but it must relate to practices which took place while it still stood: *m. Sukkah 5.4*.[10] It describes a procession towards the east gate of the temple precincts: when it reached the gate,

הפכו פניהם ממזרח למערב ואמרו אבותינו שהיו במקום הזה אחוריהם

אל ההיכל ופניהם קדמה ומשתחוים קדמה לשמש ואנו ליה עינינו . . .

---

8. Many manuscripts read an aorist participle here, but this is presumably due to subsequent Christian insistence that God no longer dwelt in the Jerusalem temple.

9. This passage was drawn to my attention by Dr Bammel, who was in the audience when a first draft of this essay was read to the meeting of the British Association for Jewish Studies in Cambridge in July 1989. οὐκ εἰδὼς καὶ ἑαυτῷ ἐχαρίσατο.

10. H. Danby, *The Mishnah* (Oxford, 1933), p. 180; J. Neusner, *The Mishnah: A New Translation* (New Haven, 1988), p. 289.

The implication seems clear: unlike those described in Ezekiel 8, they turned to face the temple and looked towards the place where God's presence was believed to be. We thus have five passages, in addition to those from Joel noted by Clements, which suggest that a belief in God's presence in the Second Temple may have been held among a wide variety of groups. It seems that this belief may have been not so much the exception as the rule, and that it is the texts and traditions which deny it which really need to be explained. I mentioned at the beginning the passage in *b. Yoma* 21b which includes the Shekinah among the five things that were missing from the Second Temple. It would be unwise to treat this as a clear statement of rabbinic doctrine on this matter. Some very different views are expressed in the admittedly late compilation in *Exod. R.* 2.2 (on 3.1). A series of biblical passages is quoted there to show, first, that God remained in the temple until it was destroyed and then withdrew to heaven—the view of R. Samuel bar Nachman—and, second, that even then he did not leave it, his presence continuing at the Western Wall— the view of R. Eliezer. No distinction seems to be made by these rabbis between the First and Second Temples, and it is reasonable to assume that what they say applies to the latter as well as to the former. The passage in *Yoma* 21b itself has a conclusion which seems to correct the 'doctrine of absence'. It says: 'They were present, but they were not as helpful [as before]'. Moreover, this passage is only one of four that list five things missing from the Second Temple (cf. *Yoma* 52b; *Songs R.* 8.9.3 [on 8.8]; *Num. R.* 15.10 [on 8.2]), and it is the only one to include the Shekinah.[11] It looks, therefore, as though it represents a rather exceptional point of view, whose basis deserves further consideration.[12]

11. Two others include the Holy Spirit, but that is usually understood to refer to the (supposed) cessation of prophecy in Second Temple times; so Abelson (see next note), p. 261.
12. See further J. Abelson, *The Immanence of God in Rabbinical Literature* (London, 1912), pp. 117-21; A.M. Goldberg, *Untersuchungen über die Vorstellung von der Schekinah in der frühen rabbinischen Literatur* (Berlin, 1969), pp. 176-96, 490-93; and for a corrective to another aspect of these passages, E. Bammel, *TLZ* 79 (1954), pp. 351-56.

THE SIBYL AND THE TEMPLE

Andrew Chester

The temple is of central importance in *Sibylline Oracles* 3 and 5, both produced in Egypt, but approximately two-and-a-half centuries apart. The bulk of the material in the former derives from the mid-second century BC, that in the latter from the end of the first or beginning of the second century AD.[1] In this essay I will first outline the relevant material and main themes in each of these two *Sibyllines*, discuss some of the issues, and finally set them briefly in comparison with the theme of the temple in *Sib. 4*, the third of the Jewish *Sibyllines* from within or around the Second Temple period.

---

1. For discussion of the dating, cf. e.g. J. Geffcken, *Komposition und Entstehungszeit der Oracula Sibyllina* (Leipzig: Hinrichs, 1902), pp. 1-30; J.J. Collins, *The Sibylline Oracles of Egyptian Judaism* (SBLDS 13; Missoula: Scholars Press, 1974), pp. 21-34, 73-76; *idem, Between Athens and Jerusalem: Jewish Identity in the Hellenistic Diaspora* (New York: Crossroad, 1983), pp. 61-72; *idem*, 'Sibylline Oracles', in J.H. Charlesworth (ed.), *The Old Testament Pseudepigrapha*. Vol. 1: *Apocalyptic Literature and Testaments* (London: Darton, Longman and Todd, 1983), pp. 354-61, 390-92; *idem*, 'The Development of the Sibylline Tradition', in W. Haase and H. Temporini (eds.), *Aufstieg und Niedergang der römischen Welt*, II.20.1 (Berlin/New York: de Gruyter, 1987), pp. 430-38. On *Sib. 3*, cf. also V. Nikiprowetsky, *La Troisième Sibylle* (Etudes Juives, 9; Paris: Mouton, 1970); V. Nikiprowetsky, 'La Sibylle juive et le "Troisième Livre" des "Pseudo-Oracles Sibyllins" depuis Charles Alexandre', in Haase and Temporini (eds.), *Aufstieg und Niedergang der römischen Welt*, II.20.1, pp. 460-542. Quotations of the Greek text below are from J. Geffcken, *Die Oracula Sibyllina* (GCS 8; Leipzig: Hinrichs, 1902).

1. *Sibylline 3: Outline of Material*

In the main collection of oracles dating from the mid-second century BC, the emphasis on the temple is constant and positive throughout, but especially so in 196-294, 545-656, 657-808 (specifically 213-15, 266-67, 273-84, 302, 564-72, 573-600, 602-18, 624-34, 657-68, 702-31, 772-75, 808). From these passages which speak of the temple (and/or refer to sacrifice and worship), the following main themes can be discerned:

1.1 The temple is described in exalted and glowing terms (e.g. 213; cf. 215-16, 266-67, 302, 565, 657-60). In 573-79, praise of the temple is set at the head of a song of praise in honour of the Jews, while the language used of the temple is in many ways parallel to the description of the Jews that follows, and can be seen as helping define their nature and raison d'être (cf. also 213-15).

1.2 Both temple and sacrifice are portrayed as central to the life and existence of the Jews (702-704), and as exercising a centripetal force upon Diaspora Jews and, in the eschatological age, especially on Gentiles (thus 616-34, 715-20; cf. 564-72) who turn to worship God and sacrifice to him.

1.3 A strong contrast is drawn between temple worship (and sacrifice) and worship of idols (548-72, 573-600, 602-34, 715-20, 772-75; cf. 32, 36ff.).

1.4 The destruction of the temple (in 587 BC) was divine punishment on the Jews for their sin and failure to observe Torah (266, 273-81).

1.5 Observance of Torah will lead to the restoration of the temple (282-94).

1.6 Observance of Torah and temple worship (in contrast to idol-worship) will result in prosperity (573-81, 586-87, 602-18).

1.7 The temple belongs centrally to the vision and prophecy of a golden eschatological age (616-23, 657-68, 702-31, 772-75).

2. *Sibylline 5: Outline of Material*

In *Sib.* 5, the emphasis on the temple, although striking, is less pervasive, and is concentrated primarily towards the end of the work (150-54; cf. 106-10, 247-52, 266-68, 351-60, 396-413, 414-33, 492-511). The main themes in these sections are:

2.1 The temple is spoken of in exalted and reverential terms (150, 397-402, 422-27, 433), often in parallel to what is said of the Jews (cf. 249, 263, 328, 381, 413).

2.2 Jerusalem and the temple are central for the Jews, and (implicitly, at least, of the temple) are set centrally within the whole earth (247-52, 266-68, 400-42, 422-27).

2.3 There is a strong contrast drawn between true temple-worship, practised by the Jews, and idol-worship, practised by the Gentiles (396-413, 351-60; cf. 267).

2.4 The destruction of the temple in AD 70 brings about the intervention of God, either directly or through the agency of a messianic figure, on behalf of the Jews, bringing divine judgment on Rome (or Nero) as responsible for the destruction (150-78; cf. 106-10, 397-433 [cf. 361-96], 434-83).

2.5 The temple and cult will be centrally important in the idyllic final age when there will be a new glorious temple, of cosmic proportions, to be built by a messianic figure (266-81, 420-33; cf. 247-52).

3. *The Temple in Sib. 3 and 5: Themes in Common and Distinctive Developments*

There is thus considerable agreement between *Sib.* 3 and 5 in the emphasis they give to the temple. The temple is portrayed in highly eulogistic terms in both; it is seen as central to the Jews and their way of life, and as integral to the vision of the idyllic eschatological age. The destruction of the temple is seen as a supreme tragedy which will bring divine judgment on its perpetrators,[2] and both also draw a strong contrast between

2. There is, however, the obvious difference that *Sib.* 3 attributes the tragedy at least partly to Israel's sin, whereas *Sib.* 5 does not. This difference is itself bound up with the fact that *Sib.* 5 is written in the wake of the catastrophe of AD 70, and the despair of the Jewish people,

true worship of God and idolatry. Some of this does of course belong to the common stock of Second Temple Jewish eschatology, as with the polemic against idolatry[3] and the importance of the temple in the final age.[4] It thus comes as no surprise that Collins[5] can speak of *Sib.* 3 as representing 'conservative eschatology', or that Sanders[6] should see *Sib.* 3 and 5 as important witnesses of restoration eschatology, looking for the renewal of the temple, in central place, in the final age. *Sib.* 3 especially looks back to this important biblical theme, and forward to its final realization.

At the same time, along with these similarities, *Sib.* 3 and 5 are also distinctive, both in relation to other Jewish texts and in relation to each other. The former is the case, in one sense at least, according to Collins's argument; while he sees *Sib.* 3 as conservative temple theology and finds parallels for it earlier (and later) elsewhere, he nevertheless argues that it is in fact atypical of Egyptian Judaism.[7] He asserts that the temple has little prominence in the literature of Egyptian Judaism otherwise. Certainly he concedes that both the *Letter of Aristeas* and Philo speak in positive terms of the temple, but he argues that nevertheless in the *Letter of Aristeas* the description of the temple is stylized and anachronistic, while in Philo the temple is allegorized and cultic worship is neither really important nor at all central for him. In the other texts available to us (apart from the *Letter of Aristeas* and Philo) there is a notable silence, or at least something very close to this, concerning the temple. The emphasis on the temple in *Sib.* 3 he sees as an attempt to link old-established biblical traditions

---

whereas *Sib.* 3, in the mid-second century BC, reflects from a distance of centuries on the disaster of 587, although its reflection may be coloured by the more recent attack on the temple by Antiochus Epiphanes in 167; cf. below.

3. Thus e.g. *1 Enoch* 99.6ff.; Ps.-Philo, *LAB* 25.7-13; 44; *Jos. Asen.* 9–12; 21.13; *Apoc. Abr.* 1ff.; *2 Bar.* 62.3; cf. also Rom. 1.25.

4. Thus e.g. *1 Enoch* 91.13; *Jub.* 1.27ff.; 4QFlor 1; *2 Bar.* 32.4; cf. G. Klinzing, *Die Umdeutung des Kultus in der Qumrangemeinde und im Neuen Testament* (SUNT 7; Göttingen: Vandenhoeck & Ruprecht, 1971), p. 84.

5. Collins, *Sibylline Oracles of Egyptian Judaism*, pp. 44-55.

6. E.P. Sanders, *Jesus and Judaism* (London: SCM, 1985), pp. 85-88.

7. Collins, *Sibylline Oracles of Egyptian Judaism*, pp. 48-49.

about the central role and eschatological significance of the Jerusalem temple with native Egyptian emphasis on the importance of temple cults for political fortunes.[8] He understands this, especially the restorative Jewish element, as belonging to the conservative Jewish priestly line in Egypt, continued in the succession of Onias IV and the priests of the temple at Leontopolis. It is by no means a contradiction, Collins claims, that those in charge at Leontopolis should express such strong support for the Jerusalem temple and its ultimate significance, since Leontopolis made no exclusive claims for itself and may not have been completely rejected by the Jerusalem authorities.[9]

In fact Collins's argument for the distinctive character of *Sib.* 3 here is not fully convincing. It is doubtful whether he does full justice to the *Letter of Aristeas* and to Philo. The description in the *Letter of Aristeas* of the Temple, its setting, design, decoration, officials and cultic practice, represents a considerable proportion of the whole work (40-43, 51-107), and is lavish and extravagant in its praise. It is certainly the case that the temple is proportionately much less prominent and central in Philo's writings, but it is given an extraordinarily positive description, and pilgrimage to the Jerusalem temple is an important theme for Philo. Indeed, the vision of the eschatological pilgrimage of the renewed remnant to Jerusalem and the temple (*De Praemiis et Poenis* 165-68) is strikingly similar to what we find in *Sib.* 3 (and 5). It is difficult to avoid the impression, then, that there is a temple ideology represented in at least some strands of Judaism in Alexandria, which gives a very real (not merely stereotyped) and elevated position to the Jerusalem temple, and that *Sib.* 3 (and 5) has its setting properly within this context.

Further, Collins admits that there is no real positive evidence for a connection between *Sib.* 3 and Onias;[10] the lack of any explicit mention of the Leontopolis temple is on this view at least a little surprising, and Collins's argument depends on

8. Collins, *Sibylline Oracles of Egyptian Judaism*, pp. 47, 50ff.
9. Collins, *Sibylline Oracles of Egyptian Judaism*, pp. 51-52.
10. Collins, *Sibylline Oracles of Egyptian Judaism*, pp. 52-53.

a number of hypothetical datings.[11] Again, one main plank of
his argument is the view that *Sib.* 3 expects an Egyptian
saviour-king;[12] but this reading of 3.652-55 is open to criticism
and alternative interpretation.[13] If, however, Collins is not
fully convincing here, then his 'solid historical foundation' for
the combination of king and temple is much less secure; and in
fact king (messiah) and temple are not in any case (*pace*
Collins) brought into relation with each other in *Sib.* 3, as distinct from *Sib.* 5. Further, to see the lack of a real parallel in
any other Egyptian Jewish work to the emphasis on the temple in *Sib.* 3 as pointing to an Oniad/Leontopolis connection is
an argument from silence, which begs the question of how
representative is the extant literary evidence from Egyptian
Judaism. In fact Collins might have cited *Sib.* 5 in favour of his
view, since this work, although post-70, still has a central
emphasis on the temple, and at 492-510 suggests a strong and

---

11. Collins, *Sibylline Oracles of Egyptian Judaism*, p. 53.
12. This is the second of four factors adduced by Collins, *Sibylline
Oracles of Egyptian Judaism*, pp. 52-53 (cf. pp. 40-44); I discuss the
other three in the rest of this paragraph.
13. Cf. H. Schwier, *Tempel und Tempelzerstörung: Untersuchungen
zu den theologischen und ideologischen Faktoren im ersten jüdisch-
römischen Krieg (66–74 n. Chr.)* (NTOA 11; Freiburg/Göttingen: Uni-
versitätsverlag/Vandenhoeck & Ruprecht, 1989), pp. 236, 242-43;
Nikiprowetsky, *La Troisième Sibylle*, pp. 133-37, 323; H. Kippenberg,
' "Dann wird der Orient herrschen und der Okzident dienen." Zur
Begründung eines gesamtvorderasiatischen Standpunktes im Kampf
gegen Rom', in N.W. Bolz and W. Hübener (eds.), *Spiegel und Gleichnis* (Festschrift für J. Taubes; Würzburg: Königshauser & Neumann,
1983), pp. 40-48 (esp. p. 43). Collins bases his interpretation on the parallel phrase in the Egyptian Potter's Oracle, presumably taking over
the argument of J. Bidez and F. Cumont, *Les Mages hellénisés, Zoro-
astre, Ostanès et Hystaspes d'après la tradition grecque* (2 vols.; Paris:
Société d'Editions, 'Les Belles Lettres', 1938), vol. 2, p. 372 n. 3,
although he does not refer to this. Schwier criticizes Collins especially
for his failure to discuss the usage of Phlegon, *Mir.* 3.7, although it
should be noted that this phrase contains the word ἀνατολαί 'ris-
ing(s)', which is precisely what Collins sees as differentiating those
passages that clearly refer to 'the East' from that which is found here
in *Sib.* 3 and in the Potter's Oracle. Nevertheless, Collins has to place a
lot of weight on a single text. I provide a fuller survey of the issues
involved here in my essay 'Jewish Messianic Hope, Mediatorial Concepts and Pauline Christology', in M. Hengel (ed.), *Paulus als Mis-
sionar und Theologe* (Tübingen: J.C.B. Mohr [Paul Siebeck], 1990).

positive connection with Leontopolis, although again this is not
certain. Even so, Collins's remaining argument, that the
Oniad/Leontopolis connection provides a specific setting for the
archaic eschatology of *Sib.* 3, is again of dubious probative
value. There could well have been other groups or circles in
second-century Egyptian Judaism that were equally or even
more conservative in their view of the temple and cult, and
their hopes for the future; Collins himself mentions the
instance of Ben Sira.[14] Nor does the view of *Sib.* 3 as representing a positive rapprochement with the Egyptian fostering of
native temple cults look so convincing in light of the attacks on
idolatry we find in *Sib.* 3, which could plausibly be seen as
attacks on the Egyptian position.

All this is not to suggest that Collins's argument is untenable,
but rather to enter qualifications and reservations about it. A
brief consideration of one indisputable feature of *Sib.* 3, its use
of themes from Isaiah 40–66, may help indicate something of
the difficulty involved in assessing the main thrust of at least
some parts of this Sibylline. Thus it clearly takes up from
Deutero-Isaiah the theme of polemic against idol-worship,
with obvious negative implications. But it also takes up themes
that are potentially more positive, concerning both Jews and
also Gentiles. Gaston[15] asserts that Deutero-Isaiah has no
place for a Hebrew messiah or a new temple, and hence in the
post-exilic writings the Zion tradition and not that of the messiah or temple is developed. Yet while *Sib.* 3 clearly does, as

14. Collins, *Sibylline Oracles of Egyptian Judaism*, p. 46; he in fact
appears to see Ben Sira as a precursor of, or closely related to, the
Oniad/Leontopolis position, but this can only be surmise, and the possibility of different groups in Egyptian Judaism, having some similar
ideological features, should not be discounted too readily. For discussion of distinctive aspects of Ben Sira, cf. e.g. M. Hengel, *Judaism and
Hellenism: Studies in their Encounter in Palestine during the Early
Hellenistic Period* (ET; London: SCM, 1974), pp. 131-53; H. Stadel-
mann, *Ben Sira als Schriftgelehrter: Eine Untersuchung zum Berufs-
bild des vormakkabäischen Sofer unter Berücksichtigung seines Ver-
hältnisses zu Priester-, Propheten-, und Weisheitslehrertum* (WUNT
2.6; Tübingen: Mohr, 1980).
15. L. Gaston, *No Stone on Another: Studies in the Significance of the
Fall of Jerusalem in the Synoptic Gospels* (SNT 23; Leiden: Brill, 1970),
pp. 105-106.

Gaston claims, use this Zion tradition (e.g. 772ff.), the dichotomy he draws between Zion and temple is untenable (even for Isa. 40–66; cf. 60.14!). Thus while Gaston[16] argues strongly against the common tendency to fail to distinguish between Jerusalem and temple, and instead simply to treat them as virtually synonymous, McKelvey[17] and Sanders[18] rightly argue otherwise; and this is still more the case for a link between *Zion* and temple. Thus *Sib.* 3, as we have seen, makes Zion/Jerusalem and temple central for the Jews and (especially drawing on Isa. 40–66 here) centripetal in effect, drawing the Gentiles towards it in the final age. As well as the temple it also takes up the theme from Deutero-Isaiah of the prophecy relating to (Cyrus as) the messiah; again, this probably points to a more inclusive and positive attitude to non-Jewish Egypt; it allows, apparently, for leadership and help for the Jews by a non-Jew, although only (as in Deutero-Isaiah) as an instrument of the God of the Jews. But since *Sib.* 3 does not passively collect traditions, but actively takes them over and modifies them for its own purpose, this does not itself settle the question of whether the messianic figure in *Sib.* 3 is Jewish or not, still less whether he necessarily comes from Egypt, although that remains a possibility.

It should also be said that if Collins is in any sense right in seeing the 'temple ideology' of *Sib.* 3 as syncretistic,[19] that is, combining the old biblical tradition with contemporary Egyptian veneration of temple cults for the political fortune they bring, then the ideology of *Sib.* 3 is clearly deliberately and self-consciously political in orientation. It is indeed difficult to see how *Sib.* 3 could not be viewed as politically oriented, in a more general sense. This, I wish to argue, is the case with *Sib.* 5 as well; but it must be stressed that these two Sibyllines show important differences as well as similarities in this respect.

These differences between the two works, and hence the distinctive aspects of both, merit further consideration. *Sib.* 3, as we have seen, in the setting of Egypt in the mid-second

16. Gaston, *No Stone*, p. 111.
17. R.J. McKelvey, *The New Temple: The Church in the New Testament* (Oxford: Oxford University Press, 1969), p. 11.
18. Sanders, *Jesus*, pp. 78ff.
19. Collins, *Sibylline Oracles of Egyptian Judaism*, pp. 46-47.

century BC, reaffirms in the strongest possible terms the importance and glorious nature of the temple, and its central place in the life of the Jews. It looks back to the destruction of the temple in 587 as a disaster; it lays the blame on Babylon, but also places the fault firmly on the side of the Jews and their failure to observe Torah (and, as we have again seen, observance of Torah leads to the restoration of the temple). Possibly *Sib.* 3 also makes allusion to the despoliation of the temple by Antiochus Epiphanes in 167, and the subsequent Maccabaean deliverance and restoration.[20] But in any case, *Sib.* 3 does not simply stop at reflection on and interpretation of a historical event. It looks also to the final age, in parallel to but going far beyond the restoration after the exile, and portrays the temple in full and more glorious form.

The question of whether or not this temple of the final age is to be characterized as 'new' has been answered in quite different ways.[21] It is difficult to dissent from Sanders's general view, that, even if the texts are not explicit on this point, to speak of God creating a temple, or of a very different, glorious temple, in the final age, necessarily implies the replacing of the old temple with a new one. For Collins, however, the eschatological temple in *Sib.* 3 is in no sense new; it is the historical temple in the earthly Jerusalem in the final age, not the heavenly temple of apocalyptic writings. Thus it belongs to history as one continuum, and excludes the apocalyptic idea of two distinct ages. This whole argument is dubious, not least in relation to the so-called apocalyptic theory of two ages;[22] there is no contradiction involved in positing a new temple on earth in the future, in continuity with the present order but at the same time representing God's eschatological transformation

20. So J. Nolland, '*Sib. Or.* iii.265-94, an Early Maccabaean Messianic Oracle', *JTS* ns 30 (1979), pp. 158-66; against this, see Collins, 'Sibylline Oracles', in Charlesworth, *OTP*, I, p. 355. If, however, Collins's argument concerning the identity of the messianic figure in *Sib.* 3 as an Egyptian king is not found convincing, his argument here will also have less cogency. Cf. further W. Horbury, 'Herod's Temple and Herod's Days', n. 12,4 in this volume.
21. Contrast e.g. Collins, *Sibylline Oracles of Egyptian Judaism*, p. 45, with Sanders, *Jesus*, pp. 85ff.
22. Cf. e.g. C. Rowland, *The Open Heaven: A Study of Apocalyptic in Judaism and Early Christianity* (London: SPCK, 1982), pp. 23-48.

of it. But it may well be that this was much less of an issue for
the writer of *Sib.* 3 than it is for modern scholarship, and that it
could speak of this great temple of the final age without considering whether this involved the destruction of the old and
the creation of a new.

In any case, the portrayal of a glorious eschatological temple
clearly reflects, *inter alia*, something of the yearning for the
fulfilment of the lavish descriptions of Deutero-Isaiah and
Ezekiel and disappointment and sense of anti-climax about
the form of the Second Temple that is reflected elsewhere in
Jewish texts.[23] It also makes clear that this new glorious temple will provoke a further attack by foreign oppressors and
divine judgment upon them, but also that Gentiles will flock to
the temple to worship God. These themes are not in fact con-
tradictory here, since *Sib.* 3 clearly expects repentance on the
part of the Jews and conversion and turning from idols on the
part of the Gentiles. Thus *Sib.* 3 calls for both fellow-Jews and
compatriot Egyptian Gentiles to turn to the God of the Jews
represented above all in the Jerusalem temple and cult. It is
thus fundamentally open in its attitude and positive in its
emphasis on God, the temple and the eschatological rewards; it
cannot be seen as exclusive or narrowly nationalistic, but it
nevertheless demands, especially of the Gentiles, a turning to
Judaism and the temple. Thus all truth ultimately resides in
Judaism and the temple; the final golden age, portrayed as
fulfilling the scriptural prophecies concerning this (767-95,
alluding to e.g. Isa. 11), will include only those who accept this.
Further, *Sib.* 3 draws very sharply the boundaries between
Judaism, the temple and Jewish sacred space, worship and
recognition of the one true God, on the one hand, and idolatry,
evil and immoral behaviour, on the other hand. It is, then, a
double-edged work, both in its emphasis on the temple and in a
wider sense.

In *Sib.* 5, by contrast, despite agreements on the positive
assessment of the temple, the attitude to non-Jews is almost

---

23. Cf. e.g. Ezra 3.12; Tob. 14.5; Jos. *Ant.* 11.80-81; cf. Gaston, *No
Stone*, p. 109; McKelvey, *New Temple*, pp. 11ff.; for positive statements
on the divine presence in the Second Temple, see the article by G.I.
Davies, above.

entirely negative. This is clear already in the condemnation of idolatry, but the most savage condemnation is reserved for the Romans (11-51, 93-110, 137-54, 162-78, 214-37, 386-433), especially for destroying the temple, and above all for Nero, who anachronistically is blamed and held personally responsible for the whole disaster. But other foreign nations (111-36, 200-13, 286-327, 333-60, 434-46, 447-83), and especially the Egyptians (52-92, 179-99 [cf. 484-511]; although 'foreign' in a circumscribed sense in this context) are condemned as oppressors. The golden eschatological age is portrayed in extravagant terms, with the temple central to it, but as far as non-Jews are concerned, the main emphasis falls on the final judgment on them; only 482-83 gives a brief glimpse of something more positive in general terms, and 484-504 specifically of the Egyptians, and the prophecy of their turning from idolatry to worship of the one true God. Even this, however, is allowed only limited scope. On the other hand, nothing is said of the failure of the Jews to observe Torah, or in any other respect, as responsible for the destruction of Jerusalem or the temple; instead it is the Romans and Nero (and more widely the Egyptians and other nations) who stand condemned for their oppression and idolatry. Nor is anything said of repentance or observance of Torah as preconditions for the restoration of the temple and the golden age to come. Instead it is a matter of the direct intervention of God, by means of a heavenly messianic figure who rebuilds the city and temple with cosmic dimensions.[24]

3.1 *Sib. 5: The Temple Built by the Messiah*

Sib. 5.414-33, then, with its theme of the messiah building the temple, sets *Sib.* 5 in further and more positive contrast with *Sib.* 3:

ἦλθε γὰρ οὐρανίων νώτων ἀνὴρ μακαρίτης
σκῆπτρον ἔχων ἐν χερσίν, ὅ οἱ θεὸς ἐγγυάλιξεν,
καὶ πάντων ἐκράτησε καλῶς πᾶσίν τ' ἀπέδωκεν
τοῖς ἀγαθοῖς τὸν πλοῦτον, ὃν οἱ πρότεροι λάβον ἄνδρες.
πᾶσαν δ' ἐκ βάθρων εἷλεν πόλιν ἐν πυρὶ πολλῷ

---

24. This point has to be made against Gaston, *No Stone*, p. 106.

καὶ δήμους ἔφλεξε βροτῶν τῶν πρόσθε κακούργων
καὶ πόλιν, ἣν ἐπόθησε θεός, ταύτην ἐποίησεν
φαιδροτέραν ἄστρων τε καὶ ἡλίου ἠδὲ σελήνης
καὶ κόσμον κατέθηχ' ἅγιόν τ' [οἶκον] ἐποίησεν
ἔνσαρκον καλὸν περικαλλέα ἠδὲ ἔπλασσεν
πολλοῖς ἐν σταδίοισι μέγαν καὶ ἀπείρονα πύργον
αὐτῶν ἁπτόμενον νεφέων καὶ πᾶσιν ὁρατόν,
ὥστε βλέπειν πάντας πιστοὺς πάντας τε δικαίους
ἀιδίοιο θεοῦ δόξαν, πεποθημένον εἶδος·
ἀντολίαι δύσιές τε θεοῦ κλέος ἐξύμνησαν.
οὐκέτι γὰρ πέλεται δειλοῖσι βροτοῖσιν δεινά
οὐδὲ γαμοκλοπίαι καὶ παίδων Κύπρις ἄθεσμος,
οὐ φόνος οὐδὲ κυδοιμός, ἔρις δ' ἐν πᾶσι δικαίη.
ὕστατος ἔσθ' ἁγίων καιρός, ὅτε ταῦτα περαίνει
θεὸς ὑψιβρεμέτης, κτίστης ναοῖο μεγίστου.

For there came from the expanses of heaven a blessed man
having a sceptre in his hands which God had delivered to him,
and he gained control over all things well, and gave back,
to all the good, the wealth which men had formerly taken.
He removed every city from its foundation with a great fire
and burned nations of mortals who had formerly done evil.
And the city which God desired, this he made
more brilliant than stars and sun and moon,
and he adorned it and made a holy temple,
splendidly beautiful in its form, and he fashioned
a great and enormous tower over many stadia
touching the clouds and visible to all,
so that all faithful and all righteous people should see
the glory of eternal God, a form desired.
East and West sang out God's renown.
For terrible things no longer befall frail mortals,
no adulteries or illicit lust for boys,
no murder, or noise of battle, but fair striving among all.
It is the last time of holy people when God, who thunders on
     high,
founder of the greatest temple, brings these things about.

The concept of the messiah building a new temple is found
only rarely in Jewish texts. Indeed, it is not completely certain
for *Sib.* 5 itself. First, what is mentioned here is not specifically
a 'messiah', but simply 'a blessed man… from the expanses of
heaven'. Such questions of definition concerning 'messianic'

figures certainly need to be raised;[25] they should not simply be brushed aside or allowed to go by default. In this case, however, while the term 'messiah' is certainly not used in the whole of *Sib.* 5 (or *Sib.* 3 either), it is clear that this heavenly figure is sent on a mission from heaven, with divine authority, to bring judgment on the enemies of the Jews and deliverance for the Jews themselves, in the eschatological age; and it is more helpful if the use of the term 'messiah' can be elastic enough to include such an agent of God's final deliverance, than if it is used more narrowly and restricted to cases where the specific term משיח (or equivalent) is found.[26] The case for seeing the 'blessed man' here as 'messianic' is further strengthened not only by noting the allusion to Dan 7.13,[27] but also by recognizing that, for the writer, this figure is fundamentally the same as the one 'exceptional man from the sky' (256), in another 'messianic' passage (256-59); and, indeed, by associating this figure also with the 'certain king sent from God' (108), again bringing divine judgment against Nero/the Romans in the further 'messianic' passage at 106-109, as also with the 'great star (which) will come from heaven to the wondrous sea' (158), again to bring divine judgment and destruction on Rome/Babylon for their treatment of the Jews in the 'mes-

---

25. Cf. e.g. J.H. Charlesworth, 'The Concept of the Messiah in the Pseudepigrapha', in Haase and Temporini (eds.), *Aufstieg und Niedergang der römischen Welt*, II.19.1, pp. 188-210; *idem*, 'From Jewish Messianology to Christian Christology', in J. Neusner, W.S. Green and E. Frerichs (eds.), *Judaisms and their Messiahs at the Turn of the Christian Era* (Cambridge: Cambridge University Press, 1987), pp. 225-64 (esp. pp. 226-30); J.J. Collins, 'Messianism in the Maccabean Period', in Neusner *et al.*, *Judaisms*, pp. 97-109 (esp. pp. 97-98).

26. The case for the narrower definition (limited, that is, to instances where the specific term 'messiah' is found) is well argued by Charlesworth, 'The Concept of the Messiah', and 'From Messianology to Christology', and the case for a somewhat wider sphere of reference for 'messiah' and 'messianic' by Collins, 'Messianism'. But there are larger and more complex issues involved here; I discuss these a little more fully in my forthcoming essay, 'Jewish Messianic Hope' (cf. n. 13, above).

27. Cf. W. Horbury, 'The Messianic Associations of "the Son of Man"', *JTS* ns 36 (1985), pp. 34-55 (esp. pp. 44-45, 48).

sianic' passage in 155-61.[28] In these latter two passages, the use of 'king' and 'star', in view of their prominent use as messianic designations in the Second Temple period, would obviously help point the interpretation of the 'heavenly man' figure of 256 and 414 in a specifically messianic direction.

Secondly, however, Gaston claims that in 414-33 it is not the messiah but God himself who builds the temple, since the 'blessed man' of 414 is specifically identified as God in 432-33.[29] Certainly in 420-27 there is potential ambiguity, since the verb 'he made' (420) could potentially refer to either God or the 'blessed man', as could the immediately following verbs, while 432-33 unequivocally attributes the preceding activity to God. Yet in view of the usage at the start of the passage, especially 'he gained sway' (416) and 'he destroyed' (418) referring to the 'blessed man', the only natural way to read 420-27 is to take it to refer to this figure introduced at 414, not to God; it is straining the sense of the passage too much to do otherwise. Nor is 432-33 any real objection, since it is obvious that the 'blessed man' is an agent of God's will and derives his power directly from God ('a sceptre in his hands which God gave him', 415), and to speak of God as accomplishing these things in no sense contradicts the portrayal of this heavenly figure as the one who performs all these tasks on earth.

Sib. 5, then, if it is correctly understood as portraying a messianic figure building a new temple, is exceptional in the context of Second Temple Judaism and related literature. It is easily possible to find evidence for God himself bringing about a new or restored temple in the eschatological age.[30] Nor do these expectations arise *de novo* in the second century BC (and in any case *1 Enoch* 89–90 probably goes back earlier than

---

28. Cf. the discussion in my forthcoming essay 'The Parting of the Ways: Eschatology and Messianic Hope', in J.D.G. Dunn (ed.), *Earliest Christianity and Judaism: The Parting of the Ways (A.D. 70–135)* (Tübingen: Mohr, forthcoming), and the further references there.
29. Gaston, *No Stone*, p. 148.
30. This theme is found in a number of texts in the pre-70 period, e.g. Tob. 14.5-6; *1 Enoch* 90.28-29; *Jub.* 1.15-17; *Ps. Sol.* 17.21-34; 11QT 29.8-10, and also in the post-70 period, e.g. *2 Bar.* 32.4; 68.5 (while it is also the case that Rev. 21.22 clearly needs to counter this expectation). Cf. McKelvey, *New Temple*, pp. 15-20, 28-34; Sanders, *Jesus*, pp. 76-90; Klinzing, *Umdeutung*, pp. 84-85.

this); they have a clear basis in biblical traditions, for example Ezekiel 40–43.[31] What is especially striking, however, is the fact that the biblical texts that speak most clearly of a (re)building of the temple, and that could be interpreted as an eschatological restoration, are those which attribute this not directly to God but to a figure which in each case lends itself to being interpreted messianically.

This is the case in 2 Sam. 7.13, where at the heart of Nathan's oracle to David it is said, 'He (David) will build a house for my name, and I will establish the throne of his kingdom for ever', and Zech. 6.12-13, 'Thus says the Lord of Hosts, Behold the man whose name is the Branch, and he shall grow up out of his place, and he shall build the temple of the Lord; even he shall build the temple of the Lord...' Both figures, 'the Branch' and David or the Davidic king, are of course interpreted messianically in the Second Temple period; in addition to these prophecies, there are are also those relating to Cyrus (designated 'his anointed', משיחו, Isa. 45.1) in Deutero-Isaiah, that he will build the temple (45.1; cf. 45.13). Hence, it would appear that the messiah and (the building of) the temple should be connected.[32] The really surprising feature of Second Temple literature is that this hardly happens at all. Indeed, in one Qumran text, 4QFlorilegium, a clear opportunity to interpret 2 Sam. 7.13 of the messiah building the temple is passed over, apparently deliberately. In the exposition of Nathan's oracle, 4QFlor 1 simply omits v. 13a; instead it concentrates on the promise of v. 11, 'Moreover the LORD tells you that the LORD will build you a house', most probably making it refer to the community itself, as well as to an actual temple of the final age. In the various discussions of this passage it has sometimes been claimed that the reference is *either* to the community *or* to a new, physical temple;[33] but at Qumran otherwise, and

31. Cf. Isa. 60.10-14; cf. McKelvey, *New Temple*, pp. 9-15; Sanders, *Jesus*, pp. 78ff.
32. Gaston, *No Stone*, p. 147.
33. For a representative sample of approaches to this text in 4QFlor, cf. e.g. Gaston, *No Stone*, pp. 163-68; McKelvey, *New Temple*, pp. 51-52; Klinzing, *Umdeutung*, pp. 80-87; Sanders, *Jesus*, p. 84; Y. Yadin, 'Le Rouleau du Temple', in M. Delcor (ed.), *Qumran: sa piété, sa théologie et son milieu* (BETL 46; Paris/Leuven: Duculot/Leuven University

52   *Templum Amicitiae*

plausibly at 4QFlor, the two belong integrally together. The publication of the Temple Scroll (subsequent to some of this debate), even if the work was not composed at Qumran, allows us to grasp the importance for the community of the expectation of a new and different temple in the eschatological age.

The theme of the messiah building the temple is certainly clear in some later Jewish texts: thus especially *Tg. Zech.* 6.12 ('And you shall say to him, "Thus says the Lord of hosts, 'This man, his name is Messiah. He will be revealed and will be exalted, and he will build the temple of the Lord'" '), *Tg. Isa.* 53.5 ('He [the messiah] will build the temple, which was profaned because of our transgressions and delivered up because of our sins'), and *Vay. R.* 9.6 (and parallels, as one interpretation of Song of Songs 4.1: 'The king Messiah whose place is in the north will come, and will build the house of the sanctuary which is situated in the south...'). The potential importance of these texts should not be brushed aside, as is done for example by Gaston;[34] it is not adequate to say of *Tg. Zech.* that it differs very little from MT. In fact, it specifically identifies the Branch as the 'Messiah', and interprets the verb 'shoot' (צמח) in a twofold way, both by יתגלי 'be revealed', itself a technical and (especially in the Targumim) specialized term for the appearance of the messiah[35] and also by יתרבי 'be exalted'. Thus the Targumist, in a short space certainly, makes the messianic interpretation of the verse plain, and it is hard to see how this sense could be missed. It is also the case that reference to the

Press, 1978), pp. 115-19; D.R. Schwartz, 'The Three Temples of 4Q Florilegium', *RQ* 10 (1979-81), pp. 83-91; and especially D. Juel, *Messiah and Temple: The Trial of Jesus in the Gospel of Mark* (SBLDS 31; Missoula: Scholars Press, 1977), pp. 172-79; G.J. Brooke, *Exegesis at Qumran: 4Q Florilegium in its Jewish Context* (JSOTS 29; Sheffield: JSOT Press), pp. 129-44, 178-93.

34. Gaston, *No Stone*, p. 149.

35. Cf. e.g. M.J. McNamara, *The New Testament and the Palestinian Targum to the Pentateuch* (Analecta Biblica, 27; Rome: Pontifical Biblical Institute, 2nd edn, 1978), p. 249; A. Chester, *Divine Revelation and Divine Titles in the Pentateuchal Targumim* (TSAJ 14; Tübingen: Mohr, 1986), pp. 184-85, 213-19; Juel, *Messiah*, pp. 186-87; cf. further E. Sjöberg, *Der Menschensohn im äthiopischen Henochbuch* (Lund: Gleerup, 1946), pp. 102-15; *idem, Der verborgene Menschensohn in den Evangelien* (Lund: Gleerup, 1955), pp. 54ff.

building of the temple, in the changed situation after the fall of the Second Temple, clearly takes on new meaning. The same holds for *Vay. R.* 9.6; in the situation after AD 70 , it cannot be the case that it simply refers to the building of the temple in the sixth century BC. And the dismissal, by Gaston and others,[36] of the crucial phrase in *Tg. Isa.* 53.5 והוא יבני בית מקדשא ('and he shall build the temple') as a gloss from Zech. 6.13 is untenable; what we have is a striking interpretation introduced into the text as an integral part of the rendering as a whole.[37] Nevertheless, it is difficult to date these texts or the tradition underlying them. It is tempting to look for a setting in the pre-135 AD period,[38] where the hopes they embody were clearly alive and their expression apparently less dangerous (or discredited) than later. But it is not possible to prove that they are that early at all, as is properly recognized by Juel[39] in his careful discussion of the texts.

There is, of course, one further text (or set of texts) from the pre-70 period which may speak of the messiah rebuilding the temple; that is, the accusation recorded in Mk 14.58 (and the parallel in Mt. 26.61; cf. Mk 15.29; Mt. 27.40; Jn 2.19; Acts 6.14) that Jesus predicted that he would destroy the temple and rebuild it in three days (the prediction of destruction of the temple attributed to Jesus in Mk 13.2; cf. Mt. 24.2; Lk. 21.6; 19.44). Not surprisingly, these texts have been discussed much more intensively than any of the others I have touched on,[40] and it is impossible to go into the whole debate here. Amongst the issues raised are whether the prophecy derives, authentically, from Jesus, and if so, whether it is simply the prophecy of destruction (which certainly seems implausible as an invention of the early church), or whether it includes that of

36. Gaston, *No Stone*, p. 149; G. Dalman, *Aramäische Dialektproben* (Leipzig: Hinrichs, 1896), p. 10; H. Hegermann, *Jesaja 53 in Hexapla, Targum und Peschitta* (Gütersloh: Bertelsmann, 1954), p. 79.
37. Cf. Juel, *Messiah*, pp. 182-83, 187-88.
38. Cf. P. Churgin, *Targum Jonathan to the Prophets* (Yale Oriental Series, 14; New Haven: Yale University Press, 1927), p. 25.
39. Juel, *Messiah*, pp. 191-96.
40. Cf. e.g. McKelvey, *New Temple*, pp. 58-74; Gaston, *No Stone*; Juel, *Messiah*, pp. 117-215; D. Lührmann, 'Markus 14,55-64, Christologie und Zerstörung des Tempels im Markusevangelium', *NTS* 27 (1981), pp. 457-74; Sanders, *Jesus*, pp. 71-76.

rebuilding also (which might be seen as a later elaboration, designed, for example, to point to Jesus' resurrection; cf. Jn 2.21-22), whether it is intended to reveal a specifically messianic self-consciousness on the part of Jesus, and whether the temple to be rebuilt is a physical temple or, for example, the community or church. I find it most plausible to see the prediction of destruction (of the Jerusalem temple) as going back to Jesus; the case of the rebuilding is less clear, and the extent to which it is 'messianic' in intent is of course caught up in the whole question under discussion here. But there are good grounds for seeing it as such. Thus Sanders, using stringent criteria of authenticity, argues for seeing the rebuilding saying as probably authentic.[41]

If so, then both *Sib.* 5.414-33 and Mk 14.58 come from within a fairly short time of each other, and represent a claim that a messianic figure will rebuild the temple. Otherwise, however, they stand far apart, above all on the question of the claim to destroy the temple. There would clearly be no point looking for a prediction of the destruction of the temple in *Sib.* 5, in the post-70 period, and the implications of this changed context must be taken into account when assessing the significance of the lack of parallels to Jesus' claim (or alleged claim) to do this.[42] Nevertheless, the question obviously arises whether a claim to destroy the temple could be understood in any sense as messianic, or even at all compatible with the role of the messiah, in the pre-70 period. Certainly, as I have noted already, there are clear indications not simply of disappointment with the actual form of the Second Temple, but also of deep dissatisfaction with its practice, and these factors, either separately or combined, helped give rise to hopes for a new and greater or more perfect temple in the future, or at the end of days.[43] It is also the case, as has properly been pointed out,[44] that those texts that look for a new, perfect temple in the eschatological (or future) age presuppose that the present temple will be destroyed or at least be no longer standing (thus,

41. Sanders, *Jesus*, p. 88; cf. p. 251.
42. Cf. Juel, *Messiah*, pp. 197-209; Sanders, *Jesus*, pp. 85ff.; against Gaston, *No Stone*, pp. 147-54.
43. Cf. *1 Enoch* 90.28-29; Tob. 14.5; *Jub.* 1.27ff.
44. Cf. Juel, *Messiah*, pp. 199-200; Sanders, *Jesus*, pp. 85ff.

for example, *1 Enoch* 90.28-29; 11QT 28–29), while *Ps. Sol.*
17.30 hints at the messiah taking purifying action against the
present corrupt city of Jerusalem (including, implicitly, the
temple).[45] But there is nothing in the pre-70 texts (apart from
the New Testament) that describes the messiah destroying
the temple (or speaks of him rebuilding it). And it cannot be
emphasized too strongly that for the writer of *Sib.* 5 the whole
idea of the messiah (or God) wilfully destroying the temple
would be anathema. It is not simply that it stands on the other
side of AD 70; there is nothing in it to suggest that it belongs in
any way to this line of criticism of the form of the temple or
conduct of the cult, or that it would have needed to be purified,
still less replaced.

It would of course be possible to attempt to understand Jesus'
prophecy (or the charge brought against him, in the Synoptic
tradition) concerning the destruction of the temple, in a more
positive way. Thus, for example, 'pull down' might be taken in
the sense of the necessary prelude to the building (or rebuilding) of a better, more glorious temple. This could correspond to
what had happened with Herod and to what is implied (as
noted above) in the case of those texts that look for a perfect
temple in the eschatological age. This view would be strengthened if the ἀχειροποίητον 'not made by hand' of Mk 14.58
were understood to imply 'divinely built', that is, especially
large and splendid (as in *Sib.* 5; cf. Dan. 2.34-36). This is
scarcely the most obvious reading of the Marcan (and Synoptic) material, however. The overriding emphasis there is
negative; the charge against Jesus apparently represents a
problem that has to be explained away as blasphemy. It is also
reflected, especially in the use of χειροποιήτοις, in the words
attributed to Stephen in his attack on the temple, in Acts 7.48
(cf. 6.14). Along with this, of course, we have the account of
Jesus' cleansing of the temple (Mk 11.15-19), which, taken in
conjunction with Jesus' sayings against the temple, is most
obviously to be understood, as Sanders argues,[46] to represent a

45. Cf. McKelvey, *New Temple*, pp. 16-17; Gaston, *No Stone*, p. 116;
Juel, *Messiah*, pp. 197-98.
46. Cf. Sanders, *Jesus*, pp. 61-71; cf. pp. 71-76, 270-71; cf. also M.N.A.
Bockmuehl, 'Why did Jesus Predict the Destruction of the Temple?',
Crux 25 (1989), pp. 11-18.

symbolic attack on the temple and sacrifices, and the temple authorities. In *Sib.* 5, by contrast, the emphasis on the temple is entirely positive in every respect. Certainly it has a vision of the temple in its perfect eschatological form, but it could scarcely be suspected of implying anything negative about the temple while it was still standing. Thus if *Sib.* 5 and Mark 14 represent two texts dealing with the role of the messiah in relation to the temple, it must be said that *Sib.* 5 has a very different understanding of the messiah. He avenges the destruction brought on his people and their temple, indeed not only avenges it but makes it good again. It would be possible to argue that vengeance is not lacking from the Marcan picture (e.g. Mk 12.9), but that, in the latter, divine vengeance is directed against the people and the temple, not towards avenging their destruction. Indeed, in *Sib.* 5 the messiah does much more than avenge; he creates a temple of massive size and beauty, to demonstrate beyond question the victory of the God of the Jews over the Romans, and to serve as a manifestation of the glory of this God.

3.2 *The Temple and the Tower of Babel*

The theme of the manifestation of God's glory in *Sib.* 5 can be seen most clearly in the description of the tower (423-27), built by this heavenly figure and reaching up to heaven; this tower could be a separate construction in its own right, but it is more obvious to understand it as part of the new, glorious temple. Sanders[47] sees in this an expression of the fulfilment of the prophecy of Isa. 2.2./Mic. 4.1 ('And it shall come to pass in the latter days, that the mountain of the LORD's house shall be established at the top of the mountains and shall be exalted above the hills, and all nations shall flow unto it'), and this is quite plausible, although in these texts it is of course the mountain (the setting of the temple, that is, not the construction) that is set on high. The emphasis on the height of the temple in *Sib.* 5 also clearly belongs to the wider context within first-century Judaism of the depiction of the sanctuary as a tower. This is what we find in, for example, *1 Enoch* 89.50, 73:

---

47. Sanders, *Jesus*, pp. 87, 370 n. 21.

'Then that house became large and spacious; a lofty tower was built on that house for those sheep, and also a tall and great tower was built on that house for the Lord of the sheep; that house was low, but the tower was raised up and lofty. Then the Lord of the sheep stood upon that tower, and they spread a full table before him... And they began again to build as before; and they raised up that tower, and it was called the high tower. And they started again to place a table before the tower, but all the bread on it was unclean and impure.' Similarly, the *Letter of Aristeas* 83-84 (cf. above) portrays Jerusalem as the centre of the land of Israel, and the temple reaching up above the rest of the city: 'we saw the city built in the midst of the whole land of the Jews, upon a hill which extended to a great height. On the top of the hill the temple had been constructed, towering above all'; but here there is no hint of allusion to Genesis 11.

It is also the case that the distinctive understanding of the temple presented here corresponds to that of the Tower of Babel in Genesis 11. This connection is perceived by McKelvey,[48] who also draws attention to the strong resemblances between *Sib.* 5 here and the allusions to Genesis 11 in *Sib.* 3. Yet McKelvey's understanding of this passage in *Sib.* 5 simply in terms of the restoration of humankind's unity is probably too general. This theme scarcely seems to be the main concern of *Sib.* 5 either here or elsewhere. Hence if justice is to be done to the implicit reference to Genesis 11 here in *Sib.* 5, and its potential significance drawn out, it will be necessary to consider the way that Genesis 11 is used in Jewish tradition more widely, along with the particular context here in *Sib.* 5.

There is a clear tradition in some later Jewish texts[49] that represents the Tower of Babel as, more than anything, an exercise in idolatry, for example, *Targum Neofiti* of Gen. 11.4: 'And they said, Come, let us build ourselves a city, and a tower whose top reaches to the heights of the heavens, and let us make ourselves an idol on the top of it, and let us put a sword in its hand, to make war against him, before we are scattered on

48. McKelvey, *New Temple*, pp. 18-19.
49. Cf. J. Bowker, *The Targums and Rabbinic Literature: An Introduction to Jewish Interpretations of Scripture* (Cambridge: Cambridge University Press, 1969), pp. 183-84.

the face of the earth'; similarly *PsJ*; so also *Ngl, VL,* which for 'an idol' have 'an idol temple'. Cf. also *b. Sanh.* 109a; *Midr. Teh.* Ps. 1.1). Certainly this tradition, in the form and texts in which we find it, cannot be traced back to anywhere near the time of the composition of *Sib.* 5, but it is possible that Ps.-Philo (*LAB* 6.1ff.) points to an interpretation of Gen. 11.2-4 that includes the theme of idolatry. Thus we find at *LAB* 6.1: 'Now come, let us build for ourselves a tower whose top will reach to the heavens, and we will make a name for ourselves and a glory upon the earth', while at 6.4 those who refuse to join in this plan say, 'We are not casting in bricks, nor are we joining in your scheme. We know the one Lord, and him we worship', and in the following verses, Abram is portrayed as being thrown into the fiery furnace by the leaders of those building the tower.

It is in any case likely enough that allusion to a tradition of this kind underlies the allusion to Genesis 11 here. Thus, in the immediately preceding section (397-413), as elsewhere in *Sib.* 5 (for example, 351-60; cf. 267), we find an attack on Gentile idolatry, especially in 403-407, starkly contrasting the worship of the Jews with that of the Gentiles. In this context (and taking account of the targumic and related traditions referred to above), it seems probable that what we have here is an implicit contrast between the Tower of Babel, representing idolatry, on the one hand, and the new temple, reaching up to heaven and portrayed as the place of pure worship of the one true God, on the other. So this new temple represents the exposure of the futility of human (that is, Gentile') rebellion against God and perversion of worship of him, and the transformation of worship. Thus the new perfect temple of the Jews, set in the new Jerusalem in the visionary eschatological golden age, will be of cosmic proportions and will reverse Babel and its effects—not in the sense of reuniting all humans with each other and making them speak a common language,[50] since it is clear that for *Sib.* 5 the Gentiles are not restored to any

---

50. Cf. the criticism of McKelvey, above; reference to the uniting of humankind in one language could of course be seen as a plausible interpretation of the Pentecost account in Acts 2, but *Sib.* 5 lacks the relevant distinctive features of the Acts narrative.

common equality with the Jews, but rather in the sense of overcoming idolatry and human usurpation of God's glory. So the 'blessed man from heaven' creates a new holy city and a temple reaching up to heaven; thus humans (that is, above all, the Jews) and God are brought together and the separation is overcome; so finally the 'greatest temple' displays the 'glory of God' to the whole world and to all Gentiles, who will see unmistakably that the God of the Jews reigns supreme.

3.3 *Jerusalem (and Temple) and the Centre of the Earth*

Finally, for *Sib.* 5, one further passage, 247-52, can be brought into consideration, even though it does not refer specifically to the temple:

ἀλλ' ὁπόταν Περσὶς γαῖ' ἀπόσχηται πτολέμοιο
λοιμοῦ τε στοναχῆς τε, τότ' ἔσσεται ἤματι κείνῳ
Ἰουδαίων μακάρων θεῖον γένος οὐράνιόν τε,
οἳ περιναιετάουσι θεοῦ πόλιν ἐν μεσογαίοις·
ἄχρι δὲ καὶ Ἰόπης τεῖχος μέγα κυκλώσαντες
ὑψόσ' ἀείρονται ἄχρι καὶ νεφέων ἐρεβεννῶν.

But whenever the Persian land shall cease from war,
pestilence and groaning, then on that day it will come to pass
that the divine and heavenly race of the blessed Jews,
who dwell around the city of God in the middle of the earth,
having built a great wall round about, as far as Joppa,
are raised up even to the dark clouds.

In this remarkable prophecy, the point again apparently is that Jerusalem (and implicitly the temple), encircled by a great wall, will be raised up towards heaven. The further notable feature here is the idea of Jerusalem as set in the centre of the earth. This theme is again rooted in scriptural tradition, for example especially Ezek. 38.12 (cf. 5.5); it is taken up from there in strikingly developed form in *Jub.* 8.19: 'And he knew that the garden of Eden was the holy of holies and the dwelling of the Lord. And Mount Sinai was in the midst of the desert and Mount Zion was in the midst of the navel of the earth. The three of these were created as holy places, one facing the other.' Jerusalem as the centre of the earth is also a theme unmistakably present in *1 Enoch* 26.1 ('And from there I went into the centre of the earth and saw a blessed place'; but the further interesting feature of *1 Enoch* 25–26 (especially 25.3: 'This tall mountain which you saw, whose summit resembles the throne of God, is his throne') is of Mount Zion reaching up into heaven. Thus just as *Sib.* 5 brings both these themes together (if only alluding briefly to Jerusalem—and temple— being set up towards heaven, a theme developed more fully in 423-27), so also does *1 Enoch* 25–26. This combination of motifs is also present in *Letter of Aristeas* 83–84, already referred to, where Jerusalem is set in the centre of the land (Israel, not the earth), and the temple reaches up high.

These traditions, common to a number of texts, as has been shown,[51] take on particular significance in *Sib.* 5. It is the case, as Hayman has pointed out,[52] that the theme of Jerusalem (or, the temple) being set at the centre or navel of the earth must be seen in the context of cosmic symbolism developed in Diaspora Judaism, and exemplified still more strongly in later texts. This cosmic symbolism is evident in relation both to Jerusalem being set at the centre of the earth and the temple reaching up to heaven in *Sib.* 5, and in the way it links both together. These themes, together with that of the messiah rebuilding Jerusalem and the temple, form important parts of what may be termed the 'temple ideology' (and ideology more widely) of *Sib.* 5. Thus Schwier[53] argues in general for the importance of Jewish temple ideology in the Second Temple period (above all in relation to the revolt of AD 66–70), and sees it at several focal points as coming, or being brought, into direct and bitter conflict with Roman religious ideology. In this respect, at least, *Sib.* 5 stands in considerable contrast to *Sib.* 3. The latter, as we have seen, certainly has considerable emphasis on the temple as set at the centre of Jewish life (213-15; cf. 266-67, 702ff., 718f., 725f.), and as an epitome of sump-

51. Cf. P. Hayman, 'Some Observations on Sefer Yesira: (2) The Temple at the Centre of the Universe', *JJS* 37 (1986), pp. 176-82. For the theme of the temple at the centre of the earth, cf. A.J. Wensinck, *The Ideas of the Western Semites concerning the Navel of the Earth* (Amsterdam: Müller, 1916), especially pp. 11-36; cf. also the discussion, and passages cited, in J. Jeremias, *Golgotha* (ΑΓΓΕΛΟΣ: Archiv für Neutestamentliche Zeitgeschichte und Kulturkunde. Beihefte 1; Leipzig: Eduard Pfeiffer, 1926), pp. 40-45.
52. Hayman, 'The Temple at the Centre of the Universe', pp. 179-80.
53. Schwier, *Tempel und Tempelzerstörung*, pp. 55ff.

tuous splendour provoking jealousy on the part of the enemies of the Jews; further, in the polemic against idolatry, it draws boundaries between (pious) Jews and others. In other respects, however, it is much more open and accommodating than *Sib.* 5; the temple in *Sib.* 3 does indeed operate a kind of gravitational pull towards itself, and the process is one-way, of Gentiles to Jerusalem. It does, however, offer the Gentiles much more clearly and fully a share in the idyllic eschatological age that God will bring about.

In *Sib.* 5, the use of the temple ideology is more negative and polemical. It makes best sense of *Sib.* 5 as a whole, and its messianic ideology in particular, to set it in context of the period leading up to the messianic revolts in Egypt and elsewhere in the Diaspora in AD 115–17.[54] Amongst other things, *Sib.* 5 is directed against Roman oppression and the destruction of the Jerusalem temple in AD 70 (and it denounces Rome and Nero for all this in the most vehement terms) and also, on Schwier's argument, against the Roman-Egyptian imperial ideology of religious-political superiority and supremacy. As distinct from elsewhere in the Roman Empire, in the case of the Jewish religion no syncretism would be possible; instead, a full-scale ideological-political-religious (and, eventually, military) battle is involved or in prospect. Thus the 'theological' themes of the messiah building the temple and Jerusalem/the temple being set at the centre of the earth belong integrally to this wider political (and related) context. That is, the writer, in defiance of all historical events, reality and plausibility, gives the Jews victory over the Romans, both militarily and ideologically, through the advent of the heavenly messianic figure who destroys the Romans and restores both Jerusalem and the temple to a form which completely surpasses their former state, and will dominate the whole world and demonstrate the

---

54. Cf. M. Hengel, 'Messianische Hoffnung und politischer "Radikalismus" in der "jüdisch-hellenistichen Diaspora". Zur Frage der Voraussetzungen des jüdischen Aufstandes unter Trajan 115–117 n. Chr.', in D. Hellholm (ed.), *Apocalypticism in the Mediterranean World and the Near East* (Tübingen: J.C.B. Mohr, 1983), pp. 655-86; Schwier, *Tempel und Tempelzerstörung*, pp. 339-42; cf. also the discussion in my forthcoming essay, 'Jewish Messianic Hope' (n. 13 above).

victory of the God of the Jews, thus confirming the (equally absurd, in human terms) situation the writer has already announced, that Jerusalem, not Rome, is the centre and hub of the whole earth. All that really matters on the world stage is brought about by the God of the Jews, and takes place in Jerusalem. The force of this ideological statement is further strengthened by the fact that it is represented as something that does not lie in the future but has already happened (as the past tense of the verb 'came' in 414 indicates). The Jews are told that God's victory on their behalf has already happened; here, as in other places, and in a not dissimilar situation, *Sib.* 5 shows close affinity with Deutero-Isaiah.[55]

4. *Sybilline 3 and 5 in relation to Sybilline 4*

Finally, it is worth examining briefly some of the striking differences between *Sib.* 3 and 5, on the one hand, and *Sib.* 4, on the other, although it is not possible to deal at all adequately with *Sib.* 4 here. In its present form, *Sib.* 4 is roughly contemporary with *Sib.* 5, but far from giving prominence to the temple, it appears to refer to it only briefly and in a mainly negative way, especially in 4-11 and 27-30.[56] Thus 4-11:

οὐ ψευδοῦς Φοίβου χρησμηγόρος, ὄντε μάταιοι
ἄνθρωποι θεὸν εἶπον, ἐπεψεύσαντο δὲ μάντιν·
ἀλλὰ θεοῦ μεγάλοιο, τὸν οὐ χέρες ἔπλασαν ἀνδρῶν
εἰδώλοις ἀλάλοισι λιθοξέστοισιν ὅμοιον.
οὐδὲ γὰρ οἶκον ἔχει ναῷ λίθον ἑλκυσθέντα,
κωφότατον νωδόν τε, βροτῶν πολυαλγέα λώβην·
ἀλλ' ὃν ἰδεῖν οὐκ ἔστιν ἀπὸ χθονὸς οὐδὲ μετρῆσαι
ὄμμασιν ἐν θνητοῖς, οὐ πλασθέντα χερὶ θνητῇ·

I am one who utters the oracles not of false Phoebus, whom vain men called a god, and falsely designated a seer, but of the great God, whom the hands of men did not fashion in the likeness of dumb idols made of stone. For he does not have as a house a stone dragged into a temple,

---

55. Cf. e.g. *Sib.* 5.80ff., 169f.; allusion to Deutero-Isaiah is even more prominent in *Sib.* 3, e.g. 13ff., 229f., 285f., 586ff., 629, 710f., 760f.
56. Cf. J.J. Collins, 'The Place of the Fourth Sibyl in the Development of the Jewish Sibyllina', *JJS* 25 (1974), pp. 365-80; *idem*, 'Development of the Sibylline Tradition', pp. 427-29.

deaf and toothless, an insult causing great suffering to people,
but one which it is not possible to see from earth, or to be
measured by mortal eyes, since it was not fashioned by mortal
hand.

And 27–30:

οἳ νηοὺς μὲν ἅπαντας ἀπαρνήσονται ἰδόντες
καὶ βωμούς, εἰκαῖα λίθων ἀφιδρύματα κωφῶν,
αἵμασιν ἐμψύχων μεμιασμένα καὶ θυσίῃσιν
τετραπόδων·

They will renounce all temples when they see them,
and altars, useless constructions of stones that cannot hear,
defiled with the blood of animals and sacrifices
of four-footed creatures.

The main thrust of these two passages, the first in particular, is a strong polemic against idolatry, a theme already
familiar to us from *Sib.* 3 and 5. Collins argues that there is
equally a radical rejection of any material, earthly temple as
fit for the worship of God; only a very different (non-earthly,
non-material) kind of temple can be countenanced. This radical attack on cult and temple, combined with the positive
enjoining of repentance and baptism in 162-70, has led to the
view that the milieu of the work is closely linked with that of
Jewish baptistic groups such as the followers of John the Baptist, or the Ebionites and Elchasaites, not in Egypt[57] but in Syria
or the Jordan valley.[58]

It has to be said, however, that there is some ambiguity in
the attitude of *Sib.* 4 to the temple, which Collins[59] probably
does not allow sufficient weight to. Thus Collins[60] renders 4.8
as 'For he does not have a house, a stone set up as a temple',
which does not correspond to the Greek text (that of Geffcken)[61] which he takes as his base, but instead (as he notes)
represents the reading of the ψ manuscript group: ναὸν λίθον
ἱδρυθέντα. The φ manuscript group also has λίθον ἱδρυθέντα

57. Thus Nikiprowetsky, *La Troisième Sibylle*, pp. 232ff.
58. So Collins, 'The Place of the Fourth Sibyl'; *idem*, 'Development of
the Sibylline Tradition', p. 429; J. Thomas, *Le mouvement baptiste en
Palestine et Syrie* (Gembloux: Duculot, 1938), pp. 46ff.
59. Collins, 'The Place of the Fourth Sibyl', pp. 367-68.
60. Collins, 'Sibylline Oracles', in Charlesworth, *OTP*, I, p. 384.
61. Geffcken, *Die Oracula Sibyllina*, p. 91.

but ναῷ, not ναόν, while the Ω manuscript group, the text printed by Geffcken (and given above) has ναῷ λίθον ἑλκυσθέντα, which Bate translates by 'a stone dragged into a temple'.[62] Thus it appears that at least the Ω and (probably) φ text should most plausibly be understood as an attack not on the Jerusalem temple but on idols and idol-worship, which does of course correspond (as I have already noted above) to the overriding emphasis of the context here. Thus Lanchester comments that in these lines the writer 'appears to condemn the ancient Semitic idea of sacred stones as the dwelling-place of a god',[63] and although it is doubtful that the reference is to a general 'ancient Semitic idea', it makes good sense of the passage otherwise. The view that the passage represents primarily a polemic against idolatry would of course be strengthened if the variant reading εἰκόν' were to be preferred to οἶκον, but it is doubtful that εἰκόν' can be considered original; it is not, however, necessary for the interpretation suggested here. Similarly, 27-30 can be understood as mainly an attack on idolatry, with its reference to 'all temples and altars'; the implication is that these are pagan temples and shrines which are to be shunned by Jews (and their Gentile sympathizers).

Further, 115-29 laments the destruction of both Jerusalem and the temple, characterizing the latter as 'the great temple

62. H.N. Bate, *The Sibylline Oracles: Books III–V* (London/New York: SPCK/Macmillan, 1918), p. 83; H.C.O. Lanchester ('The Sibylline Oracles', in R.H. Charles (ed.), *The Apocrypha and Pseudepigrapha of the Old Testament*, vol. 2: *Pseudepigrapha* [Oxford: Clarendon Press, 1913], p. 393) translates by '(For He has not as His habitation) a stone set up in a temple', apparently rendering the φ text, and notes as a variant the reading 'dragged to a temple'. But his rendering in any case differs notably from that of Collins. It is further possible that κωφότατον νωδόν τε should be rendered, with Bate, as 'deaf and dumb', rather than 'dumb and toothless', as Collins; κωφότατον is of course ambiguous, and can have the sense of either 'dumb' or 'deaf', but Bate's rendering captures better the force of the polemic against idols, while Collins's version is verging on tautology. A similar question arises at line 28 with the usage of κωφῶν; again, 'deaf' (as Bate) is probably to be preferred to 'dumb' (as Collins), although the sense here is not much affected. At line 9, Lanchester translates by 'dumb and helpless', emending νωδόν to νωθρόν, but such a change is unnecessary.

63. Lanchester, 'Sibylline Oracles', p. 393.

of God'; this should not be dismissed as a 'simple historical statement'.[64] Moreover, although Nikiprowetsky[65] is criticized by Collins[66] for going beyond the evidence of the text in asserting a causal connection between the destruction of the Jerusalem temple and the eruption of Vesuvius, the text nevertheless does appear to imply that this destruction does lead to considerable catastrophe. Thus 125-27 speaks of the Romans destroying not only the temple, but also the Jewish people and their land; these are all closely bound up together, and the immediate aftermath, and apparently consequence, is made clear in 128-29, which describes an earthquake that destroys Salamis and Paphos and floods that come over Cyprus. The portrayal of the eruption of Vesuvius follows in 130-34, then in 135-36 we read: γινώσκειν τότε μῆνιν ἐπουρανίοιο θεοῖο, εὐσεβέων ὅτι φῦλον ἀναίτιον ἐξολέσουσιν ('know then the wrath of the heavenly God, because they will destroy the blameless tribe of the godly'). Collins argues that it is this (the destruction of the Jewish people, not the temple) that is thus given as the cause of Vesuvius erupting; he admits that the 'destruction of the pious' historically includes the destruction of the temple, but argues that *Sib.* 4 here does not attach special importance to the latter. This is certainly so, but in view of the close correlation of the various terms in 125-27, it may be misleading to draw too much of a distinction here. It is also unclear whether 135-36 refers back, as the explanation of 130-34, or forward, implying that God's wrath is shown in the chaos and disasters portrayed in 137-51, throughout the world, in the form of that dreaded event, the return of Nero (137-39) and the catastrophes that follow (140-51). It is hard to reconcile what is said (or implied) of the temple in these passages with the thoroughgoing radicalism of other texts (for example, Acts 7.48; Heb. 8–9) from the post-70 period.

Nevertheless, the predominantly negative attitude of *Sib.* 4, and its lack of interest in the temple, remain striking. Thus, for example, even if 8-9 are not taken to be a rejection of the idea that God can have any kind of physical house (and

64. Collins, 'The Place of the Fourth Sibyl', p. 368.
65. Nikiprowetsky, *La Troisième Sibylle*, p. 234.
66. Collins, 'The Place of the Fourth Sibyl', p. 368.

specifically a temple; a theme unmistakably set out in Acts 7.48; 17.24 [discussed by C.K. Barrett in the present volume]), but are understood as an attack on the attempt to see God as present in or represented by the form of an idol, the following lines clearly point to the true house or temple of God as one which is non-material. Lanchester in fact translates ἀλλ' ὃν ἰδεῖν οὐκ ἔστιν ἀπὸ χθονὸς οὐδὲ μετρῆσαι ὄμμασιν ἐν θνητοῖς, οὐ πλασθέντα χερὶ θνητῇ as 'But He is one whom none can see from earth, nor measure with mortal eyes, seeing He was not fashioned by mortal hand'; if this rendering were right, it would of course move the passage as a whole still further in the direction of a polemic against idolatry and at the same time make much less plausible the view that there is any implication of an attack on the Jerusalem temple here. But the rendering is unlikely to be correct, since grammatically the antecedent of ὄν is more obviously οἶκον than (an implied) θεός, although certainly ὅς at the start of line 12 refers to God; it might, then, be seen as picking up from the ὄν of line 10, while what is said in 12 shows that 11-12 could plausibly refer to God himself and not just his temple (though the οὐ πλασθέντα χερὶ θνητῇ 'not fashioned by mortal hand' is less easily explicable in this way; cf. the use of χειροποίη-τος/ἀχειροποίητος of a temple or shrine in e.g. Mk 14.58; Acts 7.48; 17.24; Heb. 9.11, 24; *Sib.* 3.606, 618; 14.62; Jos. *Ant.* 4.55; *War* 1.419). Hence it appears most likely that the present passage disallows the possibility of God having any material habitation or temple; similarly, the reference in 29-30 to being 'defiled with the blood of animals and the sacrifices of four-footed creatures' has obvious negative implications for the actual practice of the Jerusalem cult. On balance, therefore, although the main thrust of both 4-11 and 27-30 is polemic against idolatry, they allow no positive place for the form and practice of the Jerusalem temple either.

The reason for the negative assessment of the material aspects of the Jerusalem temple and sacrificial system is in one sense obvious enough. That is, *Sib.* 4 stands only ten years or so beyond the fall of Jerusalem and the destruction of the temple; not surprisingly, the positive emphasis now falls on repent-ance, baptism and (if 179-92 is original to the oracle) final resurrection, judgment and reward of paradise for the righteous. It is of course the case that at least a substantial element of these themes, in the form of repentance, judgment and eschatological paradisal reward for the righteous, is clearly evidenced in *Sib.* 3 and 5 (cf. e.g. 3.601-18, 624-34, 669-701, 702-31, 741-66, 767-95; 5.110, 281-85, 381-85, 492ff.), but it is equally the case, as we have seen, that the themes of repentance and reward especially are bound up with those of temple and sacrifice (e.g. 3.626-29, 718, 772-75; 5.422-77, 492ff., 501-503). Hence the differences in context and usage between *Sib.* 4 and the other two *Sibyllines* indicate that they have much less in common than might be thought from the fact that these themes are found in all three. In fact there would appear to be much closer parallels for *Sib.* 4 in works which also reflect the immediate aftermath of the destruction of the temple in 70, making repentance and acts of mercy the equivalents of temple-service and shifting the positive emphasis from the physical temple to a non-material divine sanctuary. This is what we find, for example, in the sayings attributed to Johanan b. Zakkai in *ARN A*, 4: 'Once as Rabban Johanan ben Zakkai was coming out from Jerusalem, Rabbi Joshua followed after him and saw the temple in ruins. "Woe unto us!", Rabbi Joshua cried, "that this, the place where atonement was made for the sins of Israel, is laid waste!"; "My son", Rabban Johanan said to him, "Do not be sad; for we have another atonement as effective as this. And what is it? It is acts of loving-kindness, as it is said, For I desire mercy and not sacrifice [Hos. 6.6]"'; cf. similarly *ARN B,* 8 or the words that Josephus at *War* 5.458 ascribes to the Jewish rebel leaders during the siege of Jerusalem ('... that those who, as he himself said, were about to perish were not concerned for their native country, and that the world was a better temple for God than this one'), thus moving the emphasis from the doomed Jerusalem to the world itself as God's true sanctuary. Even here, however, the points of difference should not be underestimated; in these utterances the precise point of connection is made for the reinterpretation of the temple and cult, and in *ARN A* there is a poignant description of Johanan b. Zakkai's great grief and mourning on hearing of the destruction of Jerusalem and the temple. In *Sib.* 4, by contrast, none of this happens; instead, the importance of the temple is diminished by being passed over for the most part in silence (even taking 111ff. fully into consideration), while the positive themes are developed quite separately, not directly in relation to the temple.

Hence, in conclusion, it is necessary to take account of the contrast between *Sib.* 4 and the other two Sibyllines considered here, especially on the issue of the temple. As far as *Sib.* 3 is concerned, the context of the work is of course quite different (although it stands close to the despoliation of the temple in 167). In the case of *Sib.* 5, it could be claimed that whereas *Sib.* 4 is completely caught up in the aftermath of the disaster of 70, when no real hopes exist for a new, rebuilt temple, by the time of the writing of *Sib.* 5 such hopes were being entertained and are reflected in the work. Yet although difference of date may account for something of the difference of emphasis in the two works, it scarcely seems adequate to explain the contrast in the perceptions of the temple: central and positive on the one hand, peripheral and mainly negative on the other. I doubt that *Sib.* 4 is as radical in its outlook as Collins argues, or that it is as consistently negative and critical as Acts 7.48, 17.24, Hebrews and related texts; full weight should be given to 115ff., and to polemic against idolatry as a main concern. Nor can it be certain, of course, that *Sib.* 4 is a sectarian work from the milieu of baptistic groups around the Jordan, although that remains a plausible suggestion in view of our limited knowledge of the Judaism of the period. Nevertheless, even though the understanding of *Sib.* 4 needs to be qualified in these various ways, there remains a very real gulf between the attitude of *Sib.* 4 and that of *Sib.* 3 and 5. The contrast between *Sib.* 4.4-11, 27-30 and, for example, 3.773-74 'the house of the great God; there will be no other house among men' is obvious enough. A still more striking contrast with *Sib.* 4 is provided by the fervent nature of the feeling for the temple and cult as it is expressed in *Sib.* 3 and 5. In both, the temple virtually symbolizes the Jewish people and their fortunes, while in *Sib.* 5 the temple becomes a potent ideological weapon in the political and religious struggle against the Roman oppressor.

It is a pleasure to offer this essay to Ernst Bammel, as a token of gratitude for the benefits of his great learning that I have received and for the personal kindness he has always shown me. It goes without saying, of course, that the essay itself is unworthy of his own standards of scholarship; but as in the case of the temple, just as the offering is unworthy of the recipient, so also the latter may yet be prepared to receive it.

TEMPLE IMAGERY IN PHILO:
AN INDICATION OF THE ORIGIN OF THE LOGOS?

Margaret Barker

Philo's Logos is a perennial problem. As we know, Philo was
presenting his Judaism in Greek terms; much has been written on the Greek elements in his work and the philosophies to
which he related his Judaism. But has that Judaism been correctly described? Where in it did Philo find any basis for his
Logos? It is hard to accept Wolfson's view of the Logos:

> It is a matter of indifference to us whether in Judaism before the
> time of Philo the personification of the term Logos meant that
> the Word of God was already considered as a real being created
> by God or whether its personification was merely a figure of
> speech.[1]

He clearly describes a separate heavenly being, and this sets a
problem for orthodox monotheism. Thus A.F. Segal says of
Philo's doctrine:

> In doing this he has an entirely different emphasis than the
> rabbis. He is clearly *following* the Greek philosophers. Like
> them he is reluctant to conceive of a pure eternal God who par-
> ticipates directly in the affairs of the corruptible world. So he
> employs a system of mediation by which God is able to reach into
> the transient world, act in it, fill it as well as transcend material
> existence without implying a change in his essence.[2]

But was he following the philosophers? Was he not rather
relating his own faith to their ideas and describing it in their

1. H. Wolfson, *Philo: Foundations of Religious Philosophy in
Judaism, Christianity and Islam* (2 vols.; Cambridge, MA, 1948).
2. A.F. Segal, *Two Powers in Heaven* (Leiden, 1978), p. 165 (my
italics).

terms? Why, for example, if his Logos resembles Aristotle's
nous is it not Aristotle's *nous*? Time and again there seem to be
restraints on what he can say. What were they? Something
must have defined and determined what he thought. Bousset
recognized that he brought the Logos *to* the philosophies
because it was 'through and through a mythological figure',
but we have come some distance from his suggestion that the
Logos derived from the Hermes–Thoth figure of the Hellenic-
Egyptian mysteries.[3] The search is now conducted among the
angel mediators who appear in the writings of the so-called
intertestamental period.

The Logos was a 'second God'; Philo says so (*Quaest. in Gen.*
62) and elsewhere he is careful to define what he means (*Som.*
228). Our habit of reading back into first-century Judaism the
orthodoxies of the later rabbis has led us to discount the possibility that a second God could have had a place within his
Judaism. Philo was an acknowledged leader of the great Jewish community in Alexandria, and it is unlikely that he could
have *invented* a second God and still retained any credibility,
let alone led their embassy to the Emperor. I propose to bring to
Philo neither the Greek philosophies to which he related his
Judaism, nor a reconstruction of the first-century situation
based on later ideas of orthodoxy (which went to great lengths
to deny any notion of a second power in heaven),[4] but the
hypothesis that it was the ideas of the apocalyptists and the
temple imagery from the royal cult surviving in their writings
which *formed the basis of most of Philo's descriptions of the
Logos.*

There is now a renewed interest in the angels of pre-Christian Judaism, especially in the Great Angel, the Son of Man
figure.[5] There are various theories as to its origin and therefore its importance; the most significant, I believe, was Dix's
when he saw in the Great Angel a later development of the

3. W. Bousset, *Kyrios Christos* (ET; Abingdon, Nashville, 1970), pp.
399, 391 respectively.
4. This is the theme of Segal, *Two Powers in Heaven.*
5. E.g. C. Rowland, *The Open Heaven* (London, 1982); J.E. Fossum,
The Name of God and the Angel of the Lord (WUNT 36; Tübingen,
1985); L.W. Hurtado, *One God, One Lord* (London, 1988).

Angel of the Presence of Yahweh.[6] The compound nature of
the Great Angel is one of the more puzzling features, but if all
seven archangels (or all four, there are variant traditions)
were aspects of the one Great Angel, just as we know the later
angels had many names, then we should perhaps have the
beginning of an understanding.[7] It is unsympathetic and
unwise to read the angelophanies too critically; while it may be
interesting for us to make minute comparisons and see which
angels had glowing feet or wore turbans, the clear impression
given is that the same angel is intended in each case. Points of
similarity in the descriptions are not due to slavish copying of
an earlier account. Those who had or described the experience
of the Angel are unlikely to have checked carefully all previous references. Such descriptions were traditional and traditional forms would naturally have been used. To read the
accounts sympathetically we must read them as we might,
say, the accounts of visions of Mary. Those who have had such
experiences almost certainly have been influenced in their
descriptions by earlier accounts of such visions. All the
descriptions are broadly similar and recognizable even though
details differ. No one would suggest that they were visions of
different Marys.

I suspect that the Great Angel texts all refer to one heavenly
being, and this was Yahweh, who had been known as the Holy
One of Israel in the ancient cult. In this paper I shall work out
the implications of this for our reading of Philo. His Logos was
this Great Angel; he allegorized (or perhaps we should say
'demythologized') for his Hellenized contemporaries the
ancient beliefs about Yahweh and Elyon in the same way as he
did the Pentateuch.

6. G.H. Dix, 'The Seven Archangels and the Seven Spirits', *JTS* 28
(1927), pp. 233-50.

7. Segal (*Two Powers in Heaven*, p. 131) mentions a rabbinic debate
on Gen. 19.24, the punishment of Sodom and Gomorrah. The name
Yahweh appears twice; R. Judah said one of the occurences referred to
Gabriel. 'While Gabriel was not considered a separate independent
power by the rabbis, the tradition attests to the existence of exegeses
which allowed the tetragrammaton to signify a being other than
Israel's one God.'

Israel's earliest religion was not monotheistic.[8] There was an elaborate cult of heavenly beings, though only fragments of that cult now survive. It was not until the exile, under the influence of the Second Isaiah and the Deuteronomists that the great diversity of older traditions came to be combined, or rather fused.[9] The result of this was that Yahweh took over the roles which had formerly been those of both Yahweh and El Elyon, and a massive re-interpretation of the older traditions was begun. Not everyone accepted the new monotheism; those who transmitted the traditions now found in the Apocalypses retained many older beliefs, the most significant of which, for our purposes, was the belief that Yahweh was not the High God but one of the sons of God. He was a Holy One, the Holy One of Israel (Isa. 4.1 *et passim*). He was Israel's patron angel.

The Qumran text of Deut. 32.8 differs significantly from the MT, but not from the LXX.[10] The MT now says that the nations were allocated according to the number of the sons of Israel; the Qumran reading is 'the sons of El'. Since the LXX has the very similar 'angels of God', it appears that the MT has lost the idea of the sons of God, and with it, the idea that Yahweh was one of them. The implication of this older reading was known to the writer of the *Clementine Recognitions*:

> For every nation has an angel, to whom God has committed the government of that nation; and when one of these appears, although he be thought and called God by those over whom he presides, yet, being asked, he does not give such testimony to himself. For the Most High God, who alone holds the power of all things, has divided all the nations of the earth into seventy-two parts, and over these he hath appointed angels as princes. But to the one among the archangels who is greatest, was committed the government of those who, before all others, received the worship and knowledge of the Most High God (*Rec.* 2.42).[11]

8. This was the theme of my *The Older Testament* (London, 1987).
9. Segal (*Two Powers in Heaven*, p. 148) shows that the earliest arguments against the 'Two powers' heresy were based on Exod. 20.2, Deut. 32.9, and 'Isa. 44–47 generally as well as other II Isaiah passages'.
10. P.W. Skehan, 'A Fragment of the Song of Moses (Deut. 32) from Qumran', *BASOR* 136 (1954), pp. 12-15.
11. Text in *GCS* 51, pp. 76-77; translation in *Ante-Nicene Christian Library*, vol. 3 (Edinburgh, 1867), p. 220.

Here we have clear evidence from a time later than Philo of
the survival of a belief that the 'God' of Israel was in fact an
archangel, the chief of the sons of El. Note that God is named
Most High, the ancient El Elyon. It appears that those who
accepted the fusions of the Second Isaiah and the Deuteronomists regarded Yahweh and El Elyon as one and the same,
although the actual name Yahweh soon fell into disuse among
them, and was replaced either by circumlocution or by Elyon.
Those who fused the deities then named the great angel of the
older tradition Michael. This is the way in which we usually
read the Old Testament and envisage first-century Judaism;
we read Elyon as a synonym for Yahweh, thus distorting
many texts. There were, however, others who had not been
directly influenced by the innovations of the exilic period, and
they kept Elyon and Yahweh as distinct figures, Yahweh
remaining the Angel of Israel. When the two streams were
confused, there resulted two Yahwehs; the High God and his
emissary were both called by the same name, as we shall see.

    There is considerable evidence from a variety of sources and
periods to suggest that this belief in Yahweh as the angel of
Israel, the 'second God', was not confined to a small or eccen-
tric group. First, there are the two figures in Daniel 7. Emerton has shown that the imagery of the vision resembled that of
the two Ugaritic gods El and Baal. Ugaritic gods, however, had
no place in a tract written for people whose ancient religion
was threatened with extinction at the hands of pagans. This
imagery must have come from the heart of Israel's own religious heritage, and the two figures must have been Israel's
equivalents of El and Baal. They were El Elyon and Yahweh as
they had been remembered in the apocalyptic traditions, even
though it is usually assumed that the Ancient of Days must, in
Maccabaean times, have been understood to be Yahweh.[12] But
not everyone understood it that way. In the tradition which
underlies this vision, it was Yahweh who was perceived in
human form 'like a son of man'. Such anthropomorphism was
deeply rooted in Israel's tradition, and is the key to under-

12. J.A. Emerton, 'The Origin of the Son of Man Imagery', *JTS* ns 9
(1958), pp. 225-42.

standing much, both in Philo, in the Rabbis and elsewhere. The
human figure was the link between the two worlds.

Second, there persisted a controversy over the two powers in
heaven. One example will suffice. In *b. Sanh.* 38b there is a passage attributed to R. Nahman (dated late third or early fourth
century) who told of R. Idi in dispute with a heretic over Exod.
24.1, 'And he said to Moses, "Come up to the LORD"'. The
heretic said that the verse implied two deities, since the text
would otherwise have said 'Come up to me'. R. Idi had said
that the LORD meant Metatron, the angel mentioned in Exod.
23.21, of whom it was said 'My name is in him'. Segal comments:

> We learn from this defence that the heretics, in rabbinic eyes,
> were seen to confuse an angel with God.[13]

*We also learn that the angel, the second deity, was called
Yahweh.*

Third, there was a widespread belief in two Yahwehs; where
the two traditions had mingled, both the High God and the
Angel were called Yahweh. Thus Metatron has some very
interesting names in *3 Enoch*; he is called Yahoel and the
Lesser Yahweh. It is assumed that the Metatron figure was
'compounded of diverse elements', but there is another possibility: that the diverse elements were all part of an older figure,
the second deity of the older cult. The two Yahwehs appear
elsewhere in various forms. As P.S. Alexander says:

> Other texts mention both the Greater Yahweh and the Lesser
> Yahweh. The titles... functioned *independently of the Metatron
> traditions.* Thus we encounter the Great Jao and the Little Jao
> in the third-century Christian Gnostic work *Pistis Sophia*, and
> in the Gnostic *Book of Jeu.* In the Syriac *Gannat Bussame
> (Garden of Delights)* we find listed among deities worshipped by
> unbelievers 'Adonai Katon, the general of Adonai Gadol, who
> are reverenced by the Israelites.[14]

The first-century *Ascension of Isaiah* also knows of two Yahwehs. Knibb translates thus:

13. Segal, *Two Powers in Heaven*, p. 65.
14. P.S. Alexander, 'The Historical Setting of the Hebrew Book of
Enoch', *JJS* 28 (1977), pp. 156-80.

> And I saw how my LORD and the angel of the Holy Spirit worshipped and both together praised the LORD (*Asc. Isa.* 9.40).

This implies that both the Father and the Son were known as Yahweh, since *Asc. Isa.* 10.7 reads:

> And I heard the voice of the Most High, the father of my LORD as he said to my LORD Christ who will be called Jesus, 'Go out and descend through all the heavens...'[15]

Yahweh was invariably linked to the human form.

Fourth, in al-Qirqisani's account of Jewish sects he mentions the Magharians, a pre-Christian group, who understood the anthropomorphisms of the Hebrew Bible to refer not to God himself, but to the great angel who had created the world. This angel not only created; he also gave the Law, inspired the prophets and ruled as God's agent.[16]

Thus far, in texts from many traditions ranging over some seven centuries from the second BC to the fifth AD, we have discovered a second divine figure named Yahweh or the Lesser Yahweh who assumed human form and was believed to have been the human figure in the Hebrew Bible. He was the creator, the lawgiver, the one who went between earth and heaven and the general of the host. The later rabbis were opposed to this belief and argued against it; and the MT suggests that a sensitive text has been altered.

In several of the non-canonical texts Yahweh appears as the Great Angel. Sometimes he is named, sometimes not. Where he is unnamed, it is usually *assumed* that he is Michael, on the grounds that that angel elsewhere is named Michael.[17] The angel in the *Apocalypse of Abraham* is named; he is Yahoel (*Apoc. Ab.* 10.3), sent by the Eternal One to be the guide and the protector of Abraham and to have charge of his descendants

---

15. M.A. Knibb (trans.), 'The Ascension of Isaiah', in J.H. Charlesworth (ed.), *The Old Testament Pseudepigrapha*, vol. 1 (New York, 1983), hereafter *OTP*.

16. L. Nemoy, 'Al-Qirqisani's Account of the Jewish Sects', *HUCA* 7 (1930); H.A. Wolfson, 'The Pre-existent Angel of the Magharians and Al-Nahawandi', *JQR* 51 (1960-61), pp. 89-106, who rejects any link between the angel of the Magharians and Philo.

17. R.H. Charles, *The Apocrypha and Pseudepigrapha of the Old Testament,* II (Oxford, 1913), e.g. pp. 335, 421.

(*Apoc. Ab.* 10.16). Being sent implies subordination. He is identified with the angel of Exod. 23.21 (*Apoc. Ab.* 10.9), and *distinguished* from Michael (*Apoc. Ab.* 10.17). He resembles the man figure of Ezekiel's visions (who, as we shall see, *was* Yahweh), wears the turban headdress of the High Priest and carries a golden rod or sceptre. In the elaborate hymn of praise to God in *Apoc. Ab.* 17, one of the names of God is Yahoel, the same as that of the angel. A similar double naming occurs in the Slavonic *Life of Adam and Eve* and the related *Apocalypse of Moses*. The angel Joel is distinguished from Michael (*Life* 31) but identified as an archangel (*Apoc. Mos.* 43.5). Jael is also a name for God (*Apoc. Mos.* 29.4). Unnamed, the angel appears in the *Assumption of Moses* 10.1-3:[18]

> Then the hands of the angel shall be filled
> Who has been appointed chief,
> And he shall henceforth avenge them of their enemies.
> For the Heavenly One will arise from his royal throne
> And he will go forth from his holy habitation
> With indignation and wrath on account of his sons.

Here we have the chief angel as a warrior ('avenge them of their enemies') and a priest ('his hands shall be filled'), characteristics we have already encountered in other angel texts; but he is also a king. He has a throne. Comparable texts in the Old Testament (e.g. Isa. 26.21; Mic. 1.3) show that the one who came from his holy place was Yahweh. Furthermore, the *Assumption of Moses* deals with the same events as Deuteronomy 32–33. If we compare *Ass. Mos.* 10.1-3 with the text of Deut. 32.43, we find that the angel of the *Assumption of Moses* bears a strong resemblance to the Yahweh of the Song of Moses. The LXX and 4QDeut show that this text too differs in the MT.[19] 4QDeut describes Yahweh avenging the blood of his *sons* (cf. MT 'servants' but *Ass. Mos.* 'sons'), and making expiation for the blood of his people. The Yahweh of 4QDeut was a warrior priest who received the homage of the elohim

18. G.W.E. Nickelsburg (*Resurrection, Immortality and Eternal Life in Inter-Testamental Judaism* [Cambridge, MA, 1972]) concluded from this text and others that a lost tradition of the great judgment lay behind all of them which included, among other things, this great angel.

19. Skehan, 'A Fragment of the Song of Moses'.

(4QDeut 32.43b). This priestly role for the angel appears also in *T. Levi* 5.1, 6, where an unnamed interceding angel grants Levi his vision of the heavenly throne; *T. Dan.* 6.1 has an angel who is both mediator and warrior, described later in *T. Dan.* 6.5 as the Angel of Peace; *T. Ash.* 6.6 and *T. Ben.* 6.1 mention the angel of peace who guides the soul to eternal life. In the *Apocalypse of Zephaniah* the great angel of fire and bronze appears (6.15). Zephaniah thought he had seen the Lord Almighty, but the angel said his name was Eremiel (*Apoc. Zeph.* 6.15). In *Joseph and Aseneth* Aseneth is visited by a man from heaven who is 'commander of the whole host of the Most High' (*Jos. As.* 14.7) and 'chief of the house of the Most High' (*Jos. As.* 15.12). Note that God is named the Most High. Although this figure resembled Joseph, he was also the angel of fire and (this time) molten iron. He had a crown and a sceptre. He had written Aseneth's name in the Book of Life (*Jos. As.* 15.4) but his name was not to be spoken or known (*Jos. As.* 15.12).

In this group of texts the angel is a human figure, a high priest, king and warrior. He is chief of the Host of the Most High, the heavenly scribe, and the guiding angel of the faithful.

Daniel lies between the Old Testament and these non-canonical texts, forming a bridge between the angels of the apocalyptists and whatever came before them. Daniel shows the chief angel in many aspects. First, he is the Prince of the Host who is attacked by the little horn (Dan. 8.11). He loses the continual burnt offering, and the place of his sanctuary is overthrown. Since this text refers to the Jerusalem temple, the Prince of the Host must have been worshipped there. Second, he is called the Prince of Princes (Dan. 9.25); since the Princes were the angels of the nations (e.g. Dan. 10.13), this Great Angel, the angel of Israel, was their chief. Third, Daniel saw him as the angel of fire and bronze, a heavenly being in human form sent to him to reveal the future (Dan. 10.1-14). Ezekiel had seen a similar figure who was Yahweh. Daniel saw this angel clothed in linen, perhaps because he was identified with the scribe of Ezek. 9.3, or perhaps it was the garb of a High Priest in the sanctuary. The High Priest wore linen when he went into the sanctuary on the Day of Atonement (Lev. 16.4) because he was entering the presence of God, and therefore dressed as one of the angels, whom the apocalyptists describe as 'men in white garments' (e.g. *1 Enoch* 87.2; 90.22; and then, by implication, the transformations described in *2 Enoch* 22.8-10; *Asc. Isa.* 8.14; 9 *passim*). Fourth, the unnamed angel was helped in his struggles by Michael (Dan. 10.13), so he was not Michael. Finally, Daniel saw the man-like figure going up to this throne to be given dominion, glory and kingdom (Dan. 7.14). (It is important to remember that the so-called 'son of man' figure is not described in Daniel, or indeed anywhere else. Only the human form is noted, until the description in Rev. 1.13ff., where the figure is described as the angel of fire and bronze. There is, then, no reason why the figure of Daniel 7 should not have been the same as the unnamed angel.) Daniel, then, could be saying that the chief of the archangels was worshipped in Jerusalem; he was a warrior, a revealer sent down to the seer who could also go up to heaven and take his place as the agent of God's rule ('to him was *given* dominion...'). He resembled Ezekiel's Yahweh, and could have been dressed as a High Priest. All this is tentative; but the evidence of other texts adds weight to the possibility that this was Yahweh, present in a second-century apocalypse.

We must now go behind Daniel to find the Yahweh Angel in the Old Testament itself. First, there is the evidence of the LXX. The Angel of the Presence in MT Isa. 63.9 becomes Yahweh himself in the LXX. Similarly the angel in the Hebrew of Eccl. 5.6 becomes God himself in the Greek. These examples suggest that the Greek translators and the originators of the MT had *different ideas* as to how a particular heavenly being was to be described: as an angel or as Yahweh? Similarly, there are later texts in which it is emphasized that Yahweh himself acted in Israel's history, for example, at the Exodus.[20] The mighty deeds had not been done by an angel or an emissary, even though there are places, for example Judg. 2.2, where it says that the Angel of Yahweh brought Israel from Egypt. Could this emphasis in later interpretation be another indication that the Angel *had come to mean* a being other than Yahweh, while the interpreters wished to keep what they knew to have been

20. J. Goldin, 'Not by Means of an Angel and not by Means of a Messenger', in J. Neusner (ed.), *Religions in Antiquity* (Leiden, 1970).

the original meaning of the text, namely that this Angel was
Yahweh himself?

The Angel of Yahweh appears often in the Old Testament,
and there are undoubtedly some places in which a being separate from Yahweh has to be understood. The Angel of Yahweh
speaks *to* Yahweh in Zech. 1.12, for example. In other places,
such as Ps. 35.5-6 and 2 Kgs 1.3, 15, the Angel appears in isolation, and had we been told that the Angel and Yahweh were
synonymous, as Elohim and Yahweh are believed to be, the
text would still make good sense. A third type of text has Yahweh and the Angel as interchangeable terms, as though they
were synonymous. It is not easy to distinguish the Angel from
Yahweh in Zechariah 3. The three who visited Abraham (Gen.
18) present a similar problem. In the Gideon stories the two
are interchangeable (cf. e.g. Judg. 6.11ff.), as they are in the
story of Samson's parents (Judg. 13). This third type forms the
bulk of the evidence for the Angel of Yahweh and raises the
important question: Was the Angel synonymous with Yahweh,
perhaps one way of expressing a manifestation of Yahweh in
human form? The Angel is always a man figure, often a warrior. This emphasis on anthropomorphism is not stating the
obvious; many of the heavenly beings were not in human
form, for example, the living creatures of Ezekiel's vision, or
the snake-like angels of 4Q Amram and the *Apocalypse of
Zephaniah.*

Yahweh was a warrior;[21] he appears frequently in the Old
Testament either as the angel with a sword, or simply as the
one who wields the sword of judgment and vengeance. Thus in
Num. 22.23, Josh. 5.13-15, 1 Chron. 21.16, the man figure or
the angel of Yahweh holds a drawn sword. In Deut. 32.41-42
and Isa. 34.5, 6 the sword of Yahweh is the instrument of
destruction; cf. Isa. 66.16; Jer. 12.12; 47.6; Ezek. 21.3-5; 32.10.
Much later there is the account in 2 Macc. 3.24ff. of the vision
of a warrior with weapons of gold coming to the defence of
Jerusalem; cf. Isa. 37.36, where the angel of Yahweh slaughtered the Assyrians before Jerusalem.

---

21. P.D. Miller, *The Divine Warrior in Early Israel* (Harvard Semitic
Monographs, 3; Cambridge, MA, 1973).

There are also more elaborate manifestations of Yahweh, visions of the king on his throne, for example Exod. 24.10, 1 Kgs 22.19-23 and Isaiah 6, which are also the setting for Deut. 33.5 and many of the Psalms. The most detailed throne vision in the Old Testament is that of Ezekiel. He saw the chariot throne (Ezek. 1), which was represented in the temple by the chariot throne of the cherubim (1 Chron. 28.18), and on the throne he saw a human form, the angel of fire and bronze. In the later vision (Ezek. 8) the prophet saw the same figure of fire and bronze, but without the throne.[22] In Ezek. 9.4 the figure is *named as Yahweh*, the one who had come to summon the judgment upon Jerusalem. Yahweh was the bringer of judgment; the day of Yahweh was the constant theme of the prophets. The judgment was set in the heavenly temple and doubtless enacted in temple ritual (e.g. Ps. 73.17). In later texts, such as the *Similitudes of Enoch*, the Judge becomes the Son of Man, while Mt. 25.31ff. sees the Son of Man, the King and Judge, as acting for his Father. The Son of Man was the agent of a High God just as Yahweh had been. Yahweh was also the scribe: Ps. 87.6 depicts Yahweh recording the people, and Isa. 34.16 mentions the Book of Yahweh as the Book of Judgment.

The heavenly king was represented on earth by the Davidic king. We shall never fully understand what lies beneath some of the more obscure statements about the ancient kings, but we can at least look at what is there. The king *sat on the throne of Yahweh and was worshipped with him* (1 Chron. 29.20, 23; cf. Pss. 11.4; 45.7; Mic. 2.13, and the close links thought to exist between Ps. 2 and Dan. 7).[23] The king was the son of Yahweh; this is how the manifestation was described. How this sonship was achieved or symbolized we do not know. No supernatural birth was envisaged (1 Chron. 28.6), but the variant readings of Isa. 9.6 suggest angelic status. The four royal titles of the MT are replaced in one of the many Greek versions by 'The Angel of Great Counsel'. Ps. 89.19 implies that there was some sort of mystical ascent experience involved in the kingmaking, as the result of which the king was set on the holy hill (Ps. 2). A comparison with Ezekiel 28 suggests that the Davidic king joined

22. Rowland (*The Open Heaven*) emphasizes this (pp. 96-97).
23. A. Bentzen, *King and Messiah* (ET; London, 1955).

the princes of the other nations in the garden of God; cf. Daniel 7 where the ascent to heaven precedes the enthronement.[24] The earliest known account of such an ascent experience is in *1 Enoch* 14, and the setting for the ascent is clearly the heavenly temple, of which the temple in Jerusalem was the earthly counterpart. Enoch was commissioned to take a message of judgment. We know from 4QShirShabb[25] that the temple functionaries had heavenly counterparts; in the days of the monarchy the king had also had the two roles; he had been the man-like representation of Yahweh the Angel, the King of Israel. It was this ancient manifestation in the king which was remembered in all the later descriptions of the crowned and sceptred angel. Later tradition gave this role to Moses. In his drama *Exodus*, the tragedian Ezekiel described how Moses ascended to the presence of God and was there made God and King; he reigned as God's agent. Cf. Philo, *Vit. Mos.* 1.155-58.

If the king represented Yahweh, we may find in the king's roles some of those of Yahweh. The Davidic king, for example, was a priest. Whatever Ps. 110 means, it does show that the royal house was associated with the Melchizedek figure, and 11QMelch implies that this same Melchizedek was believed to function as Yahweh on the Day of Judgment, for texts which in the Old Testament refer to Yahweh, in 11QMelch refer to Melchizedek. This could have been an innovation; or it could have been a traditional understanding of those passages. Either way, the royal priesthood is associated with Yahweh.

The Davidic king was 'the firstborn, the highest of the kings of the earth' (Ps. 89.37). Yahweh (Gen. 49.24; Isa. 40.11; Jer. 31.10; Pss. 23.1; 80.1) and the Davidic king (Ezek. 37.24) were described as shepherds of the people, a pastoral image which was also used of angels. Enoch described the seventy angels and their punishment. Even two or three centuries later, Hermas mentions several shepherd angels (*Vis.* 5.1; *Sim.* 6.1). Other temple imagery also involved the dual role of the king: the menorah, for example, represented both the presence of

---

24. Cf. *The Older Testament*, pp. 115-21.
25. C. Newsom, *Songs of the Sabbath Sacrifice* (Harvard Semitic Studies, 27; Atlanta, 1985).

Yahweh with his people, and the stability of the Davidic house.[26]

The ancient Yahweh was also manifested as the Name, by which was meant something very different from what we mean by a name, although exactly what this was is not easy to define. It is one of the most mysterious of the titles, and for that reason probably one of the most important. The Name was synonymous with Yahweh in some cases; in others the word itself seems to have had special powers.

The greatest exponents of Name theology were the Deutero-nomists and their heirs; when they reformed and reformulated the theology of the ancient cult, they moved away from anthropomorphism and redefined what was meant by the Name. This association is very important. Mettinger's study concluded:

> The concept of God advocated by the Deuteronomistic theology is strikingly abstract. The throne concept has vanished and the anthropomorphic characteristics of God are on the way to oblivion. Thus the form of God plays no part in the D work of the Sinai theophany (Deut. 4.12).[27]

Solomon's prayer at the dedication of the temple is the clearest expression of the new theology, and shows the older beliefs being rejected.

> But will God indeed dwell on earth? Behold heaven and the highest heaven cannot contain thee; how much less this house which I have built (1 Kgs 8.27).

Any idea of the visible presence of God was abandoned and the older anthropomorphism was replaced by abstract ideas: 'You saw no form; there was only a voice' (Deut. 4.12). There were two reasons for this: the Deuteronomists were closely associated with the monotheism of the Second Isaiah who had identified Yahweh with Elyon and therefore 'relocated' Yahweh only in heaven rather than in the temple on Zion; and they were constructing from the ruins of the monarchy a faith to survive though it could no longer have the visible king at its

26. Cf. *The Older Testament*, ch. 9.
27. T.N.D. Mettinger, *The Dethronement of Sabaoth* (Lund, 1982), p. 124.

centre. The old concept of the human form in the temple was
no longer tenable.

> In the Name theology not only the Sabaoth designation but also
> the cherubim throne have disappeared; God himself is no longer
> present in the Temple but only in heaven. However, he is repre-
> sented in the temple by his Name.[28]

This is in clear contrast to earlier use of the Name, even by the
Deuteronomists. It had previously been synonymous with the
presence of Yahweh, not a substitute for it. In Deuteronomy 12
it is said that the cult actions take place before Yahweh (vv. 7,
12, 13); in the place Yahweh chooses (vv. 14, 18, 26); and in the
place where he causes his Name to dwell (vv. 5, 11, 21). Either
the text is riddled with contradictions, or there was a time
when these three expressions were synonymous. The presence
of Yahweh was the presence of the Name. Other texts afford
corroboration: Yahweh dwelt in the temple (e.g. Ps. 11.4; Jer.
8.19); the Name dwelt in the temple (Ps. 74.7). The Name of
the Lord could come in judgment (Isa. 30.27). The Name
seems to be a person also in Ps. 20.1-2 and in the Hebrew of Ps.
75.5. In Ps. 118.10-13 Yahweh and the Name are synonymous. The Name could be 'in' an angel (Exod. 23.20-21). The
Name as a designation for Yahweh did not cease with the
reforms of the Deuteronomists. Many later examples can best
be explained as a survival of the older practice. The *Gospel of
Truth* 38, for example, contains the statement 'Now the Name
of the Father is the Son' and goes on to show that the Name in
its visible aspect is the Son. The whole picture is complicated by
later ideas of existence and essence, but behind it there lies the
unmistakable mythology of Elyon and his sons who were
manifested in the created order. One son in particular, the
Name, was deemed to be their ruler. Similarly in the *Shepherd
of Hermas*, the Name of the Son of God and the Son of God are
synonymous; both support the whole creation (*Sim.* 9.14).

The Hermas text brings us to the second aspect of the Name;
whether thought of as a heavenly being or as the sacred letters
it was associated particularly with the work of creation.
Indeed, Yahweh itself was thought by the Targumists to mean

---

28. Mettinger, *The Dethronement of Sabaoth*, p. 123.

the Creator. TN to Exod. 3.14 explains the divine name thus: 'He who spoke and the world was from the beginning, and shall say to it: Be! and it shall be. He has sent me to you.' TJI has 'He who spoke and the world was; who spoke and all things were...'[29] The command at creation was a command to separate and thus to bring order (Gen. 1). The Name as a form of sacred letters was the key to the created order. Some traditions described it as the written seal which secured the natural order; others knew the secret Name as the key to the great oath which bound the created order. These three—separation, sealing and binding—all pass into Philo's Logos imagery.[30]

A picture, albeit indistinct, has emerged. Yahweh was the Holy One of Israel, the chief angel of the hosts of Elyon. He was a warrior, a priest and a king. He was manifested in human form. He guided Israel in its wanderings and souls up to the presence of God. He was present in the king, his son, present in the temple, and represented by the Menorah. He was the creator, the judge and the heavenly scribe. He was the Name, and the power of the Name was the key to the processes of creation. This Great Angel became Philo's Logos. Just as he allegorized the stories of the Pentateuch and put them into the language of the philosophers, so he took the mythology of the temple cult and made it his Logos. He did this by transposing the whole system into the language and thought world of Greek philosophy. Thus his heavenly archetypes are not *derived* from Plato; the ancient Wisdom traditions of Israel already had a highly developed system of heavenly counterparts, centred upon the belief in the heavenly temple and the worshipping angels. Plato's ideas formed a point of contact between the systems. Similarly, the Logos is not *derived* from

29. M. McNamara, *The New Testament and the Palestinian Targum to the Pentateuch* (Rome, 1978), pp. 103-12, lists all the various versions and discusses them.

30. Wolfson (see n. 16 above). W.H. Brownlee ('The Ineffable Name of God', *BASOR* 226 [1977], pp. 39-45) gives a history of opinions as to the meaning of the divine name. It is interesting that both Merkabah and Gnostic traditions associate the revealed God with the Creator God; see P.S. Alexander, '3 Enoch' in *OTP* (n. 15 above), p. 236. For 'sealing' see D. Sperber, 'On Sealing the Abysses', *JSS* 11 (1976), pp. 135-59, and for 'binding' see my *The Lost Prophet* (London, 1988), ch. 6.

Aristotle's Nous nor from the Stoics for whom the term meant the divine order, the reason which pervaded the universe. The Wisdom of Solomon shows that Philo's own community had had a Logos of their own for some time, and the figure is familiar. On the night of the Exodus[31]

> Thy all-powerful Logos leaped from heaven, from the royal throne,
>   into the midst of the land that was doomed,
> a stern warrior, carrying the sharp sword of thy authentic command,
>   and stood and filled all things with death,
> and touched the heaven while standing on the earth (Wis. 18.15).

In the original Exodus story it was Yahweh who destroyed the Egyptians. Note that the Logos links earth and heaven, and that the sword is well on the way to becoming the sword in the mouth of the Son of Man (Rev. 1.16). Why the Great Angel should have been called the Logos (Word) is not known, but an exactly similar term (Memra, Word) appears in the Targums as a designation for Yahweh. Philo linked the Angel/Logos of his Judaism to the Reason/Logos of the philosophers, and thus began to map the myths of his own culture onto the world of his Greek contemporaries. Hagar, he said, met the angel or divine Reason (Logos) when she fled from Sarah (*Cher.* 3). The original story (Gen. 16) says she met the Angel of Yahweh when driven out by a harsh mistress; Philo says that Hagar represents the lower culture and Sarah the stern ways of those who seek virtue. When Hagar fled, she met the Divine Reason/ Divine Logos who persuaded her to return. Similarly Balaam met the 'armed angel, the Logos of God' (*Cher.* 35). Again, the original (Num. 22) says it was the Angel of Yahweh who met Balaam with a drawn sword. When dismissing the possibility that the creator angel of the Magharians could have been the same as Philo's Logos, Wolfson said:

> Philo does not identify the Logos with the God of the Old Testament, nor does he use it as an explanation for its anthropo-

---

31. But see also C.T.R. Hayward, 'The Holy Name of the God of Moses and the Prologue of St John's Gospel', *NTS* 25 (1978), pp. 16-32.

morphic description of God... *Philo never calls the Logos an angel*.[32]

Such a statement seems incredible! Philo says that the Logos has many names:

> ... God's First-born, the Word, who holds the eldership among the angels, their ruler as it were. And many names are his, for he is called, 'the Beginning', and the Name of God, and His Word and the Man after His image, and 'he that sees', that is Israel (*Conf. Ling.* 146).*

The ruler of the angels and the Name were designations of Yahweh. The firstborn was not only a royal title; it shows that the Logos was begotten, a son of God. He was

> neither uncreated as God, nor yet created as you (i.e. human beings) (*Rer. Div. Her.* 206).

We have to envisage, perhaps, a process of creation in the divine realm, which preceded that of the material world. The Logos is

> antecedent to all that has come into existence... (*Migr. Abr.* 6);
> ... eldest and most all-embracing of created things (*Leg. All.* 3.175).

Philo's Logos was a deity of some sort; he refers to the Logos as a second God when discussing Gen. 9.6:

> For nothing mortal can be made in the likeness of the most high One and Father of the universe, but (only) in that of the second God, who is His Logos (*Quaest. in Gen.* 2.62).

Philo's name for the greater deity is the Most High and the Father, that is, the ancient El Elyon, Father of the sons of God. What was originally meant by 'humans being made in the image of God is not known, but one could guess that God was envisaged in human form by whoever said it. Such anthropomorphism caused considerable disquiet among later interpreters who had come to reject the anthropomorphisms of the

---

32. Wolfson (see n. 15 above), p. 96.
* The quotations from Philo are taken from F.H. Colson and G.H. Whitaker, *Philo* [Greek text with introductions and English translation] (10 vols.; Loeb Classical Library; London and Cambridge, MA, 1929–1962).

Hebrew Bible.[33] Philo, too, makes a characteristic shift; it was
the rational part of man, he said, which was formed as an
impression of the Logos.

The question: How many Gods?, though raised elsewhere, is
not clearly answered. When expounding the account of
Jacob's dream at Bethel, a name which he takes to mean literally 'the place of God', he says:

> And do not fail to mark the language used, but carefully inquire
> whether there are two Gods; for we read 'I am the God that
> appeared to thee', not 'in my place' but 'in the place of God', as
> though it were another's. What, then, are we to say? He that is
> truly God is One, but those that are improperly so called are
> more than one. Accordingly the holy word in the present
> instance has indicated Him Who is truly God by means of the
> articles saying 'I am the God', while it omits the article when
> mentioning him who is improperly so called, saying 'Who
> appeared to thee in the place' not 'of the God', but simply 'of
> God'. Here it gives the title of 'God' to His chief Word, not from
> any superstitious nicety in applying names, but with one aim
> before him, to use words to express facts [*or* to accommodate
> language to practical needs] (*Som.* 1.228-30).

'The God' means the true God (presumably the Most High, if
Philo is consistent) and 'God' is a term applied to other heavenly beings such as the Logos. The argument from 'the place
of God' resembles one used by the later rabbis[34] and it does suggest that Philo knew of a second deity who could be referred to
as 'the place'. When discussing Exod. 24.10, which in the LXX
differs from the MT and reads 'they saw the place where the
God of Israel stands', Philo says:

> For then they shall behold the place, which in fact is the Word,
> where stands God the never changing (*Conf. Ling.* 96).

Since Philo had here been discussing those who serve the Exis-
tent 'who in their thoughts ascend to the heavenly height', we
see how he reinterprets the mystical ascent which, for the
apocalyptists, had been the ascent to the presence of the divine
throne. Philo says that what is seen is not the King, Yahweh of

33. A. Altmann, 'Homo Imago Dei in Jewish and Early Christian
Theology', *JR* 48 (1968), pp. 235-59.
34. Segal, *Two Powers in Heaven*, p. 131.

Hosts (Isa. 6.5), nor 'the likeness as it were of a human form' (Ezek. 1.26), but the Logos. Anthropomorphism, he says, is only for the unsophisticated. Of Gen. 31.13 he says:

> Accordingly, when He says 'I am the God who was seen of thee in the place of God', understand that He occupied the place of an angel only so far as appeared, without changing, with a view to the profit of him who was not yet capable of seeing the true God (*Som.* 1.238).

He continues with an explanation of the relationship between the two Gods:

> For just as those who are unable to see the sun itself see the gleam of the parhelion and take it for the sun, and take the halo round the moon for that luminary itself, so some regard the image of God, His angel the Word, as His very self (*Som.* 1.239).

Philo seems to be criticizing *those who have identified the Logos with the Most High, that is, Yahweh with Elyon*. He recognized several heavenly beings, but only one of them was the true God.[35]

He identified the Logos with the Angel of Yahweh mentioned in Exod. 23.20; the Logos led all seekers after God until they attained 'full knowledge' and became themselves like angels.

> For as long as he falls short of perfection, he has the Divine Word as his leader: since there is an oracle which says, 'Lo, I send My messenger before thy face... for he will by no means withdraw from thee; for My name is on him'. But when he has arrived at full knowledge, he will run with more vigorous effort, and his pace will be as great as that of him who before led the way; for so they will both become attendants on the All-leading God (*Migr. Abr.* 174-75).

Here he is allegorizing. The story of the desert wanderings becomes the journey into the presence of God which others had called the ascent.

> ... Moses has already made it manifest that the sublime and heavenly wisdom is of many names; for he calls it 'beginning' and 'image' and 'vision of God' (*Leg. All.* 1.43).

---

35. Cf. the hostility to the creator God described in Gnostic texts, when he said he was the only God: *NHC* 2.4.94; 2.5.100.

'Full knowledge' for Philo is the same as the apocalyptists' wisdom, that vision of God which transforms the mystic to the angelic state. 'All who lived in the knowledge of the One are rightly called sons of God' (*Conf. Ling.* 145); in the underlying system, the sons of God were the angels, those who had the heavenly knowledge. Beneath this passage, then, we glimpse the Angel who led the seeker into the presence of God where he achieved divine status and became a son of God. This heavenly guide had formerly been Yahweh; in the approximately contemporary *Apocalypse of Abraham* it was the angel Yahoel, and in the later *3 Enoch* it was Metatron, the Lesser Yahweh. Philo identified the guiding angel with Reason; it was the Logos who brought the seeker into the presence of God. In another exposition of Exod. 23.20, the Logos is described as the judge and mediator (*Quaest. in Exod.* 13), titles which derived directly from the ancient roles of Yahweh.

One of the most complex and illuminating of the roles of the Logos is that of High Priest (*Migr. Abr.* 102).[36] His temple was the whole universe.

> For there are, as is evident, two temples of God: one of them this universe, in which there is also as High Priest His First-born, the divine Word, and the other the rational soul, whose Priest is the real Man (*Som.* 1.215; cf. *Fug.* 108).

Here Philo is adapting what we know from 4QShirShabb to have been current beliefs about the temple and its cult. 4QShirShabb, which are approximately contemporary with Philo, depict a heavenly liturgy, but they are so fragmented that much is not clear. There is no pre-eminent angel who could have been the heavenly High Priest, even though other texts, as we have seen, do describe such a figure. The High Priest was important because he could pass through the veil of the sanctuary, that is, he could pass from the material, visible world into the invisible presence of God.[37] He wore special multi-coloured robes (Exod. 28; 39), but when he entered the Holy of Holies on the Day of Atonement, he wore white garments (Lev. 16; *b. Yoma* 35a). The Pentateuch does not say

---

36. E.R. Goodenough, *By Light, Light. The Mystic Gospel of Hellenistic Judaism* (New Haven, 1935), ch. 4.
37. Alexander, '3 Enoch', *OTP*, I, p. 236.

why he dressed as he did. Philo says that every part of the dress was significant: the garments represented the world; the blue robe was the air, the flowers and pomegranate patterns were the fruits and waters of the earth, the breastplate was heaven, the twelve precious stones were the signs of the zodiac and so forth (*Migr. Abr.* 102; *Vit. Mos.* 2.117-26; *Spec. Leg.* 1.85-87). When the High Priest passed through the veil he went from the material world into the presence of God where he wore white linen. White robes were the garb of the angels, and although Philo does not say this, he hints at it when he says that the robes were made of linen, not of wool, 'the product of creatures subject to death' (*Spec. Leg.* 1.84). He also says that the High Priest puts on a robe

> of linen made from the purest kind, a figure of strong fibre, *imperishableness, most radiant light*: for fine linen is hard to tear, and is made from no mortal creature, and moreover when carefully cleaned has *a very brilliant and luminous colour* (*Som.* 1.216-17).

Thus the High Priest wears the stuff of this world when he is outside the sanctuary, and the dress of angels within it. Having said that the High Priest is the Logos, Philo then makes his transposition. What he says about the cosmic significance of the Logos must have been the original significance of the High Priest, since it is this which Philo both assumes and interprets. Others had known similar beliefs:

> For upon his long robe the whole world was depicted, and the glories of the fathers were engraved on the four rows of stones, and thy majesty on the diadem upon his head (Wis. 18.24).

The Word, he says, as the High Priest, passed through the veil from the presence of God and thus became robed in the four elements; that is, he took a material form. This must refer the older belief in a visible manifestation of Yahweh perhaps in the temple, since the Logos passes from the sanctuary, through the veil whose likeness he adopts, and thus into the visible world.

> Now the garments which the supreme Word of Him that IS puts on as raiment are the world, for He arrays Himself in earth and air and water and fire and all that comes forth from these (*Fug.* 110).

The High Priest, the outward and visible image,

> offers the prayers and sacrifices handed down from our fathers,
> to whom it has been committed to wear the aforesaid tunic,
> which is a copy and replica of the whole heaven, the intention of
> this being that the universe may join with man in the holy rites
> and man with the universe (*Som.* 1.215).

Goodenough said that such 'cosmic worship' was one clear
example of how Philo differed from the Stoics:

> The Stoic saw union or harmony with the cosmos as harmony
> with the ultimate. Philo sees it only as a way of joining in with
> the hymn of all creation to the Creator who is infinitely beyond
> the world.[38]

The Logos/High priest passes back into the presence of God as
Mediator.

> To His Word, His chief messenger (*archangelos*), highest image
> and honour, the Father of all has given the special prerogative,
> to stand on the border and separate the creature from the
> Creator. This same Word both pleads with the immortal as sup-
> pliant for afflicted mortality and acts as ambassador of the ruler
> to the subject (*Rer. Div. Her.* 205).

Discussing the veil of the sanctuary, Philo speculates about
how the Logos can become visible:

> The incorporeal world is set off and separated from the visible
> one by the mediating Logos as by a veil. But may it not be that
> this Logos is the tetrad, through which the corporeal solid comes
> into being? (*Quaest. in Exod.* 2.94).

Philo is certain about the Logos at the conjunction of the visible
and invisible worlds; what he wonders is whether this relates
in any way to the geometry of solids! The Logos was also the
Shadow, used as the means of creation:

> God's shadow is His Word, which he made use of like an
> instrument, and so made the world (*Leg. All.* 3.96).

The significance of the veil and the shadow become apparent
in the later Gnostic writings, which clearly derive from similar beliefs.

---

38. Goodenough, *By Light, Light*, p. 117.

> A veil exists between the world above and the realms that are below; and shadow came into being beneath the veil; and that shadow became matter; and that shadow was projected apart...
> It assumed a plastic form molded out of shadow, and became an arrogant beast resembling a lion. It was androgynous... he became arrogant saying, 'It is I who am God, and there is none other apart from me' (*Hypostasis of the Archons* 94-95).[39]

After this the lion-God made himself a chariot of cherubim and surrounded himself with angel ministers. The untitled work (*NHC* 2.5.98-101) is similar. It describes a veil which separates humans from those belonging to the (sphere) above. A shadow brings the lower creation into being, and thinks he is the only God. He is a lion figure who presides over a creation clearly modelled on Genesis 1. There follows an intricate account of the origin of seven androgynous powers, with names like Yao and Eloai. These seem very close to Philo's powers, and beneath the hostility we see the Great Angel of Israel whom some had identified with the High God.

The turban of the High Priest was significant; on it was a golden plate which Exod. 28.36 says bore the words 'Holy to Yahweh'. Philo knew another tradition; on the turban was a golden plate

> with four incisions, showing a name which only those whose ears and tongues are purified may hear or speak in the holy place, and no other person, nor in any other place at all. That name has four letters (*Vit. Mos.* 2.114; cf. *Migr. Abr.* 103).

Thus the High Priests bore the name Yahweh.

The Logos was also the central stem of the menorah, dividing three lamps from three lamps (*Rer. Div. Her.* 215-25). Philo argues from this fact towards Heracleitus's theory of opposites, but he must have begun with the fact that the Logos was represented by the central stem of the lamp. Earlier traditions had linked the lamp with the presence of Yahweh in the Temple, and the seven branches of the lamp were the seven eyes of Yahweh (Zech. 4.10). Philo's near-contemporary, the seer John, described these seven lamps as the seven spirits before the throne (Rev. 1.4). More interesting for this

39. English translations in J.M. Robinson (ed.), *The Nag Hammadi Library* (Leiden, 1977), p. 167.

enquiry is that the angel of fire and bronze was the central stem of the sevenfold lamp. (This surely lies behind the present 'one like a son of man in the midst of the lampstands' [Rev. 1.14].) The seven are also the eyes of the lamb (Rev. 5.6), as they had been the eyes of Yahweh. Philo knew of the plural nature of Yahweh implied by this symbolism, and used it as the basis for what he says about the Powers.[40]

The Powers are closely associated with the Logos; they too can enter matter. They were the ancient angels, both the higher ranks and the angels of the natural order. The latter are described in *Jub.* 2.2, and there are lists of these angels' names in *1 Enoch* 6 and 69. In each list most of the names are compounded with *-el*. Although we are far from understanding the roles of the angels, they do seem to represent visible and tangible aspects of God. God is One, says Philo, but around him he has the numberless Powers which all assist and protect the created order (*Conf. Ling.* 171).

> That aspect of Him which transcends His Potencies cannot be conceived of at all in terms of place, but only as pure being, but that Potency of His by which He made and ordered all things, while it is called God... holds the whole in its embrace and has interfused itself through the parts of the universe (*Conf. Ling.* 137).

These Potencies (Powers) were integral to Philo's Judaism; he distinguishes carefully between what Moses says, and the teaching of the 'Chaldaeans'. Moses says that

> the complete whole around us is held together by invisible powers which the Creator has made to reach from the ends of the earth to the heaven's furthest bounds, taking forethought that what was well bound should not be loosened: for the powers of the Universe are chains that cannot be broken (*Migr. Abr.* 181).

There is nothing in our reading of Moses which says this, a warning that there is much beneath even the familiar texts of the Old Testament which Philo knew and we do not, his Judaism's 'oral tradition', perhaps. What he says here sounds very

---

40. E.R. Goodenough, *Jewish Symbols in the Graeco-Roman Period*, vol. 4 (New York, 1953), p. 84, and L. Yarden, *The Tree of Light*, (London, 1971), plate 69, show several representations of the menorah with a prominent central shaft.

like the 'cosmic covenant', especially since the Powers are the
angels, the host of heaven whose breaking loose is the theme of
1 Enoch. Philo's Moses says:

> By Thy glory I understand the powers that keep guard around
> Thee (*Spec. Leg.* 1.45).

Moses was told that he could not see that face of Yahweh but
only what was behind him (Exod. 33.23); this was understood
to mean the angels, the Powers. There is an exactly similar
understanding of the passage in the Targum:

> And I will make the troop of angels pass by who stand and min-
> ister before me and you will see the Word of the Glory of my
> Shekinah but it is not possible for you to see the face of the Glory
> of my Shekinah (*TN Exod.* 33.23).

Thus Philo draws on a tradition of interpretation common to
his community and that which produced *Targum Neofiti*.[41] He
adapts it and says that 'the Powers around the Glory', what
humans can see of the presence of God, means their visible
form in the universe.[42] This is like the Platonic 'Forms' but
again, this is only a comparison. The original existed already in
his own Judaism (*Fug.* 165; *Mut. Nom.* 9). Yahweh the King
surrounded by his hosts is the oldest of the temple visions (Isa.
6; 1 Kgs 22). Philo must have understood the song of the
seraphim to mean that the whole earth was full of the Glory,
i.e. the Powers, of Yahweh.

These powers were closely linked to the Logos, who was
their head, just as Yahweh had been the chief of the angels.
Philo uses several illustrations for this, for example the six
cities of refuge which are 'colonies of the Logos' (*Fug.* 94). It is
interesting that he uses the six-plus-one theme again here,
reminiscent of the menorah and its branches. The nature of
these powers is also interesting; their leader is creative power,
the second is royal power, the third gracious power (at this
point there is a break in the text). Were these derived from the

---

41. There is no agreement as to its date and origin; see A.D. York,
'The Dating of Targumic Literature', *JSJ* 5 (1974).

42. M.D. Hooker ('The Johannine Prologue and the Messianic Secret',
NTS 21 [1974], pp. 40-58) suggests that Exod. 33.12-23 also forms the
background to Jn 1.14-18, the revelation of the Glory.

archangels whose names were compounded with -*el*? We should perhaps ponder the fact that Elohim, the other name for Yahweh in the Old Testament, is a plural noun, meaning angels or gods, and that it was the Deuteronomists, those who suppressed anthropomorphism and the memory of the older cult, who gave us the impossible text: 'Yahweh our Elohim is one' (Deut. 6.4). Similarly, the golden plate on the High Priest's turban represented the single behind the plurality:

> the original principle behind all principles, after which God shaped or formed the universe (*Migr. Abr.* 103).

Neither of these statements about the plurality of the Logos can have derived from the text in question. Philo illustrates from each that this was the case, and that the many Powers were ruled by, and in some way a part of, the Logos. The sacred name was the name of the Powers:

> The third [commandment] is concerned with the name of the Lord, not that name the knowledge of which has never even reached the world of mere becoming... but the name which is given to His Potencies. We are commanded not to take this name in vain (*Rer. Div. Her.* 170).

Time and again we find that the Logos is the visible, the manifested God. Discussing Deut. 4.39, 'Yahweh is God in heaven above and on the earth beneath', Philo says:

> Let no one suppose that He that IS is spoken of... What is meant is that potency of His by which He established and ordered and marshalled the whole realm of being (*Migr. Abr.* 182).

This is reminiscent of the Logos in Wisdom, which touched the heaven while standing on the earth (Wis. 18.15).

There were two chief Powers, called God (Elohim) and Lord (Yahweh), but these were but two aspects of the One. They were linked to or represented by the two cherubim of throne.

> And the two primary Potencies of the Existent, namely that through which He wrought the world, the beneficent, which is called God, and that by which He rules and commands what He made, that is the punitive, which bears the name of Lord, are as Moses tells us, separated by God Himself standing above and in the midst of them. 'I will speak to thee', it says, 'above the mercy-seat in the midst of the two Cherubim. He means to shew that the primal and highest Potencies of the Existent, the

beneficent and the punitive, are equal, having Him to divide them (*Rer. Div. Her.* 166).[43]

Philo uses the imagery of the cherubim in many ways; elsewhere it is Reason/Logos who stands between the two cherubim, to unite them.

> While God is indeed one, His highest and chiefest powers are two, even goodness and sovereignty... And in the midst between the two is a third which unites them, Reason, for it is through reason that God is both ruler and good. Of these two potencies sovereignty and goodness the Cherubim are symbols, as fiery sword is the symbol of reason (*Cher.* 27-28).

Here Philo equates the cherubim of the Garden of Eden with those of the temple which represented Eden. Between the two cherubim in the Jerusalem temple was not the flaming sword (Gen. 3.24 does not say the sword was between them) but the throne.[44] It is impossible to assess exactly what Philo does with the underlying tradition, because we can only make comparisons if evidence has survived elsewhere. The cherubim and what they symbolized remain a mystery.[45] What is clear is that Philo associates aspects of the Logos with the throne, and the two cherubim with the aspects known as Elohim and Yahweh. The gracious power is represented by the mercy seat between the cherubim. The passage in which Philo outlines this theory is not at all clear, nor is it consistent with what he says elsewhere—a warning, perhaps that he cannot be pressed too hard in his transpositions.

> ... the lid of the ark, which he calls the Mercy-seat, representing the gracious power; while the creative and kingly powers are represented by the winged Cherubim that rest upon it. The Divine Word, who is high above all these, has not been visibly portrayed, being like to no one of the objects of sense. Nay, He is Himself the Image of God, chiefest of all Beings intellectually perceived, placed nearest, with no intervening distance, to the Alone truly Existent One. For we read: 'I will talk to thee from above the Mercy-seat, between the two Cherubim' (Exod. 25.21) (*Fug.* 100-101).

43. Cf. *Quaest. in Gen.* 57; *Deus Imm.* 109.
44. The sword may have been a symbol of Yahweh for Philo.
45. See R. Patai, *The Hebrew Goddess* (New York, 1967), ch. 3.

Had he said no more, we should have concluded that the Logos was the one who spoke to Moses, that is, the Logos was Yahweh. But Philo then adds that the Logos is the charioteer to whom the occupant of the throne speaks! Both the highest Powers, it should be noted, are equal and parallel, and both are subordinate to the High God.[46]

The combined name Yahweh–Elohim which occurs so often in the Pentateuch, stands for the two Powers combined.

> Why does (Scripture) say that when Abraham was ninety-nine years old, 'The Lord God appeared to him and said, I am the Lord thy God'? It gives the appellations of the two highest powers... for by them the world came into being, and having come into being, it is governed by them (*Quaest. in Gen.* 3.39).

In the same work Philo speaks later of 'uttering a double invocation to the powers of the Father, (namely) the creative and kingly' (*Quaest. in Gen.* 4.87).

The Logos was also the royal figure, 'he who is at once High Priest and King' (*Fug.* 118). He was a human figure:

> God's Man... the Word of the Eternal...
> He is called, 'the Beginning', and the Name of God and His Word and the Man after His image, and 'he that sees', that is Israel (*Conf. Ling.* 41; 146).
> The image of God is the Word through whom the whole universe was framed (*Spec. Leg.* 1.81).

He was the Branch of Zech. 6.12, a messianic text (*Conf. Ling.* 62), and he was the viceroy appointed to sustain the universe:

> [I] sustained the universe to rest firm and sure upon the mighty Word, who is My viceroy (*Som.* 1.241; cf. *Agric.* 51).

This status was symbolized by the High Priest's diadem:

> ... the symbol not of absolute sovereignty but of a an admirable viceroyalty (*Fug.* 112).

The Logos was the key to the cosmic covenant and its stability; he is actually called 'His Logos which he calls his Covenant' (*Som.* 2.237; cf. *Migr. Abr.* 181 and *Conf. Ling.* 137).

---

46. Segal (*Two Powers in Heaven*) does not emphasize the difference between the High God and the Angel (one pair of powers in heaven) and the two equal powers described by Philo.

This must be read alongside the fact that the Logos was the head of the powers, and it was the Powers which bound the creation together.

> ... the everlasting Word of the eternal God is the very sure and staunch prop of the Whole. He it is, who extending Himself from the midst to its utmost bounds and from its extremities to the midst again, keeps up through all its length Nature's unvanquished course, combining and compacting all its parts. For the Father Who begat Him constituted His Word such a Bond of the Universe as nothing can break (*Plant.* 8-9).

Of the Logos as High Priest, Philo says:

> And the oldest Logos of God has put on the universe as a garment... 'He does not tear his garments' for the Logos of God is the bond of all things, as has been said, and holds together all parts, and prevents them by its constriction from breaking apart and becoming separated (*Fug.* 112).

The Logos was also the seal of the universe:

> The Word of Him who makes it is Himself the seal, by which each thing that exists has received its shape (*Fug.* 12; cf. *Som.* 2.45).

Philo must have known the tradition of Yahweh's name being the seal but he rejected the original magical associations such as are found in the tale of sealing the abysses. Rather than the seal which secures it, for him the seal becomes the mould which forms the shape of the universe.

The Logos also created by dividing, as did God in Genesis 1:

> ... the Severer of all things, that is his Word... (*Rer. Div. Her.* 130),

and he maintained order by keeping the conflicting powers apart:

> ... the earth shall not be dissolved by all the water... nor fire be quenched by air; nor, on the other hand, air be ignited by fire. The Divine Word stations Himself to keep these elements apart ... he mediates between the opponents amid their threatenings, and reconciles them (*Plant.* 10).

Cf. the role of Yahoel in the *Apocalypse of Abraham*:

> I am the one who has been charged... to restrain the threats of
> the living creatures of the cherubim against one another... I
> am appointed to hold the Leviathans (*Ap. Abr.* 10.9-10).[47]

The imagery underlying Philo's exposition of the Logos is
unmistakable; the temple cult of Jerusalem was the source of a
very great deal of it, and given that we only know of that cult
fragments that can be reconstructed from many sources, it
may well be that far more of his allusions and imagery could
fit did we but know the master picture. What, for example, lies
behind Philo's image of the Logos as food (*Leg. All.* 3.173)?
Commenting on Exod. 16.15, he says that the Logos is the
heavenly bread. A similar tradition must underlie Jn 7.48-51.[48]
Again, what gave rise to the picture of the Logos 'that brings
man to repentance and salvation by entering the soul and
making man aware of his sins and bidding them be cleared out
in order that the Logos might be able to perform the necessary
work of healing' (*Deus Imm.* 134-35; cf. *Rer. Div. Her.* 63-
64)?[49] Might this twofold process be based upon the twofold
ritual of the Day of Atonement (Lev. 16)? One goat rid the
people of sin and the blood of the other effected atonement. The
atoning goat was the one 'for Yahweh' (or 'as Yahweh'; the
Hebrew could mean either). The High Priest, who bore the
name of Yahweh, took the blood into the sanctuary and thus
effected atonement not only for the people but also for the
temple (cf. Deut. 32.43; Heb. 9.12).[50]

Finally, brief mention must be made of two other aspects of
the Logos—brief because they are fully covered in all works on
Philo. First, the Logos was closely connected with Moses, but
significantly in the context of the royal cult; and second, the
Logos has much in common with Wisdom, again in this context. Philo knew of the traditions drawn upon by Ezekiel the
tragedian in his *Exodus*.[51] Both writers associated Moses with

47. Cf. the role of Yahweh in Job 41.
48. P. Borgen, *Bread from Heaven: An Exegetical Study of the Concept
of Manna in the Gospel of John and the Writings of Philo* (Leiden,
1965).
49. R. Williamson, *Jews in the Hellenistic World. Philo* (Cambridge,
1989), p. 114.
50. Both, of course, could be Christian additions.
51. Eusebius, *Praep. Ev.* 9.29.

a mystic ascent, as a result of which he was given both divine and royal status.

> ... he was named god and king of the whole nation, and entered, we are told, into the darkness where God (ὁ θεός) was (*Vit. Mos.* 1.158; cf. *Som.* 2.189).

Moses was not merely a man, but one who belonged to both worlds (*Som.* 2.189; cf. *Rer. Div. Her.* 84). If Philo is consistent in his usage, 'the God' denotes the High God, and 'God' denotes the Logos. This means that Philo associated Moses with the ancient royal traditions, with the mystical ascent which lay at the heart of the ancient temple cult and was depicted in the vision of Daniel 7. A man could become 'God and King' just as the God and King could be in human form.[52]

Second, both the roles and the imagery associated with the Logos resembled those of Wisdom. The Wisdom described in Wis. 7.25 is exactly Philo's Logos:

> ... a breath of the power of God,
> And a pure emanation of the glory of the Almighty.

Since Wisdom's roles were almost exactly those of the Spirit of Yahweh in the Old Testament, this is another link between the Logos and Yahweh. The initial objection might be that Wisdom is a female figure and the Logos male, but Philo does not think this gender difference a problem. Wisdom was second after God, he said, and femininity expressed the subordinate role:

> Let us, then, pay no heed to this discrepancy in the gender of the words, and say that the daughter of God, even Wisdom, is not only masculine but also father, sowing and begetting in souls aptness to learn (*Fug.* 52).

Cf. *Rer. Div. Her.* 119, where it is the Logos who implants this seed.

Both Wisdom (Prov. 8.30) and Logos (*Migr. Abr.* 5-6) were the agents of creation. Both Wisdom (Prov. 8.22-24) and Logos were the firstborn.[53] Wisdom was created but eternal (Sir. 24.9; cf. *Conf. Ling.* 41). Wisdom penetrated all things (Wis. 7.24);

---

52. Cf. *The Older Testament*, p. 150.
53. Although Prov. 8.22 says that Wisdom was brought forth by Yahweh.

Logos was the bond of the creation (*Plant.* 9). Wisdom (Sir. 24.8) was given Israel for its special heritage; Logos was the angel of Israel. Wisdom ministered before the creator in Zion (Sir. 24.8); Logos was the High Priest. Wisdom was the guide of Israel's Exodus and wanderings (Wis. 10.15ff.). Wisdom was an angelic being who could find no place on earth and so returned to heaven (*1 Enoch* 42). Wisdom sat beside the divine throne or shared it as the consort (Wis. 8.3-4; 9.4, 10; *1 Enoch* 84.5). Most striking of all is the fact that Wisdom is a person in some texts, and in others just a body of teaching. Philo has done something similar with the Logos; although it is clearly a person, he has grafted it into the philosophical systems of his day.[54]

E.R. Goodenough observed long ago that, despite all efforts, Philo remained an enigma.

> No one seems to have tried to read Philo, if I may say so, with the grain instead of against it, to understand what Philo himself thought he was driving at in all his passionate labours.[55]

Can it be that Philo was demythologizing? We know so little of the mythology of ancient Israel (indeed it is said that there was none!) that it is virtually impossible to appreciate the extent and the genius of the transformation he effected.

It is with mixed feelings that I offer this little piece to Dr Bammel; I am happy to contribute to this volume as a token of affection and gratitude, but sad that it marks the end of an era in Cambridge.

54. It is the fashion to assume that personifications are a late development; I doubt this and think that 'gods' preceded demythologizing.
55. Goodenough, *By Light, Light*, p. 5.

HEROD'S TEMPLE AND 'HEROD'S DAYS'

William Horbury

Ancient accounts of Herod's temple often pass over the name of Herod. He is not named as builder in *Mishnah, Middoth*, by Philo in his description (*Spec. Leg.* 1.71-78; cf. *Leg. ad Gaium* 294-97), by Tacitus or Cassius Dio, or by Josephus when not following Nicolas of Damascus; the long description in book 5 of the *War* names Solomon as founder of the temple, but Herod only as builder of Antonia (Josephus, *War* 5.185, 238).

These silences can readily be ascribed to the negative views of Herod expressed by Josephus and in rabbinic and Christian sources, and reflected in Strabo's reference to Jewish 'hatred towards Herod' as the justification for Antony's execution of Antigonus (in a passage quoted by Josephus, *Ant.* 15.9-10). Other reasons for silence can be envisaged, however, including in different cases the biblically influenced and traditional character of the narratives or the writer's sense that the building was a communal achievement. Moreover, as will be seen in a moment, the silence is broken not only when Josephus follows Nicolas, but also when the story of the building of the sanctuary recurs in rabbinic narrative.

E. Bammel has drawn attention to the political value of the temple, and in particular its official oversight, for the house of Herod and Herodian supporters.[1] The accounts of Herod's temple may therefore suitably introduce some reconsideration of Herodian kingship in its Jewish setting. The concentration of historiography on Judaea and its movements of revolt

1. E. Bammel, 'The Trial before Pilate', in E. Bammel and C.F.D. Moule (eds.), *Jesus and the Politics of his Day* (Cambridge, 1984), pp. 423-24, 446; and in a review of M.D. Goodman, *The Ruling Class of Judaea* (Cambridge, 1987) (on the Herods and their adherents, see especially pp. 40-46, 122-23) in *JTS* ns 40 (1989), pp. 213-17 (215).

against Rome tends to highlight aspects of the house of Herod which were, or were regarded as, non-Jewish. Herodian kingship should also be viewed against its broader Jewish background, with fuller reference to the Diaspora and to likely differences of attitude among Jews at home as well as abroad, so that areas of merging as well as contrast gain due prominence.[2] A small step in this direction is at any rate attempted here. Some of the narratives of the building of Herod's temple in Jerusalem, and Persius's lines on 'Herod's days' in Rome, are considered as foci of positive associations between the house of Herod and the Jews of the Roman empire.

The desiderata just outlined are of course not ignored by historians, and they are prominent in the relatively short prewar treatments of the house of Herod by H. Willrich and A. Momigliano; more recently, A. Schalit has monumentally presented Herod the Great as a Hellenistic monarch imbued with Augustan ideology, but one sufficiently aware of Jewish feeling to foster a Herodian messianism as the analogue to a ruler-cult, and one whose achievements entitle him to be recognized as a king of Israel; while M. Stern, dissenting from this recognition, has nevertheless indicated many connections as well as conflicts between the Herods and their Judaean Jewish subjects.[3] In Schalit's book, however, although Hellenism is central, the claims of political history accord less prominence to the discussion of Jewish Hellenism, a debate also relevant to

2. This point is noted (with regard to Herod the Great) by M. Hengel, *The Zealots* (ET; Edinburgh, 1989), pp. 323-24 n. 68.

3. H. Willrich, *Das Haus des Herodes zwischen Jerusalem und Rom* (Heidelberg, 1929); A. Momigliano, 'Herod of Judaea', 'Rebellion within the Empire', sections iv-vii, and 'Josephus as a Source for the History of Judaea', in S.A. Cook, F.E. Adcock and M.P. Charlesworth (eds.), *The Cambridge Ancient History*, X (Cambridge, 1934, repr. 1971), pp. 316-39, 849-65, 884-87 (the general standpoint differs from that of Momigliano's post-war work; see n. 36, below); A. Schalit, *König Herodes* (Berlin, 1969; a revised and enlarged version of the text originally issued in modern Hebrew, Jerusalem, 1960); M. Stern, 'A. Schalit's Herod', *JJS* 11 (1960), pp. 49-58, and (among other writings) 'The Reign of Herod' and 'The Herodian Dynasty and the Province of Judaea at the End of the Period of the Second Temple', in M. Avi-Yonah and Z. Baras, (eds.), *The Herodian Period* (= *The World History of the Jewish People*, First Series, 7) (London, 1975), pp. 71-178.

assessment of Herodian kingship (and Schalit wrote before M. Hengel's contributions to this debate). Moreover, here and in Stern's writing the emphasis still lies mainly on Judaea, as is naturally also true of the treatment of hostility to the Herods in work on the antecedents of the Judaean revolt of 66–70 by Hengel and Goodman (see notes 1, 2, above).

The contrasting evidence for some positive Jewish recognition of Herodian kingship therefore deserves fresh attention, with some notice of the diaspora as well as Judaea, and of the overlap of attitudes between the two which discussion of Hellenism in Judaism has often indicated.[4] Estimates of public opinion must of course reckon with a probable difference between the homeland, where revolts broke out in Idumaea, Judaea, Peraea and Galilee on the death of Herod the Great, and the diaspora, where Herodian monarchs were valued as protectors of the Jews. Among Judaean and Galilaean Jews themselves, however, opinion will also have varied; it is likely that the division between rich and poor emphasized by Josephus, and the overlapping division between town and country, often corresponded to a difference in attitudes to the Herodian government.

Some Jews were supporting the house of Herod in Judaea and Galilee before Herod the Great established his reign. When he was fighting for the crown between 40 and 37 he found Jewish partisans in Galilee, Idumaea and Judaea (especially Jericho), and Jerusalem itself—where leading Pharisees urged submission to Herod—was divided (Josephus, *War* 1.291-93, 319, 326, 335, 358, parallel with *Ant.* 14.395-98, 436, 450, 458; 15.2-3). At the capture of the city the Jewish attack-

---

4. For example, E. Schürer, *Geschichte des jüdischen Volkes im Zeitalter Jesu Christi,* III (4th edn; Leipzig, 1909), pp. 188-89 ('Palestinian' Judaism can be found outside as well as inside Palestine, and 'Hellenistic' Judaism inside as well as outside); W.D. Davies, *Paul and Rabbinic Judaism* (2nd edn; London, 1955), pp. 1-16 (6-7, reciprocal interchange of thought between Palestine and the Diaspora); on a Herodian halakhic instance, E. Bammel, 'Markus 10.11f. und das jüdische Eherecht', *ZNW* 61 (1970), pp. 95-101 (divorce initiated from the wife's side, as by Herod the Great's sister Salome in her marriage with Costobar, known in Jewish Palestine as well as the Diaspora, despite its condemnation as un-Jewish by Josephus, *Ant.* 15.259).

ing forces were as hard to restrain as the Romans (*War* 1.351
= *Ant.* 14.479).[5] Thereafter, Jerusalem and Jericho will always
have had their wealthy Herodian constituency (strengthened
by the foundation of Phasaelis and Archelais in the region of
Jericho), but it is also notable that the long periods of Herodian
rule in the northern tetrarchies found response in the
nomenclature of more prosperous Jews. The name Herod is
attested in Tiberias in 66 (two leading citizens of that name are
mentioned by Josephus, *Vita* 33), and, later on, in inscriptions
at Capernaum and Beth She'arim; Philip of Bethsaida (Jn
1.45; 12.21) was perhaps, like the Herods of Tiberias, named
after the tetrarch who was also city-founder.[6] 'Herodians',
best understood as supporters of the house of Herod (with H.H.
Rowley, see note 30 below), are envisaged both in Galilee and
Jerusalem in Mark (3.6; 12.13).

Moreover, Jewish town-dwellers in particular were regularly at close quarters with gentiles, as at Jamnia and Caesarea or in the Decapolis but west of the Jordan, at Scythopolis;
and so a diaspora-like situation, in which a Jewish king could
be valued, was reproduced in the homeland. Correspondingly,
Herod the Great could be remembered as a Jewish king and
benefactor by the wealthy Jewish community of Caesarea,
who argued that this largely gentile city was theirs, since its
founder was a Jewish king (Josephus, *War* 2.266). In the diaspora itself, Babylonia and Alexandria contributed important

5. The vast majority of Jews supported Antigonus, in the judgment of
M. Stern, 'Social and Political Realignments in Herodian Judaea', *The
Jerusalem Cathedra*, II (1982), pp. 40-62 (40-41); Herodian numbers
may indeed be exaggerated in Josephus, on the basis of Nicolas of
Damascus (as in the case of Galilee, according to Schalit, *Herodes*, p.
90); but the Jewish population was clearly divided, and the significance for this point of the zeal of the Jewish captors of Jerusalem, not
mentioned by Stern, is brought out by Schalit (p. 173 n. 95).
6. For the inscriptions see B. Lifschitz, *Donateurs et fondateurs dans
les synagogues juives* (Paris, 1967), p. 61, no. 75 (= *CIJ*, II, no. 983)
(donor of column at Capernaum), and M. Schwabe and B. Lifschitz,
Beth She'arim, II. *The Greek Inscriptions* (Jerusalem, 1967), p. 17,
no. 56; these names suggest some qualification of Goodman, *Ruling
Class*, p. 122 n. 16, where the failure of ordinary Jews to take Herodian
names is contrasted with gentile willingness to take the name Agrippa
under Agrippa II, but this evidence (indicating a similar Jewish
inclination in Herodian territory) is unmentioned.

groups of Herodian adherents (see Stern, as cited in note 5, above), and Herodian supporters and nomenclature reappear in Rome (see Rom. 16.10-11 and section II (c), below). Many of Herod the Great's descendants gained added prestige from Hasmonaean high-priestly ancestry (which Agrippa I is represented as valuing particularly in Philo, *Leg. ad Gaium* 278), and the acclaim which these Herodian princes could receive from Jews both at home and abroad, in Judaea, Alexandria, the Greek islands and Italy, is loud and clear in the cases of Mariamme's sons Alexander and Aristobulus, and her grandson Agrippa I.

Recognition of the Herods has therefore left widespread traces in the evidence for the unified but varied ancient Jewish community, in which differences of standing and outlook often traversed the difference between homeland and diaspora. The texts considered below against this background come from a dossier which has often been examined. Thus, M. Stern's summary of the claims of Herod the Great to be viewed as a Jewish king largely overlaps with seventeenth-century argument for the Jewishness of Herod, itself a reaction against the treatment of Herod as an alien in patristic interpretation of Gen. 49.10 on the departure of the sceptre from Judah.[7] Here two items in Stern's summary are reviewed again, but in recent work known to the writer the narratives of the temple-building have had little consideration, the possible link between the temple and 'Herod's days' has not

---

7. M. Stern, 'The Reign of Herod', pp. 110-11; cf. F. Spanheim, *Dubia Evangelica* (2 vols.; Geneva, 1639), II, pp. 225-55, summarizing the debate initiated by J.J. Scaliger's assertion of Herod's Jewish descent (cited in n. 30, below). Justin Martyr and Eusebius (cited in n. 17, below) viewed Herod's allegedly Ascalonite origin respectively as an objection to and a support for the claim that Christ came when the sceptre had departed from Judah; this interpretation of Gen. 49.10 is made to rest, rather, on Herod's Idumaean descent in the version of Josephus's account of the deputations to Augustus concerning Herod's will in the fourth-century Christian Latin Hegesippus, *Historiae* 2.1, 2. Herod is called *alienigena* without further specification in the interpretations of Gen. 49.10 in the same sense by Rufinus, *De Benedictionibus Patriarcharum* 1.7 and Augustine, *De Civitate Dei* 18.45 (translated with further Augustinian material in Ad. Posnanski, *Schiloh* I [Leipzig, 1904], pp. 71-75).

been re-examined, and exegesis of the texts has not been connected with the broader discussion of Herodian kingship
against the Jewish background sketched above. It will be
argued that Persius is a further witness to the Jewish observation of Herodian festivals attested by Josephus, and that
these passages illustrate the function of Herod's temple as a
royal sanctuary, bring out the character and Jewish
significance of the Herodian form of ruler-cult, and confirm
the importance of the more favourable Jewish attitudes to the
house of Herod.

I. *Narratives of the Building of the Temple*

a. *Josephus*

When Josephus follows Nicolas, and presents Herod as the
king of the Jews building the Jerusalem temple (*War* 1.400-
401; *Ant.* 15.380-425), he echoes court publicity in which three
royal associations of the enterprise are heavily underlined.
First, in Herod's speech to the people beforehand, it is represented that the Jews' own king is restoring the temple to the
height originally planned by Solomon. (Regret for the fall of
Solomon's temple, which 'was high', and hope that a future
temple will be very high, are reflected at 2 Chron. 7.21; *1
Enoch* 90.29; *Sib.* 5.425.) The forefathers who rebuilt and
maintained it after the exile had to be content with the
reduced dimensions prescribed by their foreign overlords,
Cyrus and Darius and others, in a time of necessity and sub-
jection. Now, however, under Herod, there is peace, prosperity,
and friendship with the universally powerful Romans, as
opposed to servitude under the Persians and Macedonians,
and the king can perform the pious duty of restoration (*Ant.*
15.385-87).

Significantly, the Macedonians are mentioned, but the Maccabees are not. This silence is emphasized by the insertion of a
reference to the Maccabees in the tenth-century Jewish paraphrase of this speech in *Josippon* (50.15-17 in the edition by D.
Flusser, I [Jerusalem, 1978], p. 227). Here it is said that they
won freedom and kingship—the points on which Herodian
silence is to be expected—but could not rebuild the temple—a
point which was indeed made in Herodian publicity (Herod's

speech in Jericho in Josephus, *Ant.* 17.162, quoted below). It was no doubt thought better, if possible, not to mention the Hasmonaean house at all.

Secondly, and consistently with the emphasis in the foregoing on Herodian deliverance from national servitude, the rebuilt temple signified Jewish victory under a conquering Jewish king. King Herod dedicated 'barbarian spoils' which were fixed round about the whole new sanctuary, with the addition of those he had taken from the Arabs (*Ant.* 15.402). 'Barbarian' is no doubt a well-worn substitute for 'enemy' in this connection (cf. Virgil, *Aeneid* 2.504), but here it seems to have both a Roman and a Jewish reference. Herod had helped to repulse the Parthians and their allies, the barbarians particularly feared in Rome, and had taken booty from them; they are repeatedly called βάρβαροι in the previous book of the *Antiquities* (e.g. 14.341, 347, 441-45, following Roman usage, in these passages probably mediated by Nicolas, but also adopted by Josephus himself [see *War* 1.3]). Moreover, the rebuilding of the temple began in 20 BC, when Augustus visited Syria, added to Herod's territory, and by a display of force in Armenia compelled the Parthian king Phraates to restore Roman spoils and standards, a great capitulation marked by publicity including coins and many references in the poets (e.g. Horace, *Od.* 4.15, 4-8);[8] it is likely that 'barbarian spoils' are meant to recall the Herodian Jewish contribution to this vaunted achievement of the Augustan peace. At the same time, indeed, Herod was building his temple to Augustus at Paneas (Josephus, *Ant.* 15.363-65). Herod had also, however, fought traditional enemies of the Jews in his victorious war against the Nabataean Arabs, who had twice defeated Alexander Jannaeus (*Ant.* 13.375, 392; 15.147-60). Here, therefore, Herod had beaten the Hasmonaean record, and 'barbarian' could allude to enemies of the Jews, as in 2 Macc. 2.21 and 10.4, and to the Arabs in particular, as in Josephus, *War* 1.274; the spoils could legitimately recall, as Herod's speech on the temple restoration is represented as doing, Jewish victory in the context of Roman friendship.

8. See J.G.C. Anderson in *Cambridge Ancient History*, X (cited in n. 3 above), pp. 262-63.

The emphases represented in the speech and the adornment of the temple therefore stamp a Herodian impress on the themes of the deliberately unmentioned Hasmonaean Hanukkah, which recalled how the Maccabees 'put the barbarian hordes to flight,... recovered the temple..., and freed the city' (2 Macc. 2.21-22; cf. 10.1-8). Herod, king of the Jews, has given them, again and in fuller measure, victory over barbarian enemies and liberty from alien rule; and—what is more than the recovery of the temple commemorated at Hanukkah—he has restored the house of God to its former Solomonic glory. Conditions in fact answer to the zealotically tinged ideal sketch of the time of David and Solomon later given in *2 Baruch*: 'much blood of the nations that had sinned then was shed, and many offerings were offered at the dedication of the sanctuary. And peace and tranquillity reigned at that time' (*Syriac Apocalypse of Baruch* 61.2-3).

Hence, thirdly, the context is not unfitting for the claim in the speech that the temple is the king's act of piety towards God, in return for having obtained the kingdom—which, with the divine will and counsel, he has brought to prosperity (Josephus, *Ant.* 15.383, 387). The themes are at once Graeco-Roman and characteristically Jewish. Herod displays the *eusebeia* which was a prime quality of the Hellenistic monarch (as emphasized by the Jewish sages in the *Letter of Aristeas*, 255, 261, and elsewhere), which was eminently shown by Augustus, the great restorer of temples,[9] and which was later claimed by the house of Herod in the title *eusebes* adopted by Agrippa I and II; it is further presented in the *War*

---

9. Hailed, for example, as a benefactor who has put the gods themselves under an obligation, in Ovid, *Fasti* 2.59-64 (especially 63-64, 'templorum positor, templorum sancte repostor | sit superis, opto, mutua cura tui'); closer to Jewish emphasis on the priority of the divine side of the exchange (in agreement with the Stoic view that God needs nothing, *Letter of Aristeas* 211; Acts 17.25) is the recommendation of Augustus's restoration policy in Horace, *Od.* 3.6, 1-5, 'delicta maiorum immeritus lues | Romane, donec templa refeceris | ... dis te minorem quod geris, imperas'. For the Greek background of the concept of exchange of benefits see W.C. van Unnik, 'Eine merkwürdige liturgische Aussage bei Josephus (Jos. Ant. 8, 111-13)', in O. Betz, K. Haacker and M. Hengel (eds.), *Josephus-Studien* (Göttingen, 1974), pp. 362-69 (364-66).

as Herod the Great's own notable quality, when he plans the restoration and also (in a speech ascribed to him in his rebuilt temple) when, eight years later, he names his successors (Josephus, *War* 1.400, 462; cf. *Ant.* 16.132-33).[10] The restoration of the Jerusalem temple is understood in the earlier speech as part of a divine-human exchange of benefits, a Graeco-Roman concept (as exemplified in note 9, above) which had entered Jewish piety in convergence with the later biblical references to divine gifts; thus, in David's prayer in 1 Chron. 29.14, his offerings for Solomon's temple are a return of God's gifts, and the opening of Solomon's prayer at the dedication of the temple (1 Kgs 8.23 = 2 Chron. 6.14) includes in Josephus a contrasting recognition that it is impossible to recompense God in the exchange (*Ant.* 8.111, see note 9, above).

In accord with the Jewish overtones of the passage Schalit, followed by A. Hultgård and Th.A. Busink, finds a Davidic messianism behind the references to God's favour to the king; and although, as Stern shows, it is unlikely that Herod claimed Davidic descent, he is presented here as a divinely appointed and guided king who is a second and perhaps still greater Solomon (in his building, comparably, as Busink notes, his retention of the old 'Solomon's Porch' will have designedly set off the greater size and splendour of his own new work).[11] The comparison with Solomon is reinforced in the *Antiquities*, where the account of Herod's temple is preceded by the story of the Essene prophecy that he would be king of the Jews and enjoy exceptional good fortune until the end of his life, when his neglect of piety and justice would bring down the divine wrath (15.373-79); Solomon, likewise, prospered by divine providence until idolatry brought wrath upon him (1 Kgs 11 as interpreted in Josephus, *Ant.* 8.190-211). Further, Herod erected a marble monument at the tomb of David and Solomon (*Ant.* 16.182-83). Herod is therefore presented as a divinely blessed king of the Jews, a king whose work approxi-

10. Inscriptions are quoted by Schürer, *Geschichte*, revised by M. Black, G. Vermes and F. Millar (ET; Edinburgh, 1973), I, pp. 452, 475.
11. Schalit, pp. 475-76; A. Hultgård, *L'eschatologie des Testaments des Douze Patriarches* (2 vols.; Uppsala, 1977, 1982), I, p. 376; Th.A. Busink, *Der Tempel von Jerusalem von Salomo bis Herodes*, II (Leiden, 1980), pp. 1061-62; Stern, 'A. Schalit's Herod', pp. 55-58.

mates to that of the divinely promised royal deliverer of the
people—a king, that is, over whom the aureole of messianism
must hover.

Messianism in the Herodian period cannot be dissociated
from contemporary ruler-cult (see Hultgård [note 11, above],
I, pp. 326-76), and could fasten on Jewish rather than specifically Davidic origins, a viewpoint following naturally from the
importance of Pentateuchal messianic texts such as Num.
24.7 and 17 (and the absence of any Davidic reference in the
'law of the king', Deut. 17.14-20), and corresponding to the
expectation of someone 'from the country' of the Jews
(Josephus, *War* 6.312). In this presentation, then, a messianic
atmosphere is being fostered around a non-Davidic reigning
king, somewhat as appears to have occurred earlier with Hyrcanus I, or later on among the following of Bar Kochba; it is
likely that temple-building was already associated with the
messianic king.[12] Early Christian understanding of the Hero-

---

12. On Hyrcanus, Josephus, *Ant.* 13.299-300, interpreted by E. Bammel, 'ΑΡΧΙΕΡΕΥΣ ΠΡΟΦΗΤΕΥΩΝ', *TLZ* 79 (1954), cols. 351-56; on Bar
Kochba, L. Mildenberg, *The Coinage of the Bar Kokhba War* [Typos 6;
Aarau, Frankfurt & Salzburg, 1984], pp. 44-45, 75-76, 90-91, 102) allows
that messianic hopes might have been harnessed for the war effort,
but stresses that the leader presented himself and was acknowledged
as a prince rather than a messiah (a separation of the roles of ruler
and messiah which seems questionable in its sharpness; contrast
Schürer, Black, Vermes and Millar, I, pp. 543-45); on the temple, note
that the thought of a messianic temple-builder is clearly widespread
after 70 (e.g. *Sib.* 5.423-25; *Targ. Isa.* 53.5, *Zech.* 6.12-13), but that the
hope for a better God-given temple at the last had then long been current (see Tob. 14.5); Zech. 6.12 LXX and *1 Enoch* 53.6 probably indicate
that the messiah can be expected to build it. See W. Bousset and H.
Gressmann, *Die Religion des Judentums im späthellenistischen
Zeitalter* (3rd edn; Tübingen, 1926), p. 239; J. Nolland, '*Sib. Or.* iii. 265-
94, an Early Maccabaean Messianic Oracle', *JTS* ns 30 (1979), pp. 158-
66 (the restoration of the temple by Cyrus and Zerubbabel is presented
in *Sib.* 3 as a pattern for the last times), with J.J. Collins, 'Messianism
in the Maccabean Period', in J. Neusner, W.S. Green and E. Frerichs
(eds.), *Judaisms and their Messiahs at the Turn of the Christian Era*
(Cambridge, 1987), pp. 97-109 (99, restricting any significance for the
Sibyl's eschatology to the possibility that final Jewish restoration will
come through a gentile king like Cyrus; but, if an eschatological reference is allowed, the allusion to judgment more naturally suggests a
messianic figure, as stressed by H.N. Bate, *The Sibylline Oracles*,

dians as those who held Herod to be the messiah (note 30, below) was doubtless influenced by the interchangeable use of 'king of the Jews' and 'Christ' in Mt. 2.2, 4, but this use itself reflects the messianism of Jewish kingship. Later Herodian invocations of a messianic atmosphere include Archelaus's appearance enthroned in the temple, discussed below (an unsuccessful attempt), and Agrippa I's enthusiastic reception by the Jews of Alexandria (Philo, *Flacc.* 25-39; section II (d), below).

The restoration was therefore made to point, in an Augustan but also Jewish messianic manner, to Herodian Jewish victory, peace and piety, and to the divine appointment of Herod as king. This presentation fits his studied favour towards Pharisees and Essenes, mentioned with emphasis just before the account of the restoration (Josephus, *Ant.* 15.370-71). These royal aspects of the enterprise are underlined by the completion of the sanctuary on Herod's accession day, which was observed with special distinction on this occasion (Josephus, *Ant.* 15.423). It has been noted that Herod's building projects usually served not only his ardour for personal fame, but also broader purposes of state (particularly, in this case, the needs of the national economy and religion); when the king took his place as founder of the new temple on his accession day, the solemnity suggests not only awareness of these needs, but also an intention to present the house of Herod as a great Jewish monarchy.[13] Thenceforth his accession day will also have been a Herodian dedication festival comparable with Hanukkah, the themes of which had been given a Herodian impress in the publicity just surveyed.

Books III–V [London, 1918], pp. 30-31); compare discussion above by A.N. Chester (n. 20) and below by C.C. Rowland, pp. 183-89, J.P.M. Sweet, 'A House Not Made with Hands' (n. 4), and J.K. Riches, pp. 245-48.

13. E. Netzer, 'Herod's Building Projects: State Necessity or Personal Need?', *The Jerusalem Cathedra* 1 (1981), pp. 48-61; M. Broshi, 'The Role of the Temple in the Herodian Economy', *JJS* 38 (1987), pp. 31-37; K. Galling, 'Königliche und nichtkönigliche Stifter beim Tempel von Jerusalem', *ZDPV* 68 (1950), pp. 138-42 (141, accession-day dedication shows Herod as a royal patron of the temple on the pattern of the prince in Ezekiel, and, still more, of Hellenistic monarchs).

This view of the temple restoration is compatible with D.M. Jacobson's suggestion (note 10, above) that the foundation of Herodium on the site of a victory over the Jewish supporters of Antigonus and allies of the Parthians (Josephus, *War* 1.265), and Herod's burial there, were intended to present the monarch as a hero (his mausoleum becoming a kind of *heroon*). Jewish views of kingship had much conformity, as seen already, with the Hellenistic royal pattern; and the assimilation of the monarch to a hero can also be identified, as Jacobson notes, in the honour accorded to David's tomb by Herod and his Jewish subjects.

The temple was a traditional place of national assembly,[14] but the specifically dynastic themes of the new building were invoked when Herod named his successors in Herod's temple and the white-robed Archelaus greeted his new subjects there from a golden throne on a dais before he offered sacrifice (Josephus, *Ant.* 16.132-35; 17.200-12, paralleled in *War* 1.457-66; 2.1-9). Archelaus's throne on a dais may be compared with the dais provided for Solomon at the dedication of the temple, according to 2 Chron. 6.13; Josephus assumes that Solomon will have been seated there (*Ant.* 8.107). A similar dais is to be put up in the temple court for the king to read the law, seated, at the feast of Tabernacles in the sabbatical year, according to the Mishnah (*Sotah* 7.8). The Jewish and Roman traditions of Herodian piety were renewed by Agrippa I with a more sensitive *captatio benevolentiae* when he offered sacrifices of thanksgiving in due form, and dedicated in the temple the golden chain given him by Caligula (Josephus, *Ant.* 19.295); his reputation for modest hesitancy in claiming royal rights in the temple is also illustrated by the Mishnaic tradition that in the sabbatical year he read the law standing, not sitting, and that his eyes filled with tears when he read from Deut. 17.15 the command that the king should be an Israelite (*Sotah* 7.8). The royal associations of the temple were clearly considered likely to encourage support for the monarch, but the question

14. Evidence from Josephus and elsewhere is gathered by A. Büchler, *Types of Jewish-Palestinian Piety from 70 B.C.E. to 70 C.E.* (London, 1922), pp. 205-208; for the idea compare Exod. 15.17; Deut. 31.11-12; *1 Enoch* 89.50, 69; 90.29, 33, 36; *T. Benj.* 9.2.

how far these associations were accepted is underlined by the silence on Herod in the accounts of his temple noted at the beginning. Satire which may have earlier antecedents appears in R. Kahana's description of 'Herodian doves' in rows in their cote cooing 'Kyrie, kyrie'—apart from one dissenter who comes to a bad end for saying 'Kyrie *cheirie*, [slave]' (*b. Hullin* 139b; see Schürer, Vermes, Millar and Black, I, p. 310 n. 77).

b. *The Babylonian Talmud*

It is therefore notable that the strongly Herodian account in which Josephus follows Nicolas[15] finds clear echoes in Talmudic tradition. The legend that rain fell only at night during construction (Josephus, *Ant.* 15.425) recurs in rabbinic interpretation of Lev. 26.4 (*Sifra, Behuqqotay, Pereq* 1.1; *Lev. R.* 35.10; *b. Ta'anith* 23a). Moreover, an alternative version of the building of the sanctuary appears in the haggadah of the Babylonian Talmud (*Baba Bathra* 3b-4a). The final sequence of this rabbinic narrative is strikingly close to that of Nicolas's account. As presented as Josephus, *Ant.* 15.365-425, it runs as follows. (i) The king represses dissent, employs many spies, and even disguises himself to hear what his subjects are saying. (ii) He demands an oath of loyalty, gets rid of objectors, but excuses Pollion the Pharisee and Samaias and their disciples, and the Essenes. (iii) Manaem the Essene had prophesied that Herod would be king. (iv) Herod plans to rebuild the temple, and explains his purpose in a speech beforehand. (v) The temple is described at length. (vi) The new sanctuary is swiftly completed within eighteen months, on Herod's accession day; the work was expedited, because rain fell only at night.

15. G. Hölscher, 'Josephus 2', *PW* 9.2 (1916), cols. 1934-2000 (1973-82), ascribes some material in this section, including some legends with rabbinic parallels, to a Jewish author who revised Nicolas; but Nicolas represents himself as entirely at home when he speaks in defence of the Jews (*Ant.* 16.31-57; cf. 12.126), his native Damascus had a very large Jewish community with numerous non-Jewish sympathizers, especially among the women (*War* 2.559-61; did this apply to Nicolas's own family?), and the material with rabbinic parallels considered here can therefore be ascribed either to him (so, probably, 421-23, on the swift completion of the sanctuary) or to Josephus himself (so, probably, 425, on the regulated rain, a story appended from 'our fathers').

The haggadah begins with Herod's rise to power as a slave of the Hasmonaean house who kills the royal family, save for one princess; but she prefers suicide to marriage with him. Then, however (*Baba Bathra* 3b, end), it approximates to the sequence in Josephus just outlined. (i) The sages expound Deut. 17.15, teaching that the king must be an Israelite, and Herod kills them all except for Baba ben Buta, whom he blinds. (ii) He tries to trick Baba into treasonable talk, but is pleased by his prudent answers, and expresses regret (now in his own person) at having killed the sages; Baba advises him to rebuild the temple. (The story is told in the Gemara with regard to the question whether a synagogue may be pulled down before a replacement is available; just this question concerning the temple is said to have dismayed the people when they heard Herod's plan, Josephus, *Ant.* 15.388-89.) (iii) Baba advises that Roman objections can be avoided if a messenger to Rome takes three years on his mission; meanwhile the temple can be pulled down and rebuilt. (iv) Herod does so, and Roman prohibition and reproof arrive too late. (v) He who has never seen the building of Herod has never seen a beautiful building; Herod wanted to plate it with gold, but the sages said that its variegated marble was more beautiful, for it was like the waves of the sea.

Josephus and the rabbinic narrative both include, in differing order, spying by Herod in person; dissent punished by execution, with some exception; friendly converse between Herod and a sage; rapid completion of the temple by Herod; and independently expressed praise for its beauty. The Talmudic Herod is a plebeian and alien usurper, a tyrant and a man of blood—a powerful caricature placarding the condemnations which are mixed with praise in Josephus—but both narratives make Herod's personal spying and repression the background of the temple rebuilding. The stress then falls in the rabbinic narrative, as in Josephus, on the prompt execution of Herod's grand design. Further, when the brilliant marble structure is praised, it is specifically called—in striking contrast with the silences noted above—'the building of Herod'; 'he who has never seen the building of Herod has never seen a beautiful bulding in his life' (*b. Baba Bathra* 4a; compare *Sukkah* 51b).

The historical writing of Nicolas or Josephus probably played a part in the origins of this haggadah, through Jewish readers who reacted positively at least to this aspect of the presentation of Herod.[16] That the tradition concerning him cannot have been negatively fixed in tannaitic material known in Babylonia is shown not only by the transmission of this amoraic story in *Baba Bathra* 3b-4a, but also by the partly parallel *Sukkah* 51b, where 'the building of Herod' is positively treated in discussion attributed to Babylonian rabbis of a *baraitha* not mentioning Herod but concluding 'he who has not seen the temple when it was standing [literally, 'in its building'] has never seen a beautiful building'. (*Eduyoth* 8.6, on the method of rebuilding the temple with due reverence, is noteworthy as another tannaitic tradition not mentioning Herod but probably implying a favourable view of Herod's temple.) In any case, however, it is notable that *Baba Bathra* 3b-4a includes, together with condemnation of Herod as a tyrannical usurper, warm and specific acknowledgment of his achievement as temple-builder. Approbation is underlined by the claim that the king did this good work on rabbinic advice, and the warmth with which his benefaction is acknowledged contrasts with the critical tone of the application of the story in *Num. R.* 14.8, to interpret 'a sin offering in Num. 7.64—because Herod's temple was built by a sinful king. The close-

16. The swift completion of the building in *Baba Bathra* 4a need not be a sign of the lateness of the narrative (as held, because of its contrast with the many years occupied by the building of the temple as a whole, by J. Neusner, *The Rabbinic Traditions about the Pharisees before 70*, I [Leiden, 1971], p. 391); the sanctuary alone is probably in view, as in Josephus. With the proposal made in the text above, compare the argument for the indirect derivation of Hasmonaean narratives in the *Babylonian Talmud* (notably in *Qiddushin* 66a and *Sanhedrin* 19a-b) from Nicolas through Josephus presented by J. Efron, *Studies on the Hasmonaean Period* (ET; SJLA 39; Leiden, 1987), pp. 161-97, 215-18 (first read by the present writer after completion of this essay); Efron, p. 185, notes the similarity in style between *Qiddushin* 66a and *Baba Bathra* 3b. A more favourable view of Nicolas's historical value than Efron adopts is taken here, but the relationship between Josephus and the haggadah of the Babylonian Talmud is assessed similarly. The general importance of literary sources in the rabbinic transmission of folk-tales is shown by E. Yassif, 'Traces of Folk Traditions of the Second Temple Period in Rabbinic Literature', *JJS* 39 (1988), pp. 212-33.

ness of the narrative of the building of the sanctuary in *Baba Bathra* 3b-4a to Josephus, and its divergence at this point from the negative view of Herod found in the context and widely reflected in rabbinic sources, suggests that Nicolas's publicistic account of the warm reception of the work was not without foundation (as could be inferred also from the rabbinic accounts of the regulated rain, the reverent reconstruction, and the beauty of the building), and that the temple continued to be admired specifically as Herod's building.

c. *The Temple Restoration and Attitudes to the House of Herod*
Three of the criticisms placarded in *Baba Bathra* 3b and also found in Josephus would have been blunted insofar as Nicolas's presentation was accepted. First, if the house of Herod had usurped the place of the Hasmonaeans, the new Herodian building made it possible to claim that 'in the hundred and twenty-five years of their reign' the Hasmonaeans 'had been unable to accomplish anything like this for the honour of God' (Herod's speech at Jericho shortly before his death, in Josephus, *Ant.* 17.162). The themes of the Hasmonaean Hanukkah, as already noted, were subsumed in and (in respect of the new building) surpassed by the Herodian dedication.

Secondly, the dynasty of the Herods might be plebeian, but its lofty ambition, expressed in the temple building, enjoyed the divine favour (Josephus, *War* 1.400, cited above). The strength of the objection that the house of Herod was not a royal family is most clear in Josephus's *Antiquities*, where it is more prominent than the charge of Idumaean birth (see *Ant.* 14.78, 300 [contrast *War* 1.241], 403 [King Antigonus], 430 = *War* 1.313 [the old bandit of Arbela], 491). Hölscher (note 15, above) suspected in these passages the hand of the anti-Herodian Jewish reviser of Nicolas, but this description well fits Josephus himself, proud of his Hasmonaean descent (see his criticism of Nicolas, *Ant.* 16.184-87). That Josephus's view was more widely shared is suggested, however, by its attribution to Antigonus and his bandit partisan, and its appearance in the gibe of 'slave' in *Baba Bathra* 3b-4a (*'abda*)—where, again, it is more prominent than the charge of alien descent—and in *Hullin* 139b (cited in I (a), above) (*cheirios*).

Thirdly, however, Hasmonaean propaganda made the house of Herod not only plebeian, but also alien; Herod was a commoner *and* an Idumaean, in Antigonus's answer to Herod's proclamation before the wall of Jerusalem (*Ant.* 14.403). Idumaean origin, explained here by Josephus as making one a half-Jew, was by no means inconsistent with zealous Jewish patriotism, as observed with regard to the house of Herod by A. Kasher (as cited in note 17, below); but it was clearly open to suspicion (see Goodman [note 1, above], pp. 117, 222-23). This relatively mild charge was no doubt strengthened because Herod's mother was Arabian (Josephus, *War* 1.181), and was still further heightened when it was combined with the charge of plebeian origin in a story that Herod's grandfather was a slave of the temple of Apollo in Ascalon.[17] In practice, then, these charges might make Herod-

---

17. Justin Martyr, *Dial.* 52.3, and Africanus to Aristides, in Eusebius, *H.E.* 1.6, 2-3; 1.7, 11 (cf. *Chronicle*, Olympiad 186; *Dem.* 8.1); Ephrem Syrus, commenting on the Diatessaron, takes the Roman census of Lk. 2.1-3 rather than Herodian government as his witness to the fulfilment of Gen. 49.10 (see note 7, above), perhaps because, since the story of Herod and the wise men comes later in the Diatessaron, the census forms the first convenient context for noting that the sceptre had departed from Judah, in accordance with this biblical testimony; but he also calls Herod an Ascalonite; see the Syriac comments on Diatessaron 2.12 and 3.7, in L. Leloir, 'Le commentaire d'Éphrem sur le Diatessaron. Quarante et un folios retrouvés', *RB* 94 (1987), pp. 481-518 (490-93, 500-501). At the time of Herod's Arabian campaign the priests said that he was 'an Arabian, uncircumcised', according to the Slavonic Josephus, passage corresponding to the Greek of *War* 1.364-70 (ET in H.St.J. Thackeray, *Josephus*, III [Loeb Classical Library; London & Cambridge, MA, 1957], pp. 636-38; discussion by R. Eisler, ΙΗΣΟΥΣ ΒΑΣΙΛΕΥΣ ΟΥ ΒΑΣΙΛΕΥΣΑΣ [2 vols.; Heidelberg, 1929, 1930], I, pp. 340-48). Justin and Africanus are discussed by J. Jeremias, *Jerusalem in the Time of Jesus* (ET; London, 1969), pp. 331-32 (Africanus's stress on the currency of the story in Greek histories favours derivation from Ptolemy of Ascalon), Schalit, *Herodes*, pp. 677-78 (favouring Jewish anti-Herodian origin), E.M. Smallwood, *The Jews under Roman Rule* (Leiden, 1976, corrected reprint 1981), pp. 19-20 n. 50 (allowing either Jewish or Christian origin), M. Hengel, *Rabbinische Legende und frühpharisäische Geschichte: Schimeon b. Schetach und die achtzig Hexen von Askalon* (Abhandlungen der Heidelberger Akademie der Wissenschaften, Phil.-hist. Klasse, 2, 1984), p. 43 (following Schalit), and A. Kasher, *Jews, Idumaeans, and Ancient Arabs* (Tübingen, 1988), pp. 62-65, 126-30 (a Christian, not a Jewish

ian rule seem to breach the law of the king in Deut. 17.15, excluding 'a foreigner that is not thy brother' (cf. Isa. 1.26, 'I will restore thy judges as at the first', echoed in the eleventh benediction of the *Amidah*, and Jer. 30.21); rabbinic sources envisage Deut. 17.15 as troubling both Agrippa I and Herod the Great (*m. Sotah* 7.8, and *b. Baba Bathra* 3b, both cited above). The Christian connection of this charge with Gen. 49.10 corresponds to Jewish preoccupation with this verse also as a guarantee of indigenous government, as the LXX, Qumran paraphrase and the Targums suggest.[18] (The fourth-century Hegesippus, possibly a baptized Jew, takes Idumaean descent to be a reason for regarding Herod as alien [note 17, above].) Charges on this score were therefore damaging; Herod met them with a claim to descent from the foremost Jews who came out of Babylon to Judaea (Josephus, *Ant.* 14.9), but the rebuilding was clearly also intended to present the house of Herod as an illustrious Jewish dynasty.

According to a fourth criticism, not reflected in *Baba Bathra* 3b-4a, Herod favoured non-Jews above Jews in his benefactions. (Diaspora Jews probably in fact gained some toleration on account of these benefactions, as argued by A.H.M. Jones [note 49, below].) This criticism seems likely to represent Josephus's own opinion, but, once again, his opinion was probably more widely shared. In the speech of the Jewish deputies in Rome after Herod's death he is said to have adorned gentile cities at the expense of cities in his own realm (Josephus, *War* 2.85, parallel with *Ant.* 17.306). Similarly, in the narrative of his life Herod is said to have treated gentile cities so well that he seemed to be forming a defensive ring to contain his own subjects (*Ant.* 15.326-30), and characteristically to have been

story). Justin ascribes the allegation to Jews, Africanus (with a detailed narrative) to gentile historians; it may perhaps be conjectured that an Ascalonite story, which claimed the great king for the city with a touch of the anti-Jewish 'poison of Ascalon' (Philo's phrase, *Leg. ad Gaium* 205), was known both to Ptolemy the writer on Herod (probably to be identified with Ptolemy of Ascalon) and to anti-Herodian Jews.

18. Posnanski (n. 7, above), pp. 20-31; M. Perez Fernandez, *Tradiciones mesiánicas en el Targum Palestinense* (Valencia & Jerusalem, 1981), pp. 123-27 (adding reference to Neofiti and to a Qumran comment published by J.M. Allegro, 'Further Messianic References in Qumran Literature', *JBL* 75 [1956], pp. 174-87 [174-76]).

the benefactor of gentiles rather than Jews (16.158-59, in reflection on his benefactions to the Greek cities), never bestowing any gift worth mentioning on a Jewish city—by contrast with Agrippa I, who was beneficent towards his own people as well (19.328-31).

Here his benefactions in Jerusalem are unmentioned; the theatre and amphitheatre (*Ant.* 15.268) could no doubt be classed as unacceptable gifts, but his monument at the tomb of David and Solomon and, above all, the temple are striking omissions. They are mainly explained, perhaps, by the likelihood that the complaint in question stems not from Jerusalem but from Jewish communities near the gentile cities which he adorned (most fully listed by Josephus, *War* 1.422-28); his benefactions to Ascalon, for example, were perhaps resented by the mainly Jewish Jamnia, or those to Ptolemais by the neighbouring Galilaeans. It is also true, however, that even his pious Jerusalem benefactions were received coolly by some of the inhabitants. Significantly, the monument to David and Solomon was popularly explained by a story that the king was trying to plunder their tomb, and Herod is represented as complaining that his expenditure on the temple has been ungratefully received (by those involved in the attempt to remove his eagle [*Ant.* 17.162-63]). The efforts to present the temple as a Jewish benefaction will have been correspondingly great.

The differing attitudes to the house of Herod noted above in the Judaean and Galilaean as well as the diaspora Jewish population suggest that such efforts will not have been entirely vain. This view is borne out by Josephus's own transmission of Nicolas's publicity (with annotations), and by its clear echoes in rabbinic literature. There is evidence, also, for a more detached view of the house of Herod, at some distance from the Hasmonaean propaganda of the three criticisms noted first above. In the *Assumption of Moses* 6 the Hasmonaean priest-kings are criticized equally with Herod the Great, who is condemned for his cruelty but not for plebeian or Idumaean origin or for usurpation; indeed, he will judge the sinful people as they deserve. This opinion corresponds to the advice of the Pharisee Samaias during the siege of Jerusalem that Herod, who was destined to punish them, should be admitted

(Josephus, *Ant.* 14.176). In its recourse to divine providence this view has points of contact, despite its negative expression, with the heavy stress on Herod's royal destiny in Nicolas's treatment of the temple.

To summarize section I as a whole, Nicolas's history, presenting Herod as the predestined monarch, was taken over by Josephus despite his criticisms (*Ant.* 16.184-87), and is likely to have been known to other Jews at the end of the first century AD. The story of the building of the sanctuary, like some other episodes from Nicolas's Hasmonaean and Herodian history, made its way either independently or through Josephus into the rabbinic haggadah. Despite the sensitivity of the issue of the sanctity of the temple, the rabbinic forms of the story have nothing but praise for what is called 'the building of Herod'.

In Nicolas's account the rebuilding shows Herod as a Jewish king piously restoring the temple to its Solomonic glory, and as a victor who has conquered the Jews' traditional enemies and (by aiding the repulse of the Parthians) has contributed to the Augustan peace after civil war, a blessing as important to Judaea as to Italy. He appears, therefore, as a Jewish king touched by the aura of messianism. This aura will have been regularly rediffused by the celebration of his accession day, now also a feast of dedication. The temple restoration thereby reinforced the Herodian form of ruler-cult.

The main points of Hasmonaean propaganda were directly opposed to this presentation, but the persistence of favourable comment on Herod's temple in rabbinic tradition, and on Herod as temple-builder in *Baba Bathra* 4a, suggests that the court publicity reflected by Nicolas was not wholly unheeded. The attestation of views which seem to show some detachment from the Hasmonaean case, together with the evidence that Jews at close quarters with gentiles valued Herodian kings as patrons, help to indicate a climate of opinion in which the Herodian presentation, supported dramatically by 'the building of Herod', could have found some hearing.

During the period from Nicolas to Josephus, Herod's decendants, Agrippa I above all, had followed his footsteps in presenting themselves as Jewish kings and patrons. This presentation was again exemplified in literature when

Josephus's rival Justus of Tiberias composed his Herodian history of the Jewish kings, from Moses to Agrippa II (Photius, *Bibliotheca*, 33). Josephus himself, by his comparison of Herod the Great with Agrippa I, makes the obvious but important point that the criticisms levelled at Herod the Great were not all thought to apply to his successors. As has now appeared, the temple was a focus in this period for more positive views of the house of Herod as a Jewish monarchy, including what may be called a Herodian messianism.

The significance of the temple in the diaspora, where the collection of the temple tax was a prized and threatened privilege defended by Herod (Josephus, *Ant.* 16.28), means that the Herodian presentation of the rebuilding will have had an impact throughout the Jewish world. Some evidence for diaspora response to the Herodian rebuilding and the house of Herod will now be reviewed in connection with Persius's lines on 'Herod's days'. It will be suggested that Persius is a further witness to the Herodian festivals with which, as has emerged from Josephus on the temple, a celebration of the dedication of the sanctuary was now associated.

II. *Persius on 'Herod's Days'*

a. *Alternative Explanations*

If 'Herod's days' were indeed days kept in honour of a Herod, the relevant lines from Persius's fifth satire (Persius 5.179-84) allow a valuable glimpse of the prestige of Herodian princes among the Jews of Rome towards AD 60. On the other hand, Herod may simply be named as a well-known king taken to represent the Jewish people. The 'days' would then be days characteristically observed by Jews, perhaps the sabbaths shortly to be mentioned by Persius, rather than Herodian commemorations; but they would still attest a Herodian reputation for Jewish loyalty. These alternatives have long been debated, and the second is adopted in two informative recent commentaries on the passage.[19]

19. M. Stern, *Greek and Latin Authors on Jews and Judaism*, I (Jerusalem, 1974), pp. 435-37; R.A. Harvey, *A Commentary on Persius* (Leiden, 1981), pp. 177-82.

Independently of this question, the lines are an important and vivid portrayal of a Jewish quarter and a Jewish festal dinner in Rome under Nero, and one of the attestations of the attraction of Jewish rites for Romans. The Herodian problem posed by the passage is reconsidered here in the light of some evidence and discussion which is not to the fore in the comments just mentioned, including Herod's dedication of the sanctuary on his accession-day. The review of inquiry into this problem attempted below may also cast some light on the history of the interpretation of the passage as a whole, which is among the most detailed and lively Roman comments on the Jews and Judaism.

Persius 5.179-84 run as follows in the editions by W.V. Clausen (Oxford, 1956, p. 28; 1959, p. 24):

> b... at cum
> Herodis uenere dies unctaque fenestra
> dispositae pinguem nebulam uomuere lucernae
> portantes uiolas rubrumque amplexa catinum
> cauda natat thynni, tumet alba fidelia uino,
> labra moues tacitus recutitaque sabbata palles.

They may be rendered, following A. Pretor with slight adaptations:

> Then again when Herod's days come round, and lamps wreathed with violets and ranged along the greasy windowsills have vomited their murky cloud, when the tail of the tunny overlapping the red dish floats in its sauce and the white jar brims with wine, you move your lips in silence and grow pale over the sabbaths of the circumcised.[20]

These lines of the satire are part of an imaginative Stoic exhortation addressed to the man enslaved by his passions, here pictured in the grip of superstition. Jewish observances form the first example of the strange rites by which he is too readily overawed; further examples follow from the cults of Isis and Cybele. The train of thought is displayed in Dryden's vigorous version:

20. A. Pretor, *A. Persii Flacci Satirarum Liber* (new edn; Cambridge, 1907), p. 86.

Thy Superstition too may claim a share:
When Flow'rs are strew'd, and Lamps in order plac'd,
And Windows with illuminations grac'd
On Herod's Day; when sparkling Bowls go round,
And *Tunny's* Tails in savoury Sauce are drown'd
Thou mutter'st Pray'rs obscene; nor do'st refuse
The Fasts and Sabbaths of the curtail'd *Jews*.[21]

b. *The Scholia*

The alternative interpretations of *Herodis...dies* either as Herodian commemorations or as other days known to be observed by Jews first appear in outline in the scholia on Persius. The comments preserved under the name of Cornutus include varying forms of the note:

> hic Herodes apud Iudaeos regnavit temporibus Augusti in partibus Syriae. Herodis ergo diem natalem Herodiani observant. aut etiam sabbata, quo die lucernas accensas et violis coronatas in fenestris ponunt.[22]

> This Herod reigned among the Jews in the times of Augustus in the region of Syria. The Herodians therefore observe Herod's birthday. Or also the sabbaths, on which day they put in the windows lamps lit and wreathed with violets.

The excerpts from the scholia published by Buecheler and Leo and quoted above do not give a full view of the textual tradition, in part of which, for instance, another comment on Herod's days appears before that just quoted.[23] Five main forms of the text have been distinguished.[24] For this essay I have compared

---

21. *The Satires of Decimus Junius Juvenalis. Translated into English Verse by Mr Dryden, and several other eminent hands. Together with the Satires of Aulus Persius Flaccus. Made English by Mr Dryden* (London, 1697), pp. 484-85.

22. O. Jahn, F. Buecheler and F. Leo, *A. Persii Flacci D. Iunii Iuvenalis Sulpiciae Saturae* (Berlin, 1910), pp. 54-55.

23. It explains them, perhaps by assimilation to the Floralia mentioned in line 178, as 'dies cupidinei'; see Kvičala (cited in n. 25 below), p. 37.

24. Clausen (1956), p. xiv; P.K. Marshall, 'Persius', in L.D. Reynolds (ed.), *Texts and Transmission: A Survey of the Latin Classics* (Oxford, 1983), pp. 293-95; on the forms of the text of Cornutus, D.M. Robathan, F.E. Cranz, P.O. Kristeller and B. Bischoff, 'A. Persius Flaccus', in F.E. Cranz and P.O. Kristeller (eds.), *Catalogus Translationum et*

O. Jahn's edition of 1843, the editions of 1520 (representing a different form of text) and 1590 (including the scholia, from a text allied to that followed by Jahn, selected by J.J. Scaliger for publication by P. Pithou in 1585), and editions of scholia from MSS in Prague and Berne.[25] 'Cornutus' preserves much from antiquity, perhaps from commentaries on Persius such as Jerome mentions (*Adversus Rufinum* 1.16); but it also includes mediaeval additions, notably from the school of Auxerre in the ninth century.[26]

In these circumstances any attempt to distinguish ancient from mediaeval material must be tentative, but content and textual variation appear to support the following suggestions. First, in the extract quoted above, the opening comment on Herod wholly lacks New Testament allusion, and places Herod's Jewish kingdom simply in Syria (contrast Lk. 1.5 'rex Iudaeae', and the references to Judaea, Jerusalem and the land of Israel in Mt. 2.1-3, 21-22); the wording seems better suited to an ancient *grammaticus* than a mediaeval commentator. Secondly, the same is largely but not entirely true of the following comment. Its initial reference to Herod's birthday could derive from the New Testament (Mt. 14.6; Mk 6.21 on 'Herod' [Antipas]), but is just as likely to reflect general ancient custom. By contrast, the ensuing mention of 'Herodiani' almost certainly depends on the New Testament or Christian sources. The comment was accordingly ascribed to Carolin-

Commentariorum: Mediaeval and Renaissance Latin Translations and Commentaries, III (Washington, 1976), pp. 201-312.

25. O. Jahn, *Auli Persii Flacci Saturarum Liber, cum scholiis antiquis* (Leipzig, 1843) (see the comments by Clausen [1956], p. xiv); *Auli Flacci Persii Satyrographi Clarissimi opus emendatum . . .* (Venice, 1520); *A. Persii Satyrarum Liber i. D. Iunii Iuvenalis Satyrarum Lib. v. Sulpiciae Satyra i. Cum veteribus commentariis nunc primum editis. Ex bibliotheca P. Pithoei IC. cuius etiam Notae quaedam adiectae sunt* (Paris, 1590) (see Robathan and Cranz, pp. 236-37); J. Kvičala, *Scholiorum Pragensium in Persii satiras delectus* (Abhandlungen der königlichen böhmischen Gesellschaft der Wissenschaften, Sechste Folge, 6, 1873-74; Prague, 1873); E. Kurz, *Die Persius-Scholien nach der Bernerhandschriften. III. Die Scholien zu Sat. IV–VI* (Burgdorf, 1889).

26. Clausen (1956), pp. xxiii-xxiv; J.E.G. Zetzel, 'On the History of Latin Scholia, II: The *Commentum Cornuti* in the Ninth Century', *Medievalia et Humanistica* 10 (1981), pp. 19-31.

gian revision by Jahn (1843), p. cxxxv. It seems possible, however, that mediaeval accretion may be limited to the word 'Herodiani'. The sequence 'Herodis...Herodiani' is confused in the textual tradition; the order of the proper nouns can be reversed, or a second 'Herodis' can appear instead of 'Herodiani', and the Prague scholia as edited by Kvičala present a text without 'Herodiani', as follows: 'Herodis igitur diem natalem observant, ut etiam sabbata...'[27] It may be suggested that this text represents an earlier form of the tradition, and that 'Herodiani' is a gloss by a reader familiar with the New Testament; its insertion into the text caused the confusion now evident. Formerly, the subject of the sentence had been 'Iudaei', understood: 'they therefore keep Herod's birthday, as also the sabbaths...' It is also worth noting, without resting too much weight on a place (the beginning of a clause) perhaps particularly liable to alteration, that the text with 'ut' makes better sense before 'etiam', and may be more original.

To summarize, there is a case for supposing the word 'Herodiani' to be a gloss on a comment which otherwise comes from non-Christian antiquity, and which originally explained 'the days of Herod' as royal birthdays observed by the Jews. It possibly also described their observation as being like that of the sabbaths. The scholiast's reference to the sabbaths, however, was widely understood as an alternative explanation, as the reading with 'aut' attests.

In this second understanding one may suspect the operation of the tendency often found in commentary to harmonize and to explain unknowns by identification with knowns. In the scholia on this passage the puzzling 'Herodis...dies' were possibly explained by identification with the known Floralia, mentioned just before (line 178; note 23, above), as well as with the known sabbaths, mentioned just afterwards.

The scholia therefore already present the two alternative explanations noted above, although one possibly early form of the comment in question unifies the elements otherwise taken as alternatives. In any case, the reference to the Herodians is more likely to be a gloss on an old comment than a sign that

27. Persius 1520, fol. xc, verso 'Herodiani...Herodis'; Kurz, p. 38; Kvičala, p. 38.

the comment which includes it is Christian. In non-Christian antiquity, therefore, 'the days of Herod' were already explained as royal birthdays, and the identification with the sabbaths was probably also already current, perhaps as a harmonizing explanation.

c. *Later Exegesis*

How were the alternative explanations presented by later exegetes? By contrast with the *scholia*, the limited number of renaissance commentators on Persius consulted for this essay incline markedly towards explanation of 'Herod's days' as sabbaths (B. Fontius, A.A. Nebrissensis)[28] or as Jewish festivals in general (Ascensius, Johannes Britannicus, J.B. Plautius, J. Murmellius).[29]

J.J. Scaliger therefore made a fresh beginning when, in his notes on Eusebius's *Chronicle* (1606), he integrated the scholion on Herod's birthday (part of the material he had selected for Pithou) with the patristic and later view that the Herodians honoured Herod as messiah—a view which had perhaps already contributed to the appearance of 'Herodiani' in the scholia.[30] Scaliger urged that, as Persius read in the light of the scholion could be taken to attest, Herodians in the time of Nero still sacrificed in honour of Herod the Great and celebrated his birthday. Furthermore, Herod was of Jewish descent, and Christian apologists from Eusebius and Augustine onwards were therefore unjustified in maintaining that Gen. 49.10 was fulfilled when rulers and governors ceased from Judah at the accession of Herod the foreigner (notes 7, 17, above).

28. Persius 1520, fol. xc, verso; Persius 1551, p. 609A; on these commentators see Robathan and Cranz, pp. 265-67, 278.
29. Persius 1551, pp. 602B, 603D, 606C, 609D; see Robathan and Cranz, pp. 267-69, 273-78, 283-84.
30. J.J. Scaliger, *Thesaurus Temporum...*, *Animadversiones in Chronologica Eusebii* (Leiden, 1606), p. 150 (on Eusebius's annal for the year 1983 from Abraham); Jerome spoke both for this view of the Herodians (*Adversus Luciferianos* 23) and against it (in his commentary on Mt. 22.15), and it was favoured by Ps.-Tertullian, Epiphanius and others, followed by H. Grotius and other scholars, cited by H.H. Rowley, 'The Herodians in the Gospels', *JTS* 41 (1940), pp. 14-27 (15-16). It was also adopted by Cornelius à Lapide (1639) in his comments on Mt. 2.1, 15; 22.16.

These arguments evoked lively contradiction, and Scaliger's interpretation of 'Herod's days' won only qualified acceptance in contemporary commentary on Persius in England;[31] but it was adopted by two influential editors of Persius, Isaac Casaubon and Otto Jahn, although each broadened and modified it. Casaubon (to whom Scaliger inscribed a copy of his work on Eusebius [Cambridge University Library, Adv. a. 3. 4]) preferred Scaliger's association of the passage with Herod the Great, and compared the Herodian group with the Roman sodalities founded to honour emperors after their deaths by sacrifices and other commemorations (for such associations in Asia Minor see Price [note 52, below], p. 118). Casaubon allowed, however, that Agrippa I might have been intended, and that royal accession days could have been observed not just by Herodians, but by Jews in general.[32] This is of course a reasonable inference from the narrative of the dedication of the temple in Josephus. Jahn, accepting that celebrations of Herod's birthday by Herodians seem to be intended, added that Persius could hardly be expected to show accurate knowledge, and that Herod's name was particularly familiar to Roman readers (Jahn [1843], p. 208). These additional considerations are important among those which have commended the alternative interpretation of 'Herod's days' as a reference to characteristically Jewish observances.

More recent exponents of the 'days' as birthdays or accession days include J. Conington and A. Pretor (echoing Jahn's

31. T. Farnaby, *Iunii Iuvenalis et Auli Persii Flacci Satyrae cum Annotationibus* (4th edn; London, 1633), p. 184, *ad loc.* (the days are either those observed by the nation obedient to Herod, the Jews, or else Herod's birthday, celebrated like an accession day; the comment is reproduced unchanged from the first edition, London, 1612); J. Bond, *Auli Persii Flacci Satyrae Sex. Cum posthumis commentariis...* (London, 1614), p. 119, *ad loc.* (paraphrasing line 179 as referring to the sabbaths of the Jews and Herod's birthday). Bond therefore combined Scaliger's proposal with the alternative interpretation, but Farnaby left the question open.

32. I. Casaubon, *De rebus sacris et ecclesiasticis exercitationes xvi* (London, 1614), p. 48; *idem, Auli Persi Flacci Satirarum Liber* (3rd edn; London, 1647), pp. 458-59, *ad loc.*

caution), among commentators on Persius;[33] W. Schmidt, writing on birthdays in antiquity (with reference, again, to associations for their observance);[34] F.-J. Dölger, in the fifth volume of his work on the symbolism of the fish (but in the second volume he had thought differently);[35] and among writers on Jewish history and the New Testament, H. Willrich (in a relatively full treatment), A. Momigliano (in his pre-war work), A. Schalit, H.W. Hoehner, and E. Bammel.[36]

These interpretations have throughout been flanked, however, by explanations of the days as days characteristically observed by Jews. M. de Roa, writing just before Scaliger's Eusebian study appeared, was followed and echoed later in the seventeenth century by John Spencer, who preferred to take the phrase as an allusion to Jewish holidays and sabbaths; for Herod's fame as a representative of Judaism de Roa cited the statement that Pompey conferred the high-priesthood on

---

33. J. Conington, *The Satires of A. Persius Flaccus* (2nd edn; Oxford, 1874), p. 113; Pretor, pp. 86-87.

34. W. Schmidt, *Geburtstag im Altertum* (Religionsgeschichtliche Versuche und Vorarbeiten, 7.1; Giessen, 1908), pp. 70 (Roman Jews formed a kind of *collegium*), 130.

35. F.-J. Dölger, *IXΘYC* (5 vols.; I: Rome, 1910; II-III: Münster i.W., 1922; IV: Münster, 1927; V: Münster, 1943), II, pp. 94 and nn. 8-9, 95, 543 (Persius describes a sabbath fish-dinner, which gives a good idea of the Diaspora Jewish *cena pura*); V, pp. 384-85 (Persius says that the Jewish community ate fish at their festal meal on Herod's birthday in Rome).

36. Willrich, *Das Haus des Herodes*, pp. 96-97, 180 (not cited in the commentaries by Stern and Harvey [n. 19, above]); Momigliano, 'Herod of Judaea', p. 332 and n. 1 (a feast called after Herod the Great, perhaps a birthday or accession day); Schalit, *Herodes*, p. 480 n. 1128 (following Schmidt, as cited in n. 34, above, and asking additionally if the Roman Jewish *collegium* may have Herod Antipas in view); H.W. Hoehner, *Herod Antipas* (Cambridge, 1972), pp. 160-61 n. 5 (the proverbially magnificent birthdays of the Herods); E. Bammel, 'Romans 13', in Bammel and Moule (cited in n. 1, above), pp. 365-83 (368 n. 22 [the celebration of Herod's birthday by the Jews of Rome]). The great difference between Momigliano's two groups of writings on Jewish history, between 1930 and 1935 (when he affirmed the importance of Hellenism within the Jewish community) and after 1970 (when he minimized that importance) is brought out and discussed by F. Parente, reviewing A. Momigliano, *Pagine ebraiche* (ed. Silvia Berti), in *Quaderni di Storia*, Year XV, no. 29 (1989), pp. 171-78; the decision on *Herodis...dies* reflects the standpoint discerned by Parente in the earlier work.

Herod, in Strabo, *Geog.* 16.2, 46.[37] Scaliger was vigorously opposed by his Jesuit adversary N. Serarius, who gave his main attention to the questions raised concerning Christian tradition that Herod was non-Jewish, but also emphasized that the days mentioned by Persius could be understood as sabbaths and festivals, especially Tabernacles and Purim; for the name of Herod as standing for Jewish piety in Roman satire he compared Juvenal 6.159 on the barefoot celebration of sabbaths by kings in Judaea, in the context of a reference to Agrippa II.[38]

Many interpretations of this kind, however, identify the days either as sabbaths or as the days of Hanukkah. The lights and the fish menu described in lines 180-83 suit both. Sabbath lights specified as such were gently mocked by Persius's contemporary Seneca (*Ep.* 95.47), and Hanukkah lights are attested in Josephus (*Ant.* 12.325) and the Mishnah (*Baba Kamma* 6.6). Fish was a festal delicacy, especially but not only eaten on the sabbath (*m. Bezah* 2.1; *t. Bezah* 2.1 [*colias* for the festival]).

The sabbath identification is commended by the mention of sabbaths in line 184. C. Vitringa, amassing evidence on sabbath lights, accordingly held that the scholiast was deceived in his reference to birthdays; Herod (Agrippa I) was clearly mentioned as a type of the Jewish people, and Persius alluded to the sabbath lights and meal.[39] Vitringa was cited and followed by E. Schürer; in the revised English translation of Schürer's work the specific identification of 'Herodis...dies' as sabbaths has been dropped, but the passage is still treated as a descrip-

---

37. M. de Roa, *Singularium locorum ac rerum libri v... de die natali sacra at profana* (Lyons, 1604), pp. 187-88; J. Spencer, *De Legibus Hebraeorum Ritualibus et earum Rationibus* (2 vols.; Cambridge, 1727), II, p. 1123 (book IV, ch. 6, first published in this edition; Spencer died in 1693).

38. N. Serarius, *Rabbini et Herodes... Adversus Ios. Scaligeri Eusebianas Annotationes, & Io. Drusii Responsionem* (Mainz, 1607), pp. 290-91.

39. C. Vitringa, *De Synagoga Vetere libri tres* (2 vols.; Franeker, 1696), I, pp. 194-45 (book I, part 1, ch. 9).

tion of the sabbath.[40] This identification of the days is wide-spread. It was adopted in Latin lexicography by Lewis and Short (but not by P.G.W. Glare);[41] among commentators on Persius, by G. Nemethy, T.F. Brunner and R.A. Harvey;[42] in study of the Jews of Rome, by A. Berliner, H.J. Leon and R. Penna;[43] in study of Jewish symbolism, by F.-J. Dölger in his earlier discussion (note 35, above), and by E.R. Goodenough (who favours connection with the sabbath *cena pura*, but leaves open the possibility that Herod's birthday is intended);[44] and in collections of passages on the Jews in Greek and Roman authors, by T. Reinach, M. Stern and M. Whittaker.[45]

The identification of the days as the eight days of Hanukkah, commemorating the Maccabaean dedication of the temple, can be made without qualification (as by H. Vogelstein, note 46 below). It has also been suggested, however, that they marked a feast of dedication with Herodian aspects. Thus J. de Voisin held that either Hanukkah, or the feast of dedication of Herod's temple, might be in view; J. Derenbourg supposed that

40. Schürer, *Geschichte*, III (3rd edn; Leipzig, 1909), p. 166 n. 49; ET, revised by M. Black, G. Vermes, F. Millar, M.D. Goodman and P. Vermes, 3.1 (Edinburgh, 1986), p. 161 n. 60.
41. C.T. Lewis and C. Short (eds.), *A Latin Dictionary* (Oxford, 1879), p. 850, and P.G.W. Glare (ed.), *Oxford Latin Dictionary* (Oxford, 1982), p. 792, *s.v.* Herodes.
42. G. Nemethy, *A. Persii Flacci Satirae* (Budapest, 1903), p. 302, and *Symbolae Exegeticae ad Persii Satiras* (Budapest, 1924), p. 12, no. xxi (supporting the interpretation from Juvenal 6.159, as Serarius did [n. 38, above]); T.F. Brunner, 'A Note on Persius 5.179ff.', *California Studies in Classical Antiquity*, 1 (1968), pp. 63-64; Harvey, as cited in n. 19, above.
43. A. Berliner, *Geschichte der Juden in Rom von der ältesten Zeit bis zur Gegenwart* (2 vols. in 1; Frankfurt a.M., 1893), I, pp. 101-102 (noting that others identify the days as Hanukkah or a Herodian festival); H.J. Leon, *The Jews of Ancient Rome* (Philadelphia, 1960), p. 38; R. Penna, 'Les juifs à Rome au temps de l'apôtre Paul', *NTS* 28 (1982), pp. 321-47 (324).
44. E.R. Goodenough, *Jewish Symbols in the Greco-Roman Period* (13 vols.; New York, 1953–68), I (1953), p. 36; II (1953), p. 106; V (1956), pp. 42-43.
45. T. Reinach, *Textes d'auteurs grecs et romains relatifs au Judaïsme* (Paris, 1895), pp. 264-65; Stern, as cited in n. 19, above; M. Whittaker, *Jews and Christians: Graeco-Roman Views* (Cambridge, 1984), p. 71.

the festival was Hanukkah, but that Herod, well known at Rome, was named by Persius instead of the Hasmonaeans; and S. Krauss, criticizing the sabbath explanation as forced, ingeniously argued that under Herod the Hasmonaean Hanukkah was renamed the feast of Herod—the title echoed in Persius—and that in response the lights of Hanukkah were introduced, to preserve the officially discouraged recollection of the Hasmonaeans.[46] O.S. Rankin, examining Krauss's theory, could not agree that the sabbath explanation was forced, especially in view of the difficulty of Persius; he also noted that a Herodian origin for Hanukkah lights seems incompatible with 2 Maccabees, but he allowed that the construction of Herod's temple could have affected the understanding of Hanukkah significantly.[47] Section I, above, has offered some confirmation for the view shared by Krauss and Rankin, that Herod's temple stood for a dynastic outlook at odds with the Hasmonaean emphasis of Hanukkah; it has seemed likely that Herod's accession day also became a new feast of dedication.

This review of interpretation has underlined some reasons which incline many to find familiar Jewish observances reflected in Persius here. He specifically mentions the sabbaths, and the lights and the fish dinner, so vividly described, fit well-known sabbath and festival customs. These points are emphasized by Stern and Harvey (note 19, above). Nevertheless, Persius's Jewish knowledge is thought probably to be limited; but Greek and Roman perception of the Herods, as attested in Strabo and Juvenal (notes 37, 38, 42, above), would have allowed Persius to take Herod as representing the Jews and Jewish custom.

---

46. H. Vogelstein and P. Rieger, *Geschichte der Juden in Rom* (2 vols.; Berlin, 1895–96), I, p. 81; J. de Voisin, *Theologia Iudaeorum* (Paris, 1647), p. 94 (book I, ch. 5); J. Derenbourg, *Essai sur l'histoire et la géographie de la Palestine, d'après les Thalmuds et les autres sources rabbiniques* (Paris, 1867), p. 165 n. 1; S. Krauss 'La Fête de Hanoucca', *REJ* 30 (1895), pp. 24-43, 204-19 (36).

47. O.S. Rankin, *The Origins of the Festival of Hanukkah* (Edinburgh, 1930), pp. 80-86 (not mentioned in the subsequent discussions of 'Herod's days' cited here).

On the other hand, this perception is not very different from that probably held by diaspora Jews who valued royal patronage. Those who explain the days as Herodian birthdays or accession days accordingly view them against the background of Jewish support for the house of Herod, especially in the Diaspora. The probable importance of contemporary ruler cults for an understanding of the Jews' response to their monarchy was indicated by Scaliger and Casaubon. The Roman Jews who kept the days might be Herodians (Scaliger) or the community in general (Casaubon), as in the probably later and earlier forms, respectively, of the scholion discussed in section II (b), above; and this discussion also showed that the sabbath explanation may in early instances have owed much to the practice of explaining the unknown by identification with a nearby known. The possible significance of Herod's newly dedicated temple in connection with the days emerges from the explanations of de Voisin and Krauss.

The understanding of 'Herod's days' suggested below draws on the presentation of Herod's accession day, in section I, above, as a dedication festival and a focus of Herodian court theology. The interpretation offered is a modified form of that adopted by E. Bammel and expounded most fully by Willrich, whose arguments will now be summarized with some additions, including further reference to R.A. Harvey. Four aspects of the background are thereby considered in turn, as follows: Jewish-gentile relations, the bearing of gentile dynastic celebrations on Herodian observances, the Jews in Rome, and the setting in Roman satire.

d. *'Herod's Days' as Royal Birthdays or Accession Days*
Willrich (as cited in note 36, above) set the lines in Persius, first, against the general background of Jewish–gentile tension. Roman Jewish observance of Herodian birthdays or accession-days (probably monthly, in the usual Hellenistic and Roman manner) would be natural, he urged, as part of a bid for official protection; we know that Herod the Great celebrated his accession-day, and that Roman Jews organized themselves in synagogues of 'Augustesians' and 'Agrippesians'; they are likely to have paid their respects to their patrons, including the house of Herod, just as in 13 BC the Jews

of Berenice in the Libyan Pentapolis made a decree to honour M. Tittius at each new moon.[48]

The Roman synagogues mentioned are perhaps more likely to be associations of slaves and freedmen from the households of Augustus and M. Agrippa, but the general importance of the motive suggested by Willrich has been shown more recently from Josephus's procedure in recording Jewish privileges; Herod's defence of the Ionian Jews (Josephus, *Ant.* 16.28) was noted at the end of section I, above, and it has been plausibly suggested that his benefactions to Greek cities (continued by his successors) played an important part in gaining toleration for diaspora Jews.[49] Graeco-Roman observance of royal birthdays and accession days in the manner to which Willrich alluded is documented by Schürer and his revisers with evidence including the Rosetta Stone (196 BC, on the monthly birthday and accession-day of Ptolemy V) and 2 Macc. 6.7 (the monthly birthday of Antiochus IV), and, for the Herods, Mk 6.21 (Antipas) and Josephus, *Ant.* 19.321 (Agrippa I) (birthdays), and Josephus, *Ant.* 15.423, cited above (Herod the Great) (accession day).[50] How naturally *Herodis... dies* can be taken in this sense appears from a law of Valentinian

48. καθ' ἑκάστην σύνοδον καὶ νουμηνίαν, 'at each [?sabbath] assembly and new moon'; see lines 23-24 of the text republished with commentary by J.M. Reynolds in J.A. Lloyd (ed.), *Excavations at Sidi Khrebish, Benghazi (Berenice)*, I (Supplements to Libya Antiqua, 5; 1977), pp. 244-45, no. 17, and in G. Lüderitz, *Corpus jüdischer Zeugnisse aus der Cyrenaica* (Wiesbaden, 1983), pp. 151-55, no. 71; the date 13 BC is supported, and the situation is connected with the hostility (including threats to the temple tax) indicated in Josephus, *Ant.* 16.160-61, 169, by M.W. Baldwin Bowsky, 'M. Tittius Sex.f. Aem. and the Jews of Berenice (Cyrenaica)', *American Journal of Philology* 108 (1987), pp. 495-510. (I am grateful to Mr J.N.B. Carleton Paget, of Queens' College, Cambridge, for drawing my attention to this article.) The importance of new moon festivals in the Diaspora at the beginning of the Christian era is shown by T.C.G. Thornton, 'Jewish New Moon Festivals, Galatians 4:3-11 and Colossians 2:16', *JTS* ns 40 (1989), pp. 97-100.

49. Schürer, *Geschichte*, revised ET, 3.1, p. 96; T. Rajak, 'Was There a Roman Charter for the Jews?', *JRS* 74 (1984), pp. 107-23 (122-23); A.H.M. Jones, *The Herods of Judaea* (Oxford, 1938, corrected reprint 1967), pp. 104-105.

50. Schürer, Vermes, Millar and Black, I (Edinburgh, 1973), pp. 347-48 (part of n. 26).

II, Theodosius I and Arcadius (7th August, 389) in which, after
a note of special days (from the Kalends to the Easter season
and Sundays), they require like reverence 'for our days too'
(*nostris etiam diebus*)—then explained as the days on which
they were born or began to reign (Theodosian Code 2.8, 19).[51]

Secondly, Willrich asked if there were Jewish parallels for a
short-lived celebration of the kind proposed, and how it might
have related to various kings of the house of Herod. He pointed
out that the observance of Herod's birthday or accession-day
by Jews in Rome could be compared with the localized or relatively short-lived celebration of other Jewish festivals, like the
feast of the Septuagint in Alexandria. 'Herod's days' in the
time of Persius, who will hardly have written this passage long
before 60, would have been a special continuance by Roman
Jews of festal days of Herod the Great.

This identification of the Herod in question was not certain,
in Willrich's view; but he preferred it, noting that Agrippa I
and II, who were significant for the Jews in Rome, seem to be
excluded because they did not use the dynastic name
(although others applied it at least to Agrippa I; see Acts 12.1),
and that Herod of Chalcis, likewise prominent in Rome
(Josephus, *Ant.* 20.13-16, 103-104; *War* 2.217, 221-23), was
less important than Herod the Great. The latter's unpopu-
larity might seem to speak against the observance of his days
after his death, but this consideration was outweighed, in
Willrich's judgment, by the likelihood that the days had the
capacity for survival often found in festivals, and that their
discontinuance might have seemed an affront to the house of
Herod; moreover, Herod's friendship with Augustus would
have benefited the Roman Jews particularly.

Here Willrich seems justified in stressing both the likelihood
that Roman Jews honoured the house of Herod, and the
uncertain identification of the particular Herod of *Herodis...
dies*. Nevertheless, the argument that days in honour of Herod
the Great were observed after his death and are mentioned
here could be based not only (with Willrich) on his friendship
with Augustus, but also (following the lead of de Voisin and

51. P. Krueger, *Codex Theodosianus* (2 vols.; Berlin, 1923, 1926), I,
pp. 65-66.

Krauss) on his building of the temple. The completion of the sanctuary on his accession-day will have made the day thereafter also a feast of dedication, an addition which might be expected to strengthen the impetus of the day. Further, the continuation of honour to a monarch after his death is known (as already noted by Scaliger and Casaubon, notes 30, 32, above) in the royal cults of the Graeco-Roman world, notably where they are connected with dynasties rather than individuals.[52] The theory of such cultus as acknowledgment of exceptional benefactions is sympathetically outlined by Nicolas of Damascus (Fragment 125) and by Philo (*Leg. ad Gaium* 149-51), and Jews will have expected to render to their own royal benefactors, as Alexandrian Jews did to the emperor, 'all the honours which the laws permitted' (Philo, *Flacc.* 97).[53] In this context, it would not be surprising if Jews continued to keep the festal days of the founder of the Herodian dynasty and the rebuilder of the temple after his death.

Such honours commonly ceased, however, when the monarch died,[54] and hostility to Herod the Great after his death was expressed by the throngs of Roman Jews who supported the Judaean embassy of opposition to Archelaus's succession (Josephus, *War* 2.80-83). Further, accession days are replaced without affront by the equivalent days of an accredited successor. It is therefore perhaps rather more likely that *Herodis...dies* should be days of later Herodian kings. The festal days of Herod the Great had the lustre of the founder of the dynasty and the re-founder of the temple; his successors

---

52. F.W. Walbank, 'Monarchies and Monarchic Ideas', in F.W. Walbank, A.E. Astin, M.W. Frederiksen and R.M. Ogilvie (eds.), *The Cambridge Ancient History*, 2nd edn, VII.1, *The Hellenistic World* (Cambridge, 1984), pp. 97-98, on Ptolemaic and Seleucid dynastic cults; S.R.F. Price, *Rituals and Power: The Roman Imperial Cult in Asia Minor* (Cambridge, 1984), pp. 61-62, 118, on second-century celebration of the birthdays of Augustus and Livia. On ruler-cults, see further W.R. Telford, below, pp. 290-94 and nn. 132, 149.

53. That the panegyric on Augustus in Philo, *Leg. ad Gaium* 143, derives from a composition used in the Alexandrian synagogues is envisaged, following W. Weber, by E. Bammel, *Jesu Nachfolger: Nachfolgeüberlieferungen in der Zeit des frühen Christentums* (Heidelberg, 1988), p. 19.

54. Price, *Rituals*, pp. 61-62, with regard to Roman emperors.

took over this aureole with the dynastic name 'Herod', which was used by Archelaus, Antipas and Herod of Chalcis, and was applied to Agrippa I. Their festal days, too, will have been 'Herod's days'. About the year 50 Agrippa II succeeded Herod of Chalcis as protector of the temple, and it may be suggested that his birthdays or accession-days, inheriting associations with the house of Herod and with Herod's temple, were still known when Persius wrote, perhaps ten years later, by the traditional name of Herod's days.

Thus far, then, Willrich's indication of Jewish–gentile tension as a strong motive for Jewish honour to Jewish kings has been endorsed, and it has been suggested that, although there is much to be said for the proposal that the 'days' belong to Herod the Great, it is perhaps somewhat more likely that, at the time of Persius, they should have been days of the reigning Agrippa II. With this modification in view, it will now be noted that Willrich also found support for an interpretation of this type from the position of the Jews in Rome and the treatment of Judaism in Roman satire.

Thus, Willrich argued (in the third element of his case to be considered here) that the circumstances of the Jews in Rome in particular favoured his interpretation. To those already noted (their organization under the names of powerful patrons [or of the households to which they belonged], and their benefit from the friendship of Augustus and Herod) he added the presence of Herodian supporters in Rome, as in Puteoli.

This consideration opens the larger question of the importance of the gentile element among Herod's supporters. Willrich himself emphasized that, although Greeks were undoubtedly prominent in Herod's court and following, Greek or Roman names might cover Jewish personages, and he evidently held that the Roman supporters were mainly Jews.[55]

---

55. Willrich, pp. 101-102, 181; for Greek-speaking Jews connected with the Herodian family, see T. Rajak, *Josephus* (London, 1983), pp. 53-55; courtiers of Herod the Great usually taken to be non-Jews, but open to reassessment in the light of Willrich's remark, include the tutors Andromachus and Gemellus (Josephus, *Ant.* 241-43; Schürer, *Geschichte*, ET revised by Black, Vermes and Millar, I, p. 311).

Here Willrich perhaps thought especially of references in Josephus to Herod's 'friends', in the sense of close political adherents,[56] in connection with Herodian princes in Rome. The passages include Josephus, *Ant.* 16.87 (Herod's correspondence with all his friends made his son Antipater well known in Rome); *War* 1.602-606, paralleled in *Ant.* 17.80 (Herod's friends in Rome induced by Antipater and his friends to accuse Archelaus and Philip); and *War* 2.104-105, paralleled in *Ant.* 17.328-31 (Herod's friends support the welcome of the youth who posed as Mariamme's son Alexander in Puteoli and Rome). Willrich will also have had in mind, however, two further passages related to these, on the Roman lodgings of the princes: *Ant.* 15.343, on the true Alexander and his brother in Rome at the house of Pollio, 'one of those most zealous for Herod's friendship', and 17.20-21, on the Roman nurture of Archelaus, Antipas and Philip—in the case of Archelaus and Antipas (Philip's host is not mentioned) 'by a certain Jew', according to B. Niese's conjecture Ἰουδαίῳ in 17.20, where MSS give ἰδίῳ, 'by a member of the [royal] household'.

Willrich held that, especially since Herod would hardly have offended his Jewish subjects by lodging Alexander and Aristobulus with a gentile, their host Pollio was more likely to be a Jewish Herodian supporter than (as W. Otto had argued) Virgil's patron C. Asinius Pollio, consul when Herod received the title of king.[57] Willrich's position on Pollio corresponds to his view that the Roman friends in general were wealthy Jews, as is most naturally suggested by their part in the welcome of the false Alexander. Apart from general considerations, however, an identification with Asinius Pollio seems to be discouraged, as Willrich noted, by the fact that Josephus himself makes no explicit connection between the princes' host and Asinius Pollio, whom he has mentioned twice in the previous book of the *Antiquities* (14.138 [through Strabo, as 'Asinius'], 389), whereas he might have been expected to

---

56. Ptolemaic, Seleucid and Roman imperial usage of the title is documented by E. Bammel, 'ΦΙΛΟΣ ΤΟΥ ΚΑΙΣΑΡΟΣ', *TLZ* 77 (1952), cols. 205-10.

57. Willrich, pp. 184-85, against W. Otto, 'Herodes', *PW* 8, Supp. 2 (1913), cols. 69, 103.

underline the distinction of Herod's friend.[58] Further, it is
questionable whether Asinius Pollio, who was not a close
adherent of Augustus and withdrew from politics under the
principate, would have been chosen by Herod or Augustus as
the princes' host or described by Josephus as zealous for
friendship with Herod; for Herod had indeed formerly, like
Asinius Pollio, been loyal to Caesar and Antony, but had now,
unlike Pollio, transferred his allegiance to Augustus.[59]

These particular objections probably do not exclude Asinius
Pollio altogether. E. Bammel (note 58, above) observes that
Josephus regularly distinguishes between individuals of the
same name who might otherwise be confused; but there is no
such distinction here. The objection derived from Asinius
Pollio's political loyalty retains considerable force, however,
even if he was, as L.H. Feldman urged, sympathetic with
Judaism (as might be suggested by the subject-matter of the
Fourth Eclogue, which Virgil addressed to him, by Herod's
advancement in his consulate, and by his patronage of the
Alexandrian historian Timagenes, who gave a friendly
description of the Hasmonaean Aristobulus I).[60] Nevertheless,
Otto's view was independently defended by Schalit, who ques-

58. Josephus habitually, however, points out possible confusions aris-
ing from recurrences of the same name, as is noted in connection with
Volumnius (with the example of *Ant.* 17.343, on Archelaus and his
steward Archelaus) by E. Bammel, 'Die Rechtsstellung des Herodes',
reprinted from *ZDPV* 84 (1968), pp. 73-79, in E. Bammel, *Judaica:
Kleine Schriften I* (Tübingen, 1986), pp. 3-9 (p. 3 n. 2).
59. The career and outlook of Asinius Pollio are described by R. Syme,
The Roman Revolution (Oxford, 1939, repr. 1985), pp. 5-6, 291, 482-86,
512, and are likewise taken to be inconsistent with this identification by
M. Grant, *Herod the Great* (London, 1971), p. 145. The force of Willrich's argument is perhaps recognized in the doubts concerning the
identification expressed by E. Groag and A. Stein, *Prosopographia
Imperii Romani* (2nd edn; Berlin & Leipzig, 1933), A 1241, p. 253;
Asinius Pollio had been regarded as the host in the first edition.
60. L.H. Feldman, 'Asinius Pollio and his Jewish Interests', *Trans-
actions of the American Philological Association* 84 (1953), pp. 73-80,
followed by Stern, *Authors*, I, p. 213, and G. Zecchini, 'Asinio Pol-
lione', *ANRW* II.30.2 (1982), pp. 1265-96 (1279-81); Timagenes is
Strabo's authority in a description of Aristobulus quoted by Josephus,
Ant. 13.319, and taken by Stern, *Authors*, I, p. 223, to show that (by
contrast with other Alexandrian writers) Timagenes was not hostile to
the Jews.

tioned whether a Jewish host would have been viewed as of sufficient eminence to be named in this context, which emphasizes the distinction of the princes' reception (their admission, also, to the house of Augustus himself is heavily stressed).[61] Once again, the political objection to Asinius Pollio remains; but Schalit's observation could then support R. Syme's tentative suggestion that the friend was Augustus's unspeakable intimate Vedius Pollio.[62] Asinius Pollio, the Pollio last mentioned by Josephus, cannot be wholly ruled out on political grounds, however, despite his splendid isolation, given the consideration from Augustus which his eminence enjoyed. In any case, Schalit's discernment of the aims of the passage makes it likely that the host of Alexander and Aristobulus was a prominent representative of the gentile element of the Roman friends.

In the case of Malthace's sons Archelaus and Antipas, Niese's conjecture at Josephus, *Ant.* 17.20, would make their host unambiguously Jewish; but the reading of the MSS makes good sense if rendered 'a member of the household', is supported by the Latin, and should probably be followed. It then remains an open question whether this high-ranking Herodian domestic, who was perhaps also the host of Philip, was Jewish, gentile, or partly Jewish; but in any case, he was a member of the household rather than one of the group of friends.

Thus far, then, the friends of Herod in Rome appear as a mixed Jewish–gentile group, with a gentile strongly indicated in the case of Pollio, but with Jewish participation suggested especially by the friends' activity in the welcome of the false Alexander. To move beyond the considerations noted by Willrich, Roman Jews of less wealth and standing connected with the house of Herod can be discerned with fair likelihood in Rom. 16.10-11, where 'those of Aristobulus' perhaps belong to the household of a Herodian prince, the brother or the son of Herod of Chalcis; the uncle and the nephew Aristobulus are

61. Schalit, *Herodes*, pp. 413-14 n. 936; for the court-like overtones of admission to Augustus, see Syme, *Roman Revolution*, p. 385.
62. R. Syme, 'Who was Vedius Pollio?', reprinted from *JRS* 51 (1961), pp. 23-30 in R. Syme, *Roman Papers*, ed. E. Badian, II (Oxford, 1979), pp. 518-29 (529).

both mentioned in Josephus, *War* 2.221, and an Aristobulus
who is probably the nephew is mentioned with Herod of Chalcis in Claudius's letter of 45 to Jerusalem, as reproduced in
Ant. 20.13. Paul's kinsman Herodion, who is immediately
mentioned in Romans (16.11), is probably a former Herodian
slave, perhaps from this same household.[63] Herodian connections are also possible in the synagogue of the Volumnesians, if
it takes its name from Herod's friend Volumnius, procurator
of Syria in 8 BC; but the restoration of a broken inscription
which would give a synagogue named '[of the He]rodians' is
doubtful.[64] Of the individual Roman Jews named in literary
sources outside the New Testament (eight from the Herodian
period are listed by H. Solin), only Livia's slave Acme and Josephus himself have known connections with the house of
Herod;[65] but Solin's list does not include the members of the
Herodian family who lived or stayed for long periods in Rome.
Lastly, the member of the household with whom Archelaus
and Antipas lodged may have been Jewish, but this is uncer-
tian. These data give at least some indication of sections of the

63. J.B. Lightfoot, *Saint Paul's Epistle to the Philippians* (4th edn;
repr. London, 1908), pp. 174-75, followed by C.E.B. Cranfield, *A Critical
and Exegetical Commentary on the Epistle to the Romans*, II
(Edinburgh, 1979), pp. 791-92 (regarding the uncle as the likeliest of
three candidates for the identification), and P. Lampe, *Die stadtrö-
mischen Christen in den ersten beiden Jahrhunderten* (Tübingen,
1987), pp. 135-36, 148 (leaving the precise identification open). N.
Kokkinos, 'which Salome did Aristobulus Marry?', *PEQ* 118-19 (1986–
87), pp. 33-50 (35), puts the birth of Aristobulus the son of Herod of
Chalcis about AD 32/33, a date which would not rule out the nephew,
but would confirm his uncle as on the whole a liklier candidate.
64. The Volumnesian identification is accepted by Penna (as cited in
n. 43, above), p. 327, but judged dubious by Smallwood, *Roman Rule*,
p. 138, because Volumnius is not known to have been a benefactor of
the Jews; but this consideration is not so strong if the synagogue members are thought to have belonged to his household. He was a supporter
of Herod, as shown (with emphasis on Josephus, *Ant.* 16.269), by
Bammel, 'Rechtsstellung' (as cited in n. 58, above), n. 2, and as a procurator of Syria could have returned to Rome with Jewish slaves in his
household. On the 'Herodian' synagogue, see Smallwood, p. 138 n. 68.
65. H. Solin, 'Juden und Syrer im westlichen Teil der römischen
Welt', *ANRW* II.29.2 (1983), pp. 587-789, 1222-49 (658-59); Acme was
executed by Augustus for intriguing with Antipater to bring about the
death of Herod's sister Salome (Josephus, *War* 1.661).

Jewish population, notably slaves or freedmen of households with a Herodian connection, where the friends of Herod might find support.

The Roman Jews in general were known in the city for their public demonstrations.[66] Two of these have a recorded connection with the house of Herod. At the second hearing before Augustus to determine Herod's will more than eight thousand Jews thronged to the temple of Apollo on the Palatine to stand by the Judaean embassy opposing Archelaus (Josephus, *War* 2.80-83, parallel with *Ant.* 17.300-303). The friends of Herod and his sons failed to muster popular support on this occasion, no doubt because they were divided, as the Herodian family was (*War* 2.81). It was quite otherwise on the occasion soon afterwards when the friends, as already noted, supported the enthusiastic reception of the false Alexander. The young prince, as he was thought to be, was borne in a litter with a royal retinue through the narrow streets, perhaps in the quarter (probably in Trastevere) described by Persius, amid the acclamations of vast crowds of Jews (Josephus, *War* 2.101-10, parallel with *Ant.* 17.324-38). Here, as when Agrippa I was later welcomed by the Jews of Alexandria, there is the atmosphere of what may be called a Herodian messianism (section I, above).

In the *Antiquities* Josephus characteristically notes that the impostor was popular because he was thought to be the son of the Hasmonaean Mariamme. With a satire written half a century after this scene in view, it should be added that popularity derived by Herodian princes from this source went towards the strengthening of the Herodian house, for Agrippa I, his brother Herod of Chalcis, and his son and daughter Agrippa II and Berenice, all important in Rome, all shared this descent.

In sum, therefore, the evidence seems to be against the view that there was little or no connection between the Herodian princes in Rome and the Roman Jewish community.[67] The

---

66. The pressure exerted by a crowd is regarded as typically Jewish by Horace, interpreted by J. Nolland, 'Proselytism or Politics in Horace, Satires I, 4, 138-43', *VC* 33 (1979), pp. 347-55.
67. This is the opinion of Penna, 'Les juifs à Rome', p. 336 and n. 145.

Herodian friends probably included Jews as well as gentiles, some of the slaves and freedmen who were an important element in the community (Philo, *Leg. ad Gaium*, 155) are likely to have been associated with households of the Herodian family or its sympathizers, and the community as a whole could be united in acclamation of a (supposed) Herodian prince.

The Roman Jewish community was therefore a setting in which the celebration of Herodian festivals can appropriately be envisaged. Two further aspects of the acclamation scene bear this out. First, the corresponding scene at Alexandria called forth a famous Greek counter-demonstration, including satirical cries of *Marin*, 'our lord', and Philo gives a reason for it which suggests the great political advantage accruing to the Jewish population from the possession of a king: each Alexandrian Greek was as vexed because a Jew had been made a king as if he himself had been deprived of an ancestral kingdom (Philo, *Flacc.* 29). This underlines the point already noted that, against the general background of Jewish–gentile tension, the Roman Jews would be likely to pay attention to the Herodian royal family, so often represented in Rome. Secondly, the crowds recall that honour to a king was not, as has perhaps sometimes been assumed in argument on 'Herod's days', a mere official form arousing no general interest. In the case of the imperial cult it has been emphasized that the official prescriptions were not an empty formality (Price [note 54, above], pp. 117-21), and similar considerations would apply to Jewish honours.

Lastly, in the fourth element of Willrich's case to be considered here, he questioned the sabbath interpretation against the background of references to Judaism in Roman poetry. 'Herod's days', he urged, would be a strange designation for the sabbaths, which were well known to Romans (compare Krauss, as cited in note 46, above); one might perhaps expect 'Saturn's day', as in Tibullus (1.3, 18; Stern, *Authors*, I, no. 126, pp. 318-20). He did not consider, however, the strong argument from Juvenal 6.159, 'dedit hunc Agrippa sorori | observant ubi festa mero pede sabbata reges', 'Agrippa gave this [gem] to his sister, where kings keep festal sabbaths barefoot' (Serarius and Nemethy, notes 38, 42, above). Juvenal, referring here to Agrippa II and Berenice, treats Judaea as the place where kings keep the sabbath with exotic piety, and Persius might likewise coin a phrase in which the sabbaths are *the* days of a Jewish king.

This argument would be reinforced, and Willrich's point would be directly met, if 'Herod' were a metonymy for 'Jews' elsewhere in Latin verse. This has more recently been urged by Harvey (note 19, above), with reference to Horace, *Ep.* 2.2, 184, 'Herodis palmetis pinguibus'; here, in a passage on differences of taste and character, one brother is said to prefer an idle life to 'Herod's rich palm-groves', while the other, wealthy and untiring, works from dawn to dusk. Harvey takes Persius to be following Horace, and understands the phrase as equivalent to 'the rich palm-groves of the Jews'; but this seems questionable, so far as a non-specialist can judge, because the palmgroves of Herod in particular, near Jericho, were famous. Antony had given them to Cleopatra, and Octavian restored them to Herod after Actium (Josephus, *War* 1.361, 396). Further, as C. Macleod pointed out, the passage deals with ambition, and an allusion to the notable ambition of Herod in particular adds to its force.[68]

If Juvenal's line suggests that the interpretation of the phrase as an abrupt equivalent for 'sabbaths' cannot be ruled out, Horace's phrase starts the more general consideration that the knowledge of the Jews and Judaism available to Roman satirists should not be minimized. Just as Horace's reference to Herod's palm-groves seems to be precise and accurate, so his at first surprising allusion to 'tricesima sabbata' (*Sat.* 1.9, 69) probably reflects Jewish usage. Here too it has been argued that this is simply a reference to weekly sabbaths, under a fanciful name devised by the poet; but it is much more likely to refer to new moon festivals observed by the Jews of Rome (see Stern, *Authors*, I, no. 129, pp. 324-26, and Thornton, 'Jewish New Moon Festivals', cited in note 48, above). Persius's *Herodis dies* are similarly unparalleled, but appear in a context in which otherwise, like Horace, the poet shows considerable knowledge of the Jews in Rome, offering our best description of a diaspora festal meal. Even if there were not

---

68. C. Macleod, *Horace. The Epistles Translated into English Verse with Brief Comment* (Rome, 1986), p. 82.

the background of Herodian influence studied here, it would be reasonable to suppose that Persius was using an uncommon but genuine Jewish name for a festival.

The Herodian associations of the Roman Jewish community, and the far from negligible knowledge of the Jews exhibited by satirists who lived in Rome, therefore support the specifically Herodian interpretation of 'Herod's days' outlined above. They were probably royal festivals, as is suggested by independent references in Josephus and the New Testament to the celebration of Herodian birthdays and accession days. Herod the Great had linked the dedication of the sanctuary with his accession day (section I (a), above), and Herodian festivals will have continued to evoke the dynastic association with Herod's temple. The phrase *Herodis... dies* in Persius is perhaps best explained by the suggestion that the birthdays or accession-days of Agrippa II had inherited an existing designation, 'Herod's days'.

III. *Summary of Conclusions*

Herodian publicity, as echoed in the accounts of Herod's temple in Josephus's *Antiquities* and the Talmud, found a great focus in the dedication of the sanctuary on Herod's accession-day (section I, above). The restored temple, with all its 'goodly stones and votive offerings' (Lk. 21.5), was thereby incorporated into the Herodian form of ruler-cult (sections I (a) and II (d), above). Jewish observance of the Herodian festivals corresponded to the importance of the house of Herod as Jewish patrons and representatives. It has here been urged that, as was already thought in the later Roman empire to be the case (section II (a)-(b) above), the Jews of Rome under Nero kept a Herodian festival, *Herodis...dies* in Persius 5.180, probably the birthdays or accession days of Agrippa II (section II (c)-(d), above). The suggestion in this form is a variant of an interpretation of Persius put forward by J.J. Scaliger, which had been perhaps most fully expounded and defended in recent times by H. Willrich. It associates the passage in Persius with the unambiguous evidence in Josephus and the New Testament for Jewish celebration of Herodian festal days.

The Herodian form of ruler-cult, and the rôle of the house of Herod as Jewish patrons, are of course attested irrespectively of this particular interpretation of Persius. Here these subjects have been approached through the narratives of Herod's temple restoration, and the importance of the temple in dynastic publicity and for Jewish attitudes to the house of Herod has been indicated especially in three areas.

First, the temple fulfilled for the house of Herod its time honored function as a royal sanctuary. Herod the Great was presented in the temple restoration as a great Jewish king like the kings of old. Examination of Nicolas's narrative, as transmitted by Josephus (section I (a), above), has confirmed the interpretation of Herod's policy as thoroughly Augustan, yet thoroughly Jewish: an appeal to the pre-Maccabaean biblical heritage (I (c), above).[69] The talmudic echo of this presentation (I (b), above) suggests that it was not entirely rejected. It gave a strong answer to many current criticisms of Herod the Great, and its virtue as a shield of his house will have been continually renewed by the splendour of the temple restoration itself (Mk 13.1; Lk. 21.5), which proceeded continuously until about the year 64.[70]

Secondly, the rebuilt temple was incorporated into the Herodian ruler-cult. Herod the Great as temple builder was invested in Nicolas's presentation with an atmosphere of what can appropriately be called Herodian messianism (I (a) and (c), above). Later Herodian monarchs were seen to have evoked or shared this atmosphere, in a Jewish counterpart to the contemporary ruler-cults (I (c) and (c)-(d), above). The connections and contrasts between the two appear especially in the career of Agrippa I, hailed as lord among the Jews of Alexandria and as godlike in the Theatre at Caesarea. This aspect of Herodian kingship deserves further consideration among the antecedents of the cult of Christ. Here it has been of

---

69. E. Bammel, 'Sadduzäer und Sadokiden', reprinted from *ETL* 55 (1979), pp. 107-115 in Bammel, *Judaica* (as cited in n. 58, above), pp. 117-26 (118-20); he follows Wellhausen's assessment of Herodian policy, but points in addition to the Augustan background, and shows concretely how policy was put into effect.

70. Josephus, *Ant.* 20.219, discussed by Smallwood, *Roman Rule*, pp. 282-83 n. 89.

note as exibiting a Herodian king or prince at the centre of a Jewish community in Rome, Alexandria of Jerusalem. These scenes were noticed together with some of the less dramatic traces of Jewish Herodian support in the preamble of the essay, and comparable evidence from Rome was somewhat more fully considered in II (d). The Herodian form of ruler-cult, sometimes viewed merely as a concession to Graeco-Roman manners, was also a medium for the expression of national feeling. To approach it through the narratives of the temple restoration is to see its strongly Jewish aspect more plainly.

Thirdly, this approach has brought into view a number of links between the Herodian monarchy and the Jewish community, in the diaspora and in the homeland. The house of Herod, responsible for a temple which was the focus of Jewish communal life throughout the world, has appeared more clearly as a Jewish dynasty. The Herodian ruler-cult corresponded to real needs of the Jewish community for protection and for self assertion, both at home and abroad. Hence, without discounting the influence of the Zealot movement or the complexities of reaction to each individual monarch, one may in general allow for a good measure of Jewish recognition of the Herods, as suggested at the beginning of the essay.[71]

Here a penultimate word should perhaps recall the room for varying views of the house of Herod not only in the diaspora, but in Judaea itself (section I (c), above). That relatively detached element in Judaean public opinion which spoke through Samaias and the *Assumption of Moses* seems to be echoed in the laconic chronicle-tradition in the name of R. Jose b. Halafta (mid-second century). It covers the period from the kingdom of Greece to the destruction of the temple, without mentioning Roman rule or endorsing Hasmonaean propaganda, by noting two Jewish monarchies of equal duration:

---

71. So H. Vogelstein, *Rome* (Philadelphia, 1940), pp. 28-29; from this standpoint the allowance made by Goodman, *Ruling Class,* pp. 122-23, for favorable attitudes to Agrippa I and II among Jews would be endorsed, but his emphasis on Jerusalem and Judaean negative views of the Herods would be complemented by some notice of likely variations.

'kingdom of the Hasmonaean house, 103 years; kingdom of the house of Herod, 103 years'.[72]

72. *B. Abodah Zarah* 8b-9a, parallel with B. Ratner (ed.), *Seder Olam Rabba* (Wilna, 1897), p. 142 ('kingdom of Herod'); for a characterization of the two texts see E. Bammel, 'Die Blutgerichtsbarkeit in der römischen Provinz Judäa vor dem ersten jüdischen Aufstand', reprinted from *JJS* 25 (1974) in Bammel, *Judaica,* pp. 59-72 (68-69).

'KORAH' AND THE SECOND TEMPLE

J.A. Draper

1. *Introduction*

The Talmud contains a rich deposit of polemic and polemical epithets, many of which, such as בייתוסים and שחרית טובלי מינים, have already been explored, (See Amussin 1963; Neher 1957). R. Johanan b. Zakkai (T1), pupil of Hillel, blames the destruction of Jerusalem on the existence of no less than twenty-four heretical sects (מינים, *j. Sanh.* 29c). The references to sects in the Talmud are notoriously difficult to specify, not least because the earlier layers of tradition have often been reapplied and generalized until they have become unrecognizable. Nevertheless, the Talmud is important as a source for the currents of Jewish controversy in the Second Temple period. Dr Ernst Bammel has delved tirelessly and effectively into the quicksands of the Rabbinic tradition to recover historical material for the reconstruction of Christian origins,[1] and has inspired generations of his students to do the same. This paper explores one group of polemical titles in Rabbinic writings, clustered around the figure of Korah, in the light of evidence from the Dead Sea Scrolls.

---

1. The list is endless, but many articles have proved to be valuable starting points for my own studies, e.g. ''Ἀρχιερεὺς Προφητεύων', *TLZ* 79 (1954), cols. 351-56; 'Schema und Vorlage von *Didache* 16', *Studia Patristica IV* (TU 79; Berlin, 1961), pp. 253-62; 'Gerim Gerurim', *ASTI* 7 (1968–1969), pp. 127-31; 'Sadduzäer und Sadokiten', *ETL* 55 (1979), pp. 107-15.

2. *Korah as the Boundary of Acceptable Controversy*

An unascribed passage from *m. Aboth* 5.17 raises fascinating possibilities about polemical use of the name 'Korah', which have not really been explored. This passage comes from the oldest layer of the tractate, according to Strack (1931: 53-54):

> Every controversy (כל מחלוקת) that is in the name of Heaven, its outcome shall be confirmed, but [any controversy] that is not in the name of Heaven, its outcome shall not be confirmed. Which controversy was it that was in the name of Heaven? This was the controversy of Hillel and Shammai. And which [controversy] was not in the name of Heaven? Such was the controversy of Korah and all his congregation (וכל עדתו).[2]

Here it is a matter of legal disputation, which lies behind the word מחלוקת. The root meaning of חלק 'to be smooth', 'to allot', 'to divide and so to differ, to object, to oppose' (Jastrow, p. 473) has been extended to 'differentiate' and hence מחלוקת comes to mean 'partisanship, difference of opinion or controversy' (Maurer, *TDNT*, VII, pp. 959-64). The question in the passage is about the tolerable limits of disagreement within the Rabbinic community. The passage seems to derive from the period after the catastrophe of AD 70, when the re-organization of Jewish national life under the Yavnean Rabbis necessitated the redefinition of the acceptable limits of doctrinal dispute.

Legal dispute is allowed, or even encouraged by the passage, within the bounds implied by the reference to Korah, which are not amplified or clarified.

2.1 *'Those who seek controversies' in the Scrolls*
The widespread usage of the term החלקות in the Dead Sea Scrolls may help to clarify the usage of מחלוקת to some extent, since they characterize one group of opponents of the sect as דורשי החלקות.

2.1.1 *The Hymn Scrolls.* 1QH 2.14-15 is set in the context of a hymn of controversy. Traitors and wicked men mock, slander

---

2. All quotations from Hebrew texts are my translations unless otherwise stated.

and trample on the righteous Teacher (2.7-15), but to the upright of way he is 'a counsel of truth and understanding':

> And I am a man of strife (איש ריב) to those who interpret error (למליצי תעות), but a [man of p]eace to all who see what is right. And I am a spirit of zeal (לרוח קנאה) to all who seek controversies (כל דורשי חלקות) (2.14-15).

The same language recurs in 2.32:

> I thank you, O Lord, because your eye s[tands watch] upon my life and you have delivered me from the zeal of those who interpret falsehood (מקניח מליצי כזב), and you have saved the life of the poor from the congregation of those who seek controversies (עדת דורשי חלקות).

This is the language of legal controversy between Jewish sects. The expression דורשי חלקות is usually translated 'those who speak smooth things', that is, who do not take the most rigorous legal position in interpretation.This matches the sense of Isa. 30.10 (cited in CD 1.18; see below). However, the extended sense of the Rabbinic usage of מחלוקת to refer to 'controversies' seems to lie behind the Qumran usage also, as it is translated above. In both these cases, the expression occurs in the context of the Teacher of Righteousness as the only source of correct legal interpretation. In particular, the second of these passages makes דורשי חלקות parallel to מליצי כזב. Thus the primary focus of the word is not moral laxity, although perhaps that is the implication, but disagreement over the right understanding of the Torah.

A passage in 4.9-10 makes it clear that the controversies concern the Torah and that the false interpreters and the Teacher of the Hymns are wrestling for influence over God's people:

> And they, those who interpret falsehood (מליצי כזב) and prophets of falsehood, have plotted against me devilishly (בליעל) to exchange your Law which is engraved on my heart for controversies (חלקות) for your people.

The Teacher of the Hymn Scroll was engaged in legal controversies with his opponents which were beyond what could be accommodated within one community. These controversies clearly include attempts made on his life and reputation by his opponent in the legal dispute.

2.1.2 *The Commentaries.* The same terminology is used repeatedly in the Commentary on Nahum, where it is given more specific content. If 4QpNah 3–4.1.2f. is allowed as a determining historical reference, then this group of opponents would seem to be the Pharisees:

> *Whither the lion goes, there is the lion's cub, [with none to disturb it]* (Hab. 2.11): [Its interpretation concerns Deme]trius king of the Kittim who sought, on the counsel of those who seek controversies (דורשי החלקות), to enter Jerusalem. [But God did not permit the city to be delivered] into the hands of the kings of the Kittim, from the time of Antiochus until the coming of the rulers of the Kittim. *The lion tears enough for its cubs and it chokes prey for its lionesses* (Hab. 2.12): [Its interpretation] concerns the furious young lion who strikes by means of his great men, and by means of the men of his council. [*And chokes prey for its lionesses; and it fills* (Hab. 2.12)]: Its interpretation concerns the furious young lion [who executes revenge] on those who seek controversies (בדורשי החלקות) and hangs men alive, [a thing never done] formerly in Israel. Because of a man hanged alive on [the] tree, He proclaims, *'Behold I am against [you, says the Lord of Hosts']*.

This is one of the few historical references in the Scrolls and seems to refer to an incident described by Josephus in *Ant.* 13.372-82. The Pharisees rebelled unsuccessfully against Alexander Jannaeus, who took his revenge by crucifying large numbers of them. If the opponents of the Qumran community, those who seek controversies, are indeed the Pharisees, then this would be a valuable insight into the kind of מחלוקת which the Rabbis considered unacceptable. From the side of the Qumran community, at least, they were engaged in controversies with the Pharisees, which they considered beyond the bounds of the acceptable.

4QpNah 3–4.2.2 applies the text of Nah. 3.1, 'Woe to the city of blood; it is full of lies and rapine' to 'the city of Ephraim, those who seek controversies (דורשי החלקות) in the last days, who walk (תהלכו) in lies and falsehood'. The use of the root הלך is probably a deliberate reference to false הלכות. The reference to the 'city of Ephraim' probably contains an attack on the

Hasmonaean dynasty, which had usurped the high priesthood and ousted the Zadokite high priest, since they originate from Modin in Ephraim. The Pharisees had accepted their take-over of the high priesthood, while the Zadokite party had withdrawn from the temple and from Jerusalem, declaring the temple defiled by illegitimate sacrifice. The carnage of war in Nah. 3.1-3 is also applied by the commentary (3–4.2.4) to 'the rule of those who seek controversies' (החלקות ממשלת דורשי). This introduces a different note into the term, indicating that the party of the opponents was in a position of power.

A further passage in 3.3 looks forward to a time when 'those who seek controversies' will fall from power and their followers will turn instead to the community of the Scrolls, 'when the glory of Judah shall arise, the simple of Ephraim shall flee from their assembly; they shall abandon those who lead them astray and shall join Israel'. The same expectation is expressed in 3.7, where the 'seekers of controversies' will be destroyed and unable to lead the assembly into error (לתעות הקהל) again.

The fragmentary commentary on Isaiah (4QpIsa^c 2.10) also contains a reference to 'the congregation of those who seek controversies (עדת ד[ורשי] החלקות) who are in Jerusalem'. The Wicked Woman who is a type of the opponents of the community in 4Q 184 is also portrayed as seducing men by controversies (ולפתות בחלקות בני איש, 1.17; cf. 4Q 185 1–2.2.14).

2.1.3 *The Damascus Document.* CD 1.18 also uses a similar phrase to describe the time when Israel has been led astray by the 'Man of the Tongue' who waters Israel with lies and leads them astray. Isa. 30.10 is cited here as a proof text for the use of אשר דרשו בחלקות, but does not necessarily give the exact sense of the term as it was used at Qumran. The title was already in common use in the community, as we have seen. The Pharisees are 'those who seek legal controversies', whereas the members of its own community are forbidden to debate with non-members (1QS 9.16f.). Legal questions within the community were to be settled by the Zadokite priests and the 'Many' (1QSb 3.23), against whose authority even murmuring meant permanent expulsion (1QS 7.17f.).

2.2 *Korah as a Polemical Title*

Acceptable legal disputation, within the bounds of the newly emerging Rabbinic Judaism after the disastrous first war against Rome (AD 66–70), is typified by the dispute of the great Pharisaic contemporaries Hillel and Shammai at the beginning of the first century AD. Unacceptable legal disputation is typified by the legal disputation of Korah and his congregation in Numbers 16. It seems not unlikely that קרח וכל עדתו is intended as a polemical epithet for a sectarian community (עדה) of the same era as Hillel and Shammai. What is at issue in the rebellion of Korah and his congregation against Moses was not legal interpretation, despite later attempts to make the dispute turn on the issue of fringes (*b. San.* 110a, seemingly on the authority of Rab), which is deduced from the context of Numbers 15, but the issue of the high priesthood (Num. 16.10, where *TgOnk., TgJon.* and *TgNeof.* all read variations of כהנה רבתה; cf. *Num. R.* 18.8). *Exod. R.* 51.1 (159b) on Exod. 38.21 states זה קרח שהיה לוי ובקש ליטול כהונה גדולה. Moses has given the high priesthood to his brother Aaron, over the head of Korah, and this provokes the rebellion.

Since *m. Aboth* uses Korah as an archetype for the unacceptable controversy, it seems that the issue of the high priesthood would be involved in this. It seems a profitable area for investigation, as to whether the remains of Rabbinic characterization of Korah confirm the possibility that this saying from *m. Aboth* refers to a sect in opposition to the Pharisees and contemporary with Hillel and Shammai. The priestly nature of the community of the Scrolls is well known, as is the quarrel between the Wicked (High) Priest in Jerusalem and the Teacher of Righteousness, probably over the issue of the Zadokite nature of the legitimate high priesthood (Vermes 1975: 53-68; 1977: 137-62; Stegemann 1971; Burgmann 1974: 323-59; 1978: 3-72; Draper 1988: 41-63). If all these things can be linked together, then there may be grounds for thinking that *m. Aboth* 5.17 is directed against the Teacher of Righteousness and the community of the Scrolls.

3. *Korah and Those Who have No Share in the World to Come*

The name Korah occurs prominently in *m. Sanh.* 10, which contains an embryonic *contra haereses*. This chapter seems out of place in its context (Danby 1919: vii n. 2), and may well have been originally an independent unit. It forms ch. 11 in the Babylonian Talmud, while it is ch. 10 in the Jerusalem Talmud. The text begins with the presupposition that all Israel has a share in the world to come. The list of heretics is then couched in terms of those who have no share in the world to come, in other words are beyond the bounds of Israel by virtue of their beliefs or practices, such as those who deny the resurrection of the dead, those who deny the heavenly origin of the Torah, and the Epicureans, as well as those who read heretical books and utter healing charms over a wound (10.1). It is interesting to note that the same tendency to define Israel in terms of a particular group, while excluding members of other groups, can be seen in the Dead Sea Scrolls. Here כל ישראל is a title for the members of the community in 1QSa 1.1, 6; 2.12. We have already cited 4QpNah 3–4.3.3, where it is expected that the 'seekers of controversies' will be abandoned and the people will then 'join Israel', namely by joining the community of the Scrolls!

The Company of Korah appears in *m. Sanh.* 10.3, as part of a collection of groups excluded from the life to come. As the series stands in the Babylonian Talmud, it is a consecutive list drawn from the Old Testament: the Generation of the Flood, the Generation of the Dispersion, the Men of Sodom, the Spies, the Generation of the Wilderness, the Company of Korah, the Ten Tribes and the Apostate City. The Apostate City does not really fit in such a consecutive list, and Danby expresses his uneasiness at the presence of this element in the section, feeling it belongs with section 11 (1933: 398). However, there are clear indications that the list is not originally a consecutive list at all, but that it has been made to conform to such a Biblical schema at a later stage. Yerushalmi sets the passage on the Generation of the Separation *after* the Spies, and it is clear that this order is correct. The teaching of R. Nehemiah which is cited by both versions of the Talmud immediately before the Spies takes the Generation of the Flood and the Men of Sodom *together*, ignoring the passage on the Generation of the Separation which intervenes in the Babylonian Talmud. If the Biblical schema is correct it is difficult to see why anyone would have changed it. If, on the other hand, the position of the Generation of the Separation in Yerushalmi is correct, then the list must originally have had some other unifying rationale.

A further puzzling feature of the list, if it is taken as a Biblical schema, is why the various groups mentioned should have been taken together. A discussion of the Men of Sodom does not seem in place in a section seemingly discussing the limits of the community of Israel, directed in 10.1-2 towards notorious heretics and sinners *in Israel*. It seems hardly necessary to debate whether the *Biblical* Men of Sodom should have a share in the world to come! I would like to propose that the titles in 10.3 are cryptic references to a sect within Israel about which there was a debate in Pharisaic and Yavnean circles. The question about whether this sect should be accepted within the bounds of Israel was genuine and heated.

The earliest nucleus of the whole unit seems to be a controversy between R. Akiba (c. AD 110–135) and his contemporary R. Eliezer b. Hyrcanus (as often, see Neusner 1973b: 373-74). Akiba excludes the particular groups mentioned from eternal life, while Eliezer declares that they will finally be saved.

3.1 *Rabbi Eliezer ben Hyrcanus*

R. Eliezer is a somewhat enigmatic figure who acts as a bridge between the pre-70 Pharisaic movement and the Yavnean reconstruction. His sayings and life have been exhaustively analysed in the fine study by Jacob Neusner (1973), who concludes that teachings of Eliezer, where they are attested by a later Yavnean master, may be accorded considerable reliability. *M. San* 10.3 has the attestation of the third-century Tanna Joshua b. Qorha in *b. Sanh.* 110b, and is thus placed, at least in part, by Neusner among the 'better traditions' concerning R. Eliezer (1973: 157).

One of the key features of the tradition concerning Eliezer is that he came into conflict at some stage with the dominant tradition of Yavneh, so that his teaching is passed on in a way different from that of the Houses:

> The best traditions make one thing clear: at some point in his
> life, Eliezer fell under a shadow, so that it was necessary to pre-
> serve his traditions in a peculiar way—by saying he said the
> opposite of what was his true opinion... We do not know what
> happened (Neusner 1973: 297).

It has been argued that he was attracted by Christianity, but
there is no evidence for this in the traditions he presents. The
later traditions claim that Eliezer was excommunicated by his
own brother-in-law, R. Gamaliel II at Yavneh (e.g. *b. BM* 59b),
because he refused to yield on his views concerning the 'oven
of Akhnai'.

Neusner (1973: 411) finds it difficult to understand why this
story of the 'oven of Akhnai' is introduced and believes it may
be an interpolation. However, it could also be that the 'oven of
Akhnai' refers to the Biblical Achan who is destroyed by stoning and by burning at Jericho, together with his whole family.
Pseudo-Philo (*LAB* 25.1–26.1) has a haggadic story in which
the hero, Kenaz, re-enacts the story of Akhan with other law-
breakers, where the punishment is by fire alone:

> And Kenaz brought them out and said to them, 'Behold now you
> know how Achan confessed when he came out in the lot and
> how he declared everything he had done. And now declare to us
> your wicked deeds and schemes. And who knows that if you tell
> the truth to us, even if you die now, nevertheless God will have
> mercy on you when he will resurrect the dead?' And one of
> them, Elas by name, said, 'Will not death now come upon us so
> that we might die in the fire?...' And when all this had been
> said, he burned all those men in the fire and everything that had
> been found with them except the precious stones (Charlesworth
> 1985: 335-36).

Here we find a similar combination of themes to the Korah
exegesis, centring around the question of whether law-breakers might expect a share in the world to come. Akhan's oven in
the quarrel of Eliezer with Yavneh could be a reference to this
complex of ideas concerning law-breakers or heretics.
Although the word תנור, 'oven', is common in its literal use (e.g.
m. Kel. 5.3-4), it is used extensively by the prophets in a figurative sense for the wrath of God (Isa. 31.9; Hos. 7.4, 6f.; Mal.
3.19; cf. Ps. 21.10). Thus it is not impossible that such a usage
underlies *b. BM* 59b, in a reference to the 'the furnace [of

God's wrath]', and that this was later misunderstood and re-interpreted to refer to purity rules concerning ovens.

The association of the Essenes with Jericho could have provided a link with Jericho. The Essenes may be the target of other Rabbinical teaching concerning the men of Jericho in *m. Pes.* 4.8 (cf. *b. Pes.* 55b-56; see Amusin 1963: 20-21). R. Eliezer is known to have favoured reconciliation with the Samaritans (*m. Sheb.* 8.9-10; cf. Neusner 1973: 316), and seems to have favoured openness towards other sects. Perhaps his stubbornness in refusing to agree to the exclusion of the Essenes lies behind the story of his excommunication.

4. *The Groups in* m. Sanhedrin *10.3*

If the three disputes following a single principle in *m. Sanh.* 10.3, between Akiba and Eliezer, are indeed the heart of the mishnaic text, then the original list referred to the 'generation of the wilderness' (דור המדבר), the 'company of Korah' (עדת קרח) and the 'ten tribes' (עשרת השבטים). To this may, perhaps be added the 'people of an Apostate City' (אנשי עיר הנדחת), since Akiba's comment is noted here also (10.6, though Danby believes that this section belongs with what follows and that אין להם חלק לעלם הבא in 10.4 should be omitted, following Yeru-shalmi). These designations may refer to different groups, may refer to the same group, or may, of course, be simple scriptural embroidery. The last possibility is unlikely, since the study of Neusner indicates that R. Eliezer first formulated his position and then adduced Scriptural texts, rather than the other way round:

> In all, therefore, it seems highly unlikely that Eliezer normally produced laws on the basis of antecedent interpretations of Scripture. Sometimes this may have been the case; in others it is not entirely clear. But in the main the exegesis of Scriptures follows after the formulation of the law. And in most cases the law is generated entirely independent of exegesis, frequently by logical extension of established principles (Neusner 1973: 392).

The location of these Scriptural figures here in the context of a list of heretics introduced by *m. Sanh.* 10.1 suggests that the Scriptural groups are veiled allusions to more contemporary groupings. Once the consecutive Biblical pattern is abandoned

as the organizing principle for the section, there is much to
suggest that they represent one single sectarian movement, or
at least related movements. The key to the section lies in the
relationship of the groups mentioned to the desert and to
Israel's desert wanderings.

4.1 *The Generation of the Wilderness*
Akiba supports his contention that the 'Generation of the
Wilderness' should be excluded from the life of the world to
come with the Scriptural text, Num. 14.35: 'In this wilderness
they shall be consumed (יתמו) and there they shall die'. Tosefta
(13.10) adds a citation of Ps. 95.11 by Akiba, 'I swore in my
anger, they will not enter into my rest'. Eliezer counters with
Ps. 50.5, 'Gather my saints (חסידי) together unto me, those that
have made a covenant with me by sacrifice'. It is likely from
Akiba's citation that the destruction in the desert is a reference
to their known fate rather than to their future judgment.
Further, from Eliezer we might infer that this sectarian
group had a positive connection with the movement of the
Hasidim, and could be said to have made a covenant with God.
The covenant is especially related to sacrifice, according to the
proof-text. This may indicate a priestly connection. On the
other hand, 'by sacrifice' may present a problem, since the
Essene community was pledged to boycott the Jerusalem
temple, at least according to CD 6.11-21, although they may
well have used the ritual of the red heifer in community ini-
tiation (Draper 1983: 148-53). On the other hand, it is clear
that the community was dominated by Zadokite priests in
opposition to the Jerusalem cult. In any case, the Scrolls show
that they considered their community worship and life as a
spiritual sacrifice (Gärtner 1965).

4.2 *The Company of Korah*
R. Akiba argues, secondly, that the 'company of Korah will not
rise up for ever (עדה קרח אינה עתידה לעלות)', a reference to the
rebellion of Korah against the award of the high priesthood to
Aaron in Numbers 16. The miraculous opening of the ground
to swallow up the company of Korah (16.33) is interpreted as
an indication that it had forfeited its share in the world to
come. The choice of this part of the narrative in Numbers may

be linked to the history of the group Akiba is attacking. Eliezer accepts the reference to the opening of the ground, but counters Akiba's inference with a quotation from 1 Sam. 2.6, 'The Lord kills and makes alive, he brings down to Sheol and brings up'. What is significant here is the location of this text in the literature of the religious poor. 1 Sam. 2.7-8 continues, 'The Lord makes poor and he makes rich; he makes low, he also raises up. He raises the oppressed (דל) from the dust, he raises the poor (אביונים) from the ash-heap.' The title 'the poor' is commonly used in the Dead Sea Scrolls to refer to the community. Indeed, the community can be referred to simply as the עדת אביונים (4QpPs 37 2.10; cf. 1QpHab 12.3, 6, 10; 1QM 11.9, 13; 13.14; 1QH 2.32; 3.25; 5.16, 18, 22; fr. 16.3; 4QpPs37 1.9; CD 6.21; 14.14). It could be that this connection with the אביונים is what has occasioned Eliezer's use of the text.

The commentary on this passage in *b. Sanh.* 109b substitutes a comment attributed to R. Judah b. Bathyra (c. AD 130–160) for that by R. Eliezer in the Mishnah: 'They are like something lost which is sought (כאבידה המתבקשת), for it is said, *I have gone astray like a lost sheep: seek your servant; for I do not forget your commandments* (Ps. 119.176)'. Here again, the concern expressed seems more consistent with a debate concerning a current sect than debate about the Biblical Korah and his company.

4.3 *The Ten Tribes*

The reference to the company of Korah is followed by Akiba's assertion that 'the Ten Tribes are not destined to return' (אינן עתידין לחזור). This is a strange contradiction of the eschatological hope of Israel, if *m. Sanh.* 10.3 is simply a consecutive pattern drawn from Scripture. It is more comprehensible if it is taken as a reference to a sect contemporary with Akiba, which was in some way associated with the ten tribes. Exile would then be seen as a punishment for their deviation from the correct interpretation of the Torah, bringing on themselves the curses of the Covenant, and a sign that they are excluded from the world to come. Akiba cites a text specifically associated with the blessings and curses of the covenant, Deut. 29.28, in this connection, 'And He shall cast them out to another land as at this day' (כיום הזה). It is well known that the Scrolls community considered itself as the community of the covenant and that entry into the community was regarded as entry into the covenant, confirmed by a binding oath, and bringing a person under the blessings and curses of the covenant. If we are indeed in the realm of the community of the Scrolls and the Damascus Document, then this would be a telling accusation, since they were self-confessedly in exile 'in Damascus', the place of exile of the ten northern tribes after 720 BC (2 Kgs 18.11). Akiba interprets this as divine punishment. Compare *Ass. Mos.* 4.9 and *4 Ezra* 13.40-53, where 'the ten tribes' is a positive and not negative term.

Eliezer retorts with a cryptic simile: 'Like as the day grows dark and then grows light, so also after the darkness is fallen upon the Ten Tribes shall light hereafter shine upon them'. It is speculative, but the Qumran scrolls are characterized by a light–darkness dualism between the Sons of Light and the Sons of Darkness. This reference could be an ironical reference to such a well-known characteristic.

5. *Other Groups in* m. Sanhedrin *10.3*

There appears to be a growing amount of evidence linking this whole passage with the community of the Dead Sea Scrolls, or with the movement with which the Scrolls was associated. It is now important to examine the other designations in the passage to determine whether they have similar links with the Scrolls. We begin with the 'Generation of the Separation', both because of the obscurity of that title, and also because of its original location in the text immediately before the titles debated by Akiba and Eliezer.

5.1 *The Generation of the Separation*

Strangely, one of the groups for whom a share in the world to come is debated is the דור הפלגה, 'the generation of the separation'. פלג refers unequivocally to the concept of separation. It is an unusual and striking title, one unlikely to have suggested itself from Scripture.

It happens that the expression בית פלג occurs in the Damascus Document 20.22, as a self-designation for the community

of 'the men who enter the New Covenant in the land of Damascus' (CD 19.33-34; cf. 20.12-13):

> And every member of the House of Separation (ביח פלג) who went
> out of the Holy City and leaned on God at the time when Israel
> sinned and defiled the Temple, but returned again to the way of
> the people in small matters, shall be judged according to his
> spirit in the Council of Holiness. But when the glory of God is
> made manifest to Israel, all those members of the Covenant who
> have breached the bound of the Law shall be cut off from the
> midst of the camp (המחנה), and with them all those who con-
> demned Judah in the days of its trials (CD 20.22-27).

What also emerges from the passage is that the community of
the Damascus Document withdrew from Jerusalem because
they considered the temple sacrifice defiled, and considered
themselves in some sense the successors of the encampment of
the Israelites in the desert, as the use of the word מחנה indicates.
For this there are numerous other references in the Document.

The use of the term ביח in CD 20.22 seems to indicate that
there is a dispute over the interpretation of the Torah, as this
word comes to have a technical use to refer to a school or college (cf. 'House of Absalom' in 1QpHab 5.9; 'House of Judah' in
CD 4.11). פלג is probably taken from Gen. 10.25: 'To Eber were
born two sons: the name of the one was Peleg, for in his days
the earth was divided, and his brother's name was Joktan'.
There is a division in the Hebrew nation, but the line of Abraham passes through Peleg! Thus the 'generation of Pelagah'
in *m. Sanh.* 10.3 would seem to refer to the community of the
Damascus Document. It is considered to be beyond the bounds
of Israel.

5.2 *The Generation of the* מבול

The Generation of the מבול is referred by *m. Sanh.* 10.3 to the
Generation of Noah by the text Gen. 6.2, 'My Spirit shall not
abide in man for ever'. This is then interpreted in the Babylonian Talmud to imply that they have neither access to judgment nor to Spirit (לא דין ולא רוח).[3] The Scrolls community
considered itself to have received the eschatological Spirit,

---

3. The other witnesses omit this phrase.

which purified its members (e.g. 1QS 3.6-12). Although the meaning 'Generation of the Flood' is well attested in Scripture (Gen. 9.11, 15, 28; 10.1, 32; 11.11), it is not the only possible one, since מבול can also be used of destruction by fire (Jastrow, pp. 724-25). Raba (BA4) in *b. Sanh.* 108b specifically raises the possibility that it refers to a flood of fire. It could easily be linked to the destruction by fire and earthquake which overtook the company of Korah (Num. 16.35), to which reference is made later. An important indication that this is its original reference is given by its link to the Men of Sodom.

5.3 *The Men of Sodom*

As has already been indicated, the inclusion of the Men of Sodom in a list considering the acceptable bounds of Israel is startling. Moreover, their case seems to be considered together with that of the Generation of the מבול. Still more striking is the fact that there should even be a contention that they shall 'stand in the judgment' (though there is some confusion in the text here). R. Nehemiah (T3) is recorded as denying that either the generation of the Flood or the men of Sodom shall stand in the judgment, citing Ps. 1.5, 'Even so the wicked shall not stand in the judgment, nor sinners in the congregation of the righteous'. The text cited indicates that the groups concerned make the claim to stand 'in the congregation of the righteous (בעדת צדיקים)'. This is an intra-Jewish dispute, not a reference to the Biblical men of Sodom at all.

If 'the Men of Sodom' is a polemical title for a Jewish sect, regarded as beyond the bounds of Israel by the Rabbis, then the Qumran community must be the most likely target. The exact location of the territory of Sodom had long been forgotten in Second Temple times, except that it was associated with the territory around the Dead Sea. One of the cities of Sodom, Zoar, is usually located at the southern end of the Dead Sea. Legend associated the saltiness of the Dead Sea with Lot's wife as turned into a pillar of salt.

In *Egeria's Travels* (c. AD 381–384), Egeria describes a visit to Mount Nebo, east of the Jordan, from which her guides, including 'the bishop of Zoar', pointed out Jericho and the Jordan. She writes:

To our left was the whole country of the Sodomites, including
Zoar, the only one of the five cities which remains today. There
is still something left of it, but all that is left of the others is
heaps of ruins, because they were burned to ashes. We were also
shown the place where Lot's wife had her memorial, as you
read in the Bible. But what we saw, reverend ladies, was not the
actual pillar, but only the place where it had once been. The pillar itself, they say, has been submerged in the Dead Sea
(Wilkinson 1971: 107).

Egeria saw in front of her, and to her left, 'the whole country
of the Sodomites, including Zoar' of which something is still
standing, visible to her from Mount Nebo. The archaeological
remains of the Biblical Zoar were approximately one hundred
and fifty kilometres south of her, at that point, and would have
been far beyond visibility. Perhaps the ruins she could see, of
which some buildings were still standing, were the ruins of
Qumran:

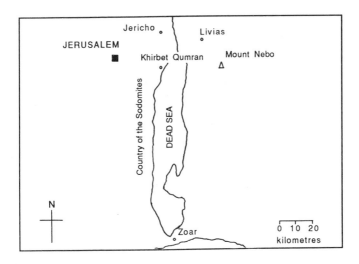

It is not clear that the city of Zoar was still extant in Egeria's day, or that its exact location was known. The 'bishop of Zoar' seems to have been resident in the vicinity of Mount Nebo, from her account. Later records describe the bishop of that city as the bishop of Sodom. Stephanus of Byzantion (seventh century AD) records the presence of Severos, Bishop of Sodom, at Nicaea in AD 325, locating also En-gedi near 'Sodom of Arabia' (IDB 1962d: 397). Thus the area east of the Dead Sea seems to have been known as 'Sodom' in the third century AD, and it seems likely that this name was current also at the time the Rabbinic tradition in *m. Sanh.* 10.3 was formulated, where it admirably suited the polemical intention. It seems that the location of Qumran next to the Dead Sea, and destruction by fire, an element linking several of the groups in *m. Sanh.* 10.3, accounts for the inclusion of the Men of Sodom in the list.

5.4 *The Spies*
The men who went into the Promised Land to spy it out for Moses in Num. 14.36-38 are also included with those who will have no portion in the world to come. Apart from their close proximity to the Korah episode, there is another link with the rest of the list, namely that they perished suddenly at God's hand. The word מגפה can refer to any form of sudden death (Jastrow, p. 730).

5.5 *The People of an Apostate City*
It may, of course, be entirely accidental that the teaching concerning the beguiled city follows these passages, but it may also be that it is a reference to a sectarian community such as that at Khirbet Qumran. They, like the people envisaged by Deut. 13.13, had gone out from the midst of Jerusalem and drawn away its inhabitants after them. The community of the Dead Sea Scrolls seem to have lived a highly visible separate existence in a 'city' next to the Dead Sea. The earliest traditions in this section seem again to revolve around Akiba, this time in debate with his contemporary, R. Jose Ha-gelili. The appellation 'Apostate City' is drawn from Deut. 13.12-18, which is cited in the Mishnah and given a midrashic exposition. However, the midrash is not attributed and it seems that it is a later development of the debate between Akiba and Jose Ha-gelili.

The emphasis is on the question of what to do *after* the city has already been destroyed. After the destruction of Qumran by the Romans in AD 68, it would be possible to speculate on whether it might be built again, since the destruction was a clear confirmation of the wrath of God against the apostates!

5.6 *Historical and Archaeological Evidence*

The archaeological excavation of Khirbet Qumran revealed that the first major occupation of the site by the sectarian community (Period Ib) ended with an earthquake and a fire. The earthquake destroyed many of the buildings and water-cisterns, the roofs fell in and walls collapsed, burying the pottery store (de Vaux 1973: 20-21). Seemingly at the same time, fire gutted the buildings (*ibid.* 21-23).

Josephus (*Ant.* 15.121-47, 370-80) describes the effect of this severe earthquake on Herod's army, encamped in the Plain of Jericho in the spring of 31 BC. They regarded it as an indication of the wrath of God, as did the Arabs, who invaded the land. The army was, only with difficulty, persuaded to continue fighting. The effect of such a calamity on the religious community at Qumran, where buildings were destroyed, perhaps with considerable loss of life, can well be imagined. It must be held as very probable that their enemies would have regarded this as proof of God's rejection of them. The memory of the calamity would have been renewed when the community re-occupied their original headquarters in 1 BC/AD 1 (de Vaux 1973: 24-36).

This historical disaster, coupled with the priestly nature of the community and their foundation by a contender for the high priesthood (Stegemann 1971; Vermes 1975: 53-68; 1977: 137-56; Burgmann 1974: 323-59; 1978: 3-72), the Teacher of Righteousness, would make 'company of Korah' a natural polemical title for the enemies of the community. The other titles found in *m. Sanh.* 10.3 all fit into the same kind of pattern.

A further calamity struck the reconstructed community at Qumran during the Jewish War, when the Romans seem to have attacked and destroyed the buildings in AD 68 (de Vaux 1973: 36-41). This disaster must have confirmed the convictions of the community's opponents that they were under

God's wrath. It also seems to be the origin of the question as to
whether the buildings of an apostate city might be built again
in *m. Sanh.* 10.3.

6. *The Company of Korah in* b. Sanhedrin *110a*

One midrashic passage, which is not attributed, seems to give
the company of Korah some definite characteristics:

> *And they rose up before Moses, with certain of the children of
> Israel, two hundred and fifty*: they were the most distinguished
> men of the community (מיוחד שבעדה); *chosen for the appointed
> times*: meaning they were skilled in intercalating the year and
> fixing new moons (שהיו יודעים לעבר שנים ולקבוע חדשים); *men of
> renown*, famous throughout the world (שהיה להם שם בכל העולם) (*b.
> Sanh.* 110a).

Here the Scriptural word 'princes' (נשיא) is replaced by מיוחד,
from the root יחד, which is used in the passive participle to
mean 'especial, particular, chosen, distinguished', although it
could also mean 'united into a community', as commonly in
the Scrolls, where it is the word the community uses to
describe itself (עצת היחד, e.g. 1QS 3.2; 5.7; 6.3, 10, 13, 14, 16; or
אנשי היחד, 5.3, 16; 6.21).

Interesting also is the understanding of מועד as referring to
seasons rather than to the assembly. The community of Korah
is given here a reputation for interest and skill in matters of
religious calendar, which is nowhere in sight in the Biblical
account. The Qumran community and the broad stream of
Essenic Judaism with which it was aligned, represented above
all by the book of *Jubilees* and *1 Enoch*, had a highly developed
solar calendar differing from that commonly used in Jerusalem. The Scrolls community claimed to have special revelation concerning the appointed times (כול הנגלות למועדי תעודיהם,
1QS 1.9), from which they dare not deviate (ולוא לקדם עתיהם ולוא
להתאחר מכול מועדיהם, 1QS 1.15).

Finally, the midrash strengthens the Biblical 'men of
renown' with the addition of 'in all the world'. Striking is the
relatively unpolemical tone of this midrash (in contrast, for
instance, with that attributed to Resh Lachish [A 2] in *b. Sanh.*
109b). While it is hard to reconcile such irenical tone towards
opponents of the Rabbis, it is harder to reconcile it towards

Korah and his company. On the other hand, as we have seen, R. Eliezer at least could talk of these opponents as חסידי who have 'made a covenant with me by sacrifice' (*m. Sanh.* 10.3).

7. The Sons of Korah

The sons of Korah escaped the debacle, according to Num. 26.11, and the writing of several Psalms is attributed to them (42; 44–49; 84–85; 87–88). The origin of this detail probably lies in the prominence of the Korahite choir in Temple worship at a certain stage. Rabbinic legend understands the 'sons of Korah' as the literal descendants of the Korah of Numbers 16. A legend recorded in *b. Sanh.* 110a envisages a special place set apart for them in Gehenna, where they sat and sang praises to God (cf. Pseudo-Philo, *LAB* 16.4). Another tradition concerning the sons of Korah occurs in the *Pesikta R.* 31.3. This work is a late collection of homiletic material, the date the collection was made being in the sixth or seventh century AD, but the material it contains may well be very early (Strack and Stemberger 1982: 273-79):

> The sons of Korah also said: Wherefore hidest Thou Thy face? (Ps. 44.25). [The Holy One, blessed be He, replied:] Was it first I who hid My face? They hid their faces first: *Our fathers... have shut up the doors of the porch, have shut up and put out the lamps, have turned away from the habitation of the Lord and turned their backs* (2 Chron. 29.6-7). Yet ye say, Wherefore hidest Thou Thy face? (Soncino, pp. 604f.).

The cry of the Psalmist in 44.25 is read as the cry of the sons of Korah, and this cry is answered by the striking choice of a text from 2 Chron. 29.6-7, the reformist Hezekiah's speech to the priests and Levites who had abandoned the Temple worship during a period of apostasy. There would seem to be no logical connection between the two texts at all, unless the connection is to be found in the polemical use of the title Korah. The 'sons of Korah' has become a polemical title for the sect under attack.

If that is so, then it indicates that the polemical title Korah has to do with a boycott of the Jerusalem temple by a priestly group. It seems that here, again, the evidence would fit the Qumran movement. The Damascus Document, which is clearly a document related to the Scrolls, even though it was found in the Cairo Genizah, states specifically:

> And all of those who enter the Covenant shall not enter into the sanctuary to kindle His altar in vain. But they shall bar the door, as God said, '*Who among you shall bar its door? And you shall not kindle my altar in vain*' (Mal. 1.10) (CD 6.11-14).

There is, of course, some debate about whether the Qumran movement did in fact practise an absolute boycott of the Temple, in the light of Josephus's statement that they 'sent votive offerings to the temple'. However, Josephus also records that they sacrificed by a different method of purification (διαφορ-ότητι ἀγνειῶν) and 'for this reason they are barred from those precincts of the temple that are frequented by all the people and perform their rites by themselves' (*Ant.* 18.19).

8. *Other Legends concerning Korah*

There are numerous other legends concerning Korah and his congregation in later Rabbinic writings, which could be connected to traditions of polemic against the Essenes. Numerous accounts connect the rebellion of Korah with the law concerning fringes from Numbers 15 (*b. Sanh.* 110a; *Midrash Tanhuma B* Vb. 4-5; Ps.-Philo, *LAB* 16.1). This must be the result of the application of the hermeneutical principle of 'juxtaposition' (סמוכין), but what may derive from earlier tradition is the underlying understanding that Korah's rebellion concerned the interpretation of the Torah. *Num. R.* 18.9 claims that Korah and his company refused to take part in controversies or answer Moses' arguments:

> This was because he was clever in his wickedness and thought: If I answer him, I know quite well that he is a very wise man and will presently overwhelm me against my will. It is better that I should not join issue with him (Soncino, pp. 718f.).

This refusal of debate or to take part in מחלוקת with the 'men of the pit' is a feature of the Qumran community:

> And [the Maskil] shall not admonish nor contend with the men of the pit, but he shall conceal the counsel of Torah in the midst of the men of falsehood; and he shall admonish the knowledge of

the truth and just judgment to those who have chosen the way
(1QS 9.16-18).

Josephus also portrays the Essenes as sworn 'to report none of
their secrets to others, even though tortured to death' (*War*
2.141; cf. 1QS 8.18; 10.24; CD 15.10).

Another Rabbinic legend concerning Korah's company is
that On, the son of Peleth, was saved by his wife's cunning
from sharing the fate of the rest of the company. She made
him drunk and sat uncovered in front of their tent when the
conspirators came to fetch him, so that they retreated in confusion (*b. Sanh.* 109b-110a; *Tanhuma* B Vb. 24). This seems
most likely to be simple legendary elaboration on the absence
of On's name from the catastrophic confrontation between
Korah and Moses, although he is mentioned as one of the conspirators in Num. 16.1. It may, however, preserve memories
of a split in the Essene movement, which is reflected in the
Damascus Document and the Scrolls (see Murphy-O'Connor
1970; 1971ab; 1974; Stegemann 1971).

9. *Possible Awareness of the Polemic in the Scrolls*

A puzzling epithet in the Scrolls and the Damascus Document
is אנשי השם קריאי מועד (1QSa 2.1f., 11, 12) or עדת אנשי השם (1QSa
2.8). CD 4.3f. interprets Ezek. 44.15 to refer to the community
in the words: ובני צדוק הם בחירי ישראל קריאי השם העמדים באחרית הימים.
Rabin (1954: 14) sees this passage as a telescoped quotation
from Num. 16.2, but fails to see the incongruity of a Jewish
community describing itself with a text relating to the congregation of Korah! The language is indeed distinctive and unique
to this episode. It could be that a title which was used *against*
the community by its opponents has come, in time, to be re-
interpreted within the community and accepted with pride. It
seems that this was how the Jesus movement came to be
called 'Christians'.

10. *Korah in the Patristic Writings*

The story of Korah continues to be used as an example in
Christian polemic. Clement of Rome (c. AD 96) holds up
Korah's fate to warn the Corinthian 'leaders of sedition and

disagreement' of the consequence of schism (*1 Clem.* 51.3-4). Irenaeus (c. 130–c. 200) warns that those who 'rise up against the truth and urge others against the Church of God' will be swallowed up by an earthquake and remain in hell, like Korah, Dathan and Abiron (*Contra Haer.* 4.26.2). Cyprian (died AD 258) uses the fate of Korah and company as a proof text to justify the action of a bishop against an insolent deacon (*Ep.* 3.1[4]), or to attack heretics who 'assert for themselves against us unlawful priesthoods' (*Ep.* 75.16[5]; cf. 69.7[6]). Epiphanius includes an account of Korah and his company in his *Panarion* (62-63; cf. *Anac.* 2.5), even linking them with the Sodomites, as in *m. Sanh.* 10.3.

Most interesting is Chrysostom's use of the Korah story in polemic against a projected rebuilding of the Temple in Jerusalem under the apostate Emperor Julian. An earthquake during the initial rebuilding led directly to the abandonment of the enterprise, because it was feared that this indicated divine wrath. The earthquake immediately conjures up Korah for Chrysostom (*Adv. Jud.* 5-6). The paucity of material on Korah in Christian writings may be a further indication that the relative abundance of material in Rabbinic writings is the result of internal Jewish rivalry.

11. *Conclusion*

It seems likely, from this examination of the material relating to Korah and his company in Rabbinic writings, that the epithet derives from polemic against a rival sect. Further, the details which remain in the tradition seem to present a strong connection with the Dead Sea Scrolls, the Damascus Document and the related Essene movements. If this is so, then the term may enable scholars to begin unravelling other references to the Essenes in Rabbinic writings.

---

4. Following the numbering of the Oxford edition of J. Fell and J. Pearson of 1682; Migne number 64.
5. Migne number 74.16.
6. Migne number 75.8.

BIBLIOGRAPHY

Albeck, C.
1971   *Einführung in die Mischna* (GT, Berlin: de Gruyter).
Amusin, J.
1963   'Spuren antiqumranischer Polemik in der talmudischen Traditio',
        in *Qumran Probleme*, ed. H. Bardtke; Deutsche Akademie der
        Wissenschaften zu Berlin, Schriften der Sektion für Altertums-
        wissenschaft, 42 (Berlin: Akademie-Verlag), pp. 5-27.
Bietenhard, H.
1982   *Midrasch Tanhuma B*, II (Judaica et Christiana, 6; Bern: Peter
        Lang).
Blackman, P.
1965   *Mishnayoth*, I–VII (New York: Judaica).
Braude, W.G.
1968   *Pesikta Rabbati*, I–II (London: Soncino).
Burgman, H.
1974   ' "The Wicked Woman": Der Makkabäer Simon?', *RevQ* 8, pp. 323-
        59.
1978   'Gerichtsherr und Generalankläger: Jonathan und Simon', *RevQ*
        9, pp. 3-72.
Charlesworth, J.H. (ed.)
1983–1985   *The Old Testament Pseudepigrapha*, 2 vols. (London: Darton,
        Longman and Todd).
Danby, H.
1919   *Tractate Sanhedrin: Mishnah and Tosefta* (London: SPCK).
1933   *The Mishnah: Translated from the Hebrew with Introduction and
        Brief Explanatory Notes* (Oxford: Oxford University Press).
De Vaux, R.
1973   *Archaeology and the Dead Sea Scrolls* (London: Oxford University
        Press).
Diez Macho, A.
1974   *Neophyti 1* (Madrid).
Draper, J.A.
1983   'A Commentary on the Didache in the Light of the Dead Sea Scrolls
        and Related Documents'. Unpublished Dissertation, University of
        Cambridge.
1988   'The Twelve Apostles as Foundation Stones of the Heavenly
        Jerusalem and the Foundation of the Qumran Community',
        Neotestamentica 22, 41-63.
Freedman, H. and M. Simon
1939   *Midrash Rabba*, I–X (London: Soncino).
Ginsburger, M.
1903   *Pseudo-Jonathan* (Berlin).
Krauss, S.
1909   *The Mishnah Treatise Sanhedrin: Edited with an Introduction,
        Notes and Glossary* (Leiden: Brill).
Lohse, E.
1971   *Die Texte aus Qumran* (Munich: Kösel).

Murphy-O'Connor, M.
  1970   'An Essene Missionary Document? CD II,14–VI,1', *RB* 77, pp. 201-29.
  1971   'A Literary Analysis of Damascus Document VI,2–VIII,3', *RB* 78, pp. 210-32.
  1972a   'The Critique of the Princes of Judah (CD VIII,3–19)', *RB* 79, pp. 200-16.
  1972b   'A Literary Analysis of Damascus Document XIX,33–XX,34', *RB* 79, pp. 544-64.
  1974   'The Essenes and their History', *RB* 81, pp. 215-44.
Néher, A.
  1957   'Echos de la secte de Qumran dans la littérature talmudique', in *Manuscrits de la Mer Morte*, ed. A. Dupont-Sommer; *Colloque de Strasbourg 25–27 Mai 1955* (Paris: Presses Universitaires de France), pp. 45-60.
Neusner, J.
  1973   *Eliezer ben Hyrcanus: The Tradition and the Man*, I–II (Leiden: Brill).
Oesterley, W.O.E.
  1919   *The Sayings of the Jewish Fathers* (London: SPCK).
Schachter, J. and H. Freedman
  1969   *Sanhedrin* (Hebrew–English Edition of the Babylonian Talmud), ed. I. Epstein (London: Soncino).
Sperber, A.
  1959–73 *The Bible in Aramaic*, I–IV (Leiden: Brill).
Stegemann, P.H.
  1971   *Die Entstehung der Qumrangemeinde* (Bonn).
Strack, H.L.
  1931   *Introduction to the Talmud and Midrash* (ET; New York: Atheneum).
Strack, H.L. and G. Stemberger
  1982   *Einleitung in Talmud und Midrasch* (Munich: Beck).
Vermes, G.
  1975   *The Dead Sea Scrolls in English* (Harmondsworth: Penguin).
  1977   *The Dead Sea Scrolls: Qumran in Perspective* (London: Collins).

THE SECOND TEMPLE: FOCUS OF IDEOLOGICAL STRUGGLE?[1]

C.C. Rowland

This essay sets out to collect and survey some texts, mainly from the apocalypses but also some other pseudepigrapha of the Second Temple period or just after, relating to the theme of the Temple and Jerusalem in the present age and the age to come. The apocalypses form a major segment of the Jewish pseudepigrapha and are a significant witness to Jewish eschatological beliefs of the period. While brief allusion will be made to the Dead Sea Scrolls, the problems posed by these texts, particularly with regard to the attitude to the Temple, demand a more detailed study than is possible here.[2]

In the table below there are various passages in which there is a differentiation between those dealing with the Temple and those which refer primarily to Zion/Jerusalem. While there may in most instances have been a presumption that Zion would have included a Temple, the fact that the book of Reve-

1. For a discussion of this theme see G. Nickelsburg, 'Enoch, Levi, and Peter: Recipients of Revelation in Upper Galilee', *JBL* 100 (1981), pp. 575-600; J.M. Ford, 'The Heavenly Jerusalem and Orthodox Judaism', *Donum Gentilicium*, ed. E. Bammel, C.K. Barrett and W.D. Davies (Oxford, 1978); H.L. Strack and P. Billerbeck, *Kommentar zum Neuen Testament aus Talmud und Midrasch*, III, p. 796; L. Gaston, *No Stone on Another* (Leiden, 1970).

2. This is particularly true since the discovery and publication of the Temple Scroll. There might even be a case for regarding the latter as an example of an apocalypse, set as it is in the context of a divine revelation to Moses on Sinai (there are some formal similarities with the book of *Jubilees*) but the complexities of interpretation of this document mean that it demands a study in its own right and will not be treated here. Some passages where a negative attitude to the Temple are expressed may be noted: 1QpHab 8.8-13; 9.3-7; 12.7-9; 4QTest 28ff.; CD 4.17; 5.6f.; 6.11f.; 12.1f.; 20.22f.

lation contemplates a new Jerusalem without a Temple makes it imperative to note that distinction. Indeed, it is worth noting that in the eschatological programme sketched, for example, in *Sibylline Oracles* 5.422 (cf. 3.286; 3.652; 5.108) there is specific reference to the Temple in the restored Zion (as also in the *Shemoneh Esreh*), though such specific reference is often absent elsewhere. It needs to be borne in mind, therefore, that a restored city might conceivably be without a Temple as in Revelation, for there would be no need of a special holy place reserved for God.

In looking at the apocalyptic material we should resist the temptation to find an apocalyptic or even late Jewish understanding of the Temple, as if the chance survival of documents which may well come from very different provenances and social milieux might witness to a uniform view of the Temple. An examination of the apocalypses hardly encourages us to suppose that there is enough cohesion in the contents of these works to offer anything approaching an 'apocalyptic' concept of *anything*. Even though we shall continue to hear talk of apocalyptic eschatology as if there were a discrete body of ideas in Second Temple Judaism linked with particular works, the view should be resisted that we can easily reduce the apocalypses, still less the pseudepigrapha, to a neat body of leading motifs.[3] Apocalypses may have a common literary form but cannot for that reason necessarily be supposed to have much else in common. It is all too often assumed that what we call apocalyptic must have been associated with particular circles in Judaism, possibly on the fringes of mainstream Jewish religion.[4] We do not know enough about the apocalypses to be able to say with any assurance that they are products of a particular group. Indeed, close analysis suggests that within this body of literature there are significant differences of concern (e.g. between *1 Enoch* and *4 Ezra*) which point to differences of function of the apocalyptic outlook in differing circumstances. Most of the apocalypses

---

3. See Rowland, *The Open Heaven* (London, 1982), particularly pp. 23ff.

4. See P.R. Davies, 'The Social World of the Apocalyptic Writings', in R.E. Clements (ed.), *The World of Ancient Israel* (Cambridge, 1989), pp. 251ff.

which we shall be examining come from a wide range of dates and circumstances. We should not be surprised, therefore, to find differences in the form of the visions and subject-matter. Apocalyptic offered a mode of discourse which would have been available to a wide range of groups with very different religious and political options. It is important to remember that it could be made to serve the needs of conservatives just as much as radicals.[5] The works which have formed the basis of this study are the Jewish apocalypses which date from the period of the Second Temple or shortly after: *1 Enoch*, Daniel, *Slavonic Enoch*, *Jubilees*, *Testament of Levi*, *4 Ezra*, *Syriac Baruch*, *Greek Baruch*, the *Apocalypse of Abraham* and Revelation, together with one or two apocalyptic pieces contained in works of different literary genre (e.g. *Life of Adam and Eve* 29). The *Sibylline Oracles* exhibit sufficient coherence of religious outlook for them to be included. Even if in their present guise they purport to be pagan oracles, their concerns and content are thoroughly Jewish and exhibit several similarities with the apocalyptic tradition.

The approach taken in this essay is to look at the material thematically. There are dangers in so doing precisely because it can link together works which are not related either in time or space and give a false sense of homogeneity. The alternative would be to attempt to treat the material chronologically. That has its disadvantages too, however. Not only are several of these works of a composite nature, but also it is not easy to determine with any degree of precision the time and place of writing in the majority of cases. Accordingly, at the risk of offering a false sense of coherence, and, with due regard for the framework imposed on disparate material by such a systematic presentation, I have set out to treat the material thematically in order to enable some general picture of attitudes to emerge from the literary remains of the period. That kind of approach is of some value when the questions being asked of the material concern the strands of thought and trends within

---

5. This point is well illustrated by a study of the way in which apocalyptic ideas functioned in different periods of history. See e.g. C. Hill, *The Antichrist* (Oxford, 1971) and N. Cohn, *The Pursuit of the Millennium* (London, 1957).

material. If we are to understand the character of the ideological struggles which were going on in the Second Temple period, then some attempt at tracing common themes and patterns is a necessary contribution to the fulfilment of that task. In so doing we can only remind ourselves that the accident of history has left us with the literary remains at our disposal, and that may distort our understanding of the centrality of the Temple and the perception of it by Jews in our period. The survey of material included here needs to be set in the context of the evidence of the importance given to the Temple in the writings of Philo, Josephus and the tannaitic literature. Philo indicates how important the Temple was for the Alexandrian Jewish aristocracy even when there was a much nearer focus of Jewish cultic activity at Leontopolis (which Philo never mentions). The inclusion of a tractate dealing with the measurements of the Temple in the Mishnah (*Middoth*) as well as records of disputes about the Temple service are reminders of what a central place the Temple (and the restoration of its worship) had. We have to rely on the hints that are available to us and run the risk that in magnifying them we are in danger of distorting the reality of the past by our hypotheses. Of course, there is no other way forward for the historian of this period. To these fragmentary comments we are indebted for some understanding of how an apocalyptic outlook coloured the views of this central organ of Jewish life.

Table of References

Solomon's Temple
1 *Enoch* 89.50; 89.67; 93.7f.; *Life of Adam and Eve* 29.5; *Syr. Baruch* 44.5f.*; 59.4; 61.2; 67.6.

The Second Temple
1 *Enoch* 26*; 89.73; Dan. 8.11f.; 8.14; 9.17; 9.25ff.; 11.31; *Life of Adam and Eve* 29.6; *Jubilees* 1.27; *Syr. Baruch* 68.5; *T. Levi* 8.17.

Indestructibility of Temple and Eschatological Assault
Sib. Oracles 3.665; 5.401; *Jubilees* 1.27; 25.21; 1 *Enoch* 56.5f.; 90.13; *Jubilees* 23.22ff.; 4 *Ezra* 13.34.

Sacrifice and Temple Questioned
1 Enoch 89.73; Slav. Enoch 45.3; T. Levi 9.9; 14.5; 16.1; Ps.
Solomon 2.3; Jubilees 23.21; Assumption of Moses 4.8; 6.1.

Temple's Destruction
Apocalypse of Abraham 27; Sib. Oracles 4.115ff.; 5.150; 5.398;
4 Ezra 10.21; 12.48; Syr. Baruch 6.7; 8.2; 8.5; 10.10; 11*;
20.2*; 85.3*.

New Temple and Jerusalem
1 Enoch 90.28f.*; 91.13; Syr. Baruch 6.8; 32.4*; Apocalypse of
Abraham 29; Life of Adam and Eve 29.7; Jubilees 1.26ff.;
4.26*; Sib. Oracles 3.702; 3.718; 5.424f.; T. Benjamin 9.2;
Tobit 14.5; Targum to Zechariah 6.12f.; Ps. Solomon
17.32f.

Heavenly Jerusalem
Slav. Enoch 55.2; Syr. Baruch 4.2ff.; 4 Ezra 7.26; 8.52; 9.26ff.;
13.36; Rev. 21.

Heavenly Temple
T. Levi 3.6; 5.1; 18.6; 4Q Širot; 1 Enoch 14.8ff.; Rev. 3.12; 7.15;
11.19; 14.15, 17; 15.5f.; 16.1, 17; cf. Heb. 9.24.

Altar in Heaven
B. Hagigah 12b; Greek Baruch 11.8; Rev. 6.9; 8.3; 9.13; 14.18;
16.7.

*References to Zion/Jerusalem which *might* imply reference to the
Temple.

Solomon's Temple

In *1 Enoch* 89–90 we have a retelling of salvation history from
creation to the coming of the kingdom. This was probably
written during the Maccabaean period (the end of the historical review in 90.6ff. focuses on the Seleucid period). In *1 Enoch*
89.50 there is a clear distinction made between the house built
for the sheep and the lofty tower built for the lord of the sheep.
This is a distinction between Jerusalem and the Temple, a fact
which is confirmed by the reference to this passage in *T. Levi*
10.5. The reference to the full table offered to the Lord indicates the proper nature of the sacrificial system at this stage in

Jewish history. A house is mentioned earlier in 89.36 and 40, where both of these passages refer to the tabernacle. Subsequently the house which Moses built for the Lord of the sheep becomes a house in which the sheep also dwelt (a reference to Zion). The tabernacle thus became the focal point of the worship of Israel in Jerusalem. In *1 Enoch* 89.67 the destruction of the house and tower are referred to (cf. Mic. 3.12).

In a section in which the history of the world is divided into ten weeks of years (93.1-10; 91.12-17) a house and a kingdom are built (93.7: clearly a reference to the Davidic dynasty). In the *Life of Adam and Eve* 29.5 (a short apocalyptic section in a pseudepigraphon which does not seem to presuppose the fall of the Second Temple) the divine plan is to establish a kingdom and habitation for the divine majesty. In *Syriac Baruch* 59.4 (a part of the vision of the black and bright waters, another historical review similar to the two examined from *1 Enoch*) Moses on the mountain is shown the likeness of Zion. This indicates a link between the settlement in Jerusalem and the foundational revelation of God's covenant establishing the Davidic decision as part and parcel of the divine plan. The measurements are to be made 'after the likeness of the present sanctuary' (Exod. 25.10; 26.30). In *Syr. Bar.* 61.2 the dedication of the sanctuary is linked with a period of rest and peace for God's people.

Second Temple

It is already clear from the Bible that the origins of the Second Temple are surrounded in controversy. The inclusion of Haggai and Zechariah in the canon represents the triumph of the point of view which looked to the re-establishment of the cult as the fulfilment of the prophetic promises.[6] There are enough hints from elsewhere that there was considerable scepticism, even opposition, if the enigmatic oracle in Isa. 66.3ff. is anything to go by.

As part of Enoch's journey he visits Jerusalem (*1 Enoch* 26; cf. *Jub.* 8.19). In *1 Enoch* 89.73 reference is made to the building of a house and the raising of a tower. Here the table placed

---

6. See e.g. O. Plöger, *Theocracy and Eschatology* (ET; Oxford, 1968).

before the tower has food on it which is polluted and impure. We may note that nothing is said about the Lord of the sheep standing on the tower here (cf. 89.50), which suggests that this temple was without the divine presence. The profanation of the Second Temple is alluded to on several occasions in Daniel (8.11; 9.17; 11.31) and its restoration predicted (8.14; 9.25). In the *Life of Adam and Eve* 29.6 the return from exile and the building of the Temple is mentioned without further comment. Zion's rebuilding features in *Syr. Bar.* 66.5 when the offerings are restored and Zion is honoured by the nations. Nevertheless the inferior quality of this restoration is noted when the text points out that the whole process was carried out 'not as fully as before' (though this might conceivably refer to the absence of a restored monarchy).

Sacrifice Questioned

In *1 Enoch* 89.73 the sacrificial offering of the Second Temple is considered inadequate (cf. 1QpHab 9.3-7; 12.7-9; 4QTest 28-30). It is worth noting that we find this reference in a work which exhibits views which may have been opposed to mainstream opinion with regard to the calendar (*1 Enoch* 82.4; *Jub.* 6.32ff.). The problem with the Second Temple according to this apocalypse dates back to its very foundation, possibly reflecting the tensions which existed at the time.[7] In the *Assumption of Moses* we have several passages in which the validity of the sacrifices offered in the Second Temple is questioned. In 4.5 the post-exilic restoration is questioned: 'And two tribes shall continue in their prescribed faith, sad and lamenting, because they will not be able to offer sacrifices to the Lord'. In 6.1 there is polemic against the Hasmonaeans who 'assuredly work iniquity in the Holy of Holies'. There is a general allusion to the essence of religion not being sacrificial offering in *Slav. Enoch* 45.3, though it seems difficult to regard this as anything other than the rather general statement in the spirit of the prophets.

---

7. See e.g. P.D. Hanson, *The Dawn of Apocalyptic* (Philadelphia, 1975).

The Indestructibility of the Temple

There is some evidence to suggest that the sort of mythology connected with the Temple and Zion in some of the psalms (e.g. Ps. 46) and in the early part of Isaiah continued well into the Second Temple period.[8] These ideas centred on the Temple as a place where God dwelt which would be inviolate. It seems to be hinted at in two passages from *Jubilees* where the Temple is regarded as an eternal building (1.27; 25.21). In *Jub.* 1.27 the building of the sanctuary is seen as something which would be eternal, as is also the case in *Jub.* 25.21. The most explicit reference to this myth comes in the fifth book of the *Sibylline Oracles* in a context dealing with the destruction of the Second Temple by the Romans (5.400). This work is not easy to date but may be as early as the second century AD, though the presence of the Nero Redivivus myth may place it somewhat earlier (5.138ff.). The myth of indestructibility seems to have been behind some of the fantastic stories preserved in Josephus's *Jewish War,* e.g. *War* 6.300 which recalls the departure of the divine *kabod* from the Temple in Ezekiel 10. Earlier Josephus tells of rash beliefs of those who expected supernatural deliverance in the moment of greatest trial, probably a reference to the Sennacherib incident (*War* 6.285, 295; cf. Isa. 38–39). In *Sib. Oracles* 3.657ff. an assault on the Temple is repulsed by supernatural means. In *1 Enoch* 90.13 (cf. 56.4) we have a passage which is surprisingly not more attested in the apocalypses, the eschatological assault on the Jews which finds some general parallel in the intensified last assault mentioned in *Jub.* 23.22ff.

The Temple's Destruction

As we might expect, the most extensive of the references to the Temple's destruction are to be found in the apocalypses which are to be dated in the immediate aftermath of 70, particularly the *Syriac Apocalypse of Baruch.* Elsewhere, in the *Apocalypse of Abraham* 27, the destruction of the Temple is justified because of idolatrous practices. In *Sib. Oracles* 4.115ff. the

---

8. See R.E. Clements, *God and Temple* (Oxford, 1965).

destruction of the Temple by Rome is explained as 'whenever they put their trust in folly and cast off piety and commit repulsive murders in front of the Temple', probably an allusion to some of the strife which Josephus describes during the siege. This book is to be dated to the end of the first century AD; there is a reference to the eruption of Vesuvius in 5.135ff. which is seen as a punishment for the desecration of the Temple. Elsewhere in the *Sib. Oracles* there are brief allusions in 5.398 (the destruction of the Temple by fire) and in 5.150. In *4 Ezra* 10.21 Ezra tells the lamenting woman about the destruction of Zion and the sanctuary and pleads with her to recognize an even greater reason for grief (cf. 12.48).

Of the passages listed above those from *Syriac Baruch* call for special attention. While it is only Zion which is mentioned explicitly in 20.2, there is a link between the destruction of the city and the fulfilment of God's eschatological promises. In two passages in 6.7 and 80.1 mention is made of the Temple vessels being hidden. In the former an angel descends from heaven, goes into the Holy of Holies and takes the veil and the holy ark as well as other items which are then committed to the earth to await the last times (6.8f.). This is a theme which emerges elsewhere in Jewish literature, e.g. 2 Macc. 2.4-8 and Josephus, *Ant.* 18.85f., the latter passage being connected explicitly with eschatologically orientated movements. In 7.1 and 8.2 we have the notion of the release of divine protection from the Temple which enables its destruction at the hand of Israel's enemies. This probably reflected the passage in Ezekiel 10 already alluded to (cf. Josephus, *War* 6.300). In 10.10 the destruction of the Temple has an air of finality about it. There seems to be little prospect of the restoration hinted at in *Epistle of Barnabas* 16 despite the imminent eschatological expectation that emerges from time to time (e.g. 20.2). Instead there is the concentration on the centrality of the Law as the vehicle of God's revelation and the means of maintaining the relationship between God and the people (see e.g. 85.3).

Building of New Temple and City

The reference to the messianic building of the Temple in *Sib. Oracles* 5.424f. is one of the few passages in the literature of this period where the messiah's task is to build the Temple (though it may be hinted at in *Ps. Solomon* 17.32f.).[9] The fifth *Sibylline* has been dated in the second century AD, but this passage which links the building of the Temple with the coming of the messiah may reflect that peculiar eschatological enthusiasm which arose when the Second Temple was destroyed and expectations of restoration and messianism intensified (e.g. *j. Berakoth* 5.1). In *Jub.* 4.26 there is a clear reference to the central role of the renewal of Zion as a focal constituent for the renewal of creation ('Mount Zion will be sanctified in the new creation for a sanctification of the earth').

In *1 Enoch* 91.13 in the *Apocalypse of Weeks*, in the eighth week, the week of righteousness, after the period when an apostate generation emerges, there is a time of bliss centred on Israel. In the next period righteous judgment is revealed to the whole world. At its close a house shall be built for the Great King for evermore, and all humankind shall look for the path of righteousness.[10] Here the building of the Temple forms part of the establishment of the earthly kingdom of righteousness. In *Syr. Baruch* 32.4 the building of Zion will be shaken in order that it may be built again. But that building will not remain for ever but will again after a time be destroyed to make way for renewal and an eternal perfection.

In *Apoc. Abraham* 29, at the end of the period of messianic woes the righteous who are left will return to the devastated Jerusalem and the Temple (ch. 27) and offer proper sacrifices (perhaps another hint that what had hitherto been offered left much to be desired). In *Life of Adam and Eve* 29.7 the building of the house of God comes after the return from dispersion. The house of God built then 'will be greater than of old' and there will be a period when the enemies of the righteous will no more be able to hurt the people who believe in God. In 14.4

---

9. Gaston, *No Stone on Another*, also adds *Targum to Zechariah* 6.12f.: 'Thus said Yahweh of Hosts: This man, messiah is his name, will be revealed and grow and build the Temple of Yahweh. He will build the Temple of Yahweh, and he will exalt its splendour and he will sit and rule on his throne, and there will be the High Priest by his throne and the kingdom of peace will be between them.'
10. The Qumran Cave 4 text reads: 'a royal Temple of the Great One in his glorious splendour for all generations for ever'.

there is a prediction of a period of destruction and desolation for the house of God. Once again the gathering of the people of God which had been dispersed will be followed by the rebuilding of the Temple. In Tob. 13.16 (which is probably to be dated c. 250 BC) there is a prediction of the rebuilding of Jerusalem 'with sapphire, emerald and precious stone'.

The character of life around the new Temple is described in *Sib. Oracles* 3.702ff. (a passage which should be compared with the description of eschatological bliss in *Jub.* 23.23ff.). This leads to the fulfilment of Isa. 2.3: 'then all the isles and the cities shall say... come, let us fall on the earth and supplicate the Eternal King, the mighty, everlasting God. Let us make procession to his Temple for he is sole potentate' (cf. Tob. 13.11).

The Animal Apocalypse in *1 Enoch* offers us one of the most important references to be considered in connection with any discussion of the eschatological Temple (*1 Enoch* 90.28-29). After the judgment of the angels of the nations[11] there is a reference to the house.[12] After the reconstruction of a new house and the acceptance by the Gentiles of the primacy of Israel (v. 30) there is a time of eschatological bliss centred on the city.

While the animal symbolism is not always easy to interpret the section on the house is quite explicit:

> And I stood up to look until he folded up that old house, and they removed all the pillars, and all the beams and ornaments of that house were folded up with it; and they removed it and put it in a place in the south of the land... And I looked until the Lord of the sheep brought a new house larger and higher than the first one; and he set it up on the site of the first one which had been folded up; all its pillars were new and its ornaments were new and larger than those of the first one, the old one which had been removed. And the lord of the sheep was in the middle of it.

---

11. On this see F. Dexinger, *Henochs Zehnwochenapokalypse und offene Probleme der Apokalyptikforschung* (Leiden, 1977) and W. Wink *Naming the Powers* (New York, 1984) who lists all the relevant material. On the heavenly temple see also R.H. Charles, *Eschatology*, pp. 179, 199. For a contrary interpretation see Strack–Billerbeck, *Kommentar*, III, p. 796, and further, R. McKelvey, *The New Temple* (Oxford: Oxford University Press, 1969).
12. This passage is alluded to in *Epistle of Barnabas* 16.3.

We may note: (1) the old house is destroyed and its various parts placed in the south of the land; and (2) God brings about a new house, larger than the first one, built in its place.

The question we have to ask is whether in this passage we have a reference to the Temple at all. If we examine this passage in the light of *1 Enoch* 89.50, we shall have reason to doubt whether it is in fact a reference to a new Temple. In that passage there is a house built for the sheep and a tower for the lord of the sheep. It would appear, therefore, that it is the *tower* which the Animal Apocalypse sees as a symbol of the Temple. The tower is also a symbol of the Temple in 89.73 where the reference to polluted sacrifices makes an identification of the tower with the Temple virtually certain. So in the description of the eschatological Zion it is possible that we might well be faced in this passage with a restored city without a Temple, as no new tower is mentioned in the new house.

Another question which arises in connection with this passage is whether we have a reference here to a heavenly Jerusalem. The main reason for supposing this is the fact that it is God who is said to have built the house. There seems to me to be insufficient evidence to develop the theory that we have here a reference to the heavenly Jerusalem. The passage is in marked contrast to *4 Ezra* 10 where there is much clearer stress on the appearance of the celestial city in a place where there was *nothing* before (cf. *4 Ezra* 7.26; *Syr. Baruch* 4.2-6). It seems preferable to suppose that what the author has in mind is *either* human agents fulfilling the divine purposes *or* a miraculous building rather than the descent from heaven of a pre-existing city (cf. Jn 2.17). We cannot rule out the possibility that this passage may have been interpreted by later readers as a reference to the heavenly Zion, but it is more likely that the original version spoke of a new city built in the last days fulfilling the divine purposes. There are similar sentiments enunciated in the *Shemoneh Esreh*, for example, the prayer to God to 'bring back worship into the Holy of Holies of thy house'. One assumes that this act would have been fulfilled by human agents in pursuance of the divine purposes.

Related to this issue but probably offering evidence of a pre-existing heavenly city/temple is *Syriac Baruch* 4.2-6 (cf. 59.4 with its allusions to Exod. 25.40; 26.30), though it is worth noting that this apocalypse is not exactly replete with references to a restored Temple. The reference to a heavenly mystery can hardly be simply the heavenly secret written on the divine palms similar to the secrets on the tablets revealed to Enoch (*1 Enoch* 93.2). The fact that the reference is made to both Paradise and the city being removed from Adam suggests that the seer has in mind both a garden and a city existing in heaven (cf. the way in which the manna is stored on high in 29.8). Similarly in *4 Ezra* 7.26 the seer is shown 'the city which is not seen... and the land which is now hidden shall be disclosed'.[13] The reference to Abraham's vision of Zion 'by night among the portions of the victims' once again connects the establishment of Zion to the founding of the nation. It reflects the type of tradition which we find in the *Apocalypse of Abraham* where this event in Gen. 15.9ff. becomes the basis for an ascent to heaven and a vision of celestial and eschatological mysteries, including the restoration of Zion and the cult.

In *4 Ezra* 9.26–10.57 there is the vision of the woman mourning the death of her son. The passage is a complex one and falls into the following sections:

Vision
(i) vision of a woman in mourning: Ezra hears that she was barren and after 30 years gave birth to a son who died on entering the wedding chamber.
(ii) Ezra's rebuke: 'For Zion, the mother of us all, is in deep grief and great humiliation. Zion ought to mourn over her children who are on their way to perdition.'
(iii) The transformation of the woman: her face shines; she utters a cry and in place of a woman a city is built.
Interpretation
(iv)
  (a) the woman is Zion (10.44).
  (b) the barrenness means the period (3000 years) before the offering was made (10.45).

---

13. Ecce enim tempus veniet, et erit, quando venient signa quae praedixi tibi, et apparebit sponsa apparescens civitas et ostendetur quae nunc subducitur terra.

(c) the birth of the son means Solomon's building of a city and the establishment of sacrifice in Jerusalem (10.46).

(d) death of the son is the destruction of Jerusalem (10.48f.).

(e) in the wake of the destruction of the city something new is required and a divine construction is initiated (10.53f.; cf. 9.24).[14]

(f) Ezra is then instructed to go in and see the splendour and vastness of the building.

There has been much dispute over this passage. Box and many others have argued[15] that the woman stands for the heavenly city and her son who dies represents the earthly city. This, however, seems to represent an oversimplification of the complexities of the passage. The woman is transformed into the heavenly, eschatological city only at the end of the vision. Until then she has been the earthly Zion. This seems the most obvious way of construing the interpretation. 10.44 states explicitly that the woman is Zion and the life of the son is the period of the cult from Solomon to the destruction by Nebuchadnezzar. Thus we are dealing in this vision with stages of Zion's history culminating in the appearance of the heavenly Zion corresponding to the transformation of the woman in the vision. It is apparent in 10.51 that the heavenly origin of what Ezra sees is emphasized. In a place where there was nothing before, the city of the Most High appears. It seems likely that at the conclusion of this passage we have material indebted to Ezekiel 40ff. This is most evident in 10.55f. where Ezra is commanded to go in and note the character of the new building (cf. Ezek. 40.4; 43.10). Even though there is no explicit reference to the Temple, the vague references to the new Jerusalem may presuppose the existence of a Temple in the new Jerusalem. The most cogent reason for this is the

14. Cf. *Syr. Baruch* 29.3 and 39.7 where we have reference to the revelation of the messiah and the messianic kingdom. On this vocabulary see the discussion of the Aramaic terminology of revelation by A. Chester, *Divine Revelation and Divine Titles in the Pentateuchal Targumim* (Tübingen, 1986).

15. See J.M. Myers, *I and II Esdras* (New York, 1974).

reference to the sacrificial system in 10.46. The replacement of the old Zion together with its cult by a heavenly city might be expected to include all that was present in the old (as is apparent in the eschatological passages in *Sib. Oracles*).

The Heavenly Temple

Already in the Bible there are hints that heaven may have contained at least a pattern of earthly entities like the cult (e.g. Exod. 25.40).[16] In *T. Levi* 3.6 we find a description of the heavenly Temple. Although there is some textual variation, mainly relating to the number of heavens, the main textual streams witness to the existence of a heavenly Holy of Holies where God dwells. There with God are archangels who offer propitiatory sacrifices to the Lord on behalf of the sins of ignorance of the righteous. They present to the Lord a pleasing odour, a rational and bloodless offering. The similarity with Rom. 12.1 raises the question of Christian influence.[17] Whatever may be the arguments for Christian influence and insertions in other parts of the Greek *Testament of Levi* there do not seem to be strong reasons for supposing that it can be found in this section. A major reason for suggesting this is that in *b. Hagigah* 12b[18] we have evidence of a very similar belief. Speaking of the fourth heaven, Zebul, it states that 'it is that in which the heavenly Jerusalem and Temple, and the altar is built, and Michael the great prince stands and offers upon it an offering'. In *Testament of Levi* the likelihood is that we have a reference to a heavenly altar of incense (cf. Exod. 30.1ff.; 37.25) similar to that alluded to in Rev. 8.3. In similar vein to *T. Levi* 3, though less explicit in its formulation, is *Greek Baruch* 11.8. Here Michael carries a large bowl, full of the virtuous deeds of the righteous which are then brought before God (14.2). Unlike *the Testament of Levi* nothing is said of a

---

16. See McKelvey, *New Temple*; J. Maier, *Vom Kultus zur Gnosis* (Salzburg, 1964) and H. Bietenhard, *Die himmlische Welt im Urchristentum und Spätjudentum* (Tübingen, 1951).

17. M. de Jonge, *The Testaments of the Twelve Patriarchs* (Assen, 1953).

18. See Rowland, *Open Heaven*, pp. 81f.

theophany, a curious absence in a work which otherwise follows the standard pattern of cosmography.

We turn now to consider a remarkable passage in the Jewish apocalypses, *1 Enoch* 14.8ff.:[19]

> And there was shown to me in my vision as follows: Behold, in my visions clouds were summoning me, and mists were calling me, and the courses of the stars and lightnings were hurrying me along and were bewildering me. The winds in my vision car-
> 5 ried me away, lifted me up and brought me to heaven. I entered until I drew near to a wall built of hailstones with tongues of fire around them, and they began to make me afraid. I entered into the tongues of fire, and I drew near to a great house built from hailstones. The walls of the house were like flat stones. All were
> 10 made of snow, and the foundations too were of snow. Its roofs were like the courses of the stars and like flashes of lightning, and between them were fiery cherubim, and their heaven was as water. A burning fire was around the walls, and the doors were burning with fire. I entered the house, which was as hot as fire
> 15 and as cold as snow, and there were no means of nourishing life there. Fear covered me and trembling overtook me. I was shaking and fearful and fell down. I continued to see in my vision, and behold, another door was opened before me. There was another house greater than the first, and the whole of it
> 20 consisted of tongues of fire. All of it excelled in its glory, splendour and majesty, so that I am not able to tell you of its glory and majesty. Its foundation was of fire. The upper part of its roof was of fiery flame. I looked and saw a lofty throne, and its appearance was of crystal and its wheel as the shining sun. There was
> 25 also a vision of cherubim. From underneath the throne there came forth rivers of flaming fire, and I was not able to look at them. The Great Glory sat on a lofty throne. His robe was as the appearance of the sun, brighter and whiter than any snow. No angel could enter the house and see his face because of his mag-
> 30 nificence and glory. No human being could look at his flaming fire which was around. A great fire stood by him and no one was near him. Ten thousand times ten thousand stood around him and before him, and his word has power. The holy angels who are near him do not depart by night nor do they leave him. Until
> 35 this time I had been prostrate on my face trembling.

---

19. Translation of the Greek from M. Black, *Apocalypsis Henochi Graece*.

Most are agreed that it comes from the earliest phase of the apocalyptic tradition. Milik[20] in his edition of the Qumran *Enoch* fragments wants to push the date of this section back to a time *before* the P reference to Enoch in Gen. 5.24. The reason for considering this heavenly ascent in the context of a discussion of references to the Temple is that the description of heaven seems to follow the geography of the cult. Thus we read in 14.10 and 15 that there are two parts to heaven, a 'great house' and a 'second house greater than the former'. Unlike the *Testament of Levi* no mention is made of a heavenly cultic activity.

The immediate context of this account of a heavenly ascent is Enoch's commission to announce judgment on the watchers and Azazel (13.1) and the request by them that Enoch should intercede with God on their behalf (13.4ff.). The watchers' petition is rejected (14.1ff.) and Enoch recounts his experience in 14.2ff. which leads to the heavenly ascent and another account of the divine rejection of the petition. Here we have an account of a mortal taken into the divine presence (parallel to other early Enoch traditions such as *Jub.* 4.20ff. which may be dependent on *1 Enoch* 14). Connections with other parts of the biblical tradition abound as the following summary indicates:

line 2 (14.80: Dan. 7.13; *T. Abraham* 10; Ezek. 8.2; 14; 2 Kgs 2.11

line 6 (14.9): Exod. 24.10; 38.22; Ezek. 1.27

line 7 'tongues': Ezek. 1; Acts 2.3; Dan. 7.9

line 9 (14.10): two houses following the two major parts of the Holy Place?

line 12 (14.11): Exod. 19.16; Ezek. 1.13

line 13: heaven as water: Ezek. 1.22; Rev. 4.6; *T. Levi* 2.7; *b. Hagigah* 15a ('When you come to the place of the marble plates, do not cry, "Water, water"')

line 19 (14.15): no veil mentioned; cf. Exod. 31.33

line 23 (14.18): Isa. 6.1; Ezek. 1.26; Dan. 7.9; Rev. 4.2; *Slav. Enoch* 22.2; *Life of Adam and Eve* 25

line 24 (wheel): 2 Kgs 2.11; Ezek. 1.16; 10.2; Dan. 7.9; 4QŠirot; *1 Enoch* 71.7

---

20. J. Milik, *The Books of Enoch* (Oxford, 1976). See also M. Barker, *The Older Testament* (London, 1988).

line 26 (14.19): fiery stream: Dan. 7.10; 4QŠirot; *1 Enoch* 71.2; Rev. 22.1

line 27 (14.22): glory: *Asc. Isa.* 11.32; *T. Levi.* 3.4; 5.1

line 27: raiment: Dan. 7.9; Isa. 6.1; Mk 9.3 and parallels; *T. Abraham* 12

line 32 (14.23): angelic attendants: Rev. 4; Dan. 7.10; *1 Enoch* 1.9.

This remarkable passage has received greater attention in recent years. Its concern with heavenly journey and its obvious indebtedness, at least in general terms, to Ezekiel 1 have made it a focus of interest for those interested in exposing the character of the mystical tradition in the Second Temple period. There seems little doubt that it offers us the earliest evidence of the expansion of Ezekiel 1. Opinion will be divided over whether it indicates a vital speculative or visionary interest. A comparison with its biblical antecedents suggests that we have come a long way from the typical prophetic commission. While the connection with Ezekiel 1 is obvious, this passage differs from other throne-theophany passages in the extent of that indebtedness.

Rejection of the Temple?

It is the book of Revelation which offers the clearest evidence of the redundancy of the Temple in the eschatological age. The celestial city *as a whole* reflects the proportions of the Holy of Holies (21.15). That connection might lead us to suppose that there is nothing other than influence of the dimensions of the tabernacle and no allusion to the Temple itself, though there are affinities with 1 Kgs 6.20. The city itself was one large holy place (just like the new Jerusalem in the Temple Scroll) from which anything unclean was rigorously excluded (21.27). With the design of the Holy of Holies forming the basis of the design of the city, the faithfulness of the new to the scriptures is ensured, while at the same time an institution which had clearly been a cause of strife in Judaism could be abandoned in favour of the unmediated access of the saints to God (21.3; 22.4; cf. *Jub.* 1.26f.). It is apparent from the references to the heavenly temple elsewhere (e.g. 11.19; 15.5; 16.1, 17) that the position taken by the book is not totally anti-cultic. In a situation where God's will is not done, the presence of the Temple in heaven is a symbol of the divine dimension to existence. The tabernacle/Temple is a reminder of obligation, and the heavenly worship represents the divine remembrance of the cost of faithful witness which will not ultimately be ignored. Indeed, the earthly temple is the basis for the inspiration of the vision of the two witnesses in Revelation 11. Measurement of the Temple offers the seer a potent way of speaking about the extent of the divine presence in a recalcitrant world.

Another feature of Revelation which may also have contributed to the absence of the Temple is imbedded in its cosmology. There is an eschatological resolution of the cosmological contrast in Revelation. Dualistic cosmology derived from the apocalyptic tradition is used to stress the transcending of the alienation of the world from God and humanity from one another. In chs. 4f. we are introduced to God's throne world, where the Almighty sits receiving the praises of heaven. In heaven there is a Temple with an altar and angels ministering, similar to what we find in *Testament of Levi*. This world above where God is acknowledged as creator and the source of messianic redemption by the heavenly host in songs of praise contrasts with the unrepentant world below. Despite the start of the eschatological woes initiated by the Lamb opening the seals, humankind refuses to repent (9.20). We have a contrast between the world above and the world below under the dominion of a regime inspired by the Devil (13.2). Revelation 6–19 tells, with several interruptions, of the overthrow of this hostile dominion, culminating in the binding of Satan and the millennium. In a new creation there is a very different cosmological pattern. In the new heavens and new earth the dwelling of God is not in the world above seated on a fiery throne (4.5), but tabernacling with people in the new Jerusalem on a throne from which flows the river of the water of life (22.1). The contrast between heaven as a haven of righteousness and an evil earth has disappeared, as also has the Temple (21.22). It is a mark of the perfection of the new creation that there is no need of a peculiar dwelling for God either in heaven or on earth.

The development of a heavenly Temple (or in *1 Enoch* 14 a description of the heavenly world which owes something to the lay-out of the cult) is not easily explained. Once again we may resort to the theory that the heavenly Temple offered a radical alternative to the inadequacies of its earthly counterpart. The presence of a heavenly throne passage from Qumran may add some weight to this belief. Other explanations seem more convincing, however. There was developing in ancient Judaism a more sophisticated cosmology in which God was believed to be enthroned in glory far above the heavens. Well before the beginning of the common era if *1 Enoch* 14 is anything to go by, some Jews had taken the step of establishing the *merkabah* of Ezekiel in a heavenly palace which only the privileged seer could view. Such a cosmological development may tell us something also of their theology. God was absent in heaven; signs of the divine presence were indirect and not immediate. Such a lack of immediacy should not blind us to the importance attached to divine immanence at particular moments in history and ritual devotion. Care should be taken not to overplay such dualistic contrast, as it is clear from the apocalypses that the whole of human history is not a random series of events but follows the plan laid down in heaven.

Concluding Comments

We do not have a great amount of material on which to base judgments about the attitudes to the Temple in the apocalyptic tradition, but the absence of much detailed discussion of the Temple is striking. This could be because this institution is taken for granted as an essential component of both this age and the age to come. In the material dating from the years immediately after the destruction of the Second Temple the relative paucity of references is noteworthy. It might have been expected that the end of the Temple would have at least led to nostalgic hopes, though a hope for its restoration is included in the *Shemoneh Esreh*. That there was a significant increase in eschatological urgency is indicated by several passages (e.g. *Syr. Baruch* 85.10; *4 Ezra* 5.50ff.; 14.10, 16). It is remarkable that the detailed prescriptions such as are found in the Temple Scroll are completely absent in the extant apocalypses. We might conclude from this that the writers of the apocalypses were against the cult. That would be too precipitous a conclusion to draw. But we need to remember that fantasizing about the details of the new age in a utopian fashion is hardly typical of the apocalypses. They show an interest in history as a whole in which *detailed* concern with the Temple would have been out of place.

The explicit concern with the heavenly Zion which we found in apocalypses from the second half of the first century AD may well derive in part at least from the catastrophe of 70. It is apparent in other subject matter in *4 Ezra, Syriac Baruch* and the *Apocalypse of Abraham* that the disaster had an effect on the content of the revelations and the concerns expressed in them. All three are virtually unique in including questions of theodicy. It should come as no surprise, therefore, that the destruction of the city led to developments in their doctrine of Zion just as it appears to have done in their emphasis on the temporary nature of the messianic kingdom and the emergence of the doctrine of the two ages.

There is some evidence of a growing concern with Zion at the expense of specific reference to the Temple. Explicit doubts about the Second Temple are occasionally expressed, for example, in *1 Enoch* 89.73 and *Syr. Baruch* 68.5. In the light of the protests raised in some of the Qumran texts about the Temple it is reasonable to suppose that some of the dissatisfaction expressed itself in the visions for the future by a concentration on Zion rather than the Temple. Still, there is nothing to compare with the hint in Stephen's speech that the whole cultic enterprise based on the Temple was flawed from the very start and was the consequence of the massive rebellion at the Golden Calf (Acts 7.40).[21]

The socio-economic context of the apocalyptic literature we have been considering was one in which the Temple played a central role in the lives of Jews both inside and outside Judaea. The regular flow of income to the Temple from all parts of the empire led to the enrichment of this institution and those who ran it. As far as Jerusalem itself was concerned, the Temple

---

21. See *Epistle of Barnabas* 16, and further M. Simon, *Verus Israel* (Paris, 1948), pp. 86, 120.

provided a central feature of the local economy. Throughout the years leading up to the First Revolt in AD 66–70 there was a programme of rebuilding which would have involved employment. More important was the regular round of sacrifices which demanded provision and was a significant component of the local economy. The removal of the Temple must have necessitated a cataclysmic shift in the pattern of life, so any one predicting its destruction was pronouncing a threat not only on an ideological focus but also on the most significant part of the Jerusalem economy. We can only with difficulty reconstruct the real-life struggles of which the literary remains are the ideological expression. There is obviously a complicated relationship between the two. Indeed, as we have seen, the apocalyptic literature cannot readily be identified as the repository of the ideas of the marginalized when only occasionally do we find critical or deviant ideas in them. The language of revelation can be used by the powerful just as much as the weak and marginalized as a way of cloaking their positions of power with the mantle of divine authority.

One of the interesting developments in biblical studies over the last decade has been the recognition that social and economic forces must be allowed their place in the understanding of religious movements. Of course, as Ernst Bammel has catalogued,[22] there has been a long history of attempts to place Jesus and the early Christians within social and revolutionary struggles for change in the last years of the Second Temple. Some of these are testimony to the ingenuity of the writers concerned and seem to have only tenuous links with the sources. Our doubts about particular solutions should not make us any less conscious of the issues that they raise. We may want to voice doubts about the whole fabric of the edifice of the 'hermeneutics of suspicion' which has dominated our reading of biblical texts in which the surface is rejected in favour of underlying tendencies. Nevertheless biblical scholarship has drunk deep of the 'spirit of the age' and in its various results has shown how productive it can be for theological as

---

22. 'The Revolutionary Theory from Reimarus to Brandon', in E. Bammel and C.F.D. Moule, *Jesus and the Politics of his Day* (Cambridge, 1984), pp. 11-68.

well as historical enquiry, in order to maintain a credible critical awareness in giving meaning to ancient religious texts. Recent scholarship with an avowedly liberationist or Marxist bent[23] which sees Jesus as part of a diffuse movement opposed to the hegemony of the Temple both ideologically and economically is an attempt to restore to our interpretative consciousness the socio-economic dimension of the struggles for power among men and women.[24] We may not want to reduce the religious to epiphenomena of class-conflict, but to deny the importance of the struggle for power is to reduce the scope of the religious to a compartment of human experience instead of allowing full weight to its social function. The literary form of our New Testament texts disguises as much as it reveals, not least in that central area of the social formation out of which and for which the texts were written. It is the task of the interpreter to restore that hidden story in a way which can ground the 'political unconscious'[25] dimension firmly in narrative we are offered and recognize the role of the text in the social and political struggles of the ancient world as well as in our own. That will demand attentiveness to what lies before us in the particularity and peculiarity of the form and language and not wholesale dismissal of its form and content. Equally, it must encompass the recognition that there is another story to be told which is never absent from the text but can disappear in our readings of it, particularly when we are tempted to see religion as merely a 'spiritual' matter.[26] Nowhere is this more true than in the discussion of the Jewish Temple. Apparently it

23. See, for example, K. Kautsky, *Foundations of Christianity* (London, 1925); G. Pixley, *God's Kingdom* (London, 1981); F. Belo, *A Materialist Reading of the Gospel of Mark* (New York, 1981); J.L. Segundo, *The Historical Jesus of the Synoptic Gospels* (London, 1986); C. Myers, *Binding the Strong Man* (New York, 1989); H. Kreissig, *Die sozialen Zusammenhänge des judäischen Krieges* (Leipzig, 1970) (most recently on the circumstances of the First Revolt, M. Goodman, *The Ruling Class of Judaea* [Cambridge, 1988]).
24. See R. Williams, *Marxism and Literature* (Oxford, 1977).
25. To quote the title of Frederic Jameson's study where some attempt is made to deal with this aspect of literary criticism (*The Political Unconscious* [London, 1981]).
26. For a further discussion of this, see Nicholas Lash, *Easter in Ordinary* (London, 1988).

is the focus of religion and not of politics. Yet the Temple was a powerful economic factor in Judaean life as well as an influential ideological symbol. There are occasional signs, however fragmentary, of peripheral movements devoted to a challenge to powerful vested interests at the centre of Jewish life. Early Christianity wrestles with and ultimately transcends the Temple by arguing for its obsolescence. This is hardly a non-controversial position in a society where power and wealth were linked particularly with one institution. A biblical study must be allowed to cast light on the social formation in which the text was created and has hitherto been read. Biblical exegesis must take care not to allow it to be divorced from the social world of today and yesterday. In this respect the emerging biblical interpretation from the so-called Third World has much to teach us.[27] The oppressive role of centres of power in the contemporary world and the fate which awaits those who challenge them have their echoes in the fate which awaited those who dared to go up to Jerusalem and of whom it could be said: 'We heard this man say, "I will destroy this Temple and in three days build a Temple not made with hands"' (Mk 14.58).

27. Its implications are recognized by Ernst Bammel in his essay already referred to.

'THE TRUMPET SHALL SOUND'
SHOFAR SYMBOLISM AND ITS RECEPTION IN EARLY
CHRISTIANITY

Markus Bockmuehl

As the friends of Ernst Bammel will know, primitive Christianity adopted many of its religious symbols from the Old Testament and from contemporary Judaism. Among these was
the trumpet, associated particularly closely with the ritual of
temple and synagogue worship. As the title of this contribution
reminds us, the trumpet also features repeatedly in
eschatological passages of the New Testament. Trumpets
announce the judgment, herald the resurrection, and accom-
pany the angels' gathering the elect from the four corners of
the earth.

There are a good many useful studies of the role of musical
instruments in the Old Testament and post-Biblical Judaism;
this is true especially for the trumpet. My contribution here is
not intended to duplicate or to reproduce such work, much of
which is readily available for example in Gerhard Friedrich's
fine article on *salpinx* or the earlier study of the *šôfār* by Sol B.
Finesinger.[1]

---

1. Gerhard Friedrich, '*salpinx*', *TWNT*, VII (1964), pp. 71-88; Sol B.
Finesinger, 'The Shofar', *HUCA* 8-9 (1931–32), pp. 193-228. The exten-
sive Freudian analysis of the *šôfār* by Theodor Reik ('Das Schofar [Das
Widderhorn]', in his *Probleme der Religionspsychologie*, I: *Das Ritual*
(Internationale Psychoanalytische Bibliothek, 15; Leipzig/Vienna:
Internationaler Psychoanalytischer Verlag, 1919), pp. 178-311; ET in
Ritual: Psycho-analytic Studies (London: Hogarth, 1931), pp. 221-361, is
less obviously relevant here; see the healthy critique by Erwin
Ramsdell Goodenough, *Jewish Symbols in the Greco-Roman Period*,
IV (New York: Pantheon, 1954), p. 167 n. 1.

Instead, the present study focuses on the symbolic significance of trumpets. After a survey of the liturgical and symbolic function of the trumpet in ancient Judaism, I want to
address one quite specific question: given the obvious connection with a rich Jewish background, what accounts for the
strikingly dissimilar treatment of trumpet symbolism in early
Christianity?

Before we begin, a definition of terms is in order. The word
'symbol' is here used in the straightforward, classical sense
(Kant, Goethe, Coleridge) of the indirect representation of a
concept or idea by means of a concrete analogy, 'above all by
the translucence of the eternal through and in the temporal'.[2]
As for the term 'trumpet', the frequent semantic proximity of
the Hebrew words (esp. *šôfār* and *ḥaṣōṣerâ*) and their respective Greek and Latin translations suggest that we may for our
purposes use it in a generic sense to denote *all* the instruments
here in view (horn, trumpet, clarion, etc.), while remaining
aware of the distinctions wherever they can be maintained.[3]

1. *The Trumpet as a Symbol in the Old Testament and in Ancient Judaism*

a. *Bible*

Both the *šôfār* (the ram's horn;[4] cf. the synonym *qeren hayyôbēl* in Josh. 6.5[5]) and the *ḥaṣōṣerâ* (the ancient trumpet
proper, straight and of bronze or hammered silver[6]) are used

---

2. S.T. Coleridge, *The Statesman's Manual*, as quoted in René
Wellek, 'Symbol and Symbolism in Literature', in Philip P. Wiener
(ed.), *Dictionary of the History of Ideas: Studies of Selected Pivotal
Ideas*, IV (New York: Scribner's, 1973), pp. 338f.

3. On the translation terminology, cf. also D.A. Foxvog and A.D.
Kilmer, 'Music', *ISBE*, III (Grand Rapids: Eerdmans, 1986), p. 43.

4. But cf. I. Abrahams, 'Trumpet', in James Hastings (ed.), *A Dictionary of the Bible*, IV (1902), p. 815, on the wide variety of possible
shapes and materials.

5. Other synonyms include *tāqôa'* (Ezek. 7.14) and *yôbēl* (Exod. 19.13).
Reik, 'Schofar', p. 179, regards the name of Jubal, the inventor of
musical instruments (Gen. 4.21), as etymologically linked with the
ram's horn.

6. Josephus, *Ant.* 3.291, describes it as a narrow tube of about 40 cm
in length, with a mouthpiece at one end and a bell-shaped flare at the

for secular and especially military purposes in the Old Testament: as a rallying call, a signal or scare tactic in battle,[7] a warning of impending attack,[8] etc. Neither was properly a musical instrument (the *šôfār* in any case less so than the *ḥ*ᵃ*ṣōṣ*ᵉ*râ*), and in view of ancient comparisons of their sound with an ass's bray[9] Friedrich is surely justified in describing the tone as 'mehr laut als schön'.[10] However, inasmuch as the chief function of both instruments was to sound a clarion alert, they could also be useful in liturgical contexts—even if, here as elsewhere, no clear differentiation between the cultic and secular spheres should be affirmed.[11]

Although it is probably impossible to maintain a consistent distinction between *ḥ*ᵃ*ṣōṣ*ᵉ*râ* and *šôfār* in Biblical usage,[12] the liturgical functions which were assigned to these instruments especially in 'P' and the post-exilic period do seem to presuppose specific applications for each. Post-exilic texts show both instruments being used in the temple liturgy, although it appears that, for a while at least, the *ḥ*ᵃ*ṣōṣ*ᵉ*rôt* (almost invariably plural) eclipsed, and perhaps replaced, the *šôfār* as the cultic instrument *par excellence*.[13] The silver trumpets were almost exclusively blown by priests.[14] They were frequently

other. It appears thus on the Arch of Titus at Rome and on coins from the Bar Kokhba war (see below).

7. E.g. Josh. 6.4ff.; Judg. 3.27; 6.34; 7.16-22; Neh. 4.14 [ET 4.20] (*šôfār*); Num. 10.9, 31.6; 2 Chron. 13.12 (*ḥ*ᵃ*ṣōṣ*ᵉ*râ*). Cf. Sol B. Finesinger, 'The Shofar', HUCA 8-9 (1931–32), p. 193, who believes the *šôfār* was originally used to repel hostile forces.

8. E.g. Jer. 6.1; Ezek. 33.3-6; Hos. 5.8.

9. B. R.H. 28b; Plutarch, *Isis et Osiris* 30 (2.362f.). *Sib. Or.* 8.117 calls it 'savage-sounding'.

10. Friedrich, '*salpinx*', p. 84.

11. Cf. Friedrich, '*salpinx*', p. 79; profane, cultic and theological meanings of the trumpet cannot be strictly distinguished.

12. Cf. esp. Hos. 5.8; 1 Kgs 1.34, 39 with 2 Kgs 11.14; etc. See further Abrahams, 'Trumpet', p. 816; Friedrich, '*salpinx*', p. 76.

13. Contrast e.g. 2 Sam. 6.15 with 1 Chron. 13.8; 15.24, 28; etc. Note, too, the striking preference for *šôfār* in the prophets, but for *ḥ*ᵃ*ṣōṣ*ᵉ*râ* in Chronicles (only once in the latter prophets, as a synonym of *šôfār*: Hos. 5.8). See n. 15 below, and cf. further Friedrich, '*salpinx*', p. 76, and Finesinger, 'Shofar', pp. 208-10, noting that the *ḥ*ᵃ*ṣōṣ*ᵉ*râ* occurs almost exclusively in later texts.

14. The only apparent exceptions are 2 Kgs 11.14; 2 Chron. 23.13; but cf. *3 Ezra* 5.62ff.

sounded in worship: Num. 10.1, 2, 10 appoints two trumpets for the daily burnt-offering (cf. 2 Chron. 29.26-28) as well as 'at your times of rejoicing' (cf. 2 Chron. 7.6; 20.28; Ezra 3.10, etc.), at appointed feasts and at the beginning of each month. In later post-exilic times there was a guild of seven priestly trumpeters who (along with players of cymbals, lyres and harps) occupied a prominent place in the Levitical orchestra.[15] The Chronicler, who specially favours the *ḥᵃṣōṣᵉrâ*,[16] features 120 priests blowing trumpets at Solomon's dedication of the temple (2 Chron. 5.12f.). As for the *šôfār*, it occurs with obvious ritual connotations, for example in David's removal of the ark (2 Sam. 6.15[17]); it also heralds the anointing of Solomon (1 Kgs 1.34) and other events of national significance.[18] Gideon's blowing of the *šôfār* is prompted by the Spirit of God (Judg. 6.34).[19] The primary religious use of the *šôfār* was at the Feast of Trumpets (the first day of Tishri, also the feast of New Year)[20] and, in the year of Jubilee, on the Day of Atonement (10th of Tishri).[21] Both instruments were sounded at King

---

15. 1 Chron. 15.24; Neh. 12.41. Cf. Adolph Büchler, 'Zur Geschichte der Tempelmusik und der Tempelpsalmen', *ZAW* 19 (1899), p. 329.

16. It occurs 3× in Sam./Kgs, 22× in Chron. (including verbal cognate).

17. 1 Chron. complements the *šôfār* with *ḥᵃṣōṣᵉrôt* here (15.28), and introduces them in 13.8. On the repeated links between the ark and the *šôfār* see Hans Seidel, 'Horn und Trompete im alten Israel unter Berücksichtigung der "Kriegsrolle" von Qumran', *Wissenschaftliche Zeitschrift der Karl-Marx-Universität Leipzig: Gesellschafts- und sprachwissenschaftliche Reihe* 6 (1956–57), p. 590.

18. E.g. the proclamation of a national fast (Joel 2.15).

19. Cf. Seidel, 'Horn', p. 589.

20. Lev. 23.23-25 (*zikrôn tᵉrû'â*, 'a memorial of trumpeting'); Num. 29.1-6 (*yôm tᵉrû'â*, 'a day of trumpeting'). Abrahams, 'Trumpet', p. 815, points out that although the *šôfār* is not explicitly mentioned, it is 'obviously intended', since aside from Num. 10.5 and Ps. 150.5 the term *tᵉrû'â* is normally connected with the *šôfār*. Cf. esp. Lev. 25.9; Ps. 81.4 (assumed by some refer to the New Year festival). Philo explicitly calls the New Year festival the feast of trumpets (*Spec. Leg.* 2.188; cf. 1.186; see further Ps.-Philo, *LAB* 13.6; Origen, *De Oratione* 27.14 [*PG* 11.415]). On trumpets at New Year in the Mishnah and Talmud, see also below.

21. Lev. 25.9. Abrahams ('Trumpet', p. 816) surmises that this may be the origin of the synagogal practice of sounding the *šôfār* at the conclusion of the Day of Atonement.

Asa's reform and renewal of the covenant (2 Chron. 15.14); and both indeed were used at times of worship and rejoicing (e.g. Ps. 98.6; 1 Chron. 15.28). Even in war the trumpets had a religious function, since they alerted God so that he would deliver his people: 'When you go into battle in your own land against an enemy who is oppressing you, sound a blast on the trumpets. Then you will be remembered by the Lord your God and rescued from your enemies.'[22]

Properly symbolic uses of trumpets are rare, and mainly limited to the *šôfār*. Nevertheless, the trumpet as a signalling instrument of course suggests the metaphorical inclusion of the object which it heralds, for example, war[23] or any other frightening event (Amos 3.6). In this sense, too, since war can be sent by God to judge his people, it is not difficult to understand the use of the horn in connection with the developing notion of a day of divine reckoning[24]—initially immanent and inner-historical, but with increasingly eschatological connotations.

In addition to the Judgment imagery, one or two other metaphorical uses are worth mentioning. Jeremiah (6.16-20) and Ezekiel (33.1-9) both use the trumpet in a simile: as the watchman must blow the trumpet when he sees impending danger, so the prophet speaks God's message of repentance.[25] The trumpet also signifies revelation in the Exodus: together

---

22. Num. 10.9; see also 2 Chron. 13.14; and cf. e.g. on 1 Macc. below.
23. Jer. 4.19-21; 42.14; Amos 2.2; Zeph. 1.16; Job 39.24f.; etc. Cf. e.g. *Sib. Or.* 5.253; 7.115f.; 8.117; *Ps. Sol.* 8.1.
24. E.g. Jer. 6.17; Hos. 5.8; 8.1; Joel 2.1ff., 15; Zeph. 1.16.
25. Cf. similarly Isa. 58.1ff.; and see below for the development of this motif in the Targums. However, references to the *šôfār* in these contexts need not imply a literal use of trumpets in the delivery of the prophetic oracles; such references may be primarily metaphorical. Contrasting earlier prophets (e.g. 1 Sam. 10.5; 2 Kgs 3.15) with later, C.H. Kraeling and L. Mowry point out that 'Of the prophets whose oracles are recorded in the Bible none is known to have used instrumental music for inspirational purposes, and some like Amos reacted violently against even the use of song in the Temple (Amos v. 23)' ('Music in the Bible', in Egon Wellesz [ed.], *Ancient and Oriental Music* [New Oxford History of Music, 1; London: Oxford University Press, 1957], p. 293).

with smoke, thunder and lightning, a *šôfār* sounds forth from Mount Sinai at the giving of the Ten Commandments.[26]

The last two texts bear a close connection to other Old Testament references in which the *šôfār* somehow designates a revelatory or redemptive action of God himself. In a passage from the well-known 'Isaiah Apocalypse', the sound of the trumpet initiates the ingathering of God's people: 'So it shall be in that day: the great trumpet will be blown; they will come, who are about to perish in the land of Assyria, and they who are outcasts in the land of Egypt, and shall worship the Lord in the holy mount at Jerusalem' (Isa. 27.13). Revealing himself in judgment of the nations and redemption of his people, 'Then the Lord will be seen over them; and his arrow will flash like lightning. The Lord God will blow the trumpet... The Lord their God will save them in that day, as the flock of his people' (Zech. 9.14, 16).[27] Finally, Yahweh's celestial rule is also heralded by the sound of the *šôfār*: 'God has gone up with a shout, the Lord with the sound of a trumpet' (Ps. 47.6).[28]

b. *Post-Biblical Judaism*
Many of these themes carry over into post-Biblical Jewish religion. We will concentrate on symbolic uses.

1. *Biblical Translations*
a. *Greek*. The authors of the Septuagint are perhaps largely responsible for the irrevocable confusion in both Jewish and Christian Greek usage between the *šôfār* and the *ḥaṣōṣ˚rā*. Both these words are frequently represented by the Greek term *salpinx*, which can moreover render *yôbēl* (Exod. 19.13), *t˚rû'â* (Lev. 23.24), *tāqôa'* (Ezek. 7.14), and (in Daniel) the Aramaic *qarnā'*. *Salpinx* also translates the constructs *qeren hayyôbēl* and *šôfar hayyôbēl* (Josh. 6.4ff.), and in one or two

---

26. Exod. 19.16, 19; 20.15 [ET 20.18]; cf. 19.13 *hayyôbēl*.
27. In view of the proto-apocalyptic imagery in these passages, it is perhaps a little surprising to find that in Daniel, the trumpet is not used (even in ch. 12), except as an instrument of pagan worship (3.5, 7, 10, 15: *qarnā'*).
28. Finesinger ('Shofar', pp. 195f.) considers that this is probably a New Year's psalm (as in fact it is used in today's New Year service). The passage also occupied Patristic exegesis, as we shall see.

other places it is introduced over and above the Hebrew text (esp. Neh. 8.15; 2 Chron. 7.6). On the other hand, *šôfār* (but not *ḥᵃṣōṣᵉrâ*) can likewise be translated with the alternative term *keratinē*. The verb *salpizein* renders the corresponding Hebrew terms *tāqaʿ*, *rûaʿ*, and *ḥṣṣr* piel, hiphil. A pronounced interest in the symbolic value of trumpets is not evident.

b. *Aramaic.* In the Targums, the Aramaic equivalents to the two main Hebrew words are *šôfrāʾ* and *ḥᵃṣoṣartāʾ*; sometimes *qarnâʾ* translates *šôfār* (e.g. Tg. Jon. Jer. 4.19, 21). The former also occurs in the *Onkelos* and *Pseudo-Jonathan* Targums to Exod. 19.13 (Heb. *yôbēl*). As in the case of LXX, I have not been able to find much evidence of symbolic usage over and above the Hebrew original. *Targum Jonathan* at Hos. 8.2 and Amos 2.2 (and cf. Jer. 6.17) explicitly connects the trumpet references of the Hebrew text (both *šôfār* and *ḥᵃṣōṣᵉrâ*) with the work of the prophets; this continues the pattern we observed earlier for Jer. 6.17 and Ezek. 33.1-9. More significant for our purposes, and in keeping with prophetic antecedents, is the *šôfār* proclaiming redemption (*pûrqân*) in Tg. Jon. Isa. 18.3.

As might be expected, the late *Targum Pseudo-Jonathan* offers a number of haggadic elaborations on the *šôfār*. Some of these may well have served to imbue it with additional symbolic value in the minds of Palestinian synagogue audiences of the Talmudic period. Here, the people at Mount Sinai are said to have heard 'the sound of the *šôfār* bringing the dead to life' (*Tg. Ps.-J.* Exod. 20.15). Using a phrase also employed elsewhere in the synagogal liturgy (and somewhat reminiscent of the reference from the Isaiah Targum cited above), the trumpet announcing the Jubilee in all the land is specifically designated 'the *šôfār* of liberty'.[29] In a curious twist (but one which is well established throughout the history of the New Year liturgy), the Feast of Trumpets, on the other hand, 'shall be for you a day of sounding the alarm to confound Satan, who is bound for you by the sound of your alarm'.[30]

---

29. *Tg. Ps.-J.* Lev. 25.9 (*šôfar ḥērûtāʾ*). Cf. n. 52 below.
30. *Tg. Ps.-J.* Num. 29.1. Cf. *b. R.H.* 16a and see below, n. 58; this belief would clearly link the use of the *šôfār* with the realm of popular magic.

2. *Apocrypha and Pseudepigrapha*
Several of these themes are taken up and developed in the Apocrypha and Pseudepigrapha; we will consider a sampling of the most pertinent references.

a. *Apocrypha*. Uses of the trumpet in Sirach and *3 Ezra* show no particular concern for symbolism, but are reminiscent of the cultic setting described in Chronicles.[31] The eschatological trumpet appears in *4 Ezra* 6.23; its function there is to introduce the final tribulation.

The most significant apocryphal work for our purposes is 1 Maccabees. As in the *War Scroll* (1QM) from Qumran,[32] the trumpet here is an important instrument of warfare: on both the Jewish and the pagan side it is used to rally and encourage the troops and to intimidate the enemy.[33] More than that, however, the Hasmonaean generals consciously engage in the blowing of trumpets on the battlefield *as a religious act* in keeping with Num. 10.9. Thus 1 Macc. 3.54 concludes an invocation to God on account of the profanation of the sanctuary and the assault of the Gentiles: '"...How shall we be able to resist them if you do not help us?" Then they sounded the trumpets and gave a loud shout.' Trumpeting is similarly combined with a loud appeal to 'Heaven' in 4.40; 5.31, 33. In the context of a war of national liberation, this suggests that their biblically derived meaning and redemptive symbolism constituted an important part of Hasmonaean religious ideology.

b. *Pseudepigrapha*. Of particular interest is the further development of the heavenly trumpet motif: it is now usually the angels who sound the instrument. The concluding chapters

---

31. Sir. 50.16 (cf. 2 Chron. 29.27 and see Büchler, 'Geschichte', p. 339, on the liturgical differences); *3 Ezra* 5.59, 62, 64, 65, 66 (cf. Ezra 3.10-13; and see n. 14 above on non-priestly trumpets).
32. This connection is also drawn by e.g. Seidel ('Horn', pp. 594, 598), although he does not sufficiently consider the theological function of the trumpets of 1QM.
33. E.g. 1 Macc. 4.13; 6.33; 7.45; 9.12; 16.8. For the mention of trumpets on the pagan side, see esp. 1 Macc. 9.12; cf. 2 Macc. 15.25.

(9–12) of the *Apocalypse of Zephaniah* (first century BC/first century AD) contain four trumpet scenes which stress the book's basic theme of the coming divine judgment. The first trumpet praises the visionary who has prevailed over the devil; the second inaugurates a vision of Hades with the souls in torment. The third trumpet is a call to the righteous to intercede on behalf of those in torment, while the final trumpet precedes an announcement of the destroying wrath of God. As in the New Testament book of Revelation, it is not clear whether the function of these trumpets is anything more than a literary device to underline the importance of the themes portrayed. They are intended to catch the reader's attention and to instill a sense of awe.

Further on the note of judgment, the *Paraleipomena of Jeremiah* feature trumpets heralding an angelic descent onto the walls of the besieged city of Jerusalem (*4 Bar.* 3.2); in an unusual picture the great angel sounds his trumpet to encourage the Chaldaeans to come and take the city (4.2). Developing earlier prophetic treatments of the Day of Judgment, the (Jewish?) Book 4 of the *Sibylline Oracles* asserts that the final apocalyptic consummation is announced by a dreadful sign 'with sword and trumpet at the rising of the sun' (4.174).

According to the first-century *Apocalypse of Abraham*, the sound of the heavenly trumpet will herald the coming of the Messiah who will gather and redeem God's people and judge the heathen (*Apoc. Abr.* 31.1). Somewhat earlier, the *Psalms of Solomon* combine the prophetic theme of an eschatological trumpet of judgment and redemption with the (in practice never implemented?) šôfār of the Jubilee:

> Sound in Zion the signal trumpet of the sanctuary; announce in Jerusalem the voice of one bringing good news; for God has been merciful to Israel in watching over them. Stand on a high place, Jerusalem, and look at your children, from the east and the west assembled together by the Lord.[34]

34. *Ps. Sol.* 11.1f.; cf. Joel 2.1; Lev. 25.9. For the trumpet accompanying the eschatological gathering of God's people, see further Isa. 27.13; *Shemoneh Esreh* 10; *Eccl. R.* 1.7; etc.; and cf. below on Mt. 24.31; 1 Thess. 4.16f.

A trumpet blown by the archangel Michael summons the angels to hear God's judgment of Adam's sin (*Apoc. Moses* 22.1, 3), but it also announces to them the joyful news of God's mercy in delivering Adam's soul (37.1). In the *Testament of Abraham* (first century AD), at the Judgment itself an angel holds a trumpet which, strangely, is used 'to test the sinners' (*T. Abr.* 12.10).

Other references could undoubtedly be adduced,[35] but the overall pattern is clear: over and above its secular and straightforwardly biblical meanings, the Apocrypha and Pseudepigrapha testify to an increasing interest in the *šôfār* as potently symbolizing Israel's aspirations for national redemption and judgment of its foes.

3. *The Dead Sea Scrolls*

At Qumran, it is almost exclusively the War Scroll (1QM; cf. 4Q491, 4Q493, 4Q496) which makes use of trumpets. *Šôfār*, *ḥᵃṣôṣᵉrâ*, and related words such as *tāqaʿ* and *tᵉrûʿâ* are all frequent in 1QM but virtually absent from all the other major Scrolls. While this discrepancy between the different documents may be difficult to account for, the main reason for the prevalence of trumpets in 1QM is its theme: it describes the final eschatological battle of God and the children of light against Belial and the children of darkness. Thus, although the subject matter is *prima facie* military, the writer's objective is intensely theological and spiritual.

Full studies of the trumpets in 1QM have been undertaken by Y. Yadin and P.R. Davies;[36] here we must concentrate on

35. Among the more unusual we might mention two passages from Ps.-Philo. In *LAB* 13.6, the Feast of Trumpets is appointed as an 'offering for your watchers' (D.J. Harrington in Charlesworth, *Old Testament Pseudepigrapha*, II, p. 321 n. (e), suspects angelic figures): 'Inasmuch as I watched over creation, so may you be mindful of all the earth'. In *LAB* 32.18, when Deborah and the people sacrifice and worship with song and trumpets, the prophetess is heard to say, 'And this will be as a testimony of trumpets between the stars and their Lord' (see 32.9, 14 for the notion of the stars as ministers of Israel; cf. Judg. 5.21 and perhaps 5.31).
36. Yigael Yadin, *The Scroll of the War of the Sons of Light against the Sons of Darkness* (trans. B. and Ch. Rabin; Oxford: Oxford University Press, 1962), pp. 87-113; Philip R. Davies, *1QM, the War*

the narrower task at hand, while relying on their foundational work. There are two main pertinent sections: 2.15–3.11 presents an Order of Trumpets ($h^a\bar{s}\bar{o}\bar{s}^er\hat{o}t$) with specific names and inscriptions (some for ceremonial and peace-time use, others for use at war), while 7.13–9.6 (cf. 16.3-9; 17.10-15) gives practical instructions on how and when the various trumpets are to be employed in battle.

There are about a dozen categories of $h^a\bar{s}\bar{o}\bar{s}^er\hat{o}t$ used by the children of light, each bearing a functionally descriptive name ('trumpets of summons' [cf. CD 11.22], 'trumpets of alarm', 'trumpets of ambush', etc.).[37] The striking theological symbolism of these trumpets, however, is apparent mainly from the inscriptions which the writer specifies for each category. All make mention of God and thereby firmly indicate this army's allegiance and orientation.[38] And quite apart from the redactional expansions which Davies has carefully identified on the trumpet inscriptions,[39] we can affirm that all of them in some way relate either to the glory of this army and God's favour toward it, or to the final judgment and redemption which are about to be accomplished.[40]

The *šôfār*, too, occupies a significant if rather less prominent place. In 1QM 7.14 and 8.9ff., while seven priests blow

---

Scroll from Qumran: Its Structure and History (Biblica et Orientalia, 32; Rome: Pontifical Biblical Institute, 1977), pp. 29-32, 75f.

37. See the tables in Yadin, *Scroll*, p. 89; Davies, *1QM*, pp. 31, 76. 4Q493 has 'trumpets of the Sabbaths' (1.13), which Joseph M. Baumgarten ('The Sabbath Trumpets in 4Q493 M^c', *RQ* 12 [1987], pp. 555-59) suggests may be the trumpets of Num. 10.10 applied to the Sabbath sacrifice.

38. Thus also Yadin, *Scroll*, p. 104.

39. Davies, *1QM*, p. 32.

40. The inscriptions read as follows (cf. Yadin and Vermes): 'Those called by God'; 'Princes of God'; 'The Army of God'; 'Summoned by God to the council of holiness'; 'The peace of God in the camps of his saints'; 'God's mighty deeds to crush the enemy and put to flight all who hate righteousness, and rescinding of grace against all who hate God'; 'Arrays of God's battalions for his wrathful vengeance on all the children of darkness'; 'Reminder of vengeance at God's appointed time'; 'God's mighty hand in war to cause all the ungodly slain to fall'; 'Mysteries of God to destroy wickedness'; 'God has smitten all the children of darkness: his wrath shall not turn back until they are finished'; 'God has gathered'; 'Rejoicings of God in the peaceful return'.

$h^a\bar{s}\bar{o}\bar{s}^er\hat{o}t$, seven Levites are appointed to march to battle with ram's horns ($\check{s}\hat{o}f^er\hat{o}t$ $hayy\hat{o}b\bar{e}l$), and to sound a battle fanfare.[41] Although no detailed information is given, clearly their purpose in war is closely related to that of the $h^a\bar{s}\bar{o}\bar{s}^er\hat{o}t$. The principal literary function of both here is to indicate the fundamentally religious, spiritual nature of this eschatological warfare, in which the trumpets of the children of light proclaim and invoke the victorious presence of God.[42]

4. *Philo and Josephus*

Josephus contributes little that is of interest. Trumpets occur frequently, but almost always in straightforward descriptive contexts of a cultic or military character.[43]

For Philo, the trumpet at Sinai symbolizes the miraculous revelation whereby the voice of God became loudly and 'equally audible to the farthest as well as the nearest'.[44] Somewhat unlike the later rabbis, Philo asserts that the $\check{s}\hat{o}f\bar{a}r$ sounded at the 'Feast of Trumpets' (New Year) reminds the Jew of the Sinaitic trumpet whose sound 'pealed from heaven and reached... the ends of the universe'; at the same time the trumpet figures in the festival as an instrument of war given 'as a thank-offering to God the peace-maker and peace-keeper'.[45]

41. Yadin (*Scroll*, p. 107) notes the similarity in both expression and number to the biblical account of the conquest of Jericho.
42. Similarly Yadin (*Scroll*, p. 113), who compares *Lev. R.* 29.4 (in contrast to secular pagan war trumpets, Israel 'know how to win the favour of their Creator with the fanfare').
Another interesting case is 4Q177 (= Catena[a]) 1-4.14f., where a *pesher* exegesis of Hos. 5.8 applies to the $\check{s}\hat{o}f\bar{a}r$. It may be that the explanation applied to the $\check{s}\hat{o}f\bar{a}r$ reads 'it is the book of the Second Law' (the Temple Scroll?), but the text is too fragmentary to permit certainty.
43. A possible exception might be *Ant.* 10.213f., where Josephus singles out the trumpet as the instrument appointed by Nebuchadnezzar to call for the worship of his idol (contrast Dan. 3.5, 10). The trumpet occurs as a military signal of victory in *Ant.* 12.410.
44. Philo, *Decal.* 33; cf. 44.
45. Philo, *Spec. Leg.* 2.189, 192.

5. *The Liturgy and Early Rabbinic Literature*

The ḥªṣōṣᵉrâ had arguably displaced the šôfār for most cultic purposes in the post-exilic period. In addition to the material presented earlier, the priestly trumpet was sounded three times every morning at the opening of the temple gates; nine trumpet blasts accompanied the morning and evening sacrifices. The commencement of the Sabbath was announced by a threefold trumpet blast from the pinnacle of the temple.[46] Another regular liturgical use of the priestly trumpet was during the joyful water-drawing at the feast of Tabernacles (*m. Suk.* 4.9; *b. Suk.* 51b), and before the slaughter of the Passover lambs (*m. Pes.* 5.5).[47]

In the traditional Jewish liturgy, however, the šôfār has clearly assumed the central position. This may derive from the apparent demise of the priestly ḥªṣōṣᵉrâ with the destruction of the Temple as well as, before and after 70, the increasing significance of the New Year liturgy under the influence of the Pharisees and their successors.[48] There is also a tradition, perhaps not unrelated, of post-70 confusion over the identity of the two instruments.[49]

In the Mishnah and Talmud, most of the references to šôfārôt and ḥªṣōṣᵉrôt show very little overt concern with the symbolic value of trumpets but are instead more strictly halakhic in orientation, i.e. they deal with practical (and technical)

46. This information from Josephus (*War* 4.582) and rabbinic literature (*m. Suk.* 5.5: *t. Suk.* 4.11f.; cf. *b. Suk.* 53b; *b. Shab.* 35b; *b. A.Z.* 70a) may have been confirmed by Benjamin Mazar's discovery in 1968 of a monumental inscription from the Southwestern pinnacle of the Temple Mount. This reads, *lbyt htqy'h lhb?*, 'for the place of trumpeting, in order to...' Aaron Demsky has recently proposed the (not impossible) reading *lbyt htqy'h lhb[dyl]*, 'for the place of trumpeting in order to distinguish'—possibly continuing with *m. Mid.* 1.1f. (*lᵉhabdîl bên qôdeš lᵉḥôl*), '...between the sacred and the profane [times]' ('When the Priests Trumpeted the Onset of the Sabbath', *BAR* 12 [1986], p. 52).

47. Cf. further e.g. *b. R.H.* 35b (feast of Jubilees); *m. Suk.* 4.5; 5.4.

48. See especially Finesinger, 'Shofar', pp. 211-13; for the possible role of the šôfār ceremony in synagogal New Year celebrations before 70, see Philo, *Spec. Leg.* 1.186; 2.188; *m. R.H.* 1.4, etc.; and cf. S. Safrai, 'Religion in Everyday Life', in S. Safrai and M. Stern (eds.), *The Jewish People in the First Century* (CRINT 1.2; Assen/Amsterdam: van Gorcum, 1976), p. 811 (citing Alon).

49. R. Ḥisda, *b. Shab.* 36a; cf. *b. Suk.* 34n.

aspects of implementation.⁵⁰ A case in point is the absolute
priority of the commandment to blow the *šôfār*, even if the
particular instrument at hand may previously have been used
for idolatrous purposes, or if it came from a devoted city (*b.
R.H.* 28a; cf. *b. Ḥul.* 89a).

This relative dearth of information in the Talmud about the
theological and spiritual significance of the *šôfār* is probably
due more to the scholarly and technical nature of much
rabbinic discussion than to an actual lack of religious interest
in the issue. An examination of more broadly based synagogal
spirituality, as expressed in liturgical texts (including the Targums, on which see §1.B.1.b above) and midrashic (esp.
homiletic) material, tends to bear this out.

In popular piety the *šôfār* was increasingly important as a
potent symbol of redemption, as 'a summons to man to repent
and to God to be merciful'.⁵¹ This is expressed in, for example,
the important daily Prayer of Eighteen Petitions, which
already in its early recension includes the request, 'Sound the
Great *Šôfār* for our freedom'.⁵² Other ancient prayers for
redemption which were accompanied by the blowing of the
šôfār include the *Hosha'na* ('O save us!'; cf. Mk 11.9f.) recited
e.g. during the feast of Tabernacles (*m. Suk.* 4.5) and the
'Anenu ('Answer us!') used in connection with public fast days
(*m. Taan.* 2.3, 5; *b. Taan.* 14a, 15b).⁵³

It was the festival of New Year (*Rosh hash-Shanah*),
however, which together with the Day of Atonement
constituted the most important liturgical occasion for blowing
the *šôfār*; the instrument was used here in conjunction with

50. A similar point is made by Goodenough, *Jewish Symbols*, IV,
pp. 171, 172.
51. Goodenough, *Jewish Symbols*, IV, p. 175.
52. *Shemoneh Esreh* 10 (*t^eqa' b^ešôfār gādôl l^eherûtēnû*); this is
followed by a prayer for the gathering of the exiles—note the apparent
allusion to Isa. 27.13. Cf. *Sifre Num.* 76.2 (ed. Horovitz, p. 71); *Tg. Ps.-
J.* Lev. 25.9 (cited earlier); and the *Musaf* Liturgy for New Year (*The
Authorised Daily Prayer Book of the United Hebrew Congregations of
the British Commonwealth of Nations* (trans. S. Singer; 2nd edn;
London: Eyre & Spottiswoode, 1962), p. 344.
53. See Joseph Heinemann, *Prayer in the Talmud: Forms and
Patterns* (Studia Judaica, 9; Berlin/New York: de Gruyter, 1977), pp.
109, 152 (139ff.).

Scripture verses relating to God's kingship, remembrance before God, and *šôfārôt* (hope for the redemption to be ushered in by the *šôfār*).[54] The blowing of the *šôfār* was believed to change God's heart from justice to compassion,[55] all the more so because, being made of a ram's horn, it was to remind him of the merits of the *Aqedah*, the binding of Isaac by his father Abraham.[56] As for the bent *shape* of the ram's horn, it came to express the need for repentance—a quality already called for in *šôfār* texts of the Old Testament (cf. n. 25 above), and increasingly associated also with the New Year.[57] There are also the beneficial magical associations of the *šôfār*, cited earlier.[58] Here, however, we have already entered well into the symbolism of the later Talmudic era. Some of these ideas have recognizable roots in the Second Temple period as examined earlier, while others appear to be later accretions.

---

54. E.g. *b. R.H.* 32a-b; *m. R.H.* 4.5; *m. Taan.* 2.3. This triad may already have been in use in the days of the Second Temple; see e.g. Heinemann, *Prayer*, pp. 94-97 n. 26. In the modern synagogue service the *šôfār* is sounded every day during the penitential month of Elul which precedes the New Year. Cf. Albert L. Lewis, 'Shofar', *EJ*, XIV, pp. 1444f.

55. E.g. *Lev. R.* 29.3 on Lev. 23.24; *Midr. Pss.* 47.2; cf. Finesinger, 'Shofar', pp. 215f.

56. Just as the entangled horns of a ram delivered Isaac, so Israel will be saved when the Lord blows the great ram's horn (Zech. 9.14; etc.); see *y. Taan.* 2.4 (65d8ff.); *b. R.H.* 16a; *Gen. R.* 56.9; also Goodenough, *Jewish Symbols*, IV, pp. 172ff.; Finesinger, 'Shofar', pp. 216-18, and the parallels cited in Strack–Billerbeck, I, p. 959.

57. E.g. *b. R.H.* 26b; cf. *Lev. R.* 29.6.

58. See above; and cf. more fully Finesinger, 'Shofar', pp. 201, 215, 219-27. In Babylonia the *šôfār* was also sounded, for a time at least, to announce the death of a person (e.g. *b. M.Q.* 27b); but Finesinger, 'Shofar', pp. 223f., and Goodenough, *Jewish Symbols*, IV, pp. 169f. (who cites the frequent depictions of the ram's horn on tombstones, above all in the diaspora) suspect that its function in these cases may be less that of announcing a death than of scaring away the evil spirits. The practice was in any case widespread in antiquity; see e.g. Johannes Quasten, *Music and Worship in Pagan and Christian Antiquity* (trans. B. Ramsey; Washington, DC: National Association of Pastaral Musicians, 1983), pp. 151-53.

The later Amoraic practice of sounding the *shôfār* for excommunication (cf. the references in Strack–Billerbeck, IV, pp. 302f. and Reik, 'Schofar', pp. 188f.) may also have magical connotations.

Before moving on to Christian trumpet symbolism, we should briefly consider one or two interesting perspectives to be gained from the symbolic use of trumpets in Jewish visual arts.

6. *Jewish Visual Arts*

Probably because of the earlier well-known reservations about realistic images, Palestinian Jewish artistic representations of trumpets do not for the most part predate the fourth century.[59] One exception consists in coins from the Bar Kokhba revolt (AD 132–135) which appear to show a pair of *ḥᵃṣōṣᵉrôt* of the kind used in the Temple.[60] But since the use of the priestly trumpet appears to have disappeared with the destruction of the Temple, the Bar Kokhba coins may in fact show our first and *only* Jewish representation of this instrument.[61]

The trumpets in ancient Jewish art, then, are almost exclusively ram's horns. Virtually always, too, the *šôfār* appears not by itself but in conjunction with other cult objects, most typically flanking a menorah with a *lûlāb* and/or *'etrôg* or incense shovel on the other side. Such representations are found on media ranging from glasses, oil lamps and amulets to tombstones and synagogue floor mosaics.[62] The actual meaning of the trumpet in a given depiction is of course difficult to determine; indeed in most cases we must rely on literary sources to help fill in the presuppositions which for Jews of the time would have brought these symbols to life. Probably many

59. Cf., perhaps, *m. A.Z.* 3.1-4 and the Amoraic debate reflected in *y. A.Z.* 3.3, 42d34f. (R. Yoḥanan).

60. Illustration in Goodenough, *Jewish Symbols*, III, fig. 696.

61. Carl H. Kraeling, however, identifies the four trumpets on Panel WB2 of the synagogue at Dura Europos as *ḥᵃṣōṣᵉrôt* (*The Synagogue* [The Excavations at Dura Europos: Final Report, 8.1; New York: Ktav, 1979], p. 129 and pl. LX). The priestly trumpets do of course also appear on the triumphal Arch of Titus in Rome.

62. See the objects discussed and listed in Goodenough, *Jewish Symbols*, IV, pp. 168f. and nn. (illustrations); p. 190 and n. 161. According to Goodenough, the earliest representation of a *šôfār* is from a capital in the synagogue of Capernaum (*ibid.*, p. 168; vol. III, fig. 478). Relevant floor mosaics include those at Beth Shean, Beth Alpha, Maon, Jericho, etc.

of the meanings we encountered above could qualify: eschatological redemption, the call to repentance, the *Aqedah*, etc. The
problem of course, is that of controls. On this issue, Goodenough writes:

> To suppose that all of this significance, or much of it, was con-
> sciously behind each representation of a shofar on a tombstone
> is as absurd as to suppose that the full scope of the mystical
> meaning of the cross is in the mind of every Catholic who buries
> his father under a cross.[63]

Nevertheless, it is equally absurd to suppose that the *šôfār* was
represented thoughtlessly, without at least some desire to give
expression to a familiar complex of ideas. As Goodenough goes
on to say, 'But the cross on the grave refers to that range of
symbolic values to some extent in every case'. It is thus in most
cases plausible, if perhaps rarely demonstrable, that the
prevalence of artistic representations of the *šôfār* in highly
symbolic (and often public!) settings reflects the widespread
popularity of the same trumpet imagery which we earlier discerned in literary sources.

This argument is strengthened wherever such imagery
appears in the context of religious synagogue inscriptions or in
conjunction with other clearly recognizable symbols. Examples include the inscription *šālôm 'al yiśrā'ēl* at Jericho as well
as the Binding of Isaac at Beth Alpha, but also perhaps the
commonplace synagogal emblem of a menorah flanked by a
šôfār and another sacred symbol (see above).[64] In this regard,
Goodenough also rightly stresses the significance of the *šôfār*
on tombstones:

> We may assume that the shofar meant for all Jews of the time
> hope of a life to come, or it would not have been put on tomb-
> stones. ... The people buried with the shofar on their graves
> were Jews who had blown the shofar and hoped for life in the
> other world through the shofar: 'Eventually they will be
> redeemed by the ram's horn'.[65]

---

63. Goodenough, *Jewish Symbols*, IV, p. 189.
64. Goodenough, *Jewish Symbols*, IV, pp. 168f. and nn. 13-20, cites
nineteen instances of the latter; note also his observations on the
Aqedah at Dura (*ibid.*, p. 189)
65. Goodenough, *Jewish Symbols*, IV, pp. 193f.

We may conclude, then, that at least from the third or fourth century, the trumpet entered Jewish visual arts as a popular expression of some of the same religious aspirations which the same symbol denoted in literary sources.

2. *The Trumpet as a Symbol in the New Testament and Early Christianity*

A quick glance over the remaining pages of this essay will show that there is rather less to be said about trumpet symbolism in early Christianity. This is due to the nature of the material, but as such it already indicates one of the main conclusions of this study, namely the relative and indeed, outside the New Testament, striking scarcity of relevant passages on trumpets. We shall have more to say about this in due course.

A. *New Testament*

Of the two words for 'trumpet' used somewhat indiscriminately in the LXX, the New Testament retains only *salpinx* (and cognate forms). This word is used eleven times, over half of which are in the book of Revelation. These instances can be quickly and easily categorized, since they fall into familiar categories.

Secular usage is present in Paul's illustration of the war trumpet in 1 Cor. 14.8: just as the trumpet's call to arms must be clear and unmistakable, so the manifestation of charismatic gifts in the church must not dull or diminish the clarity of the gospel proclamation. Another example of secular symbolism may be the trumpeters (*salpistai*) of Babel in Rev. 18.22, who, together with other musicians, craftsmen and merchants, represent the city's glory which will be destroyed. The mention of the trumpet in Heb. 12.19 is more clearly theological, but it merely reflects the sense of awe and wonder perceived in the account of Exodus 19, without further development of the original symbolism.[66]

---

66. Friedrich ('*salpinx*', p. 86) indeed may be right to see this reference as *less* symbolic, inasmuch as there appears to be no connection with the voice of God.

A more difficult instance is Mt. 6.2: 'When you engage in an act of charity, therefore, do not sound a trumpet (*mē salpisēs*) before you as the hypocrites do in the synagogues and streets in order to be praised by men'. The figurative meaning of the trumpet here is fairly clear: Jesus criticizes the public display of one's acts of charity for the sake of human recognition. However, the available sources do not permit us to determine whether this figure of speech also had a real *Sitz im Leben* in first-century Palestine.[67] It is best to assume, therefore, that the 'trumpeting' in this case is indeed figurative and perhaps symbolic, but not perhaps in a theologically significant sense.

Much more common and familiar is the New Testament's eschatological use of the trumpet. As in Isa. 27.13 and various Jewish sources we discussed (see above, §1.B.2.b), the great trumpet will sound when at the last the chosen people are gathered (by angels) from the four corners of the earth (Mt. 24.31). Similarly, the exalted Christ will, at the sound of the 'last' trumpet (1 Cor. 15.52), at the 'voice of the archangel' and 'the trumpet of God' (1 Thess. 4.16), raise the dead and transform the living, gathering them to meet him 'in the air' (1 Thess. 4.16f.). The person who blows the trumpet is thus probably God himself or the archangel, as in some of the Jewish texts we discussed; indeed there is little here that is not compatible with a first-century Jewish background.

The usage of the book of Revelation is somewhat distinct. As in the *Apocalypse of Zephaniah* (see §1.B.2.b above), angelic trumpets function repeatedly as a literary device, to stress and punctuate the scenes of the celestial drama. At the outset of his account, and again at the beginning of his vision of the open heaven, John of Patmos compares the voice of his heavenly interlocutor to that of a trumpet (Rev. 1.10; 4.1)—perhaps to allude to the power of the voice of God.[68]

---

67. Friedrich (*'salpinx'*, p. 85) surmises a possible connection with the liturgical use of the *šôfār* on public fast days; but this seems less than plausible. Evidence is lacking, too, for his additional inference (p. 86) of a synagogal practice of sounding the ram's horn when announcing large donations, to encourage others and bring the donor to remembrance before God.
68. Cf. Exod. 19.16ff. and see Friedrich, *'salpinx'*, p. 87.

Instead of the more usual single trumpet to announce the final judgment, Revelation 8–11 introduces the seven angels with seven trumpets who implement the ascending stages of the judgment over the cosmos and the nations of the earth.[69] As the drama unfolds, the divine purpose is still the call to repentance (9.20f.)—another familiar association of the sound of the *šôfār*. But while that call is not heeded, the heavenly course of events continues irrevocably to the 'completion of the mystery of God' (Rev. 10.7), viz. the fulfilment of his ultimate redemptive purposes when 'the kingdoms of this world have become the kingdoms of our Lord and of his Messiah; and he will rule forever and ever' (11.15).

The positive evidence of the New Testament use of trumpet symbolism has proved to be fairly unsurprising; all the major themes have been encountered before. There is, however, an important point to be made *e silentio*: with the exception of Rev. 18.22 (which is negative in tone), the New Testament writers never describe the *šôfār* as a real instrument for contemporary Christian use. The symbolic reference is retained and affirmed, albeit in a somewhat narrower eschatological frame. But the object itself, whether by design or by accident, no longer has an identifiable *Sitz im Leben* in the experience of the community.

B. *The Second and Third Centuries*
This New Testament evidence, together with the increasingly Gentile cultural background of the early church, had far-reaching implications for the Christian reception of trumpet symbolism.

Like the flute and several other musical instruments, the trumpet—albeit otherwise a prominent instrument of war—had an established place in the pagan cults.[70] One of the conscious struggles in the development of early Christian music, therefore, was the definition of a distinctive style of liturgy which would be clearly dissociated from idolatrous pagan rites. Contemporary philosophical criticism of religion, on the other hand, had found expression in the rejection of sacrifices

69. See Rev. 8.2, 6, 7, 8, 10, 12, 13; 9.1, 13, 14; 10.7; 11.15.
70. See Quasten, *Music and Worship*, pp. 1-50, esp. 6-8, 17, 36.

and other external aspects of the popular religions, including their use of liturgical, and especially instrumental, music. This view, first proposed by Plato and subsequently espoused by several Greek philosophers as well as by Philo of Alexandria for example, and many of the early Fathers, replaced such external forms with the inward disposition of 'spiritual worship' (*logikē thusia*).[71] This notion also came to be quite formative for the early Christian attitudes to music—partly because of the basic incompatibility between the purposes of pagan liturgical music and the Christian worship of God, and partly because it provided a convenient apologetic rationale for Christianity's distinction from the pagan cults.[72] In particular, early Christian literature (and, by implication, art) agrees in large part with the philosophers' rejection of musical instruments in worship. This subject has been amply discussed by others and is too vast to be addressed here; two brief illustrations shall suffice. In describing Christian as opposed to pagan worship, the author of the eighth book of the *Sibylline Oracles* writes:

> They do not pour blood on altars in libations of sacrifices. No drum sounds, no cymbal, no flute of many holes, which has a sound that damages the heart, no pipe, which bears an imitation of the crooked serpent, no savage-sounding trumpet, herald of wars...[73]

Clement of Alexandria writes in his *Paedagogus*, 'Leave the syrinx to the shepherds and the flute to superstitious devotees

---

71. See Quasten, *Music and Worship*, pp. 51-57, quoting numerous references.

72. Cf. Quasten, *Music and Worship*, pp. 60-62; O. Casel, 'Die *logikē thusia* der antiken Mystik in christlich-liturgischer Umdeutung', *Jahrbuch für Liturgiewissenschaft* 4 (1924), pp. 37ff., as cited in Quasten, *Music and Worship*, p. 99 n. 1; Gerda Laube-Przygodda, *Das alttestamentliche und neutestamentliche musikalische Gotteslob in der Rezeption durch die christlichen Autoren des 2. bis 11. Jahrhunderts* (Kölner Beiträge zur Musikforschung, 104; Regensburg: Bosse, 1980), pp. 267-82.

73. *Sib. Or.* 8.113-117; cf. Quasten, *Music and Worship*, pp. 59-120, esp. 59-62, 72-75.

who rush to serve their idols. We completely forbid the use of these instruments at our temperate banquet.'[74]

For present purposes, however, we must turn our attention to the symbolic use of trumpets.

Initially, we find a number of familiar uses, including re-affirmations of the eschatological trumpet motif in the context of an apocalyptic tradition being kept alive. Thus the *Didache* speaks of the three true signs of the end: the *parousia*, the sound of the trumpet, and the resurrection of the saints (16.6). The final trumpet of judgment, redemption and resurrection occurs also for example, in the Christian additions to *4 Ezra*, in the *Apocalypse of John*, and in the previously cited eighth book of the *Sibylline Oracles*;[75] it is frequently discussed, too, in the relevant Patristic commentaries. MS Moscow of the *Martyrdom of Polycarp* relates that when Irenaeus was in Rome, he heard a voice 'like a trumpet' which informed him that Polycarp had at that hour died as a martyr.[76]

Although the early fathers did not doubt that the ancient Israelites used musical instruments, that was not taken as an example for the Christian church. In part, this may be because the very Jewishness of the trumpet as a symbol (attested by its high public visibility in synagogues and on tombstones) might be grounds enough to downplay it at a time

74. *Paed.* 2.4. The opposition to instrumental (but not of course choral) music continued for a long time. The Greek church apparently *never* allowed it, while even Thomas Aquinas could still write in AD 1250, 'Sed instrumenta musica, sicut citharas et psalteria, non assumit Ecclesia in divinas laudes, ne videatur judaizare' (*Summa Theologica*, 11/2, 91.2; cf. Joseph Bingham, *Origines Ecclesiasticae; Or the Antiquities of the Christian Church*, II [London: Straker, 1840], p. 483 n. [n]).

75. *4 Ezra* 1.29; *Gk. Apoc. Ezra* 4.36; *Questions of Ezra* B 11; *Apoc. John* 1.9; *Sib. Or.* 8.239. It is, incidentally, worth noting the frequent occurrence of this motif in the Koran: Suras 6.74; 18.100; 20.102; 23.101; 27.87; 36.50; 39.68; 69.13ff.; 74.8; 78.18ff.; 79.6ff. In the *Gospel of Bartholomew* 4.12, oddly, the archangel Michael sounds his trumpet not to raise the dead but to summon the imprisoned Beliar.

76. *Mart. Pol.* 22.4 (LCL, II, p. 344).

when the church clearly felt the need to define its own distinct identity over against Judaism, too.[77]

Trumpets, and music in general, were very much seen as having played a role among God's ancient people in the past, and as playing their important part in the heavenly and future uses in the kingdom.[78] This, together with the increasing influence of the Alexandrian school of interpretation, meant that Old Testament texts encouraging the instrumental praise of God in the present were almost invariably interpreted allegorically—i.e. most often ethically.[79] Such is the case above all for the Patristic exegesis of the Psalms.

Clement of Alexandria considers that the praise 'with the sound of the trumpet' (Ps. 150.4) anticipates the trumpet of the resurrection.[80] Origen, in commenting on Ps. 81.4 (80.4 LXX), writes that just as the Israelites were once commanded to sound the trumpet on the new moon, so now the 'new people' use the trumpet of the gospel (*tē euangelikē chrōmenos salpingi*) whose sound has gone out into all the earth.[81] He offers a similar interpretation on Ps. 98(97).5f., where Origen adduces 1 Sam. 2.10 LXX to show that *elatē salpinx* (the *hªṣōṣªrâ*) stands for teaching and reproof, while *keratinē salpinx* (the *šôfār*) convicts the opponents of the truth and is a symbol of victory.[82] According to several of the Fathers, Ps. 47.5 ('God has gone up with a shout, the Lord with the sound of a trumpet', 46.6 LXX) refers to the Ascension: for when Christ

77. Dr W. Horbury has kindly drawn my attention to Chrysostom's polemic against going to see the trumpeting of the synagogue in *Contra Iudaeos* 1.5; 4.7.

78. Cf. Laube-Przygodda, *Gotteslob*, pp. 225f. (but contrast Chrysostom, who foresees no use of musical instruments in the resurrection: *Commentary on 1 Timothy* [PG 62.576]).

79. Laube-Przygodda, *Gotteslob*, pp. 226f., 268-70.

80. *Paed.* 2.4; cf. Origen, *Selecta in Psalmos* (PG 12.1684).

81. Origen, *Fragmenta in Psalmos* 80.4 (PG 12.1054). On the same passage cf. further his *Selecta in Ezechielem* (PG 13.793).

82. *Fragmenta in Psalmos* 97.5, 6 (PG 12.1054); for a comparable use of the silver *elatē salpinx* see *Selecta in Ezechielem* (PG 13.793). Elsewhere the trumpet symbolizes the sound of rejoicing (*Selecta in Psalmos, MPG* 12.1437). In Ps. 150.4 the *salpinx* of praise is said to represent the eschatological trumpet, or else 'the contemplative mind which has believed the spiritual teaching' (*Selecta in Psalmos* [PG 12.1684]).

ascended, two angels called to the apostles 'like a trumpet'.[83] For Augustine, the trumpet and other musical instruments of Ps. 150 represented the harmony of Christian lives lived in praise of God;[84] such musical worship of God is rendered with one's voice, life, and deeds.[85]

The Fathers also found allegorical trumpets in other parts of the Bible. Legal passages could be interpreted in a similar fashion: Jerome likens the silver trumpet of Num. 10.4 to the archangel's eschatological trumpet of judgment.[86] Even the seven trumpets of the Apocalypse, although in themselves symbolic and therefore often interpreted literally, could sometimes be subjected to allegorization: thus Ambrose saw the seven trumpets as denoting seven progressive stages of the proclamation of God's word: the seven angels correspondingly represented the pre-Mosaic preachers, Moses and the teachers of the Law, the prophets, Christ and the Apostles, the defenders of the church's orthodox faith, the Christian martyrs, and the preachers of the word of God.[87]

The trumpet of Christ is at times explicitly contrasted with the pagan trumpet, the invention of which was popularly ascribed to the Etruscans.[88] Thus Clement of Alexandria affirmed that Christ's trumpet is not of war but of peace, since it is the trumpet of his gospel.[89] Similarly, Christians no longer use the old psaltery, trumpet, and other instruments, but honour God with the Word of peace alone (*Paed.* 2.4). Tertul-

---

83. Commentaries by Jerome, *PL* 26.963; and Cassiodorus, *PL* 70.334; cf. possibly Justin, *Dial.* 37. See also Reinhold Hammerstein, *Die Musik der Engel: Untersuchungen zur Musikanschauung des Mittelalters* (Berne/Munich: Francke, 1962, p. 206).

84. Augustine, *Enarrationes in Psalmos* (Ps. 150) [*PL* 37.1965f.].

85. 'Cum laudatis Deum, toti laudate; cantet vox, cantet vita, cantent facta' (*Enarrationes in Psalmos* [Ps. 148] [*PL* 37.1938]); 'sic cantant canticum novum, sic dicant Alleluia, corde, ore, vita' (*ibid.* [Ps. 140] [*PL* 37.1960]); quoted in Laube-Przygodda, *Gotteslob*, p. 257 n. 5.

86. Jerome, *Epistle* 119 (*PL* 22.977).

87. Ambrose, *Expositio in Apocalypsin* (*PL* 17.933ff.). Cf. Laube-Przygodda, *Gotteslob*, p. 236, who also (p. 241) compares the exposition of Bede.

88. Tatian, *Oratio ad Graecos* 1; Clement of Alexandria, *Paed.* 2.4; *Stromata* 1.16; and cf. the references cited in Friedrich, '*salpinx*', p. 73.

89. *Protrepticus* 11.116.

lian asserted that it was unfitting that the trumpeter should disturb a deceased Christian (on this cf. above, n. 58) who expects to be raised by the angelic trumpet.[90] God does not come with war cries and trumpets, but in tranquillity.[91]

Exceptions to this consistent Christian transformation of the trumpet from a symbol into pure allegory are few indeed; the only one I have come across is the suggestion in the *Rule of Pachomius* and in John Climacus that trumpets preceded the invention of bells as the call to worship in some Oriental monastic traditions.[92] In explanation of this phenomenon, Hans Kosmala has suggested the (unlikely?) possibility of Essene influence.[93]

Although the New Testament evidence, read by itself, does not appear to envisage an ongoing Christian use of trumpets, the book of Revelation does describe the present-day use of trumpets in heaven—and of course the 'last trumpet' itself is of heavenly origin. This suggested to the early church that instrumental music, although unsuitable for earthly worship because of its idolatrous connotations in the culturally dominant paganism, was nevertheless legitimately produced in heaven for the glory of God; and the saints could expect to participate in this music in the future.

This trend in early Christian literature is fully borne out by the evidence of early Christian art. While musical instruments are generally avoided in the early period,[94] the earliest

90. Tertullian, *De corona* 11, as quoted in Quasten, *Music and Worship*, p. 184 n. 100.

91. *Pseudo-Clementine Homilies* 2.44.

92. *Rule of Pachomius* 3; John Climacus, *Scala paradisi* 19 (*pneumatikē salpinx*), as cited in Bingham, *Origines*, II, p. 488; Wetzer and Welte's *Kirchenlexikon*, V (Freiburg: Herder, 1888), 697f. Cf. the use of *salpinx* and *salpizō* for the call to worship in Theodorus Studita (d. 826), *Iambi* 10 (*PG* 99.1784B); *Poenae* 1.99 (*PG* 99.1745D).

93. Hans Kosmala, *Hebräer, Essener, Christen* (Studia Post-Biblica, 1; Leiden: Brill, 1959), p. 361. He does not, however, regard this Essene trumpet blast primarily as a call to worship but rather as an announcement that God is ready to act, signifying as it were the 'trumpet of revelation' (pp. 355-59).

94. Note, however, the occasional representations of Orpheus-Christ with a syrinx (panpipe), e.g. in the third-century Domitilla Catacombs at Rome (see Pierre du Bourguet, *Early Christian Art* [trans. T. Burton; New York: Reynal/Morrow, 1971], p. 53) or in the early fourth-

representations of trumpets relate invariably to the Israelite past or the heavenly future.[95] Thus a mosaic in the Basilica of Santa Maria Maggiore (constructed by Sextus III in 432–440) shows the trumpets used in the conquest of Jericho,[96] while the mosaic of San Michele in Affricisco at Ravenna (first half of 6th century) introduces the genre of 'tuba angels'[97] who represent the voice of God or of the angels at the coming judgment, or who are simply participants in the heavenly liturgy.[98]

3. *Conclusion*

The *šôfār* was a widespread, popular symbol of revelation, redemption and repentance in Jewish literature and art of the Second Temple and Rabbinic periods. Its priestly complement, the *ḥ*ᵃ*ṣōṣ*ᵉ*râ*, which had apparently occupied an even more significant place in Temple worship and ritual, virtually disappeared both as a ritual instrument and as a significant symbol after the year 70.

Early Christian trumpet symbolism, by contrast, is characterized by the complete *lack* of any ongoing liturgical function for the instrument. While the New Testament's silence on the use of trumpets might be merely accidental, Patristic thought on the matter, prodded by apologetic concerns and the con-

century mosaic pavement in the Cathedral of Bishop Theodore at Aquileia (illus. in André Grabar, *Early Christian Art* [trans. S. Gilbert and J. Emmons; New York: Odyssey, 1968], fig. 27).

95. But cf. the apparent image of a funerary trumpeter in the Catacomb of St Lucy at Syracuse; see Quasten, *Music and Worship*, 184 n. 100. Note further that trumpets must be carefully distinguished from representations of fruit horns or cornucopias; see e.g. du Bourguet, *Early Christian Art*, p. 125 (floral image from the Mausoleum of Santa Costanze in Rome, first half of 4th century); also Ludwig Budde, *Antike Mosaiken in Kilikien* (Beiträge zur Kunst des christlichen Ostens, 5/1; Recklingshausen: Bonger, 1969), fig. 94 (and p. 43).

96. Carlo Cecchelli, *I Mosaici della Basilica di S. Maria Maggiore* (Turin: Ilte, 1956), p. 181 and pl. 42.

97. Engelbert Kirschbaum (ed.), *Lexikon der christlichen Ikonographie*, IV (Rome: Herder, 1972), p. 607 (*tuba* is the Vulgate's equivalent of *salpinx* and *keratinē*).

98. Hammerstein, *Musik*, p. 205.

temporary philosophical critique of pagan ritual, developed into a considered opposition to all instrumental music. The remaining trumpet symbolism in the early Fathers, therefore, tends to be reduced to pure allegory, so that the respective Biblical passages come to mean anything *but* real trumpets. Instrumental music now belongs to the Old Testament past, but also to the worship of heaven and thus to the future. Thus, aside from their *ad hoc*, metaphorical use to denote the preaching of the gospel or the Christian life of worship, trumpets retain their original symbolic force in regard to only one area: the hope of the resurrection and the world to come.

THE DESOLATE HOUSE AND THE NEW KINGDOM OF
JERUSALEM: JEWISH ORACLES OF EZRA IN 2 ESDRAS 1–2

J.C. O'Neill

We know that Jesus was not the only one who warned his people that the Second Temple would be destroyed like the First unless they repented. No one would be more pleased than Ernst Bammel if we could discover an actual Jewish document from the time containing such a prophecy which we could put alongside the oracles recorded in the Gospels, 1 Thessalonians and Josephus. This is an attempt, made in his honour, to show that the first two chapters of the book known in the English Apocrypha as 2 Esdras (*5 Ezra* in Hennecke) is not a Jewish-Christian writing at all, as the scholars (with the honourable exception of Riessler and Kraft) assume, but a genuine Jewish collection of oracles, preserved by a community that had not yet heard of Jesus of Nazareth.

Prima facie, 2 Esdras 1–2 is a non-Christian Jewish writing for the simple reason that the name of Jesus does not occur. I know of no other ancient writing that lacks the name of Jesus which is Christian. By 'Christian' I mean containing oracles delivered by people who confessed Jesus Christ as Lord; of course most of the non-Christian Jewish writings we have, apart from the Dead Sea Scrolls, are copies made by Christian scribes, and in that secondary sense Christian. My critics will immediately reply that we have plenty of Christian documents (in the primary sense) lacking the name of Jesus, because we have plenty of documents that were written by Christians purporting to be Jewish seers or scribes from long ago: the *Testaments of the Twelve Patriarchs*, the Christian *Sibylline Oracles* and the *Ascension of Isaiah*, not to mention the voluminous writings ascribed to the *Shepherd of Hermas*.

If I am to make a case for 2 Esdras 1–2 I will have to do better than that.

My case is that 2 Esdras 1–2 contains at least one passage that no Christian, whether Jewish Christian or Gentile Christian, could have written; and that 2 Esdras 1–2 contains no passage that a Jew could not have written. The worst 2 Esdras 1–2 contains are some Christian scribal contaminations of the original Jewish text.

First, a passage no Christian could have written. In 1.30 we read, *ita uos collegi ut gallina pullos suos sub alas suas*, words strikingly similar to Jesus' lament over Jerusalem in Mt. 23.37 and Lk. 13.34. It is very unlikely that a Christian writer would ascribe to the Lord Almighty words referring to God's care of his people before their rebellion, knowing that Jesus had employed them at the time when God finally required of his people the blood of the prophets (2 Esd. 1.32; cf. Lk. 11.51; cf. Mt. 23.36).

That is an easy case, but it is only one, and against it scholars set a host of passages they allege no Jew who did not know of Jesus could possibly have written.

Secondly, then, passages where it is claimed the oracles must be Christian.

We can begin by setting aside a host of New Testament 'allusions'. Here is a list, but in none of these is it likely that the New Testament was the source since the phrases are common in Jewish literature apart from the New Testament.

1.26 *et pedes uestri inpigri sunt ad committenda homicidia*: Rom. 3.15 = LXX.

1.28; 2.31 *dominus omnipotens*: 2 Cor. 6.18. Oesterley thinks, 'This title of God stamps the passage as Christian', but he overlooks Isa. 5.7 as rendered by Philo, *De somniis* 2.172.

1.29 *ut essetis mihi in populum, et ego uobis in deum*: Heb. 8.10 = LXX.

1.32 *ego misi pueros meos prophetas ad uos, quos acceptos interfecistis et laniastis corpora illorum*: Mt. 23.37; Lk. 13.34.

1.32 (text of CM) *corpora apostolorum*: cf. 1.37 below.

1.33 *domus uestra deserta est*: Mt. 23.38; Lk. 13.35.

1.37 (text of C) *testantur apostoli populum uenientem cum laetitia*: Lk. 11.49 διὰ τοῦτο καὶ ἡ σοφία τοῦ θεοῦ εἶπεν, ἀποστελῶ εἰς αὐτοὺς προφήτας καὶ ἀποστόλους.

2.2 *mater, quae eos generauit, dicit illis: ite, filii, quia ego uidua sum et derelicta*: Gal. 4.26-27.

2.9 (text of CM) *quorum terra descendit usque ad infernum*: Mt. 11.23.

2.11 *dabo eis tabernacula aeterna*: Lk. 16.9 ἵνα...δέξωνται ὑμᾶς εἰς τὰς αἰωνίους σκηνάς.

2.12 *lignum uitae*: Rev. 2.7; 22.2, 14.

2.13 *petite et accipietis*: Jn 16.24; cf. Mt. 7.7; Lk. 11.9.

2.13 *iam paratum est uobis regnum*: Mt. 25.34.

2.13 *uigilate*: Mt. 24.42; 25.13; Mk 13.35, 37.

2.16 *et resuscitabo mortuos de locis suis et de monumentis educam illos*: 1 Cor. 15.52; cf. Mt. 27.53.

2.16 *quoniam cognoui nomen meum in illis*: Rev. 3.12; 14.1; 22.4.

2.18 *et paraui tibi arbores XII grauatas uariis fructibus*: Rev. 22.2.

2.20 *uiduam iustifica, pupillo iudica ...orfanum tuere*: Jas 1.27.

2.23 *et dabo tibi primam sessionem in resurrectione mea*: Mt. 20.21; Mk 10.37.

2.25 *nutrix bona, nutri filios tuos*: cf. 1 Cor. 4.15; Gal. 4.19.

2.26 *seruos quos tibi dedi, nemo ex eis interiet, ego enim eos requiram de numero tuo*: Jn 6.39; 10.28, 29; 17.12; 18.9.

2.31 *filios tuos dormientes memorare, quoniam ego eos educam de latibulis terrae et misericordiam cum illis faciam, quoniam misericors sum, dicit dominus omnipotens*: Rev. 20.13.

2.34 *requiem aeternitatis*: Mt. 11.29.

2.35 *quia lux perpetua lucebit uobis per aeternitatem temporis*: Rev. 21.23; 22.5.

2.36 *fugite umbram saeculi huius*: 1 Cor. 7.31 τὸ σχῆμα τοῦ κόσμου τούτου; Col. 2.17; Heb. 8.5; 10.1.

2.36 *accipite iocunditatem gloriae uestrae; ego testor palam saluatorem meum*: Tit. 2.13.

2.37 *gratias agentes ei qui uos ad caelestia regna uocauit*: 1 Thess. 2.12.

2.38 *numerum signatorum*: Rev. 7.3, 4.

2.38 *in conuiuio domini*: Mt. 26.29; Mk 14.25; Lk. 22.16; 1 Cor. 11.20; Rev. 19.9.

2.39 *splendidas tunicas a domino acceperunt*: Rev. 3.4, 5; 6.11; 7.9, 13, 14.

2.40 *recipe ...numerum tuum et conclude candidatos tuos*: cf. 2.38.

2.40 *Sion*: Heb. 12.22.

2.41 *filiorum tuorum...plenus est numerus*: Rev. 6.11.

2.41 *ut sanctificetur populus tuus, qui uocatus est ab initio*: Rom. 8.29, 30; Eph. 1.4.

2.42 *ego Ezra uidi*: Rev. 1.9; 4.1.

2.42 *uidi turbam magnam, quam numerare non potui*: Rev. 7.9.

2.44 *tunc interrogaui angelum et dixi: qui sunt hi, domine?*: Rev. 7.13, 14.

None of these 'allusions' compels us to think that the author or authors of the oracles in 2 Esdras 1–2 knew and used the New Testament. Why, then, do the scholars say with one voice that the little book is plainly Christian? The answer is, Because 2 Esdras 1–2 is a prophecy about how God has rejected his people Israel and given the kingdom of Jerusalem to the Gentiles. The Mother in 2.15 is the church.

I have to concede that the text, as it stands, undoubtedly gives that overall impression. Only the concluding words of the collection, *tunc dixit mihi angelus: uade, adnuntia populo meo, qualia et quanta mirabilia domini dei uidisti*, make us pause. Otherwise, in 1.24, 31, 35, 37; 2.5-7, 10-11, 33-34, we seem to have clear evidence that the writer or writers saw Israel from a perspective that could only be the perspective of a Jewish Christian. In every one of these places, however, there is evidence that scribes have slightly corrupted a text that originally told a different tale. Let us take these passages in turn. I print the text of S (*Codex Sangermanensis*) from France in the left-hand column, and the text of C (*Codex Complutensis*) from Spain in the right-hand. Variants are from A (*Codex Ambianensis*), M (*Codex Mazarinaeus*) and L (*Codex Legionensis*).

1.24

S	C
quid tibi faciam, Iacob?	*quid tibi faciam Jacob,*
noluisti me obaudire, Iuda.	*noluit obaudire me Iuda.*
transferam me	*transferam me*
ad alias gentes	*ad gentem alteram*
et dabo eis nomen meum,	*et dabo illi nomen meum*
ut custodiant	*et custodientes custodient*
legitima mea.	*legitima mea*

The singular of C, *ad gentem alteram*, may well be right and the plural of S a change by a Christian scribe to refer to the Gentiles (cf. Kraft, pp. 162-65). The *gens altera* is probably the foolish nation of Deut. 32.21. In the light of what follows in 1.28, 29, it is clear that 1.24 is still an appeal to Israel.

1.31

S	C
dies enim festos uestros	*dies festos*
et neomenias	*et neomenias,*
	sabbata
et circumcisiones carnis	*et circumcisiones*
repudiaui.	*non mandabi uobis.*

The text of C may well be the original, being an allusion to Jer. 7.22, but even the text of S is no more harsh a judgment than many an Old Testament prophet had directed against Israel without thereby implying that God had rejected it absolutely.

1.35

S	C
tradam domus uestras	*tradam domos uestras*
populo uenienti	*populo uenienti a longe.*
qui me non audientes	*et qui te non noberunt*
credunt;	*credent tibi,*
quibus signa	*et quibus signa*
non ostendi,	*non hostendo*
facient quae praecepi	*facient quae dixi*

The *me* in *qui me non audientes* of S is perhaps a Christian scribe's insertion of a reference to Jesus. The scribe meant that the church which had not heard Jesus during his ministry obeyed, while the Jews who had heard his words in the flesh did not. The speaker is more likely to be God. Could the original text have referred to Ezra, *te* in C? The people would be the generation living long after the time of the prophets (1.36), who yet obey their teaching. Of course *te* is a difficult reading, because it is easy to forget that God's oracle for the people was originally spoken to a prophet, who could be addressed as 'thee' in an oracle. In the Spanish text the oracle to Ezra is in a separate sentence from the oracle to Israel.

The words *a longe* of C indicate the people who come from the east (1.38; cf. Zech. 8.7; Bar. 4.36, 37; 5.5), probably a scattered righteous remnant in Israel.

1.37

S	C
testor	*testantur apostoli*
populi uenientis gratiam	*populum uenientem*
cuius paruuli exultant	

cum laetitia,
me non uidentes
oculis carnalibus
sed spiritu credent
quae dixi.

cum laetitia.
me autem non uidentes
oculis carnalibus
spiritu credunt
et quae dixi
audierunt
et credunt mihi.

The Spanish text (C) clearly imagines Christ to be the speaker: the apostles bear witness to peoples who have not seen Christ with the eyes of flesh but who believe in the spirit. The French text (S) could possibly be taken in the same sense but the more natural reading is to suppose that the prophet is speaking about himself: a generation to come long after his death will pay attention to his words. That is likely to be the original sense of the passage, but a final judgment must wait on the resolution of the difficult next verse.

1.38

S

et nunc
pater (corr. *frater*; A *partem*)
aspice cum gloria
et uide populum
uenientem ab oriente
quibus dabo ducatum
Abraham etc.

C

iam
pater
aspice cum gloria
et uide populum
uenientem ab oriente
cui dabo ducatum
cum Habraam etc.

If we accept the text as it stands, the speaker must be Christ. Only Christ would have the power to give Abraham, the patriarchs and the prophets as leaders to the people coming from the East. Christ addresses God as Father. That would seem to confirm the reading of 1.37 that I have rejected above. One way out would be to suppose that God is speaking and addressing Ezra as father of the nation (Metzger). Perhaps the corrector of the French text sensed the difficulty of God's calling any man father and changed *pater* to *frater*. I think the natural way to take the text is to suppose that God is the speaker. If so, v. 37, where I have argued that Ezra is the speaker, must be regarded as an entirely separate oracle. Then I am inclined to take *pater* as the insertion of a Christian scribe who supposed Christ to be the speaker, as he had already supposed in v. 37. This conjecture is supported by the Spanish text of 2.5. The text

of A is possibly original, and the occasion of *pater*: look in the
direction of glory, i.e. east (Weinel).

2.4-6

S	C
The mother speaks:	
ite, filii,	*ite, filii,*
et petite a domino	*petite a domino*
misericordiam.	*misericordiam.*
ego autem	*ego enim*
	desolata sum.
te pater	*te patrem*
testem inuoco	*inuoco*
super matrem filiorum	*super matrem eorum*
quia noluerunt	*qui noluerunt*
testamentum meum	*testamentum tuum*
seruare	*seruare*
ut des eis confusionem	*ut tu des eis confusionem*
et matrem eorum	*et matrem illorum*
in direptionem	*in direptione*
ne generatio	*ne quando generatio*
eorum fiat.	*in eis fiat.*

In the French text (S) the *ego autem* marks a change of
speaker; Christ now raises his voice to denounce those who
have not served his covenant. When we turn to the Spanish
text (C) we discover a more natural state of affairs in which
the mother continues to speak, and we also discover the
slightly unusual idiom that gave the scribe responsible for the
French text the idea that Christ had begun to speak in place of
the mother: the mother's speaking of herself in the third person, *te patrem inuoco super matrem eorum*. The Spanish text
is more likely to be the original.

2.10, 11

S	C
haec dicit dominus	*haec dicit dominus*
ad Ezram:	*ad Esdram:*
adnuntia populo meo,	*adnuntia populo meo*
quoniam dabo	*quoniam parabi*
	eis manducare
	et dabo illis
eis regnum Hierusalem,	*regnum Ierusalem*
quod daturus eram	*quod daturus eram*
Israel.	*Israel*

et sumam mihi	*ut sumant sibi*
gloriam illorum	*gloriam illorum*
et dabo	*et dabo*
eis tabernacula aeterna,	*eis tabernacula aeterna*
quae praeparaueram illis.	*quae paraberam illis*
	(M: *eis*).

This is one of the clearest passages in support of the argument
that 2 Esdras 1–2 is a Christian book. No Jew could have
written that God had completely abandoned Israel in favour of
the Gentiles. The last sentence in the French text seems to
clinch the case: God has resumed to himself the glory that used
to be Israel's in order to give it to the Gentiles. 'I will give to
these (the Gentiles) the eternal tabernacles which I had prepared for those (the Jews)'. However, the Spanish text gives a
rather different picture, reading *ut sumant sibi* in place of *et
sumam mihi*. If we read the passage as a whole in the right-
hand column, there is now no distinction between *eis* and *illis*;
both refer to God's people who inherit the Kingdom of
Jerusalem and who are a righteous remnant within Israel
rather than a new people altogether. The conclusion seems
inescapable that the French text represents a text corrupted
by a Christian scribe.

2.33, 34

S	C
ego Ezra	*ego Esdra*
accepi praeceptum	*accepi praeceptum*
a domino	*a domino*
in monte Choreb	*in monte Cobar*
ut irem ad Israel;	*ad Israel.*
ad quos cum uenirem	
reprobauerunt me	
et respuerunt	*et respuerunt*
mandatum domini.	*mandatum hoc.*
ideoque uobis dico	*uobis dico*
gentes	
quae auditis	*qui auditis*
et intellegitis:	*et intelligitis,*
expectate	*expectate*
pastorem uestrum.	*pastorem uestrum.*
requiem	*requiem*
aeternitatis	*aeternitatis vestrae*
dabit uobis	*dabo uobis*

quoniam in proximo	*quoniam in proximo*
est ille	*est*
qui in finem saeculi	*finis saeculi*
adueniet.	*et diminutio hominum.*

One single word *gentes* in the French text converts this passage into a prophecy of the utter rejection of Israel in favour of the Gentiles. The word is lacking in the Spanish text and we can only conclude that it was originally added in order to make Ezra teach the complete rejection of Israel.

I conclude that the corrupt state of the text in each of these passages forces us to choose between two hypotheses: either scribes tended to convert a text teaching the replacement of Israel by the church into a more plausible text in which a Jewish prophet warned an apostate people that a righteous portion of Israel would inherit what was promised to Israel as a whole; or scribes tended to convert a text in which a Jewish prophet warned an apostate people that a righteous portion of Israel would inherit what was promised to Israel as a whole into a text teaching the replacement of Israel by the church. There is no historical evidence that would support the idea of a school of scribes who wanted subconsciously to make Jewish Christian texts into purely Jewish texts, and there is plenty of evidence of the existence of scribes who subconsciously worked on the assumption that the church had indeed replaced Israel in God's favour. We must conclude that the passages alleged in support of the hypothesis that 2 Esdras 1–2 is a Christian book are all corruptions introduced subconsciously by Christian scribes, and that the book they were copying was originally a Jewish document. 2 Esdras 1–2 should be taken out of the collections of Christian apocryphal writings and put firmly and unashamedly into the category of Jewish apocryphal and pseudepigraphical writings.

The Jewish document has a number of interesting features. The Kingdom, meaning the Kingdom of God, occurs at 2.13, 35; the spatial force of the term is confirmed by the unique phrase, the Kingdom of Jerusalem (2.10); and the plural Heavenly Kingdoms occurs in 2.37. The Messiah is referred to as shepherd (2.34), saviour (2.36), the tall young man (2.43), the one who crowns the saints (2.46), and the Son of God (2.47). Finally, the destruction of the Second Temple is prophesied

(1.33), a precious pointer to the date of the original document, which confirms that we can use it with confidence to enrich our knowledge of Judaism at the time of the New Testament—that is, when we have purged it of the slight but momentous changes introduced into the text by the Christian scribes who have preserved it for us.

BIBLIOGRAPHY

Ball, C.J., *The Ecclesiastical or Deuterocanonical Books of the Old Testament Commonly Called the Apocrypha. Edited with Various Readings from the Best Authorities* (AV: Variorum Reference Edition; London: Eyre and Spottiswoode, 1892).

Bensley, Robert L., *The Fourth Book of Ezra: The Latin Version edited from the MSS* (Introduction by Montague Rhodes James; Texts and Studies, III.2; Cambridge: Cambridge University Press, 1895).

Duensing, H., 'Das fünfte und sechste Buch Esra', in E. Hennecke, *Neutestamentliche Apokryphen in deutscher Übersetzung* (ed. W. Schneemelcher; 3rd edn; Tübingen: Mohr, 1964), II, pp. 488-93 (5th edn; Tübingen: Mohr, 1989 [with Aurelio de Santos Otero], pp. 581-90); *New Testament Apocrypha* (ed. R. McL. Wilson; London: Lutterworth, 1965), pp. 689-95 (trans. D. Hill).

Eddrup, E.P., 'II Esdras', in *The Old Testament according to the Authorized Version. With a Brief Commentary by Various Authors. The Apocryphal Books. Esdras to Maccabees.* (London: SPCK, 1880).

Fritzsche, O.J., *Libri apocryphi Veteris Testamenti graece* (Leipzig: Brockhaus, 1871), pp. 640-45.

Gutschmid, Alfred von, 'Die Apokalypse des Esra und ihre spätern Bearbeitungen', *Zeitschrift für wissenschaftliche Theologie* 3 (1860), pp. 1-81 (24-33).

Hilgenfeld, Adolf, *Messias Judaeorum, libris eorum paulo ante et paulo post Christum natum conscriptis illustratus* (Leipzig: Reisland, 1869), pp. 183-211.

Knibb, M.A., '2 Esdras', in R.J. Coggins and M.A. Knibb, *The First and Second Books of Esdras* (The Cambridge Bible Commentary, New English Bible; Cambridge: Cambridge University Press, 1979), pp. 76-100.

Kraft, R.A., 'Towards Assessing the Latin of "5 Ezra": The "Christian" Connection', *Essays in Honor of Krister Stendahl*, *HTR* 79 (1986), pp. 158-69.

Labourt, M.J., 'Le cinquième livre d'Esdras', *RB* 6 (1909), pp. 412-34 [contains translation of the Spanish and French texts in parallel columns].

Lupton, J.H., 'II Esdras: Commentary and Critical Notes', in *The Holy Bible according to the Authorized Version (AD 1611). With an Explanatory and Critical Commentary and a Revision of the Translation by Clergy of the Anglican Church: Apocrypha* (The Speaker's Commentary, ed. Henry Wace; London: Murray, 1888), I, pp. 71-148.

Metzger, B.M., 'The Second Book of Esdras', in *The Oxford Annotated Apocrypha, The Apocrypha of the Old Testament. Revised Standard Version.*

Expanded Edition Containing the Third and Fourth Books of the Maccabees and Psalm 151 (New York: Oxford University Press, 1977).

—'The Fourth Book of Ezra with the Four Additional Chapters', *The Old Testament Pseudepigrapha* (ed. J.H. Charlesworth; London: Darton, Longman and Todd, 1983), I, pp. 516-59.

Myers, Jacob M., *I & II Esdras: Introduction, Translation and Commentary* (The Anchor Bible; Garden City, NY: Doubleday, 1974).

Oepke, A., 'Ein bisher unbeachtetes Zitat aus dem fünften Buch Esra', *ConNT* 11 (1947), pp. 179-95.

Oesterley, W.O.E., *II Esdras (The Ezra Apocalypse) with Introduction and Notes* (Westminster Commentaries; London: Methuen, 1933).

Riessler, P., *Altjüdisches Schrifttum ausserhalb der Bibel* (Freiburg and Heidelberg: F.H. Kerle, 1928), pp. 310-17, 1285-86.

Stanton, G.N., '5 Ezra and Matthaean Christianity in the Second Century', *JTS* ns 28 (1977), pp. 67-83.

Volkmar, G., *Handbuch der Einleitung in die Apokryphen. Zweite Abtheilung. Das vierte Buch Esra. Esdra propheta. Nunc primum integrum edidit ex duobus manuscriptis italae, adhibitis orientalibus prorsus recognitis, cum commentariis et glossario* (Tübingen: L.Fr. Fues, 1863).

Weinel, H., 'Das fünfte Buch Esra', in E. Hennecke (ed.), *Neutestamentliche Apokryphen in deutscher Übersetzung und mit Einleitungen* (Tübingen and Leipzig: Mohr, 1904), pp. 305-11 (2nd edn, 1924), pp. 390-94.

—'Das fünfte Buch Esra', in E. Hennecke (ed.), *Handbuch zu den neutestamentlichen Apokryphen in Verbinding mit Fachgelehrten* (Tübingen: Mohr, 1904), pp. 331-36.

APOCALYPTIC—STRANGELY RELEVANT

J.K. Riches

> He comes to us as One unknown, without a name, as of old, by
> the lake-side, He came to those men who knew Him not. He
> speaks to us the same word: 'Follow thou me!' and sets us to the
> tasks which He has to fulfil for our time.[1]

Schweitzer's famous words at the end of the *Quest* summed
up the great sense of alienation which historical studies of
Jesus had produced by the beginning of the present century—
at least in those with ears to hear! The *Quest* had been undertaken in the hope that it would lead to the restoration and
rediscovery of the human Jesus beneath the overlay of subsequent dogmatic portrayals of Christ; but the figure that had
emerged from such studies by the middle of the nineteenth
century proved to have a suspicious likeness to the ideals of the
various restaurateurs and portraiteurs—some said, to the
restaurateurs and portraiteurs themselves—and it was the
task of scholars like J. Weiss[2] to show how very different the
Jesus of first-century Galilee had been. And, as is well known,
Weiss did this by showing the extent to which Jesus drew on
first-century forms of apocalyptic language: how indeed in his
view Jesus' thought was shot through with the expectation of
an imminent cosmic crisis, in which God would intervene to
put an end to this world and to inaugurate a final, new age, in
which his reign would run supreme.

Now this was, without question, a most significant step forward in the historical understanding of Jesus—however we

---

1. A. Schweitzer, *The Quest of the Historical Jesus* (London: A. & C.
Black, 1936), p. 401.
2. *Jesus' Proclamation of the Kingdom of God* (Philadelphia:
Fortress, 1971 [1st German edn, 1892]).

may wish to qualify this interpretation of first-century apocalyptic texts, for example by consideration of the place of the
temple in Jesus' thought (see below). And it showed Jesus to be
a very different figure indeed from his liberal historians with
their belief in progress and the future of Western, European
Protestant culture. And yet it was Schweitzer's claim in his
peroration to his *Quest* that such *strangeness* was precisely
that which could enable men and women nineteen centuries
later to stand with the first disciples and hear like them the
challenge of the unknown Jesus to follow him. Was that a
merely rhetorical flourish with which to round off his great
survey? The history of Albert Schweitzer's own life would
hardly suggest that it was. The remark is, I think, worthy of
some attention. At the least it may stand as a caution against
subsequent attempts to domesticate apocalyptic—at least as it
was used by Jesus; at best it may indeed enable us to hear
Jesus' call with renewed sharpness. And the suggestion is that
we can only hear that call thus sharply when Jesus has
become truly a stranger to us and to our world.

Subsequent research into Jesus' life and teaching has been so
dominated by these questions that it is difficult to be impartial
in singling out figures for discussion who exemplify at least
some of the pitfalls against which I wish to warn. So as the
matter is not, to me at least, a matter of indifference and as a
Festschrift itself is a personal volume perhaps I may without
offence be more personal.

Some 25 or more years ago I went out with a group of fellow
students from Cambridge to work in refugee camps in Aus-
tria. It was a summer expedition undertaken with all due
enthusiasm and enjoyment and I still recall it as a time of
great happiness. But it was more: in the course of working
alongside refugees, as they built their homes after years of
upheaval and hopelessness, the terrible reality of war in
Europe began to dawn. To sit and share one's breakfast with
people who had survived the transports across Europe to
Siberia; to encounter the broken figure of the former inmate of
Mauthausen, the concentration camp not far away on the
Danube; to hear the stories of the farms and homes left and lost
far away in Eastern and Central Europe was to be made
painfully aware of the fragility of the world whose stability I

had until then taken for granted. Suddenly one became aware of the dark forces that can possess societies and destroy or subvert all normal standards of decency and humanity. One became aware of the fascination which such forces can exert, of the sheer destruction which they can wreak. But also one saw the extraordinary resilience of people, their ability to recover a sense of purpose, to struggle against all the odds to build a decent life again for their families.

To return to the confident culture of early 1960s London and Cambridge was a strange experience. I was in no mood to share its easy optimism. And in searching for ways of coming to terms with what I had seen I found strange comfort and help in the apocalyptic vision of painters like Egon Schiele, in the music of Britten and Mahler, in the films of Ingmar Bergman and Frederico Fellini. For here the dark images of death, of the beast, of the opening of the seals and the horsemen of the apocalypse were woven into the fabric of experience in such a way as to throw into sharp relief the forces of plague, destruction, cruelty, corruption on the one hand and the fragile beauty of human compassion and warmth and innocence on the other. And I recall, too, a conversation with Ernst Bammel, with his very different experience to many of my Cambridge teachers, where he directed me to that dark, yet somehow hopeful book, *Was ist der Mensch*? (Göttingen: Musterschmidt, 1960) by H.J. Schoeps, himself a powerful reminder of the need for New Testament studies to be earthed in the wider issues of theology and anthropology.

And there was a strange comfort in the way that such visions, for all their terror, were contained within a framework of belief in a God who, though he might seem distant and indeed deaf to the cries of the world, would still bring new dawns and wipe away all tears. And such hopes answered another chord: the desire to be actively involved in countering those forces which threaten the peace and stability of our world or which indeed are already at large, the wish to support and stand alongside those already engaged in the struggle for justice, peace and human dignity.

It was, I repeat, in the use of apocalyptic imagery by artists, musicians, film directors and writers that I began to find some help in coming to terms with the darker side of experience; not

240 *Templum Amicitiae*

in its interpretation by biblical scholars, to whom I was at the
same time being introduced by teachers in Cambridge. Here
the debates turned largely on the question of how far Jesus
had, or had not, appropriated contemporary Jewish apocalyptic beliefs in an imminent end to the world. The preferred
solution of scholars like Charles Harold Dodd was to acknowledge that Jesus had indeed been influenced by contemporary
apocalyptic beliefs in a radical inbreaking of divine judgment
and salvation[3] but that he had substantially reworked those
beliefs in proclaiming that such an inbreaking of divine grace
and judgment was taking place in his own life and ministry.[4]
And Dodd believed that such proclamation could be given an
enduring sense if it was *interpreted* as meaning (in more contemporary language) that in Jesus the 'absolute, the "wholly
other", had entered time and space',[5] that in him spiritual
forces had become available which would shape the culture
and constitution of Christendom at least for centuries to come.
Jesus, that is to say, proclaimed *a new understanding of history*, centred on the fact of his own life and ministry. Subsequently, scholars like Jeremias, while largely accepting Dodd's
views, would argue that he had overstressed the element of
fulfilment in Jesus' preaching, at the cost of the continued
element of expectation.[6] Others, like Cullmann, would go on to
argue that the New Testament authors had remained true to
this basic characteristic of Jesus' preaching in themselves
announcing a new understanding of sacred history: *which
was indeed at the very heart of the New Testament.*[7] Thus by
some remarkable alchemy Jesus' disturbingly strange

3. Notably in *The Parables of the Kingdom* (London: Nisbet, 2nd edn,
1936). Dodd was, of course, much indebted to Rudolf Otto's fascinating
The Kingdom of God and the Son of Man (London: Lutterworth, 1938
[German edition, 1934]).
4. *Parables of the Kingdom*, p. 49; but cf. the important qualification
of this at p. 79: 'While formally the new and original element in the
teaching of Jesus is that the Kingdom of God, long expected, has come,
there is an even more profound originality in the new content given to
the idea through His revelation of God himself'. It is significant that in
both passages Dodd refers to Otto.
5. *Parables*, p. 107.
6. *The Parables of Jesus* (London: SCM, 1963).
7. *Salvation in History* (London: SCM, 1967 [German edition 1965]).

proclamation of the imminent arrival of the Kingdom with power, of the Son of Man coming with the holy angels to put an end to history and usher in a new world, has become a doctrine of saving history, a 'Biblical theology' indeed which even claims to replace other forms of systematic and metaphysical theology. This, some might say, is domestication on the grand scale.

I cannot here enter into detailed criticism of Dodd's treatment of Jesus' parables and his interpretation of Mark 13 and the other apocalyptic predictions (which he took to refer to specific historical events in the life of Jesus and Israel), nor indeed of his more general account of contemporary Jewish beliefs about the Kingdom of God which underlies his treatment. His work was always eloquent and clear; surer, indeed, when he entered the world of Classical scholarship where he was a master than in the field of Semitic thought and philology; always using his impressive erudition to *interpret* and understand the texts with which he wrestled. But at the end of the day it has to be said that by taking Jesus' proclamation of the coming of the divine power and glory to refer not only to the *historical* events surrounding Jesus' life, but also *to the subsequent history of the Church*, Dodd deprived it of much of its cultural critical power, indeed of its power to illuminate the dark and terrifying aspects of our history. Yet it was precisely that which attracted writers and painters like Büchner, Schiele and others. Certainly, Dodd seemed largely innocent of the deep doubts about the identification of Christendom and Christianity which the First World War had raised in the minds of men like Barth and Bultmann, and there seems to be evidenced in his writing an almost constitutional inability to attend to the darker sides of Christian history which might have shaken that easy identification. His much acclaimed *The Founder of Christianity* makes this all too painfully clear when he dismisses, on the first page, the horrors of the Confessional Wars of the seventeenth century as 'some unfortunate accompaniments'[8] to the birth of Modern Europe. In short, the domestication of Jesus' apocalyptic proclamation of the coming of the Kingdom leads in this case to a screening out

8. London: Collins, 1971, pp. 1-3.

of the dark side of our history. Strange indeed, when one considers that such texts and preaching so often have their genesis in the darkest moments of a people's history, seeking as they do to illuminate the mystery of evil and to sustain *in the very presence of such oppressive force* hopes for the future.

Of course, Dodd is by no means the only scholar to have turned to these questions. We should at least mention the highly original work which Bultmann produced in his *Jesus and the Word*[9] which, as he wrote to Barth, was conceived as an attempt to address what for him was the central task of New Testament theology, namely to understand how the proclaimer, Jesus, became the proclaimed Jesus Christ.[10] He was concerned, that is, with the way in which in the Synoptics, as contrasted with John, there is more than simply the claim *that* Jesus is the revealer. What is this extra and how is it to be understood? Bultmann, like Dodd later, certainly saw Jesus' proclamation of the Kingdom of God as being sharply distinct from other more mythological forms of contemporary Jewish apocalyptic.[11] If others saw the Kingdom of God as a distant event in time in which the far God would suddenly draw near to judge and save, Jesus as he confronted men and women with the proclamation of God's will and his coming presented them with a choice: either to commit themselves totally to God's will and service *or* to turn away. Those who responded willingly would in the moment of decision experience the 'nearness' of God, as their lives were transformed and re-orientated. Those who turned away would indeed experience the remoteness, the judgment of God as they turned back in on themselves.[12] Here something of the urgency and the personal implications of the Gospel were recovered. But alongside that gain was a loss. As enthusiastically as Dodd and Cullmann had embraced an historical reference for Jesus' proclamation of

9. London: Scribner's, 1934 (German edition, 1926), not noticed by Dodd in his *Parables*, though he does refer to Bultmann's work on the history of the Synoptic tradition and makes some use of form-critical insights.
10. See *Karl Barth—Rudolf Bultmann. Briefwechsel, 1922–66* (Karl Barth, Gesamtausgabe, 5; Zürich: Theologischer Verlag, 1971), p. 63.
11. *Jesus and the Word*, pp. 98ff.
12. *Jesus and the Word*, pp. 138-40.

the Kingdom, Bultmann, following the early Barth, rejected any attempt to identify the Kingdom and the history of this world. The Word remained free, transcendent, encountered time and again through history, never itself being identified with it. It was essentially an 'event' of a different kind, an 'event' between the Word and the individual hearer not to be objectified, making use of the language of cosmic disaster and change only metaphorically to refer to the change in an individual's self-understanding.

I mention this briefly only to make one point: Bultmann is right, I think, to suggest that Jesus did not engage in great speculation about the nature of the End, of the signs of its coming: Mk 13.32 follows on neatly from Mk 13.4 and what intervenes is best accounted for as the subsequent creation of the Church, drawing on Jewish apocalyptic texts and models. He is right, too, to acknowledge that 'Jesus, like his contemporaries, expected a tremendous eschatological drama'.[13] But is it an adequate account of such beliefs to say that their '"real significance" does not in any sense depend on the dramatic events attending its (sc. the Kingdom of God's) coming, nor on any circumstances which the imagination can conceive? It interests him not at all as a describable state of existence, but rather as the transcendent event, which signifies for man the ultimate Either-Or, which constrains him to decision.'[14] It may well be that the thought of such an imminent event concentrates the mind wonderfully. But the *function* of beliefs should be clearly distinguished from their *sense*. We need to see more clearly what the sense of Jesus' beliefs about the future was and to acknowledge more fully their mistakenness. Perhaps then we can address other questions about the truth of Jesus' other beliefs and also turn again to the question of the function of Jesus' beliefs about the future. And that in turn will take us back to Schweitzer.

13. *Jesus and the Word*, pp. 29, 35f.
14. *Jesus and the Word*, p. 37.

1. *Jesus' Beliefs about the Future*

One of the difficulties with claiming that Jesus was mistaken in his belief that the new age was dawning is that of giving any specific content to that belief. The debate since Johannes Weiss has in no sense been marked by unanimity; there is deep disagreement over the originality to Jesus of many of the central texts, such as the middle section of Mark 13; and more recent attempts by E.P. Sanders[15] to derive Jesus' beliefs in the End from his actions certainly do not yield the unequivocal results that were hoped for.

One of the interesting aspects of Sanders's book on Jesus is, nevertheless, the way he focuses attention on Jesus' actions in the Temple as evidence of his espousal of Jewish restoration eschatology. The difficulty is that while we can indeed be reasonably confident that Jesus did in fact do and say something of significance in the Temple,[16] probably during his last visit to Jerusalem, we cannot be anything like so sure what such actions may have meant, nor indeed what he said and with what sense. Thus rather than starting with a list of indisputable facts, it might be better to start with a list of at least plausible claims which relate to Jesus' beliefs about the future and which, taken together, may give us some indication of his beliefs about the future, sufficient at least to suggest that they were not fulfilled.

1. Jesus called twelve disciples and seems to have attached some special significance to this number.

---

15. *Jesus and Judaism* (London: SCM, 1985).

16. *Jesus and Judaism*, p. 61: 'Despite all this, it is overwhelmingly probable that Jesus did something in the temple and said something about its destruction'. Elsewhere Sanders lists among the 'almost indisputable facts' that 'Jesus was engaged in a controversy about the temple' (p. 11) and as 'certain or virtually certain' that 'Jesus shared the world-view' that he calls 'Jewish restoration eschatology', the key facts here being Jesus' 'start under John the Baptist, the call of the twelve, his expectation of a new (or renewed) temple, and the eschatological setting of the work of the apostles' (p. 326). See further my review article: 'The Words and Works of Jesus the Jew', *Heythrop Journal* 17 (1986), pp. 53-62.

The most obvious explanation is that he anticipated some role for them in the coming kingdom: judging over the twelve tribes of Israel (Mt. 19.28). There is of course nothing unusual about radical groups picking up elements from their tradition in order to forge new patterns of leadership, constitutions, etc. The radical groups of the Reformation plundered the Old Testament freely to construct their ideal societies;[17] so too did the sectaries at Qumran.[18] If something like this is happening in the case of Jesus, then we should be alive to the possibility that what he had in mind was both quite simple in outline and also possibly quite wildly different from the then existing constitutional arrangements of the outgoing Temple-state. Just as figures like Theudas and the Egyptian[19] evoked episodes from the period before the possession of the Land, so it is also possible that Jesus may have looked back to a period before the Temple-state as an ideal world which would be restored in the new age. Such a world may or may not have included a restored Temple; if such a Temple was envisaged then of course the new world would have been significantly different from that of the tribal amphictyony.

2. Jesus predicted or threatened the destruction of the Temple and performed some kind of prophetic sign in the Court of the Gentiles.

Interpretations of the relevant sayings (Mk 13.1f.; 14.58; cf. Lk. 19.44) and of Jesus' actions in the Temple (Mk 11.15-19 pars.) vary substantially. The central question posed by Sanders's treatment is whether Jesus was referring to the

17. See the account of the Münster Anabaptists in Norman Cohn's *The Pursuit of the Millennium* (London: Paladin, 1970), esp. pp. 268f., for an account of the constitution which Bockelson introduced, drawing on Old Testament notions of the twelve Elders. He later had himself proclaimed king of the New Jerusalem.

18. This is not the place for a full discussion of the organization of the Qumran Community. It is, however, interesting to note that its documents too refer to 'twelve men and three priests' in the Council of the Community (1QS 8.1) and that the communities described in the Damascus Rule were divided up into tens according to Old Testament models derived from Exod. 18.25 (CD 13.1).

19. *Ant.* 18.85-87; 20.97-98, 169-72; cf. *War* 2.261-63; Acts 5.36; 21.38.

destruction of the Temple only—or to its destruction and restoration.

Neither the sayings nor the accounts of Jesus' actions give any conclusive answer to this question. Sayings occur in both forms: either as a *prediction* of the Temple's destruction (Mk 13.1f.), or as the *threat* of its destruction coupled with the promise of its rebuilding (Mk 14.58; 15.29; cf. Jn 2.19). Jesus' reported action—overturning a table—may well symbolize destruction,[20] but if so, would it also have symbolized its restoration? Sanders himself believes that it would have been taken to refer also to its restoration (p. 71). His case for this rests however on a broad claim that such an attack on what had been ordained by God was only conceivable on the assumption that 'destruction, in turn, looks towards restoration' (p. 71); and on the more specific and more difficult claim that such expectations of the destruction and rebuilding of the Temple were sufficiently widespread among Jews of the time to have led at least to some such interpretation of Jesus' action in the Temple (p. 88).

The arguments here are complex. On the one hand there are those like Gaston[21] who argue that there are no precedents in pre-70 Judaism for a belief in the destruction *and* restoration of the Temple:

> The future salvation was couched in terms of the new Jerusalem, even if the temple should occasionally be presupposed as part of this (Tobit, *Jubilees*). Although it might be natural, it is never explicitly said that the old temple must be removed before the new one comes (p. 119).

This involves reading a number of the relevant texts (notably *1 Enoch* 90) as referring to the restoration of Jerusalem the city, rather than to the Temple itself. By contrast Sanders, follow-

---

20. So Sanders, *Jesus and Judaism*, p. 70, where he records C.F.D. Moule's view that destruction would have been better symbolized by breaking something. See too the important discussion by A.E. Harvey, *Jesus and the Constraints of History* (London: Duckworth, 1982): 'What is being expressed in symbolic action is the divine judgment on a particular use which was being made of the temple' (p. 133).

21. *No Stone on Another. Studies in the Significance of the Fall of Jerusalem in the Synoptic Gospels* (NovT Suppl., 23; Leiden: Brill, 1970).

ing McKelvey,[22] argues that we should assume, unless there are contrary indications, that references to Jerusalem or Zion would always have been taken to be inclusive of the Temple and that expectations of a new Temple occur in Tob. 14.5; *1 Enoch* 90.28f.;[23] *Jub.* 1.15-17, 26, 28; *T. Benj.* 9.2; 4QpPs 37 3.11; 11QTemple 29.8-10; and *Sib. Or.* 3.294, 702-20, 772-74; 5.414-33.

Two things are impressive about these texts. One is that they are largely drawn from the radical fringes of Judaism, which may therefore not be wholly characteristic of more widespread popular beliefs such as would condition Jesus' audience's understanding of his actions in the Temple. The other is that with the exception of *1 Enoch* there is no specific reference to the destruction of the Temple, though it may of course, as Sanders suggests, be implied (p. 85).

The question here is what precisely is implied. It is clear that there has to be some transition between the old temple and the new one which is to be created by God. But is the image of destruction always, or indeed ever, appropriate here? Where it occurs explicitly, as in *1 Enoch* 89–90, it occurs in a context of judgment on the corruption of the cult. 11QTemple 29.8-10 speaks by contrast of God's glory dwelling upon the old sanctuary until he creates his own anew, clearly a very different context. Is the omission of any description of the passing of the old temple indicative of the desire to avoid suggestion of its destruction and hence any implications of divine judgment on it?

That is to say, evidence for belief in the destruction *and* restoration of the Temple in the first century, prior to AD 70, is not strong. There is some evidence for the belief in a renewed Temple, principally from circles associated with Qumran.

---

22. R.J. McKelvey, *The New Temple. The Church in the New Testament* (Oxford: Oxford University Press, 1969).

23. Sanders does, however, at this point avoid the main sting of Gaston's argument (*No Stone on Another*, p. 114) which is that it is the tower in *1 En.* 89 which specifically refers to the Temple and that there is no reference to such a tower in the renewed house which is brought in *1 En.* 90.28f. Sanders's attempt to turn this argument by pointing to the cultic motifs in *1 En.* 89 hardly meets the point (*Jesus and Judaism*, p. 81).

There is considerably less evidence for belief in the destruction *and* restoration of the Temple as a sign of the End, though *1 Enoch* 90.28f. remains an intriguing possibility. Apart from this there is the story in Josephus (*War* 6.300-305) of the other Jesus, son of Ananias, who prophesied the destruction of the Temple and the city in the period before its actual destruction.

A number of conclusions should be drawn from this brief review of more recent discussions of Jewish expectations concerning the Temple contemporary to Jesus. In the first place, while we may take the Qumran and other evidence as indicating that such expectations were quite within the range of ways in which first-century Jews could envisage the end, we should not make too confident judgments about how widespread such beliefs would have been. Secondly, the evidence of the Gospel Temple narratives and of Jesus' sayings is not enough of itself to substantiate claims that Jesus' action would have been understood as symbolizing not only destruction but also restoration. Thirdly, we are forced to the conclusion that on either view, viz. whether Jesus believed in the destruction and restoration of the Temple, or merely in its destruction, he was a relatively unusual figure, whom we have to read not simply as reflecting commonly held beliefs of the time but as developing such beliefs in strikingly different ways. To make such claims is often thought both to offend against good practice in the history of religion, and to be motivated by apologetic concerns. In the context of the present argument which is trying to pin down Jesus' mistakenness about the future, perhaps the latter charge may appear implausible. But the former also needs to be challenged. Refusing to acknowledge the variety of religious beliefs within a community, and the role of individuals in developing such variety, is hardly a promising starting point for any historian, least of all for a historian of religions, who must be constantly alert to the oddities and unpredictability of human religious behaviour, however difficult that may make his or her task.

That is to say: our knowledge of contemporary Jewish beliefs about the Temple does not give us any strong grounds for assuming that anyone who prophesied the Temple's destruction *would have been understood* to imply belief in its restoration; but nor does it entirely exclude that possibility. Thus perhaps we need to ask a rather more speculative question: not, did first-century Jews actually, so far as we know, believe in the destruction and the restoration of the Temple, but under what circumstances would a first-century Jew have been able to contemplate both the destruction and the restoration of the Temple?

In the broadest terms one would have to assume that such a person would have been both deeply committed to the Temple cult, seeing it as of central importance to Israel's continuing relationship to God; and that he or she would have to be deeply out of sorts with the present condition of the Temple. That is to say, for Jews to have seen both the destruction and the restoration of the Temple as consistent with the rule and justice of God they would have had to see the one as judgment and the other as the final recompense for those who had remained faithful.

Now, as we have seen, there is evidence for such beliefs occurring separately. The writer of *1 Enoch* clearly saw the destruction of the Temple as linked to the pollution of the sacrifices (89.73) and this, as Gaston argues (p. 114), is very possibly seen as an act of divine judgment. Malachi 3 threatens swift judgment against those who do not present right offerings; there is no specific mention of the destruction of the Temple, though what is envisaged by 'its purifying by fire' is not clear and might easily have suggested such thoughts. *Ps. Sol.* 8 attacks the immorality and impurity of the priesthood. Similar charges are to be found in Qumran (1QpHab 12.8f.; CD 5.6ff.), though none of this is specifically linked to prophecies of the Temple's destruction. Did Qumran believe that such an event would occur? We have seen that there is a belief in a divinely created Temple in the *Temple Scroll* but that this does not relate in any explicit way to the destruction of a ritually polluted Temple. However, it should not be forgotten that Qumran also preserved *1 Enoch* in its library and that this text too would have informed their beliefs. Thus it is not altogether impossible that at some point the community entertained belief in the destruction of the Temple as well as its restoration. Nevertheless the clearest near-contemporary example of belief in the destruction of the Temple is Jesus, son of Ananias, whose prophecies of the destruction of Jerusalem and the

Temple contain echoes of Jer. 7.34. The latter text inveighs specifically against ritual defilement and human sacrifice and prophesies mass destruction. What Jesus son of Ananias prophesied against, we do not know. Nor do we know whether he looked for any restoration beyond the coming judgment.

The relevance of all this to Jesus of Nazareth is not hard to seek. If Jesus predicted or threatened the destruction of the Temple, that would have been certainly striking and unusual but not without precedent or subsequent exemplars. If Jesus not only predicted the destruction of the Temple but also looked to its restoration, that would not only have been—quite possibly—without precedent; we would also have to suppose that what was only dimly hinted at was understood by crowds who would have no reason to make such a connection; and we would have to suppose that for Jesus the Temple was central to his conception of God and his dealings with his people. But of this latter we have remarkably little evidence, as, say, contrasted with our knowledge of Qumran. Thus it is not unthinkable that Jesus should have simply pointed to the destruction of the Temple, without any thought of its restoration. Further clarification of what Jesus might have expected must wait on considerations of other aspects of his teaching which I can do little more than list.

3. Jesus was a disciple of John the Baptist. This suggests that there is some kinship between John's and Jesus' expectations of the end. In the first place they both expected the end to come soon. John spoke of the axe already being laid to the root of the tree (Mt. 3.10); Jesus spoke of some of his hearers living to see the kingdom of God come with power (Mk 9.1). Both seem to have enjoyed a popular support and to have addressed their message to any who would hear. But equally there were contrasts which were related to the content of their message. John, the ascetic prophet, announced judgment and purification; Jesus already anticipated the joys of the coming kingdom in his invitation to sinners to share meals with him. In his small band of followers the first signs of the kingdom were to be perceived.

4. Jesus called disciples. Martin Hengel[24] has made a close comparison of Jesus' calling of disciples with other analogous phenomena in the ancient world. While arguing that there is something quite distinctive about Jesus' call, he nevertheless points to important similarities between Jesus and the charismatic prophet figures of the Zealot movement. What is of immediate significance for our study are two points: that Jesus calls people to make a radical break with the mores of their society (Mt. 8.22)[25] and that he calls them to 'go after him', much as the Zealot leaders called men to follow them in a holy war on the Romans and their puppets.[26] This is not of course to suggest that the means by which Jesus called his disciples to wage this 'holy war' were those of the Zealots. Rather the way that they were to follow was one of suffering and the cross. But it does suggest that Jesus expected his followers to take some active part in the establishment of his kingdom; and that they were to expect to take power after some kind of a struggle.

5. Jesus was a rural figure.[27] He came from Nazareth and as far as we can judge from the Gospels his active life as a healer-teacher-prophet was based on the villages and small towns in Galilee and the North, specifically avoiding the larger Hellenistic cities. Similarly we may assume that most of his followers came from such a background (though Lk. 8.1ff. mentions women from higher social circles; as women they may well have been attracted to someone who made such a radical challenge to the existing order).

The precise significance of this to our theme is far from certain. The disciples' comment in Mk 13.1, 'Look, Master, what wonderful buildings!', may express their wonder at (and

24. *The Charismatic Leader and his Followers* (Edinburgh: T. & T. Clark, 1981).
25. *Charismatic Leader*, pp. 8ff.
26. *Charismatic Leader*, pp. 20ff.
27. G. Theissen has done most to draw attention to the importance of this aspect of Jesus' milieu; see, for example, 'Die Tempelweissagung Jesus. Prophetie im Spannungsfeld von Stadt und Land', *Theologische Zeitschrift* 32 (1976), pp. 144-58; *Lokalkolorit und Zeitgeschichte in den Evangelien* (NTOA 8; Fribourg/Göttingen: Universitätsverlag/Vandenhoeck & Ruprecht, 1989), and 'Jesusbewegung als charismatische Wertrevolution', *NTS* 35 (1989), pp. 343-60.

estrangement from?) the world of the cities with their Hellenistic architecture, of which of course the Temple was an outstanding example. Theissen has suggested that Jesus' movement was inspired by such a rural animus against the world of the cities and their leadership. It is by no means implausible— drawing again on analogies with the radical Reformation and the Peasants' Revolt—to suggest that Jesus should indeed have been the spokesperson for such deep-rooted rural dissatisfaction, though there are inherent difficulties in arguing for the breakdown of social norms in rural Galilee in the first century AD.[28] If such a view were correct, it would lend support to the further belief that Jesus' threat/prediction of the destruction of the Temple was motivated by a deep rejection of its leadership and those merchant classes who controlled its trade and that what he expected thereafter would have included the assumption of leadership positions by his followers. It would not, it seems to me, have any very clear bearing on the question whether or not Jesus expected its restoration. Certainly the presence in Jerusalem of large numbers of Jewish pilgrims at the main festivals makes it abundantly clear that the city and its Temple were still the focus of widespread popular religious sentiments and aspirations. If Jesus did not predict its restoration but only its destruction, this would not easily have found popular resonance. Indeed, if the Gospel reports are to be believed, popular support for Jesus in Jerusalem was at best fickle, perhaps never very strong.

6. Like the Pharisees, and unlike the Sadducees, Jesus believed in the resurrection. Belief in the resurrection is first attested in Dan. 12.2 at a period when official Seleucid prescription of the Law meant that those who obeyed the Law, the 'righteous', were liable to punishment, indeed death. Clearly this conflicted with the widespread belief in the Old Testament that God would reward the righteous and punish the wicked *in this world*. This reversal of expectations will then, we may suppose,

---

28. As Theissen is fully aware; cf. '"Wir haben alles verlassen" (Mc. X, 28). Nachfolge und soziale Entwurzelung in der jüdisch-palästinischen Gesellschaft des 1. Jahrhunderts n. Chr.', in his *Studien zur Soziologie des Urchristentums* (WUNT 19; Tübingen: Mohr, 1979), p. 134.

have led to the belief that due apportionment of punishments and rewards would still occur, but in another dispensation, in a new age when the dead would rise to receive their deserts. Thus belief in the resurrection would entail the belief that the *present* Temple-state was part of a world that was passing away and would be replaced by something radically new. How new we can learn from Jesus' exorcisms and healings. Not only would the dead rise, but demon possession would come to an end as would disease and sickness. But it was also a belief about the end of the existing constitutional order. One can therefore understand its rejection by the Sadducees easily enough. What the nature of the new constitutional order was to be was not of course something that could simply be read out of belief in the resurrection. It may indeed have included the restoration of the Temple, with or without its present incumbents, but it will also have allowed for quite different conceptions of the coming new social order and will therefore have been subversive. And this would furnish another reason for it to have been regarded with deep suspicion by the Sadducees.

What then can we say in conclusion to this discussion about Jesus' beliefs in the End? With some certainty we can say that he looked for a radical transformation of the present order which would occur at least within the life-time of his followers. Such a transformation would restore Israel's fortunes and bring blessing to his followers and it would put an end to suffering, disease and demon-possession and even death. The coming of the new age, it is probable, was to be preceded by the destruction of the Temple as, we may suppose but with a good deal less confidence, an act of divine judgment on those who were seen as faithless rulers of the people. Whether or not Jesus expected the new order to be constituted around a restored Temple, it is very difficult to say. We certainly cannot rule out the possibility that he expected a new order of things without any Temple, based in some way on the old order of the twelve tribes with his disciples installed as leaders of the tribes.

While a good deal of this must remain tentative, some of it has a very considerable degree of probability: Jesus' belief in some radical transformation of the present order which would bring blessing, see the dead rise, the end of sickness and a new order for Israel. It does not seem to me to require extensive argument to show that subsequent events have proved Jesus mistaken in all such particulars.

2. *The Relation between Jesus' Beliefs about the Future and his Other Beliefs*

Now the problem that this raises is primarily: If Jesus believed that among those who heard him were those who would experience the fullness of God's rule before they died, must we not dismiss him—along with all the other contemporary millenarian prophets who looked for some radical restoration of Israel's fortunes—as deluded? How can we seriously attend to other aspects of his teaching about the fatherhood of God (or about love of enemies) if he was so clearly proved wrong in this case? The question might be put as follows: Are Jesus' other theological and ethical beliefs *so* related to his beliefs in the imminent future coming of the kingdom that the truth of the latter is a *necessary* condition of the truth of the former? Do we have to say: if and only if Jesus' belief in the Kingdom of God is true, is his belief in the fatherhood of God true? This may be a slightly unusual way of posing the question, but I suspect that many attempts to wrest an acceptable contemporary sense from the kingdom of God, etc., have been based on an unexamined belief that the answer to this question must be in the affirmative. I want to suggest the opposite. Having done that, I shall then go on to ask what the value to us of such beliefs in the future coming of the kingdom might be, despite their falsity.

What reasons can we then give for suggesting that Jesus' beliefs about, for example, the fatherhood of God, were not internally related to his beliefs about the future?

Let me come at this indirectly. Beliefs in some kind of radical change or fortune for Israel, linked with the idea of God's intervention were, we have seen, quite widespread at the time. Groups and individuals as distinct as the Pharisees, the Qumran community and Jesus all believed in the resurrection. Jesus himself as a follower of John the Baptist will have been introduced to such beliefs in one particular form, though exactly what, if anything, John the Baptist taught about the world which was to be ushered in by the stronger one, we do not know.

Such beliefs we have also seen varied considerably and would in their various expressions reflect the values and theological beliefs of particular groups or individuals in first-century Judaism. Thus there can be considerable variety of belief about, for example, the place of the Temple in the New Jerusalem which is to come. Certainly in subsequent Jewish Christian writings like Revelation there are explicit denials that there will be a temple in the New Jerusalem at all. Whereas *Enoch* envisages the destruction of the corrupt temple (ch. 89), 11QTemple 29.8-10 envisages the sanctification of the old Temple and its eventual replacement by another more glorious one. The most likely reading of this text is that Qumran saw the Temple cult as an integral part of the New Age and believed that such worship was to have a central and continuing place in Israel's relation with God. This in turn reflects Qumran's particular understanding of the Law, which was expressed in seeing their own worship and prayers during their period in the desert as having an atoning function,[29] and in their particular exposition of the calendar (CD 3.12-15) and indeed of the whole conduct and order of Temple worship. We might say that widespread belief in some final fulfilment of Israel's hopes *combines* in Qumran with belief in God's holiness, in the centrality of the cult, in the special understanding of the Law which had been given to the Teacher of Righteousness to produce the particular vision of the end that they had. Of course the process whereby these links were made may be complex and its social and psychological history may vary considerably. But it seems clear that logically the belief in, say, the holiness of God and the special revelation to the Teacher of Righteousness are independent of belief in some future resolution of Israel's problems.

Similarly with Jesus. Jesus' views of the end, we may conjecture, were first learnt from John the Baptist. But Jesus' con-

---

29. 1QS 11.3f.; cf. 8.4, 12 which however Knibb (*The Qumran Community* [Cambridge: Cambridge University Press, 1987], pp. 138f.) sees as evidence for the belief in Qumran that 'within the temple formed by the community a life of perfection would take the place of sacrifice'.

temporaries saw a considerable difference between him and John (Mt. 11.16-19). Such a difference will most probably have had its roots in the difference between their understandings of sin and forgiveness. John's 'stronger one' was clearly coming to administer judgment of a terrible kind. The agricultural imagery of the threshing floor and the burning of the chaff (Mt. 3.12) has its own particular terrors. Jesus' meals with sinners by contrast, disputed though their precise meaning may be,[30] rested on a particular understanding of God's forgiveness. If, as I am inclined to believe, they were meant to indicate something about the nature of the coming messianic banquet, about who would participate and on what terms, then again we can see how ideas about God's forgiveness, his ways of dealing with sinners, would have moulded Jesus' picture of the end. Again, if he indeed expected the Twelve to sit on the twelve thrones judging and ruling over the twelve tribes, we can see how beliefs about the rights and place within God's concern of the rural peasantry of Galilee have led to very surprising accounts of the final fulfilment, which would clearly not have been acceptable to all Jews.

I mention both cases to bring out the logical point, namely that Jesus' beliefs about the nature of God's forgiveness and of the worth of the—marginalized—Galilean peasantry (1) are both logically independent of his belief in *some* kind of resolution of Israel's problems, and (2) both combine with that latter generalized belief to produce a rather different picture of the end than, we may suppose, was John's. But if this is so, it follows that the truth or falsity of Jesus' belief in God's forgiveness is not logically dependent on the truth or falsity of the belief that such an end would shortly come.

3. *The Sense and Function of Jesus' Beliefs about the Future*

If this much be granted, then we may still want to ask what the sense and the function of such beliefs is, before we can ask what relevance they may have for us. The distinction between sense and function is important, though often overlooked.

---

30. See the important discussion of the matter in E.P. Sanders, *Jesus and Judaism*, ch. 6.

What we say is not the same thing as the effect of what we say, the reasons for saying it, what we hope to achieve by saying it.

As far as the sense is concerned, the belief that there would shortly be a final resolution of Israel's problems, possibly ushered in by times of great tribulation, but resulting in freedom from oppression and suffering, was clearly false, as the subsequent history of the Jewish people makes abundantly clear.

However, simply to say that it was false is not to exhaust its interest. In his important discussion of mythological eschatology,[31] Bultmann argued that myths about the future coming of God were one way of representing a widespread sense of human transitoriness and finitude. God's transcendence, which might elsewhere be presented in terms of his spatial elevation over the human sphere, is in the myths of eschatology said to reside in his future revelation of himself. Moreover talk of God's holiness and judgment in such myths also expresses the view that what distinguishes God and humanity is not simply transitoriness, futility: it is God's holiness and righteousness on the one hand and men and women's sinfulness and injustice on the other. Bultmann, with his concern to interpret myths existentially, restricted his treatment to their anthropological implications. But it is also surely right to point out that such myths give expression to a profound conviction that there is a reality which transcends the evil and oppression of this world, which indeed is fundamentally opposed to it and which will ultimately put an end to it. That is to say, talk of God's coming with power to judge this world is one way of expressing one's profound rejection of certain values and actions and of advocating certain others. The attractiveness of such language and imagery is attested to by its use by contemporary writers and artists, to whom I alluded earlier.

This provides a suitable point from which to consider the function of such beliefs. Myths of this kind may be seen in the most general terms as cultural resources by which particular communities may make sense of and shape their experience, may interpret those experiences which seem most deeply to question their inherited beliefs and which may lead them to

---

31. *Jesus Christ and Mythology* (London: SCM, 1960), ch. 2.

falter or despair. How specifically they do that will vary enormously. What we have just been suggesting is that mythological eschatology may offer very potent means for condemning certain, perhaps dominant, modes of behaviour and values and advocating others. Such myths also, in so far as they point to the future, can provide a form for discussing possible futures for the group, for an examination of its norms, indeed, *where a radical change in the whole constitution of society is entertained, for a critique or rejection of other deeply held beliefs in that culture.* But always we must be aware of the range of uses to which such beliefs may be put. It is not for us to say how they could have been used, rather to look and see how they were in fact used.

Thus, for example, in Revelation belief in a final end to this age to be followed by a world where all tears will be wiped away serves to call the churches to repentance, to encourage and to reinvigorate a suffering community. For Matthew and his community it may be that belief in a coming judgment, more or less imminent (Mt. 24f.), may be used to reinforce the rules of a group which is beginning to become settled and to establish its own rules in contrast to those of its surrounding society. But such beliefs may also serve *to open up* the possibilities of new worlds and thus stand at the beginning of new communal forms of social world construction. It is here that I would wish to locate a figure like Jesus.

The three types of use of mythological eschatology are taken from communities or individuals who are concerned to advocate or uphold certain values. What distinguishes the way in which the beliefs function in the three cases is, in the first instance, the situation in which the groups or individuals find themselves. In the first two cases the writings are addressed to young communities who are experiencing difficulties of various sorts in living up to the norms and values which they have recently adopted, which are innovative and, in large measure, 'dissonant' with the values of the surrounding culture. In Revelation persecution is making the community falter and belief in some final resolution is therefore consoling and encouraging to those who might otherwise defect. In Matthew a young community attempting to develop its own norms and values in competition with Jamnia requires certain sanctions for the enforcement of those norms. The danger here may well be that the proximity of other, perhaps quite powerfully attractive, religious norms with their roots in the same cultural milieu as Matthew's may threaten to mislead the community into adulterating (as the writer sees it) norms which it is just beginning to develop and embody in social forms.

Jesus' situation is significantly different. He too lived in a situation where the values of his community were under pressure, but his response as a prophetic, liminal figure is to reach out in search of new values which may reinvigorate the group. The values which he advocated were, I have argued elsewhere,[32] importantly innovative and he therefore had to find some legitimization for his advocacy of values which were contentious within his own community. Thus here there is a very different strategy at play. The proclamation of a new age means the parting with the old. Old rules may be abandoned in favour of the new, while still invoking the authority of the tradition for the change. Thus belief in the coming of the kingdom, the New Age, can have a subversive effect. The tradition can be invoked to legitimate that which transcends it: 'Many prophets and kings have desired to see what you have seen, and have not seen it...' (Lk. 10.24).

That is to say, belief in the end may be used not merely to reinforce and inculcate beliefs in a particular community's values. It may also be used to introduce or advocate new values, new ways of perceiving God, the world and humanity which are, if not unprecedented, nevertheless significantly discontinuous with the community's traditions. Whatever it was that Jesus was suggesting about the nature of God's forgiveness through his meals with sinners, it was clearly offensive. If indeed he predicted the destruction of the Temple, but not its restoration, then that too would have been deeply offensive to some.

There is an important sense here in which Jesus is fighting on two fronts. He, like other Jewish leaders, is opposed to the

32. See my *Jesus and the Transformation of Judaism* (London: Darton, Longman & Todd, 1980) and 'Parables and the Search for a New Community', in *The Social World of Formative Christianity and Judaism* (Festschrift H.C. Kee; Philadelphia: Fortress, 1988), pp. 235-63.

powerful alien cultural forces of Hellenism which threaten to undermine traditional Jewish mores. But he is also opposed to, and indeed seen as a threat by, other Jewish groups who developed different strategies for dealing with the erosion of Jewish norms and who had greater influence within the Jewish community. It is interesting to speculate that in advocating new norms Jesus is in a creative way drawing on values from both cultural worlds, that of Judaism and of the Graeco-Roman world. But in so doing he is reaching out to new worlds which are to come, beginning to lay the foundations for the new communities which will come after him.

In his concluding remarks to his historical survey Albert Schweizer stressed the unknownness of Jesus as that which links us to him and to his disciples. And this neatly poses the problem which besets all historical research: how to avoid on the one hand the perils of modernizing one's subject and on the other falling into pure antiquarianism where technical skill and erudition are so highly valued as to suppress any attempt at explanation and understanding. And the suggestion is sometimes made,[33] that it is in perceiving the strangeness of a subject, a period, that we learn most, as we are taken out of our own age and confronted with what is other, yet still recognizably a part of us.

But in what sense is Jesus 'unknown'? And is that 'unknownness' the same for us as it was then for the disciples? Hardly; they, we may suppose, shared his belief that the end would shortly come, as did many of their contemporaries. We can only adopt such beliefs at the price of losing all contact with reasonableness and historical experience. They met him as one unknown, an insignificant son of a Galilaean outsider; we meet him as one all too well known, as one who has shaped and been involved in 2000 years of our history. And yet, historical research does indeed dissociate Jesus from the authoritative figure of our own Christian past, and so gives him back to

33. D.E. Nineham, *New Testament Interpretation in an Historical Age* (London: Athlone, 1976).

us with all the strangeness and surprisingness of one we thought we knew and now discover we knew only darkly.

Yet while we may not share the disciples' belief in the imminent coming of the kingdom, we do share with them—if we accept his call—the same sense of taking our lead from someone who stands outside and challenges the accepted norms of our society. For there is a strange parallel between the ways in which, on the basis of belief in the end, Jesus was able to challenge his society's most cherished beliefs—and the way in which if we accept this strange Jesus he may enable us to break free from the inherited traditions which bind us.

But again we must guard against the perils of modernizing, of pressing the similarities too hard. He looked to a sudden and dramatic transformation of his world; as indeed did many others who spoke for the powerless of their age. We may stand in a very different position in relation to the management and control of change in our society. In this sense then our way will be very different from that of his first disciples; it may involve us in political debate, planning and action in ways which would simply not have been available to them. Thus the tasks Jesus sets us, as Schweitzer indeed recognized, will not be those that he set them. But they will be grounded in the same urgent insistence on the needs of the poor, the sick and the oppressed, the heavy laden.

But, suggests Schweitzer, beyond all these differences and similarities what unites us or divides us from the first disciples is the ability to hear and to respond to Jesus' words—'Follow me'—to accept them as binding and authoritative. All too often it is claimed that the historical study of Jesus sets a divide, a distance between us and him which precludes involvement, discipleship. And in this sense Schweitzer's life-long commitment to him, his own discipleship, seems puzzling, even aberrant, a *trahison des clercs*.

What I have offered by way of discussion of Jesus' apocalyptic beliefs may perhaps be regarded as an apology, if one were needed, for Schweitzer's commitment to Jesus *because* of his historical understanding of him. I have tried to show in the first place that Jesus' beliefs about the nature of God were not inextricably linked to some belief in the sudden end to the world that he shared with many of his contemporaries. And I have also tried to show that a proper understanding of beliefs about the End revealed them as playing an important part in allowing Jesus to articulate beliefs and values which ran counter to those which were current in his society. The intriguing thing about mythological eschatology is indeed its continued ability to enable writers and artists to see beyond the limitations of their present world; to see its horrors without losing hope and to see values and goods which may lead them beyond. But it is perhaps also significant that the most effective use of such language is now in the fictive or imaginative mode. Where in Western society it is taken literally, as in some religious sects, it is often linked to the most appalling lack of moral and theological sensitivity.

In what sense may Jesus and his words still call us out of our world, call us to see its darkness for what it is and to seek to embody the values and beliefs he advocated in new worlds? If we cannot be shaken out of our bondage to this world by the proclamation of the imminent end, what will move us? Here perhaps attending to the nature of charismatic leadership, of the trust and obedience given to such figures, may assist. Such leaders cannot establish their authority by appeal to accepted notions, by presenting acceptable credentials, for they seek to challenge the very foundation of the society to which they address themselves. Paradoxically they have authority in so far as they earn it, elicit it from their followers. Further, that recognition is given insofar as the charismatic leader is able to speak to their inmost hopes and fears, to illuminate them and to point men and women in directions, perhaps both painful and surprising, which may cost them their all—and which may yet hold out the promise of life, joy and peace.

Such charismatic figures are disturbing: they have the power, that is, to remind us that not even our most firmly established religious and moral traditions are inalienable possessions, but rather that they represent, at best, the best findings in humanity's never-ending search for the truth. They have the power to stir men and women to renewed efforts in the search for that truth and they do so as they set tasks beyond any individual's sole resources and yet which we cannot, if we wish to remain truly human, refuse. That is, of course, in so far as they are indeed true guides.

In this sense Jesus remains our contemporary. He has the power—and here surely Schweitzer is right to see historical studies as his ally—to challenge and disturb even our most deeply cherished beliefs, even and especially those which are linked to his name, and to set us free to follow his call to care for the needy, and the wounded, to love our enemies. And this power resides, not in some assured authority, the authority of the official texts of an official church, but in his ability to renew in us our common search for the truth and to be our guide. Precisely in our encounter with him as *the one who stands outside us and against our world* lies the possibility of that conversion.

MORE FRUIT FROM THE WITHERED TREE:
TEMPLE AND FIG-TREE IN MARK
FROM A GRAECO-ROMAN PERSPECTIVE

William R. Telford

Introduction

One of the pleasures of being invited to contribute to this
Festschrift for Ernst Bammel is to recall the period in the
early 1970s when as a postgraduate at Cambridge I had the
good fortune, as others have done, to benefit from his erudite
and exacting supervision. To a young man embarking on a
doctoral thesis, Ernst's scholarship was, and remains, awe-
inspiring, both in the breadth of his interests and in the depth
of his knowledge. One such interest is the theme of this collection, the Second Temple. Inspired by him, I was led into an
investigation which had as its overall aim the task of ascer-
taining the attitude taken to the Temple by the author of the
earliest Gospel, Mark, and the community to which and for
which he speaks. In narrower and more concrete terms, that
investigation was concerned with one of the most curious
miracle stories in the Jesus tradition, namely his cursing of the
barren fig-tree (Mk 11.12-14, 20ff.), a story which was seen as
supplying a vital clue to that attitude. The place and function
of this pericope within Mark's redactional scheme, its subsequent redaction-history within the Gospels, its origin, background and *Sitz im Leben* prior to Mark and its particular
connection with the Cleansing tradition of Mk 11.15-19
formed the basic core of the thesis.

That study under Ernst, which came happily to print,[1]
sought the answer to a twofold question. Starting from the

1. W.R. Telford, *The Barren Temple and the Withered Tree. A Redaction-critical Analysis of the Cursing of the Fig-tree Pericope in Mark's*

familiar observation that the story is split into two parts around the account of Jesus' action in the Temple, it asked what Mark might have intended this puzzling story to convey in its present context and how in turn it was likely to have been understood by the first-century reader for whom it was intended. Investigations, therefore, proceeded along two main lines. In the first place, literary-, form-, source- and redaction-critical work on the Synoptic Gospels, and on Mark in particular, were brought to bear on the pericope. In the second place, certain related motifs pertaining to the story were traced within background material supplied by the Old Testament, early Judaism and nascent Christianity. In particular, the place of the tree and especially the fig-tree within this material was examined, and their literary, religious and symbolic usage explored. Attention was given especially to the cultic dimension and note taken where fig-tree imagery was linked with temple imagery. The aim was to construct thereby a conceptual pattern or grid of related ideas and associations that would enable a modern reader to place himself or herself within the interpretative frame of reference that might have been adopted by a first-century reader of the Gospel.

It is unnecessary to repeat the detailed argument of the book but, in general, this research led me to conclude that the fig-tree story is best understood against the background of Jewish eschatology. It was conceived, I have maintained, out of elements discernible in the Old Testament and within a climate of expectation regarding the Messianic Age—in which nature will be extraordinarily responsive to the righteous, when mountains will be made low, when trees will bear fruit out of season, and so on. Within the framework of Mark's Gospel, however, linked as it is with Jesus' action in the Temple, the story has a further significance. It is intended to be an eschatological sign, prefiguring the destruction of the Temple cultus (an event of dramatic significance to the Markan community) and hence has been deliberately placed by Mark in con-

Gospel and its Relation to the Cleansing of the Temple Tradition (JSNTS 1; Sheffield: JSOT Press, 1980).

nection with these Christian traditions describing Jesus' Messianic appearance in Jerusalem.

For Mark, then, and for the tradition he used, the Judaeo-Christian associations explored in *The Barren Temple and the Withered Tree* were determinative. However, the world of Mark and his readers was not simply that of the Old Testament, early Judaism or nascent Christianity, as we are now recognizing to a far greater extent. His first-century world and theirs was also the world of the Roman Empire, an empire that stretched 'from the ocean to the Arabian desert, from the snows of Germany to the hot Sahara' and 'a power whose eye pierced everywhere'.[2] The *lingua franca* of that world was the Greek language, *koinē*, and as a result it was a world influenced and suffused since Alexander's time by Greek culture, thought and ways. The New Testament itself, despite its Semitic heritage and character, belongs nonetheless to the extensive realm of Greek literature, and more particularly to its Hellenistic phase.[3] Mark itself was written in Greek and for a readership whose mother-tongue it was or who were capable of reading it in this medium.

It follows then that no interpreter of the New Testament in general, or the Gospel of Mark in particular, can afford to ignore the Hellenistic dimension, the Graeco-Roman influences and perceptions which shaped or affected it, either at the level of its composition or in terms of its readership. Parallels in Graeco-Roman literature, education and world-view which a comparative study of Hellenism produces can be illuminating and instructive. Much recent research is highlighting the influence of the Graeco-Roman world on early Christian life and literature. Early Christianity is a product broadly of two streams of tradition, Jewish and Hellenistic, and the New Testament writings, and Mark in particular, in many ways reflect the intersection of these. Scholars are increasingly

2. F.J. Haverfield, 'The Roman Empire in the First Century', in *Peake's Commentary on the Bible* (London: T.C. & E.C. Jack, 1920), p. 612.

3. This point was strongly emphasized by Professor F.F. Bruce in a Presidential Address to the Studiorum Novi Testamenti Societas at Aberdeen, August 26, 1975. See F.F. Bruce, 'The New Testament and Classical Studies', *NTS* 22 (1975–76), pp. 229-42.

exploring the social and rhetorical interaction between the early Christian tradition, with its Jewish roots, and the Greek-speaking people of the Mediterranean world in whose communities the Christian writings were disseminated.[4] Even on Christianity's native soil, in Palestine, the mother-religion of Judaism was not hermetically sealed from Hellenistic influences.[5] The stability and prosperity established by the Roman Empire allowed considerable scope there as elsewhere for the free intercourse of ideas and beliefs as well as of trade and commerce—before, that is, the destruction of the Jewish state by Titus (AD 67–70) which constituted the most notable military interruption to an otherwise widely enjoyed *pax romana*.

All four of the Gospels, with the possible exception of Mark, were written, according to most scholars, after 70 AD, the year that witnessed this cataclysmic destruction of Jerusalem and its Temple. In his published writings, the late S.G.F. Brandon

4. Recent literature on this subject is too extensive to mention exhaustively but note should be taken, for example, of D.E. Aune, *The New Testament in its Literary Environment* (Library of Early Christianity, 8; Philadelphia: Westminster, 1987); D.E. Aune (ed.), *Graeco-Roman Literature and the New Testament* (SBL Sources for Biblical Study, 21; Atlanta: Scholars Press, 1988); A.J. Malherbe, *Moral Exhortation. A Graeco-Roman Sourcebook* (Library of Early Christianity, 4; Philadelphia: Westminster, 1986); H. Elsom, 'The New Testament and Graeco-Roman Writing', in R. Alter and F. Kermode (eds.), *A Literary Guide to the Bible* (Cambridge, MA: Belknap, 1987), pp. 561-78; P.R. Trebilco, 'Paul and Silas—"Servants of God Most High" (Acts 16.16-18)', *JSNT* 36 (1989), pp. 51-73; F.G. Downing, 'Cynics and Christians', *NTS* 30 (1984), pp. 584-93; *idem*, 'Ears to Hear', in A.E. Harvey (ed.), *Alternative Approaches to New Testament Study* (London: SPCK, 1989), pp. 97-121; *idem, Jesus and the Threat of Freedom* (London: SCM, 1987); *idem, Christ and the Cynics. Jesus and Other Radical Preachers in First-Century Tradition* (JSOT Manuals, 4; Sheffield: JSOT Press, 1987), esp. pp. 14-15 (where a variety of sayings on the temple and figs are given). In particular, on Mark's Gospel, see V.K. Robbins, 'Mark 1.14-20: An Interpretation at the Intersection of Jewish and Graeco-Roman Traditions', *NTS* 28 (1982), pp. 220-36; *idem, Jesus the Teacher: A Socio-Rhetorical Interpretation of Mark* (Philadelphia: Fortress, 1984); *idem*, 'The Woman who Touched Jesus' Garment: Socio-Rhetorical Analysis of the Synoptic Accounts', *NTS* 33 (1987), pp. 502-15.

5. See W.D. Davies, *Paul and Rabbinic Judaism* (London: SPCK, 1953), pp. 5-8.

claimed that, on internal evidence, Mark itself was written shortly after 70 AD and that it was, in fact, the destruction of Jerusalem that called forth the Gospel (a literary form that was in itself a *nouveau genre*[6]). Mark, in his view, 'was a product of the reaction of some body of Gentile Christians to the overthrow of the Jewish national state' and 'may fairly be regarded as a mirror in which may be found reflections of the mind of such Christians when they considered what that event has meant for them'.[7] In respect of its audience and provenance, moreover, he was of the firm opinion that 'the Gospel was written for a Greek-speaking, Christian community which needed to have Aramaic words and Jewish customs explained to it. These and other facts support the early tradition that Mark was composed at Rome, presumably for the use of the Church there.'[8]

Although Brandon's views on Christian origins have not been shared by all scholars,[9] most would accept that Mark's

6. More recent work has questioned this assertion. Cf. C.H. Talbert, *What is a Gospel? The Genre of the Canonical Gospels* (London: SPCK, 1978); D.E. Aune, 'The Problem of the Genre of the Gospels: A Critique of C.H. Talbert's *What is a Gospel?*', in R.T. France and D. Wenham (eds.), *Gospel Perspectives: Studies in History and Tradition in the Four Gospels*, II (Sheffield: JSOT Press, 1981), pp. 9-60; Aune, *New Testament in its Literary Environment*, pp. 17-76; and the discussion in W.R. Telford (ed.), *The Interpretation of Mark* (Issues in Religion and Theology, 7; London: SPCK/Philadelphia: Fortress, 1985), pp. 9-10.

7. *The Fall of Jerusalem and the Christian Church* (London: SPCK, 1951), p. 186.

8. 'The Date of the Markan Gospel', *NTS* 7 (1960–61), p. 127. Brandon's views on the *Sitz im Leben* and dating of the Markan Gospel are reproduced and defended in a number of works; cf. e.g. *Fall of Jerusalem*, ch. 10; the *NTS* article cited, pp. 126-41; 'Matthean Christianity', *Modern Churchman* 8 (1965), pp. 158-59; 'The Apologetical Factor in the Markan Gospel', *SE* 2 = *TU* 87 (Berlin, 1964), pp. 34-46; *Jesus and the Zealots* (New York: Charles Scribner's Sons, 1967), ch. 5; *The Trial of Jesus of Nazareth* (London: Batsford, 1968), *passim*; 'Jesus and the Zealots: Aftermath', *BJRL* 54 (1971), pp. 53-55.

9. A notable counter to his views was the collection of essays, *Jesus and the Politics of his Day* (Cambridge: Cambridge University Press, 1984) edited and with contributions by E. Bammel himself and C.F.D. Moule. See also, for example, the critical reviews of his work by C.F.D. Moule, *JTS* ns 3 (1952), pp. 106-108 (*The Fall of Jerusalem*); M. Hengel, *JSS* 14 (1969), pp. 231-40 (*Jesus and the Zealots*); W. Wink, 'Jesus and

Gospel was intended for *a Greek-speaking and predominantly Gentile Christian community* that flourished about this time.[10] The frequently occurring latinisms[11] and the explanations given of Jewish words and customs[12] would certainly seem to confirm this. A number of scholars would still also accept, moreover, that *Rome* was the place of the Gospel's origin.[13]

Revolution: Reflections on S.G.F. Brandon's *Jesus and the Zealots'*, *USQR* 25 (1969), pp. 37-59; W. Klassen, 'Jesus and the Zealot Option', *CanJT* 16 (1970), pp. 12-21; and his own evaluation of the response to his views in the *BJRL* article cited above.

10. A sample of the standard commentaries makes this clear: W.G. Kümmel, for example (*Introduction to the New Testament* [London: SCM, 1975], pp. 97-98), notes that the great majority of modern scholars agree with the tradition that Mark was composed in Rome. He himself thinks that nothing (apart from tradition and the use of Latin loan-words) points directly to Rome but that 'a Gentile Christian community in the East is much more likely'. He gives the date of composition as around AD 70. N. Perrin, too, thinks that Rome is only one possibility among others. He argues that the Gospel was written by an author who had strong links with the Palestinian form of the Christian tradition but was concerned above all with the Hellenistic Jewish Christian mission to the Gentiles. His readers were 'men and women of the church caught up in a resurgence of apocalyptic expectation occasioned by the circumstances of the Jewish War' and who were awaiting 'an imminent parousia in the period immediately following the fall of Jerusalem and the destruction of the Temple' (*The New Testament. An Introduction* [New York: Harcourt Brace Jovanovich, 1982], pp. 241-43, 257). R.H. Fuller (*A Critical Introduction to the New Testament* [London: Duckworth, 1966], pp. 106-107) proposes a Palestinian provenance for Mark. The Gospel is nonetheless a Hellenistic one, he asserts, but its traditions are also in close touch with Palestinian tradition. He suggests Antioch as a likely place of origin and a date of c. AD 68. W. Marxsen claims that the author was writing in or near Galilee by reason of the interest he takes in this area, and suggests a date between AD 67 and 69 (*Introduction to the New Testament* [Oxford: Blackwell, 1968], pp. 142-43).

11. Cf. e.g. 4.21; 5.9, 15; 6.21, 27, 37, 39; 7.4; 12.14, 15, 38, 42; 13.17; 14.5, 21, 24; 15.15, 16, 29, 39; and see V. Taylor, *Mark* (London: Macmillan, 1952), pp. 44-45.

12. Cf. e.g. 5.41; 7.2-4, 11, 34; 12.18, 42; 15.16, 22, 34, 42; Taylor, *Mark*, pp. 296 (on 5.41), 334-35 (on 7.1f., 3).

13. The classic arguments are found in B.W. Bacon, *Is Mark a Roman Gospel?* (Cambridge, MA: Harvard University Press, 1919), *passim*; B.H. Streeter, *The Four Gospels* (London: Macmillan, 1936), pp. 12, 488-99; M. Goguel, *The Life of Jesus* (London: George Allen & Unwin, 1933), p. 141; F.C. Grant, *The Gospels: Their Origin and their*

Given the Graeco-Roman ambience of the work, then, it is altogether surprising that few, if any, of the commentators upon the Markan fig-tree story have tried to cast some light on the pericope from this quarter.[14] It will be my purpose, therefore, in this article, to supplement what I have already written about the symbolic nature of the story by examining the place of the fig-tree and related motifs in the Graeco-Roman world. How would the Gentile reader, albeit steeped in the Old Testament tradition, have looked at the story? What associations would he or she have shared with the Old Testament and early Judaism regarding trees and the fig-tree? What possible additional associations might have coloured the thinking of the Graeco-Roman reader? Would he or she have shared the view of nature and of the miraculous that was reflected in the haggadic stories that I have previously examined?[15] In sum, how would he or she have understood the withering (on the part of the Christian movement's founder) of a fig-tree in the vicinity of the Jewish Holy City? To gain impressions that might supply clues to this understanding, let me first of all remark on the place in general of the fig-tree in the Graeco-Roman world, before going on to consider its symbolic associations (erotic and cultic) for Gentiles. I shall also examine the place of trees and fig-trees in Hellenistic myth, legend and omen before drawing some conclusions where this particular story (in its Temple context) and the reader of Mark are concerned.

The Fig-tree and its Fruit in Graeco-Roman Estimation[16]

The fig-tree was regarded with the greatest esteem throughout the Graeco-Roman world. Both delicious and cheap, figs

Growth (London: Faber & Faber, 1959), pp. 74-77, 116; Taylor, *Mark*, p. 32; see further scholars and bibliography cited in Brandon, *Zealots*, p. 221 nn. 3, 4.

14. This point is also noted by V.K. Robbins in respect of the commentaries on Mark in general which tend to ignore the Graeco-Roman parallels. See *NTS* 28 (1982), p. 220.

15. *Barren Temple*, pp. 186-96.

16. For *general works dealing with figs and the fig-tree*, see *Barren Temple*, p. 165 n. 17, but for Graeco-Roman material note especially: G.B. Winer, *Biblisches Realwörterbuch* (Leipzig: Carl Heinrich

were as highly prized by the Greeks and the Romans as they
were by the inhabitants of Palestine. Sister to the vine,[17] as in
the Old Testament, the fig-tree was looked upon as the tree
par excellence that had led humans from a wild and barbaric
state into a purer, softer, more civilized life.[18] Athenaeus, the

Reclam sen., 1847; henceforth *BRW*), I, pp. 366-67; H. Graf zu Solms-
Laubach, *Die Herkunft, Domestication und Verbreitung des gewöhn-
lichen Feigenbaums* (Göttingen: Dieterichsche Universitäts-Buch-
drückerei, 1882; henceforth *Solms-Laubach*), *passim*; A. Pauly and G.
Wissowa (eds.), *Real-Encyclopädie der classischen Altertumswissenschaft* (Stuttgart: J.B. Metzler, 1909; henceforth *PW*), VI, 'Feige',
ad loc.; T. Klauser, *Reallexikon für Antike und Christentum*
(Stuttgart: Anton Hiersemann, 1969; henceforth *RAC*), VII, pp. 640-58,
679-81; J. Murr, *Die Pflanzenwelt in der griechischen Mythologie*
(Innsbruck: Wagnersche Universitäts-Buchhandlung, 1890), pp. 31-35;
V. Buchheit, 'Feigensymbolik im antiken Epigramm', *RheinMus* 103
(1960), pp. 200-29; J.G. Frazer, *The Golden Bough* (London: Macmillan, 1911–15), *passim*; A.B. Cook, 'ΣΥΚΟΦΑΝΤΗΣ', *Classical Review* 21
(1907), pp. 133-36. For *study aids* to the Classical Literature, see e.g. J.
Lemprière and F.A. Wright (eds.), *Classical Dictionary of Proper
Names Mentioned in Ancient Authors* (London: Routledge & Kegan
Paul, 1949; henceforth Lemprière), and P. Harvey (ed.), *The Oxford
Companion to Classical Literature* (Oxford: Clarendon, 1937; henceforth *OCCL*). For the abbreviations of classical authors and works,
used here see Liddell and Scott's *Greek–English Lexicon* (Oxford:
Clarendon, 1968).

17. A legend attributed to the Epic poet Pherenicus tells how Oxylus,
son of Oreius, married his sister Hamadryas and fathered among
others Ampelus (vine) and Syke (fig-tree), two tree nymphs who subsequently gave their names to these trees. As a result the satirical poet
Hipponax of Ephesus (fl. c. 540 BC) called the black fig-tree sister of the
vine (συκῆν μέλαιναν ἀμπέλου κασιγνήτην; cf. Ath. 3.78b [Loeb Classical
Library; henceforth LCL], I, pp. 337-39, and *PW*, VI, p. 2145; *RAC*,
VII, p. 642).

18. 'Als wohlschmeckendes, auch dem Ärmsten leicht zugängliches
Nahrungsmittel stand im alten Griechenland die Feige in sehr hohem
Ansehen und wurde allgemein als diejenige Frucht gepriesen, welche
die ursprünglich rohen Menschen zu einem milderen, sanfteren
Leben geführt habe' (Murr, *Pflanzenwelt*, p. 31). Herodotus recounts
how a certain Lydian named Sandanis attempted to dissuade Croesus
from marching against Cyrus and the Persians by informing him that
there was nothing to be gained by conquering the inhabitants of a barren land who neither drank wine nor ate figs (Hdt. 1.71 [LCL, I,
pp. 86f.]; see Frazer, *Golden Bough*, II, pp. 315-16). Belief in the
'civilizing' influence of the fig-tree is illustrated by the Elder Pliny,
who states that if a branch of the wild fig-tree is put round the neck of a

grammarian of Naucratis in Egypt (fl. c. 200 AD) and author of the *Deipnosophistae* ('Dons at Dinner')[19] records the view of one Magnus who said that the fig-tree 'was made to be the guide of men to civilization (ἡγεμὼν τοῦ καθαρείου βίου τοῖς ἀνθρώποις ἐγένετο)'. The Athenians, he further relates, named its fruit for this reason ἡ ἡγητηρία, or the Leader, and the place where it was deemed to have been first discovered, a suburb of Athens, was named by them Ἱερὰ Συκῆ (Sacred Fig-tree).[20] Figs were carried at the head of a procession in the Greek festival of *Plynteria*, a halt being made in Ἱερὰ Συκῆ on the way.[21]

In Jewish estimation, the fig-tree was a blessing from Yahweh to his people. Among the Greeks and Romans, it was a gift from the gods. Legend attributed it to Demeter who had caused it to spring forth from the earth (at the aforementioned Ἱερὰ Συκῆ) as a gift for Phytalus, the hero who had given her hospitality.[22] Other legends name it variously as the gift of Dionysus, of the Phrygian heroine, Syke, of Athena, or of Chronos (Saturn).[23] A number of ancient cities in Greece and Italy were called after the fig-tree, with aetiological legends

---

bull, however fierce, the animal will be subdued to the extent of becoming incapable of movement (*H.N.* 23.130 [LCL, VI, pp. 500-501]). Such a belief was held by a number of the ancient writers; cf. *PW*, VI, p. 2145; *RAC*, VII, p. 656. 'The eating of figs' as a symbol of the peaceful, prosperous life can at times carry with it, however, the more disparaging notion of an existence that is soft, dissipated and devoid of aggressive vitality, a way of life suited to Lotus-Eaters (see Murr, *Pflanzenwelt*, p. 32). Patroclus, a general in the army of Ptolemy I, is said to have sent a symbolic gift of fish and figs to the Macedonian king Antigonus Gonatas (277–39 BC), these friendly offerings being interpreted by the latter to his friends as a sign prompting the Macedonians either to become masters of the sea, or to 'eat figs' (Ath. 8.334a [LCL, IV, pp. 16-17]; *PW*, VI, p. 2144).

19. See Lemprière and *OCCL*, *ad loc.*

20. Ath. 3.74d (LCL, I, pp. 320-23). For further references to Ἱερὰ Συκῆ and to the fig as the earliest cultivated fruit, see Cook, *op. cit.*, p. 134 n. 2; Murr, *Pflanzenwelt*, p. 31; *PW*, VI, p. 2145.

21. *PW*, *ibid.*, and below.

22. See, for example, Paus. 1.37.2 (LCL, I, pp. 196-99); Murr, *Pflanzenwelt*, p. 31; *PW*, VI, p. 2145; *RAC*, VII, p. 657; Cook, *op. cit.*, p. 134 and n. 2.

23. See Murr, *Pflanzenwelt*, pp. 32-34, and below.

and sagas ostensibly explaining their origins.[24] Very often it was the long-standing connection of special, peculiar or sacred fig-trees with these places that gave rise to the legends associated with them.

The fig-tree appears to have been cultivated in Greece and Italy from a very early time, as its role in these ancient legends and place-names indicates. The tree features, for example, in the foundation-myth of Rome, the legend of Romulus and Remus, as we shall presently see. Some scholars have claimed, indeed, that Greece was the cradle for the cultivation of the fig-tree (e.g. Reynier), but this is disputed. J. Murr claims the distinction for Asia Minor (whence it was introduced on to the Greek mainland about the eighth century BC),[25] while Solms-Laubach gives the honour ultimately to the Semitic peoples of Syria.[26]

---

24. Cf. e.g. the celebrated city of Olynthus in Macedonia, named, it was said, after a son of Hercules but deriving etymologically from ὁ ὄλυνθος, the name variously used for the fig-tree or its fruit (below, n. 30; Ath. 8.334e-f [LCL, IV, pp. 18-21]; Murr, *Pflanzenwelt*, p. 34; *PW*, VI, p. 2146). The city of Sykea in Cilicia was said to have received its name from one of the Titans, Sykeus by name, who had been pursued by Zeus but had taken refuge with his mother, Gē (the personification of the earth). She had caused the fig-tree to grow for her son's pleasure (or protection, εἰς διατριβὴν τῷ παιδί—the tree was believed to be able to divert lightning bolts! Cf. Ath. 3.78b [LCL, I, pp. 336-37]; Murr, *Pflanzenwelt*, p. 34; *PW*, VI, p. 2145). Strabo (c. 64 BC–AD 14) mentions an Erineus (= wild fig-tree) south-west of Troy, a place described by him as 'rugged and full of wild fig trees') (Str. 13.1.35 [LCL, VI, pp. 70-71]; *RAC*, VII, p. 643). A city, Ficana, not far from Rome and on the way to Ostia, existed, according to Livy, in the time of Ancus Martius, one of the legendary kings of Rome (Livy 1.33.2 [LCL, I, pp. 118-19]; *PW*, VI, p. 2104), and a city called Ficulea or Ficuliae, between Rome and Nomentum, is said to have been built by the Aborigines and existed at least up until the time of the Emperors (cf. Livy 3.52.3 [LCL, II, pp. 172-73]; D.H. *Antiq.* 1.16.5 [LCL, I, pp. 54-55]; Mart. 6.27 [LCL, I, pp. 372-73]; *PW*, VI, p. 2104). In respect of the aetiological legends, it is interesting to compare the hypothesis advanced by E. Schwartz regarding the origin of the Markan fig-tree story; see 'Der verfluchte Feigenbaum', *ZNW* 5 (1904), pp. 80-84; Telford, *Barren Temple*, pp. 11-12, 18, 213, 214-15, 216.

25. Murr, *Pflanzenwelt*, p. 31.

26. *Solms-Laubach*, pp. 72ff., esp. p. 77.

The ancients make reference to two distinct kinds of fig-tree, the wild fig-tree (ὁ ἐρινεός or *caprificus*) and the cultivated fig-tree (ἡ συκῆ or *ficus*).[27] The former (the male tree) is infested with insects which alone can pollinate the fruit of the cultivated tree (the female). In consequence of this, branches of fruit from the wild fig-tree were hung up on these female trees, so securing, by artificial means, 'a real marriage of the trees (caprification)'.[28] Both Theophrastus and Pliny record that a wild fig-tree may turn spontaneously into a cultivated one, or *vice versa*. If the latter should occur, it is a portent of a very serious kind.[29]

A whole variety of terms were employed for the fig-tree and its parts, a fact that again reflects the tree's importance and its long-standing cultivation.[30] The wild fig-tree produced fruit either once, twice or three times a year according to the

27. *Solms-Laubach*, p. 5; *PW*, VI, p. 2100; *RAC*, VII, p. 641.
28. Cf. Frazer, *Golden Bough*, II, pp. 314-15. For a description by ancient writers of the technique of caprification, see Thphr. *H.P.* 2.8 (LCL, I, pp. 150-55); Plin. *H.N.* 15.21 (LCL, IV, pp. 342-45), and, further, *Solms-Laubach*, pp. 23ff.; E.C.A. Riehm, *Handwörterbuch des biblischen Altertums* (Leipzig: Velhagen & Klasing, 1893), p. 442; *PW*, VI, pp. 2102, 2129-33; C. Roth and G. Wigoder (eds.), *Encyclopedia Judaica* (Jerusalem: Keter, 1971; henceforth *EJud*), VI, p. 1273; *RAC*, VII, p. 641.
29. Cf. Thphr. *H.P.* 3.1 (LCL, I, pp. 118-21); Plin. *H.N.* 17.38, 242 (LCL, V, pp. 166-69). Paul's famous analogy of the olive tree springs to mind in this connection. See A.G. Baxter and J.A. Ziesler, 'Paul and Arboriculture: Romans 11.17-24', *JSNT* 24 (1985), pp. 25-32.
30. The unripe green figs of the cultivated tree were named ὄλυνθοι and they in turn produced the first-ripe fruit, the πρόδρομος (*ficus*). The term πρόδρομος is used in Isa. 28.4 (LXX) (cf. *TDNT*, VII, p. 751 n. 3; Telford, *Barren Temple*, p. 147 and n. 97). The summer figs were called σῦκα or *fica* (sometimes *serotinae*) and the popular dried figs ἰσχάδες or *caricae*. The term ὄλυνθος was also used of the wild fig-tree or its fruit, although ὁ ἐρινός or ἐρινεός is the most common designation. The usage of these terms was not uniform, however, and different regions often employed special terms of their own. On Naxos, the σῦκα were called μείλιχα (the 'soft' or 'gentle' fruits). The term καρπός, however, designates both the fruit of the wild fig-tree (which was generally unpalatable) and that of the cultivated tree. The tree in Mark's story was doubtless intended to be a cultivated tree, since its fruit (if it had any) was deemed to be edible, and the term ἐρινός rather than συκῆ would probably otherwise have been used. See *PW*, VI, pp. 2103-12; *RAC*, VII, p. 641; *BRW*, p. 367.

ancients (they, like modern scholars, did not agree on the exact number of crops),[31] but its fruit was in the main quite unpalatable.[32] Reference is sometimes made to the winter figs of both species,[33] but these are rare, do not fully ripen, are easily shed, and are unpleasant to eat.[34]

The varieties of cultivated fig-trees and the different strains of figs in the ancient world were numerous. In Italy, for example, in Cato's day (234–149 BC) six different varieties were on the market. During the reign of the Emperor Tiberius (AD 14–27), a large number were imported from Syria, according to Pliny, and he himself could name some twenty-nine varieties in his own day.[35] Of all figs, however, it was Attic figs that were deemed the best in the world (at least according to Athenaeus!).[36] The fig-tree was believed to have been first produced in Attica, as we have noted, and Aelian reports that the Athenian's diet was figs long before he learned to eat meat.[37] The delicious Attic dried figs or ἰσχάδες, indeed, are cited as the emblem of Athens itself.[38] A story is told by Dinon, an historian of the time of Alexander, that a eunuch deliberately brought figs to the table of the Persian king Xerxes to remind him of the expedition he had planned against Athens.[39] The place of figs in such stories, legends and anecdotes, as well

31. See *PW*, VI, pp. 2112-13; Telford, *Barren Temple*, pp. 2-5.

32. *Solms-Laubach*, p. 5; *PW*, VI, p. 2101; Murr, *Pflanzenwelt*, p. 34.

33. Cf. e.g. Plin. *H.N.* 15.19.72 (LCL, IV, pp. 338-39); 23.64.129 (LCL, VI, pp. 500-501); I. Löw, *Die Flora der Juden* (Veröffentlichungen der Alexander Kohut Memorial Foundation, 2, 3, 4, 6; Leipzig/Wien: R. Löwit, 1924–34), IV, p. 238.

34. See *PW*, VI, p. 2113. According to Marcus Aurelius, a man seeking a child when he can no longer have one is insane, for 'only a madman will look for figs in winter' (M. Aurel. *Comm.* 11.33 [LCL, pp. 316-19]).

35. Cf. Plin. *H.N.* 15.19.68-73; 21.82-83 (LCL, IV, pp. 334-39), 344-47; see also *PW*, VI, pp. 2119-25; *RAC*, VII, pp. 646-47.

36. Cf. Ath. 3.74d-e (LCL, I, pp. 322-23); 14.652d (LCL, VI, pp. 524-25).

37. *PW*, VI, p. 2120.

38. εἰσέβαινον ἰσχάδες, τὸ παράσημον τῶν Ἀθηνῶν (Alexis, cited Ath. 14.652c [LCL, VI, pp. 524-25]).

39. Dinon, in his *Persian History*, cited Ath. 14.652b-c (LCL, VI, pp. 522-25).

as in cultic usage and symbolism, is prominent and the part they played in Athenian life is well documented.[40]

The fruit of the cultivated fig-tree was an item of diet in the ancient world that was enjoyed by the poor, by ordinary citizens and by the great alike.[41] Plato is said to have been a lover of figs[42] and the Emperor Caesar Augustus, though a sparse eater, was particularly fond of the first-ripe variety.[43] Figs were extremely nourishing. Athletes of ancient times were

40. It is worth remarking, for example, on the part played by the *sycophant* (συκοφάντης) in Athenian life (cf. *PW*, VI, pp. 2120-21; *RAC*, VII, p. 645; *TDNT*, VII, p. 759). The origin of the term is a matter of dispute, and was so even in the ancient world. The historian Istros (fl. c. 200 BC), for example, brought the term into connection with a ban on the export of Attic figs which he claimed existed in Attica in ancient times. This ban was in force in order that the residents alone might enjoy the figs, but inevitably there were those who engaged in smuggling. It was to those responsible, public-spirited persons who 'showed up' or denounced the smugglers, Istros claimed, that the term συκοφάντης ('fig-detectives') was first given (cf. Ath. 3.74e [LCL, I, pp. 322-23]). A second view was advanced by Philomnestos (cf. Ath. 3.74f. [LCL, *ibid.*]) who stated that 'sycophants' were those trustworthy citizens who, in ancient times, when fines and taxes were paid in figs, wine and oil, exacted such tolls from their fellow-citizens. Yet a third opinion was expressed by others (e.g. Suidas) who claimed that the term was originally used of those who, at a time when there was a famine in Attica, had accused others of plucking the figs from orchards that were sacred to the gods. In general, then, the term seems to have been employed originally with regard to those individuals who were mindful of and responsive to the welfare of either the public or the gods, whence it came in turn to be used of those who court persons of power and influence by slandering others for personal advantage. In his article, 'ΣΥΚΟΦΑΝΤΗΣ', *Classical Review* 21 (1907), pp. 133-36, A.B. Cook reviews but refutes the philological hypotheses advanced above. The second element of συκοφάντης, he claims, can only mean 'one who *shows* or exhibits', rather than 'one who *shows up* or informs against'. Hence he relates the word in its origin to the sign of the fig, an obscene gesture employed throughout the ancient world to ward off evil. To show the fig sign before an individual was therefore to imply that he or she was an evil to be averted by superstitious means and hence 'to slander' that person grossly.

41. See *PW*, VI, pp. 2135-37.

42. τὸν φιλόσυκον, οἷος ἦν Πλάτων ὁ φιλόσοφος (cf. Ath. 7.276f. [LCL, III, pp. 244-45]).

43. 'Ficos virides biferas maxime appetebat' (cf. Suet. *Aug.* 2.76.1 [LCL, I, pp. 240-41]).

said to have used them as a staple food before the boxer-trainer Pythagoras of Samos changed their diet to that of meat.[44] Zeno, the founder of Stoicism, was the subject of ridicule because he existed, it was said, only on bread, water and dried figs, and encouraged his disciples to do likewise.[45] Figs were fed to slaves and to soldiers.[46] They sustained peasants during the winter, were even used as animal fodder and yet at the same time were given pride of place as offerings to the gods at festivals such as the Saturnalia.[47]

The fig-tree, then, was a tree with as special a place in Graeco-Roman life as it enjoyed in Jewish life. Its citizens sat under it for shade, as in the Old Testament,[48] and it possessed, they said, the power to protect them from thunderbolts.[49] Its blossoming was a sign that winter was over (cf. Song 2.13) and that the sea could once again be navigated.[50] Its sap could curdle milk and was used in the preparation of cheese.[51] Its leaves and other parts were applied to wounds, tumours, boils and ulcers and, as in the Old Testament, it was held to have wide-ranging medicinal and curative properties.[52] Its fruit above all, either fresh, dried or pressed into a cake ($\pi\alpha\lambda\acute{\alpha}\theta\eta$),[53] was a delicacy esteemed by all—so much so, indeed, that for Lucian it is the symbol for luxury ($\tau\rho\upsilon\phi\acute{\eta}$) itself.[54]

---

44. Cf. Plin. *H.N.* 23.63.121 (LCL, VI, pp. 494-95).

45. See *RAC*, VII, p. 645.

46. *RAC*, VII, p. 644.

47. *PW*, VI, pp. 2135-37; *RAC*, VII, p. 647.

48. Cf. Plin. *H.N.* 17.18.89 (LCL, V, pp. 62-63).

49. Cf. e.g. Plu. *Moralia* 664c (LCL, VIII, pp. 318-19), and above, n. 24.

50. *RAC*, VII, p. 643.

51. Cf. e.g. Plin. *H.N.* 23.64.126 (LCL, VII, pp. 498-99); *PW*, VI, pp. 2137-38; *RAC*, VII, pp. 648-49; Löw, *Flora*, pp. 246-47.

52. Cf. e.g. Plin. *H.N.* 23.63.64 (LCL, VI, pp. 492-501); Telford, *Barren Temple*, p. 133.

53. See *PW*, VI, p. 2136; Telford, *ibid.*

54. Cf. Lucian, *Merc. Cond.* 24 (LCL, III, pp. 452-53). A well-known proverb, coined by the iambic poet Ananius, stated that figs were better than gold; cf. R. Eisler, *Orphisch-dionysische Mysteriengedanken in der christlichen Antike* (Vorträge der Bibliothek Warburg, 1922–23, Part 2; Berlin: B.G. Teubner, 1925), p. 109 and n. 1; Ath. 3.78f. (LCL, I, pp. 340-41): 'If one should lock up within the house much gold, a few

The Fig-Tree and its Fruit in Erotic and Cultic Symbolism

The prominent place that the fig-tree enjoyed in Graeco-
Roman society, combined with the practice by the ancients of
drawing on the animal and plant kingdom for figurative
imagery, led, as could be expected, to the fig-tree's common
and widespread employment in symbolism.[55] The fig-tree,
according to J. Murr, was to the plant kingdom what the pig
was to the animal kingdom—*the outstanding symbol of creative potency and fertility.*[56] The fact that the cultivated tree
(the female) could only produce the sweet, highly prized figs by
being fertilized through the agency of the wild fig-tree (the
male) led to the tree and its fruit, as well as the process of
caprification which produced it, being utilized as a profound
symbol or archetype for human procreation and coitus.[57] The
milky sap of the fig, named by the Romans *semen* (inter alia)
and occasionally by the Greeks σπέρμα,[58] was regarded as
having a fertilizing potency, a belief exampled elsewhere even
in more recent times.[59] According to J.G. Frazer, fertility rites
connected with the artificial fertilization of the fig-tree may
have been practised in Roman times and from a very early
period. On the seventh of July, a festival, the *Nonae Caprotinae* or *Poplifugia*, was held throughout Latium. It bore some
resemblance to the Saturnalia. Female slaves were allowed to
dress up as free women and to take remarkable liberties.

figs, and two or three men, he would discover how much better than
gold figs are.'
55. Cf. V. Buchheit, 'Feigensymbolik in antiken Epigramm',
RheinMus 103 (1960), p. 200: 'Wer sich des Reichtums antiker Symbole
von Homer an, namentlich im Tier- oder Pflanzenbereich, erinnert,
wird sich nicht wundern, dass gerade der im ganzen Mittelmeerraum
wachsende Feigenbaum und die als tägliches und billiges Nahrungsmittel hochbegehrte Feige dem antiken Menschen Anlass geboten
haben zur Entwicklung einer weiten und geläufigen Symbolik'.
56. 'Der Feigenbaum sei in der vegetativen Welt dasjenige, was das
Schwein in der animalischen ist, das ausgesprochenste Symbol der
Zeugung und Fruchtbarkeit' (Murr, *Pflanzenwelt*, p. 32).
57. Eisler (*Mysteriengedanken*, p. 108 and n. 5) describes the fig as
'das uraltvolkstümliche Sexualsymbol' and points out the resemblance
between the Hebrew word for the 'fig' (תְּאֵנָה) and that for 'coitus' (תַּאֲנָה).
58. *PW*, VI, p. 2112.
59. Cf. Frazer, *Golden Bough*, II, pp. 316-18.

Feasts were held under a wild fig-tree. The women cut branches from the tree (to beat each other with, Frazer surmises, and hence to communicate the generative virtue of the tree to the women struck by them) and offered the milky sap of the tree to Juno Caprotina, the goddess of the goat (*caper*) or of the wild fig-tree (*caprificus*). The licence allowed to both men and women on this occasion was supposed to secure the fertilization of the fig-trees by homoeopathic magic, a ritual counterpart to caprification. It is Frazer's view, moreover, that in very early times the old Latin kings personated the god of the fig-tree, an act involving both sacred marriage and subsequent death. The (violent) death of Romulus, who, legend claims, was suckled by a she-wolf under a fig-tree (the *ficus Ruminalis*),[60] was likewise celebrated on this day.[61]

A festival similar to the Roman *Nonae Caprotinae* seems also to have been celebrated by the Greeks. According to W.R. Paton, human scapegoats (φαρμακοί), chosen to take upon themselves the evils afflicting the community, were put to death at the *Thargelia*, an early harvest festival (May). The victims were given dried figs to eat, black and white figs were hung around their necks (an imitation of the process of caprification) and they were scourged on the genitals with branches of the wild fig-tree. The ritual, in Paton's view, was originally designed to assist the fertilization of the fig-trees by having the scapegoats personate the god or the spirit of the tree whose generative powers were believed to produce its fruit. In time the idea of purification and expiation came to overshadow this earlier notion.[62]

---

60. See the discussion towards the end of this article.

61. For this *Nonae Caprotinae* or *Poplifugia* Festival, cf. e.g. Varro, *L.L.* 6.18 (LCL, I, pp. 190-93); see also Frazer, *Golden Bough*, II, pp. 312-19; VI, p. 98; *PW*, VI, pp. 2109, 2149; *RAC*, VII, pp. 653-54.

62. Paton's view is set out and discussed by Frazer who links it with his own opinion regarding the *Nonae Caprotinae* festivals (Frazer, *Golden Bough*, IX, pp. 255-59, 272-73). Frazer also notes, it may be added, Paton's intriguing suggestion that the expulsion of Adam and Eve from Eden, clad only with fig-leaves about their loins, may harbour a reminiscence of a similar custom of fertilizing fig-trees by a pair of scapegoats who, like the victims of the *Thargelia*, assimilated themselves to the tree by wearing its foliage or fruit (*op. cit.*, IX, p. 259 n. 3).

Reference has already been made to the 'sign of the fig',[63] one of the commonest prophylactic gestures used in the ancient world, and one that is employed even in the present day.[64] The sign was made by thrusting the thumb between the first and second fingers of the closed hand, and is displayed also in amulets. Although recourse to 'the fig' was made by Greeks, Romans and Jews alike[65] as a charm to ward off ghosts or avert the Evil Eye, the sign had an undoubted sexual significance.[66] An obscene gesture of this kind, by diverting the eyes from whatever threatened the individual, could serve an apotropaic function.[67]

Also of phallic significance were the whole group of words denoting the fig-tree and its fruit: *ficus, ficosus, ficetum, marisca*, σῦκον, συκῆ, σύκινος, συκάζειν, συκώδης and even συκοφαντεῖν.[68] In his article in the *Rheinisches Museum für Philologie*, V. Buchheit examines a number of Graeco-Roman epigrams in which fig language appears and demonstrates convincingly the suggestive sexual symbolism that lies behind them.[69] The phenomenon of applying the imagery of seedtime, fruit and harvest to the sphere of love and sexuality is, of course, universal but in this respect the fig was and is preeminent.[70] Buchheit shows how the verb συκολογεῖν was used of sexual intercourse, the fig itself, σῦκον, of the male and female genitals, the word σύκωσις of venereal diseases, the

---

63. Above, n. 40.

64. See Cook, *op. cit.*, pp. 134-36.

65. Cf. e.g. Ovid, *Fast.* 5.433 (LCL, pp. 292-93); *b. Ber.* 55b (Soncino edn, p. 340). The Jewish sign, where the right thumb was placed in the left hand, and the left thumb in turn in the right hand, was regarded as an even stronger gesture; see *RAC*, VII, p. 651; Löw, *Flora*, p. 252.

66. One may possibly compare, for example, Suet. *Calig.* 4.56.2 (LCL, I, pp. 490-91).

67. Cf. e.g. Plu. *Moralia* 681F/682A (LCL, VIII, pp. 426-27); *RAC*, VII, pp. 650-51.

68. See Cook, *op. cit.*, p. 136.

69. Buchheit, 'Feigensymbolik im antiken Epigramm', *RheinMus* 103 (1960), pp. 200-29.

70 For a modern-day parallel, one can do no better than point to D.H. Lawrence's splendid poems, 'Figs' and 'Bare Fig-Trees' (*Selected Poems* [Harmondsworth: Penguin, 1954], pp. 44-48, 59-61), the former of which was employed in a scene in the Ken Russell film of Lawrence's *Women in Love* (1969).

adjective *ficosus* of the individual afflicted with it, and so on. The seeking and plucking of figs had a covert sexual connotation. The fig-tree offering its fruit to all is the comely maiden or prostitute offering men her charms.[71] The fig-tree with leaves but no fruit is the old prostitute whose sexual fires have been spent.[72] The individual who turns into a wild fig-tree (*caprificus*) has abandoned himself to unnatural vice.[73]

It is little wonder, then, that the fig-tree was to the ancients 'un arbre indécent'.[74] Pliny, for example, reports that in the year 154 BC a fig-tree sprang up (in the place where formerly a palm-tree had grown) on the altar of Jove on the Capitol. From that date, according to Piso, the eminent statesman and historian of the period, chastity no longer held its sway.[75]

Given the tree's widespread erotic significance, it is fair to ask if such a dimension is to be perceived in regard to the fig-tree that Jesus approached for its fruit. On the whole, it is unlikely. The lascivious association of the fig-tree is indeed very old, and there does seem to be some echo of it in Gen. 3.7.[76] Fig imagery occurs within the context of Hebrew love poetry (cf. Song 2.13), although not necessarily with sexual overtones. The Jews applied fig language to the different stages of female development,[77] and the sexual associations of the fig do enter into the Rabbinical treatment of Hos. 1.3.[78] In general, how-

71. Buchheit, *op. cit.*, pp. 204ff., 210ff.
72. Buchheit, *op. cit.*, p. 216.
73. Buchheit, *op. cit.*, pp. 218ff.
74. The description is Buffon's; see R.C. Trench, *Notes on the Miracles of our Lord* (London: Pickering & Inglis, 1846), p. 478 n. 2.
75. 'A quo tempore pudicitiam subversam Piso gravis auctor prodidit'; cf. Plin. *H.N.* 17.38.244 (LCL, V, pp. 168-69); Buchheit, *op. cit.*, p. 202; *PW*, VI, pp. 2144-45; *RAC*, VII, p. 652.
76. Telford, *Barren Temple*, p. 134 and n. 30.
77. Telford, *Barren Temple*, p. 183.
78. The fig-cake or $d^e b\bar{e}l\hat{a}$ is frequently mentioned in the Rabbinical literature, although a certain down-playing of the cultic significance of the fig and fig-cake, possibly in view of their Dionysiac associations, may perhaps be discerned. The sweetness of these cakes led to their being associated in the Jewish mind with 'bodily indulgence' and in turn (perhaps in view of their pagan cultic usage) with 'sexual indulgence'. The Talmud (e.g. *b. Pes.* 87a-87b [Soncino edn, pp. 460-61]) in a symbolic treatment of Hos. 1.3 describes Gomer, the daughter of *Diblaim*, as a prostitute since all enjoyed her as a cake of figs ($d^e b\bar{e}l\hat{a}$).

ever, the Jewish tradition knows little of this symbolic dimension or else avoids it (as we suspect) on account of its pagan origin. For this reason, it is improbable that Mark or his source, in conceiving the story, intended that it should convey such overtones. On the other hand, it is to be noted that the fig-tree as a sexual symbol is encountered in the writings of the Church Fathers and they doubtless imbibed such an association from the Graeco-Roman environment in which they lived. The notion of the tree as an emblem of concupiscence, the primeval tree seducing men (and particularly Adam) from a life of purity, was subsequently read into a number of scriptural passages, including our own.[79] There remains always the possibility, therefore, that a Gentile reader, influenced by both the Old Testament (and particularly the Genesis myth) and by his own native cultural associations, would have viewed the story in the exalted terms of a curse by the Saviour of the world upon a tree that symbolized moral decay, upon the tree, even, that had corrupted mankind's first parents. In less exalted terms, he may have viewed the tree's failure to produce figs for Jesus as an emblem for Israel or its Temple. In its show of leaves, but lack of fruit, it was no better than a spent prostitute, a very strong image indeed!

A similar piece of symbolic exegesis is given by Jerome (cf. Löw, *Flora*, p. 244). Opposition to the pagan usage of sweet cakes made from raisins and figs may be reflected in the prohibition against offerings of leavened loaves made with honey (cf. Lev. 2.11; *b. Men.* 52b [Soncino edn, p. 317]; *b. Pes.* 36b [Soncino edn, pp. 169ff.]; 119b-120a [Soncino edn, pp. 617-20]) and (in some cases) their intoxicating effect. Resistance to Dionysiac elements influencing popular Yahwism may also perhaps be detected in the Nazirite abstinence from wine and from dried or pressed figs (*b. Naz.* 4a [Soncino edn, p. 9]; 9a [Soncino edn, p. 28]; *b. Ker.* 13b [Soncino edn, p. 102]). One may possibly compare, too, the curious 'dessert (קיץ) like white figs for the altar' passage of *b. Sheb.* 12a-12b (Soncino edn, p. 53). White figs (בנות שוח), according to *b. A.Z.* 13b-14a (Soncino edn, p. 70), were forbidden to be sold to idolaters, doubtless because of the fig's close association with phallic worship. See W.A.L. Elmslie, *The Mishnah on Idolatry: 'Aboda Zara* (Texts and Studies, 8.2; Cambridge: Cambridge University Press, 1911), p. 9; *RAC*, VII, p. 663.

79. See, for example, Buchheit, *op. cit.*, pp. 202-204; *RAC*, VII, pp. 668-78.

Allied with the fig's erotic connotations, however, is the close
connection, touched on hitherto, between the tree and its fruit
and Graeco-Roman religion and culture. The cultic associations of the fig were remarked on in my examination of the
Old Testament and early Jewish evidence,[80] and it is well to
note these links in the Gentile world too. The fig-tree was particularly associated with phallic worship. Ritual phalluses,
used especially in connection with the cults of Dionysus and
Priapus, were made of fig-wood, as were the images, face-
masks, statues, etc., associated with these gods.[81] Figs were
favourite offerings to most of the gods of fertility,[82] however,
and they figure prominently in the rituals enacted at Graeco-
Roman festivals, especially the Athenian ones.[83] A cake of figs
(παλάθη ἰσχάδων) was carried at the head of the procession of
the *Plynteria*, to be offered to the goddess Athene (Minerva).[84]
Figs were associated, too, with the *Brauronia* (a festival held at
Brauron in Attica in honour of Artemis/Diana),[85] with the
Hyacinthia (in honour of Hyacinthus and Apollo)[86] and with
the Saturnalia, perhaps the most celebrated festival of all.[87]
The fig-tree's connection with both the Roman *Nonae
Caprotinae* and the Greek *Thargelia* festivals has already
been mentioned, along with the cathartic or expiatory signifi-
cance that was attached to it.[88]

80. *Barren Temple*, chs. 5 and 6.
81. See Elmslie, *op. cit.*, p. 9; Murr, *Pflanzenwelt*, pp. 32-33; *PW*, VI,
pp. 2145-46, 2148; *RAC*, VII, pp. 648, 657; Eisler, *Mysteriengedanken*,
p. 108 n. 5; Frazer, *Golden Bough*, VII, p. 4.
82. Excavations at Pompeii, for example, have uncovered burnt figs
among the remains of offerings presented at the Temple of Isis. For a
review of the archaeological evidence relating to the fig in antiquity, its
depiction in reliefs, in wall-paintings, etc., see *PW*, VI, pp. 2149-50;
RAC, VII, pp. 679-81.
83. See *PW*, VI, pp. 2148-19; *RAC*, VII, pp. 654-56; Cook, *op. cit.*,
p. 134; Murr, *Pflanzenwelt*, pp. 31ff.
84. See nn. 20, 21 above and the related text.
85. Cf. Ar. *Lys.* 641 (LCL, III, pp. 66-67).
86. Cook, *op. cit.*, p. 134 and n. 15.
87. Cf. Mart. 8.53.8 (LCL, I, pp. 460-61); Stat. *Silv.* 1.6.15; 4.9.26-28
(LCL, I, pp. 64-65, 262-63); Ovid, *Fast.* 1.185 (LCL, pp. 14-15); *PW*, VI,
pp. 2110, 2122, 2123.
88. See esp. *RAC*, VII, p. 655; *PW*, VI, p. 2149.

The deities with which the fig is associated are numerous: the Horai (or Seasons),[89] Helios,[90] Hermes,[91] Juno,[92] and even Mithras.[93] Both Athene and Demeter, as previously noted, were credited with its introduction.[94] The citizens of Cyrene, on the other hand, regarded the fig as a gift from Chronos (Saturn), and Pliny reports that a (sacred) fig-tree stood in front of the temple of Saturn in Rome up until 404 BC, before being removed for upsetting a statue of Silvanus.[95] Some doubt does surround Apollo,[96] but on Rhodes his father Zeus (Jupiter) was deemed protector of the fig-tree and surnamed Συκάσιος, Μειλίχιος or Ἔνδενδρος (since he was believed to inhabit one or more sacred fig-trees).[97] The tree figures prominently in the cult of the aforementioned Priapus.[98] J. Murr claims that the gift of the dried fig (ἰσχάς) was also linked, in ancient times, with the Asiatic 'Great Mother' goddess Cybele, the bearer being a Phrygian heroine named Syke. This Syke may, he thinks, be identified with the nymph of the same name with whom Dionysus fell in love.[99]

It is with this latter god, however, that the fig-tree was most identified in the ancient world. Dionysus (linked by the Romans with their wine god Bacchus or Liber) was the embodiment of the fruitfulness of nature, as was the closely related Priapus.[100] As such, he was the god of all the trees but

89. Cf. Ar. *Pax* 1165-68 (LCL, II, pp. 106-107); Cook, *op. cit.*, p. 134.
90. Cook, *ibid*.
91. σῦκον ἐφ' Ἑρμῇ = a lucky find. The first-ripe fruit was brought to Hermes; see *PW*, VI, p. 2143.
92. *RAC*, VII, p. 657; Murr, *Pflanzenwelt*, p. 34.
93. *RAC*, VII, pp. 657-58.
94. Murr, *Pflanzenwelt*, pp. 31, 33.
95. Cf. Plin. *H.N.* 15.20.77 (LCL, IV, pp. 342-43); Murr, *Pflanzenwelt*, p. 34 and n. 1; *PW*, VI, p. 2148.
96. Cf. Murr, *Pflanzenwelt*, p. 33; contra *RAC*, VII, p. 657.
97. Cook, *op. cit.*, p. 134; Murr, *Pflanzenwelt*, p. 32; *RAC*, VII, p. 657.
98. Cf. Hor. *Sat.* 1.8.1 (LCL, pp. 96-97), and above, n. 81.
99. Cf. Ath. 2.55a = 3.75b (LCL, I, pp. 238-39, 324-25); Murr's interpretation of this passage, *Pflanzenwelt*, p. 33.
100. For material on Dionysus, see, for example, J. Leipoldt, *Dionysos* (Angelos, 3; Leipzig: E. Pfeiffer, 1931); *RAC*, VII, pp. 656-57; *EJud*, VI, 'Dionysus, Cult of', *ad loc.*; *PW*, VI, pp. 2145-46; Frazer, *Golden Bough*, VII, ch. 1; Murr, *Pflanzenwelt*, p. 32; Buchheit, *op. cit.*, p. 201 and n. 8; B.M. Metzger, *Index of Articles on the New Testament and*

especially of the cultivated ones. Honoured by farmers and
fruit growers in particular, he was deemed to make the trees
grow and prayers were offered to him for the prosperity of the
country's fruits.[101] Dionysus had a special connection with the
vine and the fig-tree, however, being identified so closely with
the latter that one of his many epithets was Συκίτης, Dionysus
of the Fig.[102] The fig-tree was his gift to humans, his discovery
alone.[103] On the Cycladic island of Naxos, he was deemed protector of the fig-trees and named Μειλίχιον, the Naxian name
for the fig.[104] In Sparta he was also apparently called Συκίτης or
Συκ(ε)άτης.[105] The fig-tree, it was said, was created out of his
feminine parts.[106] He was believed to have taken up his abode
in certain sacred trees, and in Boeotia he was styled
Ἔνδενδρος for this reason.[107] Cultic φαλλοί, set up in his
honour, were of fig wood, as were face-masks, images and
statues of the god.[108] Sometimes he appears crowned with fig-
leaves,[109] or decorated with a necklace of figs.[110] Figs were

the Early Church Published in Festschriften (JBLMS 5; Philadelphia:
Society of Biblical Literature, 1951), p. 53.

101. Frazer, *Golden Bough*, VII, pp. 2-5.

102. Cf. Ath. 3.78c (LCL, I, pp. 338-39); Cook, *op. cit.*, p. 134; E.R.
Goodenough, *Jewish Symbols in the Greco-Roman Period* (New York:
Bollingen Foundation, 1958), VIII, p. 141; G. Dalman, *Arbeit und Sitte
in Palästina* (Beiträge zur Förderung christlicher Theologie; Gütersloh: C. Bertelsmann, 1928–42), I, p. 381; Frazer, *Golden Bough*, VII,
p. 4; *PW, loc. cit.*; Buchheit, *loc. cit.*

103. According to Sosibius, the Lacedaemonian; cf. Ath., *ibid.*; Murr,
Pflanzenwelt, p. 32.

104. Ath., *ibid.*, and above, n. 30.

105. Murr, *loc. cit.*

106. Murr, *ibid.* On the effeminate Dionysus, see Frazer, *Golden
Bough*, VI, pp. 258-59.

107. Murr, *ibid.*

108. Above, n. 81 and related text. The practice of setting up φαλλοί to
the god is connected with the Prosymnus story. When Prosymnus
showed Dionysus the way to the Underworld, it was said, he exacted
an oath from the latter that on his return he would introduce
Prosymnus to the pleasures of love. When Dionysus came back,
however, he found that Prosymnus was dead, whereupon he cut for
himself a branch from a fig-tree, shaped it into a phallus, and made a
show of fulfilling his promise to the dead man. See Clem. *Al. Protr.*
2.29, 30 (LCL, pp. 72-73); *PW*, VI, p. 2146.

109. Murr, *Pflanzenwelt*, p. 33.

offered to him as a gift,[111] and he may have played a role, according to J.G. Frazer, in the ceremony for the artificial fertilization of the fig-tree.[112]

The cult of Dionysus originated in Thrace but spread like wildfire throughout the Graeco-Roman world, 'until the god whom Homer hardly deigned to notice had become the most popular figure of the pantheon'.[113] Practically all Greeks sacrificed to Dionysus the Tree-god (Διονύσος Δενδρίτης), claimed Plutarch (writing in the first century AD) and Tacitus names him 'Father Liber, the conqueror of the East'.[114] Non-Jews of Alexandria and Rome claimed that the cult was wide-spread among Jews, and Plutarch's Bacchanalian interpretation of the Festival of Tabernacles is therefore interesting in this respect. The Roman writer claimed that the carrying of fig branches into the Temple was a major part of the festival.[115] Plutarch's description, however, is a reflection, according to Abraham Schalit, of Tabernacles as it was celebrated in the Greek diaspora at the end of the first century and the beginning of the second century AD, and not as it was celebrated in the Temple.[116] Tacitus, too, reports the belief that the Jews

110. Buchheit, *loc. cit.*
111. Buchheit, *ibid.*
112. Frazer, *Golden Bough*, VI, p. 259 and n. 1.
113. Frazer, *Golden Bough*, VII, p. 3.
114. Cf. Plu. *Moralia.* 675F (LCL, VIII, pp. 390-91); Tac. *Hist.* 5.5 (LCL, II, pp. 184-85).
115. 'A few days later (after Sukkoth) the Jews celebrate another festival, which one may simply call a Bacchanalian festival. For this is a festival on which the Jews carry fig branches and sticks adorned with ivy and carry them into the Temple. One does not know what they do in the Temple. It seems reasonable to suppose that they practise rites in honor of Bacchus. For they blow small horns as the people of Argos do during the festival of Dionysus, and call upon their god. Others, who are called Levites, walk in front, either in allusion to Lysios (Λύσιος)— perhaps 'the god who attenuates curses'—or because they call out 'Euius', i.e. Bacchus (ὁ Εὔιος)' (Plu. *Moralia* 4.671D-672B [LCL, VIII, pp. 361-67], cited in *EJud*, VI, 'Dionysus, Cult of', *ad loc.*). It is to be noted, too, that some NT scholars have suggested that the fig-tree pericope was originally associated with the Feast of Tabernacles (so W.H.P. Hatch, T.W. Manson, C.W.F. Smith); see Telford, *Barren Temple*, pp. 3, 15.
116. *EJud, ibid.*

were devotees of Father Liber.[117] A number of Palestinian towns and cities were associated with the god (e.g. Beth-Shean/Scythopolis, Rafa) and some were said to have been founded by him.[118]

A certain amount of syncretism undoubtedly did take place, and from an early period. J. Leipoldt points to the existence of a coin from Gaza of the fifth century BC, upon which Yahweh appears in a form similar to the customary Greek representation of Dionysus.[119] It is unlikely, however, that the Jews themselves were the primary agents of such syncretism. Pious Jewry on the whole shrank from making contact with and being compromised by the pagan syncretistic influences that surrounded it. Dionysiac influence, on the other hand, appears to have been stronger in Syria, and at the time of the Seleucids, for example, the Jews themselves were coerced into participation in Dionysiac feasts and processions.[120] Otto Eissfeldt, who examined the archaeological evidence for the influence of Graeco-Roman cults in Syria, presents data that indicate that the Dionysus cult had its followers in the Graeco-Roman period in places such as Gerasa, Ba'albek (Heliopolis) and Dura-Europos, although in general (he states) the religion of Syria did remain 'heimisch-syrisch' in its essential features.[121]

117. 'But since their priests used to chant to the accompaniment of pipes and cymbals and to wear garlands of ivy, and because a golden vine was found in their temple, some have thought that they were devotees of Father Liber, the conqueror of the East, in spite of the incongruity of their customs. For Liber established festive rites of a joyous nature, while the ways of the Jews are preposterous and mean' (Tac., *loc. cit.*).

118. *EJud, loc. cit.*; see sources and literature cited by M. Hengel, 'The Interpretation of the Wine Miracle at Cana: John 2.1-11', in L.D. Hurst and N.T. Wright (eds.), *The Glory of Christ in the New Testament: Studies in Christology in Memory of George Bradford Caird* (Oxford, 1987), pp. 83-112 (esp. pp. 108-11).

119. Leipoldt, *Dionysos*, p. 9.

120. See 2 Macc. 6.7; cf. also 14.33. The Seleucids were enthusiastic devotees of Dionysus. A coin of Antiochus VI (145–142 BC), for example, designates the king as an epiphany of the god (Leipoldt, *Dionysos*, p. 10).

121. See Eissfeldt, *Tempel und Kulte syrischer Städte in hellenistisch-römischer Zeit* (Anecdota Oxoniensia; Leipzig: J.C. Hinrichs, 1941),

The Dionysiac influence on early Christianity is a subject that warrants closer investigation. The parallels in particular between descriptive representations of Christ and Dionysus would make a fascinating study. Evidence that such influences did exist is presented and discussed by Leipoldt.[122] Dionysus was, after all, a dying-and-rising god.[123] Legends told of his miraculous birth, with details that form analogies with the birth narratives of the New Testament.[124] The changing of water into wine was a miracle associated with the god (cf. Jn 2.1-12)[125] and it is of note that R. Bultmann claims that the self-same miracle attributed to Jesus was taken over from the Dionysus tradition.[126] Jesus is identified, too, with the true Vine (Jn 15.1ff.), the tree that, with the fig-tree, was otherwise widely associated with this Thracian god.[127]

It would, of course, be unacceptable to stress the significance of these similarities at the expense of the profound differences that do exist, on the other hand, between both cult figures. Our concern is limited, nevertheless, to the question of what associations the Gentile reader might have brought to his or her understanding of Mark's story. The fig-tree was a tree that was widely venerated. It was the tree sacred (above all) to

pp. 31, 43, 62, 152, 152-55. The Acropolis Temple in Ba'albek, for example, has a number of Dionysiac motifs decorating its great door, and as such led the German Ba'albek expedition of 1898–1905 to claim it was a temple to Bacchus (Eissfeldt, pp. 43, 62). The Temple of Artemis in Dura-Europos likewise has Dionysiac emblems (Eissfeldt, p. 152). An Agonistic Inscription (dating from the period AD 105–114) for a statue dedicated to Gerasa's first agonothete (superintendent of the public games) intimates that it was a gift presented by a sacred guild in the service of Dionysus and the Emperor Trajan. See C.H. Kraeling (ed.), *Gerasa. City of the Decapolis* (New Haven: American Schools of Oriental Research, 1938), pp. 442-44.

122. Leipoldt, *Dionysos*, ch. 4.

123. Leipoldt, *Dionysos*, p. 50. On the dying-and-rising god, see Talbert, *What is a Gospel?* (London: SPCK, 1978), pp. 53-56, and his article, 'The Myth of a Descending-Ascending Redeemer in Mediterranean Antiquity', *NTS* 22 (1976), pp. 418-39.

124. Leipoldt, *Dionysos*, pp. 50-51.

125. Leipoldt, *Dionysos*, p. 51.

126. See Bultmann, *The History of the Synoptic Tradition* (Oxford: Blackwell, 1972), p. 238; Hengel, as cited in n. 118, above.

127. Leipoldt, *op. cit.*, p. 51.

Dionysus, who produced and protected its fruit and was known at times to dwell in it. The fig-tree had cultic significance, and Jesus' address to it was an act at home in a world where trees were objects of fear or veneration, the home of demons or gods.[128] The founder of Christianity had blasted this tree, withering it ἐκ ῥιζῶν with the breath of his lips. Given the religious dimension that surrounded it, then, one can scarcely doubt that, at the very least, Jesus' action would have been seen as *an exhibition of superior power*. The *precise* significance of the tree's withering *in the vicinity of Jerusalem* would, on the other hand, have centred, I believe, on the 'omen' character of that event and it is to this dimension that I shall now turn.

Trees and Fig-trees in Myth, Legend and Omen

'The Jews regard as profane all that we hold sacred.' So said Tacitus,[129] and in respect of the tree his judgment is in general not untrue.[130] Nevertheless, in the Graeco-Roman tales in which trees figure there exist features similar to the haggadic legends that were discussed in *The Barren Temple and the Withered Tree*. The 'atmosphere' that pervades these tales, the attitude taken to nature and the miraculous, their cosmological presuppositions are, in many respects, analogous.

The world of nature for the ancients was not regarded in the impersonal and scientific light in which it is regarded today. Nature was a sphere to be cajoled or propitiated, rather than one to be objectively exploited or manipulated as in modern times. Though often brutal, this world was nevertheless 'enchanted'. The heavens and the earth, the elements, the animals and the plants were not indifferent to the human situation. They possessed an awareness of what was happening in the human world and had a capacity to respond to the sig-

128. For an example of the self-same conception in more modern times, it is interesting to read the account given by Mrs Crowfoot and Miss Baldensperger of the veneration paid to a sacred fig-tree at Afka in Syria by both Christian and Moslem women. See *From Cedar to Hyssop* (London: Sheldon, 1932), p. 109.
129. Tac. *Hist.* 5.4 (LCL, II, pp. 178-79).
130. See Telford, *Barren Temple*, p. 139 and n. 63.

nificant events of human life. The world of nature is endowed with a will. As such, nature can offer resistance, in Graeco-Roman theodicy, to the divine Will, or refuse to succour human beings dependent on her.[131] At other times, especially in the golden ages of humanity's past and future experience, nature can respond with a wondrous alacrity or display an unmitigated responsiveness to the advent of a new dawn for humankind. She it is who will recognize the divine man and saviour figures who are expected to bring this world about.

It was such a cosmological and eschatological understanding that I have argued was reflected in the Jewish Haggadah relating to the trees. A parallel to such thinking in the Graeco-Roman world is to be seen in the legends and stories that circulated in respect of the Emperor-cult. In his book, *Der römische Kaiserkult bei Martial und Statius*, Franz Sauter has examined the expression given to this cult by these two Roman writers and has sought to trace links with and precedents for such *adulatio* in the Hellenistic and Oriental ruler-cults (*Herrscherkulte*) of earlier times. He highlights the exalted ways in which the Emperor was regarded. To the peoples of the Graeco-Roman world, the Emperor was saviour, prince of peace, the 'Liebling' of gods and men, the ruler of the world. He was compared with Jupiter or Hercules or with other such heroes or gods. To him were applied the epithets of *dominus, deus, magnus, sanctus, aeternus* or *invictus*.[132] Of particular significance is the belief that he, like the Jewish Messiah, was

131. See, for example, J.G. Kahn, 'La parabole du figuier stérile et les arbres récalcitrants de la Genèse', *NovT* 13 (1971), p. 44; F. Sauter, *Der römische Kaiserkult bei Martial und Statius* (Tübinger Beiträge zur Altertumswissenschaft, 21; Stuttgart/Berlin: W. Kohlhammer, 1934).

132. Sauter, *Kaiserkult, passim*. In addition to Sauter on the emperor cult, see L.R. Taylor, *The Divinity of the Roman Emperor* (Philological Monographs, 1; Middletown: American Philological Association, 1931); K. Scott, *The Imperial Cult under the Flavians* (Stuttgart/Berlin: W. Kohlhammer, 1936). Two recent works are also important: D. Cuss, *Imperial Cult and Honorary Terms in the New Testament* (Paradosis, 23; Fribourg: University Press, 1974); D. Fishwick, *The Imperial Cult in the Latin World. Studies in the Ruler Cult of the Western Provinces of the Roman Empire* (Etudes préliminaires aux religions orientales de l'empire romain, 103; Leiden: E.J. Brill, 1987). I am grateful to Mr Brian Yhearm for drawing my attention to these works.

the creator of a new Golden Age (*aureum saeculum*).[133] Though the idea appears earlier (in connection with Gaius Caligula, for example),[134] the first emperor with whom the expectation of an *aureum saeculum* is unambiguously associated was the young Nero, according to Sauter.[135] One may also compare the belief expressed on the part of Josephus that it was the Emperor Vespasian to whom the Jewish Messianic oracle of a world-ruler to emerge from Judaea applied,[136] and when Vespasian himself returned to Rome in 70 AD the Roman populace welcomed him rapturously as their saviour.[137] Martial depicts the Domitianic period in similarly glowing terms, the Emperor's reign having secured the favour of the gods, the liberty of the people, and the elevation of Rome.[138]

Allied with this belief that the Emperor, god upon earth, *dominus et deus*, is to inaugurate a new Golden Age is the widely held conception that the animal and plant kingdom will recognize the *numen* of the Emperor and will respond to it.[139] Wind and weather obey him.[140] Sun, moon and stars vie

133. 'Die Vorstellung vom Herrscher als dem Friedensfürsten ist unzertrennlich verknüpft mit der anderen Vorstellung, dass seine Regierung für sein Volk oder die ganze Menschheit eine Zeit des Segens und Glückes überhaupt ist. Dies ist das ständig wiederkehrende Motiv der ägyptischen und israelitischen Prophetie. Auch die hellenistischen Herrscher und deren Nachfolger, die römischen Kaiser werden in diesen Tönen gefeiert... Jeder kann in Ruhe seiner Arbeit nachgehen. Das Laster ist vernichtet, die Feinde braucht man nicht zu fürchten, jeder lebt in Freude behaglich dahin' (Sauter, *Kaiserkult*, p. 19).
134. Sauter, *ibid*.
135. Sauter, *Kaiserkult*, p. 20.
136. *War* 6.312-13 (LCL, III, pp. 466-67).
137. τὸν εὐεργέτην καὶ σωτῆρα καὶ μόνον ἄξιον ἡγεμόνα τῆς Ῥώμης ἀνακαλοῦντες (*War* 7.4.1, esp. §71 [LCL, III, pp. 522-27]).
138. *Mart.* 5.19 (LCL, I, pp. 308-309); Sauter, *Kaiserkult*, p. 21. On Martial and the cult, see also H. Szelest, 'Domitian und Martial', *Eos* 62 (1974), pp. 105-14.
139. 'Nicht nur der Mensch empfindet "die Heilige Macht" des Kaisers, sondern auch die Natur, insbesondere die Tierwelt, wird davon ergriffen und bezeugt ihre Verehrung' (Sauter, *Kaiserkult*, p. 166).
140. For example, see Sauter, *Kaiserkult*, p. 167. Of these, Sauter mentions the eulogy given by Cicero to Pompey in which the statement

with one another to catch a glimpse of him.[141] Animals behave
unnaturally in his presence, perceiving and revering the
divinity that resides in him.[142] Such beliefs are not new, claims
Sauter.[143] They represent merely the transfer to the person of
the Emperor of traditional motifs and traits that appear in
connection with the heroes and gods of ancient Greek and oriental myth and legend.[144] Parallels are to be found likewise in
Jewish[145] and Christian circles,[146] and in respect of the latter

is made that the latter's wishes have always secured (*inter alia*) even
the compliance of wind and weather (*etiam venti tempestatesque obse-
cundarint*; cf. Cic. *De Imp. Cn. Pomp.* 48 [LCL, pp. 60-61]), as also the
hymn of Philo praising Augustus as 'the Caesar who calmed the tor-
rential storms on every side' (ὁ καῖσαρ, ὁ τοὺς καταρράξαντας παντα-
χόθι χειμῶνας εὐδιάσας; cf. Ph. *Leg. ad Gaium* 21.145 [LCL, X, pp. 72-
73]). It should be commented, however, that both these instances are
invested with a rhetorical (and, therefore, metaphorical) flavour
which lessens their force as examples of *actual*, alleged miracle-work-
ing of this kind.
    141. Cf. e.g. Mart. 8.21 (LCL, II, pp. 16-17), and other examples given
by Sauter, *Kaiserkult*, pp. 167-68.
    142. Cf. e.g. Mart. 1.6, 14, 104 (LCL, I, pp. 34-35, 38-39, 94-95); 4.30
(LCL, I, pp. 250-51); 9.31 (LCL, II, pp. 92-93); 14.73 (LCL, II, pp. 464-65),
and other examples given by Sauter, *Kaiserkult*, pp. 168-69.
    143. 'Wichtig ist die Feststellung, dass Martial mit diesen Gedichten
nicht völlig Neues geschaffen, sondern nur in besonderer Zuspitzung
und bemerkenswerter Häufigkeit ein Thema verwendet hat, das seine
Vorgeschichte und sein Nachleben hat' (Sauter, *Kaiserkult*, p. 169).
    144. Pythagoras, it was said, had tamed wild animals and Empe-
docles had held back the winds (Sauter, *Kaiserkult*, pp. 166-67). To
Sauter's examples may be added Aristides' description of Asclepius
and Serapis as rulers of the winds and waves and as the rescuers of
humans from the perils of the sea. See P. Fiebig (ed.), *Antike Wundergeschichten. Zum Studium der Wunder des Neuen Testaments*
(Kleine Texte; Bonn: A. Marcus & E. Weber, 1911), XVII, pp. 21-23.
    145. According to 2 Macc. 9.8, Antiochus Epiphanes, like King
Canute, had aspired likewise 'in his superhuman boastfulness' to
command even the waves of the sea to obey him. R. Gamaliel, the
prime mover in the excommunication of R. Eliezer (see Telford, *Barren Temple*, pp. 113-14, 187), is said at a later time to have been successful, however, at the selfsame feat. According to *b. B.M.* 59b
(Soncino edn, p. 354), the Rabbi had stilled a storm that had been occasioned by R. Eliezer's anger over the affair. See P. Fiebig, *Rabbinische
Wundergeschichten des neutestamentlichen Zeitalters* (Kleine Texte;
Bonn: A. Marcus & E. Weber, 1911), pp. 10-12. A further instance is
offered by the story of the Jewish child who, when aboard a heathen

one need only point to Mark's own story of the stilling of the storm (Mk 4.35-41).

The plant world too recognizes the imperial *numen*. Martial, speaking of a plane-tree in Corduba which Julius Caesar had planted, says: 'It seems to feel who was its creator and lord; so green it is, and with its boughs it climbs high heaven' (Mart. 9.61.9, 10 [LCL, II, pp. 118-19]). Expressed here, though in a diluted form, is the belief, appearing also elsewhere, that plants and particularly trees connected with the Emperor would grow profusely, or, if he appeared, would give a sudden surge of growth, or even would revive again if already withered.[147] Sauter points to a number of examples.[148] According to Quintilian (fl. c. AD 35–c. 95), a palm is reported to have sprung up on the altar dedicated to Caesar Augustus (Quint. *Inst.* 6.3.77 [LCL, II, pp. 480-81]). The latter Emperor is likewise said to have been overjoyed when, on his arrival on the island of Capri, an old oak whose branches were withering suddenly became vigorous again. This event was greeted as a good omen (cf. Suet. *Aug.* 92.2 [LCL, I, pp. 262-63]). A further legend associated with Augustus tells of a palm tree at Munda in Spain (the site of Caesar's battle with the republican forces of Rome) which his adopted father had spared as an omen of victory. From this tree a shoot is said to have immediately sprouted and to have grown at such a rate that in a few days it had not only equalled the parent tree but overshadowed it. Doves, moreover, came to nest in its

ship in a storm (like Jonah), calmed the storm by appealing to his God. This latter tale is accredited to R. Tanḥuma (fl. c. AD 350) and forms a parallel, Bultmann thinks, to Mk 4.35-41. See P. Fiebig, *Antike Wundergeschichten*, XVII, pp. 23-24, and Bultmann, *History*, pp. 234-35.

146. The firmament is said to have stood still at the birth of Jesus, according to the Book of James, or *Protevangelium*, a pseudepigraphical infancy gospel that dates at least to the second century (*Protev.* 18.2, cited in M.R. James, *The Apocryphal New Testament* [Oxford: Clarendon, 1953], p. 46). The Buddhist tradition records a similar event at Buddha's birth (Sauter, *Kaiserkult*, p. 168).

147. 'Äussert sich hier die Wirkung des Numens in einem besonders starken Wachstum, so ist dies nur eine schwächere Abart eines weit verbreiteten Wundertypus, wonach Pflanzen und Bäume beim Erscheinen des Kaisers plötzlich hervorwachsen oder, bereits im Absterben begriffen, wieder aufleben' (Sauter, *Kaiserkult*, p. 170).

148. Sauter, *Kaiserkult*, pp. 169-70.

branches, even though this was not their customary habitat (Suet. *Aug.* 94.11 [LCL, I, pp. 270-71]).

This particular legend is discussed by W. Deonna in his article on the legends surrounding Augustus, and is interesting for several reasons.[149] The palm was of course the symbol of victory, but it was also the tree of Apollo, and Octavian was deemed to be Apollo's son. The prodigious growth of the palm-tree, therefore, is taken as an omen prefiguring the prospering of Octavian's fortunes and his future elevation to power, particularly after the battle of Actium (31 BC). Caesar himself, notes Deonna, is said to have recognized in this omen that Octavian would be the successor who would eventually overshadow him, and that he 'would decrease', as with John the Baptist in respect of Jesus, while his adopted son 'would increase' (cf. Jn 3.30).[150]

The symbolic dimension investing the story is heightened, moreover, by the mention given to the doves. The dove for the ancients was a symbolic bird, 'un oiseau prophétique', and its function in particular was to offer presages for those of regal status.[151] It was also, however, the bird of Aphrodite or Venus, from whom the Julian family traced their origins. By nesting in the palm-tree, therefore, the doves were confirming Octavian's royalty.

Legends such as these illustrate clearly the great importance that was attached in the Graeco-Roman world to the tree and its symbolic significance. Pliny, for example, devotes a section of his *Natural History* to the behaviour of trees and to the portent-value of such behaviour.[152] Theophrastus does likewise.[153] A mystical bond was deemed to exist either between certain important individuals (rulers, Emperors, and others) or between cities and the trees associated with them.[154]

---

149. See W. Deonna, 'La légende d'Octave-Auguste, dieu, sauveur, et maître du monde', *RHR* 83 (1921), pp. 32-58, 163-95; 84 (1921), pp. 77-107.

150. *Ibid.*, p. 193.

151. 'La colombe est un oiseau prophétique, qui donne spécialement des présages aux rois, des "auspicia regalia"' (Deonna, *op. cit.*, p. 194).

152. Cf. Plin. *H.N.* 17.38 (LCL, V, pp. 166-71).

153. Cf. Thphr. *H.P.* 2.3 (LCL, I, pp. 118-23).

154. See Deonna, *op. cit.*, pp. 94ff.

Plutarch tells, for example, of the cornel-tree in Rome which was said to have sprouted from the shaft of a spear thrown by Romulus, the founder of the city. Preserved as sacred by the inhabitants of Rome, this tree was the object of extreme solicitude and frequent anxiety was caused whenever it was thought that it might be withering. The tree was inadvertently destroyed in the time of Gaius Caligula (AD 37–41).[155]

Two sacred myrtles were also associated with the shrine of Romulus, one of them called the patricians' myrtle (*myrtus patricia*), the other the myrtle of the common people (*myrtus plebeia*). For many years, says Pliny, the patricians' tree was the more flourishing of the two, but from the Marsian war onwards (the civil war 91–88 BC) the position was reversed, the plebeian tree blossoming with vigour and vitality, while the patricians' tree withered away into barrenness (*paulatim in sterilitatem emarcuit maiestas*).[156]

The aforementioned Augustus was a particularly superstitious man and when a palm-tree sprang up between the crevices of the pavement in front of his house, he transplanted it to the inner court of his palace on the Palatine where the Penates were kept and worshipped. Great pains were taken by him to ensure that it would grow. Since these household gods of the Julian family had been elevated by Augustus to the status of gods of the State, and came to be worshipped as such, the open association of his own emblem, the palm-tree, with the Penates bore a significance that could scarcely be missed.[157]

The Julio-Claudian dynasty ceased with the death of Nero in AD 68 and Suetonius records that prior to this it had been the custom of Emperors of that line to plant laurel branches in a grove of such trees that had first sprung up in Livia's day (38 BC). Just before the death of each Emperor, it was said, the tree which he had planted withered. In Nero's last year, however, the whole grove withered from the root up (*silva omnis exaruit radicitus* = ἐκ ῥιζῶν; cf. Mk 11.20).[158] This parallel is a striking one, for the report of this alleged omen would have

155. Cf. Plu. *Rom.* 20.5-6 (LCL, I, pp. 154-55).
156. Cf. Plin. *H.N.* 15.36.120-1 (LCL, IV, pp. 370-71).
157. Cf. Suet. *Aug.* 92.1 (LCL, I, pp. 262-63); Deonna, *op. cit.*, pp. 94-95.
158. Suet. *Galba* 1 (LCL, II, pp. 190-91); cf. also Plin. *H.N.* 15.40.136-37 (LCL, IV, pp. 380-83).

been circulating at the very time when Mark's Gospel was in process of composition. The tree involved in this omen story is not, admittedly, a fig-tree (although we shall presently be examining similar omen stories in which our tree does figure). Its value for the Markan pericope is, however, scarcely diminished, for omen stories such as these clearly demonstrate that Gentile readers of the first century, like their Jewish counterparts, would have viewed the sudden blossoming or withering of a tree connected with an individual or city as a portent of either good fortune or disaster, of blessing (in Jewish terms) or judgment.[159]

Figs and fig-trees themselves, however, do play a prominent role in Graeco-Roman myths, legends and omen stories. A well-known instance is told with regard to the celebrated species of figs (*cauneae*) produced at Caunus, a city of Caria opposite Rhodes. When Marcus Crassus (d. 53 BC) was embarking at Brundisium upon his fateful expedition against the Parthians, a man selling Caunian figs cried out 'Cauneas, Cauneas'. This was a bad omen, it was said, warning Crassus against going (*cave ne eas*), and if he had heeded it he would not have perished.[160] The Third Punic War (151–146 BC) was said to have been finally embarked upon when Cato, an inveterate opponent of Carthage, produced a first-ripe African fig in the Senate. Responding to the senators' expressions of admiration over its size, beauty and freshness, he declared that it had been picked the day before yesterday at Carthage—so near was that country to Rome's walls![161]

The fig-tree itself is often depicted as having a sinister, dark and portentous side,[162] and this is true especially of the wild fig-

159. 'La croissance et le dépérissement de ces arbres fétiches auxquels s'attache la vie des individus et des cités est l'objet des préoccupations rituelles des citoyens ... Car un arbre fétiche qui tombe, sèche brusquement, ou au contraire, reverdit après avoir séché, est considéré comme un prodige, malheureux dans le premier cas, favorable dans le second' (Deonna, *op. cit.*, pp. 96, 97).

160. Cf. Cic. *De div.* 2.40.84 (LCL, pp. 464-67); Plin. *H.N.* 15.21.83 (LCL, IV, pp. 346-47); *PW*, VI, p. 2110.

161. Cf. Plin. *H.N.* 15.20.74-76 (LCL, IV, pp. 338-41); Plu. *Cat. Ma.* 27.1 (LCL, II, pp. 382-83); *PW*, VI, p. 2144; *RAC*, VII, p. 650.

162. R.C. Trench points out that on two occasions when the fig-tree occurs prominently in the New Testament, viz. in Lk. 13.6-9 and Mk

tree (ὁ ἐρινεός, *caprificus*).[163] We have already commented upon the fact that the reversion of a cultivated tree (*ficus*) to a *caprificus* was regarded as an omen of a particularly disturbing kind.[164] Murr draws attention to the fact that this 'düstere Auffassung' appears in as early a work as the *Odyssey* where it is said that the site beneath which the whirlpool Charybdis 'sucks down the black water' was marked by a great wild fig-tree (ἐρινεός).[165] The place Ἐρινεός, next to Eleusis, which was named after this tree, was said by local tradition to have been the spot where Persephone was carried off into the Underworld.[166] According to Pausanius, an ἐρινεός figured as a portent of coming disaster for the ancient Messenians. An oracle delivered by Pythia, the priestess of Apollo at Delphi, had declared that whenever a he-goat (τράγος) drank of the river Neda's winding stream, Messene's destruction would be at hand. The oracle's words were deemed to have been fulfilled, however, when a wild fig-tree, which the Messenians themselves called τράγος, was seen bending towards the stream and touching the water with the tips of its leaves.[167] In later times (AD 183), according to the *Acts of the Arval Priesthood*, the temple of Dea Dia had to be pulled down and completely rebuilt and reconsecrated because a wild fig-tree had sprouted on its roof.[168]

The cultivated tree, too, had its place in legend and omen. Just as the death of Nero was said to have been foreshadowed in the sudden withering of a laurel grove 'from the root up', so too the imminent death of the Emperor Alexander Severus (AD 222–235) was signalled when three fig-trees (of the kind

---

11.12-14, 20ff. and parallel, in neither case does it appear as a symbol of that which is good (*Notes on the Miracles*, p. 478 n. 2).

163. 'Beim wilden Feigenbaum ist, bei anderen unveredelten, keine oder nur schlechte Frucht tragenden Sträuchern und Bäumen, inbesondere solchen, die mit schwarzberindetem, knorrigen Stamme und Astwerk ausgestattet sind, eine unglückliche Bedeutung nicht wohl zu verkennen' (Murr, *Pflanzenwelt*, p. 34).

164. Above, p. 274.

165. Cf. *Od.* 12.103-104 (LCL, I, pp. 438-9); Ath. 3.76e (LCL, I, pp. 330-31); Murr, *Pflanzenwelt*, pp. 34-35.

166. Cf. Paus. 1.38.5 (LCL, I, pp. 204-205); Murr, *Pflanzenwelt*, p. 35.

167. Cf. Paus. 4.20.1ff. (LCL, II, pp. 270ff.).

168. See *PW*, VI, p. 2104; *RAC*, VII, p. 652.

bearing Alexandrian figs) suddenly fell down before his tent door.[169]

The most notable stories, however, are those told in connection with the fig-trees at Rome. Nowhere, indeed, according to J.G. Frazer, was the practice of venerating trees more in evidence than in the heart of the great metropolis.[170] Pliny, for example, tells of a particular fig-tree that grew in the middle of the forum and which commemorated the spot where 'when the foundations of the Empire were collapsing in portent of disaster, Curtius had filled up the gulf with the greatest of treasures, I mean virtue and piety and a glorious death'. The reference is to the incident, occurring in 362 BC, when a chasm opened in the forum, which soothsayers claimed could only be filled by throwing into it Rome's greatest treasure. A soldier, Marcus Curtius, thereupon mounted his horse and leapt into the hole, which subsequently swallowed him up.[171]

By far the most revered and the most celebrated of these Roman fig-trees was the *ficus Ruminalis*.[172] The legend that Romulus and Remus, the founders of Rome, were suckled by a she-wolf under a fig-tree has already been touched upon. The story of the twins is given by a number of Greek and Roman writers.[173] Both were sentenced to exposure and committed to the waters of the Tiber. The basket in which they lay was washed up (according to most versions of the legend) beside this fig-tree, a spot identified by tradition as lying at the foot of the Palatine Hill, at the Lupercal, where the she-wolf is said to have brought them up. In Pliny's day, nevertheless (the first century AD), a fig-tree actually growing in the forum itself was identified explicitly as the tree of the Romulus and Remus

---

169. Cf. *Hist. Aug. Al. Sev.* 60.5 (LCL, II, pp. 300-301).
170. Frazer, *Golden Bough*, II, p. 10.
171. Cf. Plin. *H.N.*, 15.20.78 (LCL, IV, pp. 342-43 and footnote by Rackham).
172. For material on this famous tree, see Frazer, *Golden Bough*, II, pp. 10, 318; *PW*, VI, pp. 2145, 2146-48; *RAC*, VII, pp. 652-53. The tree is represented on Roman coins as well as on the great marble reliefs that stand in the forum; see esp. Frazer, II, p. 10 n. 3; *PW*, p. 2150.
173. Cf. e.g. Ovid, *Fast.* 2.410ff. (LCL, pp. 86-87); Livy 1.4.5 (LCL, I, pp. 18-19); Varro *L.L.* 5.54 (LCL, I, pp. 52-53); D.H. *Antiq.* 1.79 (LCL, I, pp. 262ff.); Plu. *Rom.* 4.1 (LCL, I, pp. 98-99).

saga.[174] This tree, the *ficus Ruminalis*, was prominently displayed and worshipped as one of Rome's sacred objects and received offerings of milk down to late times.[175] Legend appears to have explained the difference of site by claiming that the tree *had uprooted itself and removed to the Comitium*[176] (the 'meeting-place' of Rome at the north-west side of the forum) at the command of Attus Naevius, an augur in the reign of Tarquin, Rome's fifth king!

The precise interrelationship in ancient tradition between the *ficus Navia* and the *ficus Ruminalis* and their relation in turn to the Romulus and Remus legend is a matter of scholarly dispute and need not detain us.[177] What is significant for our enquiry is the attitude taken to these fig-trees by the first-century Roman. The symbolic associations of these fig-trees were inextricably bound up with the fortunes of the city, and indeed the state itself. The *ficus Curtius* reminded the Roman citizen of the near-destruction of his beloved city. Pliny further records that it was 'a portent of some future event when it (the *ficus Ruminalis*) withers away and then by the good offices of the priests is replanted'.[178] Tacitus reports, even more strikingly, that in the year AD 58, the very period in which the Markan traditions were circulating orally, such a calamity occurred—the *ficus Ruminalis* withered![179] This event was

174. Cf. Plin. *H.N.* 15.20.77 (LCL, IV, pp. 340-43). Livy records that a bronze statue representing the twins being suckled by the wolf was erected in 296 BC and placed beside the *ficus Ruminalis* (Livy 10.23.11-12 [LCL, IV, pp. 444-47]; cf. also D.H. *Antiq.* 1.79.8 [LCL, I, pp. 266-67]).
175. See, for example, Plu. *Moralia* 278D (LCL, IV, pp. 92-93); Frazer, *Golden Bough*, II, p. 318.
176. So we should translate Pliny's 'miraculo ex aere iuxta dicato, tanquam comitium sponte transisset Atto Navio augurante' (Plin. *loc. cit.*). See *RAC, loc. cit.*, and Jackson's note on Tac. *Ann.* 13.58 (LCL, V, p. 103). H.R. Rackham seems to have missed this point in referring, in his translation, to the *wolf's* spontaneous migration into the forum! A bronze statue of Naevius himself, erected by Tarquin, also stood near the sacred fig-tree and remained standing at least until the time of Dionysus of Halicarnassus (fl. c. 25 BC; cf. D.H. *Antiq.* 3.71.5 [LCL, II, pp. 254-55]).
177. See esp. *PW, loc. cit.*; *RAC, loc. cit.*
178. Plin. *loc. cit.*
179. 'Eodem anno ruminalem arborem in comitio, quae octingentos et triginta ante annos Remi Romulique infantiam texerat, mortuis

regarded as a portent, although with the reblossoming of the fig-tree the city breathed again.

In view of the significance attached to the blossoming and withering of trees, can it be seriously doubted, then, how the Markan reader would have understood the fig-tree story? Indeed, if Mark's Gospel was, as Brandon and others have claimed, a *Roman* Gospel and circulated in Rome about the time of the Romano-Jewish War, then we must seriously consider whether these traditions concerning the withering of Nero's laurels 'from the root up' or the withering of the *ficus Ruminalis* played any part (in addition to Old Testament influences) in the conception of the Markan story. Such a tradition connection would, of course, be difficult to prove but might be proposed if our chief concern were that of the story's origin. Even were this too bold a position, however, one must surely take into account such omen stories when considering how a Gentile Christian would have looked upon Mk 11.12-14, 20ff. It is this background, as we have seen, that commentators to date have largely neglected. The withering of a fig-tree at the Roman metropolis was seen as a portent of disaster for that city. Would the withering of a fig-tree at the Jewish metropolis have been viewed any differently?

Final Summation

Our examination of the Graeco-Roman background concerning trees in general and fig-trees in particular can be said to have both supplemented and reinforced the attempt that I have made in my previous study to isolate the key hermeneutical factors that must be brought to bear upon the Markan Fig-tree story in its Temple context. We have examined figs and fig-trees in Graeco-Roman estimation. We have seen that the tree and its fruit was as highly prized by Greeks and Romans as it was by Jews. To the latter it was a blessing from Yahweh, and to the former likewise it was a gift from the gods. The tree was deemed instrumental in bringing civilization to

ramalibus et, arescente trunco deminutam prodigii loco habitum est, donec in novos fetus revivesceret' (Tac. *Ann.* 13.58 [LCL, V, pp. 102-103]).

humans, and the eating of figs was regarded as a symbol for luxury itself.

From this general estimation of the tree that in Mark's Gospel is cursed, we went on to consider its symbolic associations for the citizen of the Graeco-Roman Empire. Although principally an emblem for the peaceful and prosperous life, we saw that the eating of figs could in turn be associated with a soft, immoral, dissipated life. We noted the prominent use of fig language in sexual symbolism, a phenomenon deriving from the tree's pre-eminent role as the outstanding botanical symbol of creative potency and fertility. For certain of the ancients the tree was in one respect 'un arbre indécent' and its depiction as such is to be compared with the Jewish and Christian Fall tradition that this was the tree that had in the beginning led humans into sin.[180] A faint possibility existed, therefore, that a Gentile Christian reader, influenced by the Old Testament and its current exegesis, may have looked upon the story as the reversal of the Fall, the sentencing by the second Adam of the tree that had corrupted the First. On the whole, however, it was thought unlikely that such an interpretation would have been entertained as early as Mark's time. The sexual dimension of the tree, however, its abstract association with moral decay and its concrete use, among other things, as an image for the prostitute, is one thing that I do not believe should be entirely dismissed. Such an association may possibly have made Mark's identification of the fig-tree with Israel and its Temple all the more powerful, as far as the Gentile reader was concerned.

A second closely related dimension that was explored was the tree's connections with Graeco-Roman religion and cultus. Such a connection is observable also in the Jewish sphere. Figs were associated with a variety of deities and festivals, being favourite offerings to the gods of fertility. Chief among these was Dionysus, and so closely identified with the fig-tree was this, the most popular god of the pantheon, that for some he was Διονύσος Συκίτης, Dionysus of the Fig. He it was who produced and protected its fruit, and he it was who was known at times to dwell in it. To Gentile readers, then, as for their

180. See Telford, *Barren Temple*, pp. 134, 189-90 and footnotes.

Jewish counterparts, the blasting of this tree with its cultic
connections would have been viewed at the very least as an
exhibition of superior power on the part of the founder of the
Christian cult. The tree that served temple or cultus should
serve him—or no one!

The third dimension to be investigated, the place of trees and
fig-trees in Graeco-Roman myth, legend and omen, is the one
that I consider to have produced the most fruitful comparisons. Here the 'world' that was opened up to us in my earlier
study of the Jewish Haggadah revealed itself likewise in the
legends that circulated with regard to the Emperor-cult. In
the haggadah relating to Israel's Golden Ages, nature is seen
to be extraordinarily responsive to the righteous and the trees
to blossom prodigiously. Such phenomena were also a feature
of the *aureum saeculum* inaugurated by the Emperor. The
animal and plant kingdom recognizes the imperial *numen*
and responds to it. Trees grow profusely in the Emperor's
presence, or revive if already withered. Such sudden growth
or withering, we have seen, was invested in the Graeco-
Roman world with a highly symbolic significance. A mystical
bond was deemed to exist between individuals or cities and the
trees associated with them. The blossoming of a tree was a
portent of good fortune. Its sudden withering was an omen of
impending disaster.

To the Gentile Christian, Jesus too was the inaugurator of
an *aureum saeculum*. To him, no less than the the Emperor,
should nature respond. The elements should recognize his
divinity (as, for example, in the stilling of the storm). Trees
should grow profusely, or offer their fruit on his approach.
That the fig-tree should not have done so was striking indeed!
His solemn words had sentenced it and it had withered 'from
the roots'.

Regarded in isolation, this story would merely demonstrate
Jesus' superior power over nature and the gods or demons
inhabiting it. Placed by Mark in the context of Jesus' visit to
Jerusalem, the story carried a more profound message. The
tree's withering is an omen concerning the fate of the city and
its Temple. Its reduction to an emaciated skeleton is a portent
of disaster no less serious than that which accompanied the

shrivelling of Nero's laurels 'from the root up', or the withering in recent memory of the *ficus Ruminalis* at Rome.

The fact that the founder of Christianity is himself the agent
of the tree's destruction is a bold expression of his superior
power and sovereignty over the Jewish Holy City and its
Temple. In thus presenting Jesus as *cursing* the fig-tree and,
mutatis mutandis, the Temple, Mark is solemnly linking the
traumatic demise of that institution in very recent experience
with the words and actions of Jesus some forty years earlier.
His connecting of the climactic rending of the Temple veil
with Jesus' crucifixion some chapters later is a further example.

In this bold and dramatic way, therefore, Mark has prepared his readers for the events of his own time. S.G.F. Brandon's view, in this respect, was correct and yet curiously he
failed to perceive the significance of this odd story for the
Gospel's purpose and intention. The Cursing of the Fig-tree
pericope is a mirror reflecting Mark's (and the Markan
community's) estimation of and response to the Temple and
its destruction. Although anti-semitism was particularly rife
after and as a result of the Romano-Jewish War, the Gentile
world in general expressed regret over the destruction of this
magnificent institution.[181] Luke, writing some ten to fifteen
years after the passions engendered by the Jewish Revolt had
cooled, reflects a sympathetic respect for their national
shrine.[182] The response of Mark, on the other hand, who, with
his predominantly Gentile Christian community, is caught up
directly in these events, is shown to be far stronger. By having
Jesus himself curse the Temple, he and his community can be
seen to be distancing themselves from Judaism and their
movement's own Jewish roots. A judgment had indeed been

181. See, for example, Brandon, *Zealots*, p. 226 and n. 3. Josephus, it
is to be noted, goes out of his way to say that Titus and the Romans had
been extremely unwilling to risk the Temple's destruction at the siege
of Jerusalem and that in the final analysis it had been the Jews themselves who had first set a light to this renowned edifice. The very need
for such an apologia indicates a background of expressed regret and
criticism over this appalling tragedy; cf. e.g. *War* 1.10; 5.334, 360-63,
444-45; 6.120-28, 214-19, 238-43 (LCL, II, III, *ad loc.*).

182. As I have argued in *The Barren Temple*, pp. 224-33.

executed on the Jewish nation and its Temple, but Jesus, Christianity's founder, in a solemn display of sovereign power, had some forty years earlier pronounced the sentence.

TEMPLE TRADITIONS IN Q

David R. Catchpole

On just two occasions the temple is explicitly brought to the attention of the reader of Q. The first is when it serves as one of the settings for the testing of Jesus' identity as son of God (Q 4.9-12),[1] and the second is when it appears as the location of the climactic assassination in the record of 'the law and the prophets' (Q 11.51). The second of these two traditions, and the complex in which it is set in Q, is more revealing than the first concerning the religious tradition to which Q and its community belong. It will form the major concern of this study. But it would be as well to draw attention at the outset to a consideration which may scarcely be doubted, namely, that to the reader of Q the temple could hardly but come to mind as implicit in other traditions beside those two. Thus, whenever legal material with a conservative religious colouring appears (e.g. Q 11.37-52 *in toto*; 16.17), that material necessarily presupposes an appreciative attitude to the temple and its cult. Similarly, when references to Jerusalem appear (e.g. Q 13.34f.), it is not a live option to interpret such references in terms of the city or the community to the exclusion of the temple, for in a striking spectrum of texts (e.g. Tob. 14.4f.; *Jub.* 1.17, 28; Jn 11.48) we see how important inclusion and association and inseparability were felt to be.[2] This view is given classic expression in the affirmation of 2 Macc. 5.15-20 that

---

1. I follow the convention of using Lucan references to identify Q passages.
2. Cf. E. Schweizer, *The Good News according to Matthew* (London: SPCK, 1976), p. 444, commenting on Mt. 23.38: 'Whether "house" refers to the city of Jerusalem or the Temple makes no material difference'. Similarly, A. Sand, *Das Evangelium nach Matthäus* (Regensburg: F. Pustet, 1986), p. 473.

divine anger with the residents of Jerusalem brought divine disregard of the holy place: 'The Lord did not choose the nation for the sake of the holy place, but the place for the sake of the nation; therefore the place itself shared in the misfortunes that befell the nation and afterward participated in its benefits'. In similar vein, and particularly apposite for our present purpose, is the case of Jesus ben Ananios (Josephus, *War* 6.300-309) whose doom-laden cries took the varied but synonymous forms of 'Woe to Jerusalem', or 'A voice against Jerusalem and the sanctuary...a voice against all the people', or 'Woe once more to the city and to the people and to the temple'.

1. The legitimacy of attaching 13.34f. to 11.37-52 must first be affirmed.[3] Doubts about this attachment in Q derive from, first, a predisposition to accept Lucan order in principle; secondly, the argument that 13.34f. follows entirely suitably on 13.27-30 in view of the shared theme of the judgment upon Israel; thirdly, the alleged discrepancy between 11.49-51 as prospective in outlook and 13.34f. as retrospective; fourthly, the ease with which the Jerusalem oracle as a prelude to the eschatological discourse in Matthew 24 (cf. especially 24.1-3) serves the purposes of Matthaean theology.[4] Over against these considerations others may be set which support an original Q association between these traditions, i.e. first, the likelihood that the Lucan position of 13.34f. is much more bound up with its dependence upon the LkR. insertion of the non-Q material in 13.31-33, with its interest in Jerusalem as both the end of the journey of the Lucan Jesus and also the allegedly unique setting for the killing of prophets; secondly, in view of the tendency towards thematic grouping of traditions in Q (see, for example, 7.18-35), the overlap in content between 11.49-51

---

3. Cf. S. Légasse, 'L'oracle contre "cette génération" (Mt 23,34-36 par. Lc 11,49-51 et la polémique judéo-chrétienne dans la source des logia', in J. Delobel (ed.), *Logia* (Leuven: Leuven University Press, 1982), pp. 237-56 (238f.).

4. D.E. Garland, *The Intention of Matthew 23* (Leiden: Brill, 1979), pp. 26f.; D.R.A. Hare, *The Theme of Jewish Persecution of Christians in the Gospel according to St. Matthew* (Cambridge: Cambridge University Press, 1967), p. 94; O.H. Steck, *Israel und das gewaltsame Geschick der Propheten* (Neukirchen: Neukirchener Verlag, 1967), pp. 45-48.

and 13.34f. makes an original juxtaposition highly likely; thirdly, there is the inappropriateness of an oracle against Jerusalem ending a complex set by Luke in one of his typical meal-scenes; fourthly, there are verbal connections which are most easily explained as reminiscences in οἶκος (Lk. 11.51 diff. Mt. 23.35; cf. Q 13.35a), and ἥξει (Mt. 23.36 diff. Lk. 11.51; cf. Lk. 13.35 diff. Mt. 23.39); fourthly, in fact both 11.49-51 and 13.34f. contain retrospective and prospective features; fifthly, Q 17.34f. shows that there is nothing more intense and final than the judgment represented by ἀφίεται; and finally, even those writers who in general favour the originality of the Lucan order are prepared to consider exceptions to that rule.

2. In the Lucan sequence of Q material following the Woes on the Pharisees there occur the Exhortation to Fearless Confession (Q 12.2-12) and Cares about Earthly Things (Q 12.22-34), both of which appear in a quite different position in the Matthaean sequence. With the next complex, the parables about Watchfulness and Faithfulness (Q 12.39-46), we touch material which, in the Matthaean Q sequence, was in exactly the same position relative to the Woes (23.1-39 leading to 24.43-51), except that there intervened the tradition about The Day of the Son of Man (Mt. 24.26-28, 37-41, 40-41, 28/Lk. 17.22-37). However, when the parable of the Unjust Judge (Lk. 18.1-8) appears immediately after Q 17.22-37 with a secondary Lucan appendix attached referring to the question of whether 'the Son of man will find faith...', it strikingly echoes the language of Q 12.40, 42, 43. When these considerations are aggregated the natural inference is that the original Q order was Q 11.37-52; 13.34f.; 17.22-37; 12.39-46. This would mean that immediately after the Lament over Jerusalem, with its concluding reference to the one who comes in the name of the Lord, there occurred the warning against those who say, 'He is ἐν τῇ ἐρήμῳ... he is ἐν τοῖς ταμιείοις'.[5] When Lk. 12.3 diff. Mt. 10.27 includes the quite redundant phrase ἐν τοῖς ταμιείοις,[6] it

5. This represents the original Q wording: S. Schulz, *Q. Die Spruchquelle der Evangelisten* (Zürich: Theologischer Verlag, 1972), p. 278.
6. Schulz, *Spruchquelle*, p. 462: 'das den Parallelismus störende ἐν τοῖς ταμιείοις'.

looks very much like a reminiscence of the saying which, on the above hypothesis, originally occurred at this point in Q. We shall return later to discuss the implications of the original Q order for the meaning of the traditions in question.

3. The order in which the woes themselves occurred in Q may be beyond recovery. Adopting the notation of W (= washing: Q 11.39-41), T (= tithes: Q 11.42), S (= chief seats, etc.: Q 11.43), G (= graves: Q 11.44), B (= burdens: Q 11.46), P (= prophetic tombs: Q 11.47f.), and K (= keys: Q 11.52), Luke's and Matthew's sequences can be set out as W-T-S-G-B-P-K and B-S-K-T-W-G-P respectively. For Schürmann[7] these represented edited versions of an original Q sequence S-B-T-W-G-P-K, his reasons being the Mt./Lk. agreement concerning T..G..P, the belonging together of T and W (Luke having transposed in order to provide in 11.37f. a suitable introduction), the suitability of B..G as a frame for T-W, with S and K as original introduction and conclusion. In effect, that means that Matthew preserved Q in respect of T-W-G-P and Luke preserved the original relationship of S..B..K. This implicit concession to Matthew has been retracted in the recent work of Kloppenborg,[8] who revives the view of Schulz,[9] for whom Q consisted of T-W-S-G-B-P-K, i.e. only one transposition by Luke, namely, that which permitted W to serve as immediate response to the LkR. introduction in 11.37f.

Any alternative proposal has its own hazards, and perhaps the need for one is not very great, but a few considerations may perhaps be ventured. So anticlimactic is K after the use of P as the basis for an extended comment and announcement of judgment (Q 11.49-51), that its Lucan position appears to derive from its generalizing character, which arguably fitted it to conclude the complex and to substitute for Q 13.34f., following the decision to move the latter elsewhere.[10] An alternative

---

7. 'Das Zeugnis der Redenquelle für die Basileia-Verkündigung Jesu', in *Logia* (note 3), pp. 182-200 (174f.).

8. *The Formation of Q* (Philadelphia: Fortress, 1987), pp. 139f.

9. *Spruchquelle*, pp. 94f.

10. Garland (*Intention*, p. 197), recognizes the incompatibility of 11.52 and 13.34f. as endings for this complex, but opts for 11.52 on the ground that it fits Luke's (*sic*) division of the charges. It is precisely that suit-

position therefore needs to be found for K. In Matthew's presentation it stands formally as the first of the sayings which uses the actual word 'woe' (Mt. 23.13), and as a generalizing statement of basic principle it is admirably suited to do so. On the other hand, P must have come last and, in view of common (catchword) references to μνημεῖα,[11] have been preceded immediately by G. This in turn places a question-mark against B. For Luke B begins the anti-lawyer group of woes, just as for Matthew it begins the catalogue of specific charges against the scribes and Pharisees. This suggests an introductory function for B, which might again be thought appropriate in view of its touching on the very essence, rather than any specific example, of the critique of Pharisaism. What then preceded G-P? The answer must surely be T-W, since W shares with G the charge of inner uncleanness (however we reconstruct the *Vorlage* of G) and combines with T to comment on two definitive features of Pharisaic practice. We thus have an interim conclusion that the last four woes were T-W-G-P, and a decision remains only in respect of S..B..K. Of the various possible permutations of these three, K-B-S would seem to be most persuasive since, first, K refers to the kingdom, which must be taken to be a central concept for the speaker, and which is probably presupposed theologically by S; secondly, K hints at Pharisaic opposition to the (prophetic preaching of) the kingdom, and in establishing with P a certain symmetry between the beginning and the end of the complex would conform to a typical Q form; thirdly, the recognition by both Matthew and Luke of K's foundational content and role has already been noted; fourthly, a MtR. movement forward of B-S is understandable in terms of the evangelist's redesigning the whole discourse under the control of 23.2-3 while at the same time feeling the influence of the Marcan parallel for S in Mk. 12.38f.; finally, B is more closely related to K than S is to either, for B engages with a matter of fundamental principle while S

ability in the Lucan context which makes such a position at the pre-Lucan stage doubtful. The same answer can be made to H. Schürmann's tentative suggestion that Luke could well have understood K in relation to, and as a conclusion for, 11.29-51 as a whole.

11. On μνημεῖα as original, cf. Schulz, *Spruchquelle*, p. 105.

pinpoints personal behaviour. To sum up, the proposed reconstruction of the Q order is K-B-S-T-W-G-P.

4. While reconstructing the content and exploring the meaning of the various woes it is important to keep under review proposals which have been made concerning the tradition history of the complex as a whole and, correspondingly, the history of the relations of the Q community with Judaism. In the view of Schulz,[12] all the woes (not including Q 11.49-51) derived from Palestinian charismatic-eschatological Torah-sharpening prophets, and no attempt was made by him to uncover strata representing different stages in the growth of the collection. Schürmann's reconstruction was more nuanced. For him, T-W formed the original 'kernel', the viewpoint of law-abiding Jewish Christians who stressed the love commandment over against Pharisaic legalism and maintained truly the word and practice of Jesus; B..G were added by those who abandoned the ceremonial law and clashed with the Pharisaic leaders of Judaism, but had not broken totally with Judaism itself; S..P..K were added at the final 'ecclesiastical-redactional' stage of Q by those who had become anti-synagogue and had broken with Judaism. Kloppenborg's modification of this view is only slight.[13] For him, T+W belong to an *intra muros* dispute with Pharisaism, recalling the demands of the covenant and by no means rejecting the ceremonial law; B+W reject Pharisaic legal interpretation in practice but not in principle, and presuppose no formal break with Judaism; G+P+K involve an attack on the very existence of Pharisaism and therefore attest a widened gulf. More recently, Tuckett has registered hesitation about whether the material is patient of so exact a process of differentiation.[14]

4.1 K originally accused the Pharisees of neither entering nor permitting others to enter (Q 11.52b).[15] The object of the verb

---

12. *Spruchquelle*, pp. 94-114.
13. *Formation*, pp. 140f.
14. 'Q, the Law and Judaism', in B. Lindars (ed.), *Law and Religion* (Cambridge: James Clarke, 1988), pp. 90-101, 176-80 (178).
15. Reconstruction of Q text: Schulz, *Spruchquelle*, p. 110.

εἰσέρχεσθε was almost certainly 'the kingdom of heaven',[16] and the Pharisees are tacitly accepted as possessing the keys of the kingdom[17]—tacitly, but of course ironically, since in no sense could such a statement be accepted at face value. The saying presupposes that entry to the kingdom, which is synonymous with 'sharing in the age to come' (*Sanh.* 10.1), is not the automatic assumption for all Israelites, so the implication must be that it is specifically the kingdom as proclaimed in mission by Jesus or his adherents which is experiencing resistance in the name of the religious convictions maintained by the Pharisees. Those convictions, promoted through their characteristic interpretation of Torah,[18] have gone beyond the will of God and thus have frustrated his purpose as authoritatively effected by Jesus. This sense of the ultimate significance of the mission of Jesus within the purpose of God underlies what will be said in P. On the broader Q canvas, the opposition to (the preaching of) the kingdom recalls Q 16.16b, while the exclusion of those whom Jesus included recalls Q 7.34b.

4.2 B originally responded to a situation in which a corpus of traditional interpretation of Torah already existed.[19] It took up the theological choice facing the contemporary interpreter: to define in ever more detail, to impose ever more precision, to formulate ever more rules, and thus to lay ever more burdens upon those who would conform to the will of God (cf. Acts 15.10), or to ease the burdens, to limit the rules, and to highlight broad principles.[20] It is unlikely that this woe presumes

16. Schulz, *Spruchquelle*, p. 110; Schweizer, *Matthew*, p. 433; Garland, *Intention*, pp. 124f.; Schürmann, 'Zeugnis', p. 176.

17. On Pharisaic usage, see J. Jeremias, 'κλείς', *TDNT*, III (1965), pp. 747f.

18. S. Schulz, *Spruchquelle*, p. 111; Garland, *Intention*, p. 127; Sand, *Matthäus*, p. 459.

19. Reconstruction of Q text: Schulz, *Spruchquelle*, p. 107.

20. It is thus more critical of Pharisaic principles than is supposed by E. Haenchen, 'Matthäus 23', *ZTK* 48 (1951), pp. 38-62 (40), and Schulz, *Spruchquelle*, p. 108. Tuckett ('Q, the Law and Judaism', p. 98) regards this Woe as the sole exception to the general rule that the Woes concern Pharisaic behaviour. Even here he thinks that the main critique concerns '(their failure) to help other people with their burdens'.

abandonment of the ceremonial law,[21] or that it accuses the
Pharisees of resorting to casuistry in order to evade the rulings
which they recommend for others[22] (an interpretation unduly
influenced by the MtR. comment in Mt. 23.3b), or that it
charges them with teaching one thing and doing another;[23] it
is rather more likely that the underlying issue is the same as
that in K, i.e. a matter of how the will of God should be defined
in relation to the announcement of the kingdom.

4.3 S probably did, as has been assumed so far, figure in Q.[24]
This follows from the 'minor agreements' in the use of φιλεῖν
(Mt. 23.6/Lk. 20.46; subsequently changed to ἀγαπᾶν by LkR.,
cf. Lk. 7.5), repeated definite articles, and the order of the items
listed. A good case can be mounted for the substance of the
charge in Q being undue attention to 'the chief seat at suppers,
the chief seats in the synagogues, and the greetings in the
market places'. A further case can be mounted in favour of the
charge's being immediately followed in this Q context by the
saying 'Whoever exalts himself will be humbled, and whoever
humbles himself will be exalted' (Q 14.11; 18.14b): first, if Luke
dropped an original reference to 'chief seats at suppers' in
order to exploit the idea in 14.7-10, it is notable that he followed
it there with this saying in just the same way as Mt. 23.12 followed shortly after 23.6, 7b; secondly, a similar reminiscence
may be detectable in the secondary addition of Lk. 18.14b to the
parable of the Pharisee and the Tax-collector (18.9-14a), in
which terms appearing in the immediate context of the woes
like 'extortion' and 'tithes' reappear, and the Pharisaic interpretation of righteousness and sense of security in relation to
God are critically scrutinized. As far as the meaning of this
woe is concerned, the synagogue as an institution is no more
frowned on than supper and marketplace in Q 11.43, while in

21. Schürmann, 'Zeugnis', p. 175.
22. Thus, J. Ernst, *Das Evangelium nach Lukas* (Regensburg: F.
Pustet, 1977), p. 387, etc.
23. J. Schmid, *Das Evangelium nach Matthäus* (Regensburg: F.
Pustet, 5th edn, 1965), p. 320; D. Patte, *The Gospel according to
Matthew* (Philadelphia: Fortress, 1987), p. 321; Schulz, *Spruchquelle*,
p. 108.
24. Schulz, *Spruchquelle*, p. 104; Schweizer, *Matthew*, p. 431.

Q 14.11 the future 'divine passive' points, as Schulz observed,[25] to that community of equals which derives from, and is expressive of, the kingdom of God. The frame of reference for S is therefore the same as that for K+B. One may add that the future 'divine passive' will also be used in the announcement of judgment in P.

4.4 T undoubtedly referred to both the tithing of mint and also the practice of judgment.[26] The word κἀκεῖνα (11.42c) indicates that mint did not stand alone, and in view of references to dill and cummin, but not rue, in tithing *halakoth* (*Maas.* 4.5; *Dem.* 2.1), together with a typical Lucan generalization in the phrase 'every herb' (cf. Lk. 21.29), the original Q combination was probably 'mint and dill and cummin'. On the other side of the antithesis ταῦτα indicates that judgment did not stand alone; the ἔλεος/ἐλεημοσύνη[27] overlap (cf. Lk. 11.41) establishes the involvement of mercy; faithfulness, as a traditional covenant partner of judgment and mercy, probably completed the trio, rather than the love of God, which may have been generated by the recollection of Deut. 6.5 (Lk. 10.27/Mk 12.30). As far as the verbs are concerned, ἀφιέναι is more likely to be original than παρεῖναι (11.42c), and therefore similarly more original than παρέρχεσθαι (11.42b).

The form of 11.42bc is chiastic: tithes–judgment, etc.–judgment, etc. (ταῦτα)–tithes (κἀκεῖνα). Content-wise, the whole saying deals with action and not at all with teaching: ποιεῖν is the opposite of ἀφιέναι, which in turn is the opposite of the *action* represented by ἀποδεκατοῦτε. Finally, 11.42b by itself would be unclear, because it might be attacking the practice of careful tithing as well as failure to practise the fundamental covenant obligations of judgment, mercy and faithfulness. No unclarity at all is left by the combination 11.42bc. What that says is that it was good and appropriate to be careful about tithing, but it is not an alternative to the practice of judgment

25. Schulz, *Spruchquelle*, p. 105. It is, of course, a commonplace that in the great new era of the future pride and its effects will be eliminated by God; cf. *Ps. Sol.* 17.41.

26. Reconstruction of Q text: Schulz, *Spruchquelle*, p. 100.

27. Luke's is the secondary version, with a rendering which conforms extensively to Acts 10–11 (Garland, *Intention*, pp. 144f.).

314 *Templum Amicitiae*

and the rest, any more than the practice of judgment is an alternative to tithing. In the hierarchy of religious obligation judgment stands well above tithing, and persons are therefore particularly culpable if they neglect the former. Such neglect makes scrupulous care show itself as nothing better than disproportionate concern for small things, whose very smallness is painfully evident within the context of the comparison with judgment and the rest.[28] T therefore attacks Pharisaic inaction, which effectively casts a shadow over one form of Pharisaic action, one which is at the very heart of the movement's existence. But it does not attack Pharisaic teaching or principles.[29] From the point of view of the speaker, Pharisaic shortcoming involves giving more attention to the special obligations of the sect than to the general obligations of the whole people of God, and especially those obligations which have to do with the treatment of the needy, the exposed, the powerless and the vulnerable.[30] Thus the speaker adopts the characteristic perspective of the prophets (Mic. 6.8; Zech. 7.9f.) and the wise (Prov. 14.22), not only in respect of what is affirmed but also in respect of the use of a contrast between religious practices (e.g. sacrifice, Isa. 1.10-17) and covenant obligations. In turn, this means that the presuppositions of T and P are in harmony.

4.5 W arguably began as Mt. 23.25 does, apart from minor and unimportant verbal adjustments. Mt. 23.26 and Lk. 11.40f., however, differ so markedly that there has been a widespread tendency to see each as entirely MtR. or LkR., as the case may be.[31] Contrary to that inference, while there are grounds for

28. C.G. Montefiore, *The Synoptic Gospels* (London: Macmillan, 2nd edn 1927), II, p. 301: 'They observe ritual minutiae and neglect ethical fundamentals'.
29. It is widely agreed that there is no question of an attack on the law (Lev. 27.30-33; Num. 18.12; Deut. 14.22f.). Cf. P. Hoffmann, *Studien zur Theologie der Logienquelle* (Münster: Aschendorff, 2nd edn, 1972), p. 170; Kloppenborg, *Formation*, p. 140.
30. Schweizer, *Matthew*, p. 441; Patte, *Matthew*, p. 325.
31. Bultmann, *The History of the Synoptic Tradition* (Oxford: Blackwell, 1963), p. 131; Schulz, *Spruchquelle*, pp. 96f.; Hoffmann, *Studien*, p. 170.

accepting that LkR. is mainly responsible for 11.40f.,[32] it
remains likely that Mt. 23.26 essentially preserves Q material:
first, there is Mt./Lk. agreement on an imperative sequel to the
initial charge; secondly, πρῶτον links Mt. 23.26 and Lk. 11.38,
and probably indicates a LkR. reminiscence of an original Q
saying;[33] thirdly, the same can be inferred from the Mt./Lk.
agreement on an address to a single Pharisee; and, fourthly,
the oft-cited parallel in Q 6.43-45[34] suggests thematic suitability within Q. The question then concerns the meaning of this
woe.

Opinions vary as to whether the vessels are real or
metaphorical in all or any of this Woe, and in addition there is
the discussion of whether or not any current Jewish halakic
debate about the washing of vessels is in mind. Perhaps one
may venture the following proposal. Maccoby's[35] critique of
the proposal of Neusner[36] that Jesus is contributing to the
internal Pharisaic debate is in general persuasive, and his
reminder that any washing process involved total immersion
helpful. But the material is not, as he urges, metaphorical
throughout: indeed it is not metaphorical at all. The pairing of
'cup and plate' suggests that literal objects are in mind, rather
than a single vessel which might correspond to a typical person. Moreover, the situation is that they have been washed, a
situation which is accepted as far as the outside is concerned.
But the vessels have food and drink in them, and here we must
note carefully the formulation ἔσωθεν δὲ γέμουσιν ἐξ ἁρπαγῆς
καὶ ἀκρασίας. When this is compared with the similar
(probably) MtR. formulation in 23.27, ἔσωθεν δὲ γέμουσιν
ὀστέων νεκρῶν καὶ πάσης ἀκαθαρσίας, it becomes clear that
the preposition ἐκ indicates how the food and drink came to be
there, and also that descriptions of contents may point not only
to actual physical objects (cf. ὀστέων νεκρῶν) but also to the
religious status of such objects (cf. πᾶσα ἀκαθαρσία). So the
food and drink, which naturally satisfy the Jewish food laws,

32. Schulz, *Spruchquelle*, p. 96.
33. H. Schürmann, *Traditionsgeschichtliche Untersuchungen zu
den synoptischen Evangelien* (Düsseldorf: Patmos, 1968), p. 115.
34. E.g. Schürmann, *Untersuchungen*, p. 301.
35. 'The Washing of Cups', *JSNT* 14 (1982), pp. 3-15.
36. ' "First Cleanse the Inside"', *NTS* 22 (1976), pp. 486-95.

have been obtained by ἁρπαγή and have thus made the inside of the vessels unclean, though not, of course, in the conventional Jewish sense. Hence, the cleanness of the whole of each vessel, in the new trans-conventional sense, depends on an abandonment of the conduct which has produced the food.[37]

It will be noticed that W is quite remarkably like T in that, first, it is structured chiastically (outside–inside–inside–outside) and it draws attention to the problem in the second term; secondly, the practice of washing is taken for granted and even protected in much the same way as the practice of tithing; and now, thirdly, the descriptions of the offence correspond. The term ἁρπαγή and its cognates are used in Jewish literature as a vivid metaphor for the predatory activities of wolves and lions,[38] and in a transferred sense for injustice done by the rich and powerful to the poor and vulnerable.[39] It represents the unprincipled grasping of the self-seeking who prosper, enjoy good food and high living, and do not give priority to 'judgment and mercy'. So while W concentrates on what is not being done, but should be, T spells out what is being done, but should not be. Thematically, it also matches the profile in S of the upwardly mobile in human terms, as well as engaging in personal polemic of the sort we find in G.

4.6 G is represented by two versions, each of which shows an awareness of Palestinian custom (though not the same one). The Matthaean version is vulnerable to a series of criticisms: first, that whitewashing was not intended as beautification[40] but as a warning of the danger of contracting uncleanness; secondly, that the application does not fit a warning against such a danger; thirdly, that there is in Mt. 23.28 evidence of Matthaean style and interests, and probably some indebtedness to the 'inside–outside' scheme of W. The Lucan version, which picks up Num. 19.16 (cf. *Ohol.* 17.5), is probably to be

---

37. The word πρῶτον indicates explicitly in W that overriding priority which T leaves implicit.

38. Gen. 49.27; Pss. 7.2; 22.13; 104.21; Ezek. 19.3, 6; 22.25, 27; Hos. 5.14; Mic. 5.8; *T. Dan* 5.7; *T. Benj.* 11.1, 2; Mt. 7.15; Jn 10.12.

39. Job 20.19; 24.9; Ps. 10.9; Isa. 3.14f.; 10.2; 61.8; Ezek. 18.7, 12, 16; Mic. 3.2.

40. Garland, *Intention*, p. 152.

preferred.[41] What is its meaning? A strong exploitation of the metaphor of the unmarked graves would lead to the conclusion that 'it portrays them as a source of ritual defilement',[42] but moral rather than ritual defilement must be the topic once the transfer from metaphor to reality has been made. In that case G is using a different and thoroughly offensive metaphor to make the same point as W, and adding the further charge that outward appearance belies inner reality.

4.7.1 P has with some justice been accused of displaying 'the logic of polemic, not of reasoned argument'.[43] Yet it must be presumed that long-term transmission could scarcely succeed with tradition which is incoherent and unreasonable, so the attempt must be made to reach back to a *Vorlage* which was coherent and rational. Luke's version, for all that it is carefully and chiastically structured (building–killing–witnessing–killing–building), makes little contribution to this attempt, since it hinges on the absurd idea that the building of a tomb constitutes approval of the murder of the person buried in it.[44] Only in two respects does Luke help us: first, by lacking Matthew's τοὺς τάφους...καὶ κοσμεῖτε...τὸν δίκαιον (the adornment idea is similar to the alien import of whitewashing to make attractive, Mt. 23.27, while the inclusion of 'the righteous' anticipates 23.35 diff. Lk. 11.50)[45] and thus confirming that MtR. (in 23.29, contrast 23.31) has created a new synonymous parallelism out of 'you build the tombs of the prophets'; secondly, by supporting the possibility that Mt. 23.30 did indeed appear in Q, in that Luke's central 'witnessing' statement matches positionally the central statement beginning καὶ λέγετε and interpreted ὥστε μαρτυρεῖτε. It is wholly normal for Q to include statements in direct speech (cf. Q 3.8; 6.42; 12.45; 13.27) and, one may add, the presence of καί in Q

41. Schulz, *Spruchquelle*, p. 106.
42. Kloppenborg, *Formation*, p. 141.
43. Hare, *Persecutions*, p. 82.
44. Contrast 1 Macc. 13.25-30. On Luke's *non sequitur*, cf. Garland, *Intention*, p. 164; Sand, *Matthäus*, p. 461. The verb συνευδοκεῖν is LkR. (Schulz, *Spruchquelle*, p. 109) in view of the similar martyrological context in Acts 8.1; 22.20.
45. Schulz, *Spruchquelle*, p. 109.

11.49 ('For this reason the Wisdom of God *also* said...') presumes that the speech of Wisdom is a response to some earlier speech. In sum, therefore, the original P probably contained Lk. 11.47 + Mt. 23.30, a complementary two-part, descriptive statement, with emphasis upon the second part, followed by Mt. 23.31, the conclusion exploiting polemically the notion of sonship.[46]

Reconstructed thus, the final woe is notable for the pattern of argument it selects in order to inculpate its audience in the deaths of the prophets. If the members of that audience had literally brought about any such death, guilt by action, rather than guilt by association grounded in so subtle an argument, could have formed the basis of a simple, direct, and compelling charge. This does not happen. Consequently, no actual prophetic death, which might be set to the account of the Pharisees, has taken place. Their guilt rests upon association with their ancestors, based upon the Deuteronomic view of Israel's history, and now asserted by the speaker. Their resistance to this view takes the form of a refusal to express repentance in confession.[47] Over against what they say as a disclaimer of responsibility, stands what Wisdom said as an affirmation of responsibility and also of judgment.[48]

4.7.2 There is no need to rehearse the familiar arguments about the contents of Q 11.49-51.[49] Again and again Mt./Lk. verbal discrepancies have to be resolved in favour of the originality of Lk. Exceptions are the 'apostles', probably inserted to prepare for 'those who are sent' (Q 13.34) as well as to include Christian leaders within the programme here described; 'from the foundation of the world', less Semitic than Mt.'s 'upon the ground' (2 Sam. 14.14) and brought in to smooth the

46. This is a modification of the view of Hoffmann, *Studien*, pp. 162f., that the Q version approximated to Lk. 11.47 + Mt. 23.31, and a return to that of Steck, *Geschick*, pp. 28f.

47. Steck, *Geschick*, p. 281.

48. The MtR. insertion of 23.32, 33 serves as a recognition by the evangelist that 23.29-31 is not an internally complete unit, and that it has to have a new conclusion added if Q 11.49-51 is disengaged. This disengagement was itself necessitated by the transformation of a Wisdom-speech into a Jesus-speech.

49. Schulz, *Spruchquelle*, pp. 336-38.

transition to the Abel reference; and 'the house', less precise than Mt.'s 'sanctuary', and probably an anticipation of Q 13.35a.

The meaning of what is said here completes what was begun in P. The past period of Israel's rejection of the prophets is mentioned again. The speech of contemporary persons is balanced and refuted by the speech of Wisdom. The previous assertion of the final answerability of those contemporary persons, based on argument rather than actuality, receives additional and ultimate confirmation from the mouth of even higher authority. Superimposed, one might say, upon all that is the Abel–Zechariah catalogue of rejected ones (Q 11.51a) with its attached repetition of the judgment on this generation (Q 11.51b). Leaving aside all attempts to identify Zechariah as anyone other than the martyr of 2 Chron. 24.20-22, we can see in Q 11.51a a panorama of all the martyrdoms of scripture, much like the panorama of experiences of suffering from Abel onwards, which the father of the famous seven sons drew from 'the law and the prophets' (*4 Macc.* 18.10).

4.8 The Lament over Jerusalem (Q 13.34f.) hinges on the contrast between two wills: ἠθέλησα...οὐκ ἠθελήσατε (13.34b). This indicates an underlying call for realignment, i.e. a demand for repentance, in the present. The contemporary refusal of repentance is seen as a projection of that which is a settled and established tendency to kill the prophets, but it is not itself expanded into a contemporary killing. The speaker, whose echoing of imagery used elsewhere for the call of God or of Wisdom, interprets his mission as prophetic and authorized by God and/or Wisdom. In a unit of tradition distinct from Q 11.47-51 he covers the same ground, expresses the same self-consciousness, alludes to the same purpose, and finally affirms the same judgment. Doubtless ἀφίεται points to God and the future, and οἶκος points to the city, the temple, and the community as a three-in-one whole. While a certain sympathy is conveyed by the intense duplication 'Jerusalem, Jerusalem' and the general mood of sorrowful lamentation, judgment forms the climax in Q 13.35a. Superimposed upon that is the more optimistic announcement that the speaker's period of invisibility will end with a joyful welcome back to the city, the temple, and the community.[50]

5.1 The history of these traditions, and therefore the manner and extent of their mirroring the history of the Q community, can now be assessed. As they stand, the woes combine criticisms of the professional principles and the personal character and conduct of the Pharisees, but it has proved difficult to sustain subdivisions of the seven. First, we have repeatedly detected connections, i.e. K/P (4.1), B/K (4.2), S/K/B/P (4.3), T/P (4.4), W/S/T (4.5), and G/W (4.6). Secondly, recourse to intra-religious polemical texts elsewhere, e.g. *Pss. Sol.* 4, CD 1.18b–2.1, 1QH 2.6-14 and *T. Mos.* 7.4-9, serves to confirm how common and instinctive, though doubtless one-sided, is the tendency to combine personal criticisms (with higher or lower coefficients of vitriol!) and assaults on principles of interpretation of the will of God. In these texts we find on one and the same stratum attacks which correspond to those which have been traced by some to different strata of Q. Thirdly, there is the term ὑποκριτής. Its appearance in five out of seven of the Woes (i.e. all but B and S) could be, and often is,[51] attributed to MtR. But Matthew can also derive it from tradition elsewhere (Mk 7.6; 12.15), including Q (Q 6.42; 12.46), and Luke's generalized warning against the ὑπόκρισις of the Pharisees immediately after his version of the Woes (12.1) suggests a reminiscence of the use of the term in the Woes themselves. If so, it is relevant that the term encompasses an extremely broad range of meaning: from inaccurate teaching and interpretation (cf. Lk. 12.56; 13.15) to downright wickedness and lack of integrity.[52] Such a range of meaning confronts us in the Woes, but it does not impede the conclusion that they form a unity.

5.2 In principle it is possible that some of the woes have been expanded. Some contain simply an accusation and are irre-

---

50. D.C. Allison, Jr, 'Matt. 23.39 = Luke 13.35b as a Conditional Prophecy', *JSNT* 18 (1983), pp. 75-84.

51. Schulz, *Spruchquelle*, pp. 96, etc.

52. U. Wilckens, 'ὑποκρίνομαι', *TDNT*, VIII (1972), pp. 559-71.

ducible (K, B, G). Others contain a further single sentence, either indicative (S, T) or imperative (W) in form. One only (P) is much more extensive, as befits the last in the series. In the case of S, the saying Q 14.11 is demonstrably capable of existing separately, and Q 11.43 is equally clearly capable of surviving alone. So the former may owe its presence here to editorial work, though it is not clear that it must do.[53] In the case of T, Q 11.42c is regarded by some as redactional, an attempt to guard against the inference that Pharisaic interpretation of the tithing laws is being rejected.[54] Reasons have already been put forward for an alternative view of this woe, and the delicate balance and clarity of 11.42bc, over against the unclarity of 11.42b by itself, tends to make the presence of an editorial comment marginally possible but highly improbable. In the case of W, the situation is not dissimilar, that is, Q 11.39 could be self-sufficient, but in isolation it lacks clarity and coherence to such an extent that the removal of Mt. 23.26 would be damaging.

The final woe, P (Q 11.47-51), has almost certainly been expanded.[55] Q 11.51a envisages a sequence of martyrs, but a

53. In a strikingly parallel text, Sir. 1.28-30, a warning against hypocrisy and failure to fear the Lord, involves the instruction, 'Do not exalt yourself (μὴ ἐξύψον σεαυτόν) lest you fall... and the Lord will cast you down in the middle of the assembly (συναγωγή)'.

54. Hoffmann, *Studien*, p. 59; W. Schenk, *Synopse zur Redenquelle der Evangelisten* (Düsseldorf: Patmos, 1981), p. 76; Tuckett, 'Q, the Law and Judaism', p. 94. This possibility had already been mentioned by Bultmann (*History*, p. 131), though with the qualification that T and W might preserve authentic sayings of Jesus (p. 147).

55. Kloppenborg (*Formation*, p. 144) regards Q 11.49-51 as a whole as 'a secondary construction of Q redaction', on the basis of (i) a discrepancy of audience between Pharisees/scribes and 'this generation'; (ii) the unexpectedness of the apparently pre-mundane speech of Sophia in the midst of the Woes attributed to Jesus; and (iii) the difference of character between the reproaches offered by the Woes and the retribution threatened in the Sophia oracle. The problem with this analysis is that, as Kloppenborg himself rightly recalls, 11.47-51 corresponds formally to the classic woe oracle form which includes an announcement of judgment. Moreover, dislocation within 11.49-51 makes unitary redaction unlikely. Finally, the broadening of which Kloppenborg speaks has already been implicit in P, since, as has from time to time been observed (e.g. Hare, *Persecutions*, p. 83), we cannot suppose that the Pharisees alone were engaged in building tombs for the prophets.

more extensive one than the sequence of prophetic martyrs; it causes Q 11.51b to reiterate the declaration in 11.50 that blood will be required of this generation. Prophets alone were in view in Q 11.50, so the extra persons mentioned in Q 11.49 must also have been added redactionally. Other Q sayings show an interest in either 'the law and the prophets' as a whole (Q 16.16), or a range of persons more extensive than the prophets as representatives of the pre-John/Jesus period (Q 7.28a; 10.24), and while these other sayings are almost certainly pre-redactional their number suggests a special interest on the part of the editor.

5.3 It is widely agreed that the Lament over Jerusalem (Q 13.34f.) has been expanded. This expansion probably includes the phrase καὶ λιθοβολοῦσα τοὺς ἀπεσταλμένους which matches the similar addition in 11.49[56] and the creation of 11.51 and is, incidentally, further confirmation that in Q the Lament did follow the Woes. That 'And I tell you, you will not see me again until you say, "Blessed is he who comes in the name of the Lord"' (13.35b) is an expansion is extremely probable.[57] The prospect of judgment forms an appropriate ending for 13.34-35a in form-critical terms, and the hopeful note struck by 13.35b is louder than anything in 13.34-35a. Allison[58] has convincingly demonstrated that 13.35b stems from a sense that a mission calling for repentance in Israel must continue and will achieve good success. It is this mission in which the Q community is occupied. Although ostensibly addressed to Jerusalem, 13.35b is more of a concluding message to the Christian community, in the same way that the whole woe complex is ostensibly addressed to Pharisees, but in fact addressed to disciples (Mt. 23.1/Lk. 20.45 diff. Mk 12.37b).

Already before Q 11.49-51, therefore, they had become representative figures.

56. From the range of Old Testament victims of stoning, Zechariah ben Jehoiada (2 Chron. 24.20-22) is the only one who could, even in the most general sense, be described as having been 'sent'.

57. F. Neirynck, 'Recent Developments in the Study of Q', in *Logia* (note 3), pp. 29-75 (66).

58. See note 50. Less convincing is his argument that this saying is integral to the oracle and not a secondary expansion.

A further component of the message to the disciples arises from the juxtaposition of 13.35b and Q 17.23f. The one who has gone away (cf. Q 19.12) and who will come (Q 12.43; 19.15) is the Son of Man. The Son of Man's coming will not be experienced restrictedly either in the sacred settings of desert or inner rooms (of the temple?—for a journey is mentioned in connection with the desert but not with the ταμιεῖα; the word ταμιεῖον is so ordinary a description of a private room[59] that its particular meaning must be fixed by its context; it is used by Josephus, *War* 4.262 and *Ant.* 9.142, 274, of a location on the Temple site; desert and Jerusalem—viewed from a distance from the Mount of Olives—are the two locations preoccupying the charismatic-eschatological leaders, according to Josephus, *Ant.* 20.167-170; elsewhere in Q 4.3-4, 9-11 desert and temple have been paired as possible locations of christological disclosure). It will not conform to the scheme of the charismatic-eschatological prophets. He will come from heaven to Jerusalem, overwhelmingly and openly for all to see. He will only come when Jerusalem is ready to welcome him because the community there has at last, in response to the Christian mission, repented.

6. If the foregoing argument has been correct, the material in Q 11.39-52, 13.34f. and 17.23f. contains a relatively small number of editorial additions. Few and light though they are, those additions do cohere with one another and form a window through which we may view the Q community and its concerns and commitments. The underlying material to which the additions were made is just as interesting, even though the theory of successive stages of literary, and therefore experiential, development has not proved convincing. That underlying material documents the religious tradition upon which the Q community relies, and to which it is answerable.

The Woes against the Pharisees have emerged as an originally unified complex attaching supreme importance to the connection between the missions of the prophets of Israel and the contemporary prophetic preaching of the kingdom.

59. A room for eating (2 Sam. 13.10) or sleeping (Song 1.4; 3.4) or storage (Ps. 144.13; Prov. 3.10; Lk. 12.24) or hiding (1 Kgs 22.25; 2 Kgs 11.2).

Deaths occurred in the former context, no deaths have occurred in the latter. That means that we can add further strength and precision to the arguments that the Woes belong to a pre-70 AD setting by locating them even before the first Christian martyrdom. Inevitably, so early a *terminus ad quem* raises the question whether in these Woes we overhear the *ipsissima vox Jesu*.

6.1 A distinction between the outlook of Jesus and the outlook of the Woes has often been detected in T+W, in that the tithing and purity laws are accepted rather than (as in Mk 7) questioned.[60] But recent discussion of Mk 7.15 has severely damaged the view that it supports a conflict between Jesus and Torah, especially when the words εἰσπορευόμενον εἰς αὐτόν are assigned to MkR. and removed; indeed, the way in which T and W, while in no way criticizing the practices in question, nevertheless subordinate them firmly to the primary obligations of justice, mercy and concern for the poor, brings them into the mainstream of what is usually regarded as authentic tradition.

6.2 Another supposed discrepancy between the Woes and Jesus has been proposed in K. There the idea of the kingdom has been contrasted with Jesus' apocalyptic perspective,[61] and understood in terms of the community, even to the extent of recalling the watchword *extra ecclesiam nulla salus*![62] This must surely be overdrawn, partly because Jesus' debt to apocalyptic must not be exaggerated, and partly because K is most easily understood in terms of a relationship between the kingdom and 'the age to come', and from the point of view of a mission which questions the assumption that all Israelites have a share in that coming age.[63]

---

60. Hoffmann, *Studien*, p. 170.
61. Schulz, *Spruchquelle*, p. 111.
62. Haenchen, 'Matthäus 23', p. 47; Schürmann, 'Zeugnis', pp. 175f.
63. Similarly in favour of authenticity, Garland, *Intention*, pp. 127f.

6.3 Finally, there is in P the confrontation with 'this generation', which Lührmann has held to be the hallmark of Q[64] and which, if so, might not be traceable to Jesus. What is striking about the other 'this generation' sayings is that they do not belong to the final stage of the compilation of Q. The first, Q 7.31, is integral to the parable of the Children in the Marketplace (7.31f.), which is older than its secondary expansion (7.33f.). As a comment on the obduracy of the audience of Jesus in Israel, presented with a prophetic message which has both celebratory and salutary aspects, this parable rings true to the message of Jesus. It is worth considering whether Q 7.35, which does not seem very obviously integrated with 7.33f., may have been an original ending for the parable, at once a 'sting in the tail' for opponents and an assurance to those who have accepted the call (cf. the call of Wisdom to the obdurate, Prov. 1.22-27, with comment on that call, 1.28-32, and final assurance about those who are attentive, 1.33).[65] The connective καί is on any showing adversative; the metaphor of children is shared by 7.31f., 35 but not by 7.33f.; and if the children of Wisdom have 'recognized righteousness' in the call of Jesus, then he must himself be a prophet sent by Wisdom. At all events, the 'this generation' theme, while firmly endorsed by Q, can be derived from Jesus. The second such text, the composite Q 11.29f., 31f., has a much controverted tradition-history. If, as I have suggested elsewhere,[66] Q 11.29f. is a Q-redacted version of an earlier saying denouncing 'this generation' for its demand for a sign and asserting that the only sign to be expected is the sign of the (future) Son of Man (cf. Q 17.23f.), this would push the earliest stage of the development of the saying back behind the stage of Q-compilation. Authen-

64. D. Lührmann, *Die Redaktion der Logienquelle* (Neukirchen: Neukirchener Verlag, 1969), pp. 35-43.

65. If the 'children of Wisdom' (Q 7.35) are to be equated with the 'babes' (Q 10.21) (cf. Légasse, 'Mt. 23,34-36', p. 246), it would be significant that 10.21 itself belongs to an older stratum of the text than the *Kommentarwort* 10.22 and is also worth taking seriously as a possible Jesus-saying.

66. 'The Law and the Prophets in Q', in G. Hawthorne and O. Betz (eds.), *Tradition and Interpretation in the New Testament. Essays Presented to E.E. Ellis* (Grand Rapids: Eerdmans, 1987), pp. 95-109 (99-101).

ticity or otherwise would be dependent on any general solution to the Son of Man problem. Q 11.31f., on the other hand, eases its way smoothly into the authentic Jesus-material, and again presumes a certain pattern for himself, namely, a preacher of the kingdom for the final generation of Israel in the traditions of wisdom and prophecy. In the light of these parallels for the last Woe, P, it seems that at least three of the four 'this generation' texts stem from Jesus. In each case there has been considerable interest shown at the Q-editorial stage, which means that the Q community committed itself particularly to a continuation of those features of the mission of Jesus which these texts preserve. Here at least, it is a case of 'from Jesus to Q' rather than 'not Jesus but Q'.

7. The Woes against the Pharisees belong to a setting of conflict *intra muros* within Judaism. Nothing disrespectful of the definitive position of Torah and Temple is said here. But what of the specific relationship between Christians and Pharisees? Attention has recently and, I believe, rightly been drawn to the closeness of that relationship.[67] It is clear that there were many convictions held in common. How then can we explain the confrontation documented by so many traditions, including the Woes? Of course, religious groups which show least sympathy for one another often have most in common in terms of heritage.[68] It's the neighbours who are often nastiest to one another! Nevertheless, the Woes do point to a discrepancy of principle as well as a willingness to engage in personalized polemic. In the setting of the prophetic announcement of the kingdom, a missionary message to Israel about which the Pharisees remain sceptical and critical, there is a disposition to stand apart from the process of generating tradition and allegedly burdensome definitions of the will of God, and to insist on the paramount importance of the major principles of the

67. Cf. R.A. Wild, 'The Encounter between Pharisaic and Christian Judaism: Some Early Gospel Evidence', *NovT* 27 (1985), pp. 105-24; Tuckett, 'Q, the Law and Judaism', pp. 98-101, with significant modifications of Wild's treatment of Marcan material; K. Berger, 'Jesus als Pharisäer und frühe Christen als Pharisäer', *NovT* 30 (1988), pp. 231-62.
68. Berger, 'Jesus als Pharisäer', p. 232.

covenant. One corollary of this result would be that we do not (*pace* Tuckett) find evidence in these Woes of a tendency to 're-Judaize' within the Q community, nor a claim by that community to be a true part of the Pharisaic movement. The tradition seems throughout to be comfortable within Judaism, uneasy about Pharisaism, and, in view of the rarity of any comment on the authority of the law (Q 16.17), not at all pre-occupied with the problem which threatened to tear apart other early Christian communities. Of such controversies Q is aware, but can afford to pass by on the other side with just that one side-glance.

8. The Lament over Jerusalem antedates its editorial modifi-cation, but by how much? Its nearest relatives, traditionally speaking, are the Woes on the Cities of Galilee (Q 10.13-15). Indeed there is arguably more than a passing similarity of scheme[69] between Q 10.3-16 and Q 11.39-52; 13.34f.: early tradition concerned with the preaching of the kingdom and climaxing in the announcement of judgment (10.3-11; 11.39-50, 52); a transitional editorial comment preparing for what follows (10.12?; 11.51); an oracle against specific cities (10.13-15; 13.34-35a); and a saying about reception of the one who has come, or will come, with the authority of God (10.16; 13.35b). When 13.34-35b is set alongside 10.13-15, internal similarities also appear:[70] first, the address to cities; second, the historical retrospect (on Tyre and Sidon, and on Jerusalem); third, the reference to the overall mission of Jesus; forth, a sense of protracted activity (πάλαι... ποσάκις); fifth, a demand for repentance; and sixth, the proclamation of judgment. It looks as if these two Q traditions have a common origin.

Once again, the possibility of derivation from Jesus is worth taking seriously.[71] First, the Gentile mission is not presupposed

---

69. Similarly, Neirynck, 'Recent Developments', pp. 66f.
70. Cf. Garland, *Intention*, p. 70.
71. Rightly, C.E. Carlston, 'Wisdom and Eschatology in Q', in *Logia* (note 3), pp. 101-19 (117): 'There is no particular reason that Jesus might not have wept over Jerusalem (Lk. 13,34f. = Mt. 23,37-39) for rejecting his message and noted the parallel between his own rejection and the rejection of Wisdom'.

by these sayings in and of themselves.[72] Second, it is hard to see why such obscure places as Chorazin and Bethsaida, which made minimal impact on the gospel tradition, should be singled out in a secondary development. Third, the abrasive radicalism of an adverse contrast between the notorious Tyre and Sidon and any Israelite city is likely to be authentic (cf. the similar contrast with Nineveh, Q 11.32, over against the tendency of Q itself to set up contrasts between those addressed and the Gentiles to the disadvantage of the latter (Q 6.33; 12.30a). Fourth, the call to repentance is too deeply embedded in too many traditions for them all to be detached from the mission of Jesus himself. Fifth, the surveying of the whole of a person's activity in a particular place is hardly inappropriate for the person himself: when the emissaries of Jesus engage particular cities with the message and signs of the kingdom, and then feel themselves to be in general unsuccessful, they respond with a final gesture of disassociation and judgment. If the tradition in Q 10.8-11 reflects the original historical situation, it can provide a parallel and support for the two general surveys under consideration. Sixth, the evidence of prophetic self-understanding on the part of Jesus is widespread in the gospel tradition, and the evidence of a sense of overall failure is widespread too. When those two elements are brought together it is entirely unsurprising that the Deuteronomic scheme should be adopted. An authentic 'two and two' should not be prevented from making an authentic 'four'! Seventh, 'your house (will be) left to you' stands as a final prophetic word of doom over city, community and temple. This is simply a variation on the theme of Mk 13.2 and 14.58, a theme which,

---

72. Those who advocate an awareness of a Gentile mission in Q are noticeably cautious about this tradition. Lührmann (*Redaktion*, p. 87) concedes the correctness of the view of H. Conzelmann (*An Outline of the Theology of the New Testament* [London: SCM, 1969], p. 144) that the point of such passages is 'not primarily salvation for the Gentiles, but rather the threat of judgment for the Jews', and their original context the engagement of the early Christian mission with Israel. P.D. Meyer ('The Gentile Mission in Q', *JBL* 89 [1970], pp. 405-17 [417]), made no appeal to Q 10.13-15 because 'it does not seem to immediately reflect the Gentile mission but only the parenetic use of Gentiles to condemn Jewish obduracy (although the contrast is most striking here)'.

as Sanders has demonstrated, has a strong claim to authenticity.[73]

9. The Q community thus inherited some traditions which expressed, on the one hand, a critical view of the Pharisees but a continuing commitment to the covenant, the law, and the temple, and on the other hand, the expectation that Jerusalem and the temple would be abandoned by God. These were held in balance. The fate of the temple in the future was not taken to imply its religious irrelevance in the present. On the contrary, the future was taken seriously and exclusively as future. And thus we have a picture of a community whose outlook was essentially Jerusalem-centred, whose theology was Torah-centred, whose worship was temple-centred, and which saw (with some justice) no incompatibility between all of that and commitment to Jesus.

73. E.P. Sanders, *Jesus and Judaism* (London: SCM, 1985).

[ὡς] φραγέλλιον ἐκ σχοινίων (JOHN 2.15)

B.D. Chilton

Dr Bammel contributed a study to a notable volume he edited, itself in honor of C.F.D. Moule, which offers a critical perspective upon the Johannine material, suitably rearranged, as offering data of primary interest within the reconstruction of the ministry of Jesus.[1] The argument is characteristically elegant: style, erudition, and fresh insight make up a powerful challenge to the bland presumption that the Synoptic Gospels hold the key to all we might know about Jesus. The present contribution is largely complementary of Dr Bammel's argument, although in one central matter, to which the title alludes, it takes a different course. In so doing, however, it only confirms my teacher's insight, that John—correctly read—provides data every bit as important for the understanding of Jesus as the Synoptics.

The consultation of Jn 11.47, in which the high priests and Pharisees gathered in council (συνήγαγον...συνέδριον), is read by Dr Bammel as a formal proceeding, which makes the hearing before Annas in ch. 18 a purely tactical session.[2] The

---

1. 'Ex illa itaque die consilium fecerunt...', in E. Bammel (ed.), *The Trial of Jesus. Cambridge Studies in Honour of C.F.D. Moule* (Studies in Biblical Theology; London: SCM, 1970), pp. 11-40.

2. Cf. Bammel, pp. 29, 30. It might be mentioned that such a reading is supported by 12.10, where ἐβουλεύσαντο δὲ οἱ ἀρχιερεῖς ἵνα καὶ τὸν Λάζαρον ἀποκτείνωσιν employs the same verb (with postpositive καί) in order to identify the plot against Lazarus with the proceeding against Jesus. In addition, the later passage makes it apparent that the high-priestly opposition was the crux of the matter in the Johannine understanding: 'the Pharisees' in 11.47 may be a stereotypical addition. On the other hand, as we shall see, it may in fact be the case that the construal of purity which Jesus acted upon (and acted out) in his occupa-

necessary conclusion of such an approach is that the telescoping of events into a 'holy week' is more radical in the Synoptics than in John, and specifically that the decision to execute Jesus was taken considerably in advance of the dénouement before Pilate. The question naturally arises, what sort of place the occupation of the Temple (in Jn 2.13-17) would have in such a scheme. Dr Bammel himself answers that question, with reference to the textual history of the pericope. He observes that Tatian (at least according to certain witnesses), Celsus's Jew (as Origen would have it; cf. *Contra Celsum* 1.67), and Papyrus Egerton 2 place the story later in Jesus' ministry, and most likely associated it with Tabernacles in ch. 7,[3] and concludes that the occupation of the Temple and the resolution to execute Jesus occurred prior to the final Passover of his life.[4] Indeed, Dr Bammel sees an echo of that chronology in the disciples' awareness in Jn 11.7f., 16 that Judaea is for Jesus a place of mortal danger.

Dr Bammel argues for the earlier placement of the occupation against Dodd, the mediator of the claim of Johannine independence from the Synoptics to the world of modern, English-speaking scholarship. As has already been indicated, his opinion has both plausibility and, to a certain degree, some

tion of the Temple put him into conflict with both priests and Pharisees.

3. Cf. Bammel, pp. 17-20. It is the nature of the Egerton Papyrus and *Contra Celsum* that the precise location of the story in narrative terms is inferential. In addition, of course, certain traditions of the *Toledoth Jesu* would support the sort of solution Dr Bammel advocates. The usage of that material in the effort critically to understand Jesus has been another major area of Dr Bammel's contribution; but it is left to other contributors to the present volume to explore that aspect of the field.

4. Raymond E. Brown (*The Gospel according to John* [Anchor Bible; London: Chapman, 1978], I, p. 118) suggests 'that on his first journey to Jerusalem... Jesus uttered a prophetic warning about the destruction of the sanctuary... it seems likely that Jesus' action of cleansing the temple precincts took place in the last days of his life'. Brown also agrees with Bammel that the story of Lazarus has been so introduced as to cause a displacement; cf. also Robert Tomson Fortna, *The Gospel of Signs. A Reconstruction of the Narrative Source Underlying the Fourth Gospel* (SNTSMS 11; Cambridge: Cambridge University Press, 1970), pp. 145-47.

textual tradition on its side. But Dr Bammel was perhaps a little too quick to view some of the Johannine deviations from the Synoptic story of the occupation as secondary; considered from a different angle, they may appear to be part and parcel of a distinctive, and more accurate, construal of what Jesus was doing in the Temple.

An approach such as Dr Bammel's reads τά τε πρόβατα καὶ τοὺς βόας in v. 15 as 'an interpolation'; the thought is that the preceding πάντας can only have referred to the men who were trading in animals, as in Mt. 21.12 (cf. Mk 11.15; Lk. 19.45).[5] The motivation of the addition is 'an anti-cultic tendency',[6] and there can be no doubt but that there is a programmatic portrayal in the Fourth Gospel of antipathy between Jesus and the Temple, or at least between Jesus and the administration of the Temple. From the first chapter, 'the Jews' send out a delegation of 'priests and Levites' in order to interrogate John (1.19), and similar personnel become involved in proceedings against Jesus (7.32, 45; 11.47f.; 12.10; 18.13f., 19f., 35). Feasts become pre-eminent as settings of controversy between Jesus and 'the Jews', usually in connection with his signs (cf. 5.1f.; 6.4f.; 7.2ff.; 10.22f.; 11.55f.; 12.1f.), and the Temple in particular is potentially a place of violence against him (7.14f.; 10.23f.; 11.56f.). All such passages might indeed be characterized as anti-cultic, but it is not at all evident that the mention of sheep and oxen in 2.15 is a matter of the same sort of polemic.

At just this point, we must return to the stylistic oddity of v. 15. As Barrett points out, if the mention of the animals were 'a merely epexegetical phrase, we should have had πάντα, not πάντας'.[7] Barrett's conclusion was resisted, however, by Ernst Haenchen, who argued that τοὺς βόας has determined the gender of πᾶς.[8] Although Haenchen's objection is noteworthy, and although his suggestion concerning the purpose of the φραγέλλιον will be accepted below, his resistance to Barrett's

5. Bammel, p. 16 nn. 23, 27, citing Wellhausen and E. Hirsch.

6. Bammel, p. 16.

7. C.K. Barrett, *The Gospel according to St. John* (London: SPCK, 1978), p. 198; cf. also Barnabas Lindars, *The Gospel of John* (New Century Bible; London: Oliphants, 1972), p. 138.

8. In *Das Johannesevangelium. Ein Kommentar* (Tübingen: Mohr, 1980), p. 200.

analysis is not compelling. The difficulty of πάντας is not only its gender, but its position. Once the personnel, τοὺς πωλοῦντας βόας καὶ πρόβατα καὶ περιστερὰς καὶ τοὺς κερματιστὰς καθημένους, are mentioned in v. 14, πάντας is naturally taken of them, with the reference to the animals as appositive. That was certainly the decision embodied in two notable renderings, the Authorized Version and Luther's Bible. But if the position of πάντας appears to make its reference plain, why ever did the peculiar construction, employing τε and καί, follow? That construction, ἅπαξ λεγόμενον in the Fourth Gospel, is what makes the phrase seem odd as in apposition, with the result that the sense of the passage has appeared problematic.

If the phrase concerning the animals in v. 15 appears to be an aporia, it is naturally associated with another, involving the merchants of pigeons in v. 16. The claim is sometimes made, and has been made as recently as in Brown's commentary,[9] that Jesus is portrayed as treating such vendors, as providers to the poor (cf. Lev. 5.7), in a kindlier fashion than he treated the others, subsituting words for a whip. Why Jesus should be cast in the role of defending those whose wealth is derived from the poor is not explained. (In any case the supposition is implicit that the different groups of vendors and animals are part of John's tradition, and not a theological illustration. To that extent, the observation is incisive.) With Westcott, it seems wise not to attribute any commercial preference to Jesus,[10] but that only excites our curiosity: why the concatenation of sellers, changers, and animals, one mentioned after and interrupting another, in vv. 14-16?

In the absense of any substantial indication that the aporia is not to be explained in respect of the Johannine attitude toward the Temple generally, the possibility that sources are conflated in the pericope should obviously be considered.[11] The accessibility to John of an account of Jesus' occupation of the Temple along the lines of the passage in the Synoptics may be taken for granted. Mark's version (11.15b-16) and Matthew's (21.12)

9. Brown, p. 115.
10. Cf. Brooke Foss Westcott, *The Gospel according to St. John* (London: Murray, 1908).
11. Cf. Brown, p. 120, who concludes that 'an independent tradition' is reflected here.

has Jesus cast out those selling *and* buying in the Temple, and overturning the tables of the money-changers and the seats of the pigeon-sellers. The additional statement in Mark (as compared to Matthew and Luke), that Jesus did not permit anyone to carry a vessel through the Temple is, as we shall see, a probably correct inference or datum, but its uniqueness excludes it from the commonly Synoptic material.[12] If we assume that such a story was available at the time Jn 2.13-16 was written, the existence *and the order of mention* of the sellers, the money-changers with their tables, and the pigeon-vendors are entirely explicable. The deviation of the pericope from the commonly Synoptic version, and especially its additions, would then be taken as reflecting another version of the story. It would include reference only to sellers, not buyers, of sacrificial animals, specified as oxen and sheep, not only pigeons. It would also refer to a group called κερματισταὶ καθήμενοι, and to the incident of the φραγέλλιον ἐκ σχοινίων. Each of these elements should be considered seriously as historically relevant to what Jesus did in the Temple.

The claim of historicity just made is, of course, consonant with Dr Bammel's evaluation of much that is contained in the Fourth Gospel.[13] In addition, the claim is only sustainable by virtue of recourse to a principle of analysis he has developed considerably. He has resisted the fallacy of portraying Judaism as a 'background' of the Gospels, as if Judaic sources were merely a frame around a portrait which in fact defined its own points of reference, and has spoken instead of the

12. Similarly, Luke's brevity is such as practically to make it seem superfluous, although it *might* be notable that, just as in Jn 2.14, Lk. 19.45 refers only to sellers, not to buyers. That may be an indication of the circulation of the material incorporated in John at the time Luke was composed. The approach to the relationship among the Gospels which I have come to prefer is one in which Matthew, Mark, and Luke are taken to be independent documentations of apostolic catechesis, along with a collection of Jesus' mishnah (which we have come to call 'Q'), and John is taken as a deliberate, meditative supplement to such catechesis. Cf. *Profiles of a Rabbi. Synoptic Opportunites in Reading about Jesus* (Brown Judaic Studies; Atlanta: Scholars Press, 1989).
13. Bammel, p. 35.

CHILTON [ώς] φραγέλλιον ἐκ σχοινίων (John 2.15) 335

'atmosphere' of the Gospel as illuminated by those sources.[14] Each of the elements specified as possibly belonging to a second source of John is better appreciated, and seen as more vividly historical, within its Judaic environment. Indeed, the passage illustrates the general proposition that the Fourth Gospel breathes the atmosphere of early Judaism so deeply, it cannot live outside that environment.

Why should sellers be referred to alone? Buyers of any commodity are, after all, part of the merchandising a market is designed to serve. For that reason, the mention of both groups in Mark (11.15) and Matthew (21.12) is natural, and the build-up to the charge that the merchants have made God's a house a 'den of thieves' (Mk 11.17; Mt. 21.13) follows more easily. But why should the buyers be omitted in John, given its anti-cultic tendency? Any criticism of cultic commercialism would obviously be more pointed if, as in the Synoptics, buyers could be mentioned, but the second source of John knew better than to put them there, and even omitted to mention Jesus' citation of Jer. 7.11; both exclusions, for all that they would have been useful within the Johannine apologetic, are honored in the received text of the Fourth Gospel. The normal place of trade in sacrificial animals was not the Temple at all, but Hanuth on the Mount of Olives.[15] The very innovation of selling animals in the Temple was potentially scandalous, implying—as one might have thought—a reversal of the prophecy in Zech. 14.21c, and it seems specifically to have scandalized Jesus.[16]

David Flusser comes to the reasonable conclusion that the setting up of vendors at the Temple was unusual, and that the practice did not last.[17] Joachim Jeremias is able to show that 'in the Court of the Gentiles, in spite of the sanctity of the

14. Bammel, p. 36. Of course, he is speaking at this point of the *Toledoth Jesu*, a body of material he has long specialized in, but the perspective is applicable more generally.
15. Cf. Victor Eppstein, 'The Historicity of the Gospel Account of the Cleansing of the Temple', *ZNW* 55 (1964), pp. 42-58, 48.
16. Cf. Richard H. Hiers, 'Purification of the Temple: Preparation for the Kingdom of God', *JBL* 90 (1971), pp. 82-90, 83.
17. Cf. David Flusser, *Jesus* (trans. Ronald Walls; New York: Herder and Herder, 1969), pp. 108-109.

Temple area, there could have been a flourishing trade in animals for sacrifice'.[18] But Jeremias is unable to produce a single passage from early Judaic or rabbinic literature which actually states in so many words that there was such a trade. Normal traffic, as Jeremias himself shows, was focused on the Mount of Olives,[19] although other sites in Jerusalem were also involved. Jeremias's best piece of supporting evidence for his supposition of trade in the Temple,[20] the importation of cattle by Baba b. Buta (cf. *y. Betzah* 2.4), does not illustrate ordinary, commercial activity, but rabbinic interest in *how* animals were to be sacrificed, in that Baba b. Buta is said to have brought the cattle into the Temple so as to encourage the offering of animals in accordance with the teaching he supported.[21] Given that the vending of animals in the Temple was itself

18. In *Jerusalem in the Time of Jesus* (ET London: SCM, 1969), p. 49.
19. Jeremias, *Jerusalem*, p. 48.
20. Jeremias, *Jerusalem*, p. 49.
21. The relevant passages read as follows, as given in H.L. Strack and P. Billerbeck, *Kommentar zum Neuen Testament aus Talmud und Midrasch* (München: Beck, 1922), I, pp. 851-52; the first is the mishnaic discussion at issue (*m. Betzah* 2.4), the second the Gemara:

> Die Schule Schammais sagte: Man darf Friedenopfer (an einem Feiertage) darbringen, aber nicht die Hände auf sie aufstemmen; dagegen darf man (der einzelne) keine Ganzopfer (an einem Feiertage) darbringen; die Schule Hillels sagte: Man darf Friedensofper u. Ganzopfer darbringen u. die Hände auf sie aufstemmen.
> Es war daselbst Baba b. Buta (Zeitgenosse Herodes des Grossen) von den Schülern der Schule Schammais: der wusste, dass die Halakha war wie die Meinung der Schule Hillels. Einmal betrat er den Vorhof u. fand ihn verödet (weil niemand mehr auf Grund der schammaitischen Lehrmeinung an einem Feiertag ein Opfer darbrachte). Da Sprach er: Mögen veröden die Häuser derer, die das Haus unseres Gottes verödet haben! Was tat er? Er liess 3000 Stück Kleinvieh vom Kleinvieh Qedars kommen u. untersuchte sie betreffs (etwaigen) Leibesfehler u. stellte sie auf dem Tempelberg auf. Er sprach zu den Israeliten: Höret mich, meine Brüder, Haus Israel: wer will, bringe Ganzopfer, bringe sie u. stemme seine Hände auf...

Quite evidently, we are not dealing here, as Jeremias would have it, with a reference to a commercial arrangement. Indeed, the present passage is rather illuminating from another point of view: Jesus was also concerned to foment a certain understanding of sacrifice. He promulgated his teaching by excluding animals, where Baba b. Buta had provided them; such, in any case, is the argument of the present contribution.

problematic, the notion that they should be available in the Temple for consumption elsewhere or resale was, in all likelihood, unthinkable.

Victor Eppstein has suggested that the presence of vendors in the Temple should be associated with a specific innovation of Caiaphas, which Talmud places forty years prior to the destruction of the Temple (cf. *AZ* 8b; *Shab.* 15a; *Sanh.* 41a). The sources refer to the exile of the Sanhedrin from the Chamber of Hewn Stone in the Temple to Hanuth; Eppstein suggests that, in turn, the merchants at Hanuth were permitted to sell within the precincts of the Temple.[22] The presence of money-changers there can have surprised no one,[23] and Eppstein attempts to explain the overturning of their tables as an inadvertent result of the mêlée over the vendors.[24] That anything accidental or inadvertent can have taken place with furniture as massive as was used in the Temple seems implausible (cf. *Sheq.* 2.1; 6.5); more probably, the quotation from Jer. 7.11 (the saying of Jesus in the Synoptic version, cf. Mt. 21.13; Mk 11.17; Lk. 19.46) was applied to the money-changers in the course of the increasingly anti-cultic transmission of the story.[25]

22. Eppstein, 'Cleansing the Temple', pp. 42-55.
23. As the mishnaic tractate *Sheq.* 1.1, 3 makes abundantly clear, the changers were particularly prominent during Adar (the month immediately prior to Nisan), when the half-shekel was collected both in Jerusalem and the provinces. But *Bekh.* 8.7 specifies that Tyrian currency is to be used for the sacrifices of Num. 18.16; Exod. 21.32; Deut. 22.29; Exod. 22.16, 17; Deut. 22.19. Such payment was so standard that one recent handbook can claim that 'all sacred dues' were payable in Tyrian coinage (E. Schürer [M. Black, F. Millar, G. Vermes], *The History of the Jewish People in the Age of Jesus Christ* [175 BC–AD 135], II [Edinburgh: T. & T. Clark, 1979], p. 272), although at least one passage in the literature (Mk 12.41-44; Lk. 21.1-4) renders that generalization suspect. The surcharge involved in the exchange of currency for cultic purposes was fixed and its application limited (cf. *Sheq.* 1.6, 7).
24. Eppstein, 'Cleansing the Temple', p. 57.
25. An additional factor, which might have influenced the shape of the Synoptic version, is that Jesus did protest the requirement that he pay the half shekel as a tax. Cf. B.D Chilton, 'A Coin of Three Realms (Matthew 17.24-27)', *The Bible in Three Dimensions. Essays in Celebration of Forty Years of Biblical Studies in the University of Sheffield* (JSOTS 87; Sheffield: JSOT Press, 1990), pp. 269-82.

Of course, the specific reference to oxen and sheep does play into the hands of the anti-cultic tendency of the early Church, but there is no sense in which they need to be regarded as an invention of that tendency. Indeed, *any* major feast required the sacrifice of both oxen and sheep (cf. Num. 28.11–29.38). The especially high number of animals prescribed in Torah for Sukkoth (Num. 29.12-38) would make that time of year as striking for trade in the Temple as Passover, and the number of sheep would not entirely dwarf the number of oxen, as at Passover. In addition to Dr Bammel's argument for putting Jesus' occupation at Sukkoth, not Passover, an argument based upon the Fourth Gospel, it might also be mentioned that Jesus' entry into Jerusalem, with its attendant singing of the Hallel, the cries of Hosanna, festal boughs, and its reference to the Mount of Olives, is more immediately reminiscent of Sukkoth than of Passover.[26]

The scandal involved in trading on the sacred mount obviously had nothing whatever to do with the presence of animals. By definition, they were appropriate victims, pure and unblemished. If they were not, they could not have been sold, much less brought into the cultic area of slaughter, north of the altar.[27] Indeed, there would have been a certain advantage to the buyer and to the cult in Caiaphas's innovation: any damage an animal might suffer between Hanuth and the Temple, under the prevalent arrangement during the first century, would be at the buyer's cost, and—if undetected or overlooked—would result in sacrificial invalidity.[28] The scandal of the arrangement was not the animals, but the money being paid for them in the precincts of the Temple. For that reason, the uniquely Johannine, 'Do not make my father's house a house of trade' (2.16b), is precisely to the point. At first

---

26. Cf. B.D. Chilton, 'The Transfiguration: Dominical Assurance and Apostolic Vision', *NTS* 27 (1979), pp. 115-24; T.W. Manson, 'The Cleansing of the Temple', *BJRL* 33 (1951), pp. 271-82; C.W.F. Smith, 'No Time for Figs', *JBL* 79 (1960), pp. 315-27; *idem*, 'Tabernacles in the Fourth Gospel and Mark', *NTS* 9 (1963), pp. 130-46; W.L. Lane, *The Gospel according to Mark* (New London Commentary on the New Testament; London: Marshall, Morgan & Scott, 1974), pp. 390, 391.
27. Cf. *Zeb.* 5.1-5, and contrast 5.6-8.
28. Cf. *Ker.* 6.8; *Sheq.* 4.9; *Gitt.* 56a.

sight, however, the center of the controversy may seem to be absent from the story: where are the proceeds of the trade in animals? John's second source may provide reference to the money, as well as the animals, in the κερματισταὶ καθήμενοι of v. 14. Those figures have naturally been associated with the money-changers of v. 15 and the Synoptics, but there are problems with that identification. Κερματιστής is rare in documents contemporaneous with the New Testament,[29] and it appears only here within the New Testament, along with κέρμα, from which it derives. Translators generally suppose that the κερματισταί are synonymous with the κολλυβισταί of v. 15.[30] From the perspective of the received form of John's Gospel, they are undoubtedly correct: it is precisely the κέρμα of the κολλυβιστῶν which is dumped over by Jesus. But it is just what John intends to say which does not make perfect sense. The coins collected for exchange into a half shekel were not such as could easily be described as κέρμα; the collection was rather of the δίδραχμον, as at Mt. 17.24, and the amount was commonly paid for two, with the στατήρ (cf. Mt. 17.27). The στατήρ was a silver coin; the δίδραχμον was worth two Attic drachmae, and there were periods in which a δραχμή alone could buy a sheep.[31] Clearly, by the period of the Gospels, δραχμαί were not regarded as extraordinarily valuable; ten would not be entirely out of place in a widow's house (cf. Lk. 15.8, 9).[32] The coins involved in the collection of the half-

29. Cf. J.H. Moulton and G. Milligan, *The Vocabulary of the Greek Testament Illustrated from the Papyri and Other Non-literary Sources* (London: Hodder and Stoughton, 1930), p. 342; Barrett, *John*, p. 197.

30. Cf. Brown, *John*, I, p. 115. With characteristic care, however, M.-J. Lagrange showed how inferentially and narrowly based that supposition is; cf. his *Evangile selon Saint Jean* (Etudes Bibliques; Paris: Gabalda, 1925), p. 65. Lagrange also allows that the κολλυβισταί have been provided by the Synoptic tradition (p. 66).

31. Cf. W. Bauer (trans. W.F. Arndt and F.W. Gingrich, augmented by Gingrich and F.W. Danker), *A Greek–English Lexicon of the New Testament and Other Early Christian Literature* (Chicago: University of Chicago Press, 1979), pp. 192, 206, 764.

32. A more likely possession would be two λεπτά or a κοδράντης (cf. Mk 12.42; Lk. 21.2). Within the period of our concern, a quadrans was worth 32 silver denarii, and 64 denarii, according to C.H.V. Sutherland, *Coinage in Imperial Roman Policy, 31 BC–AD 68* (London:

shekel, however, were clearly not κέρμα, when it is borne in mind that a shekel was the equivalent of four δραχμαί or denarii.[33] Of course, were one paying for sacrificial animals, or changing money for that purpose, small change would be generated.[34] The appearance emerges, then, that in the received text of John, the Synoptic story of the money-changers has been cross-bred with the story of the second source, in which the cashiers of the animal-vendors had their small change poured off their tables, and the tables themselves were overturned.

The φραγέλλιον ἐκ σχοινίων, finally, clearly establishes the target of Jesus' action in John's second source. Just that point was recognized by Westcott, who recognized the σχοινία as ropes used to tether the oxen and sheep (but not, obviously, the pigeons).[35] Staffs and objects not suited to the practice of sacrifice were forbidden in the Temple,[36] but Jesus is here portrayed as using the very objects which would need to be there

Methuen, 1951), p. 199. In relation to the shekel, such coins would indeed be κέρμα.

33. The value of the shekel is given by Josephus, *Ant.* 3.8.2 §195. *Sheq.* 2.1 refers to the changing of coins into the even larger denomination, the daric, for the purposes of transport.

34. In *Sheq.* 5.3-5 a scheme is laid out, in which money for sacrifice was paid in the Temple in exchange for a seal. The seal was then good for drink offering. It may be that Caiaphas's innovation involved such an arrangement. In any case, money found near cattle-dealers (wherever located) could be deemed to be second tithe (*Sheq.* 7.2). Clearly, there was a felt affinity between money paid for sacrifice and the sacred currency.

35. Westcott, *John*, p. 91. Barrett's suggestion that the *flagellium* directly refers to 'a whip for driving cattle', although theoretically possible, is not plausible here, in that (a) it is made ἐκ σχοινίων, and (b) even P[66, 75]—among other witnesses—describe the resulting object as ὡς φραγέλλιον, not directly as a *flagellium*. Quite evidently, the text is not simply referring to a common object. Amongst more recent commentators, Ernst Haenchen may be mentioned as supporting Westcott's interpretation. Indeed, Haenchen states the point far more plainly (*Johannesevangelium*, p. 200): 'Da man Tiere nicht mit den blossen Händen treiben kann, macht sich Jesus «eine Art Geissel» (lies mit P66 und P75 ὡς φραγέλλιον) aus Stricken, mit denen die Tiere angebunden gewesen waren'.

36. Cf. *Ber.* 9.5. It is notable that the same mishnah proscribes entry with a money-belt.

in order to control the animals, so as to expel them and their vendors.[37] As Brown rightly observes, in v. 19 'Jesus is insisting that they (sc. the merchants) are destroying the Temple', and Jesus' act amounts to an attempt to prevent that destruction.[38] Far from being an attempt to prophesy the ruin of the Temple,[39] Jesus' aim was purification, along the lines of stopping illicit trade (cf. Zech. 14.21c).[40] His act did not merely illustrate a reality, it accomplished it:[41] he and his followers occupied the

37. Cf. Lagrange, *Saint Jean*, pp. 65, 66. His comment is not the less lucid for its acerbity, 'Les hommes comprennent et s'enfuient les premiers, mais Jésus expulse aussi (en plus des synoptiques) les brebis et les boeufs plus lents à s'ébranler, ce que Loisy, attentif à un certain idéal de style et indifférent à la réalité, regarde comme surajcuté'.
38. Brown, *John*, I, p. 122. Brown sees v. 19 as 'originally an eschatological proclamation', because he has been influenced in his reading by the markedly different Synoptic versions of the saying. But within John's second source, the issues are purity and decadence, not eschatology. For the use of the imperative, cf. Lagrange, p. 94, and his citation of Isa. 37.30; Mt. 23.32; Jn 13.27, and Bultmann, p. 125 n. 4, and his citation of Amos 4.4; Isa. 8.9; Jer. 7.21.
39. So, recently, E.P. Sanders, *Jesus and Judaism* (London: SCM, 1985), p. 75. Sanders's position has found a particularly lucid rejoinder in a contribution from Craig A. Evans, 'Jesus' Action in the Temple and Evidence of Corruption in the First-Century Temple', which is to appear in the *1989 SBL Seminar Papers*. The especial strength of Evans's work is that it points out the paucity of evidence for the messianic scheme of the destruction and rebuilding of the Temple which Sanders takes as axiomatic. I am grateful to Professor Evans for sending me a copy of the manuscript of the article prior to its publication. Cf. also Evans, 'Jesus' Action in the Temple: Cleansing or Portent of Destruction?', *CBQ* 51 (1989), pp. 237-70. Pp. 265-67 provide a fine, critical appraisal of Eppstein's contribution.
40. Cf. Brown, *John*, I, p. 119.
41. Cf. C.H. Dodd (*The Interpretation of the Fourth Gospel* [Cambridge: Cambridge University Press, 1953], p. 301): '...Jesus is not promising a significant event yet to come, but inviting his questioners to see in the actual occurrence of the Cleansing of the Temple the σημεῖον they desire'. Dodd unfortunately goes on to give Jesus' act a quasi-Platonic twist, 'The purging of the temple—that is, the expulsion of the sacrificial animals from its courts—signifies the destruction and replacement of the system of religious observance of which the temple was the centre: a new "temple" for an old one' (cf. Lindars, p. 137). Historically speaking, it is preferable not to see an act in respect of purity as metaphorical of anything else, be it eschatology (as

Temple in order to stop the sale of animals there, as well as the transit of vessels (Mk 11.16; cf. Zech. 14.21a).[42] What Jesus was doing in the Temple was preventing the sacrifice of animals whose trade made them ritually impure in his eyes, and the focus of his action is marked by the φραγέλλιον ἐκ σχοινίων.

Of course, it is one thing to discover the focus of Jesus' action, and quite another to hone the lenses through which it should be viewed. But at least, by knowing the point of focus, we have some idea of the appropriate orientation of our perspective. The φραγέλλιον ἐκ σχοινίων is an object which ill comports with Sanders's theory, that Jesus wished to prophesy the destruction of the Temple. Even more emphatically, it rules out the easy Platonism of making Jesus object generally to the religious system of sacrifice, as in Dodd's reading.[43] *Faute de mieux*, it might seem wise to return to the theory of the Synoptic Gospels, and portray Jesus as objecting to priestly corruption, as in Evans's suggestion. But John—or rather, the second source of John—suggests we have a tighter focus to achieve, a focus not on commercialism as a whole, but on the specifics of trading for sacrificial animals in the precincts of the Temple. To imagine Jesus attacking commercialism is appealing,[44] as the development of the Synoptic tradition would indicate, but such a characterization is simply too general to fit the particular nature of his activity.

Scholarship has persistently provided us with reading glasses, when our actual problem is that we suffer astigmatism. Studies seek to specify the alleged occasion upon which Jesus is said to have attacked the very notion of sacrifice, or its administration in the Temple, or the building where it took

in Sanders) or religious observance (as in Dodd): systemically, purity obviously has a value all its own in early Judaism.

42. The vessels, it should be observed, might indeed have been used to carry the blood of slaughtered animals; cf. (for example) *Zeb*. 5. Cf. B.D. Chilton, *A Galilean Rabbi and his Bible: Jesus' Own Interpretation of Isaiah* (London: SPCK, 1984), pp. 17, 18.

43. Cf. H. Stegemann, 'Some Aspects of Eschatology in Texts from the Qumran Community and in the Teaching of Jesus', *Biblical Archaeology Today: Proceedings of the International Congress of Biblical Archaeology. Jerusalem, April 1984* (ed. A. Biran; Jerusalem: Israel Exploration Society, 1985), pp. 408-26.

44. Cf. *Thomas l.* 64 (end).

place. The result is that we comfortably read Jesus' entire
ministry as an anti-cultic enterprise, conveniently think of
him in prophetic, didactic, and/or messianic terms, and sub-
sume any appearance of interest in sacrifice *per se* within
some combination of those categories. How else can Jesus be
conceived of in an age in which 'sacrifice' is only positively
meaningful as a metaphor, within the realm, say, of war,
sport, or parenthood? That very question is a symptom that
our vision is, historically speaking, astigmatic. The tradition of
Jesus' theology, as reflected in all four Gospels, is simply too
redolent of concern for the institutions of sacrifice to be consistent with the implicitly or explicitly anti-cultic portraits of him
which are current.

Matthew represents Jesus as insisting that sacrifice should
be offered—in the Temple—after one is reconciled with one's
neighbor (Mt. 5.23, 24), and as commissioning his followers
with an authority to forgive (16.19;[45] 18.18). The cleansing of
lepers, an emphatically priestly function, is a persistent theme
within the Synoptics at various levels (cf. Mt. 8.1-4/Mk 1.40-
45/Lk. 5.12-16 [cf. Mt. 10.8]; Mt. 11.5/Lk. 7.22; Lk. 17.14, 17),
and purity is also presented as a global issue (Mt. 15.1-20/Mk
7.1-23; Lk 11.37-44; Mt. 23.23-27). The practical matter of
how money is to be raised for the Temple and sacrifice is also
reflected as a concern of Jesus in the Synoptics (Mt. 17.24-27;
Mk 12.41-44/Lk. 21.1-4; Mt. 23.23/Lk. 11.42). Throughout,
the essential stance of Mt. 23.16-22, which portrays the Temple as the source of sanctification, rather than as an object of
sacrificial activity, is clearly maintained. Jesus is consistently
portrayed in the Synoptic Gospels as construing purity in
terms of what the worshiper willingly does in respect of God's
presence in the Temple, rather than as characteristic of or
inherent within objects. That stance is so closely associated
with Jesus, it is also adduced in the controversy concerning the
sabbath (Mt. 12.1-8/Mk 2.23-28/Lk. 6.1-5).

45. The priestly aspects of this saying, which become apparent under
comparison with *Targ. Isa.* 22.22, are investigated in B.D. Chilton,
'Shebna, Eliakim, and the Promise to Peter', *Targumic Approaches to
the Gospels. Essays in the Mutual Definition of Judaism and Christianity* (Studies in Judaism; Lanham: University Press of America),
pp. 63-80.

The Synoptic portrayal has obviously been conditioned by the thinking of early Christianity, but it is not within our present purpose to discuss the extent to which that is the case. Even in the absence of such discussion, the data must make it seem odd in the extreme to suppose that Jesus was not characteristically concerned with what and who was fit for sacrifice. Such a supposition is the astigmatism we need to correct. The geographical references within the narrative of Jesus' passion in all four Gospels make it highly probable that Jesus' concern for the traffic in the Temple was not an incidental or symbolic flash in the pan, but part of a programmatic intention to assure the fitness of sacrifice. He stays in Bethany,[46] on the east side of the Mount of Olives, and is therefore in a position to know of the arrangements for selling sacrificial animals. Indeed, the Mount of Olives itself features prominently, as the starting point of the triumphal entry,[47] as the location of his discourse against the Temple,[48] and as the place of his arrest.[49] Jesus takes up a position in all four Gospels which is cognate with his occupation of the Temple: he dwells where fitting sacrifices may be acquired. That is where the authorities who resented his incursion tracked him down. His trail had been marked by a φραγέλλιον ἐκ σχοινίων.

---

46. Cf. Mt. 21.17 (and the reference to nearby Bethpage in v. 1); 26.6; Mk 11.1, 11, 12; 14.3; Lk. 19.29 (and, after the resurrection, 24.50); Jn 11.1, 18; 12.1.

47. Mt. 21.1; Mk 11.1; Lk. 19.29.

48. Mt. 24.3; Mk 13.3; cf. Lk. 21.37.

49. Mt. 26.30; Mk 14.26; Lk. 22.39. Of course, reference to Gethsemane (Mt. 26.36; Mk 14.32) and to the Johannine garden (18.1) should be associated with the same complex of material.

ATTITUDES TO THE TEMPLE IN THE ACTS OF THE APOSTLES

C.K. Barrett

References in Acts to the Jerusalem Temple constitute a problem to which attention has often been drawn.[1] Did the author of Acts, did the early Christians whose story he claims to tell, regard the Temple as a good thing, or a bad thing? Did they make use of it, or not? If they used it, for what purpose did they use it? Did they treat it simply as a convenient place of assembly or did they share in its official activities? Did they recall, imitate, or disown the action in which Jesus is said to have cast out the traders (Lk. 19.45f.)?[2] Did they recall, quote, or retract the prophecies of the destruction of the Temple that are attributed to him (Lk. 21.5f.; cf. 19.44)?[3] If it should appear that conflicting views are expressed in Acts, how is this to be explained? Is it because different opinions were held by different groups within the early church, and were correctly represented by Luke? Is it because attitudes to the Temple changed in the course of time? Is it because Luke drew on different sources and did not trouble to coordinate them? A further set of questions arises as soon as we look into the background of Acts—and this to some extent we are bound to do if we are to understand Acts itself. What views of the Temple were current among Jews at the time of the origins of Christianity? Were these uniform, or were there differences between, say, Palestinian Jews and Diaspora Jews? Is any light thrown upon

1. E.g. W.G. Kümmel, *Die Theologie des Neuen Testaments* (NTD Ergänzungsreihe, 3; Göttingen: Vandenhoeck & Ruprecht, 1969), pp. 112f.
2. The story is told at greater length and with greater emphasis in the other gospels: Mt. 21.12f.; Mk 11.15-19; Jn 2.13-17.
3. Luke does not include this feature of the mockery of the crucified Jesus (Mt. 27.40; Mk 15.29).

the question by the destruction of the Temple in AD 70, after which time all Jews were obliged to live without the Temple, as, perhaps, some Christians had already chosen to do? And what of Leontopolis?[4] and, more remotely, of Elephantine[5] and the Samaritan Temple on Gerizim?[6] We must ask further what Christian parallels there are to the view, or views, of the Temple that we find in Acts. These may help us to place Acts not only chronologically but in relation to the developing pattern of Christian practice and belief.

An impressive list of questions; and there are few of them to which satisfactory answers can be given, or could be given even if this sketch were greatly expanded. It will be best to begin by surveying the evidence in Acts. The following include perhaps not all but at least the most important relevant passages.

1. *1.13*. On their return from the Mount of Olives, where they had witnessed the Ascension, the Eleven went up into the ὑπερῷον, where they (and apparently some others—1.14) were staying. There are a few passages in the LXX[7] where ὑπερῷον is used of a chamber in the Temple, and it has been suggested that the Christians were able to make use of such a room. Cf. 2.2. This view is improbable; 3.1 represents Peter and John as entering the Temple rather than residing in it. It is however not impossible (cf. Lk. 24.53); if true it would suggest both that the Christians were content to be in the Temple and that the Temple was at least tolerant of them.

2. *2.2*. The Twelve (see 2.14) are now said to be (on the Day of Pentecost) in an οἶκος. The word may mean *house* or *room*; καθήμενοι may mean *dwelling* or *sitting*. οἶκος is used by Josephus in *Ant.* 8.65 for both the Temple and chambers contained within the Temple. It is not impossible (though not very likely)

4. Josephus, *Ant.* 13.62-73; *War* 7.423-32.
5. There is a summary of the evidence in E. Schürer, *The History of the Jewish People in the Age of Jesus Christ* (rev. edn by G. Vermes and F. Millar; Edinburgh: T. & T. Clark, 1973–1987), 3.38-40.
6. Josephus, *Ant.* 13.256.
7. 1 Chron. 28.11 (and 20, *si v.l.*); 2 Chron. 3.9—Heb. עליה; Jer. 20.2; Ezek. 41.7—Heb. עליון.

that we should again think of the Christians as having some
sort of meeting place in the Temple; it is certain that the Temple courts would make a suitable scene for the speech that follows; crowds attending the feast would undoubtedly congre-
gate in the Temple. It is worth noting, however, that Peter's
speech makes no allusion to the Temple.

3. *2.46*. Luke's summary describes the Christians' constant
attendance at the Temple: 'Die Christen waren vorbildliche
Juden!'[8] Verse 42 will refer to observance of the Jewish hours
of prayer; these were observed in the Temple but elsewhere
also. According to Jeremias,[9] 'κατ' οἶκον is contrasted with "in
the Temple", in the sense of "at home", as in Philemon 2. The
sense is not "in their own homes", as it is [sic] shown by the
presence of all the apostles. See also Acts 12.12; 2.1-2; 1.15,
where we find the whole community foregathered.' This is not
wholly correct; it is not said that all the apostles were present,
nor is the whole church present at 12.12. The inference,
therefore, that the church had at this stage its own meeting-
house, capable of being set alongside and contrasted with the
Temple, is anything but secure. Luke's words are consistent
with corporate activity in the Temple, and family—perhaps
extended family—meals at home. What the Christians did
when they met in the Temple is not stated. Luke is probably
composing his own summary[10] and at this point had no precise
activity in mind; he did however wish to associate the Christians with, rather than detach them from, the institutions of
Judaism.

4. *3.1*. Peter and John were going up to the Temple at the
afternoon[11] hour of prayer. It is implied, though not actually
stated, that they were going there to pray. 'En outre, de nom-
breux Israélites se pressaient au Temple, à l'heure des
sacrifices; ces rites de boucherie nauséabonde, primitivement

8. G. Schille, *Die Apostelgeschichte des Lukas* (ThHkzNT; Berlin:
Evangelische Verlagsanstalt, 1984), p. 122.
9. J. Jeremias, *Jerusalem in the Time of Jesus* (ET; London: SCM,
1969), p. 131 n. 20.
10. Using traditional material such as occurs at 3.11.
11. D adds τὸ δειλινόν.

accomplis dans le silence, étaient aux environs de l'ère chréti-
enne, surtout aux jours de fête, entourés de musique, de chants
et de prières: des psaumes, le décalogue, le šema', la bénédic-
tion sacerdotale, d'autres prières, en particulier la première
ébauche des dix-huit bénédictions; en tout cela le peuple avait
sa part, poussant les acclamations qui lui revenaient, se
prosternant à certains moments, se recueillant, plein
d'angoisse, tant que le prêtre brûlait les parfums dans le
sanctuaire'.[12] It seems unlikely that Luke's interest is confined
to time (it was afternoon) and place (the lame man begged at
the Temple gate; the Christians frequented Solomon's Portico—3.11; 5.12); he probably had traditional material behind
him. He represents the apostles as doing precisely what devout
Jewish laymen, who had the privilege of residence in
Jerusalem, would do.

5. *3.11*. Solomon's Portico. At 3.2 the beggar was said to sit at
the Beautiful Gate of the Temple; this gate cannot be identified
with certainty. A variant reading[13] makes it impossible to
establish the topographical relation between the Gate and the
Portico, though it is probable that the Old Uncial text is what
Luke wrote and that he believed the Portico to be inside the
Gate. For our present purpose the matter is unimportant;
Luke represents Christians as gathering somewhere within
the perimeter of the Temple. They (presumably) chose to use
it; no one (until ch. 4) objected to their doing so. Cf. 5.12.

6. *4.1f.* Peter and John are arrested by the Jewish authorities,
who include the στρατηγὸς τοῦ ἱεροῦ, who was responsible for
public order in the Temple. These verses raise a number of
important issues which however are not relevant and need not
be mentioned here, where we are concerned primarily with
the Temple. Verse 2 suggests that the authorities were vexed
by the proclamation of resurrection, in which, so far as they
were Sadducees, they did not believe (23.6); that the unacceptable doctrine was associated with Jesus would no doubt accen-

---

12. J. Bonsirven, *Le judaïsme palestinien au temps de Jésus-Christ*
(Paris: Beauchesne, 1934, 1935), II, p. 119.
13. In D (h mae).

tuate its offensiveness. Verse 7, however, suggests that the Council was concerned to investigate not the teaching but the miraculous act that had taken place. The presence of the στρατηγός suggests an offence against public order. It is doubtful whether Luke himself analysed the material in this way; he would probably, if asked, have allowed that all the strands mentioned contributed to the situation that he described. He does not say that the action and speech of the apostles were found more provocative because they happened in the Temple, though the fact that they did so would bring the Temple police on the scene as activity outside the Temple enclosure would not have done. We can say little more than that the apostles were operating close to the centre of Jewish affairs—both physically and doctrinally.

7. *4.5.* The point just made is reinforced by the fact that the Sanhedrin met in the לשכת הגזית, a room in the Temple.[14] There is a tradition[15] that forty years before the fall of Jerusalem the meetings of the Sanhedrin were transferred to the חנות, or חניות. The trustworthiness of this tradition is questionable; fortunately for us the scene of the meeting is less important than that of the offence.

8. *5.12.* See above; Solomon's Portico was already mentioned as a Christian meeting place in 3.11. As at 2.46 Luke is probably using an element of tradition in the construction of his summary. The use of such a place may suggest that the Christians had no centre of their own, but the common practice in the Mediterranean world of meeting in the open air must be borne in mind. This is sufficient to discount the remark of Schille (*Commentary*, p. 157): 'Man geht bereits an die Eroberung des Tempelplatzes!'—which, if it were true, would greatly increase the interest of this paper.

9. *5.20f.* The apostles are to return to the Temple and resume there their proclamation of the Gospel. If Luke once more has in mind Solomon's Portico he does not say so; the point here is

14. *Yoma* 25a; Josephus, *War* 5.144.
15. *Shab.* 15a; *RH* 31a; *Sanh.* 41a; *AZ* 8b.

probably the simple one that official disapproval is to cause no withdrawal; the former provocation is to be repeated. The apostolic Gospel is described as τὰ ῥήματα τῆς ζωῆς ταύτης; it is possible that there is an allusion to the occasional description of the Temple as ביח חיינו;[16] but it is in fact unlikely that either Luke or his readers were aware of the term. If they were, Luke would be making the claim that the Gospel realized what the Temple adumbrated. In v. 26 the στρατηγός and the ὑπηρέται reappear; it may be implied that the apostles might not have been charged if they had not been (v. 25) ἐν τῷ ἱερῷ ἑστῶτες, thus creating a disturbance within the Holy Place. This however is not consistent with the rest of the narrative.

10. *5.27.* Cf. 4.5.

11. *5.42.* For ἐν τῷ ἱερῷ and κατ' οἶκον, cf. 2.46. This verse also is part of a summary, almost certainly Luke's own editorial work. This is important because it means that we have here his own opinion. The life and teaching of the early Christians had two foci, the Temple and their own οἶκος, or rather (taking κατά distributively) their own οἶκοι, specifically Christian centres.

12. *6.13, 14.* The opposition to Stephen did not originate in the Temple and among its officials but in a Hellenist synagogue;[17] it focused however upon Stephen's alleged attitude to Moses, the Law, and the Temple. It is possible that Luke is here combining two threads of narrative (see v. 11), but our present task does not require us to attempt to disentangle them.

In v. 13 it is alleged that Stephen is continually speaking against the Holy Place. מקום, אתרא, and τόπος were all on occasion used to refer to synagogues, but there can be no doubt here (see the next verse) that the reference is to the Temple. The allegation that Stephen has spoken against the Temple is amplified in v. 14: Stephen has alleged that Jesus will destroy it.

---

16. *Lev. R.* 19; other references in M. Jastrow, *A Dictionary of the Targumim, &c.* (New York, Berlin, London: Choreb, Shapiro, Valentine, 1926), p. 455.

17. For synagogues in Jerusalem see the summary evidence the new Schürer (n. 5), II, p. 445.

This recalls a synoptic passage that Luke does not reproduce in his account of the trial of Jesus,[18] though he retains (21.6; cf. 19.44) the prediction that the Temple will be destroyed. Those who make the allegation against Stephen are described as μάρτυρες ψευδεῖς. The description is Luke's, and it means that in his opinion the witnesses were lying; this probably means not only that they had not heard what they said that they had heard but also that it was something that Stephen would not have said because he did not believe it. Luke is probably motivated by the belief that no accusation against a Christian, leading to the death penalty, could possibly be true. This leads him into difficulties which can only be resolved by asking (as Luke himself did not do), what destruction means: abolition or fulfilment? What Stephen (or the traditions Luke used in telling the story about Stephen and writing his speech) thought about the Temple must be found in ch. 7, not in ch. 6.

13. *7.46-50*. It would be desirable, but is manifestly impossible, to consider the whole of Stephen's speech (7.2-53) in order to evaluate fully his attitude to Law and Temple. There are no words against Moses and the Law (cf. 6.11, 13). Moses was sent by God as a ruler and redeemer, and was thus an image of Christ (7.35, 37);[19] the Law he received on behalf of his people is described as living oracles (7.38). The fault lay not in him but in them, who made and worshipped a calf (7.41) and served the host of heaven (7.42). These observations of the idol worship of the people of God prepare the way for v. 44. In the wilderness the fathers had for worship a tent; this was a good thing. It signified God's presence with his people but did not confine him to a locality. God commended it, and provided a pattern for it (Exod. 25.40). Verse 45 is loosely expressed but indicates that the use of the tent persisted through the occupation of Canaan up to the time of David.

18. Mt. 24.2; 26.61; Mk 13.2; 14.58; 15.29; cf. Jn 2.19; *Gospel of Thomas* 71.
19. Luke does nothing to bring this out. Joseph and Moses typology may lurk somewhere in the tradition, but he was not greatly interested.

David proposed to provide a σκήνωμα for the house[20] of Jacob. This appears to be a verbal reference to Ps. 131(132).5, which supplies the word σκήνωμα, and an allusion to the narrative of 2 Sam. 7.1-29, where David's proposal, though at first approved, is disallowed by the prophet Nathan who, however, adds (without any mark of disapproval) that David's son Solomon would build the house. Whatever Nathan may have thought, Stephen's disapproval seems clear.[21] The house contravened the prophetic principle of vv. 49f. Idols may dwell in a house made by human hands, but not the Most High.[22] The point is pressed home by the quotation of Isa. 66.1f. Other interpretations of this passage will be mentioned below; for Stephen (Luke) the crucial word appears to be that which has been used in v. 47, οἶκος. No οἶκος is capable of containing (in any sense) the Creator of heaven and earth; the most that humans may give him is a σκηνή[23] in which they may worship the God who both inhabits and transcends the whole of his own creation. The existence of an οἶκος, in which someone—God (since it is built for him)—οἰκεῖ, dwells, can only point away from and not towards the truth. It is difficult not to find Stephen guilty of speaking ῥήματα κατὰ τοῦ τόπου τοῦ ἁγίου (6.13).

14. *8.4-25.* In this paragraph Philip evangelizes the Samaritans. Only a negative observation is in place: the Samaritans had had a temple on Mount Gerizim; it was destroyed by Hyrcanus (Josephus, *Ant.* 13.255f.). There is no allusion to it in Acts.[24]

---

20. There is a difficult textual problem here, but οἴκῳ is the harder reading and should be preferred to θεῷ.

21. The alternative is to take Luke's meaning to be: Solomon built him a house, but of course this operation must be understood in the light of the principle stated in vv. 48-50. This does less justice to the strongly adversative ἀλλά and the probably adversative δέ.

22. ὁ ὕψιστος is in an emphatic position.

23. It may be that David's intended σκήνωμα would also be permissible.

24. Cf. Jn 4.20.

15. *8.27*. The Ethiopian eunuch had visited Jerusalem for the purpose of worshipping.[25] This must have meant a visit to the Temple, since non-sacrificial worship could be offered to the God of Israel anywhere; but this, for a man who was not a born Jew and could not have been accepted as a proselyte (Deut. 23.1)[26] was impossible. It is true that hope was held out to the eunuch in Isa. 56.3-5, but this was a matter of eschatological promise, not of Temple regulations. One can ascribe προσκυνήσων only to ignorance or oversight on Luke's part.

16. *15.16-18*. At the Council of Jerusalem James quotes Amos 9.11f.[27] The passage is referred to here because it is possible that the tent of David (τὴν σκηνὴν Δαυίδ) may refer to the Tabernacle that was still in use in David's time (cf. 7.45f.). This is improbable; and though there may be a reference to the eschatological pilgrimage of the Gentiles to Mount Zion,[28] their 'seeking the Lord' does not necessarily imply a visit to the Temple.

17. *15.20, 29; 21.25*—the so-called Apostolic Decree. This passage is referred to because the Decree may reflect the essential elements of Judaism (apart from circumcision) as it was understood and practised in the Diaspora by Jews who could not include attendance at the Temple among the requirements of their religion.[29]

18. *17.24, 25*. Isa. 66.1f., quoted at 7.49f., with other similar OT passages, lurks behind the Areopagus speech, though it is given Greek dress and ornament and reflects the manner of Hellenistic Judaism. In its context the argument clearly refers to the objects of pagan religion to be found in Athens; logically it

---

25. The future participle προσκυνήσων must mean this.
26. LXX 23.2; cf. *Yeb.* 8; *Nid.* 5.9. In some passages the Hebrew סרים is a social rather than a physiological term, denoting a person in high office, but this man's official position is described separately.
27. With a hint perhaps of Isa. 45.21.
28. See J. Jeremias, *Jesus' Promise to the Nations* (SBT 24; London: SCM, 1958), pp. 55-73.
29. See my *Freedom and Obligation* (London: SPCK, 1985), p. 102.

would apply equally to the Temple of Jerusalem;[30] God can no more be confined within the Temple than the Parthenon, and needs Jewish lambs and bulls no more than Greek. Did Luke notice this? Did he take the argument to be limited strictly to its immediate setting?

19. *18.18.* It is not clear whether it was Paul or Aquila who had taken the vow—presumably a Nazirite vow. The vow maker would be able to conclude the vow only in the Temple, and it is surprising, though not impossible, that he should have shaved his head while still absent from Jerusalem. That a vow needed to be absolved in the Temple probably confirms the view that the ἐκκλησία mentioned in 18.22 is the church of Jerusalem. To take a vow seems to imply acceptance of the religious framework of Judaism, including the Temple.

20. *19.21.* Paul's determination to visit Jerusalem is probably to be connected not with a desire to visit the Temple but with his collection for the poor (though Acts does not mention this, except distantly at 24.17).

21. *20.16.* The desire to visit Jerusalem for Pentecost probably does imply a visit to the Temple; Pentecost was still the name for a Jewish festival, not a Christian.[31]

22. *21.20-30.* Paul arrived in Jerusalem amid rumours that he was teaching apostasy from Judaism. To disprove these rumours he was to see to the purification of four men who had taken vows; they were to shave their heads and Paul was to meet the cost of the sacrifices they had to offer. The process was almost complete when Jews from Asia, seeing Paul in the Temple, gathered a crowd and attempted to lynch him on the grounds that he was everywhere teaching against the people, the Law, and the Holy Place, and had brought Greeks into the Temple and had thus profaned (κεκοίνωκεν) it. Several assertions are involved in this narrative. (a) Paul was willing to

30. The word χειροποίητος is used in both passages.
31. The earliest references to Pentecost as a Christian observance seem to be in Tertullian and in *Apostolic Constitutions* 5.20.

take part in proceedings that involved participation in the Temple cultus, including sacrifice. (b) He did this in order to prove that he observed the Jewish Law. He thus rebuts in advance, as he will do again later (24.12, 17, 18; 25.8), the charge that he had profaned the Temple. The accusers mistakenly supposed that he had brought Trophimus not only to Jerusalem but into the Temple. (c) Paul is thus represented in the Acts narrative as a loyal, obedient, observant, but misunderstood Jew. The question that arises is whether this is a historically correct account of the Paul whom we meet in his epistles. The question is relevant to us only so far as it bears on the question whether Luke introduces into his work elements which, whether intentionally or not, give a false understanding of the early Christian attitude to the Temple. Did he represent this as more favourable than it was? Or, better, did he represent it as more uniform that it was? For it is quite possible that the attitude that he describes was that of James and his elders (21.18) but not that of Paul. Certainly, in this passage we have the work of one who was concerned to affirm that the Christian who had the reputation of being the most radical treated the Temple with the greatest respect.

23. *22.17-21.* Paul, addressing the Jerusalem mob, recounts his conversion and call. The unique feature in this account[32] is that after his encounter with Ananias Paul returns to Jerusalem and prays in the Temple, where God charges him to go to the Gentiles. Again the question of historicity arises, but Luke's account is unambiguous. (a) Paul's first step after conversion and baptism is to visit the Temple and pray there; he has not ceased to be a Jew. (b) It is in the Temple, the heart of Judaism, that he is committed to evangelize the Gentiles; the Christian mission fulfils Judaism.

24. *22.30; 23.1.* For the meeting place of the Sanhedrin see above on 4.5.

25. *23.2-5.* The High Priest commands Paul to be struck on the mouth; Paul replies angrily; it is pointed out that he is address-

---

32. When compared with those in Acts 9 and 26.

ing the High Priest disrespectfully; he replies that he did not know that the person commanding him to be struck was the High Priest. It is not agreed[33] whether this reply was seriously intended or ironical. If the latter, Paul shows that he cares little for the Temple and its officials; if the former, it shows an exaggerated respect. The former is in closer accord with these chapters as a whole; whether it is true to the historical Paul is another question.

26. *24.6.* Paul is accused of having tried to profane the Temple (ἐπείρασεν βεβηλῶσαι). Cf. 21.28; the different verb makes no difference to the sense.

27. *24.12, 17, 18.* These verses take up again Paul's answer to the charges brought against him. Neither in the city, nor in the synagogues, nor in the Temple was he guilty of creating an uproar or even of arguing (διαλεγόμενον)—he had done less than Peter! He had been in a state of ritual purity (ἡγνισμένον) and had been bringing alms and offerings.[34] Again, Paul is the good, observant Jew.

28. *25.8.* To his assertion that he has not offended against the Law or against Caesar Paul adds that he has not offended against the Temple.

This rapid survey of the most important references and allusions to the Temple in Acts manifests a considerable variety of attitudes. At one extremity there is the claim that the Christian mission proceeds from the Temple itself (22.21); this is probably to be seen also in preaching in the Temple on the Day of Pentecost—certainly soon afterwards. Allied to this is full acceptance of the services afforded by the Temple; Paul enters into its sacrificial system, paying the charges of men who had taken a vow and receiving the same rite of purification. The charge that he had brought Gentiles into parts of the

33. Few today think that Luke understood the words ironically; he was representing Paul as a law-abiding Jew.

34. προσφοράς—the word used, along with προσφέρειν, of sacrificial offerings in the technical sense at 21.26.

Temple reserved for Jews is rejected as false; though he had
had a Gentile friend in the city he had not taken him across
the barrier. Those who went up to the Temple for prayer (3.1)
might have prayed privately. They recognized that the Temple was a house of prayer, but so far as Luke's express language goes they could have prayed in the synagogue; he does
not say that they offered, or had the intention of offering, sacrifice. Next comes the use of the Temple as a convenient
meeting place, a use which leads to trouble with the Temple
authorities. Finally there is an attack on the Temple as an
institution that should never have been brought into being. It
was part of Israel's perversion into idolatry of its true God-
given system of worship.

It is natural to ask whether there is any analogy to this
strangely mixed set of attitudes. It is hard to find one.

In Palestinian Judaism, where Jews lived within easy reach
of the Temple, no parallel can be found. The quotation from
Bonsirven (note 12 above) depicts, in as favourable terms as
may be, the attitude of the Israelite to the Temple; at least, it
describes the religious attitude of the religious Jew. The Temple was a national as well as a religious centre, and the bloody
internecine conflicts of the last months before the fall of
Jerusalem in AD 70 bear their own testimony to a loyalty and
patriotic devotion as intense as they may have been ethically
misguided. Up to a point we may recognize the attitude of
Peter and John, and of those who liked to listen to their chosen
teachers; certainly not the attitude of Stephen. Nor is this to be
found among reactions to the loss of the Temple. The Temple
could no longer be regarded as indispensable to the existence of
Judaism, but the problem raised by its disappearance was one
that could be dealt with on the basis of the revelation that was
anterior to the Temple; it had generated the Temple and it
could generate substitutes for the Temple. The OT contained a
strong non-cultic, indeed an anti-cultic strand in addition to all
the regulations for the cultus of Tent and Temple, and it was
natural to emphasize this non-cultic element. This was done
notably by R. Johanan ben Zakkai.

> Once as Rabban Yohanan ben Zakkai was coming out of
> Jerusalem, Rabbi Joshua followed after him, and beheld the
> Temple in ruins. Woe unto us, Rabbi Joshua cried, that this

place, the place where the iniquities of Israel were atoned for, is laid waste. My son, Rabban Yohanan said to him, be not grieved. We have another atonement as effective as this, and what is it? It is acts of lovingkindness, as it is said, 'For I desire mercy and not sacrifice' (Hos. 6.6). [35]

Moreover there was at first (and that will mean, up to the time when Acts was written) a strong hope that the Temple would be speedily restored. 'Man hofft auf ein plötzliches wunderbares Geschehen, durch das der Tempel restituiert wird. Diese Erwartung äussert sich in der Forderung der Gelehrten an die Priester, keinen Wein zu trinken, um bei der bald bevorstehenden Erneuerung des Tempels sofort wieder dienstfähig zu sein.'[36] This is reflected in the fourteenth and seventeenth of the Eighteen Benedictions.

> 14. To Jerusalem, thy city, return in mercy, and dwell therein as thou hast spoken; rebuild it soon in our days as an everlasting building, and speedily set up therein the throne of David.

> 17. Restore the service to the oracle of thy house; receive in love and favour both the fire-offerings of Israel and their prayer; and may the service of thy people Israel be ever acceptable unto thee.[37]

These were the prayers of the Synagogue; and the Synagogue increasingly took the place of the Temple. 'Bis dahin wurde nicht nur in den Synagogen, sondern auch im Tempel gebetet, viele gingen dorthin und nahmen an den Gebeten teil, von jetzt ab war die Synagoge die einzige Stätte, an der die Gemeinde ihren Gottesdienst verrichtete.'[38]

Reference to the Synagogue, with which after AD 70 all Jews must be content, suggests the situation of Diaspora Judaism. The attitude of Jews who lived in places remote from the

---

35. *Aboth R. Nathan* 4, translation quoted from J. Neusner, *A Life of Rabban Yohanan Zakkai* (Studia Post-Biblica, 6; Leiden: Brill, 1962), p. 142.

36. *Yoma* 38a; H. Wenschkewitz, *Die Spiritualisierung der Kultusbegriffe Tempel, Priester und Opfer im Neuen Testament* (Angelos-Beiheft, 4; Leipzig: Pfeiffer, 1932), p. 28.

37. S. Singer, *The Authorised Daily Prayer Book* (London: Eyre and Spottiswoode, 1912), pp. 49, 50.

38. I. Elbogen, *Der jüdische Gottesdienst in seiner geschichtlichen Entwicklung* (repr. Hildesheim: Olms, 1967), p. 251; see also pp. 245-50.

Temple is not easy to describe and cannot have been uniform. One may however begin from the fact that the Temple was financed by the contributions made by Jews throughout the world by means of the Temple tax. The cost of the sacrificial victims offered was immense and it is clear that the average Jew felt that he must pay his share. To say, however, that the majority of Jews supported the Temple financially is not to say that all felt a profound religious attachment to it. The tax was a national tax, a mark of one's Jewishness. In some cases, at least, but it is impossible to estimate them numerically, it will have been a token of patriotism rather than of piety—though it is important to remember that for many Jews the two motivations went hand in hand; there was no competition but mutual support between them. The average moderately religious Jew in the Dispersion cannot have felt any antipathy to the Temple or he would not have supported it and visited it when he could, as many did, for the Pilgrim Feasts. At the same time he must have recognized that his religion could not depend on his presence in the Temple; he must find a way of practising Judaism that was independent of the building and of the sacrificial system that was its *raison d'être*.

To understand this position (and to express it in the few words that are all that can be used here) we are to a great extent dependent on Philo; this is unfortunate, because, though Philo was undoubtedly a loyal Jew, he was anything but an average, representative one. He is, however, important because, notwithstanding his use of different terminology and concepts, his attitude, like that which we find in Acts, is a double one. No one has done more to bring out the allegorical, 'spiritual' significance of the Law, but he has little patience with those who neglect its requirement of external obedience. He makes this point in relation to (among other things) the Temple in *De Mig. Abr.* 89-93: We shall neglect the purity of the Temple (τῆς περὶ τὸ ἱερὸν ἁγιστείας) and tens of thousands of other things if we attend only to the things that are signified by their deeper, hidden sense (τοῖς δι' ὑπονοιῶν δηλουμένοις) (92). To Philo this is clearly unthinkable. External observances must be observed. Conversely, in *Spec. Leg.* 1.66-298 Philo gives a detailed account of the structure of the Temple, of its furniture, of the rules for priests, and of the sacrifices that they offer;[39] but he begins with the recognition that we must believe that the loftiest and true temple of God is the whole universe (τὸν σύμπαντα κόσμον) (66), and allegorizes almost every detail that he gives. It is worth noting that he describes the Temple of Jerusalem as χειρόκμητον (67), and argues that because God is one there can be only one temple.[40] There is thus in Philo a twofold attitude to the Temple, as there is in Acts, but it is a different twofoldness, with nothing corresponding to Stephen's affirmation that a house made by human hands is not merely inadequate as a dwelling-place for God but is positively misleading. There may be an allusion to Isa. 66.1 in *Spec. Leg.* 1.66; there is a clearer one at *De Conf. Ling.* 98: he says that the world of sense is as it were God's footstool,[41] but the passage is not used as it is in Acts 7. The world of sense is described as God's footstool to show that creation does not contain the cause of its own being, and that the world is under God's direction.

At Qumran also there was a double attitude to the Temple, but again it was different from that of Acts. This has often been observed, and must here be sketched in the greatest brevity. The Qumran Sect was profoundly concerned with the Temple in its holiness and in every detail of its operation. It suffices to refer to the *Temple Scroll.*[42] It was not because the Sect undervalued the Temple that they (including members who were priests) cut themselves off from it, but because it had fallen into the hands of a priesthood that did not observe what the Sect believed to be the correct rules of purity and followed the lunar calendar, rather than the solar calendar by which the Sect determined the dates of the Festivals. It was fundamental to the Sect that it should separate from these 'men of falsehood' (אנשי העול) and adhere to 'the priests who keep the

---

39. Cf. the *Mishnah* tractate *Middoth*.
40. This may be a veiled attack on the Temple at Leontopolis.
41. 'He says', φησί. It is not clear who 'he' is.
42. See J. Maier, *Die Tempelrolle vom Toten Meer* (Uni-Taschenbücher, 829; München and Basel: Reinhardt, 1978), pp. 12f., noting eleven stages of increasing holiness, from 'Das Heilige Land' to 'Der innerste Kultdienstbereich: Das Allerheiligste, der Sitz der Gottesgegenwart'.

covenant' (הכוהנים שומרי הברית).[43] The latter would in due course supplant the former as an early result in the eschatological War.[44]

All this constitutes an essentially simple story. The Temple is in itself a right, divine institution. It is at present perverted into wickedness by priests who are guilty of both liturgical and moral error. At the appointed moment good priests will over-throw the bad ones. It is only on a very superficial level that this bears any resemblance to the two attitudes found in Acts.

Enough has now been said to illustrate the fact that the treatment of the Temple found in Acts has no adequate paral-lel in Judaism. That Peter and John should go to the Temple to pray is easy enough to parallel; that Paul should take part in Temple rituals raises problems enough when we ask whether the Paul of the epistles would have behaved in this way, but it is only what thousands of Jews in all parts of the Empire would have done. But to use Isa. 66.1 in the way in which Stephen does, to allege that a permanent οἶκος was never commanded or desired by God, to make the universal statement that no human-made buildings constitute his dwelling and that he is not to be worshipped by material gifts: these things may be paralleled in the OT but scarcely in contemporary Judaism. The paradoxical—or, perhaps, thoughtless—combination of the positive and negative principles is without analogy.

What was the attitude of other early Christians to the Tem-ple? For Paul there is very little direct evidence. The Temple itself he scarcely mentions. There is an allusion to the activities of priests in 1 Cor. 9.13, and a reference to the ναὸς θεοῦ in 2 Cor. 6.16 which leads immediately to the claim that we (Christians) ναὸς θεοῦ ἐσμεν ζῶντος; this recalls 1 Cor. 3.16f. and 6.19, where the Christian community and the individual Christian are said to be God's ναός. Paul speaks unfavourably of the festivals (Gal. 4.10); he mentions Passover explicitly (1 Cor. 5.7) and may allude to the Day of Atonement (Rom. 3.25), but in such a way as to suggest that the former Jewish sacrifices have been replaced and transcended by the sacrifice of Christ. The Gospels contain something of the dual attitude of

43. 1QS 5.2.
44. 1QM 2.1-6.

Acts. The doom of the Temple is foretold (see above); this is not a condemnation of the Temple itself but of those who abuse it. Its sacrificial system is taken for granted in, for example, Mt. 5.23. Jesus visits it in his youth (Lk. 2.46) and at the other end of the story, after the resurrection, his disciples are to be found there διὰ παντός (Lk. 24.53). The cleansing of the Temple (Mk 11.15-17, and parallels), though, like the rending of the veil (Mk 15.38, and parallels), a portent of disaster,[45] attacks the abuse rather than the proper existence of the Temple: My house shall be called a house of prayer for all the nations. The same may be said of Hebrews. The Temple and its ritual will disappear when that which is perfect is come (Heb. 8.13), but it was in its time a valid forecast of that which is to be.

What is lacking elsewhere in the NT is the bitter attack on the Temple made by Stephen and the consequent paradox of favourable and unfavourable attitudes. The nearest parallel in early Christian literature is provided by the *Epistle of Barnabas*, and this contains so many problems that it is impossible to discuss it seriously here.[46]

Like Paul, Barnabas sees in the sacrificial system of the Temple a preliminary manifestation of the crucifixion of Jesus. ἀκούσατε πῶς περὶ τούτου πεφανέρωκαν οἱ ἱερεῖς τοῦ ναοῦ (*Barn.* 7.3). This relates to the statement that Jesus σταυρωθεὶς ἐποτίζετο ὄξει καὶ χολῇ; the argument is both detailed and tortuous in a way that Paul's treatment of Passover is not. The priests and their operations have only a typological value.[47] The only true temple is the Christian, or perhaps the community of Christians: ναὸς γὰρ ἅγιος... τῷ κυρίῳ τὸ κατοικητήριον ἡμῶν τῆς καρδίας (6.15). This may need some qualification; it is spiritual Christians who may be so regarded: γενώμεθα πνευματικοί, γενώμεθα ναὸς τέλειος τῷ θεῷ.[48] They attain this state by practising the fear of God and

45. See my essay in *Jesus und Paulus. Festschrift für W.G. Kümmel zum 70. Geburtstag* (ed. E.E. Ellis and E. Grässer; Göttingen: Vandenhoeck & Ruprecht, 1975), pp. 13-20.
46. See especially the article 'Barnabas, Nerva, and the Yavnean Rabbis' by P. Richardson and M.B. Shukster, *JTS* ns 34 (1983), pp. 31-55.
47. The word τύπος occurs at 7.3.
48. 4.11. Cf. Philo, *Somn.* 1.149, σπούδαζε οὖν, ὦ ψυχή, θεοῦ οἶκος γενέσθαι, ἱερὸν ἅγιον, ἐνδιαίτημα κάλλιστον.

observing his commandments. The Temple of the Jews could thus suggest that which itself was not. Barnabas deals with the matter in ch. 16. Unlike Stephen he does not refer to the story of David and Solomon. How (historically) the Temple came into being he does not tell. But it was a mistake, and like Stephen he quotes Isa. 66.1 (and 40.12) to prove it. His application of the rhetorical questions, ποῖον οἶκον οἰκοδομήσετέ μοι; ἢ τίς τόπος τῆς καταπαύσεώς μου; is clear, and is made explicit by the words that immediately follow: ματαία ἡ ἐλπὶς αὐτῶν (16.2). The error of the Jews was to build their hope upon the house rather than upon God. πλανώμενοι οἱ ταλαίπωροι εἰς τὴν οἰκοδομὴν ἤλπισαν, καὶ οὐκ ἐπὶ τὸν θεὸν αὐτῶν τὸν ποιήσαντα αὐτούς (16.1). 16.2 begins with an interesting sentence: σχεδὸν γὰρ ὡς τὰ ἔθνη ἀφιέρωσαν αὐτὸν ἐν τῷ ναῷ. σχεδόν is probably to be taken with the nearest words, ὡς τὰ ἔθνη; Barnabas hesitates to equate Judaism with heathenism, but he comes close to doing so. ἀφιεροῦν normally means[49] *to hallow, consecrate*, and Bauer–Aland,[50] taking the word in this sense, and ἐν as instrumental, understand the sentence to mean '*sie haben ihn durch den Tempel geweiht*, statt umgekehrt die Weihe d. Tempels auf Gott zu gründen'. It may well be better to take both the ἀπό (in ἀφιεροῦν) and the ἐν in their local sense: the Jews (according to Barnabas) have shut God away in the holiness of a shrine, keeping him safely out of earshot;[51] compare Windisch's rendering,[52] 'Sie haben ihn ja doch beinahe wie die Heiden in den Tempel (wie) in einen heiligen Bezirk eingeschlossen'. They have reduced God to holy insignificance.

The rest of *Barnabas* 16 contains the most interesting and difficult historical problem of the epistle. The Jews themselves (αὐτοί) and the servants of their enemies (οἱ τῶν ἐχθρῶν ὑπηρέται) are jointly engaged[53] in building a new temple (16.4).

49. So Liddell and Scott, p. 289.
50. Col. 252.
51. Cf. Jer. 7.1-15, where the prophet accuses his people of being so obsessed with the Temple that they refuse to hear God's word.
52. H. Windisch, *Der Barnabasbrief* (HNT Ergänzungsband; Tübingen: J.C.B. Mohr [Paul Siebeck], 1920), p. 387.
53. There is a variant reading which by omitting καί gives αὐτοὶ οἱ τῶν ἐχθρῶν ὑπηρέται; the Jews are not now involved. The variant is the easier reading, and though certainty is impossible there is much to be said for the more difficult.

364 *Templum Amicitiae*

To what does this refer? This fascinating question must be set aside; the new temple will be as false as the old; the only valid temple is the spiritual temple consisting of Christians who have received the forgiveness of their sins, put their hope in the Name, and become new, created afresh from the beginning; ἐν τῷ κατοικητηρίῳ ἡμῶν ἀληθῶς ὁ θεὸς κατοικεῖ ἐν ἡμῖν (16.8). But we may see here what puts the heat into Barnabas's exegesis and argument. It is well enough to treat the old material temple as an allegory of the new spiritual temple; it is a different matter when a new alliance threatens to rebuild the old material temple.

The new temple was not built; Christian reaction cooled down and the notion of a Christian spiritual temple returns. A clear index of this—all that can be considered here—is found in Justin's use of Isa. 66.1. In 1 *Apol.* 37 it is one of four prophecies, all from Isaiah, which illustrate the way in which the Spirit speaks in the person of the Father.[54] Nothing is said about the meaning or application of the verse, of which only part is given. In *Trypho* 22 part of the verse, somewhat out of order, is quoted to prove that God is not in need of a house or of sacrifice but provided the Temple in order to keep the Jews from idolatry.

Conclusions from this study may be stated briefly but with some confidence.

(1) There are passages in Acts that assume that Jewish Christians will naturally continue to use the Temple as they did in their pre-Christian lives. Not only is the Temple a proper place in which to meet for religious discourse and for prayer, the old sacrificial system continues in use, and that even by Paul. People take vows, and the vows must be discharged in the proper form. There are also passages, or at least there is a passage, in which the most radical of all views is maintained. The Temple ought never to have existed at all. God did not intend it, and made the matter clear through his prophets. He who inhabits the whole universe that he himself created needs neither house nor victuals. The Temple was part of that Jew-

54. Elsewhere, of the Son, and of a particular prophet.

ish record of disobedience that culminated in the rejection and death of Jesus of Nazareth. So Stephen in the speech contained in ch. 7. In ch. 17 Paul's attack on Athenian religiousness (δεισιδαιμονία) is expressed in terms that are equally applicable to Jewish religion. God who made the world and all the things that are in it, being Lord of all, does not dwell in shrines made with hands, nor is he worshipped by human hands as if he needed anything, since he himself gives to all humanity life and breath and all things. It is indeed arguable that Luke did not intend these words to apply to the Temple in Jerusalem, but he does not explicitly make the exception.

The two lines of thought lie side by side, and no attempt is made to reconcile them.

(2) There is good reason to think[55] that both Stephen's speech and Paul's speech on the Areopagus were derived by Luke from sources originating with Hellenistic Jews who had become Christians. It is probable that the attacks on temples contained in these speeches were made originally by Hellenistic Jews. They had good reason to attack heathen temples, and it would be understandable if, though some Jews in the Dispersion thought of the distant Temple with wistful longing, others treated it as sour grapes: We can do without it and it would be better if it were not there—it only leads the residents of Palestine into narrow, localized, and completely inadequate ideas of God and of the service of God. The difficulty is that we cannot parallel this thought, and in particular this way of interpreting and using Isa. 66.1[56] in Hellenistic Jewish sources. This is perhaps capable of explanation. It may be that those Jews who took this line were few and that a high proportion of them, being more loosely attached than others to Judaism, became Christians. It may be too that the combined effect of the rise of Christianity and the fall of Jerusalem was to lead

---

55. See my essays in *Studien zum Text und zur Ethik des Neuen Testaments. Festschrift zum 80. Geburtstag von H. Greeven* (ed. W. Schrage; BZNW 47; Berlin and New York: de Gruyter, 1986), pp. 57-69, and *New Testament Christianity for Africa and the World. Essays in Honour of H. Sawyerr* (ed. M.E. Glasswell and E.W. Fasholé-Luke; London: SPCK, 1974), pp. 69-77.
56. Which seems to have been seldom quoted.

Diaspora Jews to close ranks; perhaps, in some cases, if they could not defend the Temple as an institution, at least to keep silence about it.

(3) Whatever sources Luke may have used he has allowed to remain in his work what appears on the surface as contradiction. What is the correct attitude of Christians to the Jewish Temple? It is hard to answer this question on the basis of Acts. This may be due to negligence or oversight. There is other evidence[57] that suggests that Luke may not have been able to give his book a final revision. There is, however, a better answer than this. What Luke allows us to read about the Jewish Temple is parallel to what he says about Jews and Judaism in general. His account of the Jews has a negative side. The story of Paul's ministry is a story of turning from the evangelization of Jews to Gentiles, from the synagogue to the agora. So it is in Pisidian Antioch (13.46) and in Corinth (18.6); finally and conclusively in Rome (28.28: τοῖς ἔθνεσιν ἀπεστάλη τοῦτο τὸ σωτήριον τοῦ θεοῦ· αὐτοὶ καὶ ἀκούσονται). From this it has been concluded that Luke had finished with the Jews; there might be a few individual conversions, but corporate Judaism was now excluded from the Gospel and from salvation.[58] This, however, is only part of what Luke wishes us to know. The Jews are the sons of the prophets and of the covenant (3.25); the Gospel is the fulfilment of what God promised in the OT, which remains authoritative (*passim*). Even after Pisidian Antioch and Corinth, Paul will begin work in the synagogue (e.g. 14.1; 18.19); why not after Rome? Most important of all perhaps is the decision that Gentile Christians must accept a mild and modified Judaism (15.29; 21.25), dictated to them, on the basis of pragmatic argument (15.21) from Jerusalem. Along with this goes a picture of a mild and modified Paul.

Luke is not (at least in this respect) negligent, though the reader may think it possible to express Luke's intention in less ambiguous terms. He means to say to Judaism both Yes and

---

57. Especially linguistic; some of the sentences in Acts are almost impossible to construe.
58. This aspect of Acts has been emphasized to the exclusion of others by J.T. Sanders, *The Jews in Luke–Acts* (London: SCM, 1987).

No. Neither his Yes nor his No is as sharp and clear as Paul's Yes and No, but they are not unrelated to them; they lie behind the compromise of Acts 15, which itself should be seen as the work of Christian Hellenistic Judaism. The OT is right, of course; but it must be rightly understood. Judaism is the heir of the OT; but to fulfil itself it must become Christian, and if it fails to accept the invitation to do so it disinherits itself. The OT could and must be understood as a Christian book, but the Temple could only be destroyed because it could not be taken over as a Christian institution.

'Chrétiens ont droit, et païens ont tort.' Luke is convinced of this, and that Jews come somewhere between the two, though in the end 'not right' must mean 'wrong'. What he says about the Temple is an index of this.

A HOUSE NOT MADE WITH HANDS

J.P.M. Sweet

The aim of this essay is to trace possible references in Paul's letters to the saying about the Temple attributed to Jesus at his trial. It is a journey through minefields: what did Jesus really say about the Temple? How much did Paul know about the earthly Jesus, and how are the possible echoes of Jesus' sayings in his letters to be understood? But no follower of Ernst Bammel should shy away from minefields.[1]

1. *Jesus' Temple-saying*

We heard him say, 'I will pull down (καταλύσω) this Temple that is made with hands (χειροποίητον), and in three days I will build (οἰκοδομήσω) another, not made with hands (ἀχειροποίητον, Mk 14.58; cf. 15.29).

Matthew shortens and softens: 'I can pull down the Temple of God and in three days build it' (26.61; cf. 27.40). Luke omits the charge, but later has false witnesses say that Stephen had said that Jesus would 'pull down this place' (Acts 6.14).

Even if these words do not represent exactly what Jesus said, or even what his accusers said he said, there is general agreement that Jesus did predict the destruction of Jerusalem and the Temple, that he enacted a symbolic interference in the Temple courts (whether or not it can correctly be called a 'cleansing'), and that this was a material factor in his trial and death. There is less agreement that he predicted a new Tem-

---

1. His *Jesu Nachfolger* (Heidelberg: L. Schneider, 1988) came to my notice only after this article was written; he may well think it blows up my view of Mt. 16.18. I am grateful to him for stimulus and encouragement over nearly thirty years; and to William Horbury for many illuminating suggestions and references for this article.

ple, but E.P. Sanders[2] has shown how the facts of Jesus' life—
his baptism by John, his call of the Twelve, his action in the
Temple—place him within Jewish 'restoration eschatology',
with its themes of God's imminent final intervention to impose
his rule (the 'kingdom of God'), the regathering of the twelve
tribes of Israel, the renewal of Jerusalem and the Temple, and
the ingathering of the Gentiles.

The point of his words will then have been not necessarily a
criticism or condemnation of the Second Temple but rather
the imminence of the New Age, in which God would bring in a
new Temple. The coming of the new meant the end of the old.
Views on the exact character of the new were fluid, but there is
evidence that, in some circles at least, the new Temple was
conceived as a community. Nathan's prophecy (2 Sam. 7) was
interpreted thus at Qumran: the fragment which Vermes
calls 'a Midrash on the Last Days' (4QFlor) speaks of God
building for himself 'a sanctuary of men, where they offer up
as incense the works of thanksgiving',[3] and in the Community
Rule the Council of the Community 'shall be an Everlasting
Plantation, a House of Holiness for Israel, an Assembly of
Supreme Holiness for Aaron' (8.5).[4]

2. *Jesus and Judaism* (London: SCM, 1985), chs. 1–3. He respectfully
dismisses Ernst Bammel's doubts about the eschatological thrust of
Jesus' message (p. 117 n. 84).

3. G.J. Brooke, *Exegesis at Qumran. 4Q Florilegium in its Jewish
Context* (JSOTS 29; Sheffield: JSOT Press, 1985), ch. 2, argues
convincingly for taking *miqdaš 'adam* as 'sanctuary of men', not
'among men' or 'human-made', and for reading 'works of
thanksgiving (*todah*)', not 'works of law (*torah*)' as Vermes does. See
also B. Gärtner, *The Temple and The Community in Qumran and the
New Testament* (Cambridge: Cambridge University Press, 1965), pp.
30-42.

4. B.F. Meyer, *The Aims of Jesus* (London: SCM, 1979), pp. 179ff., follows Otto Betz in claiming that the Qumran interpretation of 2 Sam. 7
reveals the logic, usually held to be lacking, behind the High Priest's
question, following the charge that Jesus had said he would rebuild
the Temple, 'Are you the Messiah?' ('Die Frage nach dem messiani-
schen Bewusstsein Jesu', *NovT* 6 [1963], pp. 20-48, and *Was wissen wir
von Jesu?* [Stuttgart-Kreutz, 1965]; ET, *What do we Know about Jesus?*
[London: SCM, 1968], pp. 87-93). But in fact 4QFlor omits the crucial
words, 'he will build a house for my name' in 2 Sam. 7.13, and it is
God, not the son of David, who will build the house, the 'sanctuary of
men'.

Further, in 2 Samuel 7 there is a pun on the word 'house':
God deprecates David's plan to build him a house, but promises
that he will build David a house—a dynasty—but when 2
Samuel 7 is developed in 1 Chronicles 17 and in the Targum,
this house is understood not as a royal family but as a kingdom
and as a religious community.[5] In this light Jesus' promise to
build his ἐκκλησία on Peter as foundation need no longer be
thought anachronistic or incompatible with his proclamation
of the Kingdom of God. This is not to say that either the
promise to Peter or the Temple-saying reported in Mark is
authentic in every detail. A powerful case can be made for Mt.
16.17-19 as a Matthaean midrash, but the midrash could go
back in outline to Jesus himself, and reasons can be suggested
for its omission by Mark. Likewise in the Temple-saying the
word 'made-with-hands' (χειροποίητος) is septuagintal, with
no exact Hebrew or Aramaic equivalent, and ἀχειροποίητος

It might seem that before AD 70 'in den Erwartungen des neuen
Tempels der Messias keine Rolle spielt' (D. Lührmann, 'Markus
14.55-64', *NTS* 27 [1981]), p. 465; cf. D. Juel, *Messiah and Temple*
(Missoula, 1977), ch. 9. Passages where the Messiah is mentioned
reflect the post-70 situation, e.g. Zech. 6.12, 'a man named the Branch
(ṣemaḥ)... will build the temple of the Lord', which becomes in the
Targum, 'Behold a man, Messiah is his name... and he will build the
temple of the Lord'; and *Or. Sib.* 5.414-33, 'A blessed man came from
heaven, who beautified God's city and made a holy temple and
fashioned a tower reaching to heaven... It is the last time of holy
people, when God, who thunders on high, founder of the greatest
temple, accomplishes these things'.
However, 4QFlor is still evidence for eschatological interpretation of
Nathan's prophecy before 70, and ṣemaḥ was already a Messianic title
at Qumran (4QFlor, and 4QPB, interpreting Gen. 49.10, unless Gärtner is right to take it as a symbol representing the community; *Temple
and Community*, pp. 35ff.); while *Or. Sib.* 5 shows that God and Messiah can stand in parallel as builders, not in mutual exclusion (cf.
Ezek. 34.11, 23 where God and David act as shepherd). Certainly a
claim to be Messiah would not automatically involve building a new
Temple, but a promise to build a new Temple could hardly fail to be
seen as a Messianic claim. If it were true that the Messiah had no part
in contemporary expectation with regard to the New Temple, the claim
to be acting as God's agent in this respect would be to claim even more
than Messianic status.
    5. See S. Aalen, '"Reign" and "House" in the Kingdom of God in the
Gospels', *NTS* 8 (1962), pp. 23-40.

seems to be a New Testament coinage (though Dan. 2.34, 35, ἄνευ χειρῶν, is close), but it looks as if Jesus did say something like this, perhaps in the form of John's conditional version, 'Destroy this Temple, and in three days I will raise it up' (Jn 2.19), and reasons can be suggested for Luke's omission of the accusation.

This is not to claim that Jesus' concerns were narrowly ecclesial; rather his concern was God's immediate presence with his people, for which Temple language was one form of expression. I hope to show the likelihood that Paul knew, and assumed his hearers knew, both the Peter tradition and the Temple-saying, and that Paul too was primarily concerned with God's presence and Spirit overriding human institutions, which is what 'made without hands' implies.

2. Paul's Allusions to the Temple-saying and to the Promise to Peter

a. For we know that if the earthly tent we live in is destroyed (καταλυθῇ), we have a building (οἰκοδομήν) from God, a house not made with hands (ἀχειροποίητον), eternal in the heavens (2 Cor. 5.1).

This is the closest echo of Mk 14.58; 'we know' (οἴδαμεν) might point to a well-known saying. But οἴδαμεν in Romans and 1 Corinthians refers to general truths and things held in common, and the application here to the destiny of the individual is at first sight remote from Jesus' concerns. As we shall see, however, such reapplication of Jesus-tradition is typical of Paul, and the shared vocabulary does suggest dependence, provided we can make sense of the reapplication (see section 3a).

At this point, before going on to other possible allusions, we should tackle the question of dependence: which way? The gospels in their present form are all later than Paul's letters and cannot be assumed to have preserved Jesus-tradition in the form in which he might have known it. In some cases indeed scholars have argued for the dependence being on

Paul, and M.D. Goulder[6] has made an interesting case for the almost immediate collection and circulation of Paul's letters, and their liturgical use in a lectionary cycle. (The weak link seems to me the apparent ignorance of Paul's letters in Acts.) Goulder has examined a large number of links between Matthew and Romans, 1 and 2 Corinthians, Galatians and Ephesians, but while some cases are evenly balanced many seem to me to point in (for him) the wrong direction. Just as it is always possible to devise a case for Mark's dependence on Matthew in any given instance, but in the great majority of cases it is much less plausible than Matthew's use of Mark, so with Paul and the Jesus-tradition. While agreeing that the evangelists' presentation of the tradition has been coloured by church development and experience, in which Paul and his letters were a major factor, and that there are instances where the priority may lie with Paul—for example the church discipline passage in Matthew 18—I still think that in the passages I am concerned with it is more likely that Paul was alluding to traditions which were later used by the evangelists. This is certainly the case with 2 Cor. 5.1 and Mk 14.58.

The individual reference of 2 Cor. 5.1 is indeed far removed from Jesus' saying, but in the next chapter Paul says 'we are the Temple (ναός) of the living God' (6.16), just as in 1 Corinthians he can refer to both community and individual as the Temple (ναός) in which God's spirit dwells (1 Cor. 3.16; 6.19).

b. 1 Corinthians 3 seems to bring in also the tradition about Peter as the foundation (θεμέλιον) of the community. It is not immediately clear in 1 Corinthians 1–4 what the groups based on Apollos and Cephas (let alone Christ) represent. But 1 Cor. 1.18 begins an attack on the Corinthian cult of wisdom, which claimed Apollos as figure-head, with the oblique weapons of word-play and innuendo: 'the word of the cross is folly to those who are perishing (ἀπολλυμένοις)... it is written, "I will destroy (ἀπολῶ) the wisdom of the wise"'. In 3.1-6

6. *The Evangelists' Calendar* (London: SPCK, 1976), pp. 218-40); see also *Midrash and Lection in Matthew* (London: SPCK, 1974), ch. 8, 'Matthew and Paul'.

Apollos is still the centre, and Paul comes back to him at 4.6; presumably he represents those who are 'puffed up', over against the apostles (4.9), which would include Cephas, who has already been mentioned again along with Paul and Apollos at 3.22.

We may suppose, then, that 3.10ff. centres on the Cephas group. The direct influences in Corinth had been Paul as initiator and Apollos as encourager, but there were probably people in Corinth who were not happy with either, and who were looking to Cephas (who may indeed have been to Corinth)[7] as the rock on which Christ had promised to build his church, and were wanting to move the community in a more conservative Jewish-Christian direction. Paul's attack is again oblique. He moves from the image of himself and Apollos as gardeners, planting and watering as fellow-workers under God, to the community as 'God's garden, God's building (οἰκο-δομή)';[8] and then traverses the claims made for Cephas by asserting that he, Paul, has laid for them the foundation, which is Christ and none other (cf. Rom. 15.20), and that others should take care how they build on it. The Corinthians are God's Temple (ναός), and 'if anyone destroys[9] God's Temple, God will destroy him' (3.16, 17).

How exactly would anyone destroy God's Temple? Presumably by flouting his Spirit who lives in the holy community, so it is tempting to take it as a reference to immorality. But there is no hint of that until ch. 5, and Paul does not say that people are making the Temple unholy, but that God will destroy those who destroy his Temple, because it is holy—set apart for him, not a human institution. So it is more likely that the reference

---

7. See C.K. Barrett, 'Cephas and Corinth', in *Essays on Paul* (London: SPCK, 1982), pp. 28-39, reprinted from O. Betz, M. Hengel and P. Schmidt (eds.), *Abraham unser Vater* (Leiden: Brill, 1963).

8. The transition may be helped by Jer. 1.10 '... to pluck up and to break down, to destroy and to overthrow, to build and to plant', which is probably also in mind along with Jesus' saying; see below.

9. φθείρει. It might help my thesis if Paul had said καταλύει. But this may be a traditional statement, one of E. Käsemann's 'sentences of holy law' ('Sätze Heiligen Rechtes im Neuen Testament', *NTS* 1 [1954/55]; ET in *New Testament Questions of To-day* [London: SCM, 1969], pp. 66-81); and φθείρειν has useful connotations of 'corrupt', 'seduce'.

is to 'jealousy and strife', 'fleshly' behaviour, living on the purely human level (κατὰ ἄνθρωπον, 3.3)—giving too much weight to humans (3.21) instead of to Christ. As we shall see, the word 'made with hands', though it may have a Platonic sense in Hellenistic circles, represents in its biblical use 'human-made' over against 'God-made'.

As concerns the Cephas tendency, it is not a question here of rebuilding the old edifice, as at Gal. 2.18; there is no sign of Judaizing in the full sense in 1 Corinthians. Rather it is a matter of building unworthy materials on to the true foundation—materials that are 'fleshly' (σαρκικά) and will not survive the test of the Last Day. This could cover both human wisdom teaching and outward aspects of Judaism, as in Romans 14, things that do not belong to the New Age of the Spirit.

At this point I should face two objections to my line of argument. First, can one simply assume that building (οἰκοδομή) and Temple (ναός) are the same thing? R.J. McKelvey[10] says that the image of the Temple is fused with that of the building for the first time at Eph. 2.20-22. On the contrary, following Paul Minear,[11] I take it that biblical imagery is kaleidoscopic: one image can merge into another—city, temple, house, building, community, mother, daughter, bride. Distinct definition and demarcation are a western trait. Secondly, the frequent connection in the Old Testament of pulling down and plucking up, building and planting, as at Jer. 1.10, suggests an objection to seeing allusions in this area to sayings of Jesus. Paul's Old Testament citations and allusions are notoriously so much more frequent and obvious than his supposed references to Jesus-tradition that it may seem better to look no further than scripture and current Jewish idiom for the source of Paul's terms, a source shared by Jesus also. But must it be either/or? Why not both/and? The case for Paul's knowledge of Jesus' sayings was over-pressed in the past, which led to a minimalizing backlash,[12] but recent work has

10. *The New Temple* (Oxford: Oxford University Press, 1969), p. 108.
11. *Images of the Church* (London: Lutterworth, 1961), ch. 3. Mk 13.1-2 refers to the Temple as οἰκοδομαί.
12. See V.P. Furnish, 'The Jesus–Paul Debate: From Baur to Bultmann', *BJRL* 47 (1965), pp. 342-81.

greatly strengthened the case, granted that Paul uses this material quite differently from scripture, in a subtle, almost subterranean way.[13]

c. In 1 Corinthians 3 the argument develops in terms of the different work (ἔργον) which people build on to the foundation as God's συνεργοί, and this leads us to another possible reference to the Temple-saying, in Romans: 'Let us then pursue the things that make for peace and mutual building up (οἰκοδομῆς). Do not for the sake of food pull down the work (κατάλυε τὸ ἔργον) of God' (14.19, 20). The 'strong' Christian is warned not to 'pull down God's work', the community in which all are welcome simply on the basis of faith (14.19); note the same oscillation between individual and community as in the Corinthian letters. The word οἰκοδομή in v. 19 reminds us of Paul's discussion of 'food' in 1 Corinthians 8 and 10, where though the context is different (idolatry rather than ascetic practice) the theme is the same: that which builds up the community, or love (cf. Rom. 14.15). We may surmise that one root, if not the only root, of all Paul's 'building up' language is in Jesus' sayings about Peter and about the Temple.

d. Peter's commission and Jesus' Temple-saying seem to come together also in Galatians.
i. It has often been suggested that in Galatians 1 Paul describes his call in terms deliberately reminiscent of the presumably well-known tradition of Peter's commission, as told in Matthew 16. The linguistic parallels are striking. His gospel came to him not from human beings 'but through a *revelation* of Jesus Christ'; 'When he who separated me from my mother's womb and called me through his grace was pleased to *reveal* his *Son* in me, that I might preach the good news of him among the Gentiles, immediately I did not confer with

13. See e.g. D.C. Allison, 'The Pauline Epistles and the Synoptic Gospels', *NTS* 28 (1982), pp. 1-32; P. Stuhlmacher, 'Jesustradition im Römerbrief?', *ThB* 14 (1983), pp. 240-50. M.B. Thompson, 'The Example and Teaching of Jesus in Rom. 12.1–15.13' (unpublished Ph.D. dissertation, Cambridge, 1988), gives a thorough discussion of the whole question, with balanced but positive conclusions. I suggest below one reason for paucity of allusion.

flesh and blood...' (1.12, 15, 16). In Matthew's Gospel Jesus greeted Peter's confession, 'You are the Messiah, the *Son* of the living God', with the words, 'Blessed are you, Simon Barjonah, because *flesh and blood* has not *revealed* it to you, but my Father who is in heaven' (16.16, 17). He continued, 'You are Πέτρος and on this πέτρα I will build my ἐκκλησία...' Paul's mission among the Gentiles could be seen as parallel with Peter's ecclesial responsibility.

But will this do? 'Separated me from my mother's womb and called me by his grace' is a palpable reference to the calls of Jeremiah (Jer. 1.5) and the second Isaiah (Isa. 49.1); indeed Paul often applies 'servant' language to himself. But again must it be either Old Testament or Jesus? Why not both/and? But a more serious objection is that this section of Matthew is missing in Mark, and while good reasons can be given why Mark should have chosen not to record it if he had known it, the passage is so midrashic and so Matthaean that it might seem easier to suppose that if there was dependence it was of Matthew on Paul. But if the midrash is based on Isa. 28.16, 17, like the passage from the Qumran Community Rule quoted above, there is no reason why it should not go back in germ to Jesus, who drew deeply on Isaiah. David Wenham[14] has restated the case for Paul's (and the Galatians') knowledge of the tradition which appears, however Matthaeanized, in Matthew 16: Paul takes Peter's primacy for granted, and argues for his own apostolic commission by comparison with the undisputed commission of Peter (Gal. 1.18; 2.7, 8); this must have been based on the authority of Jesus, and Matthew

---

14. In D. Wenham (ed.), *The Jesus Tradition outside the Gospels* (Gospel Perspectives, 5; Sheffield: JSOT Press, 1985), pp. 24ff. He takes up the arguments of J. Chapman in *Revue Bénédictine* 29 (1912), and the contrary arguments of A.-M. Denis in *RB* 64 (1957) and P. Refoulé in *RevSR* 38 (1964), which were countered by A. Dupont in *RSR* 52 (1964). The linguistic arguments for and against the priority of Gal. 1.16 are evenly balanced, but at the very least they leave the question open; and in view of Paul's difficulties in Galatians it is hard to believe that Peter's authority needed the support of a tradition framed in terms of Paul's account of his own commission. For the general question of dependence see above.

16 is the only passage which gives such authority.[15] It is formally possible that Matthew created the story from Paul's
words, in order to bolster Petrine authority against Pauline
Christians, if Paul's letters were indeed known in Matthew's
area. But it is far easier to see it the other way round, since we
know Paul is defending his apostleship over against that of the
Jerusalem 'pillars', and there is the strange shift at Gal. 2.7, 8
from Paul's regular term Κηφᾶς to Πέτρος. This is best
explained by his need to make clear to Greek-speaking Galatians that this Κηφᾶς was the same as the Peter whose commission from Christ, as the πέτρα on which his church was to
be built, had no doubt been drummed into them by the Judaiz-
ers.

ii. There is support for this approach in the reference to the
'reputed pillars' (οἱ δοκοῦντες στῦλοι εἶναι, Gal. 2.9), as
expounded by C.K. Barrett in his article, 'Paul and the "Pillar
Apostles"',[16] which I summarize. He argued from Paul's
ironic use of δοκεῖν (four times, 2.2, 6, 9) with its *double enten-
dre* of 'reputation' and 'appearance as opposed to reality', that
the title 'pillars' was not of his choosing but came from the
Jerusalem church. Its most plausible background is in apocalyptic, with its hope of a new Jerusalem and new Temple going
back to Isa. 54.11ff. The promise to the Philadelphians, 'He
who is victorious—I will make him a pillar in the Temple of
my God' (Rev. 3.12), belongs to the same conception of the
church as the eschatological Temple of God, already being
built here on earth. Jesus very probably shared this conception,
with his prophecies of doom for unrepentant Israel and its
Temple and his hints of a new order transcending Israel's
institutions; and Christians believed that the leading apostles
occupied, or would occupy, positions of fundamental importance in the New Age. In the Old Testament and Rabbinic

15. This is not to insist on the Matthaean setting of the story. Jesus
commissions Peter for pastoral responsibility at Lk. 22.32 and Jn 21.15-
17, not for mission; but the building of the new Temple-community
implies the ingathering of the Gentiles, and is thus parallel to Paul's
mission in Gal. 1.16.
16. In J.N. Sevenster and W.C. van Unnik (eds.), *Studia Paulina*
(Haarlem: de Erven F. Bohn, 1953), pp. 1-19.

writings the distinction between 'pillar' and 'foundation' is slight (biblical imagery is kaleidoscopic).

Paul clearly regarded the pillars as very important—he had to consult them (Gal. 2.2)—but he also insists on his own independent commission (Gal. 1.1; 2.6): hence his repeated use of δοκεῖν and his insistence on the overriding activity of God (2.8), who does not go by outward appearances (2.9). Later he uses the symbolism of the new City to support his doctrine of Christian freedom (4.25-27), with no mention of apostolic foundation. The new Israel (6.16) is not united to the old by a group of exclusively Jewish pillars but by God's own continuous activity. In fact the argument of 2.11-21 is sharpened in the light of the ascription of the term 'pillar' to Peter. 'The meaning of the obscure verse 18 seems to be that Peter (by his vacillating action) was not building up a new Israel, but the old, though this had previously been destroyed by Peter's own recognition that justification was to be found only in Christ' (Barrett, p.18).

iii. The argument is sharpened even further if we recognize Paul as implying that Peter was failing to build up (οἰκοδομεῖν) not a new Israel but a new *Temple*, and was instead rebuilding the old Temple, which he had pulled down; and that he had pulled it down not simply by recognizing that Christ was the only source of justification but fundamentally by sharing Christ's death in order to live for God (2.19). It was at Christ's death that the curtain of the Temple was torn in two (Mk 15.38 and parallels), a sign of God's departure and its obsolescence.

Most commentators assume that the obscure v. 18 refers to Peter's behaviour at Antioch, and his rebuilding the wall of legal observance which by eating with Gentiles he had pulled down; but none so far as I know has connected it with Jesus' Temple-saying, probably because of the currency of the terms 'pull down' and 'build' in various metaphorical senses, particularly in connection with law. The builders of Ps. 118.22 were interpreted as teachers of the Law; καταλύειν is used in 2 and *4 Maccabees* of abolishing laws and constitutions, and of course at Mt. 5.17. The question of the validity of the Law is so central in our passage that it seems perverse to look further.

Yet multiple reference is typical of Paul.[17] Israel, Jerusalem, Temple and Law are all integrally related. If we see v. 18 as an echo of Jesus' well-known Temple-saying, prepared for by the earlier hints of Peter as foundation or pillar of the eschatological Temple-community, then Paul's argument takes on a deeper subtlety. He is moving implicitly from the status of the Law, which for many Jewish Christians was non-negotiable, to the status of the Temple—the whole 'edifice' of Judaism which he and Peter had both pulled down in so far as they were 'in Christ', identified with him in his death (his rejection by Judaism) and in his resurrection (Judaism's rejection by God). He is putting law in a wider context, in which it no longer calls the shots.

The 'I' of v. 18 is agreed to be general, including Peter and the Jewish Christians as well as Paul—but Peter could not have agreed, and Paul's Galatian opponents would not recognize Peter as having agreed, that he had pulled down the Law. Paul himself denied later that he was abolishing the Law (Rom. 3.21), and Jesus certainly had not pulled down the Law (even if Mt. 5.17, 'think not I came to pull down [καταλῦσαι] the Law' is not original), as E.P. Sanders has shown.[18] But Jesus had said something about the Temple, which could be understood as a sentence of destruction and replacement, and the Christian communities saw themselves as the new Temple which he would build.

We must look more closely at the drift of Paul's argument.

> We ourselves who are Jews by birth and not Gentile sinners, yet who know one is not justified by works of the Law but through faith in Jesus Christ, even we have believed in Christ Jesus, in order to be justified by faith in Christ... But if in seeking to be justified in Christ we turned out to be ourselves sinners, is

17. Cf. P. Vielhauer, *Oikodome* (Wiesbaden: O. Harrassowitz, 1939), pp. 88-90. Ernst Bammel, commenting on the threat to 'temple and nation' (τόπος καὶ ἔθνος) at Jn 11.48, collected passages which 'express the duality of temple and city, or temple and people' (*The Trial of Jesus* [ed. E. Bammel; London: SCM, 1970], pp. 21-24). Jer. 1.10 may also be in mind.

18. *Jesus and Judaism*, ch. 9. But he argues that Jesus' attitude to the Law cannot be separated from his attitude to the Temple, which shows, not that he opposed the Law, but that for him the whole Mosaic dispensation was not final (pp. 251-52).

Christ then an agent of sin? God forbid! For it is if I build up again the things I pulled down that I prove myself a transgressor (Gal. 2.15-18).

Verses 17 and 18, and the connection between them, are the main problem. It is generally agreed that 'sinners' (ἁμαρτωλοί) in v. 17 picks up the same word used in v. 15 of the Gentiles outside the Law: Christians by seeking to be 'justified in Christ' and not by legal observance are found in the same boat with the Gentiles. Is Christ then an agent of sin (ἁμαρτία), in the sense of Gentile law-ignoring behaviour? No—such behaviour does not for Christians constitute sin, for it is if I build up again what I had pulled down that I show myself up as a transgressor.

But why 'transgressor'? J. Lambrecht points out in his thorough study of Gal. 2.11-21[19] that παραβάτης and παράβασις normally in Pauline usage refer to a specific law or command; he thinks that παραβάτης in v. 18 cannot, therefore, be taken in the same sense as ἁμαρτωλός and ἁμαρτία. He suggests three possibilities:

a. 'By reimposing the barriers I had pulled down I acknowledge that in pulling them down I had transgressed the Law.' This, he admits, fits ill with v. 19, where the γάρ would lose explanatory force.
b. We might connect the transgression not with καταλύω but with οἰκοδομῶ. Since there is no transgression where there is no Law (Rom. 4.15), and the Law was added with a view to transgressions (Gal. 3.19), restoration of the Law will inevitably lead to transgression. But this again fits uneasily with v. 19, and συνιστάνω, 'show myself up', implies present rather than future transgression.
c. Does the transgression then consist precisely in the 'building again'—in the restoration of the Law negating God's initiative in Christ (v. 21)?

Verse 19 then follows on: 'I prove myself a transgressor, for through the Law I died to the Law that I might live for God'. If I rebuild the Law I am rejecting God's grace and saying Christ has died in vain (v. 21). Verses 18-21 then form a neat

19. 'The Line of Thought in Gal. 2.14b-21', *NTS* 24 (1978), pp. 484-95.

unit, framed by 18b and 21a. But this attractive explanation founders, he thinks, on the Pauline use of παραβάτης with reference to a specific law or command. But is this so? ἁμαρτωλός has been used for those outside the Law in v. 15 (echoed in v. 17, on the usual understanding). And if one is under 'the law of Christ' (Gal. 6.2)—not ἄνομος θεοῦ, but ἔννομος Χριστοῦ (1 Cor. 9.21)—then to go back on Christ makes one a transgressor of this law. To be wholly consistent he should have repeated ἁμαρτωλός, but that would have been tedious and παραβάτης brings out the 'Law-less' aspect of ἁμαρτία in this passage (it has a similar sense in Rom. 7.7ff.).[20]

Meaning depends on context, and the context is decisive for this interpretation. The whole passage can now hang together. Verses 15-17 refer to Antioch, and v. 18 supports the preceding statement: we can deny that Christ promotes sin because for Christians it is if we go back on God's work in Christ that we show ourselves up as sinners. Sin is refusing to acknowledge God and give him thanks (Rom. 1.21), failing to live by faith, *coram Deo*, rather than failing to live by divine institutions which God's own action has overtaken.

Here, then, is the point of using words which, while appropriate with regard to the Law, actually evoke the Temple: Paul is trying to win over the Galatians by putting before them an argument based on that by which he tried to win over Peter and the other Jews who had 'joined in his hypocrisy' (2.13). To win over as opposed to demolishing an opponent you have to approach obliquely: you have to make concessions to your listeners if you are to take them with you, as Eta Linnemann showed in her study of Jesus' parables.[21] So Paul does not deny Gentile sinfulness, but moves to a Christian definition of sin. He does not devalue the Law, but evokes an evaluation of Judaism as a whole, centred here on the Temple, and in the next chapter on Abraham and the whole history of God's

20. 4QFlor 5 says the sanctuary which the Lord will build will not be desolated again, as the former sanctuary was because of Israel's sin: Jewish Christians no doubt feared that breaking the Law would desolate the New Temple. Perhaps παραβάτης was a current taunt, reflected in Matthew's account of the handwashing controversy (Mt. 15.2).
21. *Die Gleichnisse Jesu* (Göttingen: Vandenhoeck & Ruprecht, 1961); ET, *The Parables of Jesus* (London: SPCK, 1966), pp. 18-30.

dealings with Israel, taking up the Jewish Christians' own texts. This evaluation Peter and company can and should accede to because it is based on what God has done in the death and resurrection of Christ.

If Paul had said, 'If I reinstate the Law which I had demolished', he would not have drawn his hostile hearers in. They would not have felt included in his 'I'; they would not agree that they, or Jesus, had demolished the Law (cf. Mt. 5.17; 23.2, 23). This may help explain why Paul cites Jesus so seldom and refers to him so allusively: Jesus belonged to Judaism; his life was not part of the New Creation which God brought into being through his death. That is why Paul centres on his death and resurrection. Jesus did not 'declare all meats clean' (Mk 7.19), or Peter would not have needed a vision to tell him that God had changed the rules, so Paul could not say that he had declared all meats clean—he could only say, 'I know and am persuaded in the Lord Jesus (the risen Lord) that nothing is unclean in itself' (Rom. 14.14).

Paul's dominant concern is 'new creation' (Gal. 6.15): what God is doing, his grace at *work* (Gal. 2.8, 9) in himself and the Pillars; God's Spirit *working* miracles (Gal. 3.5)—an emphasis picked up in the account of Peter's vision and of the acceptance of Gentiles on equal terms at Antioch (Acts 10.47; 11.17, 21, 23). Galatians is marked by the contrast of spirit and flesh, God's gracious action and outward appearances. This leads us back to 2 Corinthians 4 and 5 where Paul is also concerned with outward appearance and inward reality.

3. *(Not) Made with Hands*

a. *2 Corinthians 5*

We look not to the things that are seen but to the things that are unseen; for the things that are seen are transient, but the things that are unseen are eternal. For we know that if our earthly house or tent is pulled down (οἰκία τοῦ σκήνους καταλυθῇ), we have a building (οἰκοδομήν) from God, a house not made with hands (οἰκίαν ἀχειροποίητον), eternal in the heavens (2 Cor. 4.18–5.1).

This passage as it continues is another minefield. At first sight Paul has deserted his Hebraic idea of the resurrection of the body in 1 Corinthians 15 for a Hellenistic dualism of body and spirit. But his fear of what to the Greek would be the glorious nakedness of the soul divested of the body (2 Cor. 5.3), and his longing to put on the new dwelling on top of the old, 'in order that what is mortal may be swallowed up by life' (5.4; cf. 1 Cor. 15.53, 54), show that he is still in the same Hebraic territory, even if he is kaleidoscopically mixing his metaphors.

The point of bringing in Jesus' Temple-saying here is again to subordinate the impressive and oppressive appearances of the old age to the hidden realities of the new. 'Paul's ideas are not developed as polemic against some hypothetical gnostics; nor is he making the same point as in 1 Cor. 15. Rather he is affirming the eschatological character of the transformation already begun, and weaving a new set of images out of traditional material.'[22] He is in fact opposing a *theologia gloriae* with his customary 'eschatological reservation'; the full possession of the heavenly existence or building must wait on earthly dissolution. Our physical body, like the earthly Temple, is under sentence of demolition; as a dwelling it is more like a *tent*, a familiar metaphor for the body which also evokes the Temple as the place of God's presence and glory, but with the suggestion of flimsiness (cf. 2 Cor. 4.7—treasure in earthen vessels).

On the other hand we already have a heavenly dwelling or clothing awaiting us, the Temple-community of the New Age, which is none other than the body of the risen Christ,[23] with

22. Frances Young and David F. Ford, *Meaning and Truth in 2 Corinthians* (London: SPCK, 1987), p. 133. One traditional term taken up in a new positive sense is the expression 'eternal house' for the grave. R. Penna, 'Les juifs à Rome au temps de l'apôtre Paul', *NTS* 28 (1982), p. 335 n. 129, notes an epitaph in which the grave is οἶκος αἰώνιος and dismisses the suggestion that it might refer to the heavenly temple. The phrase was common in antiquity, and he notes biblical analogies: Ps. 49.12; Eccl. 12.5; Tob. 3.6. Contrast the αἰώνιοι σκηναί of Lk. 16.9.

23. 'It is this present inclusion in the resurrection Body of Christ, the eschatological community, that is the ground (οὖν, v. 6) for our having "confidence" ... it cannot be "put on" in its completeness till He is all in all' (J.A.T. Robinson, *The Body* [London: SCM, 1952], pp. 78-79). The individual Christological interpretation of the Temple-saying at Jn 2.21 and the community interpretation are two sides of one coin.

whose death we are identified in our afflictions (4.10-14). It is in heaven, and will come from heaven (5.1, 2), as will Jesus our deliverer (1 Thess. 1.10), the saviour who will transform our body of humiliation to be conformed to his body of glory (Phil. 3.20). The reference is both corporate and individual; the evocation of Jesus' Temple-saying brings a corporate emphasis into what might seem merely individualistic. It is also the charter for a non-natural God-centred hope ('from God... not made with hands') in the midst of the hostile appearances of this age. Church and Christian are both God's work (ἔργον), and 'he who has worked (κατεργασάμενος) us into this state is God, who has given us the Spirit as a pledge of what is to come' (2 Cor. 5.5).

b. *Stephen's speech*
The theme of God's work over against human devices and institutions is evident in the biblical background of χειροποίη-τον. The word occurs several times in the LXX translating a Hebrew term for idols, worthless nothings (*'elil*), and the prophets frequently mock the human manufacture of heathen gods. Solomon's temple, by contrast, though undeniably built by human hands, was covered by divine instructions (2 Sam. 7.13), and human handiwork was kept to the minimum (1 Kgs 6.7). It could in that sense be regarded as God-made, as in the song of Moses by the Red Sea: 'Thou broughtest them in and didst plant them in the mount that is thy possession, the dwelling place, O LORD, of thy own making, the sanctuary, O LORD, which thy hands prepared; the LORD shall reign for ever and ever' (Exod. 15.17). This text was taken up at Qumran in the midrash on 2 Samuel 7 to which we have already referred, but it was applied to the 'sanctuary of men' which God would build in the last days, and the only reference to a building (2 Sam. 7.13a) was omitted from the quotation.

At Qumran there was opposition not to the present Temple but to the present priesthood, and it is clear they did not see their House of Holiness as a total and permanent replacement for the Temple. But to a Hellenistic Jew familiar with the interpretation of Nathan's prophecy in terms of a household rather than a house, as taken up by Jesus and perhaps even more radically exploited by Diaspora Jews,[24] the way would be open to see the Temple itself as not God's will, indeed as χειροποίητον. The word at Mk 14.58 may be a gloss, in the sense of 'human-made'; ἀχειροποίητον would then mean 'the work of God' rather than 'spiritual' in a Platonic sense.[25]

The gloss might seem to stem from the Hellenists of Acts 6, in view of Stephen's applying the term to Solomon's Temple (Acts 7.48). This was in a speech purporting to be an answer to the charges brought by 'false witnesses saying, "This man does not cease speaking against this holy place and the Law, for we have heard him saying that this Jesus of Nazareth will pull down (καταλύσει) this place, and change the customs which Moses delivered to us"' (Acts 6.12-14). Luke of course fails to mention the accusation by false witnesses against Jesus which Mark and Matthew record, and Morna Hooker has suggested that Luke was right: 'Is this in fact a dispute between church and synagogue which the other evangelists have transferred to the lifetime of Jesus? Does Mark perhaps give this away by his use of the terms χειροποίητος and ἀχειροποίητος?'[26] However, the evidence for Jesus having in some way threatened the Temple and envisaged its replacement by a community remains strong, and Luke may have omitted the accusation because his sources connected the perception of the Temple as χειροποίητον with Stephen.

Stephen's speech and the whole episode are so Lucan that it may be doubted if he had sources. But Stephen's attack on the

24. As suggested by M. Simon, *St. Stephen and the Hellenists* (London: Longmans, 1958), pp. 84-94; cf. C.K. Barrett's essay in this volume.

25. Apart from Mk 14.58 and 2 Cor. 5.1, the word is found only at Col. 2.11: the περιτομὴ ἀχειροποίητος is being buried and raised with Christ in baptism, again not philosophical dualism but biblical eschatology: what God is doing in the New Age. Likewise χειροποίητος is close to σαρκικός, belonging to this age, as applied to the rite of circumcision which identifies the Jews, περιτομὴ ἐν σαρκὶ χειροποίητος (Eph. 2.11). There is no necessary reference to the Temple-saying, but ἀχειροποίητος is so rare that the author can hardly have been unaware of it. The echo helps to root Christians, who have forgone Jewish ritual, in the ritual of the New Age.

26. 'Traditions about the Temple in the Sayings of Jesus', *BJRL* 70 (1988), p. 16.

Temple as idolatrous is so sharp, even though Luke has said the charges against him were false, and so contrary to the attitude to the Temple in the rest of Luke–Acts,[27] that it must be based on fact.

In the historical survey which culminates in the quotation from Isaiah 66, the word 'made with hands' has been prepared for as far back as v. 40:

> ... saying to Aaron, '*Make* us gods...'; and they *made* a calf... and offered sacrifices to the idol, and rejoiced in the *work of their hands*... 'You took up the tent of Moloch and the star of the God Rephan, the images (τύπους) which you *made* to worship...' The tent of testimony was with our fathers in the desert, according as he who spoke to Moses commanded him to *make* it after the image (τύπον) which he had seen... David found grace before God and asked to find a tent-dwelling (σκήνωμα) for the house of Jacob. But Solomon built him a house. But the Most High does not live in things *made by hands*. As the prophet says, '... What sort of house will you build for me, says the Lord, or what is the place of my rest? Did not my *hand make* all these things?' (Acts 7.40-50).

This is strong meat, but the point of 'made with hands' as Luke presents the scene is not simply idolatry in the sense of worshipping images, but rather human self-assertion[28] which refuses to recognize God's revelation and God's work—not so much idolatry as the refusal to acknowledge God which leads to idolatry (Rom. 1.18ff.). Stephen exploits Ps. 131(132).5 to claim that with David it was not a matter of human making but finding what God wanted, and that this was a σκήνωμα for the house(hold)[29] of Jacob, not a house. David's tent would

---

27. See G.W.H. Lampe's Ethel M. Wood Lecture, *St. Luke and the Church of Jerusalem* (London: Athlone, 1969).

28. M. Simon (*Hellenists*, p. 89) points out that in Philo, while the term normally refers to idolatry, it can refer as in secular Greek to human-made as opposed to natural—'calamities artificially provoked by man's destructive energy' (*Spec. Leg.* 1.184; 3.203; *Flacc.* 62). It is used in a neutral sense of the sanctuary (*Vit. Mos.* 2.88).

29. The variant reading θεῷ for οἴκῳ is manifestly a case of *lectio facilior*, in harmony with Ps. 131(132).5. Some scholars nevertheless prefer it because of the awkwardness of the shift to οἶκος meaning 'house' in the next line. But that is the point! It is the same pun that goes back to Nathan's prophecy in 2 Sam. 7.

have been just as much 'manufactured' as Solomon's house; the point of the tent is that God revealed its pattern on the mount (7.44), the holy place of revelation (7.33) over against 'this holy place', which Stephen has been accused of speaking against (6.13).[30] Angels and prophets, revelation and recognition (or failure to recognize) are stressed throughout, and Luke sets the whole speech accordingly: Stephen's face was like an angel's (6.15), and at the end, before he was rejected like the prophets, he was full of the Holy Spirit and saw the heavens opened.

Whatever may have been the view of Stephen, the target in Acts is not the Temple but the Jews who reject the work of God's hand and resist the Holy Spirit. The Temple and its sacrifices are no more identified with idolatry than the Law is identified with pagan religion at Gal. 4.8-10. With the word χειροποίητος Luke in effect turns against the Jews their own critique of pagan religion, which appears on Paul's lips in Athens: 'God who made the world... does not dwell in temples made by hands (ναοῖς χειροποιήτοις), nor is he served by the hands of men...' (Acts 17.24, 25). By their rejection of Jesus and his witnesses they are putting themselves in the position of pagans who fail to perceive God's hand and work. Just before the Stephen episode Luke has had Gamaliel say:

> If this plan and this work (ἔργον) is of men (ἐξ ἀνθρώπων) it will be pulled down (καταλυθήσεται—like the temple made with hands), but if it is of God (ἐκ θεοῦ) you will not be able to pull them down (καταλῦσαι αὐτούς—they are God's handiwork), lest you turn out to be fighting against God (Acts 5.38, 39).[31]

To sum up, there is a background for 'made without hands' which stems from the Hebrew Bible, not Hellenistic spiritualizing, and which fits well Jesus' own sense of God's reve-

---

30. The significance of the tent is that God revealed it, not that it is mobile or desert-based (the desert is the place of apostasy as well as revelation). It is the 'tent of witness' (7.44), linked with the 'ecclesia in the desert' (7.38) which is echoed by the ecclesia in Jerusalem (8.1, 3). God's household and its witness are implicitly contrasted with a human-made building and its sacrifices. Luke shows no interest in the idea of the church as the New Temple.

31. Cf. J.-F. Collange, *Énigmes de la Deuxième Épître de Paul aux Corinthiens* (Cambridge: Cambridge University Press, 1982), p. 185.

lation and work in bringing in a new order, centred on people not buildings. It is in this sense the gloss at Mk 14.58 would have been understood, even if the idolatrous flavour of χειρο-ποίητον may have influenced Matthew and Luke to omit it.

4. Perceptions of the Second Temple

According to Acts, Jerusalem and the Temple were central not only for the earliest church but also for Paul. Professor Barrett has written on attitudes to the Temple in Acts, but we may ask what was Paul's perception on the evidence of his letters, and what finally was Jesus' perception, in the light of the possible Pauline allusions which I have examined. It is possible, though often difficult, to distinguish an attack on an institution from an attack on those who run it, or to distinguish rejection of an institution from the quest for something better which puts it in the shade—as, for Paul, the glory of Moses' dispensation was 'deglorified' by the surpassing glory of the Spirit's (2 Cor. 3.10). Eschatology, unless it is purely escapist, must seem subversive to those whose stake is in the status quo. Thus it is possible to have respect for the Temple, as the place where God said his name should dwell, and for the Law as holy, just and good, and to combine such respect, on the one hand, with fierce criticism of the present administration whose failure may lead God to demolish his own institution (cf. biblical prophecies of God's deconstruction of the cosmos which humans have corrupted), and on the other hand, with looking for God's 'fulfilment' of the earthly institution which (it may be believed) he has already set in motion.

I have suggested that for Paul the Temple symbolized the whole of Judaism as a divine institution and thus could include the Law, which on its own was an unmovable mountain, and that Jewish Christians could be helped to let go of the Law if they could be led to see it as part of a greater whole which Christ by his death and resurrection had replaced, and as part of a history in which it was subordinate to God's promise to Abraham, whose seed is Christ. Implicit, then, is the belief that the earthly Temple is, like the Law, a pointer to the heavenly eschatological reality which is even now taking shape in Jesus' *ecclesia*, with its apostolic pillars and builders.

In that sense the present Temple is earth-bound, like the present Jerusalem, which is in bondage and is not to be confused with the Jerusalem above (Gal. 4.25, 26). But this does not cancel respect for the present Temple, city and Law while waiting for the End; indeed the events of the End can still be connected with the earthly Temple (2 Thess. 2.4) and earthly Zion (Rom. 11.26), as many commentators understand those passages. The loyally Jewish Paul of Acts—visiting Jerusalem, keeping festivals, worshipping in the Temple—may not be entirely a Lucan fiction; compare his respect for the Law as God-given, however sharp his condemnation of those who tried to rebuild what they had pulled down.

There is likewise no need to doubt John's picture of a Jesus who attends the festivals, and Matthew's of a Jesus who upholds Temple and sacrifice while attacking those who abuse them (Mt. 23.16-22; 5.23, 24), just as he upholds the Law while attacking those who abuse it. His action in the Temple can still be seen as a 'cleansing' (directed against the people of Israel who worship there but do not respond to God's visitation; cf. Lk. 13.1-5; 19.44), in spite of E.P. Sanders's argument that it was simply an acted sign of coming destruction to make way for the New Temple.[32] But just as Jesus points beyond the Law to God's immediate presence and demand, so he points beyond the Temple to the new 'sanctuary of men'[33] which he is building, and which will stand firm through the birth pangs of the New Age, when city and Temple will be utterly destroyed. Something more than Solomon, the builder of the first Temple, is here; something greater than the Temple itself (Mt. 12.6, 42).

To sum up, we may guess that Jesus shared the common perception of the Second Temple as the place of God's presence and the centre of salvation, but that he perceived God to be doing something new, commissioning him to regather the lost sheep of the house of Israel, and building a house or community of people, founded on his twelve disciples with Peter as

32. *Jesus and Judaism*, pp. 61-71, opposed by Morna Hooker in *BJRL* 70 (1988), pp. 17, 18, taking 'cave of robbers' in its context in Jer. 7.5-15. It was an attack not on sacrifice or on commerce, but on the religiosity which they served.
33. 4QFlor; see notes 2 and 3.

their head—a temple of God's making to replace the physical temple which, with Jerusalem itself, was under sentence of destruction. There is some confirmation that such was his perception if Paul did indeed allude to Peter's commission and the temple-saying as well-known traditions, in the way I have suggested.

Paul's own attention was fixed on the New Temple, the *ecclesia* of God, and its building up, but there is no need to doubt his respect for the Second Temple, or for the Law, as God-given and as pointing forward to the New Age. Other Christians, like Stephen, may have been less respectful, seeing the physical temple as a frustration of God's will that a household rather than a house should be his dwelling. Stephen's attack, however, as presented by Luke, was primarily on those who ignored God's revelation and resisted his Spirit, and we must remember that 'I will have mercy and not sacrifice' does not mean that sacrifice *with* mercy is rejected. If the household were in order there would be no quarrel with the house.

Christians no doubt varied in their perceptions but most, if not all, would have accepted that at the death of Jesus the curtain of the Temple was torn in two. The Second Temple had been proleptically pulled down and 'after three days' the New Temple was proleptically in place. The old could still be honoured, but it must not be rebuilt.[34]

34. Some Christians may, like people at Qumran, have expected God to bring a new Temple at the Last Day, but it is significant that in the Revelation the New Jerusalem contains no temple (21.22). 'The Lord God Almighty is its temple, and the Lamb'; its dimensions are cubical, like the Holy of Holies (22.16), and it incorporates all peoples (22.24). The function of a temple as a place of meeting and atonement has been totally fulfilled.

οἵτινές ἐστε ὑμεῖς:
THE FUNCTION OF A METAPHOR IN ST PAUL

D.R. de Lacey

The commonplace observation that Paul can call the church God's Temple should serve only to emphasize the importance to us of understanding what rôle the Temple would formerly have played in his faith and experience. That in turn may illuminate and clarify his various applications of the image. What is in his mind when he makes this identification? Why does he express it at this point, and in this way? What effect does he expect it to have on his audience; what function does it play in his argument? Here we consider the function of one such application, in 1 Cor. 3.16. This occurs in the long and coherent argument which opens our 1 Corinthians, and which extends from 1.10 to at least 4.21. Paul appears to tackle three related issues: the proper basis of Christian existence (not the apostles, the figureheads of the Corinthian factions, not even baptism, but the gospel), the proper content of that basis (not earthly wisdom but the Spirit of God, the mind of the crucified), and the proper status of the figureheads (not leaders of rival factions but co-operators in the service of God). In this last, Paul abruptly moves at 3.9 from the analogy of a field (the figureheads only labourers together in it) to that of a building. But this building turns out to be a temple, the Temple of God. Although this is not stated until 3.16, we suggest that the image was already in Paul's mind from the outset and that its introduction is a deliberate step in the argument towards which he has been consciously moving from at least 3.1. To understand why he does so we shall first explore the functions of the Temple more generally within the spirituality of Judaism.

1. *The Temple in Judaism*

The primary model of worship embodied in the Temple cultus could be viewed as that of 'giving God his due'; most clearly seen in the prophetic protests against its abuse.[1] It is one which focuses more on the community than on the individual; more on the external act than on the inner experience. The very design of the Temple bespeaks this fact: 'interior space... was divided in such a way that one would be hard put to find separate, personal areas. The architectural presupposition... is that *crowds* will be present.'[2] At the heart of the Temple liturgy lay the sacrificial system explicated in the Torah and administered by the hereditary priesthood. Lay Israelites came to the Temple to present their offerings or sacrifices, and to prostrate themselves—these were the essence of Temple-worship, and any other religious activities were incidentals. Haran comments:

> In the Temple... prayer was considered a gesture of secondary order. There it was a substitute for sacrifice, a kind of 'offering of the poor' ... sacrifice could not usually be done without, while prayer was optional.[3]

Cohen puts it even more forcefully: 'The cult is silent, except for the squeals of the animals'.[4] These are rhetorical overstatements no doubt, but serve to highlight the external and community aspects of the cultus. No particular effect on the worshippers is to be expected—save that of a purity explicitly formulated in exclusively cultic terms. For the worshippers, we may say, the cultus served only to enable them to

---

1. Most particularly in Haggai and Malachi. B. Malina, *The New Testament World* (London: SCM, 1983), p. 142, uses the analogy of client-gifts to a patron.

2. J.F. Strange, 'Archaeology and the Religion of Judaism in Palestine', *ANRW* II.19.1, pp. 646-85 (657; italics represent *Sperrdruck* in the original).

3. M. Haran, 'Temple and Community in Ancient Israel', in M.V. Fox (ed.), *Temple in Society* (Winona Lake: Eisenbrauns, 1988), pp. 17-25 (22).

4. S.J.D. Cohen, 'The Temple and the Synagogue', in T.G. Madsen (ed.), *The Temple in Antiquity* (Provo, UT: Brigham Young University Press, 1984), pp. 151-74 (155). Only in Lev. 16.21 is there any reference to a verbal confession over the head of the victim.

participate in the cultus. Hence the basis for it must be sought outside the consciousness of the worshippers. It clearly presupposes a presence of God in the Temple, a presupposition which goes back at least to the idea of Yahweh 'causing his name to dwell' in the place of his choice (Deut. 12.11, 21, 26; 14.24; etc.). How such a view could be coupled with a belief in the transcendence of God is admirably seen in Solomon's dedicatory prayer in 1 Kings 8: it opens with the words 'I have built thee an exalted house, a place for thee to dwell in for ever'; but later this is rephrased as 'I have built the house for the *name* of the LORD'; with the acknowledgment, 'Behold, heaven and the highest heaven cannot contain thee; how much less this house which I have built!' Solomon therefore prays that 'thy eyes may be open night and day toward this house, the place of which thou hast said, "My name shall be there", that thou mayest hearken'; and later, 'hear thou in *heaven* thy dwelling place, and do'. The author of this prayer has clearly thought deeply over the issues of immanence and transcendence, and begun (or continued) a path of spiritualizing, yet without eviscerating, the concept of the presence of God. Thus in captivity the people are to 'pray to thee toward their land, which thou gavest to their fathers, the city which thou hast chosen, and the house which I have built for thy name'; and God hears again from his proper dwelling-place, in heaven.[5]

In this sense one may accept McKelvey's conclusion: 'without the presence of God there can be no temple';[6] and hence one may say that a major rôle of the Temple is that it *defines worship*, attracting to itself every aspect of Israelite religion. Even the domestic rite of Passover becomes attached to this place;[7] and personal prayers and other acts of devotion

5. Interestingly, the Chronicler adds a closing invocation, 'Arise, O LORD God, and go to thy resting place, thou and the ark of thy might' (1 Chron. 6.41).

6. R.J. McKelvey, *The New Temple* (Oxford: Oxford University Press, 1968), pp. 100f.

7. Only in Deut. 16 within the canon, and it is overwhelmingly likely that Passover was also celebrated outside Jerusalem. This was certainly true at Elephantine in the fifth century (though the temple there perhaps makes this a special case), and there are hints in later literature of celebrations elsewhere in the Land (e.g. in Jericho in *m. Pes.*

are directed towards it.[8] For this reason in his brief but suggestive article Haran[9] argues that when personal, non-Temple religious practice develops, it is understood by analogy with these cultic acts, and this is indeed the major impact of the cultus. Even in the Psalms, prayer is *likened* to sacrifice[10] as if it were a derivative activity. Haran's thesis may however be rather too neat to stand without further elaboration. The later rabbinic doctrine of *kawwanah* is already implicit in much of the prophetic attack on unthinking adherence to the liturgy; and the psalter contains manifest awareness, as in Psalm 51, of the priority of the clean heart and right spirit over sacrifice.[11] For all the emphasis in Samuel and Kings on the central place of the Temple in the life of God's people, there is little there on the significance of the sacrificial system which it embodied. From the prayers of Hannah with which the work opens to the activities of Hezekiah towards its close, prayer is constantly emphasized over above sacrifices as Israel's primary response and major responsibility. Josiah's reforms include a grand Passover, but no other sacrifices are mentioned. Indeed, the idea of 'sacrifice' seems to be much more prevalent before the turning-point of the building of the temple by Solomon than after it;[12] and in Solomon's great prayer of dedication there is no reference to the place being a house of sacrifice, despite the number of sacrifices which the king

10). But we have very little hard evidence of Jewish attitudes to the festivals away from Jerusalem.

8. E.g. Dan. 6.10; Ps. 138.2; cf. Ps. 5.7. Synagogues were provided with the means for worshippers to orient themselves towards Jerusalem; see Strange, 'Archaeology'.

9. Haran, 'Temple and Community in Ancient Israel'.

10. Haran cites Pss. 141.2; 119.108; 51.19; the list could easily be extended.

11. As noted above, cultic cleansing in any event only covered a very restricted range of specific impurities.

12. Although the vocabulary of sacrifice is broad, some impression may be gained from looking at the term זבח. The actual root זבח (apart from מזבח) occurs 30× in 1 Samuel, 3× in 2 Samuel, 8× in 1 Kings and 5× in 2 Kings, a total of 46, of which many do not refer to the Temple but to the במה. In the RSV 'sacrifice' occurs 25×, 2×, 14× and 13× respectively. At best 3 of these in 2 Kings (20.1; 16.15; possibly also 17.36) refer even indirectly to the orthodox Temple cultus. The Chronicler adds a few extra references, but not so as materially to alter the general picture.

actually offered on that occasion.[13] Already within the Old Testament there is a long tradition of spirituality which while related to the cultus uses different models of worship.[14]

It is thus more reasonable to postulate a complex combining of models, from a very early stage, than to suggest a neat chronological progression from the external rite towards the internal disposition of the heart. We need also to recall that the books of Kings and Chronicles are themselves tendentious documents and may be actively combating attitudes which were unwilling to put the centralized cultus at the heart of the faith. The Exile added a further dimension to Israelite spirituality. The significance of the cultus and the possibility of worship apart from it had now to be re-evaluated; and the Temple and the Holy City became powerful symbols of self-identity in an alien world. The Second Temple in its disappointing beginnings served only to heighten the spiritual,[15] and in many cases eschatological, aspects of this attitude. By the first century the battle was decisively won: Temple and Yahwism lay inseparably together.[16]

13. Cf. Cohen, 'The Temple and the Synagogue', p. 154: 'in 1 Kings 8, after building an elaborate slaughterhouse, King Solomon offers a long invocatory prayer which speaks only about prayer toward or at the temple, and says nothing about the sacrificial cult'.

14. For instance, that of personal encounter seen in Ps. 27.8: 'Seek ye my face!' It is noteworthy that the historiographers place the cultus fairly late in the day: not until Cain and Abel is sacrifice mentioned in Genesis, and *Jubilees* marks Adam's sacrificing—of spices only—as beginning 'from the day he covered his shame'.

15. This is an unfortunate word since it can be taken to suggest a dualism which was probably foreign to mainstream Jewish thinking, or to imply a specific link with the notion of the Holy Spirit, a concept which had very specific connotations within the mental world of first-century Judaism. Since, however, there is no convenient alternative, it will be used here though with caution.

16. On centralization of the cultus see also M. Haran, *Temples and Temple-Service in Ancient Israel* (Oxford: Clarendon, 1978). On the existence of other temples in Judaism see below, note 30. J. Neusner (*A History of the Jews in Babylonia* [Leiden: Brill, 1965], I, p. 36) notes that Herod built more than one Temple. After AD 70 (or perhaps better AD 135) the situation changed even more radically than at the Exile. For this reason alone rabbinic attitudes to the Temple need handling with the utmost caution.

There is a second way in which the cultus indirectly influences all of Jewish spirituality. Recent interest in sociology has served to increase our awareness of its significance. As the dwelling-place of God, the Temple stood at the centre of the universe, the navel of the world.[17] Hence it mirrors the cosmos[18] and defines sacred space and the realm of the holy. It follows that there can only be one Temple,[19] which thus acts as a unifying force for the Jewish faith. Such a perspective reinforces the one above, making it well-nigh imperative that all Jewish worship is in some way or another related to the Temple,[20] and frequently we find future hope expressed in terms of a new and glorious Temple. This is a very natural development from the Exile and destruction of Jerusalem, and the pitiful inadequacy of the Second Temple in its earliest stage. However, it remains as a powerful category even for those who look beyond the material world to some kind of more 'spiritual' culmination of their hopes.[21] It also remains power-

17. In *Jub.* 8.19 three holy places are identified: Eden the dwelling of God, Sinai, and 'Mount Zion in the midst of the navel of the earth'. A similar cosmic model seems to underlie *1 Enoch* 24–26. Later on, significant events in Israel's history get located there, from the binding of Isaac (as already suggested by 2 Chron. 3.1) to the events of the eschaton.

18. And in 11QTemple the ideal Temple covers precisely the area of the whole of the Holy City (M. Broshi, 'Dimensions', *BAR* 13 [1987], pp. 36f.). Josephus also interprets the Temple furniture in cosmic terms: *Ant.* 3.180ff. See also Ezek. 43.7; Philo, *Flacc.* 46.

19. Josephus, *Ant.* 4.201, ἐν ἑτέρᾳ δὲ πόλει μήτε βωμὸς μήτε νεὼς ἔστω· θεὸς γὰρ εἷς καὶ τὸ Ἑβραίων γένος ἕν; *Ap.* 2.193 εἰς ναὸς ἑνὸς θεοῦ; cf. also Philo, *Spec. Leg.* 1.67, ἐπειδὴ εἷς ἐστιν ὁ θεός, καὶ ἱερὸν ἓν εἶναι μόνον. For a practical demonstration of the significance of this, see F. Dexinger, 'Limits of Tolerance in Judaism: The Samaritan Example', in *Jewish and Christian Self-Definition*, II. Note that Josephus can affirm the above even though he is aware of the existence of (at least) the Heliopolis temple—a sure indication that there is a significant element of spiritual interpretation in his attitude.

20. A concrete expression of this is seen in the provisions made in synagogues for prayer to be offered towards the Holy City; see Strange, 'Archaeology', for details.

21. Already in Ezekiel the new Temple appears to be other-worldly, given the architectural impossibility of the specifications given. We may see how the Temple dominates hope in groups like that responsible for 11QTemple without having to decide whether a this-worldly fulfilment was expected or not.

ful even when the Temple is no longer seen as the specific dwelling-place of the deity. According to a later tradition, the Shekinah never dwelt in the Second Temple.[22] This may represent a hostility to, or at least an ambivalence towards, the Temple of the pagan Cyrus, restored by the Edomite Herod, but it is more likely to reflect the widespread view that in this 'present evil age' God was no longer actively involved in this world's affairs but communed with humans only on an individual level. If so it represents not an anti-Temple polemic but part of a wider theodicy, combined with the absence of the ark and the Shekinah. If so, then positive attitudes to the Temple become even more pointed: it marks the focal point of the meeting of a *deus absconditus* with his faithful people.

What actually occurred in the Temple? Our sources provide numerous details, by no means always in agreement; where they are less clear is on the significance which these rituals had in the minds of the worshippers. The problem is compounded for us by our cultural alienation from the enthusiastic bloodletting which characterized so much of what occurred; yet our sources indicate that it engendered awe and worship in the participants.[23] Full, and disappointingly uncritical, descriptions of the details will be found in the standard literature[24] and need not be rehearsed here. But it is worthy of note that the reality was probably a great deal more complex than such descriptions may imply. To perform the necessary rituals in accordance with the stipulations of the Pentateuch is no straightforward matter, as our sources themselves indicate

22. A.M. Goldberg, *Untersuchung über die Vorstellung von der Schekhinah in der frühen rabbinischen Literatur—Talmud und Midrasch* (Berlin: de Gruyter, 1969), p. 287. See G.I. Davies, 'The Presence of God in the Second Temple and Rabbinic Doctrine', in this volume.

23. It is not coincidental that the visions of Isaiah and Luke's Paul are located in the Temple.

24. CRINT, the new Schürer, etc.; see also Y. Yadin, *The Temple Scroll* (London: Weidenfeld & Nicolson, 1985). The most extensive discussions on the Temple in ancient literature are to be found in *Middoth, Tamid, Yoma* and *Shekalim*; Josephus, *Ant.* 15.380ff.; *War* 5.184ff.; 11QTemple. These are tendentious, and by no means always in agreement. Archaeology is increasingly providing other information.

on a closer reading. Rabbinic writings witness to deep suspicion and hostility between the Pharisees and Sadducees on many matters of ritual,[25] a factor which it would be facile to interpret in terms of wilful Sadducean perversity.[26] Doubtless their interpretation of the Torah and ritual were as coherent and cogent as those of any other sect within Judaism.[27] Much of Jewish sectarianism could be interpreted as rival attempts to interpret the Torah and to combine the cultic and personal aspects of Israelite religion.[28] There were those for whom the Temple ritual of the time was so flawed[29] that adherents felt themselves obliged to withdraw completely from all or part of it. This led to an immediate demand for a theology to justify this action and to cope with the absence of the prescribed rituals for dealing with impurities and approaching the deity. The Samaritans solved this problem one way, with a rival sanctu-

25. It is perhaps only fortuitous that on what was perhaps the major bone of contention—the calendar—they found themselves in agreement. The Pharisaic claim that they were able to *overrule* the Sadducaean priests on this matter is improbable in the extreme.

26. The Sadducees need and deserve comparable championing to that given the Pharisees by E.P. Sanders and (more especially) J. Neusner.

27. The *Tendenz* of our sources, from the Books of the Maccabees (see 1 Macc. 1.11; 2 Macc. 4; etc.) to the Talmud, is uniformly hostile. It is notoriously difficult to apprehend aright the motives of one's enemies, perhaps especially when one suspects them of heresy.

28. See esp. A. Green, *Jewish Spirituality: From the Bible through the Middle Ages* (London: Routledge & Kegan Paul, 1986), Introduction (esp. p. xiii), for a valuable discussion of aspects of Jewish faith too often ignored. For all its weaknesses, M. Smith, *Parties and Politics*, gives valuable insights into the psychological and religious backgrounds to Jewish sectarianism. See also J. Blenkinsopp, 'Interpretation and the Tendency to Sectarianism: An Aspect of Second Temple History', in E.P. Sanders *et al.*, *Jewish and Christian Self-Definition*, II (Philadelphia: Fortress, 1981), pp. 1-26.

29. It is not necessary to suppose that the basis for accusations of corruption was primarily moral laxity on the part of the priests, even if that was how it was perceived, e.g. at Qumran. Issues of prohibited degrees of marriage and the length of a menstrual period are essentially questions of interpretation, not of fact. We need not suppose that the priests were insincere in their view of such matters. There were also problems of priestly succession: the Maccabees were not of high-priestly line, and indeed for the authors of *1 Enoch* 89.73f., *T. Mos.* 4.6-8 (probably, though see Priest's comments in Charlesworth) and 1QpHab the Second Temple was profane from its inception.

ary;[30] and the Essenes another, by (effectively) extending the metaphorical application of the language of the cultus while (apparently) still hoping for a restoration of true Temple worship at some future date.[31] It is likely that the majority of diaspora Jews, with minor variants, may have developed, or followed, comparable rationalization (or spiritualization) in their attitude to the cultus.

However, the Pharisaic approach could afford to be more nuanced. On central matters of ritual they were in reasonable agreement with the Sadducaean Temple authorities. Yet they too re-interpreted the cultus, by taking (effectively) as their founding charter Exod. 19.6: 'you shall be to me a kingdom of priests'. Thus their own 'priestly' service extended beyond the Temple (where in any event they had no right to minister) and into the home, making the whole of the City, indeed the whole of the Land,[32] as holy as the Sanctuary itself. In this sense every meal was a sacrifice; every act part of the Temple

---

30. On the Samaritans see F. Dexinger, 'Limits of Tolerance', and on their Temple see Strange, 'Archaeology', esp. p. 649. (The situation with the Samaritans is of course more complex than the text above might be taken as suggesting.) The same may also be true to some extent of the various other Jewish temples known to us, from Elephantine and Arad to the Tobiad temple at Araq el-Emir and the Oniad temple at Leontopolis. See also Josephus, *Ant.* 14.260, on Jewish sacrifices as (apparently) a normal part of life in Sardis. The extent of Jewish temple-building and sacrifice outside the Land is a neglected aspect of Jewish spirituality sadly beyond the scope of this essay. See M. Hengel, *Judaism and Hellenism* (London: SCM, 1974), and M.E. Stone, *Scriptures, Sects and Visions* (Oxford: Blackwell, 1982), for a brief discussion. Whether sacrifice was offered at Qumran remains uncertain. Suffice it to note that the establishment of such priestly institutions do not appear (in contrast to the Samaritan case) to have led to schism.

31. On Qumran see in particular Yadin, *The Temple Scroll*; M.A. Knibb, *The Qumran Community* (Cambridge: Cambridge University Press, 1987).

32. Indeed, once the principle is established, its application could be world-wide. Thus the later Rabbis in Babylon could simultaneously decree the world outside the Holy Land to be unclean with corpse-uncleanness and continue their liturgical rites within that world. It need therefore come as no surprise that Paul could be both a Tarsian and a Pharisee.

liturgy. Sacred space and sacred time now pervade the whole of life.

Such democratization of the liturgy has paradoxical results. Not only does it widen the worshipper's experience of sacred space; it also reduces the significance of the archetypal sacred space, at least in principle. For if everywhere is as holy as the Sanctuary, then the Sanctuary is no more holy than anywhere else.[33] We should not assume, however, that such attitudes in general led to other institutions being viewed as rivals to the Jerusalem Temple. The application of Temple-imagery to buildings such as synagogues appears to be later;[34] and apart from the Samaritan case even the other Jewish temples do not appear to have been seen in this light.[35] What we might expect, however, is that the Jerusalem Temple becomes an ideal, a part of the intellectual furniture, a spiritual rather than geographical centre to the faith; and that particularly for those who for whatever reason live away from the Holy City. Indeed, when God is not seen as in any sense localized in the Temple (not even by the presence of the Shekinah) some such reinterpretation is imperative, and so for the Pharisee the Temple and its ritual become the models for that holiness which now pervades all of life.[36]

One final feature of the Second Temple may not be insignificant for our purposes. Josephus, *Ant.* 20.219, dates the comple-

33. And so in the Apocalypse of John there is no need for a Temple at all, ὁ γὰρ κύριος ὁ θεὸς ὁ παντοκράτωρ ναὸς αὐτῆς ἐστιν καὶ τὸ ἀρνίον. Here, doubtless in the light of conflict between Jew and Christian, the spiritualization is set in opposition to the physical.
34. See Strange, 'Archaeology', pp. 656f., on the plainness of the Second-Temple synagogues: 'In terms of its archaeology... early synagogue Judaism in the Land stands in stark contrast to Temple Judaism...'
35. See Stone, *Scriptures, Sects and Visions*, who notes how for instance the Elephantine community appealed to both Jerusalem and Samaria for assistance. The Temple tax provided a concrete means for diaspora Jews to identify with the Jerusalem Temple.
36. J. Neusner (*The Rabbinic Traditions about the Pharisees before 70* [Leiden: Brill, 1971]), notes how 'purity' is the main concern of the traditions which survive from this period, a purity clearly seen in a religious perspective, hence holiness. It is worth emphasizing that contracting impurity is inevitable since it is often involuntary; and that much of the Temple ritual serves precisely to remove it.

tion of the Temple to about AD 63, so that Herod's reconstruction work was still in progress at the time that Paul was active.

2. *The Temple in Paul's Thinking*

As a self-proclaimed Pharisee (Phil. 3.5) Paul may presumably be identified with the pattern of belief sketched above. The fit seems good.[37] He uses of himself priestly language which would have been abhorrent had there been any intention to take it at all literally. Although he sees nothing unusual in his own statement that there was a lapse of at least fourteen years between two visits to the Holy City (*ergo*, to the Temple), Jerusalem clearly remains of religious significance to him.[38] However one rates Luke as an historian, there is at least nothing incongruous or implausible in his picture of a Paul who rejects the observance of the Torah as a condition for his converts, while both remaining a Pharisee[39] and continuing to worship in the Temple. Paul's debt to his background[40] scarcely needs defending.

Let us then turn to 1 Corinthians 3, to see what light an awareness of Paul's Pharisaism might shed on his argument.

9   θεοῦ γάρ ἐσμεν συνεργοί· θεοῦ γεώργιον, θεοῦ οἰκοδομή ἐστε.

37. There is of course one major area in which we see a radical departure from his former thinking, as Barrett highlights: 'Paul is nowhere more un-Jewish than in this μηδὲν ἀνακρίνοντες. His whole life as a Pharisee had been essentially one of ἀνάκρισις, not least into foods' ('Things Sacrificed to Idols', *NTS* 11 [1964–65], pp. 138-53 [146]). But it is unfair to conclude, as Barrett does, that Paul had therefore ceased to be a Jew (*ibid.* and in his *1 Corinthians, ad* 9.20f.; 10.25). He remains a Jew—even remains a Pharisee—but with this extra factor in his thinking: that in Christ all is made pure.
38. The collection witnesses to a concern not just for the nation but also for the focal point of its faith. In Gal. 4 the present Jerusalem is in bondage; but only because (as with the Temple) the concept of the true Jerusalem has been transferred to the Church.
39. The function of Acts 26.5 can scarcely be to deny that he is now a Pharisee, otherwise the argument falls to the ground.
40. Given the nature of our sources, almost every modern work on Paul and Judaism is effectively a study of the relationship between Paul and *Pharisaism*.

10 κατὰ τὴν χάριν τοῦ θεοῦ τὴν δοθεῖσάν μοι ὡς σοφὸς ἀρχιτέκτων θεμέλιον ἔθηκα, ἄλλος δὲ ἐποικοδομεῖ. ἕκαστος δὲ βλεπέτω πῶς ἐποικοδομεῖ·
11 θεμέλιον γὰρ ἄλλον οὐδεὶς δύναται θεῖναι παρὰ τὸν κείμενον, ὅς ἐστιν Ἰησοῦς Χριστός.
12 εἰ δέ τις ἐποικοδομεῖ ἐπὶ τὸν θεμέλιον χρυσόν, ἄργυρον, λίθους τιμίους, ξύλα, χόρτον, καλάμην,
13 ἑκάστου τὸ ἔργον φανερὸν γενήσεται, ἡ γὰρ ἡμέρα δηλώσει· ὅτι ἐν πυρὶ ἀποκαλύπτεται, καὶ ἑκάστου τὸ ἔργον ὁποῖόν ἐστιν τὸ πῦρ ὑαὐτὸρ[41] δοκιμάσει.
14 εἴ τινος τὸ ἔργον μενεῖ ὃ ἐποικοδόμησεν, μισθὸν λήμψεται·
15 εἴ τινος τὸ ἔργον κατακαήσεται, ζημιωθήσεται, αὐτὸς δὲ σωθήσεται, οὕτως δὲ ὡς διὰ πυρός.
16 οὐκ οἴδατε ὅτι ναὸς θεοῦ ἐστε καὶ τὸ πνεῦμα τοῦ θεοῦ οἰκεῖ ἐν ὑμῖν;
17 εἴ τις τὸν ναὸν τοῦ θεοῦ φθείρει, φθερεῖ τοῦτον ὁ θεός· ὁ γὰρ ναὸς τοῦ θεοῦ ἅγιός ἐστιν, οἵτινές ἐστε ὑμεῖς.
18 μηδεὶς ἑαυτὸν ἐξαπατάτω· εἴ τις δοκεῖ σοφὸς εἶναι ἐν ὑμῖν ἐν τῷ αἰῶνι τούτῳ, μωρὸς γενέσθω, ἵνα γένηται σοφός.
19 ἡ γὰρ σοφία τοῦ κόσμου τούτου μωρία παρὰ τῷ θεῷ ἐστιν· γέγραπται γάρ, ὁ δρασσόμενος τοὺς σοφοὺς ἐν τῇ πανουργίᾳ αὐτῶν.

The juxtaposition of gardening to building in v. 9 looks harsh at first sight, though there are enough examples of the two ideas in parallel to render it unremarkable,[42] particularly if the concept of the church as the Temple was already in the

41. *Om* P46 א D Ψ m latt.
42. καὶ κληθήσονται γενεαὶ δικαιοσύνης, φύτευμα κυρίου εἰς δόξαν. καὶ *οἰκοδομήσουσιν* ἐρήμους αἰωνίας, ἐξηρημωμένας πρότερον ἐξαναστήσουσιν (Isa. 61.3f.); *οἰκοδομήσατε* οἴκους καὶ κατοικήσατε καὶ *φυτεύσατε* παραδείσους καὶ φάγετε τοὺς καρποὺς αὐτῶν (Jer. 36.5; cf. v. 28); Ἐὰν καθίσαντες καθίσητε ἐν τῇ γῇ ταύτῃ, *οἰκοδομήσω* ὑμᾶς καὶ οὐ μὴ καθέλω καὶ *φυτεύσω* ὑμᾶς καὶ οὐ μὴ ἐκτίλω (Jer. 49.10); καὶ *κατοικήσουσιν* ἐπ᾽ αὐτῆς ἐν ἐλπίδι καὶ *οἰκοδομήσουσιν* οἰκίας καὶ *φυτεύσουσιν* ἀμπελῶνας καὶ *κατοικήσουσιν* ἐν ἐλπίδι, ὅταν ποιήσω κρίμα ἐν πᾶσιν τοῖς ἀτιμάσασιν αὐτοὺς ἐν τοῖς κύκλῳ αὐτῶν (Ezek. 28.26; note the possibility of eschatological interpretation of this passage); οὐ *φυτεύσεις* σεαυτῷ ἄλσος, πᾶν ξύλον παρὰ τὸ θυσιαστήριον κυρίου τοῦ θεοῦ σου οὐ ποιήσεις σεαυτῷ (Deut. 16.21); τί οὖν λεκτέον; ὅτι πρέπει τῷ θεῷ *φυτεύειν* καὶ *οἰκοδομεῖν* ἐν ψυχῇ τὰς ἀρετάς. φίλαυτος δὲ καὶ ἄθεος ὁ νοῦς οἰόμενος ἴσος εἶναι θεῷ καὶ ποιεῖν, δοκῶν ἐν τῷ πάσχειν ἐξεταζόμενος (Philo, *Leg. All.* 1.48). These, and other passages cited in this article, were identified with the help of an Ibycus Scholarly Computer searching the corpus of the *Thesaurus Linguae Graecae.*

forefront of Paul's mind. Several factors combine to suggest that this was in fact the case.

1. The presence of God in or among his people, while not demanding the application of Temple-imagery, certainly predisposes towards it. We need only note how the two go together in 2 Cor. 6.15 and 3.16. Thus the fact that Paul has already affirmed the presence of God in the community[43] makes plausible the suggestion that the οἰκοδομή should be seen from the start as a Temple. Certainly, as soon as Paul asks himself *what* God is building, there can be very few options for the answer. Not only is the Temple the defining focus of all sacred space, but for a Pharisee the faithful are seen as a kingdom of priests, and where else should priests be found?

2. The analogy is not so uncommon as to be unexpected. It is found elsewhere in the early Christian tradition[44] and probably also in the Qumran writings.[45] More significantly, it occurs later on in this very epistle, but applied in a different way. If it were not already a part of Paul's conceptual furniture, then this double coining would manifest an unprecedented mental fecundity. But the οὐκ οἴδατε in each case suggests rather that the image was assumed by Paul to be already familiar— which suggests that it did not just occur to him as he began to pen v. 16. If, as some suppose, 2 Cor. 6.13–7.1 represents a fragment of an earlier letter, we need look no further to discover why Paul might assume their knowledge of the idea.

3. The fact that Paul sees no need to defend or explain the analogy when he comes to it, despite the fact that his subsequent argument depends on its acceptability, suggests that he knew it to be uncontentious.

4. The vocabulary used by Paul even before v. 16 suggests that the Temple is in mind. Paul describes his own role as that

---

43. Cf. 2.12ff.

44. 1 Pet. 2 uses a text also dear to Paul. See McKelvey for a fuller discussion.

45. See B. Gärtner, *The Temple and the Community in Qumran and the New Testament* (Cambridge: Cambridge University Press, 1965); Knibb, *The Qumran Community*, though the discovery of the Temple Scroll perhaps makes such an interpretation of the Qumran attitude less certain. See Mr Sweet's essay in this volume.

of a σοφὸς ἀρχιτέκτων. This, while not a technical term,[46] clearly indicates that something more than a private dwelling[47] is in mind. He also refers to the ἔργον of the builders, to φθορά and ζημία. In a recent article J. Shanor argues that this reflects the 'standardized and conservative' vocabulary of ancient building-contracts for temples.[48] One might argue that such contracts are not specific to *temple* construction, but Paul clearly has a religious, not to say cultic, edifice in view. Then there are the building materials. Again, the comparable OT language would lead us to think in terms of the Temple.[49] If so an interesting point emerges. Commentators generally assume that Paul contrasts two sets of triads, the first proper building materials, the second not.[50] The major problem with such an approach is of course that wood is a much more reasonable building material than gold for the average building, even for the rich, and thatch must have been a common

---

46. The only other instances of this phrase in the CD-ROM corpus of the *Thesaurus Linguae Graecae* are: ταῦτα μὲν δὴ θεμελίων τρόπον προκαταβεβλήσθω, τὰ δὲ ἄλλα τοῖς σοφῆς ἀρχιτέκτονος, ἀλληγορίας ἑπόμενοι παραγγέλμασιν ἐποικοδομῶμεν (Philo, *Somn.* 2.8); and ὡς οὖν εἶδε τόπον εὐφυΐᾳ διαφέροντα... εἰπών ὡς "Ομηρος ἦν ἄρα τά τ' ἄλλα θαυμαστὸς καὶ σοφώτατος ἀρχιτέκτων, ἐκέλευσε διαγράψαι τὸ σχῆμα τῆς πόλεως (Plutarch, *Alex.* 26.7).

47. Cf. Barrett's 'his own badly-constructed house' in his commentary on v. 15.

48. J. Shanor, 'Paul as Master Builder', *NTS* 34 (1988), pp. 461-71. The phrase 'standardized and conservative' occurs in footnote 1.

49. καὶ ἰδοὺ ἐγὼ κατὰ τὴν πτωχείαν μου ἡτοίμασα εἰς οἶκον κυρίου χρυσίου ταλάντων ἑκατὸν χιλιάδας καὶ ἀργυρίου ταλάντων χιλίας χιλιάδας καὶ χαλκὸν καὶ σίδηρον, οὗ οὐκ ἔστιν σταθμός, ὅτι εἰς πλῆθός ἐστιν· καὶ ξύλα καὶ λίθους ἡτοίμασα, καὶ πρὸς ταῦτα πρόσθες. καὶ μετὰ σοῦ εἰς πλῆθος ποιούντων ἔργα τεχνῖται καὶ οἰκοδόμοι λίθων καὶ τέκτονες ξύλων καὶ πᾶς σοφὸς ἐν παντὶ ἔργῳ. ἐν χρυσίῳ, ἐν ἀργυρίῳ, ἐν χαλκῷ καὶ ἐν σιδήρῳ οὐκ ἔστιν ἀριθμός (1 Chron. 22.14-16); κατὰ πᾶσαν τὴν δύναμιν ἡτοίμακα εἰς οἶκον θεοῦ μου χρυσίον, ἀργύριον, χαλκόν, σίδηρον, ξύλα, λίθους σοομ καὶ πληρώσεως καὶ λίθους πολυτελεῖς καὶ ποικίλους καὶ πάντα λίθον τίμιον καὶ πάριον πολύν. καὶ ἔτι ἐν τῷ εὐδοκῆσαί με ἐν οἴκῳ θεοῦ μου ἔστιν μοι ὃ περιπεποίημαι χρυσίον καὶ ἀργύριον (1 Chron. 29.2-3). This is a more plausible supposition than Conzelmann's 'fabulous building' (*in loc.*).

50. To Godet the contrast is between the houses of the rich ('Oriental palaces and temples presented to the eye only the most precious materials') and the houses of the poor.

roofing.[51] Only for a temple would this particular list make sense:[52] Paul's implication that 'wood, hay and stubble' are unacceptable materials would else fail.

5. The building is to be tested by fire, a standard part of the imagery specifically linked to eschatology.[53] Although it is admittedly the *work* rather than the building which is tested by fire, it may be significant that the only edifice mentioned in heavenly visions is, of course, the Temple.

It therefore seems not unreasonable to suppose that the image of the church as the Temple of God has shaped Paul's conception of θεοῦ οἰκοδομή from the outset. Certainly, had he used the phrase οἶκος θεοῦ in v. 9, few would have doubted that he had the Temple in mind. But he inverts the order and uses οἰκοδομή. The word-order is dictated by the parallel with θεοῦ γάρ ἐσμεν συνεργοί[54] and for our purposes is thus of little significance. Is it possible that οἰκοδομή could be used to express that part of the semantic range of οἶκος which approx-

51. Cf. *Historia Alexandri Magni, Recensio* ε, 33.9.

52. Cf. Bengel, *ad loc.*, who misses the LXX allusion in the λίθους τιμίους but comments on the ξύλα, 'In mundo multa recte aedificantur ex ligno; sed non in aedificatione Dei', and compares Rev. 21.18f. That ξύλα is included in the materials for the Temple is a slight problem, but Galen, *De simplicium medicamentorum temperamentis ac facultatibus* 11.672 includes χόρτον, καλάμοι and ξύλα in a list of dry things, suggesting that their collocation is at least a natural one.

53. From Mal. 3.19 on. It is also part of Stoic belief; cf. Cicero, *De natura deorum* 2.118. Some of Paul's words are found (in different order) in *T. Abr.* 13.13, and C.W. Fishburne ('1 Corinthians iii.10-15 and the Testament of Abraham', *NTS* 17 [1969-70], pp. 109-15) supposes direct dependence. But apart from problems of dating, more obvious sources lie closer at hand. If 2 Thessalonians is authentic, then the idea of eschatological fire is integral to Paul's gospel (cf. esp. 2.5!). Hence we may agree with Conzelmann that Paul is 'not painting an apocalyptic scene' without denying the existence of apocalyptic imagery here.

54. Where the order clearly indicates emphasis, though we cannot simply assume that the emphasized word is the first (*pace* many commentators, e.g. G.D. Fee who asserts: 'the emphasis is altogether on God'). See my 'Word-Order and Emphasis', in F. Poswick (ed.), *Bible et Informatique: Méthodes, outils, résultats* (Genève: Slatkine, 1989).

imates to 'dwelling-place'? The answer may well be Yes,[55] though such a strong condition is not necessary for the argument presented here. We need only suppose that it could serve as a half-way point: in Paul's mind but not yet expressed. If he wished to couple with the Temple-idea his picture of the continuing work of the labourers (as in the picture of the γεώρ-γιον), his choice of the term οἰκοδομή is scarcely surprising.

What then are Paul's intentions and strategy? For most of 1.10–3.8 he has been defending his own position on the Faith and the status of its ministers. Up to this point there has been no instruction specifically addressed to the reader since 1.10;[56] but now there are both direct and indirect appeals for action.[57] Most commentators see these as addressing a variety of issues in Paul's agenda, notably that of σοφία,[58] but it may be that he is more single-minded. 3.10-12 emphasizes the importance of building on the right foundation, that of the person of Jesus;[59] and 3.18-21 specifies the false σοφία of the congregation as boasting ἐν ἀνθρώποις. In 4.5-7 the 'judging' which is condemned consists at least in part of choosing one over against another; and the final request is to follow Paul himself, and to support the power of the gospel over against mere words. Taken together, these passages strongly suggest that Paul's overriding concern remains that of the factions and their attitudes to the figureheads. If so, it would not be unreasonable to suppose that the attack on σοφία is an implicit attack on one of the factions—not, probably, on the figurehead himself[60] but on

---

55. Note especially the phrase τὰς οἰκοδομὰς τοῦ ἱεροῦ in Mt. 24.1, though the plural here may (as it would in English) modify the semantic range.

56. 1.26 is scarcely an exception.

57. 3.10-12, 18-21; 4.5-7, 16-21.

58. See e.g. Fee for one such approach, and details of others.

59. Fee implies that the question of the foundation has become unimportant by 3.12, which makes Paul's emphasis on it somewhat strange, and by neat sleight-of-hand redefines the foundation as 'the gospel itself, with its basic content of salvation through Jesus Christ' (p. 139). This allows him to add 'we may rightly assume that he intends them to hear "Jesus Christ and him crucified"' (*ibid.*) and in a footnote to claim that this is 'more in keeping with the context of the argument as a whole'. The larger 'whole' suggests otherwise.

60. Paul has already said that he and Apollos share a common goal in vv. 5-8; it is implausible in the extreme, therefore, to suppose that he

the attitude of those within the Corinthian church who attached themselves to him. It is remarkable that this factionalism is viewed by Paul as the greatest of the problems in Corinth,[61] and Welborn[62] thinks it represents to Paul 'a mirror of the cosmic conflict between the rulers of this age and the power of God'. That may be, though more prosaic possibilities lie closer at hand.[63] If Paul saw himself threatened by the Apollos-group then the Temple-image provided an ideal instrument for defusing the situation and developing his argument. By focusing on the self-identity of the church as the worshipping community, this model allows him to shift the focus of attention from the activities of the figurehead apostles to those of the local leaders who are causing the factions, and to move from defence to attack.[64] In three conditional clauses Paul presents his readers with three possible options: building with permanent materials and receiving due payment,

---

believed that Apollos had presented himself as in any way a rival (see G. Sellin, 'Das "Geheimnis" der Weisheit und das Rätsel der "Christuspartei" (zu 1 Kor 1–4)', *ZNW* 73 [1982], pp. 69-96). Not so does Paul deal with heresiarchs! Given that the issue focuses on supposed 'wisdom' and hardly at all on identifiably Jewish issues, it is also improbable that the opponent in view is Cephas (see P. Vielhauer, 'Paulus und die Kephaspartei in Korinth', *NTS* 21 [1974–75], pp. 341-52). The Corinthians would certainly be justified in seeking more concrete indications of how Peter could be accused of building on a different foundation before renouncing his leadership.

61. Not only does he tackle it first, and at great length, but the implicit warning in 3.17 is more severe than any other addressed to Christians, and comparable only with the attitude to Jewish opponents in 1 Thess. 2.16. *Pace* Héring, it is less likely that Paul's mind has already run on to the problems of chs. 5 and 6, given that the warnings there are far less severe.

62. L.L. Welborn, 'On the Discord in Corinth: 1 Corinthians 1–4 and Ancient Politics', *JBL* 106 (1987), pp. 85-111 (109).

63. Throughout his commentary (though not, remarkably, at this point) Fee presents the view that the whole of 1 Corinthians is an apologetic letter of defence in the face of a personal attack on his credentials.

64. Several scholars see little significance in Paul's change to this particular image; cf. McKelvey, *New Temple*, 99: it is 'by way of intensifying his warning'; and Fishburne, '1 Corinthians iii'. Fee rightly notes the changed function of the argument, though differing from the position argued here.

building with impermanent materials[65] and being fined, or damaging the very Temple of God[66] and suffering destruction.

Given the significance which Paul has placed on the one foundation laid by himself, it is likely that this third option corresponds to attempting to lay, or build upon, another foundation. In the application of the analogy this would mean enticing Christians away from Jesus Christ to follow instead those who assembled themselves under a figurehead as teacher of σοφία.[67]

We may therefore surmise the following strategy in this passage. By means of somewhat forced discourse links, Paul combines a number of ideas which easily cohere around the central concept of a Temple: the importance of building with appropriate materials, the significance of its uniqueness as the *locus* for true worship, the fearsomeness of the sanction against damaging this work of God, the demand for holiness. So without the need for specific accusations his implied threat allows him to move toward correcting the situation while avoiding explicit censure of named individuals.[68] By not identifying the tenor of his metaphor Paul also leaves the threat numinously open-ended. Coupled with the following μηδεὶς ἑαυτὸν ἐξαπατάτω it invites the reader to consider all possible ways in which he might be harming the church and its worship. It therefore provides a possible basis for the specific issues to be tackled later[69] while affirming in the strongest possible terms Paul's anathema on all who encourage or even tolerate partisanship or schism. In our world of denominationalism

---

65. Paul's point seems to be not so much that the materials are *shoddy* (see above at note 51) as that they are *inappropriate* for this particular building.
66. See Shanor, 'Master Builder', p. 462, for this sense of φθείρειν.
67. Fee interprets the argument in terms of σοφία itself rather than the factions; but the latter makes more natural sense of Paul's points.
68. It is noteworthy that Paul rarely names those he attacks, however explicit his attack may otherwise be (Euodia and Syntyche are remarkable exceptions). In a shame-culture this is an important way of preserving face all round.
69. Though when the image of Temple is resumed in ch. 6, it is in a very different way.

where we can complacently say, I am of Cranmer, and I of Luther,[70] perhaps we need to hear Paul's words afresh.

One of my first assignments when a raw undergraduate in the Divinity Faculty was an essay on early liturgy for Dr Bammel. As representatives of two very different traditions we met each other with (on my side at least) a deal of suspicion and uncertainty. I trust that I have learned somewhat since, and that in this return to issues cultic and liturgical I may have demonstrated something of my debt to a teacher who helped me in my own attempts to build on the one Foundation.

לחיים!

70. Or even suppose that we solve the problem by uniting just a few of the denominations while leaving others outside.

HEBREWS AND THE SECOND TEMPLE

Barnabas Lindars, S.S.F.

I

The temple in Jerusalem is not mentioned in Hebrews. This is strange, because the argument of the whole epistle turns on the contrast between the sacrifice of Christ and the sacrificial ordinances of the law of Moses. Detailed references are made to priesthood and sacrifice, but these (with one possible exception)[1] are always taken from Exodus and Leviticus. The place of worship is always denoted by the terminology of the tent in the wilderness.

This observation has been taken as a factor in determining the date and provenance of Hebrews, and also has a bearing on the basis of interpretation of the theology of the letter as a whole. With regard to the date, it is frequently argued that Hebrews must have been written after AD 70. The temple would surely have been mentioned rather than the tent, if actual ceremonies were referred to. The descriptions are entirely theoretical, and no attempt is made to relate them to actual practice. On the other side it is pointed out that Hebrews uses the present tense, so that he does not suggest that the sacrifices are now obsolete. But this argument does not carry much weight, because the Mishnah tends to slip into timeless present when describing what was formerly done in the tem-

---

1. The mention of the ashes of a heifer in 9.13 is out of line with the rest of the context, where all details belong to the Day of Atonement, as prescribed in Leviticus 16. But according to Maimonides (*Mishneh Torah* 8.8.1.4) it was customary for the high priest to be cleansed with water containing the ashes on two days during the week before the Day of Atonement. This connection between the ashes, prescribed at Num. 19.9, and the Day of Atonement is confirmed by *m. Parah* 3.1, among other earlier sources.

ple. Thus this consideration is inconclusive, and ought to be left out of the discussion. It does, however, point to the ambiguity of the argument, because the reason why the temple is not referred to must still be explained, whether Hebrews was written before the destruction or not. In fact a good case can be made for the decision to refer only to the provisions of the Law on the grounds that the author needed to contrast sacrifice under the old covenant with the sacrifice of Jesus, which inaugurates the new covenant. Thus his argument required attention to the Law which gives the theoretical basis for sacrifice rather than the temple in which it was currently put into practice.

Similarly, the exclusively theoretical and scriptural references to sacrifice have been taken as evidence that either the author or the group of readers whom he seeks to correct, has no interest in the historical temple (whether it is still standing or not), but wishes to spiritualize the Law as the basis of divine knowledge. In this case the theology of Hebrews is related to some form of incipient Gnosticism. Käsemann argued that this was the position of the author himself, who used the Law to commend the Christian life as the soul's heavenly pilgrimage.[2] Koester maintained that this was the false idea held by the readers, who failed to take into account the implications of the sacrificial death of Jesus.[3] In either case the argument of Hebrews is held to have no relation to the historical temple, even if it is regarded as still standing at the time when the letter was written.

The traditional interpretation of Hebrews, however, assumes that the temple is still in full operation, and claims that the whole object of the author is to prevent the readers from denying their newly acquired Christian faith and reverting to Jewish worship. This I believe to be basically correct, though it needs some modification. I have argued elsewhere[4] that the real problem is that the readers are deeply troubled by the con-

2. E. Käsemann, *Das wandernde Gottesvolk* (Göttingen, 1958).
3. H. Koester, *Introduction to the New Testament* (Philadelphia, 1982), II, pp. 272-76.
4. B. Lindars, 'The Rhetorical Structure of Hebrews', *NTS* 35 (1989), pp. 382-406; *The Theology of the Letter to the Hebrews* (Cambridge, forthcoming).

sciousness of sin (9.9; 10.2). Though at their conversion (2.2-4; 10.32-34; 13.7) they had received the 'foundation of repentance from dead works and of faith towards God' (6.1), they were not prepared for the possibility of falling into sin in the interval before the parousia, which they were led to believe was imminent (10.25, 37). Now that this has happened, they are at a loss to find anything in their Christian practice which can put them right with God. We have to remember that feelings of guilt involve the emotions, and require some form of practical expression. In these circumstances there would be a strong pressure from within themselves to resort to the Jewish methods of atonement which have served them in the past.

If this is correct, the problem of Hebrews' total failure to mention the temple and the existing cultus becomes more acute. I shall suggest, however, that there are good reasons for the omission, and that it does not preclude the supposition that the temple held a very strong place in the emotions of the readers before their conversion, even if (as seems probable) they live far away from it in the Diaspora. Such is the hold of the temple on their imagination that they are bound to look longingly at their past association with it when faced with the problem of the need for atonement for their sins. I shall try to show that there are good grounds to claim that Hebrews is a valuable addition to the sources which have a bearing on Jewish attitudes to the temple in New Testament times.

This essay is offered with respect and friendship to Ernst Bammel, and can suitably start with a reference to a brief article in which he has given eloquent expression of the regard in which the temple was held by Diaspora Jews, entitled 'Nicanor and his Gate'.[5] This is concerned with the identity of the man who presented the famous doors of a gateway on the east side of the temple as rebuilt by Herod the Great.[6] These doors were made of bronze, which shone like gold, and inspired

5. E. Bammel, 'Nicanor and his Gate', *JJS* 7 (1956), pp. 77-78 (reprinted in *idem, Judaica: Kleine Schriften*, I [WUNT 37; Tübingen, 1986], pp. 39-41).
6. This need not be referred to as the 'third' temple for our present purpose, as the rebuilding incorporated at least part of the second temple and the worship continued without a break, so that it was to all intents and purposes the same.

Tiberius Julius Alexander, the alabarch of Alexandria, to overlay all the other doors of the temple gates with silver and gold. Nicanor also came from Egypt, and the story is told that the precious doors were made there and were nearly lost in transit. A great storm blew up, and the sailors hurled one of the doors into the sea to lighten the ship. Nicanor then offered to go overboard himself with the second one, but at that moment the storm suddenly ceased. On arrival at Joppa the other door was found under the ship unharmed. Bammel suggests that Nicanor's offer was a gesture of despair, as the doors represented all his spare wealth. He identifies Nicanor with an Egyptian merchant, whose correspondence with Marcus Julius Alexander (probably a son of Tiberius Julius Alexander) has come to light in the papyri. Nicanor is likely to have been a proselyte, who showed his enthusiasm for his new faith by means of a costly gift to the temple, and he no doubt planned to end his days in Jerusalem in strict observance of the Law, like Queen Helen of Adiabene.[7] His donation was made some time before AD 50.

II

We must now look at the situation of the readers of Hebrews in more detail, so as to gauge more accurately their relationship with the temple. I have suggested above that the real issue is the need felt by these Christians for an objective practice of purification from sin. Possibly on account of the delay of the parousia they have lost confidence in their relationship with God through Christ because of the barrier erected by post-baptismal sin. They need a method of atonement which can put right their day-to-day sins and remove the recurring sense of guilt. Their Christian practice appears to make no provision for this. So they are tempted to resume the methods of atonement provided by the Law which they had previously practised. This need not entail denial of their Christian faith, because they could still accept that the sacrifice of Christ is the starting point of their relationship with God, and will be the

7. Josephus, *Ant.* 20.49-53, 95.

decisive factor at the coming judgment. The problem is how to cope with sin in the present.

But for the leaders of the Hebrews church (13.17) their return to Jewish practices, involving some degree of re-admission to the Jewish community which they had left on becoming Christians, is a fatal step and is bound to lead to apostasy (6.4-6). It seems that the Hebrews church required a complete break from the synagogue from the beginning. This may be referred to in 10.32-34, describing the hardships which followed on their conversion, including imprisonment of some members and confiscation of property. Both could be due to the disruption within families caused by the uncompromising position taken up by the founders of the Hebrews church (2.3-4; 13.7), who may well have been a group of Hellenistic Jewish converts from the community around Stephen at Jerusalem (Acts 6.8-14; 8.1, 4).

It is not clear how far the first Christians maintained the Jewish laws in relation to purity. Hengel has argued that they regarded the atonement sacrifices as superseded by the sacrifice of Christ from the first.[8] Acts tends to show a law-abiding attitude on the part of Jewish Christians. Paul is willing to compromise for the sake of the common life in mixed congregations. The one thing which he will not allow under any circumstances is that Gentile converts should be required to Judaize. It is obvious, however, that a Jewish-Christian group which repudiates the laws of purity must involve a sharper break with Judaism than might occur in other circumstances.

The above scenario for Hebrews explains the two special points which are central to the argument of the letter and are reinforced with the most solemn warnings (6.4-12; 10.26-31). These are the two facts that (a) the death of Christ as a sacrifice for sin is the sacrifice of the new covenant, which renders the sacrifices under the Law of the old covenant obsolete; and (b) the sacrifice of Christ is permanently effective, so that nothing else needs to be done to cope with sin in the present, in spite of the delay of the parousia. This leaves the practical difficulty, that Christianity has no specific means of dealing with day-to-day sins, unresolved. In my view Hebrews provides the

8. M. Hengel, *The Atonement* (London, 1981), p. 56.

answer to this problem in its concept of the life of faith, which has its practical expression in the 'sacrifice of praise' of the Christian liturgy (10.23-25, 39; 13.15-16).

If the above interpretation of Hebrews is correct, it can be assumed that the converts are Hellenistic Jews, probably in the Diaspora, who have been brought up to hold the Jerusalem temple in great veneration, and would see Nicanor's costly gift of doors of bronze as an outstanding example of personal devotion. For such people the sheer fact of the existence of the temple and its cultus was deeply meaningful. They felt that they had a personal stake in it through their annual payment of the half shekel tax (Exod. 30.13). Though they might go to the temple only rarely, if ever, they could pay for sacrifices to be offered there in connection with personal vows. The synagogues in the Diaspora provided meetings designed to help the sense of solidarity with the worship of the temple. Especially at festival times Diaspora Jews could feel that they were part of what was going on through dinner parties held at the synagogues.[9]

These things were not forgotten when they accepted Christian faith. No doubt their conversion was accompanied by a strong emotional impulse, which at the time made it easy to put aside their feeling for the temple, as they now looked to Jesus, the pioneer and perfecter of their faith (12.2), and acknowledged that here they had no lasting city, but they sought the city which is to come (13.14). But the problem of atonement for daily sins suggests that they have now lost their first confidence and no longer have the conviction that they will always be able to resist temptation. Of course it was a mistake to think that they would be able to do so, but such confidence is a well-known feature of the experience of those who have undergone religious conversion, and indeed converts to a new cause often maintain an exceptionally high standard of moral purity for a considerable time. The author of Hebrews, however, is sufficiently experienced to know that this cannot be kept up for ever. In spite of his reputation as a rigorist, he does know that people are bound to fall into sin from time to

9. E. Schürer, *The History of the Jewish People in the Age of Jesus Christ*, III/1 (rev. edn; Edinburgh, 1986), pp. 144-45.

time, and he is prepared to deal with them with sensitivity and pastoral care. His ideal of the merciful high priest (2.17; 4.14-16; 5.2) is paralleled in contemporary Jewish sources, and owes something to meditation on the Jesus tradition, notably the Gethsemane tradition.[10] But it very likely also reflects his own pastoral caring, as one who knows that sins are bound to occur (12.1-11) and wants to help the leaders of the Hebrews church in the exercise of their spiritual responsibility (13.17).

Furthermore there can be no denying the fact that the readers of Hebrews are expected to be familiar with the laws of the Pentateuch in the Septuagint version. However, it does not follow from this that the temple is no longer standing, or that they have no interest in it. What it does suggest is that both author and readers took it for granted that the temple and its worship corresponded with the pentateuchal laws. We shall see also that the argument of Hebrews requires attention to the laws because it is concerned with the revealed will of God. The worship of the temple puts the laws into practice, but it is the laws which are primary from this point of view, and it is to them that recourse should be made to discover what constitutes an atonement sacrifice.

Finally, though the date of Hebrews is a question which lies outside the scope of this essay, the onus of proof must be on those who support a date later than the destruction of the temple in AD 70. Whereas a reference to this event can be detected in Mt. 22.7, Lk. 21.20 and Jn 11.48, there is no such possible allusion in Hebrews. Nevertheless the argument of the letter would have gained greatly in force if the author had been in a position to mention it. For these Christians are not indifferent to the fate of the temple. On the other hand, for the author the temple is part of the whole structure of the old covenant which 'is becoming obsolete and... ready to vanish away' (8.13). It would have been an irresistible impulse to point out that the temple, sacrifices and priesthood had all ceased to exist, if that had already happened. What better sign could there be that the old covenant was 'becoming obsolete'?

10. Cf. R.A. Stewart, 'The Sinless High-Priest', *NTS* 14 (1967–68), pp. 126-35; W. Horbury, 'The Aaronic Priesthood in the Epistle to the Hebrews', *JSNT* 19 (1983), pp. 43-71, esp. 59-66.

Hebrews would certainly see this as the work of God, preparing for the end.

III

Thus it comes about that, though the temple as such is never mentioned in Hebrews, there is a *prima facie* case for the assumption that the argument is conducted in full awareness of the importance of the sacrificial cultus at a time when it was still very much a going concern. It is simply taken for granted that the description of the tent and the regulations for sacrifice in Exodus and Leviticus apply to the present temple. It will now be shown that the existing temple is the real point of reference wherever the tent in the wilderness is mentioned, and similarly all references to priesthood and sacrifice are intended to be seen in relation to the actual practice of the temple service.

The situation in Hebrews is to some extent comparable to rabbinic references to the Second Temple, though the rabbinic discussions are expressly concerned with the conditions which used to obtain before the temple was destroyed. These conditions are often referred to in a timeless way when theoretical points are under consideration, so that the fact that they really refer to the past may seem to be forgotten. But this is not so in reality, and the text easily reverts to the past when the point at issue requires reference to actual practice.

It is also significant that the rabbinic descriptions do not list the laws which governed the conduct of the temple service, but explain how they were carried out in practice. The Mishnah is not *torah* but *halakah*. In the tractate *Yoma* the regulations of Leviticus 16 for the Day of Atonement are taken for granted throughout. The description gives a great deal of valuable detail about how they were carried out before the destruction. Further deductions are drawn from these statements in the Talmud. Sometimes the description drops into the language of the Pentateuch in a way which is not strictly applicable to the second temple. Thus in *m. Yoma* 5.1-4 the ark is mentioned several times in connection with the cleansing of the holy of holies, because it was notionally there. However 5.2 tells us that, since the loss of the ark at the Exile, the place was marked by a flat stone, called the *šetiyyah* ('foundation'). The further explanation in *y. Yoma* 5.42c, that it was so named because 'from it the world was founded', perhaps indicates that it was identified with the rock now protected by the Dome of the Rock.[11] Apart from this necessary deviation there is no suggestion that there could be any difference between the pentateuchal laws and the practice of the second temple.

It is also worth noting that, because the Day of Atonement involves the high priest in a complicated ceremonial duty which is done only once a year, and because (with frequent changes of high priest in New Testament times) this was often the first time in a particular high priest's experience, it was not expected that he would always get it exactly right. Provision is made to give him the help that is needed to perform such an unfamiliar action. In particular, if he makes a mistake he is to go back to the point where the error was made and repeat the action properly.[12] For a modern person the thought of interrupting an act of worship by going back and repeating part of it to get it right may seem grotesque. But the temple service depended on precise observance of the Law, and to leave a mistake uncorrected would be intolerable.

This fact illuminates the argument of Hebrews, because it reinforces the point made above that, to meet the need of the readers, the author must show that the death of Jesus actually satisfied the revealed requirements for an atonement sacrifice. Thus, uniquely in the New Testament,[13] the Day of Atonement

11. This might be the meaning of the text, even if the identification of the *šetiyyah* with the rock is wrong. The exact relation of the temple building to the rock remains an unsolved problem; cf. M. Avi-Yonah, 'Jerusalem of the Second Temple Period', in Y. Yadin (ed.), *Jerusalem Revealed* (New Haven and London, 1976), p. 13.

12. *M. Yoma* 5.7.

13. Paul's use of ἱλαστήριον in Rom. 3.25 has been taken since Origen to imply the use of the Day of Atonement in exposition of the death of Christ, but this depends on the doubtful suggestion that ἱλαστήριον means the mercy seat as in Exodus and Leviticus and Heb. 9.5. The only close parallel is *4 Macc.* 17.22, where it is used in a similarly metaphorical way to denote the martyr's death as a proptiatory sacrifice, and neither refers to the mercy seat nor makes allusion to the Day of Atonement. Most recently J.D.G. Dunn (*Romans* [Word Biblical Commentary; Waco, 1988], I, pp. 171-73) rejects 'mercy seat', but

is chosen as the basis of proof that the confession that 'Christ died for our sins according to the scriptures' (1 Cor. 15.3) can be substantiated. The Day of Atonement was the supreme annual ceremony of atonement in the temple. It also had great popularity as one of the most widely observed days of the calendar throughout the Jewish world. It was valued as the catch-all ceremony to atone for unatoned sins of the whole of the previous year. It was thus directly relevant to the problem of post-baptismal sins which caused so much distress to the persons addressed in Hebrews. No Jews could be unfamiliar with the central features of the ceremony, even if they never visited Jerusalem. The arrangements are briefly recalled in Heb. 9.1-5. Thereafter the author refers only to such details as are necessary to his exposition of the atoning efficacy of Christ's death.

The essential point for the argument of Hebrews is that the one historic sacrifice of Jesus has permanent efficacy, so that there is no longer any need for repeated acts of atonement to deal with sin. It is thus necessary to show that the death of Jesus fulfils the essentials for a sacrifice for sin, but also that it surpasses the limitations of the sacrifices prescribed under the old covenant. The author takes as his model the cleansing of the sanctuary on the Day of Atonement, which was done by the sacrifice of a bull on behalf of the high priest himself and the sacrifice of a goat on behalf of the people (both are alluded to in 9.12-13). In both cases the high priest performs the blood ritual in the holy of holies, and this is the only time in the whole year when the innermost sanctuary is entered. This act symbolizes direct access to God. It is important to remember that this is not a matter of typology, but the actual meaning of the rite, as the ark (or its substitute the šetiyyah) was the place where God had promised to meet with his people (Exod. 25.32). So also Jesus' death as a sacrifice fulfils this provision of the Law. Acting like the high priest, he sacrificed the victim (himself), and brought its blood into the holy of holies, inas-

retains the allusion to the Day of Atonement. But this reads far too much into the implications of one word. Paul's expression is sufficiently explained by the use of περὶ ἁμαρτίας in Isa. 53.10 and the clear allusion to Isa. 53.12 in Rom. 4.25.

much as through the shedding of his blood he entered into the presence of God in heaven. But unlike the ceremonial of the Day of Atonement, his entry into the sanctuary is permanent, so that there is no need to repeat the process, and all the sacrifices under the old covenant are rendered obsolete. This explains why Hebrews omits to mention the scapegoat, which vividly symbolizes the removal of the people's sins,[14] but does not lead to the concept of a permanent relationship with God.[15]

The contrast between obsolescence and permanence presupposes that the regulations for the Day of Atonement are not merely theoretical, but are carried out in practice (cf. 9.9). But there is a further practical side to the argument, in that these regulations provide the standard for the concept of atonement, the pattern to which the death of Jesus must conform, if it is to be regarded as an atoning sacrifice. In my view it is misleading to speak of this as typology, if by that is meant the observation of correspondences between the old covenant and the new. It is much more a matter of timeless concepts, the definition of the conditions which must be fulfilled if an action is to be regarded as an atonement sacrifice. The argument is essentially practical, because it is concerned with what needs to be done to effect the removal of sin for all time.

These facts provide the key for understanding the references to priesthood and sacrifice in Hebrews. Timeless references are based on the information given in the Pentateuch, but the author regards them as still (temporarily, 8.13) operative, and so he has in mind their practical contemporary expression in the service of the temple. There is no suggestion that the laws and the contemporary practice might differ, or that they belong to different orders of being. The fact that the Pentateuch refers to the tent in the wilderness presents no problem, because everyone knows that that was a temporary model and that the historical temple is the real thing. One can speak of the tent and mean the temple without fear of misunderstanding, because everyone makes the necessary mental adjustment automatically.

---

14. Cf. *m. Sheb.* 1.6; *m. Yoma* 6.2.
15. The scapegoat is first used as a type of Christ in *Barn.* 7.6-11.

So, when priesthood is mentioned for the first time in Heb. 2.19, the model which at once springs to mind is the ideal of priesthood in the service of the temple. At this very early stage in the argument of the epistle it is only a metaphor, and its full importance for the theology of Hebrews is not yet apparent. The idea of priesthood has, however, been already prepared for by the use of cultic language at the very beginning of the epistle, when the death of Jesus is briefly referred to in these words: 'When he had made purification for sins' (1.3). The use of καθαρισμὸς τῶν ἁμαρτιῶν in connection with the death of Jesus occurs in the New Testament only here and in 2 Pet. 1.9. The verb καθαρίζω nearly always carries with it either literal or metaphorical reference to cleansing by ceremonial washing rather than atonement as a result of sacrifice. But the sacrificial reference does appear in Tit. 2.14 and 1 Jn 1.7, 9, and possibly also Eph. 5.26. Hebrews uses καθαρίζω in 9.14, 22, 23; 10.2 in the context of the atoning effect of the blood ritual of the atonement sacrifices, which is fully achieved only in the death of Jesus. In view of the great importance of the ceremonial of the Day of Atonement for the central argument of Hebrews, it is not fanciful to see a deliberate allusion to it already in 1.3, and indeed a specific echo of Lev. 16.30, which sums up the whole purpose of the ceremony: ἐν γὰρ τῇ ἡμέρᾳ ταύτῃ ἐξιλάσεται περὶ ὑμῶν καθαρίσαι ὑμᾶς ἀπὸ πασῶν τῶν ἁμαρτιῶν ὑμῶν ἔναντι κυρίου, καὶ καθαρισθήσεσθε. The exact phrase as in 1.3 is found only in Exod. 30.10 with reference to the annual cleansing of the altar of incense (ἀπὸ τοῦ αἵματος τοῦ καθαρισμοῦ τῶν ἁμαρτιῶν τοῦ ἐξιλασμοῦ ἅπαξ τοῦ ἐνιαυτοῦ καθαριεῖ αὐτό).

Thus the cultic metaphor is applied to the sacrificial death of Jesus at the outset of the epistle. The context requires that it should be taken as a way of referring to his death, so that it is a condensed way of saying, 'When he had died a death which effected purification of sins for the people'. The phrase thus presupposes that the readers are fully aware of the basic proclamation that 'Christ died for our sins according to the scriptures' (1 Cor. 15.3), so that it is not even necessary to mention the death as such to convey the meaning. There is no risk that they might not understand the phrase (in spite of being 'dull of hearing' on this very issue, Heb. 5.11). No one would suppose that Jesus literally performed a cleansing ceremony before taking his seat on high. Moreover, as the Greek phrase is not commonly used as a technical term in Greek literature, there could be no mistaking the allusion to the cleansing ceremonies prescribed in the Jewish Law. The author can take it for granted that the readers will understand this. They would also know that cultic ceremonies of purification employing sacrificial blood were performed only by priests. Thus the mere assertion that Jesus 'made purification for sins' carries with it the implication that his death was a priestly act.

All this is expressed in 1.3 in only four Greek words, but they have been most carefully chosen to drop a hint, but at this stage no more than a hint, of the argument to be deployed later.[16] But although the next two chapters are concerned mainly with other matters of theology, which are necessary as the basis for the main argument later, the concept of atonement is not allowed to fall out of sight. So in 2.11 the author refers to the death of Jesus as an act of sanctification, pointing out that ὅ τε γὰρ ἁγιάζων καὶ οἱ ἁγιαζόμενοι ἐξ ἑνὸς πάντες. Though the verb ἁγιάζω is not necessarily sacrificial, denoting only transference of something to the sphere of the holy by contact with that which is holy, it can be deduced from 9.13-14 that the author intends it to be an oblique reference to the death of Jesus as a sacrifice. So the function of Jesus as ὁ ἁγιάζων is that of a priest, in accordance with numerous passages where the word is used in Exodus and Leviticus. And the particular aspect of priesthood which justifies the metaphor at this point is its representative character. It was necessary for the purpose of atonement that Jesus should die as a sacrificial victim, and he could not do this unless he were human and like all other human beings subject to death. Though the Levitical priesthood involves separation from the rest of the people as a priestly caste, the priests share the same weaknesses as the rest of humanity. This is recognized in the ceremonial of the Day of Atonement, in which the high priest first performs the blood ritual on behalf of himself (implicitly for the whole priesthood of which he is the head) by the sacrifice of a bull,

16. Cf. Lindars, 'The Rhetorical Structure of Hebrews', p. 391.

and then repeats the process on behalf of the people by the sacrifice of a goat. So again, as in 1.3, the metaphor is only briefly expressed, but carries implications which are relevant to the central argument.

After such preparatory hints the application of the metaphor of priesthood to Jesus in 2.17 appears completely natural. Jesus shared the mortality of the human condition ἵνα ἐλεήμων γένηται καὶ πιστὸς ἀρχιερεὺς τὰ πρὸς τὸν θεὸν εἰς τὸ ἱλάσκεσθαι τὰς ἁμαρτίας τοῦ λαοῦ. The idea is still metaphorical, but the language is again drawn from Leviticus 16, especially vv. 30 and 34, except for the descriptive adjectives. Significantly ἐλεήμων is most frequently an attribute of God himself in the Septuagint, often co-ordinate with οἰκτίρμων. Thus, whereas the previous verses have stressed the priesthood of Jesus on its human, representative side, here there is a hint of its other side as a mediating agency for the mercy of God who forgives sins (cf. ἔλεος in 4.16). The other adjective, πιστός, is added in anticipation of the theme of Moses, who was πιστὸς ἐν ὅλῳ οἴκῳ αὐτοῦ ὡς θεράπων (3.5 = Num. 12.7), which immediately follows (3.1-6).[17]

The notion of agency is continued in 3.1 with the description of Jesus as τὸν ἀπόστολον καὶ ἀρχιερέα τῆς ὁμολογίας ἡμῶν. The first designation picks up the thought of Jesus as God's spokesman (1.2), reflecting God himself (1.3), which is one element in the confession of faith. The second summarizes his function as the effective agent of atonement through his sacrificial death, which is an equally important item in the primitive kerygma. Thus nothing at this stage suggests that the priesthood of Jesus is more than a metaphor.[18] The same is true of the fuller description in 4.14-16, which closes the first division of the argument of the epistle. The theme of sharing the weakness of human nature is given fresh emphasis in the

17. This also anticipates the exhortation to maintain faith at the conclusion of the argument, and is one of several important structural links between chs. 2–3 and 11–12; cf. the chiastic analysis of A. Vanhoye, *La structure littéraire de l'Epître aux Hébreux* (Paris, 1963).

18. This is true, even if the conjunction of apostle and high priest was already current in connection with the Day of Atonement, as suggested by *m. Yoma* 1.5 and the poetry of Yose b. Yose (cited by Horbury, 'The Aaronic Priesthood', p. 65).

light of the testing which Jesus has himself endured. It is
widely held that the application of this theme to Jesus at this
point makes allusion to the traditions behind the Gospels,
which are expressed in the Temptations (Mt. 4.1-11 = Lk. 4.1-
13) and Gethsemane narratives (Mt. 26.36-46 = Mk 14.32-42
= Lk. 22.40-46; cf. Jn 12.27).

It is now clear that there are crucially important characteristics in the Hebrews concept of priesthood which are not
derived from Exodus and Leviticus but from the correspondence of Jewish ideas known from later sources with the
broader background of Christian thought about the sacrificial
death of Jesus. This does not necessarily imply that the
metaphor of priesthood was already applied to Jesus.[19] In my
view the gentle way in which the idea is introduced in
Hebrews suggests just the opposite. The author is preparing
the ground for an idea that is vitally necessary for his purpose,
but which he does not expect to be familiar to his readers
(5.11–6.1). As part of this preparation he draws into the
exposition of priesthood ideas that are already current in connection with Jesus' death. The Gethsemane tradition is one of
these. Almost certainly another is the widespread use of the
Suffering Servant prophecy of Isaiah 53, to which there is a
clear allusion in 9.28.

These observations explain the appealing depiction of priesthood which immediately follows in 5.1-4. This gives the norm
for the appointment of 'every high priest'. The facts—his
function of offering sacrifices and sin-offerings on behalf of the
people, the need to offer them on behalf of himself as well as
the people, the calling of God as the essential basis of appointment—are selectively chosen from Exodus and Leviticus as
essential points which can be shown to be duly observed in the
claim that Jesus too is a real high priest (5.5-10). The quali-
ties—his pastoral sympathy and self-effacing refusal to put
himself forward—are derived from the convergence of Jewish
sources with the Jesus tradition. However, this is a timeless
passage about what is ideally always true in the appointment
of a high priest. The author expects the readers to agree that

---

19. This is commonly argued by commentators; cf. also M. Rissi, *Die
Theologie des Hebräerbriefs* (WUNT 41; Tübingen, 1987), p. 55.

this is the norm. He is most careful not to present an unkind or grudging picture of priesthood, which would put the readers on the defensive, in view of their deeply felt need for the benefit of atonement for post-baptismal sins. They will, of course, be told that the sacrifices of the old covenant are superseded, so that they are making a grievous mistake in seeking association with the existing temple and its cultus. That is the burden of the central argument in chs. 7–9. But the author cannot make this point successfully if he has alienated the readers by speaking slightingly of the actual worship of the temple. He is not arguing that the temple and its personnel should be reformed. His aim is far more radical, and requires the most careful persuasion to convince his readers.

So there is no mention here of the hereditary character of the Levitical priesthood, as if that might imply an inferior man-made institution, though he will bring up this point in another connection in 7.11-14. The political factors which so often dictated the choice of high priests in New Testament times are disregarded. The notorious conduct of some of the Hasmonaean high priests is not mentioned. So what is claimed here for 'every high priest' is idealistic and far removed from the sadly unsatisfactory reality. But that is intentional, for the reason just indicated. The author is putting forward a 'best case' model, so as to make the true nature of the priesthood of Jesus stand out by contrast. The priesthood of Jesus after the order of Melchizedek qualifies him to be the high priest of the sacrifice of the new covenant. Even on the best showing, the Levitical priesthood cannot achieve what is effected by the sacrifice of the new covenant, because it is bound by the limitations of the old covenant.

It must be noted, further, that Hebrews does not present two contrasting pictures, but two contrasting practices. 5.1-4 presents a single ideal picture, and it is then shown that Jesus, in his own priestly order of Melchizedek, conforms to it just as much as the Levitical high priests. Moreover the difference between them is not that of type and antitype but of function. The Levitical priesthood exists to perform the sacrifices of the old covenant, but Jesus is the high priest of the new covenant. It is not suggested that the sacrifices of the old covenant do not happen. The point is that they have ceased to be relevant because of the historic event of the sacrifice of the new covenant in the death of Jesus. The fact that they continue, instead of ceasing altogether, as the logic of the argument would seem to require, explains the ambiguity which is present throughout Hebrews, and indeed the whole of the New Testament. The intimate connection between the historic death of Jesus and the imminent parousia, which actually closes the present era, creates ambiguity everywhere. It is the parousia which really begins the new world, though the decisive act by which it is inaugurated has already taken place in the death of Jesus, so that the Christians are left in a position of suspense. Hebrews is most insistent that there is no need of further acts of atonement during this time of waiting: 'So Christ, having been offered once to bear the sins of many, will appear a second time, not to deal with sin but to save those who are eagerly waiting for him' (9.28). But in fact the worship of the temple, together with the whole Jewish code of practice for dealing with the consciousness of sin, continues to be available during this period of waiting.[20] The whole argument of Hebrews is addressed to the urgent need to stop the readers from resorting to this practice in their anxiety to cope with their troubled consciences (9.9, 14; 10.2).

Once it is realized that Hebrews is concerned with practice in relation to the new covenant, it becomes clear that the author's aim is not to inculcate an inward and spiritual religion as opposed to an outward and ritualistic religion, but to persuade the readers to leave behind the current Jewish practice of atonement and to participate fully in the Christian celebration of the new covenant (13.13, 15). The old sacrifices are ineffective because they are time-bound, needing constant repetition. They thereby fail to produce the condition promised in the prophecy of the new covenant, in which God promised that he would 'remember their sins no more' (Jer. 31.34). This prophecy is quoted at length in 8.8-12, before the contrast between old and new sacrifices is explained in ch. 9, precisely to

20. It is probable that 9.8, ἔτι τῆς πρώτης σκηνῆς ἐχούσης στάσιν, is purely logical, seeing that the temple service is due to be superseded by the new covenant, but the timeless present strongly suggests that the temple is still in operation at the time of writing.

make this point. It is picked up again at the conclusion of the argument in 10.17, with the comment, 'Where there is forgiveness of these, there is no longer any offering for sin' (10.18). The old practice is no longer needed.

The problem which faces the readers is that they have lost confidence during the time of waiting, because they feel that their Christian life offers no suitable practice to deal with their renewed sense of sin. It is not sufficiently realized by students of Hebrews that the solution to this problem is the real climax of the argument. This is given in the long section in the life of faith (10.19–12.29). But faith for Hebrews is not merely a mental attitude. The author is not expecting the readers to sit still and do nothing. He knows that faith in the continuing efficacy of the sacrifice of Christ must be accompanied by action, if it is to be related to the readers' present need. However, he does not propose any new ceremony. The practice which they need is already available in the liturgy, which they are neglecting. So he exhorts them to return to the Christian assembly (10.25) in which the faith is expressed. It is in the continual celebration of the act of God in Christ that the permanent efficacy of that act is realized, and the need for the old rites of purification disappears. So the answer to their problem is that they should 'continually offer up a sacrifice of praise to God, that is, the fruit of lips that acknowledge his name' (13.15). The explanation that the sacrifice consists in verbal acknowledgment is necessary, because otherwise the readers might think that the offering of the sacrifice of praise is meant literally, i.e. that they are being advised to offer the *todah* (Lev. 7.12-15; 22.29-30). In fact it is most probable that there is a literary allusion to Ps. 116.17 (LXX 115.8), which refers to the θυσίαν αἰνέσεως. The Christians' *todah*, however, is the assembly in which they 'proclaim the Lord's death until he comes' (1 Cor. 11.26), not the *todah* sacrifice of the temple service.

This possible misunderstanding on the part of the readers makes sense if the temple sacrifice remains a live option for them, either through personal visits to join in its worship or through paying expenses for the offering of sacrifice. One last point which enhances this impression still further is the careful use of tenses in Hebrews 9. In 9.1-2 the past tense is used to denote the regulations which were laid down for the construction of the tent and the holy of holies according to the old covenant. Again in v. 6 the past tense is used to denote the completion of these arrangements (τούτων... κατεσκευ- ασμένων), but from that point the timeless present is used to indicate the normal practice. At the same time it is made clear that these provisions are only temporary arrangements of limited value 'until the time of reformation' (9.8-10). At this juncture the argument turns to the contrast of the truly effectual sacrifice of Christ, but the timeless present is still used for the temple service (9.11-14). However, the author has to show that the death of Christ not only functioned as the final atonement sacrifice, but also inaugurated the new covenant. It is thus necessary to include the contrast with the sacrifice which accompanied the inauguration of the old covenant by Moses (9.18-21). Here past tenses are used. When the argument returns to the model of the Day of Atonement, the author reverts to the timeless present once more (9.22,[21] 25), and this is continued in the broader considerations of 10.1-4, 11. All this makes much better sense if the timeless presents correspond with current practice in the temple than would be the case if the temple were already destroyed. For then the reference would have to be to a spiritualized Jewish worship whose liturgical expression is nowhere described in the epistle. In fact the only spiritualized worship in view is the Christian *todah*, and that depends, not on the distinction between outward and inward, nor on a Platonic distinction between matter and forms, but on the temporal distinction between the era of the old covenant and the inauguration of the new covenant. The sacrifices of the old covenant failed to effect permanent reconciliation with God, and so had to be constantly repeated. The sacrifice of the new covenant has opened the way to a perma-

---

21. The statement that χωρὶς αἱματεκχυσίας οὐ γίνεται ἄφεσις is often taken to imply that the author has only limited knowledge of the laws dealing with purification and assumes that it is the slaughter of the victim which effects forgiveness. But the word probably means sprinkling of blood, not shedding of blood, and so refers to the essential part played by the blood ritual in both the Sinai covenant and the Day of Atonement; cf. T.C.G. Thornton, 'The Meaning of αἱματεκχυσία in Heb. ix 22', *JTS* ns 15 (1964), pp. 63-65.

nent state of reconciliation, and this is maintained through the constant celebration of that sacrifice in the liturgy and fellowship of the church (13.15-16).

IV

The author of Hebrews knows that Christians have to maintain a constant struggle against sin (12.4).[22] This is bound to be so until they reach 'perfection', i.e. the completion of the whole process of redemption.[23] Thus his complaint is not that his readers have the consciousness of sin, but that they are doing the wrong thing in order to cope with it. In his view, by reverting to Jewish practices they are denying the whole basis of Christian faith. It is clear that the form of Christianity which came to the Hebrews church (2.3-4; 10.32-34; 13.7-14) required a complete break with Jewish practice. It is very likely that it stemmed from the radical position of the Hellenists represented by Stephen in Acts 6. The Hebrews church would then be a Jewish group in the Diaspora evangelized as a result of the persecution mentioned in Acts 8.1-4 and 11.19-26. The argument of Hebrews, if viewed by an antagonist, could well be described as maintaining that 'this Jesus of Nazareth will destroy this place, and will change the customs which Moses delivered to us' (Acts 6.14). In their first enthusiasm after conversion the readers rejoiced to be free from sin and reconciled to God through Christ in readiness for the parousia, which they eagerly awaited (9.28). Now they are burdened with the sense of sin once more, as the time of waiting lengthens out. They know what they used to do to come to terms with guilt. But apparently their Christian practice makes no provi-

---

22. The apparent rigorism of 6.4-6 and 10.26 is due to the author's fear that the readers are about to commit apostasy, and so to deny the whole meaning of the gospel of forgiveness which they have embraced. They would therefore be self-excluded from the scope of redemption. The erroneous application of these passages to 'mortal' sins stems from Tertullian, *On Modesty* 20, writing with puritanical rigorism in his Montanist days. For the history of interpretation of the passage, cf. R.C. Sauer, 'A Critical and Exegetical Reexamination of Hebrews 5.11 to 6.8' (unpublished PhD dissertation; Manchester, 1981).

23. Cf. D. Peterson, *Hebrews and Perfection* (Cambridge, 1982).

sion for atonement in the interval before the parousia. This is why they are tempted to resort to the Jewish practices which they had abandoned.

Some idea of what this might involve has been given above. There would be both private and public aspects. Privately they would be careful to observe the laws of purity which were customary in their former Jewish life. They would also observe the days of fasting, especially the Day of Atonement, when fasting was enjoined on all Jews everywhere (*m. Yoma* 8.1). But this might not be enough to remove the stain of sin and restore the sense of wholeness when serious offences were involved. For this to be achieved some form of connection with the temple would be needed, because full restoration required the appropriate sacrifices. The ideal would be to go to Jerusalem and make a personal sin-offering immediately. However, *m. Temurah* 4.3 presupposes the case where a person sets aside money for a sin-offering, but there is some delay before it can actually be purchased and offered. No doubt Jews in the Diaspora sent money for sacrifices even if they could not go to Jerusalem in person. In any case some offences at least would be covered by the regular sacrifices at the new moon, which were offered for unintentional sins (*m. Sheb.* 1.5), and of course the Day of Atonement cleared off the back-log of una-toned sin for the whole of the previous year. In this connection a suspended trespass-offering (i.e. one due, but not yet per-formed) was met by the sort of total amnesty provided by the Day of Atonement, and was therefore regarded as no longer due (*m. Ker.* 6.4).

A further point arises from the system of the suspended sacrifice. If there was likely to be long delay before it could be offered, the less devout would be tempted not to bother about it. One may well ask what it was intended to achieve, if every-thing needed to make restitution for offences and to restore purity at home had already been done. But it was the sacrifices of the sin-offering and the trespass-offering which restored the worshipper to full participation in the temple itself, giving entitlement to eat the hallowed things, or sacrificial meats, so that until this was done the restoration of the sinner was not complete.[24] So again, for a fully satisfying sense of atonement from sin, the devout Jews of the Diaspora would wish to fulfil all the obligations, so as to be competent to eat the hallowed things, even if there was no likelihood of travelling to Jerusalem to do so in the near future. The devout Jew would not feel right until this was done.

The urgency of Hebrews suggests that the readers were Jews of this kind, who would not be satisfied until they had fulfilled all the obligations for complete reconciliation according to the Law. The author has to tackle the question of sacrifice seriously, because it is not just a matter of theory and symbolism but a matter of practice which is crucial to their religious allegiance. They are in effect being asked to choose between their fairly recent decision for the Christian way, which for them had entailed a clean break with their past Jewish practice, and return to the whole Jewish system, which they had been led to believe had been rendered obsolete by Christ (8.13; 10.18). Participation in the synagogue meetings would tend to draw them back into the Jewish society from which they had separated themselves so painfully, often at the cost of disruption of family and friendships. This would explain their tendency to absent themselves from the Christian assembly (10.25). It is not going too far to suggest that they found themselves under strong emotional pressure to return to full Jewish practice. Their friends and relations in the synagogue would be anxious to win them back, and would have the best motives to exert emotional pressure. There are plenty of signs in Hebrews that the author needed to use all his rhetorical skill and powers of persuasion to hold them in the Christian community.

The seriousness of the problem is thus not due to philosophical disputes but to deep-seated feelings, which cannot be satisfied by intellectual arguments alone. It is the felt need for a tangible form of reconciliation for sin which has driven these converts to look back to their Jewish past. The composition of Hebrews is aimed at recovering their confidence in the permanent efficacy of the sacrifice of Christ by means of an

24. Cf. *m. Toh.* 14.3 for the three stages required for the restoration of the cleansed leper.

argument which is likely to make the maximum emotional impact on them from this point of view. They are addressed as people for whom the pentateuchal laws have the real authority of self-evident truth, who value the contemporary expression of these laws in the service of the temple, and who feel deeply the emotional power of the temple as the focus and spiritual centre of all devout Jews everywhere. The presentation of the Christian case has to make an equally powerful emotional appeal.

On this showing the letter to the Hebrews should be added to the evidence for the profound importance of the temple for the religion of Judaism in New Testament times. There may have been many Jews who found the traditional sacrifices barbarous and unacceptable and would be glad to be rid of them, just as there were among the pagans.[25] There must also have been those who deplored the politics and the secular aims of the circles around the high priests. There were those like Jesus himself who saw its magnificence and wealth as a barrier to the proper valuation of the religion of the poor.[26] But for many people, and probably for the vast majority of Jews, the temple was valued as the assurance that God was in the midst of his people wherever they might be. The mere fact of the *tamid*, offered every morning and evening, gave a sense of confidence. The glowing description of the high priest Simon in Sir. 50.1-21, which catches the impact of the temple worship so vividly, must have affected the imagination of Jews far and wide. The idealization of the temple in the *hekaloth* literature and in the liturgical documents from Qumran attests the imaginative power of the temple even among those who excluded themselves from it on grounds of conscience.

If, as I have argued above, Hebrews is to be dated before the fall of Jerusalem, it is still necessary to think of a fairly late

25. Cf. J.W. Thompson, 'Hebrews and the Hellenistic Concepts of Sacrifice', *JBL* 98 (1979), pp. 569-78.
26. For an original interpretation of the cleansing of the temple from this point of view, see R.J. Bauckham, 'Jesus' Demonstration in the Temple', in B. Lindars (ed.), *Law and Religion* (Cambridge, 1988), pp. 72-89.

date, probably between AD 65 and 70.[27] Hebrews then shows by
implication the continuing power of the temple on the Jewish
religious consciousness right up to the end, and this gives the
lie to any suggestion that it could easily be dispensed with or
that the task of renewing Judaism which faced Johanan ben
Zakkai and other Pharisaic leaders was anything but extremely formidable.

Nicanor's gift of doors for the temple gives striking evidence
of the importance of the temple for Diaspora Jews, in this case
for a proselyte, if Bammel's suggestion is correct. The readers
of Hebrews are likely to have valued the temple equally before
their conversion. When the consciousness of sin leaves them
feeling unable to find peace with God within their Christian
faith and life, it is to the worship of the temple that their
thoughts return. Such was the hold of the temple on their
imagination, and so it must have been for countless Jews
before disaster struck.

27. The chief criterion is the advanced christology of 1.1-4, which is
closely parallel to Col. 1.13-20. Colossians is generally dated about AD
65 by those who deny Pauline authorship. On the other hand signs of
Early Catholicism are lacking in Hebrews; cf. B. Lindars, 'The Rhetorical Structure of Hebrews'.

BETTER PROMISES: TWO PASSAGES IN HEBREWS AGAINST
THE BACKGROUND OF THE OLD TESTAMENT CULTUS[1]

Robert P. Gordon

While the Letter to the Hebrews gives little away as to the
identity and location of either its writer or its addressees, a
certain amount can be gleaned about the circumstances of
those whom tradition early named 'the Hebrews'. They were
second- or third-generation Christians in the sense that they
were at some distance from the Christ-event which had been
preached to them and which now formed the basis of their
faith. Because of their Christian profession they had been subjected to public humiliation, persecution, and confiscation of
property. We may judge from the references in 10.34 and 13.3
that some of their friends had been imprisoned, and that some
of these were still in prison at the time of writing. So far their
privations had fallen short of martyrdom, but the statement in
12.4 that they had 'not yet resisted to the death (lit. "blood") in
the conflict with sin' hints at the prospect of greater demands
being laid upon them. It is also clear that the writer regarded
his readers as currently in a trough of spiritual torpor, for
whatever reason. That they were Christian converts from
Judaism has been disputed, but it seems very likely. Whether
they were emphasizing their Jewish heritage to the detriment
of their Christian commitment,[2] or were struggling with a

1. This paper was read at the Annual General Meeting of the Irish
Biblical Association at Tallaght, Co. Dublin, on 22nd April, 1989. I am
pleased to offer it as a contribution to the Festschrift in honour of Dr E.
Bammel on the occasion of his retirement.
2. As was argued by William Manson in the 1949 (1950) Baird Lec-
tures (*The Epistle to the Hebrews. An Historical and Theological
Reconsideration* [London: Hodder and Stoughton, 1951]).

temptation to return to the Jewish fold, is a finer point; ultimately the positions may not be greatly different.

This is as much as may be deduced from the several brief references to the addressees' circumstances as they occur in the letter (2.1-4; 5.11f.; 6.9f.; 10.32-34; 13.7). That there were religious or intellectual factors contributing to their present state need not be doubted, but whether these are to be regarded as the root or the fruit of the problem is more difficult to judge. There are, on the other hand, quite strong hints as to the psychological condition of 'the Hebrews' in a number of references which deserve highlighting in this particular connection. The 'fear of death' evidently was regarded by the author as a sizeable obstacle to a continuing commitment on the part of his readers. The idea first appears in 2.14f. where the death of Christ is seen as that by which the wielder of the power of death was destroyed and those who through fear of death had been held in lifelong slavery were given their freedom.[3] In 5.7 the divine Son is portrayed as one who in his earthly life 'offered up prayers and petitions with loud cries and tears to him who could save him from death'; and he, moreover, was heard 'because of his humble submission'. In this case the solidarity of Christ with his people even, or especially, at their most vulnerable point is very strikingly expressed. And significantly, salvation from death is here not escape from the encounter but posthumous deliverance. That is also part of the message of ch. 11. The leading theme of this chapter is, to be sure, the necessity and the inspirational power of faith, but there is an ancillary theme which can be overlooked only with difficulty, viz. that faith overcomes death in whatever form it presents itself, and in any one of a number of ways. By faith Abel still speaks, even though dead (v. 4), by faith Enoch was translated so as not even to see death (v. 5), by faith Abraham, although 'as good as dead', became the progenitor of a host of descendants (v. 12), by faith the same Abraham received his son Isaac back from the dead—in a figure (v. 19), by faith the dying Jacob blessed Joseph's sons and worshipped (v. 21), by faith Joseph at the end of his life gave instructions about his

---

3. Already in 2.9 it had been stated that Christ entered into death 'so that by the grace of God he should taste death for everyone'.

bones (v. 22), by faith Israel's firstborn escaped the judgment
of death in Egypt, the Israelites drowning in the Red Sea, and
Rahab destruction with the rest of Jericho (vv. 28-31). Others
stopped lions' mouths, quenched flames, escaped the sword,
received their dead back again (vv. 33-35a); yet others
embraced death to gain a better resurrection, were stoned,
were sawn in two, or were put to death by the sword (vv. 35b-
37). The supreme example of suffering and overcoming is,
nevertheless, Christ himself who 'in anticipation of the joy set
before him endured the cross, despising the shame' (12.2). It is
at this point that the readers are reminded that their suffering
has not so far resulted in martyrdom. For the present they
should remember that God uses suffering as a discipline for
his children, and this discipline, it is claimed in what functions
as a minor climax in the argument, does not issue in death but
in life: 'Should we not *submit all the more to the father of
spirits and live?*' (v. 9). Life and not death, if they could grasp it,
is the outcome of God's paternal dealings with the faithful. The
development of this sub-theme in chs. 11–12 serves, then, to
nerve the faint endeavour of those who have been enjoined in
10.35-39 to persevere in the Christian faith. Even death must
yield before the author and finisher of faith (12.1f.).

Twice in the section on Moses in ch. 11 mention is made of
the fearlessness of faith, first in relation to Moses' parents and
then in relation to Moses himself. The parents are said not to
have feared the king's edict (v. 23), and Moses, less obviously,
is declared not to have feared the king's anger when he for-
sook Egypt (v. 27). Since in the first century βασιλεύς was used
for 'emperor' as well as 'king' (cf. 1 Pet. 2.13, 17) it is reasonable to inquire whether these references are meant to have a
contemporary application, especially since v. 27 most naturally refers to Moses' hurried departure from Egypt when he
realized that the Pharaoh sought to kill him—hence NEB's
targumizing, 'By faith he left Egypt, and not because he feared
the king's anger'.[4] If the writer is so intent on saying that

4. That it is Moses' first 'exodus', and not *the* Exodus, that is considered in v. 27 is supported by the fact that the keeping of the passover is
not mentioned until v. 28. It is also questioned whether disregard of

Moses was activated by faith rather than by fear of the Pharaoh is it not because he wishes to raise the issue of fear of the king-emperor with his readers? And if all that I have said so far seems particularly suited to William Manson's thesis that Hebrews is addressed to Jewish Christians living in Rome in the period between the Claudian expulsions around AD 49 and the Neronian persecutions of the 60s I would not wish to disagree.[5] While this, by its very specificity, goes beyond the evidence of the letter itself, it provides an historical context more agreeable to the content of Hebrews than any other of which I am aware.

Whatever its exact causes and manifestations, it is undoubtedly a problem of arrested development that is addressed in Hebrews. That the Christian believer is far from being disadvantaged through lack of an Old Testament-type cultus is, in the circumstances, something that the author sees fit to argue from a number of standpoints and at some length. The main business of this paper is to discuss two passages, in chs. 6 and 9, and to note the ways in which the Old Testament is used in order to secure this point, that in Christ there is promise of better things, things that, according to the better reading at 9.11, may even be said to have come already.

In Hebrews 6 the discussion revolves about two 'impossibilities' (cf. ἀδύνατον, vv. 4, 18) of central importance to the author's argument. The long sentence beginning in v. 4 introduces the first, namely that it is impossible to renew to repentance those who have once been enlightened so long as they are crucifying anew the Son of God. Even so, the writer voices the confidence that his readers are in a better state (vv. 9f.). In vv. 13-20 things take on a still more cheerful aspect as the discussion turns to another kind of impossibility, that of God going back on his promise to his people for whose sake he had confirmed

---

pharaonic anger is a relevant consideration on the second occasion (though compare Exod. 10.28f.).

5. Manson, *op. cit.*, pp. 162-67. See also F.F. Bruce, 'Hebrews: A Document of Roman Christianity?', in W. Haase and H. Temporini (eds.), *Aufstieg und Niedergang der römischen Welt (ANRW)* II.25.4 (Berlin, 1987), pp. 3496-521.

his promissory word with an oath. Verses 1-12 and 13-20 are therefore rotating about different axes. It is the second of these 'impossibilities', and a particular element within it, in vv. 18f., that concerns us here.

The writer characterizes himself and his readers in v. 18 as those 'who have fled to take hold of the proffered hope'. This hope is then likened in v. 19 to an anchor of the soul, 'both sure and stedfast' (AV). In many discussions of these verses the figure of the anchor is back-read into v. 18, sometimes to the exclusion of any other metaphorical content, as in Otto Michel's paraphrase: 'Die Exegese denkt etwa an ein Schiff, das aus der hohen See in den Hafen geflüchtet ist, wo es nun geborgen vor Anker liegt'.[6] Occasionally καταφυγόντες in v. 18 is interpreted independently of the nautical metaphor that follows, in which case a reference to the Israelite institution of the cities of refuge may be entertained (cf. Num. 35.6-28; etc.).[7] According to the ancient legal provision, an unintentional homicide was entitled to flee to one of the appointed cities and enjoy its protection until the death of the ruling high priest. G.W. Buchanan, on the other hand, divests κατα-φυγόντες of any idea of literal flight, preferring the meaning 'have recourse' and explaining that 'the people who flee to an oath are the ones who can gain support from it'.[8]

The separation of v. 18 from the nautical metaphor of v. 19 is, in my view, entirely justified by the improved sense which then becomes possible, and the reference to the cities of refuge heads in the right direction even though it fails to account fully for the terms of the verse. The associated ideas of 'fleeing' and 'laying hold' suggest that the writer had more specifically in mind the seeking of sanctuary at the altar in Old Testament times, a provision that is mentioned independently of the cities of refuge tradition. Surprisingly, in a survey of a score of commentaries on Hebrews I have been able to find only one

6. *Der Brief an die Hebräer* (KEKNT; 12th edn; Göttingen: Vandenhoeck & Ruprecht, 1966), p. 253.

7. E.g. C. Spicq, *L'Epître aux Hébreux. II. Commentaire* (Paris: Gabalda, 1953), p. 163; H.A. Kent, *The Epistle to the Hebrews. A Commentary* (Grand Rapids: Baker, 1972), p. 121.

8. *To the Hebrews. A New Translation with Introduction and Commentary* (Anchor Bible, 36; Garden City, NY: Doubleday, 1972), p. 115.

commentator who envisages a reference of this sort: 'The notion of Abraham's strong faith, reaching out a hand to the strong grasp of God's oath, reminds him of men fleeing for refuge, perhaps into a sanctuary, and laying hold of the horns of the altar...'[9] The basic text for this idea is Exod. 21.13 where the unintentional homicide is appointed 'a place to which he shall flee', and the exact nature of this provision becomes clear when it is laid down in the next verse that anyone found guilty of deliberate killing is to be removed from the altar and put to death. As is well known, there are two illustrations of this institution at work, in 1 Kings 1–2. When Adonijah realized that his bid for the throne had failed, and that his life was in jeopardy, he 'rose, went and took hold of the horns of the altar' (1 Kgs 1.50). A closer verbal correspondence is furnished by the account of Joab's sanctuary-seeking in 1 Kings 2, when he feared for his life because of his part in the Adonijah coup:

> And Joab fled to the tent of the Lord and took hold of the horns of the altar (v. 28).

The effort was unavailing, however, and Solomon did not put down an opportunity to rid himself of a dangerous man.

This institution, we submit, lies behind Heb. 6.18f., and it provides an apt figure for Christian refuge-seeking in Christ. As the examples from 1 Kings 1–2 show, the exercise of the right of asylum was not limited to the unintentional homicide: Adonijah and Joab feared for their lives on other grounds. It is unnecessary, therefore, to ask in what way, from the viewpoint of Hebrews, the Christian may be compared with the unintentional homicide in Hebrew law.

So far the question of vocabulary has largely been skirted, but it requires some comment. If Heb. 6.18f. has in view the Old Testament altar asylum should we expect some verbal echoes of the Greek version of Exodus 21 and 1 Kings 1–2? Several commentators have noted that καταφεύγειν features in

---

9. T.C. Edwards, *The Epistle to the Hebrews* (Expositor's Bible; London: 1888), p. 107. Spicq (*op. cit.*, p. 163), includes 1 Kgs 1.50; 2.28 among his references, but makes nothing of them. See also H.W. Attridge, *The Epistle to the Hebrews* (Hermeneia; Philadelphia: Fortress, 1989), p. 183 (the volume was published after this paper was written).

sections on the cities of refuge (Deut. 4.42; 19.5; Num. 35.25; Josh. 20.9), but it is also used in Exod. 21.14 of an *intentional* homicide who flees to the altar of God in vain hope of sanctuary. Philo also uses this verb in his discussion of Exodus 21 in *De Fuga* 78-81 and *De Specialibus Legibus* 3.88-91. In 1 Kgs 2.28 the simple verb φεύγειν describes Joab's flight to the altar. There is no parallel occurrence of κρατεῖν in the Old Testament texts that refer to grasping the horns of the altar; the Septuagint has ἐπιλαμβάνειν and κατέχειν to describe respectively Adonijah's initial grasping and subsequent clinging to the altar (1 Kgs 1.50), and κατέχειν is used of Joab's similar action (2.28f.). The occurrences of κατέχειν in the present tense in 1.51 and 2.29 are noteworthy in that they indicate the kind of clinging that may be suggested in the use of κρατῆσαι in Heb. 6.18.[10]

For all that, the kind of allusion that we are envisaging hardly depends for its viability upon verbal correspondence with one or other of the relevant Old Testament texts. Moreover, G. Howard has shown just how often *quotations* in Hebrews diverge from the Septuagint or the Massoretic text or both.[11] If this is the situation with quotations a comely tolerance over allusions is called for.

The author of Hebrews possibly takes the comparison with the ancient sanctuary asylum a step further than has so far been mooted. In two of the three Old Testament passages already considered the removal of a suppliant from the altar is mentioned, as a contingent measure in Exodus 21 and as an actual occurrence in 1 Kings 2; for the protection of the sanctuary could be denied on legal grounds (Exod. 21.14), or could be disregarded irrespective of legal considerations (1 Kgs 2.34). (The vulnerability of the institution is highlighted in a different kind of way in Amos 3.14 where God says that when he destroys the altars of Bethel the altar-horns will be cut off and fall to the ground. The more likely signification of this threat is that all possibility of turning to God for help. of

10. Cf. H. Braun, *An die Hebräer* (HbNT 14; Tübingen: Mohr, 1984), p. 190, comparing Heb. 4.14.
11. 'Hebrews and the Old Testament Quotations', *NovT* 10 (1968), pp. 208-16.

seeking sanctuary at the altars of Bethel, would be cut off—
this in keeping with the 'twelfth-hour' [H.W. Wolff]
perspective of Amos.)

Seeking sanctuary by grasping the horns of the altar was
familiar practice, therefore, in ancient Israel, but the suppliant
was not thereby guaranteed his safety. The altar to which he
had access was also accessible to those who might disregard a
man's legal right. It is not entirely clear from the Old Testament references where such an altar might be located,[12] but
this is largely unimportant since the writer of Hebrews would
not have contemplated the possibility of anyone but the Jewish
high priest entering the most holy place in the tent of meeting.
Whether the altar in question be envisaged in the forecourt or
the outer compartment of the tent (cf. 1 Kgs 2.30?), to lay hold
upon a hope that entered εἰς τὸ ἐσώτερον τοῦ καταπετάσματος
was literally to enter a new sphere.

In this reading of v. 19, then, Christian hope reaches right
into the most holy place and enjoys a sacrosanctity that the old
Jewish system could not provide. With such an understanding
of the verse there is less cause than before to press the reference to the anchor so that it is made to reach into the heavenly
adytum. Even less do we have grounds for contrasting, with
Chrysostom, Calvin and others, the ordinary ship's anchor
which goes down into the sea and the Christian anchor of hope
which ascends into the heavenly realm.[13]

In Hebrews 9 a contrast in terms of effectiveness is drawn
between the sacrificial order associated with the Old Testament tent of meeting and the sacrificial death of Christ. In vv.
6-10 the limitations of the old ritual are noted. Even when the
Israelite high priest entered within the most holy place on the
annual Day of Atonement he could do no more than present
animal blood first for himself and then for the sins of igno-

---

12. Cf., however, J. Gray, *I and II Kings* (3rd edn; OTL; London:
SCM, 1977), p. 96, commenting on 1 Kgs 1.50: 'The location of the altar
is not mentioned, but doubtless it was by the tent which housed the ark
(v. 39)'.

13. Spicq (*op. cit.*, p. 164), goes so far as to appeal to Hebrew cosmology, according to which there was a supra-terrestrial ocean above the
firmament.

rance (ἀγνοημάτων) committed by the people of Israel. There was nothing within this system that could clear the conscience of the worshipper; only externalities were affected by the tabernacle-temple ritual. In portraying Christ as the high priest of the Christian economy, on the other hand, vv. 11-14 assert that his offering of himself has cleansed the consciences of his people from 'dead works' and has fitted them for the service of the living God (v. 14). Encouraged by this straight-forwardly contrastive mode of presentation, writers on these verses are invariably drawn into some sort of comment on the limited purview of the Old Testament sacrificial system which is summarized in Leviticus 1–7. Seldom, if ever, is the discussion brought face to face with the passage in the Old Testament which actually sets out the two categories of sin which appear to be basic to the development of thought in Heb. 9.6-14. The passage in question is Num. 15.22-31, the *locus classicus* in the Old Testament for the distinction between sins of ignorance, for which atonement could be made by means of pre-scribed sacrifices (vv. 22-29), and high-handed sins which, because there was no atonement possible for such, carried the death penalty (vv. 30f.). This distinction may be echoed in Ps. 19.12f. where the psalmist asks, 'Who can understand his errors (*šᵉgî'ôt*)?' (v. 12), and then prays, 'Keep your servant also from presumptuous sins (*zēdîm*)' (v. 13).[14] The Qumran *Community Rule* makes use of these same categories when it prescribes penance for two years for a sin of inadvertence but expulsion for the person who sinned deliberately (*bᵉyād rāmâ*, cf. Num. 15.30).[15] Elsewhere in Hebrews there is implicit recognition of this category distinction. At 5.2 the Jewish high priests are said to be able to bear with 'the ignorant who stray', which appears to deal in our first category of sins of inadvertence, while at 10.26 the possibility of atonement by sacrifice is rejected for those 'sinning wilfully' (ἑκουσίως ἁμαρτανόντων)

14. See the discussion by J. Milgrom, 'The Cultic *šgg* and its Influence in Psalms and Job', *JQR* ns 58 (1967–68), pp. 120f., and cf. D.J.A. Clines, 'The Tree of Knowledge and the Law of Yahweh (Psalm xix)', *VT* 24 (1974), p. 13 n. 3.

15. 1QS 8.20–9.2. See P. Wernberg-Møller, *The Manual of Discipline, Translated and Annotated with an Introduction* (Studies on the Texts of the Desert of Judah, 1; Leiden: Brill, 1957), p. 132.

after having received the knowledge of the truth.[16] There is
good reason, therefore, to give ἀγνοημάτων in 9.7 its natural
sense of 'sins of ignorance'. The view that it is to be interpreted
broadly as an equivalent of ἀμαρτία because Lev. 16.34 may be
taken to mean that the Day of Atonement covers *all* the sins of
Israel (see below), or because of the claimed equivalence of
ἀμαρτία and ἀγνόημα in the Septuagint and in some extra-bib-
lical texts[17] seriously weakens the contrast which the author
of Hebrews is seeking to establish.

The relevance of the two categories of Num. 15.22-31 to the
argument of Heb. 9.6-14 may become more apparent upon a
consideration of the meaning of the expression 'dead works' as
it occurs in 9.14 and also in 6.1 ('not laying again the foundation of repentance from dead works and of faith towards
God'). In 9.14 there is an obvious contrast between *dead* works
and the service of the *living* God.[18] The former are done in
independence of God and accordingly lack the quality or grace
of divine life. This, however, is not normally thought to
exhaust the significance of the expression, and there are three
main interpretations which recur in the secondary literature.
Many writers, it may be observed, do not limit themselves to
one line of explanation.

1. The view that the 'dead works' are the works of the
(Jewish) law is well represented by R.J. Daly, according to
whom 'obedience to the dead works of the law is replaced by
the new cultic principle of service (*latreuein*) to the will of the
living God'.[19] B.F. Westcott expressed a similar understanding
of the 'dead works' of 6.1: 'The writer of the Epistle is thinking,
as it seems, of all the works corresponding with the Levitical
system not in their original institution but in their actual relation to the Gospel as established in the Christian society. By the
work of Christ, who fulfilled, and by fulfilling annulled, the

16. Contrast the use of ἀκουσίως in translation of BH *šegāgâ* ('sin of
inadvertence') in LXX Lev. 4.2; Num. 15.24; etc.
17. Cf. Calvin, *Commentary, ad loc.*; T. Hewitt, *Hebrews. An Introduction and Commentary* (TNTC; London, 1960), p. 143. See also Spicq,
op. cit., p. 253; Braun, *op. cit.*, p. 256.
18. Cf. Braun, *op. cit.*, pp. 160, 271.
19. *The Origins of the Christian Doctrine of Sacrifice* (London: Darton, Longman & Todd, 1978), p. 70.

Law, the element of life was withdrawn from these which had (so to speak) a provisional, and only a provisional, vitality.'[20] This is a more sophisticated version of the 'dead works' = 'works of the law' interpretation, nevertheless the counter-argument that works of the law would be unlikely to give a person a guilty conscience—unless the issue is approached from a different angle, as in, say, Romans 7—seems to be adequate refutation of the 'works of the law' interpretation in whatever form it is presented.[21]

2. J. Moffatt understood 'dead works' to be those moral offences from which a person had to break away in order to become a Christian.[22] Moffatt, like many others, was also inclined to see in the reference to 'dead works' an analogy with 'dead bodies', a source of ritual defilement according to priestly law.[23] More recently G.W. Buchanan has referred the 'dead works' of 6.1 to the pre-Christian experience of the addressees in Hebrews: '"Dead works" referred to the life Christians had lived before they were baptized into the community. "Dead" described those people who were outside of the covenant, living as other pagans.'[24] And he too draws on the analogy of corpse contamination.

3. Possibly the most favoured line of interpretation is that which thinks in terms of 'works that lead to death', which is the translation (or paraphrase) given by NIV. Comparison is usually made with *Didache* 5.1 and its exposition of 'the way of death', by which is understood 'the way that leads to death'. Again, *4 Ezra* 7.119 asks, 'For how does it profit us that the eternal age is promised to us, whereas we have done *the works that bring death*?' This is R.H. Charles's translation of *mortalia opera* and it makes for a convincing contrast with the

---

20. *The Epistle to the Hebrews. The Greek Text with Notes and Essays* (London: Macmillan, 1889), p. 144.

21. Cf. D. Peterson, *Hebrews and Perfection. An Examination of the Concept of Perfection in the Epistle to the Hebrews* (SNTSMS 47; Cambridge: Cambridge University Press, 1982), p. 139.

22. *A Critical and Exegetical Commentary on the Epistle to the Hebrews* (ICC; Edinburgh: T. & T. Clark, 1924), p. 74.

23. Cf. P.E. Hughes, *A Commentary on the Epistle to the Hebrews* (Grand Rapids: Eerdmans, 1977), p. 361.

24. *Op. cit.*, p. 103.

promised 'immortal age', which, *4 Ezra* laments, is denied the descendants of Adam.[25] The Pauline statement that 'sin pays wages and they are death' (Rom. 6.23) provides a conceptual, if not a close verbal, parallel from within the New Testament.

If 'dead works' are those that have death as their entail the distinction between the two categories of sins of ignorance and high-handed sins is the more clearly visible in Heb. 9.6-14. But the distinction is there just so that it can be shown to have been dissolved through Christ's high priestly ministrations. For an oblique commentary on what is happening in Heb. 9.6-14 we can turn with profit to rabbinic sources. 'Great is repentance, for deliberate sins are accounted [to the repentant sinner] as errors', says Resh Lakish in *b. Yoma* 86b, and the same idea can be illustrated from a couple of references in the Targum to the Prophets. *Tg. Hosea* 3.1 does not pretend to treat in literal fashion the acquisition of the adulterous woman whom the prophet was commanded to love. Predictably, in the Targum the adulterous woman is Israel in its idolatry. 'Nevertheless', says the Targum, 'if they repent they shall be forgiven and they shall be like a man who has acted inadvertently and has spoken a word in his wine'.[26] Thus even the sin of idolatry may, if repentance supervenes, be treated as a sin of inadvertence. The second Targumic reference is Hab. 3.1. In the MT the chapter is headed, 'A prayer of Habakkuk the prophet *'al šigyōnôt*'. The untranslated term is of a type familiar in the Psalter, but of uncertain meaning. The Targum clearly links *šigyōnôt* with the Hebrew *šᵉgāgâ* ('sin of inadvertence', cf. Vg *pro ignorationibus* and the renderings of the Greek minor versions), hence its otherwise improbable account of the MT: 'The prayer which Habakkuk the prophet prayed when it was revealed to him concerning the extension which is given to the wicked, that if they return to the law with a perfect heart they will be forgiven, and all their sins which they have committed before him will be like sins of inadvertence'. These rabbinic

---

25. *Apocrypha and Pseudepigrapha of the Old Testament in English*, II (Oxford: Clarendon, 1913), p. 591.
26. The reading *bhmryh* ('in his wine') is preferred to the variant *bhbryh* ('against his fellow') in view of the underlying Hebrew; cf. MT and *Targum Isa.* 28.7.

passages, while putting more of a premium upon repentance (though compare Heb. 6.1), are addressing from the Jewish side the issue which engages the author of Hebrews in 9.6-14.[27]

Our passage states clearly that the activity of the Jewish high priests on the Day of Atonement was concerned with the sins of ignorance committed by the people of Israel, but this is significantly different from what is said in Leviticus 16 on the subject. There the high priest makes atonement for the most holy place 'because of the uncleanness and rebellion of the Israelites, in respect of all their sins' (v. 16), he lays his hands on the head of the live goat and confesses over it 'all the wickedness and rebellion of the Israelites' (v. 21), and the result of the atonement ritual is that Israel are made clean from all their sins (v. 30; cf. v. 34). Such an understanding of the function of the Day of Atonement appears to be represented in rabbinic sources. According to *m. Yoma* 8.8, 'Repentance atones for minor transgressions against both positive and negative commands while for graver sins it suspends punishment until the Day of Atonement comes and effects atonement'. And in *b. Ker.* 7a the view is expressed that, with three notable exceptions, the Day of Atonement atones for all the sins mentioned in the Torah, whether repentance is in evidence or not. It could, perhaps, be argued in relation to these statements, formulated as they were when there was no temple and no cultic observance of the Day of Atonement, that it is the spiritual exercises that effect the change,[28] though in *m. Yoma* 8.8 repentance is noticeably in play before the annual fast.

By comparison, the author of Hebrews is positively reductionistic in his assessment of the significance of the Day of Atonement. As we have already noted, there is no reason to

27. For further references and discussion see G. Larsson, *Der Toseftatraktat Jom hak-Kippurim. Text, Übersetzung, Kommentar. I. Teil, Kapitel 1 und 2* (Lund: Studentlitteratur, 1980), pp. 141-44. I am most grateful to Dr Horbury for drawing my attention to Larsson's study.

28. A rabbinic view noted by F.F. Bruce, *Commentary on the Epistle to the Hebrews* (New London Commentaries; London: Marshall, Morgan and Scott, 1965), p. 196 n. 63.

treat ἀγνόημα as equivalent to ἁμαρτία; the writer limits the efficacy of the Day to *sins of ignorance*. This desire to show the limitations of the so-called Levitical order even on its most holy day is also apparent in the contrasting references to conscience in vv. 9 and 14. Then as if to cap this line of argument the writer declares in v. 15 that Christ's death necessarily had retrospective effect, setting people free from *deliberate sins* (παραβάσεων) committed under the first covenant. Hebrews 9 might, as to the point at issue, be compared more readily with the truncated version of the Day of Atonement given in Ezek. 45.18-20, according to which the priestly ministration would be on behalf of 'everyone who errs and is foolish' (v. 20). The author of Hebrews may have had in mind some of the Old Testament's own statements about the limited efficacy of animal sacrifices (Ps. 51.16f.; Mic. 6.6-8; etc.), but he may well have considered it of more immediate significance that Leviticus 16 concludes a section beginning with ch. 11 and consisting of food laws (ch. 11) and instructions on ritual purification (chs. 12–15). This much may lie behind the statement in 9.10 that the 'gifts and sacrifices' were only concerned with 'food and drink and various ceremonial washings'.[29]

The approach to Heb. 9.6-14 adopted in this paper has assumed that an Old Testament categorizing of sins into two main classes provides the basis for the writer's argument about the superiority of Christ's sacrifice over what had preceded in Jewish ritual. It is quite distinct from, yet not necessarily incompatible with, another emphasis represented by, for example, J.W. Thompson in an article entitled 'Hebrews 9 and Hellenistic Concepts of Sacrifice'.[30] Thompson thinks that the author of Hebrews is operating with a dualistic anthropology which corresponds to the heaven–earth duality, from which it follows that only 'the earthly side of human existence' is served by an earthly cultus. The metaphysical assumptions of vv. 11-14 in particular are thought to be characteristic of the

29. Manson (*op. cit.*, p. 158) suggests that this circumscription of the Old Testament cultus relates to the situation of the addressees, for whom Jewish teachings on food and drink were a 'danger'.
30. *JBL* 98 (1979), pp. 567-78.

Platonic tradition and, of course, Philo can be quoted to the effect that the Levitical cultus availed for the cleansing of the body but did not affect the soul.[31] Nevertheless, even though it may be conceded that our author is well versed in the language and thought of Platonism, with or without the direct assistance of Philo, a strong case can be made out for the Old Testament as a sufficient matrix of Heb. 9.6-14. Even v. 23, which Thompson wishes to link with v. 13 and its reference to outward purity, does not go beyond the concept of heavenly prototype and earthly counterpart that is attested in the ancient near east and that may well be reflected in 'the pattern shown in the mount' of Exod. 25.9, 40 (cf. Heb. 8.5).[32] It would be a foolhardy *Alttestamentler* who would seek to deprive the 'Alexandrine' section of Hebrews of all its Alexandrinisms, yet the mere fact of the ancient author's preoccupation with redemption rather than cosmology ensures that the argument will be subjected to a constant pull towards the ordinances and institutions of the Old Testament, even if only for contrastive purposes.

> It is characteristic of the Epistle that all the arguments from the divine worship of Judaism which it contains are drawn from the institution of the Tabernacle. These, which are treated as the direct embodiment of the heavenly archetype, are supposed to be still preserved in the later forms and to give force to them. They were never superseded even when they were practically modified.

Thus does B.F. Westcott comment on one of the more eye-catching features of the Letter to the Hebrews.[33] Other considerations may have played their part. The author may have reckoned that the tabernacle (or 'tent of meeting') suited better his conception of the Christian life as a pilgrimage, or he may have been attracted by the idea of heavenly prototype and earthly counterpart,[34] which is more prominent in the tabernacle tradition than the temple, though properly agreeable

31. *Spec. Leg.* 1.269-71.
32. Cf. also Num. 8.4; 1 Chron. 28.19.
33. *Op. cit.*, p. 233.
34. Cf. R.J. McKelvey, *The New Temple. The Church in the New Testament* (Oxford: Oxford University Press, 1969), p. 147.

with either. At the same time, it is very clear that the form of Jewish worship envisaged in Hebrews is not pristine in the sense that it reflects merely the data of the relevant biblical texts; elements from later times are also represented.[35] This is important because it confirms what should be otherwise clear from the argumentation of the letter, namely that, despite the 'archaizing', it is the service of the Second Temple—whether by now in its last phase or already extinct—that the author rejects as *passé*. It is a small matter, in the end, whether Heb. 6.18f., or even Heb. 9.6-14, is tied to the tabernacle or to the temple. In neither case, from the author's point of view, could the old institution achieve what was now available in Christ. Both belonged to a system that was obsolete and ageing and 'ready to vanish away' (8.13).

35. See W. Horbury, 'The Aaronic Priesthood in the Epistle to the Hebrews', *JSNT* 19 (1983), pp. 43-71.

THE 'SANCTUARY' IN THE FOURTH *ODE OF SOLOMON*

P. Cameron

Introduction

According to Harris and Mingana, 'This *Ode* is the most important in the whole collection on account of the historical detail with which it appears to commence'.[1] More accurate would have been: 'This Ode may be the most important in the whole collection, if the detail with which it commences is historical'. But further, its importance will depend not only on whether the reference in the opening verses to the sanctuary is historical, but also, if the reference is historical, on its identification. There is, unsurprisingly, considerable difference of opinion on both questions.

Of course the reason why the answers to these questions are potentially important is that there is such difference of opinion on every aspect of the *Odes of Solomon* as a whole: date, place, authorship, original language are all legitimately disputed. If the reference at the beginning of the fourth *Ode* could be shown to be historical and identifiable, then perhaps the question of date could be settled, and even (by implication, and in decreasing order of probability) the questions of religious milieu, geographical location, and language.

That would be a great advance. Until there is a consensus on at least some of these matters, the *Odes of Solomon* are likely to continue to be treated as they have been since their discovery by Rendel Harris in 1909—as a quarry. They have provided supporting material for innumerable theories, but rarely have they been examined and appreciated in and for themselves. Their status is analogous to that of a statue from

---

1. J.R. Harris and A. Mingana, *The Odes and Psalms of Solomon* (Manchester, 1920), II, p. 221.

the ancient world which has suddenly come on the market, unaccompanied by any reliable record of where it was found or in what circumstances: no one knows where or when or by whom it was sculpted, or even whether it is the original or a copy. That is what happens when something is recovered by treasure-hunters rather than by archaeologists, and in such a situation the scholars tend to resemble the treasure-hunters: they appropriate the object and see whether they can profit by it. A scholar whose speciality is Hittite sculpture may pronounce the sculpture Hittite—and then perhaps rewrite the history of Hittite sculpture. A scholar with a Chinese background may insist that it is Chinese.[2] No one will have eyes only for the sculpture itself and its beauty.

This has been the fate of the *Odes of Solomon* as a collection, and of the opening verses of the fourth *Ode* in particular: what was seen as a possible control has itself been ransacked. Harris[3] thought the reference was to attempts to continue temple worship, probably at Leontopolis—the *Ode* should therefore be dated soon after AD 73 and the writer was 'if not Jewish, at least Jewish in sympathy'. Harnack[4] agreed that the allusion was to rivalry between the two temples of Jerusalem and Leontopolis, but deduced that the *Ode* must have been written while they were both standing, i.e. before AD 70; and further, that given the 'certainly Jewish' reference in *Ode* 4.1-3 (he found another at 6.8), and given the equally certain Christian references elsewhere, the *Odes* as a whole consist of a Jewish *Grundschrift* which has been subjected to Christian interpolations. For Gunkel,[5] the 'holy place' was paradise, and the *Ode* entirely Christian. For Loisy too,[6] it was paradise, but an actual paradise—the present community of

---

2. This is not so farfetched as it sounds: see L. Woolley, *Digging up the Past* (Harmondsworth, 1960), p. 21.

3. J.R. Harris, *The Odes and Psalms of Solomon* (Cambridge, 1909), pp. 54ff., 91.

4. A. Harnack, *Ein jüdisch-christliches Psalmbuch aus dem ersten Jahrhundert* (Leipzig, 1910), pp. 75ff.

5. H. Gunkel, 'Die Oden Salomos', *ZNW* 11 (1910), pp. 291-328 (296f.).

6. A. Loisy, 'La mention du Temple dans les *Odes* de Salomon', *ZNW* 12 (1911), pp. 126-30.

believers. Bernard[7] understood it somewhat similarly, but specifically in terms of baptism, which he finds everywhere in the *Odes*: 'The thought of our Odist is... of the unique dignity of the Church, the company of the baptized'. For Bauer[8] it was the community of believers or the believer himself.

In the face of such diversity (and such confidence), one has to ask what, if anything, puts any of these assertions above the status of mere assertion. What grounds, for example, does Harris have for saying, 'It is clear that the Temple in the *Ode* is a real Temple'?[9] On the other hand, does the opposing argument,[10] that the reference is to a spiritual or allegorical temple, really find support in the alleged absence of other historical references in the Odes—or can this simply be stood on its head, so that if the reference in the fourth Ode *is* historical, we should then look for more historical references elsewhere, for example in the Odist's 'persecutors' (5.4; 29.10), in the 'wars' (9.9; 29.9), and of course in 6.8? What criteria are available in deciding how to account for this foundling?

Clearly it must first of all be looked at as a self-contained entity and as far as possible understood and appreciated in itself. One would not be justified in looking for possible parallels to the head of the statue, while ignoring the relation of the head to the other parts of the body. That means both that the fourth *Ode* must be viewed as a whole, and that its connections with the rest of the *Odes* must be examined. Some scholars of course have attempted to do this. Loisy, for example, draws attention to the structure of the *Ode* and to what appears to be an echo of the beginning at the end;[11] Gunkel refers to the apparent rejection of the temple-cult in *Ode* 20;[12] and of course everyone appeals to the other reference to the temple in the sixth *Ode*.

None of this, however, is quite satisfactory or sufficiently rigorous. The reference to the temple in the sixth Ode is, if possi-

7. J.H. Bernard, *The Odes of Solomon* (Cambridge, 1912), p. 50.

8. W. Bauer, in *Neutestamentliche Apokryphen* (3rd edn; ed. E. Hennecke and W. Schneemelcher; Tübingen, 1964), II, p. 580 n. 4.

9. *The Odes and Psalms of Solomon*, II, p. 222.

10. See e.g. Bernard, *The Odes of Solomon*, p. 49.

11. *ZNW* 12 (1911), p. 126.

12. *ZNW* 11 (1910), p. 297.

ble, even more problematic, so that it is a classic case of *ignotum per ignotius*;[13] *Ode* 20 may not be any less Jewish than the criticisms of the cult by the Old Testament prophets; and as far as the structure of the fourth *Ode* itself is concerned, there is more to consider than the beginning and the end—the question is the coherence of the imagery throughout.

Indeed this appears to be the problem with practically all the *Odes*: their coherence. It is not just that the speaker changes suddenly and without warning or confirmation in mid-*Ode*; and it is not just that a particular image is often obscure or even impenetrable in itself; the major difficulty is in relating each image to what precedes and what follows, and in discovering the pattern or unity of the *Ode* as a whole—assuming indeed that there is such a pattern of unity to be discovered.

Now underlying this problem is the question of translation. Gunkel had some trenchant things to say about the quality of the existing translations of the *Odes*:

> Nur beiläufig erwähne ich, dass die deutschen Übersetzungen ziemlich nüchtern und prosaisch klingen. Ist es wirklich dem exakten Orientalisten unmöglich, auch dem Geiste der Lieder gerecht zu werden und dem deutschen Leser etwas von der pathetischen oder innerlichen Schönheit der Oden zu zeigen? Mögen künftige Übersetzer von Luther lernen und den Schätzen von Poesie, die hier an den Tag gekommen sind, ihr Recht geben!

He also remarks on 'wie viel Sonderbares oder völlig Unverständliches, um nicht zu sagen Unsinn, finden wir überall' in the translations.[14]

That was in 1911. Unfortunately things do not seem to have greatly improved. In contrast with the proliferation of translations of the canonical scriptures into contemporary language, there appears to be no English translation of the *Odes* which does not use 'thou' and which does not sound 'ziemlich nüchtern und prosaisch'. The first three verses of the fourth *Ode*, for example, in what is probably the most frequently cited

---

13. For a discussion of the problems raised by the sixth *Ode*, see J.A. Emerton, 'Notes on Some Passages in the Odes of Solomon', *JTS* ns 28 (1977), at pp. 507-12.

14. *ZNW* 11 (1910), pp. 292f.

recent English translation, that of Charlesworth, read as follows:[15]

> No man can pervert Thy holy place, O my God;
> Nor can he change it, and put it in another place.
> Because he has no power over it;
> For Thy sanctuary Thou designedst before Thou didst make special places.
> The ancient one shall not be perverted by those which are inferior to it.

Of course it is understandable that the scholarly translator, translating for other scholars, should want to produce as neutral and untendentious a translation as possible. But there are two unfortunate consequences. One is that the *Odes* remain in practice inaccessible to the non-scholar—and considering all the scholarly noises about the beauty and poetry of the *Odes*, that *must* be unfortunate. The other is that such flat and antiquated translations give the impression, even to scholars, of being more neutral than they actually are—and of course it is not just Syriac-speaking scholars who comment on the *Odes*. Those who do not have Syriac take such translations as the basis for exegesis, whereas they are—as all translations are—themselves the result of exegetical decisions, whether entirely conscious or not.

What I propose to do now, therefore, is not so much to avoid this circularity—that is impossible—as to articulate it, and at the same time to try to do justice to the fourth *Ode* as a poetic unity, by offering first as neutral (though intelligible) a translation as I can, second some exegetical comment (necessarily brief), and finally a revised, and I hope slightly more literary translation in the light of the exegesis. Whether this will solve the questions we began with, remains to be seen.

Provisional Translation

1   No one changes your holy place, my God,
      And there is no one who will change it and put it in another place,

---

15. J.H. Charlesworth, *The Odes of Solomon* (Oxford, 1973), p. 22.

2 Because there is no authority over it.
   For you designed your sanctuary before you made places:
3 The ancient will not be changed by the things which are
   inferior to it.
   You have given your heart, Lord, to your believers:
4 You will never be idle.
   And you will not be without fruits.
5 For one hour of your faith
   Is better than all days and years.
6 For who will put on your grace and be deprived?
7 Because your seal is known,
   And your creatures are known to it,
8 And your hosts possess it,
   And the chosen archangels put it on.
9 You have given us your fellowship:
   It was not that you lacked us,
   But we lacked you.
10 Sprinkle on us your sprinklings,
   And open your rich springs which supply us abundantly with
   milk and honey.
11 For there is no regret with you
   That you will regret anything you have promised.
12 And the end was revealed to you.
13 For whatever you have given you have given for nothing,
   So that you will not draw back again and take them back.
14 For everything has been revealed to you as God,
   And has been established from the beginning before you.
15 And you, Lord, made everything.

Exegesis

Verses 1-3. The significant thing about the first three verses is
the three-fold use of the root *ḥlph* and the noun *'athrâ*. To
some of the early commentators—always on the lookout for
an excuse to emend—this repetition was 'highly suspicious'.[16]
It is, however, a distinctive feature of the style of the *Odes*,[17]

16. E.g. W.E. Barnes, 'The Odes of Solomon', *JTS* 11 (1909–10), p. 617.
17. On this see Harris and Mingana, II, pp. 101ff.; J.A. Emerton,
'Some Problems of Text and Language in the *Odes* of Solomon', *JTS* ns
18 (1967), at pp. 373f.; and most fully J.H. Charlesworth, 'Paronomasia
and Assonance in the Syriac Text of the *Odes* of Solomon', *Semitica* 1
(1970), pp. 12-26. Oddly enough, Charlesworth does not refer to *Ode* 4.1-
3.

and a feature which is not always simply ornamental (though it can be—cf. e.g. 6.9): passages like 11.1-3 indicate that the repeated use of the same root is intended to produce a progression of ideas which would otherwise be very difficult to express, and which is of course almost impossible to capture in translation. In the present passage the subtlety is increased, because one of the words which appear to change their meaning with their place in the sequence has the basic meaning 'to change' (*ḥlph*), and the other has the basic meaning 'place' (*'athrâ*).

The first appearance of *'athrâ* is qualified by the suffix and the adjective 'holy'—'your holy place'; and the second by the adjective 'other'. In v. 2 the word occurs in the plural and is contrasted with *qûdshākh*, which seems to be used synonymously with 'your holy place'.

The two instances of *ḥlph* in v. 1 are both in the shaphel: the first is an absolute sense, the second explicited by 'and put it in another place'. In the first line of v. 3 the form is the eshtaphal, and the context in that line demands the meaning 'be usurped' or something like it.

The intention of the writer therefore seems to have been to progress from the general to the particular, and from the abstract to the concrete. He begins, in other words, with the general proposition that God's holy place is unchangeable (v. 1a); he then justifies that proposition by explaining that the holy place is not of the sort that can be picked up and put down somewhere else (v. 1b)—it is not subject to that kind of physical control (v. 2a); that assertion he supports by the argument that the holy place, the sanctuary, was thought of or planned by God before he created any (physical) place at all (v. 2b); and (as everyone knows) the elder takes precedence over the younger (v. 3a). The holy place, that is to say, is 'unchangeable' both because it is not an ordinary (physical) place and because it is older than any (physical) place.

The translator has to try to bring out both the progression and the implicit contrasts in the three-fold use of each root. In the case of *'athrâ* he is really obliged to use the word 'place' three times: the different shades of meaning can only be indicated by the qualifiers, as they are in Syriac. In v. 1a the adjective *qaddîshâ* is etymologically related to *qûdshâ* in v. 2b, and if the latter is to be translated 'sanctuary' (the word can mean simply 'holiness'—it is used elsewhere in the *Odes* only in conjunction with *rûḥâ*, 'spirit of holiness' = 'holy spirit'), then 'sanctified' would be a possible translation of the former. It sounds a little unnatural, however, so 'sacred' is probably better; at least it shares several letters with 'sanctuary'. In v. 1b 'some other place' is better than 'another place'; the implication is not just that the 'sacred place' cannot be moved to a different location, but that the very idea of 'location' is misconceived. In v. 2b the plural *'athrawâthâ* has to be translated 'any place'; the English plural 'places' is in the context an instance of what Gunkel meant by 'Sonderbares, oder völlig Unverständliches, um nicht zu sagen Unsinn'. In the Syriac there is an obvious assonance between *'ethra'îth* and *'athrawâthâ*; the translation of the first by 'planned' goes some way towards preserving this.

The position with the root *ḥlph* is different. To use the word 'change' three times would miss the point altogether: an English root has to be found which can both capture the idea of physical removal and indicate that there is a word-play in the original. Perhaps 'plant' is best. In v. 1a what is being denied is that the sacred place is movable: unfortunately there is no word 'unplant'—'uproot' will have to do. In v. 1b the notion is of being 'transplanted', and in v. 3a of being 'supplanted'. The revised translation of vv. 1-3 will therefore read:

No one, my God, can uproot your sacred place,
There is no one who can transplant it and set it down in some
    other place—
Because it is not subject to physical control.
For you planned your sanctuary before you made any place,
And the elder will not be supplanted by the younger.

Verse 3b. This looks at first sight like a change of gear, but it cannot be: it is the second half of a couplet, and it presumably continues the thought of the first three verses. Harris and Mingana draw attention to 2 Chron. 7.16: 'Now I have chosen and consecrated this house that my name may be there forever; my eyes and my heart will be there for all time' (RSV). But there is a difference between God's name, eyes and heart being in the temple, and—the thought in *Ode* 4—God giving his heart to believers. After all, he could not be said to give his name and his eyes to believers. So that what is involved here in the idea of God's heart, is not something which is contained or present in the 'sacred place', but rather something which is synonymous with it. Verse 3b, in other words, sums up the content of the preceding verses, and confirms the non-physical nature of the 'sacred place'.

Verse 4. The same combination of *bṭl* and *pi'rā* is found in *Ode* 11.23, there in conjunction with *'athrā*. But *'athrā* in 11.23 has the meaning of 'room' or 'space' in paradise, and it is paradise which is there characterized as 'never idle' but 'filled with fruit'. Moreover, this paradise appears to be a present possession which is given to the believer by God (11.12). The implication therefore here is that in speaking of the heart of God being given to believers (another image for the 'sacred place'), the writer is thinking in terms of the paradise described in *Ode* 11.

Verse 5. This sounds like an echo of Ps. 84.10: 'For a day in thy courts is better than a thousand elsewhere' (RSV), where 'courts' is paralleled in the second half of the verse by 'the house of my God'. But the significant thing is that in the *Ode* the word *haimānûthā* is substituted for the reference to the temple. In every other occurrence in the *Odes*, this word means 'faith in God' rather than 'God's faithfulness', and there is no reason to think that it means anything else here.[18]

Verses 1-5. It therefore appears that while vv. 1-3a describe the sacred place in negative terms, i.e. as non-physical, vv. 3b-5 continue the description positively: the sacred place is the heart of God, it is given to believers, it has some connection with what is elsewhere called paradise, and it consists in faith (not in a building).

Verse 6. Some of the commentators speak of the 'apparent discontinuity' between vv. 5 and 6,[19] but the *geir* seems to indicate that v. 6 gives the grounds for the preceding statement in v. 5. That is to say, the reason why an hour of faith is qualita-

---

18. Only J.A. Emerton ('The *Odes* of Solomon', in Sparks, *Old Testament Apocrypha* [1984], p. 692) translates it as 'thy faithfulness', and he gives the alternative 'faith in thee' in a footnote.
19. E.g. Harris and Mingana, p. 223.

tively so different is that whoever puts on God's grace will lack nothing. The basic sense of *ṭlm* is 'to oppress, or deceive', but in the ethpeel it has the additional meaning 'to lack, to be deprived of'. The root appears elsewhere in the *Odes* only at 33.12, again in the ethpeel, where it probably means 'shall not lack anything', because the parallel is 'but shall possess immortality/incorruption'.

Verse 7. This verse in turn either (a) gives the grounds for the proposition in v. 6 that those who have put on grace will lack nothing, or (b) elucidates what is meant by 'putting on'; which of these is correct depends on the interpretation of *ḥtm'*. The word *ḥathmâ* means a 'seal', or 'signet-ring', or 'sign'; the word *ḥthāmâ* means 'the act of sealing or signing', and is used also of making the sign of the cross. The only manuscript of *Ode* 4 is of course unpointed, so that it could be either, and in any case they appear to have been used interchangeably. The only other occurrence in the *Odes* is at 23.8, 9, where it is used in the context of a letter, and therefore must mean 'seal' rather than 'sign'. But there is no such controlling context here. Bernard of course understands it as the seal of baptism,[20] but the reference to archangels in v. 8 makes this problematic—though Harris and Mingana offer an excursus on the circumcision of angels.[21]

The verbs which govern the noun *ḥtm'* in vv. 7 and 8 can hardly be said to clarify its meaning: it is capable of 'being known', of 'knowing', of 'being possessed' (by powers), and of 'being put on'[22] (by archangels). The last of these is scarcely compatible with either baptism or the sign of the cross, and the second seems to suggest some sort of agent or hypostatization, perhaps along the lines of *Ode* 23—though to appeal to that *Ode* would certainly entail *obscurum per obscurius*. It might be better to understand the word as referring to some kind of objective guarantee of God's grace, the recognition of which ensures that the believer lacks nothing.

Whatever the precise meaning of *ḥtm'*—if indeed it has a precise meaning—it appears that vv. 6-8 continue the argu-

---

20. At pp. 51f.
21. At pp. 224ff.
22. The same verb which is used in v. 6 for 'putting on grace'.

ment by further describing this gift from God (variously referred to as his sacred place, his sanctuary, his heart, his faith, his grace), or by explaining how believers receive it.

Verse 9. And in this verse there is yet another image, *shawthāphūthâ*, which means 'fellowship' or 'participation' or 'partnership', but which is also one of the words for the eucharist, for holy communion. It appears again in the *Odes* at 21.5, again describing the relationship between the believer and God, and in a context of 'putting on light' and being constantly in God's presence. The rest of v. 9 itself brings out the mutuality of the relationship implied by *shawthāphūthâ*, by stressing that it is not because of any lack or need on his part that God has allowed us to share in it: it is the reciprocity involved in *shawthāphūthâ* which makes such a disclaimer necessary.

The progression of ideas, therefore, from v. 1 onwards finds its culmination in this word. Looked at negatively, God's sacred place is not something physical; looked at from his side, it is his heart, which is always fruitful; looked at from our side, it is our faith, it is the grace we put on; looked at from both sides, it is communion between God and man.

Verses 10-15. With v. 10 there again seems to be a change of gear, both formally and in content. The mood suddenly shifts from the indicative to the imperative, and the 'rains', 'fountains', and 'milk and honey' seem to be foreign to the context.

But as far as the form is concerned, the following verse makes it clear that the imperatives in v. 10 are not so much hesitant petitions for more favours, as confident assertions that God will act in accordance with his promises—so confident that they are expressed in the form of commands. Just as the sacred place was planned before anything else, and nothing can change that (vv. 1-3), so with all God's gifts: they are all freely given, they are never retracted; everything, from beginning to end, has been established before God, who created everything.

As for the 'rains' of v. 10, the mention of anything liquid will inevitably conjure up baptism, and Bernard argues that v. 10b is likewise a reference to the 'administering of milk and honey to the newly baptized, to symbolise their entrance into "the land flowing with milk and honey", the land of promise which the chosen people reached after passing through the waters of the Jordan'.[23]

There are, however, other possibilities. The idea of water is a necesssary one in any vision of paradise emanating from the Middle East, and it appears more than once in the Paradise *Ode* 11, whose connections with this *Ode* have already been referred to. The word *mabû'â*, used here in v. 10 in the plural, appears at 11.6, and there is the (certainly not baptismal) *potamos charas* in the part of *Ode* 11 which is uniquely preserved in Papyrus Bodmer XI.

Moreover, the content of the promises which Bernard finds here operating only as symbols of baptism could just as well be the primary reference. After all, the word 'promise' occurs in v. 11, and it is becoming increasingly clear that the subject of the entire *Ode* is the sacred place, its origin conceived by God in the beginning, and its final end manifest to him. Now the content of God's promises to his people Israel is of course traditionally summed up as a land flowing with milk and honey, and the importance of the rains is closely bound up with this. For example, Deut. 11.9: 'that you may live long in the land which the Lord swore to your fathers to give to them and to their descendants, a land flowing with milk and honey...'; 11.11: 'a land... which drinks water by the rain from heaven...'; 11.14: 'he will give the rain for your land in its season, the early rain and the later rain...'; 11.16: 'Take heed lest... the Lord shut up the heavens so that there be no rain, and the land yield no fruit'.

On this understanding, the 'rains' and the 'milk and honey' of v. 10 are simply another way of describing the sacred place; the *Ode* is permeated with its developing imagery from beginning to end.

Revised Translation

1 No one, my God, can uproot your sacred place,
   There is no one who can transplant it and set it down in some other place—

2 Because it is not subject to physical control.
   For you planned your sanctuary before you made any place:
3 And the elder will not be supplanted by the younger.
   You have given your heart, Lord, to your faithful ones:
4 You never lie fallow,
   And you are never barren.
5 For one hour of your faith
   Is better than any number of days or even years.
6 For who puts on your grace and lacks anything?
7 Because your seal is known,
   And your creatures are known to it;
8 Your forces are armed with it,
   The elect archangels themselves put it on.
9 You have brought us into your fellowship—
   Not because you needed us,
   But because we needed you.
10 Let your rains drop down on us,
   Open your teeming springs and shower milk and honey on us.
11 For you are not one to feel regret,
   Or retract anything that you have promised:
12 The outcome has been revealed to you.
13 For whatever you have given, you have freely given:
   You will not vacillate or take anything back again.
14 For all things have been revealed to you as God,
   And prepared before you from the beginning.
15 And you, Lord, made all things.

Implications

The structure and the inner logic of the fourth *Ode*, together with parallels in the other *Odes*, strongly suggest: first, that the sacred place or sanctuary of vv. 1-2—far from being an isolated reference at the beginning—forms the subject-matter of the entire *Ode*; second, that what is in mind is not the Temple, or indeed anything physical at all; third, that its nature is hinted at in a series of images which draw attention to different facets, and accordingly any simple identification of the sacred place with 'the church', or 'the believer', or 'paradise' (present or future) would be unwise.

Even to say that the *Ode* involves a spiritualization of the 'sanctuary' might be misleading, but if the above interpretation is on the right lines, there are interesting parallels with the conversation between Jesus and the Samaritan woman in John 4. Most obviously, there is the woman's statement at 4.20 that according to the Jews the place (*topos/ 'athrâ*) where God should be worshipped is in Jerusalem, whereas the Samaritans worship him 'on this mountain'; and the reply of Jesus in vv. 21f. that the time is coming when people will worship God neither on that mountain nor in Jerusalem, but 'in spirit and in truth'. But there are other coincidences: there is the theme of water—particularly, in v. 14, the *pege hudatos* (cf. *Ode* 4.10); there is the woman's implicit claim (in v. 12) that what is older (Jacob) takes precedence over what is—apparently—younger (cf. *Ode* 4.3); there is the woman's testimony in vv. 29 and 39 that Jesus is omniscient (cf. *Ode* 4.14); and there is in v. 22 the notion of God being 'known' (cf. *Ode* 4.7). The implications of these coincidences may be worth exploring.[24]

24. See in this connection J.H. Charlesworth and R.A. Culpepper, 'The Odes of Solomon and the Gospel of John', *CBQ* 35 (1973), pp. 298-322. The only parallel they suggest between *Ode* 4 and John 4 is *Ode* 4.10b/ Jn 4.14.

LAW AND TEMPLE IN ORIGEN[1]

C.P. Bammel

The question of the proper attitude to be taken to the Old Testament Law much occupied Christian writers of the second century. Jews, Judaizing Christians and even pagans might attack Christian failure to obey the law. Thus Justin in the *Dialogue with Trypho*, which is addressed to a certain Marcus Pompeius, perhaps a pagan enquirer (141; cf. 8), represents Trypho and himself as in agreement that the chief Jewish complaint against Christians was their failure to live according to the law (10), and he also describes Jewish Christians who tell Gentile converts that they will not be saved unless they observe the law (47). The Jew quoted by Celsus reproaches those who after being deluded by Jesus have abandoned the law of their fathers,[2] and Celsus repeats this accusation.[3] The author of the *Epistle to Diognetus* replies to the question why Christians do not worship in the same manner as the Jews (3.1). On the other hand the views of Marcion and the Gnostics, who relegated the Old Testament God who gave the law to an inferior level, demanded a response from those who maintained his identity with the Father of Christ. Marcion himself in his *Antitheses* used the contradictions between

---

1. I apologize for the shortcomings of this paper. Paradoxically they must be taken as a tribute to the honorand of this volume. Preparing it without his knowledge and hence without the benefits of direct consultation, I have been doubly aware of the debt I owe to him on other occasions.

2. Origen, *Contra Celsum* 2.1ff. On Celsus's Jew, cf. E. Bammel, 'Der Jude des Celsus', *Judaica: Kleine Schriften*, I (Tübingen, 1986), pp. 265-83, especially pp. 274-76 on this accusation.

3. Origen, *Contra Celsum* 5.25 and 33; cf. 3.5.

the law and the gospel to argue for two Gods,[4] and perhaps the most interesting discussion of Moses' law is the letter of the Valentinian Ptolemy to Flora, which is directed against two contrary sets of opponents, those who regard the law as ordained by God the Father and those who attribute it to the devil. Ptolemy himself ascribes it, or rather the part of it that is not of human origin, to the creator god, a god of justice who hates evil.[5] The extent of Christian embarrassment may be seen in concessions such as the theory of the Clementine *Homilies* that certain false chapters had been added to the written law subsequent to the time of Moses himself (2.38ff.; 3.3ff., 47ff.; cf. 16.10ff.) or the view favoured by the *Didascalia* and by Irenaeus that the legislation imposed after the worship of the golden calf was intended as heavy bonds or a yoke of bondage and was abolished by Jesus. They even apply Ezek. 20.25 'I gave them statutes which were not good' to this legislation.[6]

For those who continued to worship the Old Testament God the destruction of the Jerusalem temple too demanded an explanation.[7] The answers to the two problems were sometimes linked.[8] The desire to vindicate divine providence and to

4. According to Tertullian, *Adversus Marcionem* 1.19.

5. Epiphanius, *Panarion*, 33.3-7.

6. Irenaeus, *Adversus Haereses* 4.26 (Harvey); *Didascalia* (ed. H. Connolly; Oxford, 1929), pp. 12-15, 216-19, 222-30; cf. pp. lix-lx, lxiii-lxv for a comparison with Irenaeus.

7. Pagan critics attacked the Jewish God for his desertion of his worshippers (cf. e.g. Minucius Felix, *Octavius* 10.4; Celsus in Origen, *Contra Celsum* 8.69), and the failure of the Jewish revolts has been seen as a factor in the development of Gnostic dualism.

8. For Christian and Jewish reactions in general, cf. G.W.H. Lampe, AD 70 in Christian Reflection', in E. Bammel and C.F.D. Moule (eds.), *Jesus and the Politics of his Day* (Cambridge, 1984), pp. 153-71; H.J. Schoeps, 'Die Tempelzerstörung des Jahres 70 in der jüdischen Religionsgeschichte', *Aus frühchristlicher Zeit* (Tübingen, 1950), pp. 144-83, H. Windisch, 'Der Untergang Jerusalems (anno 70) im Urteil der Christen und Juden', *Theologisch Tijdschrift* 48 (1914), pp. 519-50, and C. Thoma, 'Auswirkungen des jüdischen Krieges gegen Rom (66–70/73 n. Chr.) auf das rabbinische Judentum', *Biblische Zeitschrift* ns 12 (1968), pp. 30-54, 186-210. The patristic view that the destruction of the temple was intended as a punishment will not be discussed here.

demonstrate the continuity of salvation history favoured a picture which gave positive but limited validity to those parts of the law which Christians no longer observed.[9] One of the most fruitful solutions[10] was the view that the ceremonial law[11] consisted of types and symbols intended only to be observed literally for a limited time until their fulfilment in Christ's incarnation.[12] To this was added the claim that the destruction of the Jerusalem temple brought the era of literal observance finally to a close.[13] The idea that the earthly temple and sacrifices had now been superseded was indeed developed prior to the destruction of the temple[14] and the preference for spiritual worship has pre-Christian roots in both Jewish and pagan thought, as Christian apologists were well aware.[15] Second-century writers make use of the claim that since the

9. For this reason the educative role of the law is often stressed; cf. for example Irenaeus, *Adversus Haereses* 4.24.2 and 25.3; Clement of Alexandria, *Paedagogus* 1.7.59.1 and 1.11.96.3f. (citing Gal. 3.24).

10. On the various criticisms of the law and attempted solutions, cf. W. Horbury, 'Old Testament Interpretation in the Writings of the Church Fathers', in M.J. Mulder and H. Sysling (eds.), *Mikra* (Assen and Philadelphia, 1988), pp. 758-61; M. Simon, *Verus Israel* (Paris, 1948); Schoeps, *art. cit.*, pp. 159ff. M.F. Wiles, *The Divine Apostle* (Cambridge, 1967), pp. 49-72, discusses the attitudes to the law developed in patristic exegesis of the Pauline epistles. Cf. also R.E. Taylor, 'Attitudes of the Fathers towards Practices of Jewish Christians', *TU* 79 (1961), pp. 504-11.

11. The term is used here for convenience. Early Christian writers usually specify 'the law concerning sacrifices, etc.'

12. This view appears in the *Epistle of Barnabas* and the letter of Ptolemy to Flora and is taken up by many later Christian writers including Clement of Alexandria. It is interesting to find that Irenaeus, while accepting it, nonetheless attacks his Gnostic opponents for overworking their use of typology (*Adversus Haereses* 4.32 [Harvey]).

13. Cf. G.W.H. Lampe, *art. cit.*, pp. 170-71; H.J. Schoeps, *art. cit.*, pp. 153ff.

14. Cf. Lampe, *art. cit.*, pp. 157-58; O. Cullmann, 'L'opposition contre le Temple de Jerusalem, motif commun de la théologie johannique et du monde ambiant'.

15. Cf. for example R.A. Kraft, *The Apostolic Fathers. 3: Barnabas and the Didache*, pp. 84, 130. According to Justin, *Dialogue with Trypho*, 117, contemporary Jews themselves were using the argument that God preferred the sacrifices of prayer offered by diaspora Jews to the temple sacrifices at Jerusalem.

destruction of the temple literal observance of the law has been impossible. Because the period of validity of the law was intended to be limited, it was laid down that sacrifice could be offered only in one place and the destruction of that place fore-ordained.

Elements of this argument are present already in the *Epistle of Barnabas*—the Old Testament sacrifices are types of Christ (7–8), the destruction of the temple was prophesied (16), the Christians are the spiritual temple of God (4.11; 16.7-10)—but the exposition of the limited validity of temple worship is missing, being replaced by the more negative idea that the people had already lost the covenant when Moses broke the two tablets because of their worship of the golden calf (4.7-8; 14.1-3).

The view of a historical development is particularly clear in Peter's speech in the Clementine *Recognitions*. Subsequent to the worship of the golden calf, in order that the people might be prevented from sacrificing to idols, Moses allowed them to sacrifice to God alone and appointed that there would be one place only in which this would be lawful (1.36-37, referring to Deut. 12.11). This was done however with a view to the fact that at the appropriate time the true prophet would teach them to cease from sacrificing (instituting baptism instead) and give warning of the destruction of the temple (1.37-38; cf. 1.64). The idea of the ceremonial law as symbolic is absent here.

Similarly Justin in his *Dialogue with Trypho* states that it was because of the people's sins that God allowed the temple to be called his house (22 end); the observation of sabbath, sacrifices, offerings and feasts was enjoined because of the hardness of the people's hearts (43, 46). All these things were types and symbols intended to end with the coming of Christ (40–43). God ordained that the passover lamb should be sacrificed in only one place, knowing that the time would come when that place would be captured and all the offerings cease (40). Justin divides the law into what is naturally good, pious and right-eous, and what was appointed because of the hardness of the people's hearts (45) and represents Trypho as admitting that, as regards the latter category, the offering of sacrifices is no longer possible (46).

The same general picture emerges in Irenaeus, *Adversus Haereses*, in the context of the refutation of Gnostic criticisms of the God who gave the law and of the fact that he allowed the destruction of Jerusalem,[16] and a similar one in Tertullian.[17] Irenaeus, who is not writing against Jews or Jewish Christians, omits the argument that obedience to the law is impossible because of the destruction of the temple, whereas Tertullian does emphasize the commandment that sacrifice should be offered to God in only one place (*Adversus Iudaeos* 5; cf. 8 end, on the cessation of sacrifice, and 13, on the destruction of Jerusalem and its consequences).

The *Didascalia* states that the Lord caused the destruction of the temple and altar by the Romans and the cessation of sacrifices and asserts that the 'second legislation' with regard especially to the punishment of the wicked and idolaters and the performance of sacrifices, libations and sprinklings of ashes cannot be performed by those in dispersion under Roman rule. To attempt to follow this legislation is to fall under a curse, as is shown by Deut. 27.26 (Gal. 3.10).[18]

The approach of Origen is characterized by the fact that he regards all the writings of the Old Testament, both law and prophets, as divinely inspired and uses the distinction between letter and spirit or literal and spiritual understanding to solve any difficulties.[19] The coming of Jesus has, in his view, re-

---

16. 4.5-6 (Harvey): the law ended with John (Lk. 16.16) and Jerusalem was abandoned once her function had been fulfilled; 4.26-32: the people were subjected to a yoke of bondage after the worship of the golden calf; pure sacrifice (like that of Abel) is now offered to God by the church throughout the world; the earthly offerings and sacrifices were the types of heavenly things.

17. Cf. *Adversus Marcionem* 18: sacrifice was allowed to prevent idolatry; *Adversus Iudaeos* 2: Moses' law was temporary; 5: earthly and spiritual sacrifice were symbolized by the offerings of Cain and Abel; earthly sacrifices were to be offered in one place only, spiritual sacrifices in every land; 8: after the Jewish defeat libations and sacrifices ceased; 13: the Spirit dwelt in the temple before the advent of Christ, who is the true temple of God.

18. *Didascalia* (ed. H. Connolly), pp. 238-40.

19. *De Principiis* Book 4 is devoted to this topic. On Origen's exegesis cf. H. de Lubac, *Histoire et Esprit: l'intelligence de l'Ecriture d'après Origène* (Paris, 1950). On his views concerning the observance of the

moved the veil which had concealed the spiritual nature of the law of Moses.[20] Unlike certain earlier writers he does not regard parts of the law in a negative light[21] or state that Jesus abrogated the old law by replacing it with a new one.[22] Thus when Celsus attacks the Christians on the grounds that Jesus gave laws in opposition to those of Moses, Origen refutes him at some length as having failed to go beyond the literal meaning of the Old Testament,[23] and uses the distinction between letter and spirit to explain the 'statutes which were not good' of Ezek. 20.25.[24]

Origen often expounds his own characteristic view with particular reference to the impossibility of literal obedience to the law since the destruction of the temple.[25] A good brief account of his approach is given at the beginning of his tenth *Homily on Leviticus*. Those of the church, he says, receive Moses as a divinely inspired prophet who wrote in symbols about future mysteries. The things written or done in the law and prophets as types of the future were like the clay model which a sculptor makes of a bronze, silver or gold statue, no longer any use after the statue is completed. Thus the former great royal city of Jerusalem and its celebrated temple were destroyed after the advent of the true temple of God, and the former high priest, altar and sacrifices had no place after the true high priest had come and the true lamb had offered himself. Those who think that they ought to obey the law with

law, cf. N.R.M. de Lange, *Origen and the Jews* (Cambridge, 1976), pp. 89-96.

20. *De Principiis* 4.1.6; cf. 2 Cor. 3.14

21. See above p. 473. This does not mean that he did not differentiate different parts of the law.

22. Cf. Justin, *Dialogue* 11 and 43, declaring that Christ himself is the eternal law; Tertullian, *Adversus Iudaeos* 3 and 6; also the rejection of the law in *Epistle of Barnabas* 3.6.

23. *Contra Celsum* 7.18ff. (ed. P. Koetschau; GCS *Origenes* 2 [1899], pp. 169.10ff.).

24. *Contra Celsum* 7.20 (ed. Koetschau, pp. 171.31–172.22); *Homilies on Exodus* 7.2 (ed. W.A. Baehrens; GCS *Origenes* 6 [1920], pp. 206.19–207.6).

25. Origen's attitude to the destruction of the temple and many related topics are discussed in the excellent book of G. Sgherri, *Chiesa e sinagoga nelle opere di Origene* (Milan, 1982); cf. in particular pp. 93-110 on the destruction of Jerusalem and the temple.

respect to the fasts of the Jews should take note of Paul's words in Gal. 5.3 and obey the whole law, go up to Jerusalem thrice a year and so on—but this is impossible, since there is no altar or priest.[26]

Particularly striking is the allegorical exposition of Moses' death at the beginning of the second *Homily on Joshua*.[27] Jerusalem is destroyed, the altar abandoned, there are no sacrifices, offerings or drink-offerings, no priests, high-priests, or services of Levites, no one appears before the Lord thrice a year or offers gifts in the temple or sacrifices the Paschal lamb or eats unleavened bread or offers first-fruits or consecrates firstlings, but these have all been replaced by the spiritual service of Christianity. Origen here refers to a lost apocryphal book for a description of two figures of Moses, the one alive in the spirit, the other dead in the body, and interprets these as referring to the spiritual law and the letter of the law.

According to *Homily on Joshua* 17 the 'shadow and example of heavenly things' (Heb. 8.5), which existed on earth as long as the temple cult was carried out at Jerusalem, has been brought to an end with the destruction of the temples at Jerusalem and on Mount Gerizim. Thus Jesus' prediction in Jn 4.21-24 has been fulfilled. Jesus himself is the true temple, the true high-priest, and the true lamb of God.[28]

Interpreting Rom. 7.1-4, Origen states that the letter of the law appeared to be alive as long as the type and image of heavenly worship was carried out at Jerusalem, but since Jesus' incarnation and the destruction of Jerusalem together with the temple and altar it has been dead. There are no sacrifices, no priesthood, no services carried out by Levites, nor can the law any longer punish murderers or adulteresses. It is no longer possible for every male to appear before the Lord three times a year, nor to sacrifice the Paschal lamb, no sheaves of first-fruits or offerings are presented, there is no purification

26. *Homilies on Leviticus* 10.1 (ed. Baehrens, pp. 440.18–442.22).
27. *Homily on Joshua* (ed. Baehrens; GCS *Origenes* 7 [1921], pp. 296.10–297.19).
28. *Homily on Joshua* (ed. Baehrens, pp. 400.15–401.10). Cf. also 26.3 (pp. 462.17–463.16), and *Commentary on Matthew* 12.20 and 16.3 (ed. E. Klostermann; GCS *Origenes* 10 [1935], pp. 113.24–114.29 and p. 468).

of leprosy or impurity.[29] A similar list appears in the exposition of Gal. 3.24ff. by Jerome, who is no doubt following Origen's lost exegesis here.[30] The phrase in Romans 8.3, τὸ ἀδύνατον τοῦ νόμου ἐν ᾧ ἠσθένει διὰ τῆς σαρκός, Origen explains as referring to the impossibility of literal obedience to the law. Before the fall of Jerusalem the law was weak according to the flesh. Now that there is no temple, altar or place to sacrifice it is altogether dead.[31]

Sometimes this picture is elaborated with special reference to contemporary Judaism. In his *Homilies on Numbers* Origen interprets Moses' marriage with the Ethiopian woman in Num. 12.1ff. as referring to the union between the spiritual law and the church. The synagogue, represented by Miriam, attacks Moses, because the spiritual law does not teach the church to observe the circumcision of the flesh, the sabbath, new moons or sacrifices.[32] Like Miriam in Num. 12.12-15, the people of the Jews, who had previously enjoyed the honour of possessing the high priests, priests, Levites, the temple, prophets and even receiving divine visitations, has been temporarily repudiated, without any of these privileges, and scattered throughout the earth.[33] In the passage just quoted from *Homilies on Joshua* 17, Origen states that the cessation of the temple cult was divinely planned in order to remove an obstacle to conversion to Christianity. He appeals to the Jews visiting Jerusalem not to lament over its ashes, but to look up and seek the heavenly Jerusalem, the heavenly altar and the high priest after the order of Melchisedek (Heb. 5.10). It is by the mercy of God that their earthly inheritance has been removed, that they may seek an inheritance in heaven.[34] The same argument, but without the appeal to the Jews, appears in

29. *Commentary on Romans* 6.7 (ed. C.H.E. Lommatzsch; Berlin, 1836–37, II, pp. 34-35). A similar interpretation is given in *Homilies on Genesis* 6.3 (ed. Baehrens; GCS *Origenes* 6 [1920], p. 69), with a challenge to 'those friends and defenders of the letter' to keep the letter of the law if they can.
30. *Commentary on Galatians* 2 (PL 26 [1845], 368 B-C); cf. also 375C on Gal. 4.8-9.
31. *Commentary on Romans* 6.12 (ed. Lommatzsch, II, pp. 67-68).
32. 6.4 (ed. Baehrens; GCS *Origenes* VII, p. 36.5-16).
33. 7.4 (pp. 44.1-23); cf. 7.3 (pp. 41.25–42.1).
34. 17.1 (ed. Baehrens; GCS *Origenes* VII, pp. 401.13–402.6).

the tenth *Homily on Leviticus*. Divine providence allowed the destruction of the city and temple to prevent admiration for the cult and ministry impeding the realization that the truth has now replaced the type.[35] Origen's attitude to the temple cult therefore is positive.[36] In his *Homilies on Numbers* he again exclaims on the magnificence and propriety of the temple cult and the fact that if it had continued in existence it would have prevented faith in the gospel.[37] In the *Contra Celsum* he explains the superiority of the Jews to other races in having only one temple, one altar, one place for burning incense, and one high priest.[38]

Most often Origen treats the destruction of the temple as the confirmation of a new era of spiritual observance inaugurated by the incarnation. In considering the arguments of Judaizing Christians, however, who think that the law should still be followed literally, he distinguishes between the situation during and shortly after the lifetime of Jesus and the subsequent cessation of the temple cult. The most interesting discussion occurs in an excursus on circumcision in the *Commentary on Romans*. Reflecting on the clash between Rom. 2.25 and Gal. 5.2 on the question of circumcision he admits that Peter and Paul did observe the law in certain respects and that circumcision may have been helpful for Jewish converts reluctant to give it up.[39] He also repeats arguments which had persuaded some gentile Christians to accept circumcision.[40] In order to investigate the question whether circumcision is still useful, he sets about examining the Old Testament instructions in order to see whether proselytes or foreigners are included in them. If the contents of the law are divinely inspired, he argues, these details are significant, and indeed the instructions to refrain

---

35. 10.1 (ed. Baehrens, p. 442.2-9).
36. Cf. *Comm. ser. in Matt.* 29 (ed. E. Klostermann; GCS *Origenes* XI [1933], p. 55.5-7), on the divine presence in and protection of the temple prior to its destruction.
37. 23.1 (ed. Baehrens, p. 210.13-27).
38. 5.44 (ed. Koetschau, p. 47.13ff.).
39. 2.13 (ed. Lommatzsch, I, pp. 120-21). Brief extracts from this discussion are preserved in Greek in Catena 10.19ff. (ed. A. Ramsbotham; *JTS* 13 [1911], pp. 217-18).
40. *Loc. cit.*, p. 124.

from blood and things that have been strangled, which are repeated in the Apostolic Decree (Acts 15.29) and still observed by gentile Christians, do include foreigners (Lev. 17.10-12, 13-14).[41] As regards sacrifices, the law about these which mentions foreigners does not say that they have to perform them but only how to if they do. As long as the temple was still standing gentiles did offer sacrifice there and indeed Jesus instructed the ten lepers to show themselves to the priest and make an offering, although one of them was a foreigner (Lk. 17.11-18, contaminated with Mt. 8.4).[42] Since its destruction, however, this has not been possible even for Jews, because it is only permitted in the one place. The same applies to the commandment that a proselyte who celebrates the Passover must be circumcised. The law commands that the Passover sacrifice take place in the Jerusalem temple, but this is now impossible. There is therefore no point in arguing about circumcision.[43]

Origen makes a similar admission concerning the period of Jesus' lifetime and immediately after in the *Contra Celsum*.[44] In reply to the accusation of Celsus's Jew referred to above, that Christians have abandoned the law of their fathers, he expounds the view that it was only after the resurrection that Jesus instructed his disciples in the spiritual interpretation of the law. According to *Homilies on Jeremiah* the intermediate time between the crucifixion and the destruction of the temple was allowed for repentance in particular for those of the Jews who were going to believe as a result of the signs and wonders done by the apostles.[45]

The time of transition, however, could only be of limited duration. As is clear from the passages cited above Origen considered that in the long term the continuance of the temple cult would have been a hindrance to conversion for both Jews and Gentiles. He reflects further on the matter in the *Contra*

41. *Loc. cit.*, pp. 124-29.
42. *Loc. cit.*, pp. 129-30.
43. *Loc. cit.*, pp. 130-31.
44. 2.1-2 (ed. Koetschau, pp. 126.12–129.24).
45. 14.13 (ed. E. Klostermann; GCS *Origenes* III [1901], p. 118.19-22).

Celsum[46] in his reply to Celsus's attack on the contradiction between the legislation of Jesus and that of Moses. Acknowledging the difference between the former manner of life of the Jews following Moses and the present way of life of Christians following Jesus' teachings, he argues that it would not have been suitable for converted Gentiles to live according to the letter of the law of Moses, since they were under Roman rule, nor could the Jews retain the structure of their society intact if they were going to follow the way of life according to the gospel. The Christians could not have killed their enemies or law-breakers according to the law of Moses, since even the Jews who want to do so are unable to follow the law in this respect. The ancient Jews on the other hand, who had their own constitution and territory, would have been entirely destroyed if they had not been allowed to fight their enemies and punish wrongdoers. The same divine providence which formerly gave the law and now has given the gospel of Jesus Christ has destroyed the city, temple and temple cult, not wishing the Jewish customs to prevail any longer, and has granted increase to the Christians, so that the Gentiles might be aided by Christ's teaching.[47]

During his time at Caesarea Origen was in contact with Jews[48] and Judaizing Christians.[49] He knew of their views and provides some interesting information about them. His observations on the significance of the destruction of the temple in the context of the question of the proper attitude to be taken to the Mosaic law are not simply the repetition of the commonplaces of his predecessors but are developed in awareness of rival arguments within the framework of his own biblical and historical expertise and desire to vindicate the unity of the two

46. 7.26 (ed. Koetschau, pp. 176.30–178.2). The passage makes interesting use of the terms πολιτεία and πολιτεύεσθαι, which is lost in a translation or paraphrase.
47. Cf. also *Contra Celsum* 4.32 (ed. Koetschau, p. 302.8-13), and 4.22 (p. 292.9-16), where Origen does speak of new laws given to the Christians.
48. Cf. de Lange, *Origen and the Jews*; H. Bietenhard, *Caesarea, Origenes und die Juden* (Stuttgart, 1974).
49. Cf. de Lange, *op. cit.*, pp. 36, 86-87; A. von Harnack, *Der kirchengeschichtliche Ertrag der exegetischen Arbeiten des Origenes*, I = *TU* 42.3 (1918), pp. 49, 68.

testaments and the beneficence of divine providence. His advocacy of 'spiritual interpretation' as a solution to the problem of
Old Testament interpretation did not destroy his interest in
historical events and their significance.

The subject continued to be treated by later writers. Eusebius
in his *Proof of the Gospel* gives a long and detailed exposition of
the fact that the law of Moses could only be observed by Jews
living in their own land.[50] Moses gave it to heal the Israelites
from idolatry but enacted in his foresight that its ordinances be
celebrated only in the Jerusalem temple. When the temple
was destroyed it was abolished and those attempting to obey it
became subject to the curse of Deut. 27.26.[51] He quotes this
verse no less than four times.[52] The *Apostolic Constitutions*
(6.25) also refer to this curse in showing that the sacrifices
according to the law can no longer be performed and the death
penalty no longer be inflicted since the defeat by the Romans,
as does Epiphanius in repeating the same stock argument
against the Nazaraeans.[53] John Chrysostom in his *Homilies
against the Jews*, attacking the Judaizing practices of Christians at Antioch, maintains that God allowed sacrifice for a
time in Jerusalem only as a concession to weakness but led the
Jews away from this practice by means of the destruction of
the city.[54] Inveighing against Julian's claim of Jewish support
in favour of animal sacrifice and his attempt to rebuild the
Jerusalem temple he asserts that the Jews themselves had
admitted that sacrifice was only allowed at Jerusalem.[55] In
reply to the same claim by Julian in his work *Against the
Galilaeans* Cyril of Alexandria repeats yet again that sacrifice

---

50. *Dem. Ev.* 1.3ff., with a summary at the beginning of 1.5.1 (ed. A.
Heikel; GCS *Eusebius* VI [1913], pp. 10.27ff., 20.16-19).
51. 1.6.31-40 (ed. Heikel, pp. 27.19–29.8).
52. 1.3.2, 1.3.25, 1.3.39, 1.6.37 (pp. 11.11, 14.35-6, 17.1-2, 28.20-22).
53. *Panarion haer.* 29.8.1.
54. 4.6 (*PG* 48.879-881; ET by P.W. Harkins, *Discourses against Juda-
ising Christians* = FC 68 [Washington, DC, 1979], pp. 88-91); cf. also
3.3.6-7 and 4.4.3-8 (*PG* 48.865end-866, 876-77; ET pp. 57-58, with note 43,
and 81-84).
55. 5.11.4-10 (*PG* 48.900-901; ET pp. 137-40); cf. also *Adv. Judaeos et
Gentiles Demonstratio* 16ff. (*PG* 48.835ff.).

was allowed in only one place so that it might cease when the temple was destroyed.[56]

The remarks of the early Christian writers who have been cited above differ in detail according to the context of their reflexions and to whether they have pagan, Jewish or Judaizing Christian opponents in mind, and some of the earlier ideas were later dropped as being too extreme, but gradually a main stream of argumentation was worked out which could be repeated whenever occasion arose. This has been illustrated almost entirely from Greek writers. Unfortunately it has not been possible to consider Jewish reactions.[57] In conclusion reference may be made to a Westerner, Augustine, whose development of his own characteristic view on the subject has been examined by the honorand of this volume.[58] In attempting to show the role of the Roman destruction of Jerusalem in the divine plan for human history Augustine expounds the theory that the Jews were excluded from their homeland and dispersed throughout the rest of the world in order that they might act as witnesses to Christianity by means of their independent preservation and custody of the Old Testament scriptures.[59]

56. *Contra Julianum* 9 (*PG* 76.981B) replying to Julian's claim cited at 970C-D.
57. On these cf. the works listed in note 8 above. For examples of Jewish accommodation to the destruction of the temple by means of the substitution of other values and actions for the temple and cult, cf. note 15 above, Thoma, *art. cit.*, p. 199, and Bietenhard, *Caesarea, Origenes und die Juden*, p. 50.
58. E. Bammel, 'Die Zeugen des Christentums', to appear in H. Frohnhofen (ed.), *Die Anfänge des theologischen Vorurteils. Judaistische, neutestamentliche und frühchristliche Forschungen* (Hamburg, 1990).
59. Cf. e.g. *City of God* 4.34; *Sermon* 5.5 (ed. C. Lambot, CCL 41 [1961], pp. 55-56).

BIBLIOGRAPHY OF ERNST BAMMEL*

'Karl Barth und die Deutschen', *Schwäbisches Tagblatt*, 13.XI.1945, pp. 1f.

Gagerns Plan und die Frankfurter Nationalversammlung (Frankfurt: W. Kramer, 1949).

Frankfurt und Berlin in der deutschen Revolution (Bonn: H. Scheur, 1949).

'Pontius Pilatus', *Einkehr. Bremer Kirchenzeitung*, 9.IV.1950, pp. 41f.

'Kaiphas und der Prozess Jesu', *Coburger Neue Presse*, 22.III.1951.

'Gamaliel, der Lehrer des Apostels Paulus', *Einkehr. Bremer Kirchenzeitung*, 26.VIII.1951, p. 75.

'1852—Kirchentag in Bremen', *Einkehr. Bremer Kirchenzeitung*, 7.IX.1952.

'Zur Vorgeschichte des Wittenberger Kirchentags', *Monatshefte für evangelische Kirchengeschichte des Rheinlands* 1 (1952), pp. 33-37.

'Pilate and Syrian Coinage', *Journal of Jewish Studies* 2 (1951), pp. 108-10.

'Φίλος τοῦ Καίσαρος', *Theologische Literaturzeitung* 77 (1952), cols. 205-10.

'Zum jüdischen Märtyrerkult', *Theologische Literaturzeitung* 78 (1953), cols. 119-26.

'Der Pakt Simon-Gagern und der Abschluss der Paulskirchenverfassung', *Festschrift Ludwig Bergsträsser* (Düsseldorf, 1954), pp. 57-87.

'Ἀρχιερεὺς Προφητεύων', *Theologische Literaturzeitung* 79 (1954), cols. 351-56.

'Zum Kapitalrecht in Kyrene', *Zeitschrift der Savigny-Stiftung, Römische Abteilung* 17 (1954), pp. 356-59.

'Die Bruderfolge im Hochpriestertum der herodianisch-römischen Zeit', *Zeitschrift des Deutschen Palästina-Vereins* 70 (1954), pp. 147-53.

'Herkunft und Funktion der Traditionselemente in 1 Kor. 15.1-11', *Theologische Zeitschrift* (Basel) 11 (1955), pp. 401-19.

'Nicanor and his Gate', *Journal of Jewish Studies* 7 (1956), pp. 77-78.

'Der achtundzwanzigste Adar', *Hebrew Union College Annual* 28 (1957), pp. 109-113.

* Reviews are mentioned only when some contribution to the subject of the book reviewed has been attempted.

'Die Schatzung des Archelaos', *Historia* 7 (1958), pp. 497-500.

'Die Neuordnung des Pompeius und das römisch-jüdische Bündnis', *Zeitschrift des Deutschen Palästina-Vereins* 75 (1959), pp. 76-82.

'Is Luke 16.16-18 of Baptist's Provenience?', *Harvard Theological Review* 51 (1958), pp. 101-106.

'Höhlenmenschen', *Zeitschrift für die neutestamentliche Wissenschaft* 49 (1958), pp. 77-88.

'Zu IQS 9.10f.', *Vetus Testamentum* 7 (1957), pp. 381-85.

'Judenverfolgung und Naherwartung. Zur Eschatologie des Ersten Thessalonicherbriefs', *Zeitschrift für Theologie und Kirche* 56 (1959), pp. 294-315.

Rev.: J. Jeremias, *Heiligengräber in Jesu Umwelt* (Göttingen, 1958), *ELKZ* 13 (1959), p. 272.

'Kirkisanis Sadduzäer', *Zeitschrift für die alttestamentliche Wissenschaft* 81 (1959), pp. 265-70.

'Πτωχός', *Theologisches Wörterbuch zum Neuen Testament*, VI (Stuttgart, 1959), cols. 888-915 (= *Theological Dictionary of the New Testament*, VI [Grand Rapids, 1968], cols. 888-915).

'Das Gleichnis von den bösen Winzern (Mk 12,1-9) und das jüdische Erbrecht', *Revue internationale des droits de l'antiquité*, 3rd Series 6 (1959), pp. 11-17.

'Gottes Διαθήκη (Gal. 3.15-17) und das jüdische Rechtsdenken', *New Testament Studies* (1959-60), pp. 313-19.

'Ein Beitrag zur paulinischen Staatsanschauung', *Theologische Literaturzeitung* 85 (1960), cols. 837-40.

'"Any Deyathiqi partially cancelled is completely cancelled"', *Journal of Semitic Studies* 5 (1960), pp. 355-58.

Rev.: F. Rehkopf, *Die lukanische Sonderquelle* (Tübingen, 1959), *ELKZ* 14 (1960), pp. 348f.

'Emil Schürer, der Begründer der Wissenschaft vom Spätjudentum. Zu seinem 50. Todestag', *Deutsches Pfarrerblatt* (1960), cols. 225-27.

Rev.: *Judentum, Urchristentum, Kirche. Festschrift J. Jeremias* (= BZNW 26; Berlin, 1960), *ELKZ* 15 (1961), p. 226.

'Matthäus 10.23', *Studia Theologica* 15 (1961), pp. 79-92.

'The Organisation of Palestine by Gabinius', *Journal of Jewish Studies* 12 (1961), pp. 159-62.

'Versuch zu Col. 1.15-20', *Zeitschrift für die neutestamentliche Wissenschaft* 52 (1961), pp. 88-95.

'A New Text of the Lord's Prayer', *Expository Times* 73 (1961-62), p. 54.

'Paul and Judaism', *The Modern Churchman* 6 (1962-63), pp. 279-85.

'Das Wort vom Apfelbäumchen', *Novum Testamentum* 5 (1962) (= *Tabula gratulatoria E. Stauffer oblata*), pp. 219-28.

'Schema und Vorlage von Didache 16', *Texte und Untersuchungen* 79 (1962), pp. 253-63.

'Problems of the Eschatology of Jesus', *The Modern Churchman* 6 (1962–63), pp. 150-64.

'Zur Frühgeschichte der Mandäer', *Orientalia* 32 (1963), pp. 220-25.

Rev.: R. Aron, *Die verborgenen Jahre Jesu* (Frankfurt, 1962), *Theologische Literaturzeitung* 83 (1963), cols. 355f.

'Nomos Christou', *Texte und Untersuchungen* 88 (Berlin, 1964), pp. 120-28.

'The Commands in 1 Peter 2.17', *New Testament Studies* 11 (1964–65), pp. 279-81.

'Erwägungen zur Eschatologie Jesu', *Texte und Untersuchungen* 88 (Berlin, 1964), pp. 3-32.

'Die Oktoberversammlung des Jahres 1871 "*Und fragten nach Jesus.*"', *Festschrift für E. Barnikol* (Halle, 1964), pp. 251-67.

'Overbeck über seine Freunde', *Theologische Zeitschrift* (Basel) 21 (1965), pp. 113-17.

'"John did no Miracle"', *Miracles. Cambridge Studies in their Philosophy and History*, ed. C.F.D. Moule (London, 1965), pp. 181-202.

'Die Täufertraditionen bei Justin', *Texte und Untersuchungen* 93 (1966), pp. 53-61.

Rev.: B. Blumenkran, *Juifs et chrétiens dans le monde occidental 430–1096* (Paris, 1960), *Theologische Literaturzeitung* 89 (1966), cols. 351-54.

Rev.: R.T. Herford, *Die Pharisäer* (Köln, 1961), *Theologische Literaturzeitung* 89 (1966), cols. 585f.

'Christian Origins in Jewish Tradition', *New Testament Studies* 13 (1966–67), pp. 317-35.

'Der Tod Jesu in einer "Toledth Jeschu"-Überlieferung', *Annual of the Swedish Theological Institute* 6 (1967–68), pp. 124-31.

'Der historische Jesus in der Theologie Adolf von Harnacks', *Tutzinger Texte* 1 (1968), pp. 71-97 [ET in *The Modern Churchman* ns 19 (1975–76), noted below].

'Excerpts from a New Gospel?', *Novum Testamentum* 10 (1968), pp. 1-9.

'Jesus and "Setting up a Brick"', *Zeitschrift für Religions- und Geistesgeschichte* 20 (1968), pp. 364-67.

'Die Rechtsstellung des Herodes', *Zeitschrift des Deutschen Palästina-Vereins* 84 (1968), pp. 73-79.

'Gerim Gerurim', *Annual of the Swedish Theological Institute* 7 (1968–69), pp. 127-31.

Rev.: D. Daube, *Collaboration with Tyranny in Rabbinic Law* (Oxford, 1965), *Theologische Literaturzeitung* 87 (1968), cols. 833-35.

'Origen Contra Celsum I.41 and the Jewish Tradition', *Journal of Theological Studies* ns 19 (1968), pp. 211-13.

'Galater 1.23', *Zeitschrift für die neutestamentliche Wissenschaft* 59 (1968), pp. 108-12.

'Rest and Rule', *Vigiliae Christianae* 23 (1969), pp. 88-90.

'Judentum, Christentum und Heidentum: Julius Wellhausens Briefe an Theodor Mommsen 1881–1902', *Zeitschrift für Kirchengeschichte* 4/18 (1969), pp. 221-54.

'Seventeen Apostles', *Journal of Theological Studies* ns 20 (1969), pp. 534f.

Rev.: K. Deschner (ed.), *Jesusbilder in theologischer Sicht* (München, 1966), *Zeitschrift für Religions- und Geistesgeschichte* 21 (1969), pp. 80f.

Rev.: R.M. Grant, *Gnosticism in Early Christianity* (2nd edn, New York, 1966), *Zeitschrift für Religions- und Geistesgeschichte* 21 (1969), pp. 279f.

'Markus 10.11f. und das jüdische Eherecht', *Zeitschrift für die neutestamentliche Wissenschaft* 61 (1970), pp. 95-101.

'Das Ende von Q', *Verborum Veritas. Festschrift für Gustav Stählin* (Wuppertal, 1970), pp. 39-50.

'What is Thy Name?', *Novum Testamentum* 12 (1970), pp. 223-28.

' "Ex illa itaqule die consilium fecerunt…" ', in *The Trial of Jesus. Cambridge Studies in Honour of C.F.D. Moule*, ed. E. Bammel (= Studies in Biblical Theology, 2/13; London: SCM, 1970), pp. 11-40.

'Crucifixion as a Punishment in Palestine', in *The Trial of Jesus*, pp. 162-65.

Rev.: J.D. Derrett, *An Oriental Lawyer Looks at the Trial of Jesus and the Doctrine of Redemption* (London, 1965), *Theologische Literaturzeitung* 85 (1970), cols. 824f.

Rev.: P. Gerlitz, *Ausserchristliche Einflüsse auf die Entwicklung des christlichen Trinitätsdogmas* (Leiden, 1963) *Zeitschrift für Religions- und Geistesgeschichte* 22 (1970), pp. 277f.

Rev.: H.J.W. Drijvers, *Bardaisan of Edessa* (Assen, 1966), *Zeitschrift für Religions- und Geistesgeschichte* 22 (1970), p. 279.

Rev.: E. Lövestam, *Spiritus Blasphemia. Eine Studie zu Mk. 3.28f par Mt. 12.31f. Lk. 12.10* (Lund, 1968), *Journal of Theological Studies* ns 22 (1971), pp. 192-94.

'The Baptist in Early Christian Tradition', *New Testament Studies* 18 (1971–72), pp. 95-128.

'Christus Parricida', *Vigiliae Christianae* 26 (1972), pp. 259-62.

Die Reichsgründung und der deutsche Protestantismus (Erlanger Forschungen, 22; Erlangen, 1973).

'Südosteuropäische Gesandte in der Paulskirche', *Korrespondenzblatt des Arbeitskreises für Siebenbürgische Landeskunde* 67 (1973), pp. 31-38.

'Fabula Seductoria', *Bulletin of the Institute of Jewish Studies* (London) 1 (1973–75), pp. 13-18.

'A New Variant Form of the Testimonium Flavianum', *The Expository Times* 85 (1973–74), pp. 145-47.

'Joh. 7.35 in Manis Lebensbeschreibung', *Novum Testamentum* 15 (1973), pp. 191f.

Rev.: M. Green, *Evangelism in the Early Church* (London, 1970), *Theologische Literaturzeitung* 82 (1973), cols. 529-32.

'Jesus und der Paraklet in Johannes 16', in *Christ and the Spirit in the New Testament* (C.F.D. Moule Festschrift), ed. B. Lindars and S. Smalley (Cambridge, 1973), pp. 199-217.

'p$^{64(67)}$ and the Last Supper', *Journal of Theological Studies* ns 24 (1973), p. 189.

'Zum Testimonium Flavianum', *Josephus-Studien. Festschrift O. Michel*, ed. O. Betz, K. Haacker and M. Hengel (Göttingen, 1974), pp. 9-23.

'Joasar', *Zeitschrift des Deutschen Palästinavereins* 90 (1974), pp. 61-68.

'Die Blutgerichtsbarkeit in der römischen Provinz Judäa vor dem ersten jüdischen Aufstand', *Journal of Jewish Studies* 25 (1974) (= *Studies in Jewish Legal History in Honour of David Daube*, ed. B.S. Jackson), pp. 35-49.

'The Jesus of History in the Theology of Adolf von Harnack', *The Modern Churchman* ns 19 (1975–76), pp. 90-112 [ET of article in *Tutzinger Texte* 1 (1968), noted above].

Rev.: W.-W. Graf Arnim, *Siedlungswanderung im Mittelalter*, I-III (Bonn, 1971–84), *Zeitschrift für Religions- und Geistesgeschichte* 28 (1976), pp. 188f.; 39 (1987), pp. 368f.

'Israels Dienstbarkeit', in *Donum Gentilicium. New Testament Studies in Honour of David Daube*, ed. E. Bammel, C.K. Barrett and W.D. Davies (Oxford, 1978), pp. 295-305.

'Der Text von Apostelgeschichte 15', *Bibliotheca Ephemeridum Theologicarum Lovaniensium* 48 (1979), pp. 439-46.

'Sadduzäer und Sadokiden', *Ephemerides Theologicae Lovanienses* 55 (1979) (Analecta Lovaniensia biblica et orientalia, 5/41), pp. 107-15.

'Albert Schwegler über Jesus und das Urchristentum', *Zeitschrift für Kirchengeschichte* 4/29 (1980), pp. 1-10.

Rev.: J.E. Wilson, *Gott, Mensch und Welt bei Franz Overbeck* (Bern, Frankfurt, 1977), *Zeitschrift für Kirchengeschichte* 88 (1981), pp. 410f.

'Preparation for the Perils of the Last Days: 1 Thessalonians 3:3', *Suffering and Martyrdom in the New Testament*, ed. W. Horbury and B. McNeil (Cambridge, 1981), pp. 91-100.

'*Schabbat* 116a/b', *Novum Testamentum* 24 (1982) (= Festheft D. Derrett), pp. 266-74.

'Paulus, der Moses des Neuen Bundes', Θεολογία (Athens) 54 (1983), pp. 399-408.

Rev.: D.L. Mealand, *Poverty and Expectation in the Gospels* (London, 1980), *Journal of Theological Studies* ns 28 (1984), pp. 511f.

Rev.: R.v. Thadden, *Fragen an Preussen* (München, 1981), *Zeitschrift für Kirchengeschichte* 86 (1983), pp. 205-207.

Rev.: E. Geldbach, *Der gelehrte Diplomat. Zum Wirken C.C.J. Bunsens* (Leiden, 1980), *Zeitschrift für Kirchengeschichte* 86 (1983), pp. 444-46.

Rev.: Kurt and Barbara Aland, *Der Text des Neuen Testaments* (Stuttgart, 1982), *Theologische Revue* 80 (1984), cols. 300f.

'The Revolution Theory from Reimarus to Brandon', in *Jesus and the Politics of his Day*, ed. E. Bammel and C.F.D. Moule (Cambridge, 1984), pp. 11-68.

'The Poor and the Zealots', in *Jesus and the Politics of his Day*, pp. 109-28.

'Jesus as a Political Agent in a Version of the Josippon', in *Jesus and the Politics of his Day*, pp. 197-209.

'The Feeding of the Multitudes', in *Jesus and the Politics of his Day*, pp. 211-40.

'The *Titulus*', in *Jesus and the Politics of his Day*, pp. 353-64.

'Romans 13', in *Jesus and the Politics of his Day*, pp. 365-83.

'The Trial before Pilate', in *Jesus and the Politics of his Day*, pp. 415-51.

'Der Nachfolger', *Friede über Israel* 68 (1985), pp. 1-15.

'Niebuhr und England', *Bonner Historische Forschungen* 52 (Bonn, 1985), pp. 131-75.

Rev.: G. Besier, *Preussische Kirchenpolitik in der Bismarckära*, *Zeitschrift für Kirchengeschichte* 84 (1985), pp. 121-23.

Rev.: J.J. Kelly, *Baron Friedrich von Hügel's Philosophy of Religion* (Löwen, 1983), *Zeitschrift für Kirchengeschichte* 84 (1985), p. 123.

Rev.: W. Gericke, *Das Buch 'De Tribus Impostoribus'* (Berlin, 1982), *Theologische Literaturzeitung* 110 (1985), cols. 620f.

'The Cambridge Pericope. The Addition to Luke 6.4 in Codex Bezae', *New Testament Studies* 32 (1986), pp. 404-26.

'Jesus und ein anderer', in Ernst Bammel, *Judaica, Kleine Schriften*, I (= WUNT 37), Ernst Bammel (Tübingen: J.C.B. Mohr [P. Siebeck], 1986), pp. 157-74.

'Pilatus' und Kaiphas' Absetzung', in *Kleine Schriften*, I (Tübingen, 1986), pp. 51-58.

'Der Jude des Celsus', in *Kleine Schriften*, I (Tübingen, 1986), pp. 265-83.

'Die Versuchung Jesu nach einer jüdischen Quelle', in *Kleine Schriften*, I (Tübingen, 1986), pp. 253-56.

'Die Zitate in Origenes' Schrift wider Celsus', *Innsbrucker Theologische Studien* 19 (1987), pp. 2-6.

'Der Zeuge des Judentums', *Zu Alexander, Festschrift Gerhard Wirth*, I (Amsterdam, 1987), pp. 279-88.

'Rückkehr zum Judentum', *Augustinianum* 27 (1987), pp. 317-29.

'Glaube im Judentum', *TRE* XIII, pp. 304f.

'Die Anfänge der Kirchengeschichte im Spiegel der jüdischen Quellen', *Augustinianum* 28 (1987), pp. 367-79.

'Das Judentum als eine Religion Aegyptens', *Religion im Erbe Aegyptens. Festschrift Alexander Böhlig*

Jesu Nachfolger (Heidelberg: Lambert Schneider, 1988).

Rev.: J.A.T. Robinson, *The Priority of John* (London, 1985), *Journal of Theological Studies* ns 39 (1988), pp. 200-204.

Rev.: R. Kampling, *Das Blut Christi und die Juden. Mt. 27.25 bei den lateinischsprachigen christlichen Autoren bis zu Leo d. Gr.* (Münster, 1984), *Theologische Revue* 84 (1988), cols. 369f.

Rev.: A. Altmann, *Von der mittelalterlichen zur modernen Aufklärung* (Tübingen, 1987), *Theologische Literaturzeitung* 114 (1989), cols. 27f.

Rev.: H.H. Schade, *Apokalyptische Christologie bei Paulus* (Göttingen, 1981), *Journal of Theological Studies* ns 40 (1989), pp. 577f.

Rev.: M. Goodman, *The Ruling Class of Judaea* (Cambridge, 1987), *Journal of Theological Studies* ns 40 (1989), pp. 213-17.

'Prophetie und Deutung', *Augustinianum* 29 (1989), pp. 601-10.

'Eine übersehene Angabe zu den Toledoth Jeschu', *New Testament Studies* 35 (1989), pp. 279f.

'Die Anfänge des Sukzessionsprinzips im Urchristentum', *Augustinianum* 31 (1990), pp. 63-72.

'Rufins Einleitung zu den Klemens zugeschriebenen Wiedererkennungen', *Antichità Altoadriatiche* (Udine, 1991).

'Die Zeugen des Christentums', *Die Anfänge des theologischen Vorurteils. Judaistische, neutestamentliche und frühchristliche Forschungen* (ed. H. Frohnhofen; Hamburg, 1990).

Rev.: M. Liebmann, *Theodor Innitzer und der Anschluss. Oesterreichs Kirche 1938, Historische Zeitschrift* 251 (1990).

Rev.: M. Hengel, *The Johannine Question* (London, 1990), *Journal of Theological Studies* ns 42 (1991).

'Hirsch und Wellhausen', *Christentum und Wahrheitsbewusstsein. Studien zur Theologie Emanuel Hirschs* (Theologische Bibliothek Töpelmann; ed. J. Ringleben; Berlin: de Gruyter, 1991).

'Die Apokryphen-Zitate bei Origenes', *Origeniana Quinta* (ed. R.J. Daly; Leuven, 1991).

'Vom Sinn der "Judaistik"', *Festschrift H. Schreckenberg.*

'Staat und Kirche im zweiten Kaiserreich', *Der Kulturprotestantismus* (ed. H.M. Müller; Gütersloh, 1991).

'Die rheinisch-westfälische Kirchenordnung und ihr Einfluss auf die preussische Landeskirche', *RhV.* 56 (1991).

Jesus and the Sabbath Law (Sheffield: JSOT Press, 1991).

Judaica et Paulina, Kleine Schriften, II (Tübingen: J.C.B. Mohr [P. Siebeck], 1991).

'Gregor d.Gr. und die Juden', *Augustinianum* 32 (1991).

'Die Tempelreinigung bei den Synoptikern und im Johannesevangelium', *Bibliotheca Ephemeridum Theologicarum Lovaniensium* 60 (1991).

Rev.: D. Flusser, *Entdeckungen im Neuen Testament*, I (Neukirchen-Vluyn, 1987), *Theologische Literaturzeitung* 116 (1991).

INDEXES

INDEX OF BIBLICAL REFERENCES

OLD TESTAMENT

NEW TESTAMENT

MISHNAH

BABYLONIAN TALMUD

PHILO

23.130   272

Plutarch
Alexander
26.7   404

Cato Major
29b

Isis et Osiris
30 (2.
362f.)   201

Moralia
278D   299
664C   277
4.671D-
672B   286
675F   286
681F/
682A   280

Romulus
4.1   298
20.5-6   295

Quintilian
Instutio Oratoria
6.3.77   293

Seneca
Epistulae
94.47   131
Statius
Silvae
1.6.15   283
4.9.26-
28   283

Strabo
13.1.35   273
16.2, 46   131

Suetonius
Aug.
2.76.1   276
92.1   295
92.2   293
94.11   294

Calig.
4.56.2   280

Galba
1   295

Tacitus
Historiae
5.4   289
5.5   286

5.13   35

Annales
13.58   299, 300

Tatian
Oratio ad Graecos
1   222

Theodosian Code
2.8, 19   136

Theophrastus
Historia Plantarum
2.8   274, 294
3.1   274

Tibullus
1.3, 18   144

Varro
De Lingua Latina
5.54   298
6.18   279

Virgil
Aeneid
2.504   109

Eclogues
4   140

CHRISTIAN

Ambrose
Expos. in Apocal.
17.
933ff.   222

*Apostolic
Constitutions*
5.20   354
6.25   475

Thomas Aquinas
11/2,
91.2   220

Augustine
De Civ. Dei
4.34   476
18.45   107, 128

Enarr. in Psalmos
150   222

Sermones
476

Epistle of Barnabas
3.6   469
4.7-8   467

4.11   467
6.15   362
7-8   467
7.3   362
7.6-11   420
14.1-3   467
16   183, 195,
363, 467
16.1   363
16.2   363
16.3   185
16.4   363
16.7-10   467
16.8   364

INDEX OF AUTHORS